WARREN COUNTY, TENNESSEE CEMETERY BOOK 2: G - L ANNOTATED

Gardens of Memory through Lytle Cemetery

by
Mrs. Almetia Cunningham
and Mrs. Martha Holt

Edited and Compiled
by
Mrs. Betty M. Majors

Heritage Books
2024

HERITAGE BOOKS

AN IMPRINT OF HERITAGE BOOKS, INC.

Books, CDs, and more—Worldwide

For our listing of thousands of titles see our website
at
www.HeritageBooks.com

A Facsimile Reprint
Published 2024 by
HERITAGE BOOKS, INC.
Publishing Division
5810 Ruatan Street
Berwyn Heights, MD 20740

Heritage Books by Betty M. Majors:

Warren County, Tennessee Cemetery
Book 1: Adcock Cemetery to Fuston Cemetery
Almetia Cunningham and Martha Holt, edited and compiled by Betty M. Majors

Warren County, Tennessee Cemetery
Book 2: Gardens of Memory to Lytle Cemetery
Almetia Cunningham and Martha Holt, edited and compiled by Betty M. Majors

International Standard Book Number
Paperbound: 978-0-7884-8981-5

TABLE OF CONTENTS

PREFACE

After compiling the inscriptions from the tombstones in the cemeteries of
Warren County, Tennessee, the authors have attempted to include the
parents, spouse and often the marriage date of each of the deceased.
Information has been gathered from obituaries, funeral home records, death
certificates and family material. Facts obtained from these sources are
placed in brackets following the tombstone inscription. Maiden names of
mothers are enclosed in parentheses. All marriage dates given are for
marriages performed in Warren County unless otherwise noted.

Many burials which were without markers have been found and are included.
This information if preceded by an *. Often spelling varies from
inscription to other source, and additional names for the deceased are
found. Since a question often exists as to which of these spellings or
names is correct, both have been included.

As with any undertaking of this magnitude, errors will arise. The authors
would appreciate any corrections or additions be sent to the editor, Mrs.
Betty M. Majors, 111 Oak Park Drive, Tullahoma, Tennessee, 37388. These
changes will be published in an addendum in the last volume of this
series.

ACKNOWLEDGEMENTS

The authors wish to thank all those persons who have shared their
knowledge of the cemeteries contained herein, and who have contributed
family information of inclusion in this volume.

DEDICATION

To the memory of A.C. Hillis, in appreciation of his contribution to this
and other publications of the records of Warren County, Tennessee. His
love of the county, and his tireless efforts to place information about
this county in print, should be an inspiration to us all.

GARDENS OF MEMORY

Located: On Hwy 55 in Morrison, TN.

TURNER, Sissie L. Pack. 31 Oct 1900-16 Jun 1981. [Daughter of John W.
        and Isabell (Watts) Pack, wife of Charles William Turner.]

TURNER, Charles W. 10 Nov 1872-11 Mar 1958. [Son of James Thomas and
        Jeanette (Middleton) Turner, husband of Sissie L. Pack.]

CANTRELL, Jackie A. 2 Dec 1899-14 Jul 1982. [Daughter of Richard and
        Dela (_____) Arnold, wife of James Richard "Peanut" Cantrell.]

CANTRELL, James R. 6 Oct 1897-25 Jan 1991. [Son of George Lawrence and
        Josie (Hardcastle) Cantrell, husband of Jackie Arnold. Married
        25 Dec 1919.]

OWEN, Warren Edward. 9 Mar 1933-3 Jan 1968. [Son of J.B. and Mary
        (Todd) Owen, husband of Dorothy Smoot.]

KIRBY, Thurman G. Born 1 Mar 1913-

HENEGAR, H. Lucille.   1926 -   . [Daughter of Charlie D. and Essie
        (Baley) Medley, wife of Perry Corder Henegar.]

HENEGAR, Perry Corder. 26 May 1919-10 Oct 1977. WWII. [Son of James T
        and Ada (Garner) Henegar, husband of Lucille Medley.]

BAKER, Malchus C. 31 Aug 1919-   . [Malchus Clinton, son of
        James Austin and Lola Ather (McGiboney) Baker, husband of Vera
        McCormick, married 5 May 1941.]

BAKER, Vera M. 17 Jun 1921-   . [Vera McCormick, wife of Malchus
        Clinton Baker.]

BAKER, John W. 24 Oct 1916-11 Jan 1993. [Son of James Austin and Lola
        Ather (McGiboney) Baker, husband of Helen M. Reeder.]

BAKER, Helen M. 2 Mar 1916-   . [Helen Marie Reeder, wife of John
        William Baker, married 20 Feb 1937.]

MESSICK, Brady. 14 Feb 1945-14 Dec 1987. [Son of Clinton and Lida
        (Merriman) Messick, husband of Christine Soltysik.]

MESSICK, Clinton. 10 Aug 1912-2 Nov 1986. [Son of Chrisley and Ella
        (Wilson) Messick, husband of 1) Flowdy _____ and 2) Lida
        Merriman.]

MESSICK, Lida. 1924 -   . [Lida Merriman, wife of Clinton Messick.]

MATTINGLY, Edith L. 12 Jul 1914-   . [Edith Jenitta, daughter of
        Vach L. and Minnie (Bouldin) Lankford, wife of Clarence
        Mattingly.]

MATTINGLY, Treva Willodene. 10 Apr 1935-5 Feb 1961. [Daughter of
        Clarence and Edith (Lankford) Mattingly, single.]

LANKFORD, Vach L. 11 Apr 1882-25 Dec 1959. [Son of William and Rachel
        (McCorkle) Lankford, grandson of Silas and Mary Lankford,
        husband of Minnie Novella Bouldin.]

LANKFORD, Minnie B. 23 Oct 1892-2 Nov 1970. [Daughter of Thomas and Elvana (Curtis) Bouldin, granddaughter of William and Jemima (Williams) Bouldin, granddaughter of William Washington and Latisha (Dodson) Curtis, wife of Vanchel Lankford, married 4 Aug 1907.]

UNDERHILL, Frank T. 16 Dec 1895-27 Feb 1969. [Son of James Holiday and Pairlee (Bailey) Underhill, grandson of George W. and Malissa (Rigsby) Underhill, married 1) Lula Page and 2) Amanda Pearson]

UNDERHILL, Frank Jr. 1931 -   . [Son of Frank Sr. and Lula (Page) Underhill, husband of Sadie M. _____.]

UNDERHILL, Sadie M. 1929-   . [Wife of Frank Underhill, Jr.]

UNDERHILL, Lula. 27 May 1898-12 Sep 1980. [Daughter of Alex and Emaline (Roberson) Page, wife of Frank Underhill, Sr.]

McDOWELL, Charley T. 17 Mar 1909-24 Aug 1970. [Charlie Tarlton, son of Manson Bryan and Mary Alice (Richey) McDowell, husband of Willie May Muncey.]

McDOWELL, Willie May. 28 Jan 1909-21 Jan 1970. [Daughter of Jim and Elva (McBride) Muncey, wife of Charlie Tarlton McDowell.]

McDOWELL, Mildred C. 1914 - 24 Apr 1981. [Mildred Cleveland McDowell, daughter of Manson Bryan and Mary Alice (Richey) McDowell.]

FRAZIER, Richard T. 28 Aug 1912-13 Sep 1976. [Son of Robert and Ella (Pedigo) Frazier, husband of Ruth Barker.]

FRAZIER, Ruth B. 2 May 1916-   . [Ruth Barker, wife of Richard T. Frazier.]

BARKER, Henry Clay, Jr. 31 Dec 1920-2 Nov 1992. WWII. [Son of Henry Clay, Sr. and Edna (Wimberly) Barker, husband of Florine Wiles.]

BARKER, Florine Wiles. 19 Nov 1922-   . [Wife of Henry Clay Barker, Jr., married 21 Jul 1943.]

GILLEN, William C. 15 Nov 1902-4 Oct 1976. WWII. [Son of John and Bertha (Tetzke) Gillen, husband of Lillian Barrett.]

GILLEN, Lillian. 12 Jul 1900-20 Oct 1984. [Daughter of James and Ella (Hollandsworth) Barrett, wife of 1) Sam Dennis who died in 1963 and 2) William C. Gillen.]

JOINES, Orvel C. 5 Feb 1903-17 Nov 1990. [Son of John Harrison and Tennec Indiana (Chumbley) Joines, husband of Dillie Elkins.]

JOINES, Dillie W. 1909 -   . [Dillie W. Elkins, wife of Orvel Clayton Joines, married 9 Aug 1925 in Cannon County, Tn.]

BAILEY, Barry Lynn. 22 Feb 1958-22 Feb 1958. [Son of Billy and Lois (Starkey) Bailey.]

BAILEY, Lois M. 1934 -   . [Lois M. Starkey, wife of Billy E. Bailey.]

BAILEY, Billy E. 1929 -   . [Son of William Schuyler and Stella (Bratcher) Bailey, married 1) _____ _____, and 2) to Lois Starkey.]

BAILEY, Stella B. 27 Apr 1900-10 Sep 1975. [Daughter of Samuel Forest and Lillie (Emery) Bratcher, wife of William Schuyler Bailey.]

BAILEY, W.S. 29 Sep 1898-16 Oct 1977. [William Schuyler, son of Tolbert B. and Abbie (Belcher) Bailey, husband of Stella Bratcher.]

ALLEN, Fannie M. 20 Jan 1889-4 Nov 1979. [Fannie Myrtle, daughter of John and Laura (Sinclair) Wilson, wife of Samuel Neal Allen.]

ALLEN, Samuel N. 7 Nov 1879- June 1977. [Son of Elijah and Parlina (Mullican) Allen, husband of 1) Bettie Fuston and 2) Fannie Myrtle Wilson.]

ARGO, Jennie B. 17 Apr 1907-   . [Jennie Braxton, wife of Tom Argo.]

ARGO, Tom. 7 Jul 1891-28 Jul 1979. [Son of Joseph and Lina (Hobbs) Argo, husband of Jennie Braxton, married 17 May 1925.]

JOHNSON, Albert James. 26 Jul 1941-8 Jul 1977. VIETNAM. [Son of Bill and Lucinda (Tate) Johnson, husband of Linda Sue Haston.]

LANCE, Helen H. 1935 -   . [Wife of Billy E. Lance.]

LANCE, Billy E. 1936 -   . [Son of Bill and Ada (_____) Lance, husband of Helen H. _____.]

HENSLEY, Ada Lance. 1917 -

LANCE, Bill. 1913- Mar 1964.

LANCE, Tammy. Dec 1959. Infant daughter of Kenneth and Phyllis (_____) Lance.

LANCE, Marie Laster. 1905 - Feb 1963. [Marie Ethel Laster, first wife of Leonard Lance.]

BLACK, Gladys S. 1898 - 28 Nov 1981. [Dora Gladys, daughter of William and Dora (Mitchell) Stewart, wife of Thomas Jefferson Black.]

BLACK, Thomas J. 25 Sep 1893-31 Oct 1959. [Thomas Jefferson, son of Marcus L. and Margaret (Vaughn) Black, husband of Dora Gladys Stewart.]

DAVIS, Mack M. 27 Oct 1911-5 Sep 1989. [Mack Millian, son of Madison Scott and Georgia (Hitchcock) Davis, husband of Gladys Loree Black.]

DAVIS, Loree B. 1917 -19 Oct 1990. [Gladys Loree, daughter of Thomas Jefferson and Dora Gladys (Stewart) Black, wife of Mack Millian Davis.]

OWENS, Cheryl Lynn. 13 Sep 1967 [only date on stone]. [Infant daughter of Bluford and Sandra (_____) Owens.]

SIMMONS, Sherman D. 1936 -   .

SIMMONS, Agnes A.   1938 -   .

TURNER, Richard L. 1919 -   . [Husband of 1) Mattie Irene Parish
         and 2) Elese (Conley) Walker.]

TURNER, Mattie I. 6 Sep 1920-25 Jun 1984. [Daughter of Lon B. and Mattie
         Irene (_____) Parish, wife of Richard L. Turner, married 27 Apr
         1937.]

ROSS, Wesley Brown. 8 Apr 1931-16 Jan 1980. KOREA. [Son of Charlie and
         Ophie (Crawford) Ross, husband of 1) _____ _____ and 2)
         Laurene Veal.]

ROSS, Laurene M.   15 Jul 1933-   . [Daughter of Amos Alvin and
         Netta Treva (Stipe) Veal, married 1) Allen Douglas Spurlock, 2)
         Wesley Brown Ross and 3) John Robert Porter.]

GREEN, Lonnie.   25 Sep 1909-23 Feb 1979. WWII. [Son of Wiley and
         Florence (Young) Green, husband of Novella Young.]

GREEN, Novella. 6 May 1921-   . [Wife of Lonnie Green.]

YOUNG, Lassie M. 21 Jun 1894-10 Apr 1979. [Daughter of Jim H. and Mattie
         (Campbell) Kirby, wife of William Hill Young.]

YOUNG, William H. 25 Jul 1874-19 Oct 1965. [William Hill, son of William
         Hillard and Fannie Frances (Wilks) Young, married 1) _____
         _____ and 2) Lassie May Kirby.]

YOUNG, Willard Edward. 24 Jun 1917-22 Jun 1987. [Son of William Hill and
         Lassie (Kirby) Young, husband of Eva Brown (div.)]

FLORA, Faye Frazier. 21 Nov 1940-21 Jul 1989. [Daughter of Richard and
         Ruth (Barker) Frazier, wife of Bruce Flora.]

CARTER, Edward T. 1925 - 7 Dec 1985. WWII. [Son of Jessie W. and Nora
         (Case) Carter, husband of Helen Sweeny.]

CARTER, Helen M. 10 Jun 1930-   . [Helen M. Sweeny, wife of Edward
         T. Carter.]

WILLIAMSON, Mary L. 1907 -   . [Mary Lorene, daughter of Jesse
         Petway and Ella Lee (Jacobs) Bryan, wife of James Nicholas
         Williamson.]

WILLIAMSON, Jim N. 1904 - 17 Feb 1967. [James Nicholas, son of Henry and
         Betty Ann (Whitlock) Williamson, husband of Mary Lorene Bryan.]

FREEDLE, Luther Mark. 22 Jun 1924-1 Jan 1988. WWII. [Son of Mark and
         Annie B. (Lance) Freedle, husband of Mary Ruth Faley.]

FREEDLE, Mary R. 1928 -   . [Mary Ruth Faley, wife of Luther Mark
         Freedle.]

EARLE, J. Pat. 19 Apr 1909-22 Oct 1986. [James Patterson, son of Jeff
         and Annie (Cagle) Earle, husband of Iva H. _____.]

WEST, Hester L. 1902-14 Apr 1968. [Husband of Daisy Cantrell, married 8
         May 1920.]

WEST, Daisy C. 1903-17 Apr 1983. [Daughter of Rev Felix and Mary (Luna) Cantrell, married 1) Hester L. West and 2) to Charlie D. Cope in Jan 1979.]

HUGHES, W.C. 28 Feb 1935-   . [Son of William Calvin Sr. and Angie V. (Phillips) Hughes, married 1) Nellie _____ and 2) to Nannie Lou (Crim) Durham.]

HUGHES, Nellie H.   1934 -   . [First wife of William Calvin Hughes, Jr., married 20 Apr 1955 (div.)]

HUGHES, Nannie Lou.   - 5 Jun 1994. [Daughter of John and Hallie Belle (Green) Crim, married 1) to _____ Durham and 2) to William Calvin Hughes.]

PATTON, James Porter. 1895 - 18 Jul 1979. [Son of John B. and Georgia (Felts) Patton, husband of Sarah Brown, married in 1939.]

PATTON, Sarah B. 1912 -   . [Sarah Brown, wife of James Porter Patton.]

WALKER, Sterling H. 14 Feb 1890-14 Apr 1966. [Son of Sam and Sarah (Hatton) Walker, husband of Jewell Foster.]

WALKER, Jewell. 1906 -   . [Jewell Foster, wife of Sterling H. Walker.]

FERGUSON, John A. 1914-9 Jun 1982. [Son of Peter and Catherine (O'Brien) Ferguson, husband of Mattie Ruth Norris.]

FERGUSON, M. Ruth. 24 Jun 1912-26 Dec 1991. [Mattie Ruth, daughter of William Alford and Mary Hoida (Miller) Norris, married 1) on 22 Jul 1927 to Cantrell Mills and 2) to John A. Ferguson.]

CLARK, Benton. 20 Nov 1898-9 May 1972. [Son of J.B. and Mary Elizabeth (Martin) Clark, husband of Chloe Allen, married 11 Jul 1921.]

CLARK, Chloe. 1901 -   . [Chloe Allen, wife of Benton Clark.]

CARTER, Jessie W. 19 Jul 1896-26 Oct 1976. [Son of Alexander O. and Amanda (Coppinger) Carter, husband of Nora Vida Case.]

CARTER, Nora V. 23 Jul 1901-25 May 1992. [Daughter of Walter Clark and Lucinda (Peden) Case, wife of Jessie W. Carter.]

YOUNG, Tom. 26 Feb 1924-24 Apr 1981. WWII. [Son of O. M. and Leona (Gilley) Young, husband of Ardith Ethel Payne.]

YOUNG, Ardith. 1921 -   . [Ardith Ethel Payne, wife of Tom Young.]

YOUNG, Thomas Dudley. 8 Oct 1949-15 Dec 1970. VIETNAM. [Son of Tom and Ardith Ethel (Payne) Young.]

COPPINGER, Marvin. 31 Dec 1918-24 Apr 1978. [Son of Wiley and Lucy (Smartt) Coppinger, husband of Dorothy Charlene Panter.]

COPPINGER, Charlene. 13 Nov 1924-   . [Dorothy Charlene, daughter of John Cooper and Cleo (Kesey) Panter, wife of 1) Marvin Coppinger and 2) Bearl Tucker, married 1 Sep 1982.]

Gardens of Memory, cont.

ELAM, Scovie L. 25 Dec 1910-30 Aug 1989. [Son of Jessie L. and Annie (Cunningham) Elam, husband of Hersie Barnes.]

ELAM, Hersie B. 1913 - 16 Oct 1988. [Daughter of James Porter and Mary Jane (Espy) Barnes, wife of Scovie L. Elam.]

ELAM, Jessie L. 29 Sep 1885-16 Jan 1968. [Jessie Lilburn, son of James "Jim" Buchanan and Rachel Ann (Shelton) Elam, husband of Sallie Ann Cunningham.]

ELAM, Sallie Ann. 6 Mar 1891-9 Jul 1990. [Daughter of Fletcher and Jane (Bottoms) Cunningham, wife of Jesse Lilburn Elam.]

TENPENNY, Georgia L. 9 Dec 1915-17 Nov 1989. [Daughter of James T. and Ada Alice (Garner) Henegar, wife of Homer Franklin Tenpenny.]

TENPENNY, Homer F. 27 Sep 1913-12 Jun 1971. Homer Franklin, son of Ernest and Eppie (Davenport) Tenpenny, husband of Georgia L. Henegar.]

BELECKI, Ruby E. 1902 - 30 Jun 1987. [Ruby Etta, daughter of James T. and Ada Alice (Garner) Henegar, wife of Leo J. Belecki.]

BELECKI, Leo J. 1898 - Jan 1994. [Son of Adam and Anastasia (Witkowski) Belecki, married 1) _____ _____ and 2) to Ruby Etta Henegar on 5 Dec 1945 in Detroit, Michigan.]

WHITLOCK, Laura Ethel. 1910-   . [Laura Ethel Lassiter, wife of James Polk Whitlock.]

WHITLOCK, James Polk. 1 Jan 1895-12 Apr 1976. [Son of James Thomas and Mahaley (Starkey) Whitlock, husband of Laura Ethel Lassiter.]

HINES, Lemmer P. 13 Jan 1899-5 Mar 1982. [Blanche Lemmer, daughter of Frank and Betty (Hill) Perry, wife of Urby U. Hines.]

HINES, Urby U. 29 Dec 1886-15 Mar 1960. [Son of William and Mollie (Wilburn) Hines, husband of Blanche Lemmer Perry, married 28 Sep 1914.]

SANDERS, Tommye E. 1906 -   . [Tommye Roberts, married 1) to _____ Eldridge and 2) to James Pope Sanders in 1950.]

SANDERS, J. Popie. 1891 - Apr 1977. [James Pope, son of Lavander Pope and Flora (Stiles) Sanders, married 1) to Ella Mai Lusk and 2) to Tommye (Roberts) Eldridge.]

HUGHES, Infant. 17 Jun 1969. [Infant of Donnie and Johnnie (Boren) Hughes.]

HUGHES, Angie. 1908 -   . [Angie V. Phillips, wife of William Calvin Hughes, Sr.]

HUGHES, Calvin. 5 Nov 1911-24 Jun 1980. [William Calvin, son of Johnnie N. and Ocie (Owens) Hughes, husband of Angie V. Phillips.]

WARREN, Alma O. 26 Nov 1913-3 Jun 1986. [Daughter of Thomas J. and Margaret Malinda "Maggie" (Curtis) O'Neal, wife of J. Ed Warren.]

WARREN, J. Ed. 9 Jan 1910-29 Jun 1976. [Son of John Tubb and Lela Mai (Jones) Warren, husband of Alma Grace O'Neal.]

McGIBONEY, Kathleen H. 5 Oct 1912-21 Jul 1987. [Daughter of Rector L. and Violet (Hitchcock) Haston, wife of Omar Cephas McGiboney, married 10 Jul 1933.]

McGIBONEY, Omar C. 8 Oct 1910-28 Mar 1981. [Son of Robert William and Millie (Baker) McGiboney, husband of Kathleen Haston.]

BAILEY, Louis Arnold. Born and died 14 Jun 1960, age 5 hours, 46 minutes. [Son of Hugh Edward and Mildred (Brewer) Bailey.]

POWERS, Howard T. 14 Nov 1934-   . [Husband of Jo Ellen Prater.]

POWERS, J. Ellen. 5 Jan 1934-   . [Daughter of Jim and Margaret Alice (St.John) Prater, married 1) on 25 Jan 1950 to Carl Morrison and 2) on 14 Mar 1954 to Howard T. Powers.]

REYNOLDS, Johnie E. 31 Dec 1902-19 Mar 1994. [Son of John B. and Mareania (Robins) Reynolds, married 1) Lora Jane Winningham and 2) Hazel Dove Safley.]

REYNOLDS, Lora Jane. 2 Mar 1905-20 Jun 1977. [Daughter of James and Della (Franklin) Winningham, wife of Johnie E. Reynolds.]

REYNOLDS, Franklin Cordell. 1933 - 19 Aug 1983. [Son of Johnie E. and Lora Jane (Winningham) Reynolds, husband of Roberta Stewart.]

COOPER, J.W. 1919 - 21 Jan 1991. [Son of James T. and Wilda Ruby (Truell) Cooper, husband of Theonia R. _____.]

COOPER, Theonia R. 1919 -   . [Wife of J.W. Cooper.]

HINES, Franklin. 1930 -   . [Son of Urby and Blanche Lemmer (Perry) Hines, husband of Mary Etta Hillis.]

HINES, Mary. 1927 -   . [Mary Etta Hillis, wife of Franklin Hines.]

TODD, Rance. 11 Feb 1878-25 Nov 1968. [Son of Hiram and Cornelia (McCabe) Todd, husband of Elizabeth Sophrena Todd.]

TODD, Elizabeth. 9 Jun 1885-20 Oct 1969. [Elizabeth Sophrena, daughter of Allie and Betty (St.John) Todd, wife of Rance Todd.]

JORDAN, Robert Lee. 9 Oct 1892-24 Apr 1975. [Son of W. Albert and Florence (Kelton) Jordan, husband of Elizabeth Gladys Lively.]

JORDAN, Elizabeth L. 1 Sep 1895-11 Oct 1964. [Daughter of Samuel Tiller and Ruth Jane (Spangler) Lively, wife of Robert Lee Jordan.]

DULANEY, Ernest Shelton. 22 Apr 1903-11 Apr 1963. [Son of James Warren and Harriet "Hattie" (Green) Dulaney, husband of Julia Lee Bain, married 9 Aug 1928.]

TENPENNY, Gregory Keith. 1957- 10 Aug 1990. [Son of Homer F. and Georgia (Henegar) Tenpenny, husband of Kathy Willene Northcutt, married 3 Jun 1988. Funeral home record has birth date as 17 Jun 1957.]

TENPENNY, Kathy Willene. 1 Jul 1962-   . [Daughter of William Ray
        and Joyce (Rogers) Northcutt, married 1) Gregory Keith Tenpenny
        and 2) _____ _____.]

DYER, William Ross. 22 Apr 1920-23 Sep 1992. [Son of William Jefferson
        and Maud (Sadler) Dyer, husband of Ethel Morgan.]

DYER, Ethel Morgan. 11 Jun 1919-   . [Wife of William Ross Dyer.]

ELAM, Infant. Born and died 16 Mar 1973. [Infant daughter of Michael R.
        and Sharon Grace (_____) Elam.]

SHIRLEY, Alton L. 17 Apr 1892-10 Jan 1969. [Son of John B. and Mollie
        (Wiser) Shirley, husband of Lela Dawson.]

HALL, Rilla Ozelle. 1919 -   . [Daughter of Ernest and Nellie
        (Shirley) Barnes, wife of 1) Paul Richard Hall and 2) Woodrow
        Wilson.]

HALL, Paul Richard. 23 Jun 1917-26 Nov 1970. WWII. [Son of Henry and
        Mamie (Helton) Hall, husband of Rilla Ozelle Barnes.]

BARNES, G.W. "Jack". 6 Jan 1925-1 Jan 1960. [Son of Ernest and Nellie
        (Shirley) Barnes, husband of Annie Crouch.]

BARNES, Nellie. 14 Jun 1899-   . [Daughter of John B. and Mollie
        (Wiser) Shirley, wife of Ernest Lee Barnes.]

BARNES, Ernest Lee. 19 Mar 1900-5 Mar 1966. [Son of James Porter and
        Mary Jane (Espy) Barnes, husband of Nellie Shirley, married 29
        Sep 1918.]

PHILLIPS, David Leon. 15 Dec 1945-13 Mar 1977. [Son of Earl and Ruth
        (Page) Phillips, husband of Judy Rogers, married 5 Jun 1963.]

HAYES, Jimmie Sue. 17 Sep 1972-19 Sep 1972. [Daughter of Morgan and
        Bonnie Sue (Phillips) Hayes.]

PHILLIPS, Earl D. Died 7 Feb 1994 age 77 years. [Son of John and Della
        (Russell) Phillips, husband of Virginia Ruth Page, married 5
        Nov 1936.]

PHILLIPS, Ruth. No dates. [Virginia Ruth Page, wife of Earl D.
        Phillips.]

PEPPER, Garry Wayne. 17 Jan 1949-23 Jan 1974. [Son of Leonard and Joetta
        (Wiseman) Pepper.]

JORDAN, Mary D. 1 Aug 1929-   . [Mary Harriet, daughter of Ernest
        Shelton and Julie Lee (Bain) Dulaney, wife of Robert Kelton
        Jordan, Sr.]

JORDAN, Robert K. Sr. 14 May 1928-23 Sep 1981. KOREA. [Son of Robert
        Lee and Elizabeth (Lively) Jordan, husband of Mary Harriett
        Dulaney, married 12 May 1946.]

CANTRELL, Lorene. 1908 -   . [Leffie Lorene, daughter of Thurman
        and Olivia A. (_____) Cantrell, wife of Leonard Clyde Cantrell]

CANTRELL, Clyde. 16 Nov 1906-27 Dec 1993. [Leonard Clyde, son of

Cleveland Avant and Julia (Estes) Cantrell, husband of Leffie Lorene Cantrell.]

STROUD, Ora Lee. 24 Jun 1896-17 Oct 1968. [Daughter of Robert and Anna (Meadows) Bailey, wife of C. Grady Stroud.]

STROUD, C. Grady. 1890 - 18 Jan 1980. [Son of George W. and Margaret (Brown) Stroud, husband of Ora Lee Bailey, married 21 Oct 1931.]

HOLCOMB, Dan. 1919 - 3 Jan 1986. WWII. [Son of H.J. and Mattie (Sutherland) Holcomb, married 1) _____ _____, 2) Georgia Smith, and 3) Sue Phifer.]

CRADDOCK, June H. 1910 - .

CRADDOCK, Robert C. 1910 - .

STEWART, Hugh West. 28 Nov 1925-19 Feb 1989. WWII. [Son of Evin and Lucille (West) Stewart.]

WOODLEE, Ollie Jones. 1914 - 11 Sep 1993. [Daughter of S.R. and Ova (Triwick) Jones, wife of John Edward Woodlee.]

WOODLEE, John Edward. 6 Apr 1909-25 Feb 1979. [Son of John L. and Malisia (Lane) Woodlee, husband of Ollie Jones.]

COPELAND, Mayo C. 19 Jun 1914-15 Aug 1981. [Mayo Clayton, son of Roscoe T. and Ethel (Crabtree) Copeland, husband of Ophia Evelyn Moffitt (div).]

COPELAND, Ethel R. 1896 - 28 Dec 1984. [Ethel Roxie, daughter of Floyd and Lucinda (Carter) Crabtree, wife of Roscoe Talmadge Copeland.]

COPELAND, Roscoe Talmadge. 1884 - Oct 1967. [Son of Thomas Carr and Mattie Elizabeth (Smith) Copeland, husband of Ethel Roxie Crabtree.]

COPELAND, Marshall Lee. 26 Oct 1921-21 Jan 1990. [Son of Roscoe and Ethel Roxie (Crabtree) Copeland, husband of Clara Juanita Bell, married 16 Jun 1944.]

GARRETT, Oren R. 1906-Nov 1964.

PATTON, Lorraine. 24 Feb 1929- . [Lorraine Scholtz, wife of Thurman Edward Patton.]

PATTON, Thurman Edward. 29 Apr 1928-10 Jun 1993. WWII, KOREA, VIETNAM. [Son of James Hershel Sr. and Annie Mai (_____) Patton.]

CRIM, Armenta. No dates. "Born happy, Departed happy."

BELL, John J. 1902 - Dec 1957. [Husband of Minnie Chambers.]

BELL, Minnie B. 1902 - 14 Aug 1993. [Daughter of Fergus and Maggie (Troglen) Chambers, wife of John J. Bell.]

ATNIP, Billie A. 1927 - .

Gardens of Memory, cont.

ATNIP, E. Daphine. 1928 -   .

ATNIP, James Carl. 1956 -   .

THOMAS, Lon Greg. 1915 - 27 Oct 1988. [Husband of Frances Jordan.]

THOMAS, Frances W. 1917 -   . [Frances W. Jordan, wife of Lon Greg
        Thomas.]

REED, Robert L. 2 May 1892-13 Mar 1969. [Robert Lee, son of Jones and
        Fannie (Allen) Reed, husband of 1) Martha Lynn and 2) Thena
        Wilson.]

REED, Martha L.   19 Mar 1881-13 Oct 1961. [Daughter of William and
        _____ (_____) Lynn, wife of Robert Lee "Bob" Reed.]

REED, Cecil A. 1915-11 Aug 1993. [Son of Robert L. and Martha (Lynn)
        Reed, husband of Wauleen Smith.]

REED, Wauleen S. 1922 -   . [Wauleen Smith, wife of Colonel Cecil
        Arvis Reed.]

CANTRELL, Howard. 25 Feb 1913-14 Jul 1992. [Son of Burgess Harold and
        Minnie (Mullican) Cantrell, husband of Georgia Alberta Parsley,
        married 21 Jan 1940.]

CANTRELL, Alberta P. 1922 -   . [Georgia Alberta, daughter of
        William G. and Pearl (Wilson) Parsley, wife of Howard
        Cantrell.]

CANTRELL, Tara Kay. 3 Feb 1971-3 Feb 1971. [Daughter of James Howard and
        _____ (Thomas) Cantrell.]

WOOD, Jessie M. 1900 -   . [Husband of Mattie Eunice Ferrell.]

WOOD, Mattie E. 10 Sep 1905-20 Apr 1974. [Mattie Eunice, daughter of
        J.E. and Emmaline (Howell) Ferrell, wife of Jessie M. Wood.]

AKINS, James F. "Jimmie" . 5 Apr 1943-19 May 1967. VIETNAM. [Son of
        Helen (Ferrell) Akins, husband of Linda Summers.]

SMITH, Collier C. 21 Jan 1911-10 Jan 1991. [Son of Haskell and Agnes May
        (Womack) Smith, husband of Odera Craddock.]

SMITH, Odera C. 1918-29 Aug 1985. [Daughter of Haley F. and Ruby
        (Harris) Craddock, wife of Collier C. Smith.]

SWINDELL, Daniel Loyde. 3 Aug 1904-19 Nov 1973. [Son of Hatton and Elva
        (Morris) Swindell, husband of Edith Gillette.]

WILKINSON, Robert Lee. 29 Nov 1898-9 Jan 1971. [Son of Cleveland and
        Tabitha Ann (Jaco) Wilkinson, husband of Mary Etta Potter.]

WILKINSON, Mary Potter. 7 Jul 1900-19 Jan 1987. [Mary Etta, daughter of
        Leander K. and Rebecca (Patton) Potter, wife of Robert Lee
        Wilkinson.]

PRATER, Glenn D. 1917-Dec 1974.

CHAPMAN, Laura Cornelia. 26 Oct 1896-15 May 1969. [Daughter of Charles

Gardens of Memory, cont.

Amos and Cynthia Allie (Watkins) Moore, wife of Tom A. Chapman
married 7 Apr 1915 (div.)]

CHAPMAN, Roy E. 22 Feb 1916-4 Apr 1980. [Roy Edward, son of Tom A. and
Laura Cornelia (Moore) Chapman, husband of Nora Lee Turner.]

CHAPMAN, Nora Lee. 21 Mar 1921- . [Daughter of Jim and Eula
(_____) Turner, wife or Roy Edward Chapman.]

WILSON, Sharon Goodlett. 22 Oct 1941-13 Dec 1962. [Daughter of Clifford
and Marjorie (Walker) Goodlett, wife of Stanley Cecil Wilson.]

MILLER, Levoy "Bill". 14 Jan 1926-20 Feb 1978. [Son of Worth and Dora
(Scott) Miller, husband of Dorotha Boyd.]

MILLER, Dorotha Boyd. 1924 - . [Wife of Levoy Miller.]

WALSH, Nola C. 20 Sep 1895-24 Aug 1977. [Daughter of Alonza and Lizzie
(Milstead) Pugh, second wife of William Walsh.]

LANCE, Clowdy Hebron. 16 Sep 1910- . [Husband of Ruth Simons.]

LANCE, Ruth S. 3 Dec 1909-14 Sep 1992. [Daughter of James Hannibal and
Martha Elizabeth (Quick) Simons, wife of Clowdy Lance.]

TALLEY, Catherine L. 1910 - .

TALBERT, Mary Lou. 1911 - . [Mary Lou Burks, wife of Aubrie L.
Talbert.]

TALBERT, Aubrie L. 1907 - 23 Apr 1982. [Son of Lee Roy and Octia (Moore)
Talbert, husband of Mary Lou Burks.]

TALBERT, Octia Moore. 3 Oct 1884-6 Apr 1949. [Octia Susanna, daughter of
William and Adeline (Burks) Moore, wife of Lee Roy Talbert.]

TALBERT, Lee Roy. 28 Sep 1885-7 Mar 1960. [Husband of Octia Moore.]

DAVENPORT, Pauline. 1919 - 18 Jul 1991. [Daughter of Charlie C. and Lou
Ann (Cherry) Couch, married 1) to Richard Davenport and 2) to
Willie I. Womack who died in 1975.]

DAVENPORT, Richard. 16 Aug 1920-26 Feb 1965. [Son of Arthur and Betty
(Certain) Davenport, husband of Pauline Couch.]

CANTRELL, Gary Lynn. 3 May 1950-8 Oct 1972. [Son of Brackett and Hazel
Nadine (Overall) Cantrell. Single.]

CANTRELL, Hazel Nadine. 7 Jun 1932-22 Nov 1993. [Daughter of Bright and
Minnie (Bratten) Overall, wife of Brackett Cantrell.]

MAHAR, Pamela Jo. 1957-5 Aug 1977. ["Pammy", daughter of Paul and _____
(_____) Mahar.]

UNDERWOOD, Delton. 1913 - .

UNDERWOOD, Charles W. 1916 - .

STUBBLEFIELD, R. Douglas. 26 Feb 1933-5 Jan 1963. [Son of Bill and Belle
Z. (Turner) Stubblefield.]

11

Gardens of Memory, cont.

STUBBLEFIELD, Bill W. 4 Dec 1905-2 Nov 1988. [Son of George and Belle (Ware) Stubblefiled, husband of Belle Z. Turner.]

DOWNS, Laura B. 1907 - . [Wife of Bill Downs.]

DOWNS, B.M. 17 Oct 1903-17 Feb 1977. [Bill Morris, son of J.W. and Alice (Walker) Downs.]

PERRY, Garry Steven. 10 May 1952-27 Jul 1974. [Son of Royce L. and Sepal (Youngblood) Perry. Single.]

ROGERS, Willie Thomas. 7 Jun 1914-23 Feb 1991. US Army. [Son of William Silas and Mary Bell (Tosh) Rogers, husband of Dorothy Jewell Walls, married 27 Aug 1949 in Rossville, GA.]

ROGERS, Dorothy J. 18 Jan 1930- . [Dorothy Jewell, daughter of John and Nancy (Fuson) Walls of DeKalb County, TN, wife of William Thomas Rogers.]

MARTIN, Wilson. 13 Feb 1893-26 May 1975. US Army. [Son of Homer and Tilly (Williams) Martin, husband of Wilsie Le _____.]

MARTIN, Wilsie Le. 1893 - Jan 1969. [Wife of Wilson Martin.]

FLATT, Lee William. 13 Jan 1913-20 Mar 1990. [Son of Jefferson Douglass and Ova (Birdwell) Flatt, husband of Catherine Pruett.]

FLATT, Catherine Pruett. 1919 - . [Wife of Lee William Flatt.]

PRATER, Sam A. 16 Jun 1893-5 Jul 1963. [Sam Arley, son of Moses Ulyssis and Tennessee (Collins) Prater, husband of Mary Ellen Lowe.]

PRATER, Mary E. 8 Jun 1893-28 Jul 1974. [Daughter of John and Jennie (Burnett) Lowe, wife of Sam A. Prater.]

WETZEL, Eugene L. 20 Jun 1911-31 Oct 1974. US Marines. [Son of Alonzo and Minnie (Bridges) Wetzel, husband of Ronalda Wright.]

WETZEL, Ronalda W. 24 May 1916- . [Ronalda Wright, wife of Eugene L. Wetzel.]

SIPE, John Paul. 15 Jul 1930-27 Nov 1982. KOREA, VIETNAM.

DODSON, Charles Clinton. 26 May 1878-25 Mar 1964. [Son of James Campbell and Martha (Haston) Dodson, husband of Sue Grissom.]

DODSON, Sue G. 1887 - 15 Apr 1969. [Daughter of Joe and Sally (Holder) Grissom, wife of Charles Clinton Dodson.]

QUINN, Leslie L., Sr. 21 Mar 1885-5 Jan 1962. [Son of Lemuel Q. and _____ (_____) Quinn, husband of Nellie Finley.]

QUINN, Nell F. 1892 - Feb 1964. [Nell Finley, wife of Leslie L. Quinn, Sr.]

GANN, Cora Estelle. 3 Jun 1929- . [Daughter of Delbert Clifford and Cora (Green) Cantrell, wife of William Hoyt Gann.]

GANN, William Hoyt. 4 Feb 1916-7 May 1994. [Son of Harrison and Amanda (Parsley) Gann, married Cora Estelle Cantrell on 10 Jun 1949.]

Gardens of Memory, cont.

PHILLIPS, Evelyn Elizabeth. 1916 - Sep 1972.

PHILLIPS, James Robert. 1914 - Feb 1978.

BARLOW, Wilma S. 9 Apr 1931-3 Feb 1990. [Wilma Sue, daughter of Herman and Lizzie (Caldwell) Cutts, wife of Johnnie W. Barlow.]

BARLOW, Johnnie W. 1926 -   . [Husband of Wilma Sue Cutts.]

COPPINGER, William A. 23 Jun 1909-28 Jul 1987. [Son of Gilbert and Martha (Hobbs) Coppinger, husband of Amy Lee Stoner.]

COPPINGER, Amy Lee. 18 Jul 1911-13 Feb 1986. [Daughter of Jesse and Martha Abigail (Coppinger) Stoner, wife of William A. Coppinger.]

COPPINGER, Jesse Willie. 8 Apr 1930-4 May 1992. [Son of Willie A. and Amy Lee (Stoner) Coppinger, husband of Lavern Brady.]

COPPINGER, Lavern. 6 May 1933-   . [Daughter of Walter T. and Mary Ethel (Christian) Brady, wife of Jesse Willie Coppinger.]

FLATT, Lola D. 2 Apr 1915-   . [Lola Davis, wife of Hulon D. Flatt.]

FLATT, Hulon D. 2 Dec 1914-14 Jun 1981. [Son of Jefferson Douglass and Ova (Birdwell) Flatt, husband of Lola Davis, married in 1940.]

WEBB, Muriel D. 26 May 1930-30 Dec 1977. [Muniel Dean, daughter of Herman and Vera (Holder) Wilson, wife of Billy Ray Webb.]

WEBB, Billy Ray. 5 Jan 1928-   . [Son of Andrew Jackson and Shellia Elfleta (Cantrell) Webb, husband of Muriel Dean Wilson.]

WALKER, Frances. 23 Jan 1930-   . [Daughter of Andrew Jackson and Shellia Elfleta (Cantrell) Webb, wife of Edward Walker.]

WALKER, Edward. 3 Mar 1928-   . [Husband of Frances Webb.]

GARRETT, Nellie M. 1907-23 May 1990. [Nellie Parker, wife of William Thomas Garrett.]

GARRETT, William T. 24 Sep 1901-24 Oct 1977. WWI. [Son of Virgil and Mary (Adams) Garrett, husband of Nellie Parker.]

COPENHAVER, Bess M. 7 Jun 1908-   . [Wife of Harry V. Copenhaver.]

COPENHAVER, Harry V. 7 Apr 1907-   . [Son of Henry Valentine and Mollie Eliza (Duncan) Copenhaver, husband of Bell M. _____.]

JULIAN, Florence M. 8 Aug 1921-   . [Daughter of William Jefferson and Maud (Sadler) Dyer, wife of Lloyd Julian.]

JULIAN, Lloyd. 2 Aug 1917-20 Nov 1983. [Son of Will and Mary (Watkins) Julian, husband of Florence M. Dyer.]

HILLIS, Melvin. 30 Jan 1914-14 Nov 1985. [Son of Garmon and Laura Ann (Roberts) Hillis, husband of Mildred Clendenon.]

Gardens of Memory, cont.

HILLIS, Mildred.   17 Sep 1921-   . [Daughter of James Newton and
        Nettie (Bouldin) Clendenon, wife of Melvin Hillis.]

GRIMMETT, Nancy L.   1896 - 17 Apr 1973. [Nancy Viola Lewther, wife of
        George Bayless Grimmett.]

GRIMMETT, George B.   16 Jan 1876-26 Jul 1970. [Son of Thomas and Betty
        (Bayless) Grimmett, husband of Nancy Viola Lewther.]

GRIMMETT, Charles E.   27 Sep 1927-13 May 1969. [Charles Edwin, son of
        George B. and Nancy (Lewther) Grimmett.]

LOCKE, W.C. 1915 -   .

LOCKE, Nora E. 1919 -   .

TUCK, E.J. 3 May 1900-13 Nov 1965. [Son of Ed and Annie (Braizer) Tuck,
        husband of Violet Lillian Greer, married in 1924.]

TUCK, Violet Lillian Greer.   [No other information]

IRBY, Mary Ruth. 1919 - 4 Jan 1974. [Daughter of Sidney and Emma Nevado
        (_____) Davis, wife of Unice Irby.]

MADEWELL, James Willard. 11 Sep 1914-2 Feb 1981. WWII. [Son of Arthur
        and Ethel (McBride) Madewell, husband of Mildred Elizabeth
        Holman.]

MADEWELL, Mildred E.   31 May 1909-18 Jun 1991. [Daughter of George and
        Catherine (Detzel) Holman, wife of James William Madewell.]

BRATCHER, Abbie C. 11 May 1902-16 Dec 1944. [Abbie Coleen, daughter of
        Colonel Thurman and Kate (Bailey) Holder, wife of John E.
        Bratcher, Sr.]

BRATCHER, John E. Sr. 4 Mar 1900-3 Apr 1965. [Son of Thomas W. and
        Hannah (Paris) Bratcher, husband of Abbie Coleen Holder.]

STEWART, Jessie M. 1912 -   . [Jessie M. Bratcher, second wife of
        Leburn R. Stewart.]

STEWART, Leburn R.   17 Feb 1906-6 Mar 1975. [Son of Tim and Hattie
        (Hollingsworth) Stewart, married 1) Nannie Lee Bratcher who is
        buried at Blues Hill Cemetery and 2) Jessie M. Bratcher.]

CANTRELL, G. Fate.   27 Aug 1909-   . [Husband of Annie Lucille
        Newby.]

CANTRELL, A. Lucille. 19 Jul 1912-9 May 1976. [Annie Lucille, daughter of
        Luther and Eula Vic (Jones) Newby.]

HALL, Irvin Q.   14 Aug 1889-15 Nov 1976. [Son of Willard and Anna
        (Mattox) Hall, husband of Mattie Ruth Davis.]

HALL, M. Ruth. 1907-25 Nov 1992. [Mattie Ruth Davis, wife of Irvin Quincy
        Hall.]

WHITEAKER, Leonard. 1925 -   . [Son of Smith and Gertrude (Perry)
        Whiteaker, husband of Alice L. Hillis.]

WHITEAKER, Alice L. 1930 - . [Daughter of Solomon and Nannie Lou (Hillis) Hillis, wife of Leonard Whiteaker.]

CAMPBELL, Taylor B. Jr. 1927 - 21 May 1994. WWII. [Son of Beecher and Luphema (Tenpenny) Campbell, husband of Lourene Scott.]

CANTRELL, Elizabeth E. 1919 - . [Elizabeth E. Malone, wife of George Lawrence Cantrell, Jr.]

CANTRELL, George L. 1917 - 3 Aug 1991. [Son of George Lawrence, Sr. and Joie Ann (Hardcastle) Cantrell, husband of Elizabeth Malone.]

RUFFIN, Harold C. 1908 - 2 Jul 1991. [Husband of Lorraine Angela Vandorne.]

RUFFIN, Lorraine A. 1920 - . [Lorraine Angela Vandorne, wife of Harold C. Ruffin.]

DAVIS, Wandalee. 1932 - .

DAVIS, Reuben L. 1928 - .

MUNCEY, Doris B. 10 May 1926-Dec 1993. [Doris Elizabeth, daughter of Moscow and Lula Azzaline (Thompson) Bogle, wife of Lester Doak Muncey.]

MUNCEY, Lester D. 1923 - 9 Jun 1994. [Lester Doak, son of George Washington and Maggie (Pepper) Muncey, husband of Doris Elizabeth Bogle, married 6 Nov 1943.]

NORTHERN, Leatrice B. 26 Nov 1909- .

NORTHERN, Paul A. 21 Sep 1905- .

NOVAK, Francene Catherine. 13 Sep 1953-3 Apr 1972. [Daughter of Wilburn and Rosemary (Bauer) Novak.]

NEAL, Phillip Van. 25 Aug 1963-4 Aug 1970. [Son of W.A. and _____ (Priest) Neal.]

NEAL, Frank A. 1903 - 15 Jul 1971. [Son of Melvin Russell and Charlie Florence (Bennett) Neal, husband of Lizzie Mae Blanks.]

NEAL, Lizzie M. 1903 - 9 Dec 1987. [Daughter of Edward A. and Martha Ella (Richardson) Blanks, wife of Frank A. Neal.]

NOVAK, Nicholas Charles. 28 May 1898-15 Jan 1985. [Son of Frank and Catherine (Link) Novak, "He had been wed for 63 years to the former Grace Soetibier."]

NOVAK, Grace Jane. 27 Jul 1898-16 Dec 1988. [Daughter of Henry and Matilda (Landing) Soetibier, wife of Nicholas Charles Novak.]

CHASTAIN, William Kenneth. 21 Jan 1912-21 Jan 1989. WWII. [Son of Henry and Hassie (Farless) Chastain, husband of Elizabeth Madewell.]

CHASTAIN, Elizabeth M. 31 Jan 1927-7 Sep 1976. [Daughter of Arthur and Ethel (McBride) Madewell, married 1) _____ _____, 2) George Carson Newby, 3) Howard Martin, 4) Carl Gulley, and 5) to William Kenneth Chastain.]

Gardens of Memory, cont.

CROUCH, Charles. 23 Dec 1899-10 May 1982. [Son of Samuel Mack and Mary Eunice (Snipes) Crouch, husband of Aline Stone.]

CROUCH, Aline Stone. 11 Nov 1906- . [Wife of Charles Crouch.]

BRADLEY, Cloris. 29 Apr 1915-28 Jan 1992. [Daughter of Clarence and Bessie (Wolfe) Bradley. Single.]

BRADLEY, Bessie W. 24 Dec 1893-29 Feb 1976. [Daughter of John M. and Fannie (Holley) Wolfe, wife of Clarence Bradley.]

BRADLEY, W.W. "Doc". 1913 - 26 May 1965. [Woodrow Wilson, son of Clarence and Bessie (Wolfe) Bradley, husband of Lourine (Thrower) Crosslin.]

BRADLEY, Lourine Thrower. 1912 - 19 Mar 1971. [Daughter of James Thomas and Mary Emeline (Stubblefield) Thrower, wife of 1) William Justin Crosslin, married 23 May 1929 and 2) W.W. Bradley, married 28 Aug 1939.]

CROSSLIN, Charles Lee. 16 Dec 1934-18 Jun 1970. KOREA. [Son of William Justin and Lourine (Thrower) Bradley Crosslin.]

WILLIAMS, Sidney Lee. 18 Apr 1886-19 Sep 1978. [Son of Sidney Sherwood and Olive Alice (_____) Williams.]

PRIOR, Roger A. 12 Sep 1892-12 Sep 1985. [Roger Arlington, son of Howard H. and Margaret Jan (Bradley) Prior, husband of Nelma K. _____.]

PRIOR, Nelma K. 1894 - 9 Sep 1979. [Wife of Roger Arlington Prior.]

YOUNGBLOOD, Leonard H. 1 May 1924- . [Son of Robert and Sammie (Tittle) Youngblood, married 1) Bettie Hillis, 2) Juanita Chisam, 3) Martha Sue (Ferrell) Dodd on 20 Jan 1968, and 4) Sandra McCord.]

YOUNGBLOOD, Juanita C. 23 Sep 1933-21 Jan 1966. [Daughter of Tom Lee and Nannie (Webb) Chisam, second wife of Leonard Youngblood.]

YOUNGBLOOD, Martha Sue. 25 Jan 1935-30 Sep 1969. [Daughter of J.B. and Jennie Mai (Tassey) Ferrell, married 1) _____ Dodd and 2) Leonard H. Youngblood.]

KEEL, Charles Edward. 6 Feb 1927-16 May 1990. WWII. [Son of Byron and Rena (Jarrell) Keel, husband of Louise Boyd, married 21 Apr 1945.]

KEEL, Louise Boyd. 13 Jul 1925 - . [Daughter of Alf and _____ (_____) Boyd, wife of Charles Edward Keel.]

RIGSBY, James Dewey. 23 Aug 1926- .

RIGSBY, Barbara Ann. 9 Jul 1933- .

BROWN, John L. 15 Apr 1892-18 Feb 1958. [Son of Harvey L. and Mary E. (Richards) Brown, husband of Grace B. Jones.]

BROWN, Grace B. 16 Oct 1896-19 Nov 1970. [Daughter of George and Ida (Thompkins) Jones, wife of John L. Brown.]

Gardens of Memory, cont.

BROWN, Paul Wayne. 22 Jan 1941-23 Mar 1941. [Son of John L. and Grace B.
        (Jones) Brown.]

PENNINGTON, Jodie Fred. 13 Jun 1905-6 Jan 1987. US Army. [Son of Joseph
        and Alice Elizabeth (_____) Pennington, husband of Flossie
        Meadows, married 4 Dec 1933.]

PENNINGTON, Flossie. 1910 -   . [Flossie Meadows, wife of Jodie
        Fred Pennington.]

MAYFIELD, Dessie B. 1922 - 27 Apr 1979. [Daughter of Robert and Sammie
        (Tittle) Youngblood, wife of Carl J. Mayfield.]

MAYFIELD, Carl J. 1920 -   . [Husband of Dessie B. Youngblood.]

RADER, Louise M. 1911 -   .

RADER, Joe B.   1910 - Dec 1973.

PERRY, John B. 9 Aug 1900-30 Dec 1983.   [John Boyd, son of Frank and
        Elizabeth (Hill) Perry, husband of Mamie Ruth Hasting, married
        20 Aug 1928.]

PERRY, Mamie R. 30 Apr 1907-13 Apr 1986. [Mamie Ruth Hasting, wife of
        John Boyd Perry.]

GILISPIE, Adolphus D. 1920 - 29 Aug 1993. [Son of Levi and Lucy (Farley)
        Gilispie, husband of Mary K. _____.]

GILISPIE, Mary K. 1922 -   . [Wife of Adolphus D. Gilispie.]

TEMPLETON, Audrey Aileen. 12 Nov 1919-10 Apr 1984. [Daughter of Victor
        and Daisy (McElroy) Johnson, wife of Joseph Allen Templeton.]

TEMPLETON, Joseph A. 3 Sep 1915-27 Oct 1987. [Husband of Audrey Aileen
        Johnson.]

SWIFT, Flossye E. 1911 - 23 Jul 1983. [Daughter of John Wesley and Norie
        Bell (Carr) Higginbottom, wife of Claude M. Swift.]

SWIFT, Claude M. 30 Sep 1907-29 May 1987. [Son of Daniel and Annie Lowe
        (Dunn) Swift, husband of Flossye E. Swift.]

LASSITER, Alton. 1904 - 8 Jan 1974. [Alton Parks, son of Bob and Nancy
        (Parker) Lassiter.]

SINKS, Albert. 10 Jun 1908-9 May 1974. US Army. [Son of Will and Amanda
        (Ballard) Sinks, husband of Bessie Elise Rhea.]

SINKS, Bessie Elise.   Died 25 Mar 1991. [Daughter of Isaac and Frankie
        Lee (Smart) Rhea, wife of Albert Sinks.]

CARR, Nobel R. 1918 -   .

CARR, Meda B. 1921 -   .

ADAMSON, Ewell Estelle. 1902 - 28 Oct 1986. [Ewell E. Cunningham, wife
        of 1) _____ Payne, 2) Horace C. Hogan (married 16 Feb 1922),
        and 3) Jesse Walling Adamson (married 21 Jun 1974).]

ADAMSON, Jesse W.   21 Jun 1902-16 Aug 1976.   [Son of Bethel Allen and
        Zadie (Hildreth) Adamson, husband of 1) Annie Laura Warren and
        2) Ewell Estell Cunningham.]

ADAMSON, Annie L. 14 May 1910-2 Feb 1967. [Daughter of Jessie Walter and
        Ollie May (Lentz) Warren, wife of Jesse Walling Adamson.]

ADAMSON, Norman W. 1938 -   . [Son of Jesse Walling and Annie Laura
        (Warren) Adamson.]

ADAMSON, Peggy A. 1943 -   .

CHAMBERS, Harry G.   1924 - 20 Jan 1988. WWII. [Son of James Allen and
        Sara Elizabeth (Bell) Chambers, husband of Velma Copeland.]

CHAMBERS, Velma R. 1924 - 30 Sep 1990. [Daughter of Roscoe and Ethel
        (Crabtree) Copeland, wife of Harry G. Chambers.]

HALL, Johnnie J. 1905 - 12 Feb 1993. [Johnnie Jackson, son of James
        Alexander and Martha Rebecca (Haley) Hall, husband of Artie
        Deberry.]

HALL, Artie Deberry. 1909 -   . [Wife of Johnnie Jackson Hall.]

CANTRELL, Robert Herman. 24 Dec 1894-16 Feb 1988. WWI. [Son of Berry Y.
        and Mae (Childress) Cantrell, husband of Emma Mai Pennington.]

CANTRELL, Emma Mai. 28 Mar 1899-27 Jan 1978. [Daughter of Joseph and
        Allie (Davey) Pennington, wife of Robert Herman Cantrell,
        married 9 Sep 1917.]

GIPSON, Amanda Renee. 10 Feb 1975-26 Sep 1984. ["Daughter of Mrs. Jane
        Drake Gipson and daughter and stepdaughter of Jim and Clara
        Gipson, all of Manchester.]

HENNESSEE, Icie Lavone. 19 Feb 1903-10 Sep 1977. [Daughter of Will and
        Allie (Milstead) Nunley, wife of Arcie Womack Hennessee,
        married 21 May 1921.]

MAYNARD, K.T. 1937 - Apr 1989. [Son of Wortie B. and Edna (Williamson)
        Maynard.]

MAYNARD, W.B. 1910 - 15 Jan 1985. [Wortie B., son of Kelly and Liza
        (Eubanks) Maynard, husband of Edna Williamson.]

MAYNARD, Edna W. 1910 -   . [Wife of Wortie B. Maynard.]

MYERS, Johnny Estell. 27 Jun 1910-23 Apr 1983. [Son of James Monroe and
        Rutha (Walling) Myers, husband of Theresa Taft.]

MYERS, Theresa T. 18 Mar 1913-2 Jun 1992. [Daughter of Thomas M. and
        Maud Emily (Graham) Taft, wife of Johnny Estell Myers.]

REED, Lucy Emma. 22 Sep 1926-1 Jun 1980. [Emma Louvina, daughter of
        Organ B. and Cleo Beatrice (Boyd) Davis, wife of William
        Sanford Reed.]

REED, William S. 1925 - 8 Jun 1993. [William Sanford, son of Sanford
        and Annie Mae (Herring) Reed, husband of Emma Louvina "Lucy"
        Davis.]

KELSEY, Stanley T. 1942 - 21 Mar 1992. [Son of Vester B. and Christine (Southard) Kelsey, husband of Nancy Louise Greene, married 23 Dec 1961.]

KELSEY, Nancy L. 17 Jun 1941 -   . [Daughter of Sammie A. and Mildred Lucille (McWhorter) Green, wife of Stanley T. Kelsey.]

KELSEY, Christine S. 1923 - 5 Mar 1990. [Daughter of William and Mary Elizabeth (Ferguson) Sourthard, wife of Vester B. Kelsey.]

KELSEY, Vester B. 7 Sep 1914 -   . [Husband of 1) Mary Christine Southard, and 2) Roberta (Crawley) Turner.]

WYATT, Michael D. 10 Jul 1943-13 May 1970. [Son of Theodore R. and Bea (_____) Wyatt, husband of Jewel Adams.]

PARKER, Beulah J. 23 Dec 1888- 28 Apr 1978. [Daughter of Nort and Caroline (Brown) Stroud, wife of Robert T. Parker.]

PARKER, Robert T. 3 Oct 1886-11 Jun 1978. [Son of Jim and Dovie (McAfee) Parker, husband of Beulah J. Stroud.]

VANDAGRIFF, Willard. 13 Mar 1917-14 May 1985. [Son of James Drew and Willie Flora (Wilson) Vandagriff, husband of Robbie Parker.]

POWELL, E. Elizabeth. 1926 -   . [Elizabeth Watson, wife of Willard F. Powell.]

POWELL, Willard F. 2 Jul 1925-24 Jan 1975. US Navy. [Son of Willard Franklin and Wilma (_____) Powell, husband of Elizabeth Watson.]

KEITH, Helen Thomason. 19 Aug 1922-6 Oct 1984. [Daughter of Guy D. and Georgia Elizabeth (Meury) Thomason, wife of _____ Keith.]

THOMASON, Georgia Elizabeth. 1903 - 14 Jan 1975. [Daughter of Frank and Bessie (Tarter) Meury, wife of Guy D. Thomason.]

THOMASON, Guy D. 1902 - 19 May 1983. [Son of Nelson and Mamie (Barlow) Thomason, husband of Georgia Elizabeth Meury, married Jan 1921.]

YOUNGBLOOD, Ernest M. 17 Oct 1920-2 Aug 1988. US Army. [Ernest Main, son of Robert and Sammie (Tittle) Youngblood, husband of 1) Melvina Austin and 2) Ollie _____.]

YOUNGBLOOD, Melvina A. 18 Oct 1917-10 Jul 1975. [Daughter of Joseph Edward and Rachel Evelee (Medley) Austin, granddaughter of William and Mary (Dodson) Medley and Granddaughter of Thomas and Mary E. (Miller) Austin, wife of Ernest Main Youngblood.]

PARSON, Calvin A. 6 Aug 1919-11 Jul 1990. [Son of Conger and Mary (Wicker) Parson, husband of Marjorie Allison.]

FRAZIER, Spencer Otis. 5 Oct 1910-27 Mar 1991. [Son of Robert and Martha (Puckett) Frazier, husband of Margie Lou Allison.]

FRAZIER, Margie Lou Allison. 31 Aug 1908-   . Daughter of James Dow and Virgie Caline (Austin) Allison, wife of Spencer Otis Frazier.]

Gardens of Memory, cont.

QUINN, Charles Vance. 6 Feb 1911-5 Aug 1985. [Son of David R. and Bertha (Melton) Quinn, husband of Martha Pauline Simrell.]

QUINN, Martha Pauline. 25 Apr 1911-31 Mar 1986. [Daughter of Henry and Beulah (Blankenship) Simrell, wife of Charles Vance Quinn.]

WATSON, Paul F. 1928 -   . [Husband of Janice L. Jones.]

WATSON, Janice L. 1933 - 22 May 1992. [Janice Louise, daughter of Harry Lee and hazel (Arnold) Jones, wife of Paul F. Watson.]

RUSSELL, J.T. 1916 - 3 Dec 1988. [John Tillman, son of W.M. and Clara (West) Russell, husband of Sue Redmon.]

RUSSELL, Sue R. 1918 - 2 Jul 1992. [Daughter of Henry and Rowena (Pennington) Redmon, wife of John Tillman Russell.]

BECK, Charles Robert. 23 Jun 1899-12 Jun 1975. [Son of William Bedford and Gordo (Lee) Beck, husband of Della Mae Chafin.]

BECK, Della Mae. 11 Sep 1902-7 Nov 1983. [Daughter of Henry and Abbie (_____) Chafin, wife of Charles Robert Beck.]

ROWLAND, Paul J. 30 Oct 1928 -   . [Son of Levon and Flora Belle (Green) Rowland, husband of Billie Joyce Moore, married 7 Dec 1951.]

ROWLAND, Billie J. 9 Feb 1934 -   . [Billie Joyce, daughter of William and Georgie Meade (Hayes) Moore, wife of Paul J. Rowland.]

WENZEL, Bernard H. 15 Mar 1906-12 Dec 1991. [Bernard Henry, son of Fredrick and Lena (_____) Wenzel, husband of Flora Belle (Green) Rowland.]

WENZEL, Flora B. 21 Dec 1907-27 Oct 1975. [Flora Green, married 1) Levon Rowland on 29 Oct 1927, div.) and 2) Bernard Henry Wenzel.]

CLEMONS, Robert W. 4 Apr 1902-7 Jan 1975. [Son of Alex and Nancy Elizabeth (Johnson) Clemons, husband of Willie Irene Rogers.]

CLEMONS, Willie Irene. 29 Sep 1920-4 Nov 1980. [Daughter of Ira and Nora (Lee) Rogers, wife of Robert Williams Clemons.]

TALLEY, Raleigh M. 1921 -   . [Son of Claude and Maude (Thompson) Talley, husband of Hazel Dyer.]

TALLEY, Hazel D. 1924 - 14 Mar 1988. [Daughter of Jeff and Maude (Sadler) Dyer, wife of Raleigh M. Talley.]

HASTON, Edward James. 7 May 1926-2 Dec 1981. KOREA. [Son of Edgar Lee and Lola Mae (Morris) Haston, husband of Rosemary Manis.]

HASTON, Rosemary Manis. 17 Dec 1928-   . [Wife of Edward James Haston.]

DRIVER, Garlin Elwood. 8 Jun 1916-20 Dec 1983. [Son of Henry P. and Effie L. (Love) Driver, husband of Vada Lorene _____.]

DENTON, Ray O. 11 Nov 1904-26 Jun 1993. [Ray Overton, son of James

William and Flora Ann (Clark) Denton, husband of Grace Katherine Butcher.]

DENTON, Grace K. 26 Dec 1906 - . [Wife of Ray Overton Denton, married 25 Nov 1926.]

CRAVEN, John William. 11 Dec 1916- . [Husband of Sarah Mai Melton, married 27 Dec 1939.]

CRAVEN, Sarah Mai. 23 Dec 1923-14 Apr 1986. [Daughter of Willie and Emma (_____) Melton, wife of John William Craven.]

CRAVEN, Tracy Louise. 2 Dec 1967-21 Jan 1972.

HYATT, Clara Edna. 25 Oct 1929-26 Jan 1969. [Daughter of Arch Edley and Lucy (Ward) Hillis, wife of Lawrence E. Hyatt.]

HONEYCUTT, George Larry. 16 May 1958-16 May 1958. [Son of William Luther and Emma Lorine (Leath) Honeycutt.}

HONEYCUTT, William L. 14 May 1910-12 Feb 1980. WWII. [William Luther, son of William and Sallie (Harvey) Honeycutt, husband of Emma Lorine Leath.]

HONEYCUTT, Emma L. 1917 - . [Emma Lorine Leath, wife of William Luther Honeycutt.]

TALLEY, Claude B. 20 Apr 1884-19 Mar 1965. [Claude Barbee, son of Thomas and Jane (Baker) Talley, husband of Maude E. Thomison.]

TALLEY, Maude E. 14 Oct 1888-17 Nov 1975. [Daughter of Charlie and Mary Lodema (Walker) Thomison, wife of Claude Barbee Talley.]

CAMPBELL, Millard Mahlon. 15 Aug 1893-27 Jul 1966. WWI. [Son of William Huffman and Nora (Rhodes) Campbell, husband of Bertha Savanah York.]

CAMPBELL, Bertha. 17 Feb 1899-13 Mar 1966. [Daughter of Alton and Bunie (Whitman) York, wife of Millard Mahlon Campbell.]

HARRIS, Lula Allison. 16 Nov 1918- . [Daughter of James Dow and Virgie Caline (Austin) Allison, wife of Bill Harris (div.)]

ALLISON, Albert A. 1910- .

ALLISON, James Dow. 11 May 1886-2 Oct 1974. [Son of William Carter and Lou (Gracey) Allison, husband of Virgie Caline Austin.]

ALLISON, Virgie Caline. 23 Apr 1887-10 Dec 1967. [Daughter of Albert and Avo (Davis) Austin, wife of James Dow Allison.]

WINTON, Andy J. 22 Jan 1882-13 Jun 1963. [Son of Samuel Houston and Ara (Lawrence) Winton, husband of Dessie Jane Bryan.]

WINTON, Dessie Jane. 4 Apr 1886-2 Sep 1980. [Daughter of George Abner and Sarah Ann Isabel (Braley) Bryan, wife of Andy J. Winton.]

MOFFITT, Pauline S. 5 Jan 1925- . [Daughter of Andrew Marshall and Emma (Haley) Scott, wife of B.F. Moffitt.]

Gardens of Memory, cont.

MOFFITT, B.F. 22 Mar 1920-15 Apr 1987. WWII. [Son of Herbert and Ruth
          (Stubblefield) Moffitt, husband of Pauline Scott.]

CAMPBELL, Mazel L. 28 Mar 1915-31 Oct 1976. [Mazel Louise, daughter of
          Harrison Joseph and Della Elizabeth (Paris) Gilbert, wife of
          Willie Selmer Campbell, married 19 Aug 1930.]

CAMPBELL, Willie S. 1910 - 30 Oct 1983. [Son of John D. and Annie (King)
          Campbell, husband of Mazel Louise Gilbert.]

MARTIN, Cyrus Haston. 24 May 1894-17 Feb 1969. WWI. [Husband of Sallie
          Elizabeth Locke, married 9 Oct 1919.]

MARTIN, Sallie. Died 1 Aug 1979. [Daughter of Will and American (Denton)
          Locke, wife of Cyrus Haston Martin.]

MARTIN, Elwood.   [No other information.]

HUTCHINGS, Mary Ann Moore. 1 Nov 1904-25 Sep 1986. [Daughter of Will and
          Elizabeth (Robinson) Moore, wife of Curry Sylvanus Hutchings.]

HUTCHINGS, Curry Sylvanus. 14 Nov 1894-28 Dec 1975. [Son of Amon and
          Catherine (Barkley) Hutchins, husband of Mary Ann Moore.]

GRIFFIN, Llewllyn. 1922 -   . [Daughter of Curry Sylvanus and Mary
          Ann (Moore) Hutchings, wife of Carl Elmo Griffin.]

GRIFFIN, Carl Elmo. 1919 -   .

SCOTT, Thomas Franklin. Died 15 Jun 1991. [Son of Douglas E. and Kitty
          (Rittenberry) Scott, husband of Josephine George.]

SCOTT, Thomas Edward. 19 Sep 1950-1 Aug 1958. [Son of Thomas Franklin
          and Josephine (George) Scott.]

WALKER, Evelyn L. 9 Jun 1923-   . [Married 1) _____ Rutledge and
          2) Lloyd B. Walker.]

WALKER, Lloyd B. 20 May 1915-27 Dec 1983. [Son of Thomas and Metta
          (Basher) Walker, husband of 1) Lela Pearl Watson and 2) Evelyn
          (_____) Rutledge.]

WALKER, Lela Pearl. 8 Jun 1914-1 Jul 1960. [Daughter of Earnest and
          Belle (Brady) Watson, first wife of Lloyd B. Walker.]

WALKER, James L. 27 Apr 1939-17 Dec 1977. [James Lloyd, son of Lloyd B.
          and Lela Pearl (Watson) Walker.]

BELL, Sarah Frances. 1940 -   . [Sarah Frances Craven, wife of
          William Carl Bell.]

BELL, William Carl. 1939 - 3 Sep 1987. [Son of John and Minnie
          (Chambers) Bell, husband of Sarah Frances Craven, married 27
          Jun 1959.]

WOODLEE, Velma. 18 May 1919-   . [Daughter of Joe and Tennessee
          Wilburn (Yell) Kidd, wife of Willie Andrew Woodlee.]

WOODLEE, W.A. 18 Nov 1914-18 Oct 1976. [Willie Andrew, son of J.J. and
          Esther (Martin) Woodlee, married Velma Kidd on 21 Dec 1938.]

LOVE, Tommy. 29 Sep 1926-3 Nov 1965. WWII. [Son of Thomas Riley and Hattie (Mullican) Love, husband of Mildred Morris.]

LOVE, Mildred. 1932 - . [Mildred Morris, wife of Tommy Love.]

CANTRELL, Fredrick R. 1899-30 Apr 1978. [Husband of Ola Betty Mae Pinegar.]

CANTRELL, Ola B. 1897-10 Dec 1977. [Ola Betty Mae, daughter of James and Martha (Young) Pinegar, wife of Fredrick Rudolph Cantrell.]

LAWSON, Betty Joyce. 5 May 1934-26 Jul 1982. [Daughter of Frederick R. and Ola Betty (Pinegar) Cantrell, married 1) Lawrence Avery Lawson and 2) Leon Cunningham.]

LAWSON, Lawrence Avery. 17 Nov 1931-24 Sep 1991. [Son of John and Verna (Medley) Lawson, husband of 1) Betty Joyce Cantrell and 2) Sharon King.]

LAWSON, Verna M. 1912 - . [Verna Mae Medley, wife of John W. Lawson.]

LAWSON, John W. 9 Mar 1905-14 Nov 1979. [Son of John Crockett and Avo (Medley) Lawson, husband of Verna Mae Medley.]

DRIVER, Henry P. 1889 - 23 Oct 1977. [Son of Milas W. and Sally (Johnson) Driver, husband of Effie Love.]

DRIVER, Effie L. 1893 - 30 Dec 1985. [Daughter of Jim and Sylvapia (Young) Love, wife of Henry P. Driver.]

DUNHAM, Arnold B. 1 Aug 1912-17 Nov 1988. [Son of George W. and Cleo (Brown) Dunham.]

DUNHAM, Rufene. 15 Oct 1915-25 Nov 1988.

YOUNG, Sandra Lorene. 13 Jan 1937-19 Dec 1981. [Daughter of James N. and Nancy Audrey (Robinson) Tittsworth, married 1) _____ Fernandez and 2) Larry Young.]

YOUNG, Pamela Annette. 23 Nov 1970 only date on stone. [Infant daughter of Larry and Sandra Lorene (Tittsworth) Young.]

LOVE, James Landon. 1919 - 3 May 1971. [Son of Willie Robert and Sarah (Smith) Love, husband of Josie Marjorie Cantrell.]

LOVE, Josie Marjorie. 1918 - . [Daughter of Zollie Adran and Shirley (Love) Cantrell, wife of James Landon Love.]

BOGLE, "Dot" Lee. 1923 -Sep 1964. [Dorothy McGee, wife of ____ Bogle.

GRIFFITH, Media V. 1 Jul 1900-3 Jun 1990. [Daughter of T.R. and Martha (Young) Vaughn, wife of Ernest T. Griffith.]

GRIFFITH, Ernest T. 1889 - Jan 1970. [Son of Paten and Hanna (Cantrell) Griffith, husband of Media Vaughn.]

TAFT, Laura Edna Churchwell. 25 Apr 1915-2 Jul 1990. [Daughter of John Henry and Mattie Marcella (Tyler) Churchwell, wife of William

M. Taft.]

TAFT, William M.   11 Feb 1911-28 Dec 1961.   [Husband of Laura Edna
          Churchwell.]

HASTON, Lola A. 1906 -   .   [Lola Mai Morris, wife of Edgar Lee
          Haston.]

HASTON, Edgar L. 28 Oct 1896-19 Feb 1976. [Son of Tommy and Eva (Drake)
          Haston, husband of Lola Mai Morris, married in 1923.]

LINDQUIST, Carl E. 10 Dec 1927-17 Aug 1973. US Navy. [Carl Edwin, son
          of David and Ida (Helstrom) Lindquist, husband of Jacquelyn
          Temoney.]

WATSON, Fred Brown. 24 Jan 1918-21 Nov 1961. WWII. [Son of J.E. Sr. and
          Elizabeth (Bell) Watson, husband of Sally Ruth Gillentine.]

GILLENTINE, Cora C. 12 Sep 1892-4 Mar 1931. [Cora Halbert Christian,
          wife of George Frank Gillentine.]

GILLENTINE, Frank. 10 Feb 1891-27 Nov 1960. [Son of Joseph and Mary Vida
          (Campen) Gillentine, husband of Cora Halbert Christian.]

GILLENTINE, Grover Hoyte. 7 Oct 1921-25 Jan 1966. WWII. [Son of George
          Frank and Cora Halbert (Christian) Gillentine. Single.]

KEENER, Landon B. 15 Jul 1942-27 Jan 1977. [Landon Brady, son of Brady
          and Leona (Dill) Keener.]

PACK, Othel D. 8 Aug 1899-10 May 1977. [Son of Sam and Leona (Parsley)
          Pack, married 1) Loretta Mai Sparkman and 2) Margaret Cowan.]

HARVEY, Frank Dubart. 15 Oct 1918-15 Sep 1972. WWII.

HARVEY, Frances Lorraine. 1921 -   .

WATTS, Margaret Ann. 6 Nov 1951-24 Jun 1984.   [Daughter of Avery and
          Betty (Cantrell) Lawson, wife of Gordon D. Watts.]

CLENDENON, James P. 4 Jun 1922-11 Feb 1989. WWII. [Son of Frank and
          Oshia (Christian) Clendenon, husband of Catherine Phillips.]

NEAL, Schuyler Glenn. 22 Jul 1906-12 Sep 1988. Marine Corps. [Son of
          Johnny and Josephine (Close) Neal.]

BOND, Willie B.G. 1913 - 8 Apr 1979. [Willie Brown, daughter of William
          Henry and Ada (Overall) Griffith, wife of _____ Bond.]

TITTSWORTH, L. Ray.   1918 -   .   [Husband of Lillie Gertrude
          Griffith.]

TITTSWORTH, Gertrude G. 1920 - 2 Jun 1979. [Daughter of Fate and Ada
          (Overall) Griffith, wife of L. Ray Tittsworth.]

MULLICAN, Kristy Lee. 19 Aug 1976-4 Dec 1976.   [Daughter of Sammie and
          Linda (Drewer) Mullican.]

MULLICAN, Cloy L. "Trader". 21 Jun 1913-5 Jun 1973.

Gardens of Memory, cont.

MULLICAN, Freda G. [No other information.]

HILL, Clay B. 28 Mar 1897-9 Mar 1973. [Clay Brown, son of Demps and Nola (Hoskins) Hill, husband of Lizzie Abigail Bost.]

HILL, Lizzie B. 27 Dec 1904-9 May 1992. [Lizzie Abigail, daughter of Jeff and Matilda Frances (Smith) Bost, wife of Clay Brown Hill.]

MORGAN, Kevin Dale. 1 Sep 1970-2 Dec 1972.

WALKER, Claud Jr. 13 May 1925-4 Jan 1994. [Son of Claud Sr. and Cumilla (Fuson) Walker, husband of Robbie Greer, married 47 years.]

WALKER, Robbie Greer. 8 Nov 1927-   . [Wife of Claud Walker Jr.]

TURMAN, Walter Victor. 31 Oct 1909-25 Dec 1992. US Marines. [Son of Walter and Ruby (Farmer) Thurman, husband of Frances Barnhill.]

BELL, Mark E. Sr. 23 Sep 1912-27 Dec 1982. [Mark Edwin, son of Walter Robertson and Belle (Shelton) Bell, husband of Audrene Crawley Walling.]

BELL, Audrene Crawley. 1920 -   . [Wife of 1) E.V. Walling and 2) Mark Edwin Bell.]

*GILBERT, Della Elizabeth, died 27 Jul 1966, age 71 years, 10 months and 19 days. Born Warren County 8 Sep 1894 to J. Frank and Georgia (Thompkins) Paris. She was married to Harrison Gilbert who died in 1963.

BRAXTON, Joe T. 1932 -   . [Son of Herman and _____ (_____) Braxton, husband of M. Elizabeth Turner.]

BRAXTON, M. Elizabeth. 1937 -   . [Daughter of Oscar Earl and Willie (Hurt) Turner, married Joe Thomas Braxton on 19 Jan 1958.]

GILBERT, Verna Mae. 27 Feb 1913-17 Aug 1961. [Daughter of Harrison Joseph and Della Elizabeth (Paris) Gilbert, wife of Homer McClary.]

REED, Elsie L. 21 Mar 1917-4 Mar 1977. [Daughter of Harrison Joseph and Della Elizabeth (Parris) Gilbert, wife of Meadows Reed.]

REED, Meadows. 1911-1 Apr 1994. [Son of Robert Newton Sr. and Mary Ethel (Meadows) Reed, husband of Elsie Gilbert.]

TRISLER, Georgia E. 16 May 1927-25 Mar 1984. [Georgia Elizabeth Gilbert, wife of James Frederick "Shorty" Trisler.]

TRISLER, James F. 21 Nov 1918-11 Sep 1988. WWII. [James Frederick "Shorty", son of Samuel Wesley and Mary Elizabeth (Grow) Trisler, husband of Georgia Elizabeth Gilbert.]

PATTON, Henrietta G. 2 Apr 1919-   . [Josie Henrietta, daughter of Alaska Elcana and Josie Estella (Pryor) Golden, wife of Clarence D. Patton.]

PATTON, Clarence D. 20 May 1913-23 Feb 1988. [Son of John B. and Mamie (Beckwith) Patton, husband of Josie Henrietta Golden, married

Gardens of Memory, cont.

24 Feb 1940.]

WALKER, Jessie A. 11 Jun 1907-   . [Wife of Vernal Walker.]

WALKER, Vernal. 18 Apr 1906-23 Jun 1980. [Son of Claude and Cumilla
        (Fuston) Walker, husband of Jessie A. _____.]

PRIEST, Ocie. 1907 -   .

PRIEST, Seamon. 1908 -   . [Son of Joe and Alice (Reed) Priest.]

CLARK, Ada F. 9 May 1938 only date on stone.

PRIEST, Nola B. 1919-25 May 1994. [Daughter of Frank Luther and Elba L.
        (Boren) Bost, wife of Kenneth Ray Priest.]

PRIEST, Kenneth R. 8 Jun 1926-17 Jan 1985. [Son of Joe and Alice (Reed)
        Priest, husband of Nola Bell Bost.]

DUGAN, Charlie Grady. 1 Dec 1917-4 Aug 1988. WWII. [Son of Jesse
        Alvin and Nettie (Hussey) Dugan, husband of Violet _____.]

*HARDING, Shelah Robert. 28 Jun 1958-27 Dec 1958. [Infant son of Douglas
        Burke and Betty Jo (Grissom) Harding.]

LAMY, Alcide Joseph. 28 Jul 1908-4 May 1980.

PENNINGTON, Claude Black. 1894 - 22 Jul 1970. [Son of Joseph and Allie
        (Davy) Pennington, husband of Mattie Belle Alley.]

PENNINGTON, Mattie B. 4 Oct 1901-4 Mar 1972. [Daughter of Verhaden
        and Maggie (Hendrix) Alley, wife of Claude Black Pennington.]

PENNINGTON, Hilda Iola. 6 Apr 1924-3 Mar 1962. [Daughter of Hubert and
        Bessie (Taylor) Nunley, wife of Clifton Cantrell Pennington.]

WOMACK, James J. 1921 -   .

WOMACK, Tennie E. 1921 -   .

ROBINSON, Frank. 1912-16 Jun 1988. [Son of Elbert William and Martha
        Carolyn (Self) Robinson, husband of Naomi W. _____.]

ROBINSON. Naomi W. 1923 -   . [Wife of Frank Robinson.]

ROBINSON, Elbert W. 10 Jan 1883-4 Sep 1963. [Son of John and Amanda
        (Lawrence) Robinson, husband of Martha Carolyn Self.]

ROBINSON, Martha C. 11 Jan 1887-28 Jun 1965. [Martha Carolyn, daughter
        of James and Mary (Henderixon) Self, wife of William Elbert
        Robinson.]

BELL, Leighmon M. 1910 -   . [Husband of Elsie Robinson.]

BELL, Elsie R. 28 Apr 1914-16 Aug 1976. [Daughter of Elbert William and
        Martha Carolyn (Self) Robinson, wife of Leighmon M. Bell.]

ROBINSON, Staley H. 1906-21 Aug 1985. [Son of Elbert William and Martha
        Carolyn (Self) Robinson, husband of Gladys M. Jordan.]

Gardens of Memory, cont.

ROBINSON, Gladys M. 1908 - 30 Aug 1987. [Daughter of Claude and Dora
        Bell (Owens) Jordan, wife of Staley Robinson.]

JORDAN, Jesse B. 21 Feb 1913-   . [Husband of Georgia Lankford.]

JORDAN, Georgia L. 22 Sep 1908-8 Jan 1984. [Daughter of Robert and
        Bertha (Dabbs) Lankford, wife of Jesse B. Jordan.]

TRAIL, Nova Lee. 15 Dec 1910-5 Jan 1986. [Daughter of William C. and
        Mary (Hutson) Reeder, wife of George Cheatham Trail, Sr.]

TRAIL, George C. Sr. 20 Sep 1906-12 Oct 1982. WWII. [Son of Peter B.
        and Sophronia Alice (Turner) Trail, husband of Nova Lee
        Reeder.]

ROBINSON, Elbert, IV. 1959 - Mar 1959.

ROBINSON, Alton E. 13 May 1921-13 Feb 1971. WWII. [Son of Elbert
        William and Martha Carolyn (Self) Robinson, husband of Dorothy
        Jean Wilson.]

ROBINSON, Dorothy Jean. 1928-27 Feb 1986. [Daughter of Sterling Brown
        and Janie (Perry) Wilson, wife of Alton E. Robinson.]

YORK, Cecil Burgess. 25 Jul 1914-28 Sep 1970. WWII, KOREA. [Son of A.B.
        and Delia (Temples) York, married 1 Nov 1941 to Jessie Lee
        McCaig.]

MARTIN, Ella M. 1893 - 18 Sep 1991. [Ella Mae, daughter of John and Jane
        (Kidd) Millraney, wife of Sam Martin Sr.]

MARTIN, Sam Sr. 18 Oct 1889-14 Mar 1967. [Son of Rance and Harriet
        (Moffitt) Martin, husband of Ella Mae Millraney.]

MOORE, Shannon D. 1970 - Jan 1990.

MOORE, Homer C. 21 Sep 1921-7 Aug 1991. [Son of B.G. and Ada (Blanks)
        Moore, husband of Margie Masters.]

BOYD, Thomas Ramsey. 28 Mar 1933-18 Sep 1988. KOREA. [Son of Joseph
        Tallman and Sara (Ramsey) Boyd, married Kathryn Webb in Oct
        1955.]

BOYD, Joseph Tallman. 18 Jl 1912-2 Jul 1993. [Son of Fernando C. and
        Sara Jane (Maxwell) Boyd, husband of Sara Ramsey.]

BOYD, Sara R. 10 Jan 1913-   . [Daughter of Lytle and Leola Johann
        (_____) Ramsey.]

LORANCE, Michael Edward. Died June 1968.

KELL, Sarah Othala. 14 Apr 1904-28 Dec 1989. [Daughter of Claude and
        Sarah Ellen (Rowland) Kell, wife of 1) _____ Greer and 2)
        LeRoy Kell.]

JORDAN, Magness. 11 Jul 1924-   . [Husband of 1) Daphne Geneva
        Hughes and 2) Betty Jo Neal.]

JORDAN, Geneva. 28 Jun 1927-5 Jan 1982. [Daughter of Martin Luther and
        Henriette (Whitlock) Hughes, wife of Magness Jordan.]

JORDAN, Mike. 3 May 1959-22 Jan 1993. [Son of Magness and Geneva (Hughes) Jordan, husband of Deborah Vaughn.]

JORDAN, Deborah. 25 Jun 1958-   . [Deborah Vaughn, wife of Mike Jordan.]

CARNEY, Thomas B. 31 Jul 1901-24 Oct 1969. [Thomas Butler, son of Thomas Butler and Allie (Fletcher) Carney, husband of Frances Lassetter.]

CARNEY, Frances L. 1907 -   . [Daughter of ___ and Minnie (_____) Lassetter, wife of Thomas B. Carney.]

JONES, Donald Lynn. 20 May 1957-24 Nov 1959. [Son of Lavern and Nonnie Ethel (Smith) Jones.]

JONES, Mildred Lavoun. 3 Nov 1934-31 Dec 1945. [Daughter of Francis Marion and Hilda (Davenport) Jones.]

JONES, Hilda C. 1907-22 Oct 1993. [Hilda Cloise, daughter of Isaac Perry and Susie (Tenpenny) Davenport, wife of Francis Marion Jones.]

JONES, Marion. 1902 - 25 Aug 1978. [Francis Marion, son of Albert and Rachel (Johnson) Jones, husband of Hilda Cloise Davenport.]

CUMMINGS, Dallas. 7 Aug 1881-29 May 1970. [Son of Warren and Josie (Smith) Cummings, husband of Sallie Gunter.]

CUMMINGS, Sallie. 1895 - 7 Oct 1992. [Daughter of Caldean D. and Mary E. (English) Gunter, wife of Dallas Cummings.]

PATTON, Ola Mae. 24 Mar 1916-29 Sep 1986. [Daughter of Dallas and Sally (Gunter) Cummings, wife of Flavil Patton.]

PATTON, Flavil. 21 Oct 1907-   . [Son of Frank and Alice (Green) Patton, husband of Ola Mae Cummings, married 16 May 1933.]

HOBBS, Flossie Mae. 17 Jul 1900-6 Aug 1976. [Daughter of Henry and Nettie (Jennings) Martin, wife of Grover L. Hobbs.]

HOBBS, Grover L. 12 Jul 1896-17 Mar 1980. [Son of Jim and Mary (Fults) Hobbs, husband of Flossie Mae Martin.]

TAYLOR, H. Raymond. 1907 - 16 Jun 1993. [Harry Raymond, son of Andrew Jackson and Sally (Goosby) Taylor, husband of Lorena _____.]

KNIGHT, Paul D. 1947 -   . [Married 1) _____ _____ and 2) Cindy Dawn Wilson.]

KNIGHT, Cindy D. 1963 - 2 May 1988. [Daughter of Harold and Malinda (Rhoden) Wilson, second wife of Paul D. Knight.]

BOND, William Jennings. 12 Jun 1896-25 Aug 1970. WWI. [Son of William Henry Harrison and Fannie (Tyree) Bond, husband of Anna Ellen Little, married 28 May 1925.]

BOND, Anna E. Little. 1905 - 5 Dec 1989. [Daughter of Erasmus and Sarah (Eubanks) Little, wife of William Jennings Bond.]

RICHARDSON, Novella Ponder. 1905 - 24 Apr 1993. [Daughter of Enoch and

Eliza (Lockhart) Ponder, wife of Milford Richardson.]

RICHARDSON, James Morris. 27 Jan 1929-12 Apr 1993. [Son of Milford and
Novella (Ponder) Richardson, married 1) Sarah _____ and 2)
Elaine Howser on 3 Dec 1988.]

RICHARDSON, Elaine H. 20 Oct 1941-   . [Elaine Howser, married 1)
Ben Parker, 2) _____ Greer and 3) James Richardson.]

PARKER, Terry Lynn. 28 Jul 1969-24 May 1990. [Son of Benjamin Franklin
and Elaine (Howser) Parker. Single.]

SCOTT, Roy L. Sr. 21 Nov 1919-22 May 1978. [Roy Lenous, son of George W.
and Tennie (Bond) Scott, husband of Ailene Moore.]

SCOTT, Ailene M. 1922 -   . Ailene Moore, wife of Roy Lenous Scott.]

TENPENNY, Bertie L. 20 Feb 1930-   . [Bertie Lucille, daughter of
Georgie and Minnie Louella (Hillis) Wiseman, wife of 1) James
Ernest Tenpenny and 2) Jim Dillard Rutledge, married 24 Aug
1972.]

TENPENNY, James E. 7 Dec 1924-6 Feb 1970. KOREA. [James Ernest, son of
Ernest Lemuel and Bessie (Pittard) Tenpenny, husband of Bertie
Lucille Wiseman, married 2 Jun 1951.]

KEITH, Ruth T. 12 Apr 1911-11 Sep 1969. [Daughter of Robert and Melissa
(Woods) Tenpenny, wife of J.B. Keith.]

KEITH, J.B. 27 Feb 1914-4 Apr 1963. [Son of Isaac and Nancy (Raymond)
Keith, husband of Ruth Tenpenny.]

SMITH, Matilda Watley. 28 Sep 1903 -   . [Wife of C.E. Cudge
Smith.]

SMITH, Cudge. 19 May 1892-18 Mar 1980. WWI. [Son of John and Ann
(Nerney) Smith, husband of Matilda Watley.]

PEARSALL, Alice M. 1912 -   . [Alice M. Smithson, wife of
Fletcher C. Pearsall.]

PEARSALL, Fletcher C. 2 May 1910-29 Aug 1981. [Son of Claude and Ada
(Hamley) Pearsall, husband of Alice Smithson, married 26 Nov
1930.]

THURMAN, Georgie Lena. 18 Apr 1901-28 Jun 1991. [Daughter of John M. and
Elizabeth (Green) Smith, wife of Harold Thomas Thurman.]

THURMAN, Harold Thomas. 1905 - 1932. [Husband of Georgie Lena Smith.]

GROVE, Jennifer Carol. 4 Jan 1966-4 Jan 1966. [Daughter of John W. and
Betty Sue (Thurman) Grove.]

BOULDIN, Clyde "Crackerjack". 30 Dec 1905-   . [Son of Andrew
Jackson and Rachel (Nunley) Bouldin, husband of 1) Ida Velma
Perry (div.), 2) Darathee L.Hannen (div.) and 3) Lula Rhea.]

BOULDIN, Elbert "Sonny". 1930 -   . [Elbert Floyd, son of Clyde and
Velma Ida (Perry) Bouldin, husband of Vera Maxine _____.]

29

Gardens of Memory, cont.

BOULDIN, Vera Maxine. 1933 - 16 Apr 1977.   [Wife of Elbert Floyd
          Bouldin.]

HOBBS, Tennie P. 6 Oct 1900-27 Feb 1987. [Daughter of Jimmie and Nancy
          (Wanamaker) Wanamaker, wife of Hervie Hobbs.]

HOOPER, Rhoda Kaye. Oct 1959 only date on stone. [Infant daughter of
          Howard and Ruth (_____) Hooper.]

SWANN, Celia Mae. 4 Sep 1913-   . [Celia Mae Hendrixson, second
          wife of Barney Swann, married 1 Oct 1933.]

SWANN, Barney. 1 Jun 1902-19 Nov 1985. [Son of Sam ad Ida (Smithson)
          Swann, husband of 1) Electie Young and 2) Celia Mae
          Hendrickson.]

SWANN, Electie. 19 Jan 1904-26 Dec 1932. [Daughter of William Calvin
          and Annie (Teal) Young, first wife of Barney Swann.]

PEARSON, Lawrence E. 1906 - May 1963. [Husband of Elizabeth _____.]

PEARSON, Elizabeth. 1905 - Jun 1990. [Wife of Lawrence E. Pearson.]

KINNEY. Elmer R. 1920 - 31 Aug 1992. WWII. [Son of Bruce and Livina
          (Hallett) Kinney, wife of Vesta Blair.]

KINNEY, Vesta L. 1921 -   . [Daughter of Virgle and Beulah (Brady)
          Blair, wife of Elmer R. Kinney.]

KELLEY, Carden Hubert. 1908 - 5 Feb 1967. [Son of B.F. and Clara (Bluhm)
          Kelley, husband of Mary Wilma Smith.]

KELLEY, Mary Wilma. 1918 -   . [Mary Wilma Smith, wife of Carden
          Hubert Kelley.]

PEEKS, Mary E. 1934 -   .

DAY, Lori Ann. Born and died 4 Feb 1974. [Daughter of Roger Owen and
          Georgia Illa (Mixon) Day.]

MORRISON, Thelma H. 17 Jul 1898-28 Mar 1982. [Daughter of David and Emma
          (Jackson) Hickerson, wife of Joseph Sutton Morrison.]

DAVIS, Felix B. 24 Aug 1911-14 Jul 1990. [Felix Butler, son of Aubrey
          and Beulah (Earls) Davis.]

RAINS, Mary Emma. 19 Jul 1891-16 May 1965. [Daughter of J.B. and Rachel
          Ann (Shelton) Elam, wife of Oscar Rains.]

RAINS, Oscar. 20 May 1883-27 Dec 1973. [Son of R.K. and Susie (Akers)
          Rains, husband of Mary Emma Elam.]

RAINS, Marie G. 11 Apr 1928-   . [Daughter of Barney and Electie
          (Young) Swann, wife of Jimmy Edison Rains.]

RAINS, Jimmy E. 28 Jul 1917-25 Dec 1993. [Son of Oscar and Mary Emma
          (Elam) Rains, husband of Marie G. Swann.]

TAYLOR, Elsie. 12 Jan 1923-   . [Daughter of Jesse and Myrtle
          (Page) Holt, wife of Floy Taylor.]

TAYLOR, Floy. 6 Aug 1918-18 May 1994. [Son of Grady and Henrietta (Mullican) Taylor, husband of Elsie Holt.]

GRIBBLE, Dee S. 1903 -   . [Dee Ida Stotts, wife of Oscar N. Gribble, married 7 May 1927.]

GRIBBLE, Oscar Newell. 10 Apr 1889-12 Dec 1974. US Army. [Son of James Alexander and Sarah Ann (Cook) Gribble, husband of Dee Ida Stotts.]

SHORT, James F. 7 Aug 1915-2 Jul 1982. WWII. [James Fletcher, son of Isaac Newton and Catherine (Jent) Short, husband of Marie Roper.]

AUSTIN, Orville. 27 May 1909-1 Nov 1986. [Son of Joseph Edward and Rachel Evelee (Medley) Austin, husband of Ora Mae Holt, married 11 Sep 1935.]

AUSTIN, Ora Mae. 9 Sep 1920-14 May 1962. [Daughter of Jess and Myrtle (Page) Holt, wife of William Orville Austin.]

RAINS, Lonnie M. 1921-25 Jun 1980. [Son of Oscar and Mary (Elam) Rains, husband of Dorothy Chandler.]

RAINS, Dorothy C. 1931-   . [Dorothy Chandler, wife of Lonnie M. Rains.]

CHANDLER, David P. 1879 - May 1964. [Husband of Lula J. _____.]

CHANDLER, Lula J. 1888 - Jan 1964. [Wife of David P. Chandler.]

PRATER, James M. 24 Nov 1898-3 Dec 1974. [James McKinley, son of William Jasper and Martha Ellen (Holt) Prater, husband of Ruth Bathsheba Cantrell.]

PRATER, Ruth B. 11 Jan 1902-8 Oct 1989. [Ruth Bathsheba, daughter of Duke McDonald and Nancy Evaline (Luna) Cantrell, wife of James McKinley Prater.]

PENNINGTON, Josephine M. 25 Apr 1925 -   . [Wife of Clyde A. Pennington.]

PENNINGTON, Clyde A. 30 Sep 1924-   . [Husband of Josephine M. _____.]

HUNNICUTT, Thelma J. 1914 -   . [Thelma Jenkins, wife of Chester A. Hunnicutt.]

HUNNICUTT, Chester A. 27 Oct 1905-26 Jul 1979. [Son of George and Annie Lee (Bagwell) Hunnicutt, husband of Thelma Jenkins.]

PATTERSON, Alma E. 1906 - 10 Dec 1993. [Daughter of Firm Thomas and Nancy Lodema (Hillis) Johnson, wife of Herbert Bethel Patterson.]

PATTERSON, Herbert Bethel "Pat". 23 Jul 1900-25 Jan 1973. [Son of Jim and Jennie (Cunningham) Patterson, husband of Alma E. Johnson.]

PATTERSON, James T. 22 Jan 1927-27 Sep 1980. WWII. [Son of Herbert Bethel and Alma E. (Johnson) Patterson.]

REED, Louise. 24 Jun 1904-30 Mar 1992. [Daughter of James Dan and Sarah Ann (Callahan) Jones, wife of Robert Newton Reed.]

SOUTHARD, Gloria Annette. 1931 - 4 Oct 1983. [First wife of Bobby Southard.]

EWING, William Warren. 18 Jul 1913-26 Jan 1966. [Son of Dave and Margaret (Collingsworth) Ewing, husband of Mildred Wilson.]

EWING, Mildred Culley Wilson. 1916 - 22 Oct 1992. [Daughter of John Bearl and Roxie (Culley) Wilson, wife of William Warren Ewing.]

ROGERS, Herman B. 1908 - 27 Aug 1971. [Son of Jeff and Velma (Moore) Rogers, husband of Velma McCorkle.]

ROGERS, Velma M. 1909 - 12 Nov 1970. [Daughter of J.M. and Harriet (Christian) McCorkle.]

ROGERS, James Morgan. 29 Mar 1933-3 Jul 1959. KOREA. [Son of Herman B. and Velma (McCorkle) Rogers.]

WOODS, James M. 27 Mar 1906-19 Jun 1986. [Son of Richard Luther and Rowena (Porter) Woods, husband of Mattie Redmon.]

WOODS, Mattie G. 23 May 1905-19 Jan 1990. [Daughter of Felix and Ella (Williams) Redmon, married James M. Woods on 18 Dec 1926.]

WOODS, Tina B. 21 Aug 1957-20 Sep 1957. [Tina Belinda, daughter of James Mitchell and Patricia Ann (Jarrell) Woods.]

SULLIVAN, Jonas William. 30 Jul 1971-19 Jan 1972. [Infant son of William T. and Charlotte Faye (Woods) Sullivan.]

SULLIVAN, Charlotte F. 26 Nov 1945 - . [Charlotte Faye, daughter of James and Mattie (Redmon) Woods, wife of William T. Sullivan, married 7 Jun 1963.]

SULLIVAN, William T. 24 Feb 1944-16 Aug 1987. [Son of James A. and Thelma (Jones) Sullivan, husband of Charlotte Faye Woods.]

WILSON, Harry C. 2 Jan 1923-25 Jan 1974. WWII. [Son of Marvin E. Sr. and _____ (_____) Wilson.]

SMITH, Dorothy Marie "Dot". 1929 - 12 Nov 1978. [Daughter of Herman and Velma (McCorkle) Rogers, wife of John Eugene Smith.]

SMITH, John Eugene "Buzz". 1920 - . [Son of Otto and Callie (Walker) Smith, husband of 1) Dorothy Marie Rogers and 2) Charlene Mayes.]

BROWN, Onmon L. 1905 - 6 Dec 1963. [Son of John Shelby and Sally (Hudgens) Brown, husband of Frances Tuck.

HUTCHINS, Louise T. 23 Dec 1924-23 Jun 1989. [Daughter of Ernest and Loe (_____) Lanoo, wife of 1) _____ McMurray, and 2) Claiborne W. Hutchins.]

HUTCHINS, Claiborne W. 13 May 1923 - . [Husband of Louise T. Lanoo.]

Gardens of Memory, cont.

STRIEGEL, Blanche B. 1913 -   . [Wife of Theodore E. Striegel.]

STRIEGEL, Theodore E. 1908-14 Jan 1984. [Son of John and Ida (Kramer) Striegel, husband of Blanche B. _____.]

GRAELL, Julius. 1901-Apr 1988. [A native of France, husband of Ruth Harris.]

GRAELL, Ruth. 1906-23 Feb 1985. [Daughter of James and Viola (Faulkner) Harris, wife of Julius Graell.]

OUBRE, Celia A. 26 Jun 1913 -   .

GILLESPIE, David D. 13 Apr 1900-19 Apr 1971. [Son of John and Mattie (_____) Gillespie, husband of Chole Rodriguez.]

GILLESPIE, Soledad. 1921 -   .

BROWN, Shelby Edward. 30 Apr 1935-5 Nov 1990. KOREA. [Son of Onman L. and Frances (Tuck) Brown.]

SMARTT, Robert White III. 1960 - Jul 1982. [Son of Robert White, Jr. and Joan (Dudney) Smartt.]

BONEY, Jessie Smartt. 28 Dec 1876-4 Dec 1959. [Daughter of George Madison and Cornelia Adelaide (_____) Smartt, wife of Robert Madison Boney, married 18 Jun 1914.]

SMARTT, Alma Roggli. 19 Jan 1886-22 Sep 1960. [Daughter of John and Louise (Zulliger) Roggli, wife of Robert White Smartt, married 3 Sep 1913.]

SMARTT, Robert White. 4 Jul 1973-28 Nov 1968. [Son of George Madison and Cornelia Adelaide (_____) Smartt, married 1) Susan Annie Fancher on 31 Oct 1905 and 2) Sarah Alma Roggli on 3 Sep 1913.]

SMARTT, Annie Fancher. 3 Mar 1881-4 Jun 1910. [Susan Annie Fancher, first wife of Robert White Smartt.]

BROCK, John L. 9 Mar 1901-21 Dec 1986. [John Lafayette, son of S.G. and Eola (Coots) Brock, husband of Lucille Simpson.]

BROCK, John C. 21 Jun 1931-3 Sep 1987. KOREA. [Son of John L. and Lucille (Simpson) Brock, husband of Billie G. Tittle.]

BROCK, Billie Gray Tittle. 18 Sep 1934-   . [Daughter of William R. and Georgia Mai (Moore) Tittle, wife of John C. Brock, married 25 Jul 1953.]

BENNETT, Elmer F. 28 Jul 1897-4 Apr 1966. [Son of Walter and Nora (Lovell) Bennett, husband of Velma Grace McAfee.]

BENNETT, Velma Grace. 27 Dec 1905-27 Jun 1989. [Daughter of Jessie Bilbra and Mary Emma (Lister) McAfee, wife of Elmer Forrest Bennett.]

DRIVER, Kizzie M. 21 Nov 1916-   . [Kizzie M. Trusty, wife of Troy Houston Driver.]

DRIVER, Troy Houston. 9 Mar 1914-7 Nov 1975. WWII. [Son of Henry P. and

Effie (Love) Driver, husband of Kizzie M. Trusty.]

MATHIAS, Terry Michael. 1957-1957. [Son of John Robert and Sara (Buie) Mathias.]

MATHIAS, John R. 6 Apr 1924-4 May 1965. [John Robert, son of Carl and Lillie (Goostree) Mathias, husband of Sarah Buie.]

TAYLOR, Randa Gustava. 1903-6 Nov 1982. [Daughter of James Franklin and Lou Dora (Cunningham) Howard, wife of Herman Banks Taylor, Sr.]

TAYLOR, Herman Banks. 14 Feb 1905-10 Mar 1966. [Son of Andrew Jackson and Sara Katherine (Goolsby) Taylor, married Randa Gustava Howard on 8 Nov 1925.]

CARTER, Addie Elzo. 24 Sep 1909-   .

CARTER, Lemmuel Harvey. 22 Aug 1908-   .

MANTOOTH, Monnie C. 8 Jan 1904-13 Sep 1987. [Daughter of Elias and Mattie (Kendrick) Murray, wife of Clyde C. Mantooth.]

MANTOOTH, Clyde C. 25 Sep 1902-6 Feb 1985. WWI. [Son of Samuel Houston and _____ (_____) Mantooth, husband of Monnie Viola Murray.]

WEBB, Bryan W. 1898 - 20 Dec 1993. [Bryan William, son of Andrew Jackson and Samantha (Green) Webb, husband of Nancy Boyd.]

WEBB, Nancy B. 1903 - 9 Jul 1988. [Daughter of Robert and Malvin A. (McBride) Boyd, wife of Bryan William Webb.]

HOLLINS, Ted Eldred. 1 Jan 1930-   . KOREA, VIETNAM. [Husband of Louise Webb.]

HOLLINS, Louise Webb. 30 Mar 1926 -   . [Daughter of Bryan Willian and Nancy (Boyd) Webb, wife of Ted Eldred Hollins.]

TAYLOR, Bobby Gene. 19 May 1942-   . [Husband of Susan Webb.]

TAYLOR, Susan Webb. 1 Nov 1941-14 Sep 1985. [Daughter of Bryan and Nancy (Boyd) Webb, wife of Bobby Gene Taylor.]

TATE, Richard Morton. 1910 - 4 Oct 1991. [Son of Willie Clyde and Bessie (Morton) Tate, married 1) Emma Lou Slaughter and 2) Irene Harris.]

TATE, Irene H. 1924 -   . [Irene Harris, second wife of Richard M. Tate.]

SMITHSON, Robert Lee. 4 Jul 1904-15 Oct 1984. [Son of Ed. W. and Mollie (LeFever) Smithson, husband of Mary Dollie Newby, married 16 Jun 1931.]

SMITHSON, Mary "Dollie" 17 May 1910-17 Mar 1976. [Daughter of Joe Sam and Callie (Denby) Newby, wife of Robert Lee Smithson.]

MASON, Donald Richard. 1929 - Jul 1991. [Son of George L. and Ester Louise (Rhodes) Mason, husband of Melba Jean _____.]

MASON, Melba Jean. 1943 -   . [Wife of 1) _____ Tate and 2)

Gardens of Memory, cont.

Donald Richard Mason.]

BASHAM, Kenneth Ray. 1958 - 11 Oct 1988. [Son of Billy Ray and Mattie
Helen (Ward) Basham.]

BASHAM, Helen W. 1933 -   . [Mattie Helen Ward, wife of Billy Ray
Basham.]

BASHAM, Billy R. 1932-   . [Billy Ray, husband of Mattie Helen
Ward.]

SUMMA, Elbert G. 1907 -15 Jul 1990. [Son of Victor Michael and Nazareth
Mary (_____) Summa, husband of Mary _____.]

SUMMA, Mary E. 1909 -   . [Wife of Elbert G. Summa.]

TAYLOR, Howard. 1925 -   .

TAYLOR, Harriet. 1927 -   .

CARTER, Charles R. 2 May 1911-21 Jul 1964. [Son of Robert B. and Mary
(McCormick) Carter, husband of Ruby Ivey (div.)]

HOPKINS, Carlene. 1942 -   .

HOPKINS, Charles E. 1941 -   .

McCOWAN, Jason Paul. 27 Apr 1972-27 Dec 1986. [Son of Jimmy and Charlene
(_____) McGowan.]

YORK, Clance Z. 28 Oct 1914-21 May 1981. [Son of Landon and Mary Frances
(Smith) York, husband of Jeanette B. _____.]

YORK, Jeanette B. 25 Apr 1924-   . [Wife of Clance Z. York.]

DAVENPORT, Doran E. 1915 -   .

DAVENPORT, Mary C. 1918 -   .

CAPSHAW, Clarence R. 11 Jun 1936-11 Jan 1990. [Son of James Benton and
Connie Avo (Hillis) Capshaw, husband of Sarah E. Biles.]

CAPSHAW, Sarah E. 15 Nov 1937-   . [Sarah E. Biles, wife of
Clarence Riley Capshaw.]

STONE, Ronald Frank. 13 Feb 1937-13 Jul 1989. VIETNAM. [Son of Orris B.
and Amma (_____) Stone, husband of Joyce E. _____.]

DAVENPORT, Jennie Ruth. 19 Mar 1964-19 Mar 1964. [Daughter of Michael
Lee and Patsy Dee (Chesser) Davenport.]

DAVENPORT, Michael L. 16 Feb 1939-20 Aug 1974. US Air Force. [Husband
of Patsy Dee Chesser.]

DAVENPORT, Patsy C. 1937 -   . [Wife of Michael Lee Davenport.]

YOUNG, Oshie Pedigo. 25 Jul 1899-28 Jun 1990. [Daughter of Harve and
Fannie (Phelps) Pedigo, wife of Johnnie William Young.]

MARTIN, Floey. Born 1910- no other information.

WILLIAMS, Jackie C. 4 Mar 1934-31 Dec 1993.

MULLICAN, Jackie Elaine. 27 Apr 1954-29 Jun 1964. [Daughter of Mack and Jackie (Williams) Mullican.]

AUSTIN, Lawrence W. 12 Jul 1924-3 May 1990. WWII. [Lawrence William, son of Lawrence W. and _____ (_____) Austin, husband of Louise Cantrell.]

AUSTIN, Louise C. 1918 -   . [Louise Cantrell, wife of Lawrence William Austin.]

TRAPP, Otis L. 1916 -   .

TRAPP, Clara A. 1919 -   .

FISHER, Laura M. 18 Jul 1905-30 Jul 1972. [Daughter of Landie and Nancy Ellen (Clark) Moore, wife of Orville Stewart Fisher, married 21 Sep 1921.]

FISHER, Orville S. 8 Aug 1897-16 Jul 1971. WWI. [Son of Irvin and Mary Leona (Dodson) Fisher, husband of Laura Mae Moore.]

FULTS, Agnes A. 25 Sep 1922 -   .

MILLER, Shirley A. No dates. [Shirley Ann Allen, wife of Charles Lee Miller.]

MILLER, Charles Lee. 7 Sep 1939-5 Dec 1980. US Air Force. [Son of Arthur and Edna (_____) Miller, husband of Shirley Ann Allen.]

PEDIGO, Thurman L. 1935 -   .

PEDIGO. E. Frances. 1936 -   .

PEDIGO, Mable. 1917 - 1 Apr 1987. [Daughter of William Riley and Allie (Maxwell) Gambrell, wife of Toy Ralph Pedigo.]

PEDIGO, Toy R. 1913 - 20 Sep 1987. [Son of Pleasant M. and Lillian (Reeder) Pedigo, husband of Mable Gambrell.]

TILTON, Joshua B. 29 Jan 1979-17 Aug 1984. [Joshua Burnett, son of Craig and Cindy (Underhill) Tilton.]

WOODS, Michael E. 1948 -   .

WOODS, Peggy A. 1951 -   .

TODD, Sterling Brown. 1926 - 2 Apr 1988. [Son of Vance and Mollie (Higgins) Todd, husband of Melvena Basham.]

TODD, Melvena Basham. 1929 -   . [Wife of Sterling Brown Todd.]

BOGLE, Virginia. 1921 - 21 Aug 1993. [Daughter of Johnnie N. and Ocie (Owens) Hughes, wife of _____ Bogle.]

BIGBEE, Wallace B. 1933 -   . [Husband of 1) Ilalie "Malie" Tucker and 2) Pat (Miller) Bonner.]

Gardens of Memory, cont.

BIGBEE, Ilalie T. 12 Apr 1931-2 Jan 1989. [Daughter of Ottie Robert and
        Sylvia (Campbell) Tucker, wife of Dr. Wallace B. Bigbee.]

HICKS, Bob P. 1918 -   .

HICKS, Mary Lou. 1916 -   .

WOMACK, Dorotha J. 31 Jan 1928 -   .

WOMACK, Johnny C. 8 Apr 1927 -   .

HICKS, Ronnie Price. 15 Sep 1948-14 May 1972. VIETNAM.

HARDISON, Clyde B. 8 Nov 1918-2 Aug 1966. [Clyde Baxter, son of Guy and
        Lura (McCord) Aldridge Hardison, husband of Frances Martin.]

HARDISON, Frances M. 1925 -   . [Frances Martin, wife of Clyde
        Baster Hardison.]

HARDING, James E. 10 Jun 1928-5 May 1992. [Son of James Lewis and Tommie
        (Thomas) Harding, husband of Cleva Dell Frater.]

HARDING, Cleva D. 5 Aug 1932 -   . [Cleva Dell Prater, wife of
        James Earl Harding.]

DORRIS, James J. 1912-6 Jul 1987. [Son of James W. and Decia (Gribbs)
        Dorris, husband of Irene Lee (_____).]

DORRIS, Irene Lee. 1917 -   . [Wife of James J. Dorris.]

SMITH, Eleanor W. 15 Feb 1932-4 Jan 1976. [Daughter of A.E. and Mamie
        (Summerour) Williamson, wife of Lynwood Smith III.]

MINER, Melissa Jane. 29 Jun 1983-20 Jul 1992. [Daughter of Tom and Laura
        Lee (McWhorter) Miner.]

RONE, Altus R. 1913 - 17 Apr 1978. [Son of A.R. and Anna (Fagan) Rone,
        husband of Grace Watson.]

RONE, N. Grace. 1915 -   . [Grace Watson, wife of Altus R. Rone.]

SMITH, William Lynwood Jr. 29 Mar 1907-1 Mar 1979. WWII. [Son of
        William Lynwood Sr. and Edith (Robinson) Smith, husband of
        Elizabeth Wilkie.]

HARRIS, Clarence L. 1917-26 Nov 1990. [Son of James Tyra and Della
        (Newby) Harris, husband of Reba Jo Vaughn.]

HARRIS, Reba J. 1924 -   . [Reba Jo Vaughn, wife of Clarence L.
        Harris.]

ARMES, Wayne K. 1929 -   . [Husband of Marie Lashie Hunt.]

ARMES, Marie H. 20 Jan 1924-24 Dec 1989. [Daughter of Charles and Maude
        (Lashie) Hunt, wife of Wayne K. Armes.]

DAVIS, Bertie M. 13 May 1923-10 Sep 1988.

TATE, Glenn E. 5 Apr 1912-11 Jun 1991. WWII. [Son of Clyde and Bessie
        (Morton) Tate, husband of Mary Graham who died in 1976.]

TITTLE, Herman C. 14 Nov 1916-19 Apr 1982. WWII. [Herman Cantrell, son of Tillman C. and Lana Mae (Turney) Tittle, husband of Delma Talley.]

MILLER, Howard P. 1912 - 14 May 1993. [Son of Oscar L. and Irene (Maugham) Miller, husband of Irene Fisher.]

MILLER, Irene F. 1918 -   . [Irene Fisher, wife of Howard P. Miller.]

HOWELL, James Otto. 17 May 1908- 1994

MARKOWSKI, Virginia Faye. 1926 -   .

MARKOWSKI, Edward C.   1928 -   .

FRANKS, Jewel B.   16 Mar 1921-   . [Daughter of Dexter and Josephine (Butler) Farris, wife of Letrell L. Franks.]

FRANKS, Letrell L. 3 Jan 1923 -   . [Son of James Marvin and Carria (Leatherwood) Franks, husband of Jewel B. Farris.]

FRANKS, Christopher Lee.   10 Oct 1969-12 Oct 1969. [Son of Leborn and Clara (Strickland) Franks, grandson of Letrell L. and Jewel B. Franks and grandson of Odis Strickland of Red Bay, AL.]

EDWARDS, Earl C. 1916-15 Apr 1990. [Son of John and Jennie (Elam) Edwards, husband of Margaret Morrison.]

EDWARDS, Margaret M. 1923 -   . [Margaret Morrison, wife of Earl C. Edwards.]

HENDRIXSON, William B. 1908 -   .

HENDRIXSON, Mattie J. 1921 -   .

GRETZINGER, Benjamin I. 24 Feb 1924-20 Aug 1966. WWII. [Son of _____ and Mary M. (Landgraver) Gretzinger, husband of Juanita McClain.]

SPAIN, Marshall Stacy. Born and died 5 Apr 1974. [Son of Tommy and Benita (Gretzinger) Spain.]

ROBERTS, Mildred L. 1922 - 24 Feb 1987. [Mildred Lee, daughter of Ballard and Cora (Hillis) Huntley, wife of Carl L. Roberts.]

ROBERTS, Carl L. 1926-25 Feb 1992. [Son of Houther and Lizzie (Hillis) Roberts, husband of Mildred Lee Huntley.]

YOUNG, Donnie Robert. 17 Aug 1943-11 Jul 1987. VIETNAM. [Son of Robert Felix and Ruby (Vaughn) Young, husband of Loretta Lynn Ritchie.]

YOUNG, Loretta Lynn R.   21 Apr 1954-   . [Loretta Lynn Ritchie, wife of Donnie Robert Young.]

ARGO, George Sanders. 23 May 1925-2 Apr 1985. WWII. [Son of Vick and Emma Lou (McGee) Argo, husband of Lillian Smith.]

GRISWOLD, Norma Jean. 1925 - Dec 1972. [Wife of Walter H. Griswold.]

Gardens of Memory, cont.

GRISWOLD, Walter H.   5 May 1920-21 Jul 1991.   WWII.   [Son of William Houston and Gussie (Woodlee) Griswold, husband of Norma Jean _____.]

JACOBS, Dorothy Mae Anderson.   17 Aug 1936-5 Jul 1994.   [Wife of 1) Henry I. Whittley (div.) and 2) Charles A. Jacobs.

ORSBORN, Doris C.   1912-4 Dec 1991.   [Daughter of Frank and Eva (Couch) Cronin.]

GUNTER, Joseph Fisher.   15 Mar 1917-29 Jun 1989.   WWII.   [Son of Edgar and Mary (Hawkins) Gunter, husband of Ruby Mae Jones.]

GUNTER, Ruby M.   17 Feb 1920-9 Feb 1990.   [Ruby Mae, daughter of Orville Lee and Lodie (Ward) Jones, wife of Joseph Fisher Gunter.]

PETERS, Jack Denton. 24 Jan 1929-13 May 1987.   KOREA.   [Son of Dale Denton and Edith (Davis) Peters, husband of Frances Webb, married 19 Dec 1951.]

PETERS, Frances Webb.   1931 -   .   [Wife of Jack Denton Peters.]

TEMPLETON, Wilson C. "Temp"   22 Nov 1927-27 Dec 1985.   KOREA.   [Son of William and Rachel (Barlow) Templeton, husband of Velma Neely.]

DILLON, James Aud, Sr.   15 Jan 1894-13 Dec 1969.   WWI.   [Son of James Edward and Mary Ann (Compton) Dillon, husband of Sarah Elizabeth Lester, married 25 Nov 1923.]

DILLON, Sarah Elizabeth Lester.   14 Jan 1896-24 Dec 1980.   [Daughter of Dr. Bailey Peyton and Nancy Alice (Dunn) Lester, wife of James Aud Dillon, Sr.]

DAVIS, Bertie M. 13 Mar 1923-10 Sep 1988.   [Bertie Mae, daughter of Charlie and Alta (Mathis) Rhody, wife of 1) _____ Hester and 2) _____ Davis.]

ROBEY, Gloria Thelma.   23 May 1928-6 Apr 1992.   [Daughter of Henry William and Della (_____) Payne.]

BYRD, Benjamin Franklin.   22 Jun 1932-20 Feb 1992.   KOREA.   [Son of Raymond and Clara (Ruelle) Byrd.]

GUDGER, William H. Sr.   2 Dec 1930-14 Nov 1971.   [Son of Harry G. and Laura (Keilberg) Gudger, husband of Margaret Yarbro.]

HOLLANDSWORTH, Elmer L.   1913 -   .

HOLLANDSWORTH, Bonnie L.   1920 -   .

SULLENS, Ricky Howard.   29 Jul 1957-2 Jan 1990.   [Son of Jessie Noel and Martha Ross (LeFevers) Sullens.]

SULLENS, Martha E.   1935 -   . [Martha Ross LeFevers, wife of Jessie Noel Sullens.]

SULLENS, Jessie Noel.   29 Aug 1931-28 Apr 1980.   KOREA.   [Son of Walter and Annie Frances (Stembridge) Sullens, husband of Martha Ross LeFevers.]

Gardens of Memory, cont.

HIGDON, James W. 1930 -   . [James Wayne, son of John C. and Elsie
          May (Rogers) Higdon, husband of Wilma J. McCormick.]

HIGDON, Wilma J. 19 Feb 1932-19 Mar 1989. [Wilma Jean, daughter of Emmit
          and Virgie Elizabeth (Campbell) McCormick, wife of James Wayne
          Higdon.

DAMRON, Ronald E. 1921 -   .

DAMRON, Mary M.   1921 -   .

RIGSBY, James Haskell. 1914 -   .

RIGSBY, Agnes D.   1918 -   .

DURHAM, James C. 8 Jul 1922-29 Sep 1988. WWII. [James Clifton, son of
          Andrew Jack and Ella Mae (Simons) Durham, husband of Ethelene
          Lindsey.]

DURHAM, Ethelene G.   11 Jun 1925-   . [Ethelene Grace "Tiny"
          Lindsey, wife of James Clifton Durham.]

HOOVER, Ronnie L. 20 Nov 1952-   . [Ronnie Lanier, son of Dalton L.
          and Leoma (Darnell) Hoover, husband of Etta Elaine Hudson,
          married 18 Feb 1971.]

HOOVER, Etta Elaine. 24 Nov 1953-   . [Daughter of Austin Peay
          "Jack" and Berchie Mozell (Billings) Hudson, wife of Ronnie
          Lanier Hoover.]

RASCOE, William H. 23 Jun 1915-18 Dec 1982. [William Henry, son of Edgar
          and Myrtle (Sparkman) Rascoe, husband of Mable Naomi Woods.]

RASCOE, Mabel N. 3 Sep 1919-21 May 1991. [Daughter of Ocies and Bertha
          (Elrod) Woods, wife of William Henry Rascoe.]

DAVIS, Gladys P. 1922 -   . [Gladys Potter, wife of Edward Thomas
          Davis.]

DAVIS, Edward Thomas. 19 Dec 1921-31 Oct 1984. WWII. [Son of Gilbert W.
          and Josie (Webb) Davis, husband of Gladys Potter.]

JUDKINS, Sam C. 9 Mar 1912-15 Jul 1991. [Sam Cordell, son of Thomas
          Henry and Callie Ann (Young) Judkins, husband of Ruby Hardy.]

JUDKINS, Nancy L. 1957 -   .

JUDKINS, Howard R. 1920 -   .

BALDWIN, Cecil C. 1910 -   . [Husband of Mary Catherine Dillon.]

BALDWIN, Mary C. 13 Aug 1911-1 Aug 1991. [Daughter of John Claude and
          Lula Esta (Hitchcock) Dillon, wife of Cecil C. Baldwin.]

COWART, Lois E. 15 Feb 1918-19 May 1991. [Lois Emma Jean, daughter of
          Euless and Emma Pearl (Ferrell) Hockett, wife of Benjamin F.
          Cowart.]

SCOTT, T. Lenier. 1933 -   .

SCOTT, B. Gail. 1943 -   .

COLEMAN, Rex A. "Pappy" 1922 - 31 Oct 1989. [Son of Almer and Beulah
        (Haynes) Coleman, husband of Sandra Rose.]

ROBERTS, Myrtle Troy. 1905-23 Jul 1989. [Daughter of I.M. and Sally
        (Romans) Davis, wife of 1) _____ Sisco and 2) Cecil Roberts.]

SAVAGE, Edward. 19 Jan 1939-21 Oct 1990. VIETNAM. [Son of Vance Smart
        and Georgia (Barnhill) Savage.]

VERPLANK, Margaret Dorothy. 1924 - 2 Dec 1993. [Daughter of Joseph and
        Clara (Georgi) Dany, wife of Grover Verplank.]

HOLLIS, Dewey Franklin. 8 Oct 1933-30 Aug 1991. [Son of Arthur and
        Aldena (Lance) Hollis, husband of Peggy Bowman.]

HOLLIS, Peggy Jo. 23 May 1936 -   . [Peggy Jo Bowman, wife of Dewey
        Franklin Hollis.]

WATSON, Rebecca Lynn. Died 7 Feb 1994, age 16. [Daughter of Robert
        Ernest Jr. and Dinah (____) Watson.

WATSON, Robert E. 1943 - 1991.

McMILLEN, Claude Alton. 1926-20 Jul 1993. [Son of Listeth W. and Susan
        (Bates) McMillian, married 1) _____ _____ and 2) Elizabeth
        Adcock.

McMILLEN, Elizabeth Adcock. 1929 -   . [Second wife of Claude Alton
        McMillen.]

TURNER, Michael Ray. 20 May 1970-3 Aug 1991. US Navy.

BARODY, Donald Ernest. 28 Jun 1924-8 Aug 1993. WWII, KOREA. [Son of
        Joseph and Maude Mae (Denno) Barody.]

TAYLOR, Vernon Floyd. 27 Apr 1924-9 Dec 1990. WWII. [Son of Andrew
        Jackson and Anna (Brown) Taylor.]

TAYLOR, Dorothy Ann. 3 Jul 1929-   ]

SMITH, Mary Frances. 7 Sep 1932-22 Aug 1991. [Daughter of Enoch and
        Lillie (Winton) Northcutt, wife of Phillip Smith, Jr.]

BELL, Kenneth Francis. 8 Oct 1918-31 Oct 1991. WWII. [Son of Henry J.
        and Hattie (Arnold) Bell, husband of Gladys _____.]

HITCHCOCK, Houston H. 24 Jul 1921-10 May 1992. WWII. [Houston Horace,
        son of Horace Edward and Sophia Electra (____) Hitchcock,
        husband of Ivena B._____.]

HITCHCOCK, Ivena B. 1925 -   . [Wife of Houston Horace Hitchcock.]

*BILES, Bobbie Inez. Died 17 Jan 1991, age 60. Daughter of Enoch and
        Lillie (Winton) Northcutt, wife of Harrison E. Biles, Sr.

JONES, William. No other information.

HANES, James M. Died 13 Jan 1994. [Son of James Everett and Virgie May

(Jones) Hanes, husband of Bernice Smith.]

BOREN, Nelson.   Died 15 Feb 1994. [Son of Gilbert and Dolly (Green) Boren, husband of Jane Miller.]

McDOWELL, Thomas A. 1 Sep 1912-24 May 1972. WWII. [Thomas Arnold, son of Mason Bryan and Mary Alice (Richey) McDowell, married 1) Magnolia Fults on 6 Jun 1936 and 2) Martha Lee Roberts on 17 Sep 1949.]

HARMON, William Claud. 6 Mar 1928-6 Aug 1990. WWII. [Son of Andrew and Jenny Sue (Rucker) Harmon, huband of Wylene Mitchell.]

HARMON, Wylene. 20 Apr 1932 -   . [Wylene Mitchell, wife of Willie Claud Harmon.]

PARSLEY, Homer E. 22 Apr 1894-19 Oct 1965. WWI. [Son of Owen and Minnie (Pack) Parsley, husband of Inez McGuire.]

PARSLEY, Inez M. 1898 - 28 May 1980. [Daughter of James Allen and Josie (Austin) McGuire, wife of Homer E. Parsley.]

PARSLEY, Othel O. 1904 - 14 May 1970. [Son of Owen and Minnie (Pack) Parsley, husband of Maudie Mae LaFever.]

THOMISON, James M. 1922-   . [Husband of Nellie Grove.]

THOMISON, Nellie G. 1925 -   .

COPE, Auston. 1918 -   .

COPE, Marie. 1923 -   .

RANKER, Kathy Sue. 13 Sep 1958-31 Mar 1967. [Daughter of Ed Ranker and Patricia (Luckenbaugh) Moore.]

MOORE, Patricia C. 1938 - 3 Jun 1984. [Patricia Charmaine, daughter of Paul and Velma (Naill) Luckenbaugh, wife of Malcolm Raymond Moore.]

MOORE, M. Raymond. 1940 -   . [Husband of Patricia Charmaine Luckenbaugh.]

CLENDENON, Bouldin. Born and died 12 Jan 1939. [Son of Harace and Levesta (Lankford) Clendenon.]

CLENDENON, Levesta L. 23 Apr 1909-11 Jan 1988. [Daughter of Vach L. and Minnie (Bouldin) Lankford, wife of Harace Clendenon.]

CLENDENON, Harace. 22 Jan 1905-25 Apr 1980. [Son of Marion and Adel (Curtis) Clendenon, husband of Cora Levesta Lankford, married 28 Jul 1926.]

HAYES, Sharon B. 1943 - 8 Oct 1980. [Mary Sharon, daughter of George L. and Emma (Bratten) Brown, wife of Johnny W. Hayes.]

HAYES, Johnny W. 1939 -   . [Husband of Mary Sharon Brown.]

HASTON, Rector L. 13 Jun 1886-26 Oct 1973. [Rector Lesley, son of Cyrus Edward and Lodema (Johnson) Haston, husband of Violet H.

Hitchcock.]

HASTON, Violet H. 6 Oct 1882-24 Jul 1973. [Daughter of Loranzo Dow and
    Frances (York) Hitchcock, wife of Rector L. Haston, married 19
    Jul 1908 in Van Buren County, TN.]

WEST, L. Shelton. 1927 -   .

WEST, Carolyn. 1929 -   .

RHODY, Charlie E. 13 May 1884-31 Dec 1971. [Charlie Edgar, son of Henry
    and Mary (Dutton) Rhody, husband of Alta Mathis.]

RHODY, Alta M. 20 Feb 1888-3 Jun 1973. [Daughter of Bluford and Mary
    (Dirting) Mathis, wife of Charlie Rhody.]

ARGO, James C. 15 Jan 1914-1 Aug 1990. [James Corbly, son of Jim D. and
    Lillie (Rogers) Argo, husband of 1) Jessie Ruth Freeze and 2)
    Stella (Jones) Huffman.]

ARGO, Jessie F. 12 Jun 1914-30 Aug 1982. [Jessie Ruth, daughter of
    Elijah Lankford and Eula (Sanders) Freeze, wife of James Corbly
    Argo.]

ROGERS, Dion. 13 Oct 1892-5 Feb 1973. [Son of John H. and Lizzie (Kesey)
    Rogers, husband of Eliza Irene Bonner, married 14 Apr 1918.]

ROGERS, Eliza. 23 Nov 1891-16 Jan 1969. [Eliza Irene, daughter of
    William Carroll and Mary Ann (Christian) Bonner, wife of Dion
    Rogers.]

BURTON, Ben Hooper. 18 May 1914-21 Feb 1993. WWII. [Son of Byrd and
    Lena (LaFever) Burton, husband of Mildred _____.]

BURTON, Mildred. 28 Feb 1915-   . [Wife of Ben Hooper Burton.]

ARGO, Jim D. 22 Dec 1885-22 Mar 1971. [Son of William and Fannie (Fults)
    Argo, husband of Lillie Rogers, married 2 Nov 1910.]

ARGO, Lillie R. 10 Oct 1890-12 Feb 1972. [Daughter of John and Lizzie
    (Kesey) Rogers, wife of Jim D. Argo.]

BYARS, Smith. 18 Mar 1910-20 Jun 1980. [George Smith, son of James H.
    and Melissa (Mullican) Byars, husband of Martha Willie Cope.]

BYARS, Willie. 30 Sep 1911-16 Aug 1991. [Martha Willie, daughter of
    Abner Lee and Zora Belle (Martin) Cope, wife of George Smith
    Byars.]

CAMPBELL, Elbert C. 10 Mar 1915-3 Jul 1992. [Elbert Cleveland, son of
    Beecher and Lou Phema (Tenpenny) Campbell, husband of Dorothy
    Beatrice Jennings.]

CAMPBELL, Beatrice Jennings. 1 May 1928-   . [Daughter of Jess and
    Lillie (Cagle) Jennings, wife of Elbert Cleveland Campbell,
    married 27 Jul 1946.]

GLENN, John Arthur. 23 Aug 1930-8 Aug 1964. [Son of Arthur O. and Nannie
    Lee (Green) Glenn, husband of Virginia Burris.]

Gardens of Memory, cont.

GLENN, Betty Ruth. 22 Mar 1929 only date on stone. [Infant daughter of
        Arthur Odis and Nannie Lee (Green) Glenn.]

GLENN, Nannie Lee. 1902 -   . [Nannie Lee Green, wife of Arthur
        Odis Glenn.]

GLENN, Arthur O. 12 Feb 1908-24 Apr 1989. ["Red", son of John and Bitha
        Marie (Denton) Glenn, husband of Nannie Lee Green.]

NEWBY, Ruth. 8 Nov 1910-20 May 1989. [Ruth Haston, wife of James
        P.Newby.]

NEWBY, James P. 1 Oct 1910-16 Oct 1977. [Son of G.C. and Elizabeth
        (Askew) Newby, husband of Ruth Haston.]

MAYFIELD, Billy M. 14 May 1927-20 May 1984. WWII. [Son of Joe and
        Carrie (Marshall) Mayfield, husband of Marie Turner.]

MAYFIELD, Marie T. 1922 -   . [Marie Turner, married 1) William
        Blair Swann on 17 Aug 1940 and 2) Billy Marshall Mayfield.]

NEAL, Dexter L. 1911 -   . [Husband of Mary Hannah Adcock.]

NEAL, Hannah. 1909 - 16 Jun 1989. [Mary Hannah, daughter of Norman and
        Betty (Cantrell) Adcock, wife of Dexter L. Neal.]

TAYLOR, Thelma. 1911-11 May 1990. [Thelma Norene, daughter of Joe Norman
        and Betty (Harvey) Adcock, wife of Clyde Taylor.]

BUMBALOUGH, Near Frances. 1882 - Oct 1972.

BUMBALOUGH, Sarah Ann. 1885 - Oct 1962.

UPTON, Eugene. 25 Jul 1961-26 Jul 1961. [Turner Eugene, infant son of
        Turner Keisling and Barbara (Hill) Upton.]

HILL, Clarence B.   17 Sep 1906-6 May 1974. [Clarence Benjamin, son of
        Marion F. and Susan (Clendenon) Hill, husband of Ida May
        Cantrell.]

HILL, Ida (Mae). 3 Jul 1909-16 Mar 1977. [Daughter of Robert and
        Sally (Earls) Cantrell, wife of Clarence Benjamin Hill, married
        15 Dec 1924.]

PHILLIPS, Lela A. 21 Aug 1906-24 Feb 1989. [Daughter of John and
        Malissie (Kilgore) Curtis, wife of Arthur Lester Phillips, Sr.,
        married 6 Aug 1922.]

PHILLIPS, Arthur Lester, Sr. 31 Aug 1901-1 Dec 1990. [Son of James
        Brownlow and Deliah Belle (Allison) Phillips, husband of Lela
        A. Curtis.]

CHISAM, Yvonne Lynne. 6 May 1959-16 Dec 1965. [Daughter of John T. and
        Betty Jo (Prater) Chisam.]

ROBINETTE, Elmer Gray. 8 Jan 1917-6 Jun 1987. [Son of Auburn and Estella
        (McMillian) Robinette, husband of Josephine (Smoot) Webb Duke.]

JOHNSON, Silas Oziar. 13 Nov 1928-25 Aug 1967. KOREA. [Son of Cecil and
        Novella (Harris) Johnson, husband of Wilma Robinette.]

Gardens of Memory, cont.

ROBINETTE, Stella T. 6 Aug 1896-15 Oct 1972. [Daughter of Neal and Alice (Thomas) McMillan, wife of Auburn L. Robinette, married 10 Jan 1915 in Virginia.]

ROBINETTE, Auburn L. 20 Feb 1891-24 Oct 1973. [Son of Daniel and Nancy Margaret (Bledsoe) Robinette, husband of Estella McMillan.]

DOTSON, Vernice. 6 Jan 1912-12 Apr 1977. [Son of Grover and Mattie Gertrude (Gipson) Dotson, husband of 1) Mollie Faye Newby and 2) Edna Wilson.]

DOTSON, Mollie Fay. 21 May 1915-27 Feb 1971. [Daughter of Andy Thomas and Allie (Mullican) Newby, first wife of Vernice Dotson.]

STUDER, Paul J. 1925 -   . [Husband of Norma Miller.]

STUDER, Norma J. 1925 -   . [Norma J. Miller, wife of Paul J. Studer.]

STUDER, John B. 14 May 1949-23 Mar 1989. US Army. [John Budd, son of Paul J. and Norma (Miller) Studer. Single.]

PRATER, Joe. 1 May 1917-9 Nov 1979. WWII. [Son of Porter and Maude (Jaco) Prater, wife of Emma Lee Youngblood.]

PRATER, Emma Lee. 18 May 1918-   . [Daughter of Robert and Sammie (Tittle) Youngblood, married 1) to James Carr on 4 Jan 1935 and 2) to Joe Prater.]

COOPER, Edwin W. 3 Dec 1912-9 May 1971. Edwin Woodrow, son of Thomas L. And Orthie (Duke) Cooper, husband of Minnie L. Campbell.]

COOPER, Minnie L. 18 Mar 1913-   . [Minnie L. Campbell, wife of Edwin Woodrow Cooper.]

GREGORY, Lorene D. 16 Feb 1920-   . [Lorene Denton, wife of George D. Gregory.]

GREGORY, George D. 18 Aug 1923-7 Oct 1974. US Army. [Son of Luke and Georgia (Nolan) Gregory, husband of Lorene Denton, married 8 Sep 1943.]

HOOVER, Dalton L. 19 Nov 1933-   . [Son of Lawrence R. and Ila Mai (Reeder) Hoover, husband of Leoma Frances Darnell, married 3 Jun 1950.]

HOOVER, Leoma Frances. 1931 -   . [Daughter of Frank and Leah (Wooten) Darnell, wife of Dalton L. Hoover.]

FOX, Catherine M. 3 Oct 1967 only date on stone. [Catherine Mae, daughter of Raymond and _____ (_____) Fox.]

FOX, O. Richard. 1942 - Aug 1961.

FOX, Birdie M. 1918-Jan 1990. [Birdie Mae McDonald, wife of Jack Wesley Fox.]

FOX, Jack W. 1911-12 Jun 1978. [Jack Wesley Fox, husband of Birdie Mae McDonald.]

Gardens of Memory, cont.

SMOOT, Reva Enole. 23 May 1924-   . [Daughter of Auburn and Stella
        (McMillan) Robinette, wife of Rayford Ray Smoot.]

SMOOT, Rayford Ray. 9 May 1920-27 Sep 1991. [Son of George and Cora
        (Brown) Smoot, husband of Reva Enole Robinette.]

DAVENPORT, Elsie Blanks. 4 Oct 1905-13 May 1993. [Daughter of James
        Martin and Ollie (Davenport) Blanks, wife of Raydon Coleman
        Davenport.]

DAVENPORT, Raydon Coleman. 15 Oct 1901-24 Feb 1969. [Son of Joseph Isaac
        and Alice Arlelia (_____) Davenport, husband of Elsie Blanks,
        married 15 Nov 1925 in Cannon County, TN.]

SHARPE, C.B. Sr. 7 Oct 1908-24 Sep 1991. [Clifton Birt, son of George
        and Nora Jane (Allen) Sharpe, husband of 1) Effie Mai Stewart
        and 2) Iona (Stewart) Luna.]

SHARPE, Effie Mai. 18 Nov 1911-25 Mar 1980. [Daughter of Willie Archie
        and Martha (Young) Stewart, wife of Clifton Birt Sharpe, Sr.]

SHARPE, Clifton B. 21 Mar 1929-31 Dec 1986. [Son of Clifton B. Sr. and
        Effie Mai (Stewart) Sharpe.]

WEDDINGTON, R. L. 24 Feb 1929-15 Oct 1986. [Roy Laymon, son of Roy and
        Daisy Susie (Hunt) Weddington, husband of Hazel Bost.]

WEDDINGTON, Hazel. 1929 -   . [Daughter of Frank Luther and Elba L.
        (Boren) Bost, wife of Roy Laymon Weddington.]

WEDDINGTON, Roy. 28 Sep 1895-2 Mar 1967. [Son of Clay and Fannie (Pharm)
        Weddington, husband of Daisy Susan Hunt.]

WEDDINGTON, Daisy Hunt. 17 Dec 1897-18 Sep 1974. [Daisy Susan, daughter
        of William and Sallie (Bohannon) Hunt, wife of Roy Weddington.]

WEDDINGTON, Luther V. 26 Aug 1920-22 Feb 1970. WWII, KOREA. [Luther
        Virgil "Blue", son of Roy and Daisy Susan (Hunt) Weddington,
        husband of Maggie Lee Hillis (div.).]

SHERRILL, Roger. 1927-1 Feb 1988. [Son of Gaines and Hattie (Reed)
        Sherrill, husband of Mabel Cunningham.]

SHERRILL, Mabel G. 1933 -   . [Mabel Cunningham, wife of Roger
        Sherrill.]

SCOTT, Zelma L. 17 Nov 1923 -   . "Beloved wife."

ANDERSON, Claude E. 18 Nov 1904-14 Apr 1989. [Claude Elson "Cricket",
        son of Claude and Bertha (Wright) Anderson, husband of 1) _____
        _____, and 2) Lois Pauline (Hillis) Walker.]

ANDERSON, Lois. 1911 -   . [Lois Pauline Hillis, wife of 1) _____
        Walker and 2) Claude Elson "Cricket" Anderson.]

CAGLE, Hugh. 1910 - 16 Aug 1993. [Son of Edmond and Mollie (Rogers)
        Cagle, husband of Ruby E. York.]

CAGLE, Ruby E. 1916 -   . [Ruby E. York, wife of Hugh Cagle.]

Gardens of Memory, cont.

RIGSBY, Audie M. 1916 - .

RIGSBY, Addie F. 1921 - .

TOWNSEND, Larry R. 1941 - 19 May 1988. [Larry Reed, son of Mrs. Ruby Davis, husband of Sheron Rigsby.]

TOWNSEND, Sheran R. 1944 - . [Sheran Rigsby, wife of Larry Reed Townsend.]

STROUD, Ruth Denton. 10 Mar 1922-12 Apr 1989. [Daughter of Green V. and Bessie (Darnell) Denton, wife of James Givin Stroud.]

STROUD, James G. 1918 - . [James Givin, son of James T. and Edna (Woodside) Stroud, husband of Ruth Denton.]

TALLEY, Carletta B. 6 Sep 1925-8 Jul 1992. [Daughter of James Cleveland and Sarah Elizabeth (Stroud) Blackburn, wife of Clyde Alton Talley.]

TALLEY, Clyde Alton. 16 Feb 1924-15 Aug 1983. WWII. [Son of Claude and Maude E. (Thompson) Talley, husband of Carletta Blackburn, married 31 May 1946.]

JOHNSON, Mildred L. 1910 - . [Mildred L. Talley, wife of James Louis Johnson.]

JOHNSON, James Louis. 17 Jun 1913-7 Dec 1989. WWII, PERSIAN GULF. [Son of James E. and Alice (Dodson) Johnson, husband of Mildred L. Talley.]

FORD, Charles (Steve). 1944 - Dec 1972.

FORD, Jane Lowry. 1 Mar 1926-8 Apr 1982. [Daughter of Randolph T. and Mildred (Hutchings) Lowry, wife of Charles Ford, married 22 Oct 1943.]

WEDDINGTON, Carl Gene. 26 Jul 1947-29 Jan 1977. [Son of Robert Carl and Pauline (Bost) Weddington, husband of Arlene Scott (div.).]

WEDDINGTON, Pauline B. 1922 - . [Daughter of Frank Luther and Elba L. (Boren) Bost, wife of Robert Carl Weddington.]

WEDDINGTON, Robert Carl. 26 May 1926-20 Sep 1978. WWII. [Son of Roy and Daisy (Hunt) Weddington, husband of Pauline Bost.]

BOST, Charles Franklin. 2 Mar 1932-16 May 1977. KOREA. [Son of Frank Luther and Elba L. (Boren) Bost, husband of Virginia Bonner.]

TALLEY, Jack R. 15 Dec 1935-5 Apr 1990. US Army. [Jack Reece, Sr., son of John Robert and Thelma (Taylor) Talley, husband of Melba Sharp.]

LOWRY, Randolph T. 17 Jul 1902-18 Oct 1990. [Randolph Taylor, son of Frank and Nolia (Taylor) Lowry, husband of Mildred Annie Hutchings, married 28 Mar 1925.]

LOWRY, Mildred H. 1907 - . [Mildred Annie Hutchings, wife of Randolph Taylor Lowry.]

Gardens of Memory, cont.

PADGETT, Wilbert T. 20 Aug 1929- . [Wilbert Thurman, husband of Lillian Louise Roberts, married 12 Nov 1949 in Rossville, GA.]

PADGETT, Lillian L. 10 Dec 1928- . [Lillian Louise, daughter of Elisha and Hallie (Bouldin) Roberts, wife of Wilbert Thurman Padgett.]

HUNTER, James C. 2 Jun 1920-11 Feb 1987. WWII. [Son of John W. and Cora (Goldtrap) Hunter, husband of Maggie Ruth Lowery.]

HUNTER, Maggie Ruth Lowery. 1933 - . [Wife of James C. Hunter.]

HILL, Fred Leslie. 6 Feb 1919-12 Oct 1993. WWII. [Son of Fred Clay and Hattie Mae (Stewart) Hill, husband of Wilma Bumbalough.]

HILL, Wilma E. 1922 - . [Wilma Bumbalough, wife of Fred Leslie Hill.]

BOUNDS, Olla. 23 Jan 1926- . [Olla Belle, daughter of Webster P. and Sallie Belle (Fisher) Hutchins, granddaughter of Webb and Liza (Luna) Hutchins and granddaughter of Lawson and Mary E. (Robinson) Fisher, wife of Malcolm Franklin Bounds.]

BOUNDS, Malcolm. 7 May 1922- . [Malcolm Franklin, son of Charlie I. and Annie (Adcock) Bounds, grandson of James and Sarah (Phillips) Adcock and grandson of William C. and Talitha H. (Gribble) Bounds, husband of Olla Belle Hutchins.]

SMITH, D.M. Sr. 7 Jul 1909-21 Dec 1978. [Son of Tom and _____ (_____) Smith, husband of Mary Ellen _____.]

KING, Jacob T. 1981-25 Sep 1992. [Jacob Troy, son of David R. and Jackie D. (Bain) King.]

KING, David R. 18 Nov 1948- . [Son of Jessie H. and Lillian Virginia (Hines) King, husband of 1) Linda E. Miller (div.) and 2) Jackie D. Bain.]

MARTIN, George Alvin. 25 Sep 1922-10 Sep 1973. [Son of George Anderson and Eva (Haley) Martin, husband of Louise Teeters.]

WHITAKER, Sidney L. 1 Jul 1922-28 Feb 1979. WWII. [Son of Sidney and Leona (Rogers) Hunter Whitaker, husband of Frances Ruth Smith.]

GORDY, James E. 1900-18 Nov 1979. [Son of James Taylor and Lula Bell (Dempsey) Gordy, husband of Hassie Loring Mathis.]

GORDY, Hassie L.M. 1914 - . [Hassie Loring Mathis, wife of James E. Gordy.]

WINTON, Alfred. 1928 - 12 Feb 1992. [Son of Hence and Ettie (Gross) Winton, husband of Maxine Gordy.]

WINTON, Maxine. 1935 - . [Daughter of James E. and Hassie Loring (Mathis) Gordy, wife of Alfred Winton.]

KING, Jessie M. 1957 - Jun 1982.

DAVIS, George S. 27 Jan 1922-7 Mar 1987. WWII, KOREA, VIETNAM. [George

Smith, son of George Smith, Sr. and Octa May (McBride) Davis, husband of Frances Ruth Pack.]

DAVIS, Frances R. 13 Feb 1929-   . [Daughter of Othel and Loretta Mai (Sparkman) Pack, wife of George Smith Davis.]

PACK, Loretta Mai. 23 Jul 1903-16 May 1994. [Daughter of Frank and Dolly (Griffith) Sparkman, first wife of Othel D. Pack.]

STEWART, Robert L. 12 Jan 1910-9 Jan 1974. [Robert Lee, son of Samuel and Edora (Flanning) Stewart, husband of Bertha Choate.]

FISH, John Wiley. 1907 - Dec 1973. [Husband of Ceva Lillian Raymond.]

FISH, Ceva Lillian. 1907-12 Feb 1991. [Daughter of Bob and Lucy Ann (Biggs) Raymond, wife of John Wiley Fish.]

ROGERS, Rufus A. 20 Apr 1908-2 Sep 1960. [Rufus Anson, son of William Silas and Mary Belle (Tosh) Rogers, husband of Louise Watley.]

ROGERS, Louise W. 8 Dec 1916-19 Mar 1983. [Daughter of Arthur Benjamin and Maude (Crawford) Watley, wife of Rufus Anson Rogers.]

CLENDENON, P. Eston. 13 Jan 1907-22 Sep 1979. [Paul Eston, son of James Newton and Nettie (Bouldin) Clendenon, husband of Ruby Jean Cass, married 25 Nov 1928.]

CLENDENON, Ruby J. 30 Nov 1904-21 Nov 1983. [Ruby Jean, daughter of Richard Martin and Louvenne Elizabeth (Hobbs) Cass, wife of Paul Eston Clendenon.]

HODGES, Ira. 1902-8 Jul 1983. [Son of John W. and Hattie (Moody) Hodges, husband of Flossie _____.]

COOK, Clayton. 5 Sep 1928-   . [Son of L.A. and Dicy Elva (Golden) Cook, husband of Mary Ellen Williams.]

COOK, Mary Ellen. 7 Oct 1933-   . [Daughter of William Toy and Ida (Martin) Williams, wife of Clayton Leroy Cook, married 8 Apr 1950.]

HARRIS, Charles T. 1950 -   .

HARRIS, Angel D. 1960 -   .

PRYOR, Mack Dean. 1912 -   .

PRYOR, Martha T. 1912 -   .

MARTIN, Bradford A. Jr. 1983 - 3 Oct 1983. [Seven week old son of Bradford Allen and Gwendolyn (Staples) Martin.]

SOLOMON, Luther Artman. 24 Jun 1922-24 May 1991. [Son of Joseph Alfred and Dora Alice (Kidd) Solomon, husband of Lela Belle Wallace.]

PARKER, Wayland M. 1917 -   .

PARKER, Laura I. 1916 -   .

LAYNE, Spergeon E. 21 Feb 1921-   . [Son of Frank and Daisy

Gardens of Memory, cont.

(Tate) Layne, husband of Virginia Reline Sitz, married 20 Jun 1940.]

LAYNE, Virginia Reline. 29 Jan 1925-   . [Daughter of Rellie and Jane (Caldwell) Sitz, wife of Spergeon E. Layne.]

MADEWELL, Odie A. 1929-24 Nov 1980. [Odie Avin, son of Arthur and Ethel (McBride) Madewell, husband of Naomi Wilmore.]

MADEWELL, Naomi. 1926 -   . [Naomi Wilmore, wife of Odie Avin Madewell.]

NORTHCUTT, William Ray. 22 Oct 1940-   . [Son of Thurman Lee and Georgia Mae (Reynolds) Northcutt, husband of Thelma Joyce Rogers, married 12 Aug 1961.]

NORTHCUTT, Joyce Rogers. 6 May 1942-   . [Thelma Joyce, daughter of Rufus Anson and Louise (Watley) Rogers, wife of William Ray Northcutt.]

BROOKS, Ethel Morgan. 1901 - 4 Jul 1977. [Wife of Walter S. Brooks.]

BROOKS, Walter S. 1902-24 Dec 1968. [Walter S., Sr., son of Albert Milton and Annie Elizabeth (Shaffer) Brooks, husband of Ethel Morgan.]

KIRBY, Johnny Ray. 2 Apr 1961-31 Mar 1978. [Son of Junior Floyd and Kiyomi (Murai) Kirby.]

KIRBY, Kiyomi. 1932 -   . [Daughter of Mrs. Taka Murai of Japan, wife of Junior Floyd Kirby.]

KIRBY, J. Floyd. 1937 -   . [Son of T.G. and _____ (_____) Kirby, husband of Kiyomi Murai.]

GOODMAN, Rozelle. 1917 -   . [Rozelle Sliger, wife of John Walker Goodman.]

GOODMAN, John W. 5 Jan 1923-2 Jul 1974. [Son of George and Mary (_____) Goodman, husband of Rozelle Sliger.]

SLIGER, Clara R. 14 Feb 1886-23 Mar 1960. [Daughter of John and Hattie (_____) Richardson, wife of Joseph Andrew Sliger.]

SLIGER, Joe A. 14 Jun 1888-14 May 1972. [Son of Andy and Harriet (Saylors) Sliger, husband of Clara Richardson.]

MAXWELL, Josie P. 1916 -   . [Josie Pack, wife of Grady M. Maxwell.]

MAXWELL, Grady M. 1911 - 5 Jun 1993. [Son of John and Atlas (LaFever) Maxwell, husband of Josie Pack.]

SAIN, Ruby S. 3 Apr 1895-23 Oct 1989. [Ruby Irene, daughter of Asa Faulkner and Mary Ellen (Hix) Stubblefield, wife of Fred Wesley "Pop" Sain, Sr.]

SAIN, Fred W. Sr. 11 Oct 1892-26 Dec 1982. [Fred Wesley, son of James Lafayette and Lillian (Judkins) Sain, husband of Ruby Irene Stubblefield.]

SAIN, Raymond L. 1 Jan 1932-6 Jun 1963. [Son of Fred Wesley Sr. and Ruby Irene (Stubblefield) Sain, husband of Colene Akers.]

KENNAMER, Patsy A. 1938 -   .

KENNAMER, J. Harvey. 1934 -   . [Son of Jewell and Ella (Bridges) Kennamer.]

KENNAMER, Ella. 1911 -   . [Ella Bridges, wife of William Jewell Kennamer.]

KENNAMER, Jewell. 3 Sep 1905-10 Sep 1992. [William Jewell, son of Abe and Maggie (Walls) Kennamer, husband of Ella Bridges.]

GRIBBLE, Annie M. 16 Apr 1912-7 Dec 1992. [Annie Marie, daughter of Isaac Newton and Annie Marie (Clancy) Smoot, wife of Joe Butler Gribble.]

GRIBBLE, Joe Butler. 20 Feb 1897-8 Aug 1971. WWII. [Son of Dock Jackson and Julia (Miller) Gribble, husband of Annie Marie Smoot.]

WILLIAMS, Samuel D. Sr. 14 Apr 1933-16 Jan 1972. US Air Force.

SLATTEN, Rayburn. 1901 - 11 Jul 1973. [Rayburn Van, husband of Clara R. Turner.]

SLATTEN, Clara R. 1907 - 15 Apr 1981. [Daughter of James Irvin and Hanna (Allen) Turner, wife of Rayburn Van Slatten.]

CLOUSE, W. Reed. 9 Sep 1900-15 Mar 1982. [Willie Reed, son of Newt and _____ (_____) Clouse, husband of Thelma Shaw.]

CLOUSE, Thelma S. 22 Jul 1905-11 Aug 1988. [Daughter of Addison Sr. and Minnie (Bates) Shaw, wife of Willie Reed Close.]

POTTER, J.C. 1 Oct 1930-4 Jun 1984. [Son of Ernest Samuel and Lucinda (Boren) Potter, husband of Ruth Wyatt.]

POTTER, Ruth W. 1926 -   . [Ruth Wyatt, wife of J.C. Potter.]

REED, George David. 1922-26 Jun 1993. [Son of Sam and Haley (Harris) Reed, husband of Dorothy Mai Tenpenny.]

REED, Dorothy Mai. 1926 -   . [Dorothy Mai Tenpenny, wife of George David Reed, Sr.]

NEWBY, H.M. "Jack". 1916 -   . [Hiram M., husband of Martha Lee Jordan.]

NEWBY, Martha Lee. 1917 - 4 Oct 1983. [Daughter of Robert L. and Gladys Elizabeth (Lively) Jordan, wife of Hiram M. Newby.]

RAWSON, George E. Jr. 1956 - 20 Mar 1979. [George Edward, son of George E., Sr. and _____ (_____) Rawson.]

CLARK, Eula G. 12 Jun 1893-2 Jan 1964. [Daughter of Nichlos Charles and Lucy Jane (Stewart) Golden, wife of Magness Clark.]

CLARK, Magness. 8 Dec 1895-4 Jul 1971. WWI. [Husband of Eula Golden.]

Gardens of Memory, cont.

OSMENT, John E. 6 Sep 1892-24 Mar 1972. [Son of Andrew and Victoria
    (Stone) Osment, husband of Jennie Barrett.]

OSMENT, S. Clifton. 1922 -   .

OSMENT, Pauline. 1936 -   .

PHILLIPS, W.V., Sr. 1909 -   . [William Virgil, husband of Ola Mae
    Womack.]

PHILLIPS, Ola Mae. 1911 - 14 Jan 1994. [Daughter of Jacob Ervin and Leth
    (Haley) Womack, wife of William Virgil Phillips.]

PHILLIPS, Charles Wayne. 1 Sep 1944-27 Feb 1978. [Son of William Virgil
    and Ola Mae (Womack) Phillips.]

CROTHERS, Kayla M. "Our Baby." 10 Oct 1990.

REDMON, Mary H. 23 Feb 1927-   . [Mary Helen Brown, wife of John Roy
    Redmon.]

REDMON, John R. 8 May 1929-31 Oct 1990. KOREA, VIETNAM. [Son of Leonard
    Payne and Mary Ella (Hardcastle) Redmon, husband of Mary Helen
    Brown.]

LUNA, Jamie J. "Punkin". 21 Oct 1977-16 Jun 1978. [Jamie Jenell,
    daughter of Burgess Wayne and Nancy Kay (Pennington) Luna.]

STONER, Leida Wanamaker. 21 Oct 1913 -   . [Daughter of James and
    Nancy (Wanamaker) Wanamaker, wife of Robert Clinton Stoner.]

STONER, Robert (Clinton). 24 May 1914-18 Dec 1989. [Son of Jess and
    Martha Abigail (Coppinger) Stoner, husband of Leida Wanamaker.]

PENNINGTON, Judy Gail. 19 Aug 1948-15 Aug 1981. [Daughter of Gaston and
    Ruby (Jones) Pennington, wife of _____ Goodwin.]

HALL, Pauline E. 21 June 1915 -   . [Daughter of Clarence E. and
    Minnie Pearl (Parsley) Freeze, wife of Thurman Alvin Hall.]

HALL, Thurman Alvin. 19 Aug 1912-21 Jan 1985. [Son of James A. and
    Martha (Haley) Hall, husband of Edna Pauline Freeze.]

TAYLOR, Daniel C. 1917- 7 Jul 1988. [Daniel Clayton, son of Stephen and
    Ellen (Sowders) Taylor, husband of Marie Cupp.]

DIXON, Helen R. 16 Sep 1938-   . [Wife of Harry Lee Dixon.]

DIXON, Harry Lee. 13 Feb 1933-23 Apr 1994. KOREA. [Son of John W. and
    Dora E. (Pennington) Dixon, husband of Helen _____.]

BROWN, Tony C. 25 Feb 1960-30 Aug 1980. [Tony Costella, son of Charles
    D. Womack and Eva Brown. Single.]

PARKER, Darlene Renee. 18 Jul 1964-26 Aug 1964. [Daughter of Cecil
    Howard and Patricia M. (Coppinger) Parker.]

WALKER, Alean. 2 Jun 1893-22 Jan 1976. [Daughter of Gordon and Tennie
    (Smith) Cantrell, wife of Joe Walker.]

WALKER, Joe.   1 Jan 1890-27 Oct 1972.   [Son of A. Gordan and Sallie (Purser) Walker, husband of Alene Cantrell, married 6 Dec 1914.]

SIMMONS, Joyce.   3 May 1934 -   .   [Joyce Ann, daughter of Joe and Alean (Cantrell) Walker, wife of Howard Simmons.]

SIMMONS, Howard.   2 Nov 1935-10 Aug 1972.   [Husband of Joyce Ann Walker, married 25 Dec 1955.]

CANTRELL, Clara N.   1935 -   .   [Clara Jones, wife of Joe A. Cantrell.]

CANTRELL, Joe A.   1930 - 22 May 1993.   [Son of Burgess Harold and Minnie (Mullican) Cantrell, husband of Clara Jones.]

PATTERSON, Connie Sue.   5 Jun 1968-12 Aug 1976.   [Daughter of William C. and _____ (White) Patterson.]

SUMMERS, Jesse Tom.   8 Sep 1888-12 Nov 1964.   [Son of Robert and Palmer (Givens) Summers, husband of 1) Mary Edna _____ and 2) Rachel Jones.]

SUMMERS, Mary Edna.   1895 - 1923.   [First wife of Jesse Tom Summers.]

AUSTIN, Dillard C.   1914 -   .   [Son of Joseph Edward and Rachel Evelee (Medley) Austin, husband of Frances Summers, married 2 Jan 1937.]

AUSTIN, Frances.   1920 -   .   [Frances Summers, wife of Dillard C. Austin.]

REYNOLDS, Robert A.   1928 -   .

REYNOLDS, Reba I.   1931 -   .

BOUNDS, Lee Austin.   19 May 1913-23 Jan 1991.   [Son of Charles Isham and Nancy Ann "Annie" (Adcock) Bounds, husband of Mary Novella Mullican.]

BOUNDS, Mary Novella.   1924 -   .   [Daughter of Dallas and _____ (_____) Mullican, wife of Lee Austin Bounds.]

YOUNGBLOOD, Lebron.   7 Apr 1916-6 Feb 1989.   WWII.   [Husband of Dollie Lorene Phillips.]

YOUNGBLOOD, Dollie.   3 Dec 1913-30 Nov 1988.   [Daughter of S.B. and Belle (Collins) Phillips, wife of Lebron Youngblood.]

CANTRELL, Zollie A.   2 Mar 1887-16 Mar 1985.   [Zollie Adron, son of James Buchannon and Sarah Elizabeth (League) Cantrell, husband of Shirlie Love.]

CANTRELL, Shirlie Love.   1899-6 Jun 1980.   [Daughter of Martin Luther and Katherine (Anderson) Love, wife of Zollie A. Cantrell.]

CORBETT, James Earl.   1 Apr 1926-29 Jul 1990.   WWII, KOREA.   [Son of James Roy and Hannah (Twilley) Corbett.]

WOODS, John B.   1932 - 4 Apr 1988.   [Son of Lucious and Jennie (Carr)

Gardens of Memory, cont.

Woods, husband of Shirley _____.]

STRODE, Jennifer Leann. 8 Sep 1983-9 Oct 1983. [Daughter of Ed Hill and
        Vivian Strode.]

STRODE, Christopher Adam. 8 Sep 1983-24 Feb 1984. [Son of Ed Hill and
        Vivian Strode.]

PHILLIPS, John F. 1940-29 Jul 1989. [John Floyd, son of William And Ola
        Mae (Womack) Phillips, husband of Dorothy _____.]

PHILLIPS, Dorothy. 1939-   . [Wife of John Floyd Phillips.]

FISHER, Roy (Feie). 24 Dec 1888-22 May 1964. [Leroy Fisher, husband of
        Carrie Neal.]

FISHER, Carrie. 27 Oct 1895-11 Jul 1970. [Daughter of Ed and Martha
        (Taylor) Neal, wife of Leroy Fisher.]

MULLICAN, W.E. (Edd). 1900 - Oct 1972. [Husband of Rachel Farless.]

MULLICAN, Rachel Farless. 17 Nov 1904-20 Apr 1963. [Daughter of Obie and
        Ida (Cunningham) Farless, wife of Edd Mullican.]

BELL, Michael David. 10 Sep 1971-11 Sep 1971. [Son of Thomas Wayne and
        Sandra Kay (Jordon) Bell.]

BELL, Janet Kay. 2 Jul 1978-2 Jul 1978. [Daughter of Thomas Wayne and
        Sandra Kay (Jordon) Bell.]

WILLIAMS, Fred D. 25 Nov 1917-15 Sep 1990. WWII.

DAVIS, Tinia Marie. 1955 - Oct 1960.

UNDERHILL, John W.   1898 - 20 Jun 1979. [Son of James Holiday and Parlee
        (Bailey) Underhill, grandson of George W. and Malissa (Rigsby)
        Underhill and grandson of William and Martha E. (Melton)
        Bailey, husband of Mattie Lee Winnett.]

UNDERHILL, Mattie Lee W. 1900-23 Feb 1985. [Daughter of W.C. and Liza
        (Holder) Winnett, wife of John W. Underhill.]

CANTRELL, James R. 6 Oct 1930-   . [James Reed, son of Zollie
        Adron and Shirley (Love) Cantrell, husband of Bobbye M. Oakes,
        married 27 May 1961.]

CANTRELL, Bobbye M. 29 Apr 1939-22 Mar 1993. [Daughter of Hunter and
        Bessie (Ward) Oakes, wife of James Reed Cantrell.]

MARTIN, Elmer. 1910 -   . [Husband of Marjorie A. Savage.]

MARTIN, Marjorie A. 1917 - 17 Dec 1992. [Daughter of Hillis and Belle
        (Locke) Savage, wife of Elmer Martin.]

DARDEN, Ottie Louis. 2 Dec 1901-10 May 1972. [Husband of Grovene
        Howard.]

DARDEN, Grovene Howard.   No dates.   [Daughter of Evan L. and Martha
        Alice (Wheeler) Howard, wife of Ottie Louis Darden.]

HOWARD, Alice W. 1885-Sep 1970. [Martha Alice, daughter of John and Julie (West) Wheeler, wife of Evan L. Howard.]

CASSETTY, Charles L. 1917 -   . [Husband of Evelyn Howard.]

CASSETTY, Evelyn H. 1923-1 Aug 1989. [Daughter of Evan L. and Martha Alice (Wheeler) Howard, wife of Charles "Steamboat" Cassetty.]

RIGSBY, Elizabeth C. 17 Jan 1925 -   . [Mary Elizabeth, daughter of Green Fletcher and Nettie Mae (Lowery) Certain, wife of Marvin Leonard Rigsby.]

RIGSBY, Marvin Leonard. 30 May 1921-12 Sep 1978. WWII. [Son of Ernest and Martha (Duncan) Rigsby, husband of Elizabeth Certain.]

RIGSBY, Everett E. 1914 -   . [Everett Elston, son of Ernest Holiday and Martha Eleanor (Duncan) Rigsby, husband of Mary Lynn Bounds, married 1 Feb 1946.]

RIGSBY, Mary Lynn. 6 Dec 1927-   [Daughter of Charles Isham and Nancy Ann (Adcock) Bounds, wife of Everett Elston Rigsby.]

MEDLEY, Dollie B. 12 Jan 1901-18 Jun 1971. [Dollie Bertha, daughter of W.A. and Maggie (Gevens) Carter, wife of Codie Medley.]

MEDLEY, Codie. 5 Feb 1901-6 Oct 1990. [Son of George and Katherine (Burton) Medley, husband of Dollie Bertha Carter.]

HENDRIX, Joseph J. 14 Jun 1920-2 Nov 1989. [Joseph Jonathan, son of Jonathan and Rosa (Perkins) Hendrix, husband of Frankie Warren, married 29 Jun 1945.]

HENDRIX, Frankie W. 14 Mar 1925-   . [Frankie Warren, wife of Joseph Jonathan Hendrix.]

GRIBBLE, Larry Q. "Moe". 1940-20 Jul 1983. [Son of Cellie Lee and Jennie (Starkey) Gribble.]

WOODS, Maggie B. 1938 -   . [Daughter of Cellie Lee and Jennie (Starkey) Gribble, wife of _____ Woods.]

FLOYD, Lucille. 11 Apr 1935-10 Mar 1991. [Daughter of Taylor and Sarah Jane (Thomas) Jones, wife of William H. Floyd (div.)]

FLOYD, Emma Alene. 12 Apr 1963-29 Nov 1964. [Daughter of William and Lucille (Jones) Floyd.]

POTTER, Grady A. 21 May 1914-30 Jan 1993. [Grady Alden, son of Leslie and Eva (Johnson) Potter, husband of Dorothy _____.]

POTTER, Dorothy B. 13 Jan 1924-   . [Wife of Grady A. Potter.]

EVANS, Ronnie. 1943-17 Jul 1988. [Ira Ronald "Ronnie", son of Nolan and Beulah (Gilbert) Evans, husband of Betty Taylor.]

EVANS, Betty. 1944 -   . [Betty Taylor, wife of Ira Ronald Evans.]

JONES, Terry Chester. 18 Jun 1947-11 Dec 1976. VIETNAM. [Son of Chester E. and Virginia Ruth (Watson) Jones.]

JONES, Chester E. 1918 - 28 Mar 1983. [Son of Joseph L. and Bettie (Knight) Jones, husband of Virginia Ruth Watson, married 24 Dec 1936.]

JONES, Virginia Ruth. 1922 - . [Daughter of Charles Louis and John Ann (Patterson) Watson, wife of Chester E. Jones.]

WATSON, Charles Louis. 1901 - . [Husband of John Ann Patterson, married 25 Dec 1921.]

WATSON, John Ann. 1908 - 29 Jan 1983. [Daughter of Shela and Mary (Miller) Patterson, wife of Charles Louis Watson.]

HIBDON, Calvin C. 1931 - 12 Oct 1992. [Son of W.B. and Noravella (Bratcher) Hibdon, husband of Reba Winona _____.]

HIBDON, Reba W. 1930 - . [Reba Winona _____, wife of Calvin C. Hibdon.]

CANTRELL, William E. 1921 - .

CANTRELL, Margaret T. 1926 - .

LANCE, Henry D. 1930 - .

LANCE, Agnes U. 1933 - .

GROVE, Elmer. 1908 - . [Husband of Mildred Eubanks.]

GROVE, Mildred. 1 May 1911-5 Feb 1992. [Daughter of Herman and Christbelle (Kirkley) Eubanks, wife of Elmer Grove.]

STROUD, Barry K. 1954 - .

STROUD, Barbara J. 1950 - .

HOLLAND, J.W. 12 Feb 1881-15 Jul 1965. [James William, son of Allen and Ellen (Chambers) Holland, husband of Lillie Shrum.]

HOLLAND, Lillie S. 1888 - Mar 1958. [Lillie Shrum, wife of James William Holland.]

SMITH, James Franklin, Jr. 25 May 1915- 10 Aug 1978. WWII. [Son of Oscar and Lena (_____) Smith, husband of Leona Byars.]

GOLDEN, Susie C. 12 May 1908-24 Jun 1966. [Susie Mai, daughter of Walker C. and Lucinda (Peden) Case, wife of John Rolfe Golden.]

GOLDEN, John Rolfe. 24 Aug 1907- . [Son of Elkanah D. and Kissie (Green) Golden, married 1) Susie Mai Case on 30 Dec 1941 and 2) Lottie Geneva (Curtis) Hitchcock and 3) Lourene Morgan.]

GOLDEN, Gladys Barbee. 27 Dec 1903-10 Nov 1992. [Daughter of John and Ellen (Malone) Barbee, wife of Charles Compton Golden, married 23 Dec 1923.]

GOLDEN, Charles C. 25 Jan 1902-18 Nov 1970. [Charles Compton, son of Elkanah D. and Kissimer (Green) Golden, husband of Gladys Barbee.]

TALLEY, Jack Reece Jr. 16 Aug 1964-3 Jun 1990. [Son of Jack Reece Sr. and Melba Jean (Sharp) Talley, husband of Donna Earles.]

ROBERTSON, Teresa Lynn. 29 Jan 1977-14 May 1983. [Daughter of Katrina (Holland) White Robertson and Kenneth D. White.]

NUNLEY, Rice A. 17 Mar 1905-3 Feb 1981. WWII. [Son of Commodore and Alpha (Smartt) Nunley, husband of 1) Juanita Madewell and 2) Louise Bishop.]

PENDLETON, John L. Jr. 19 Nov 1947-6 May 1972. VIETNAM.

GREEN, Joseph Samuel. 11 Feb 1893-13 Oct 1972. [Son of Mathew Compton and Eliza Elliot (Kirby) Green, husband of Flaura White, married 17 Nov 1918.]

GREEN, Flaura White. 13 Aug 1896-6 Jun 1981. [Daughter of John Henry and Flaura (Robinson) White, wife of Joseph Samuel Green.]

HANFORD, Naomi. 1920 only date on stone. [Daughter of Joseph Samuel and Flaura (White) Green.

GOLDEN, Allen Ward. 3 Aug 1913 - . [Son of Elkanah D. and Kissimoer (Green) Golden, husband of Flora Jane Grizzell, married 29 May 1934.]

GOLDEN, Flora Jane. 21 Apr 1914- . [Daughter of Isaac John and Julie Ann (Sanders) Grizzell, wife of Allen Ward Golden.]

MASON, Stephanie Renee. 15 Jan 1983-10 Sep 1983. [Daughter of Phillip and Dorothy B. (Woodley) Mason.]

HILL, Grady Howard. 22 Aug 1929-22 Sep 1970. [Son of James William and Bessie (Anderson) Hill, husband of Mary Albie Sims.]

HILL, Joseph Lee. 1958 - Nov 1960.

LAFEVER, Arthur J. 24 Aug 1912-5 Nov 1973. WWII.

BUTCHER, Bill F. 9 Feb 1936 - . [Husband of Jean E. Rhea, married 19 Sep 1955.]

BUTCHER, Jean E. 23 May 1932-14 May 1993. [Daughter of Isaac and Frances (Smartt) Rhea, wife of Bill F. Butcher.]

ABSTON, Mary Jane. 26 Aug 1957-9 Feb 1958. [Daughter of Enzena Abston.]

REED, Michael Brent Jr. 10 May 1986-23 Feb 1988. [Son of Michael Brent and Faye (Shields) Reed.]

ROLLEY, Charles Irwin. 30 Jan 1920-2 Oct 1991. WWII. [Son of Paul and Margaret (_____) Rolley, husband of Lois Cleta Wright.]

ROLLEY, Lois Cleta. 1921 - 9 Jan 1985. [Daughter of George Washington and Catherine (____) Wright, wife of Charles Irwin Rolley.]

WOLF, Hazel M. 1919 - 9 Aug 1992. [Hazel Marie, daughter of Harry Miles and Edna Mae (LaCrone) Sands, wife of 1) _____ Samuels and 2) Caleb Alvin Wolf II.

WOLF, Caleb A. 1929 -   . [Son of Joseph Laban and Mary Kathleen (McCord) Wolf, husband of Hazel M. Sands.]

ELROD, Madie B. 17 Dec 1909-12 Oct 1992. [Daugter of William John and Martha Ella (Hale) Bess, wife of William Davis Elrod.]

FUQUA, Fred A.   13 Sep 1905-5 Jul 1987. [Son of Albert and Ferbie (Lambert) Fuqua, husband of Lucille Agness Bryant.]

FUQUA, Lucille A. 10 Jun 1915-9 Dec 1983. [Daughter of John and Mollie (Whitaker) Bryant, wife of Fred A. Fuqua.]

FUQUA, Kaytella A.   31 Oct 1938-20 Dec 1969. [Daughter of Guy and Madeline (Massey) Mitchell, wife of Charles Fuqua.]

BROWN, J.B. 1919 -   . [Husband of Mary Ethel (Buchanan) Grayson, married 4 Oct 1971.]

BROWN, Ethel. 6 May 1896-20 Oct 1991. [Mary Ethel, daughter of Henry and Dora (Cunningham) Buchanan, wife of 1) Alexander Grayson who died in 1964 and 2) J.B. Brown.]

ATNIP, Herman Tanley. 28 Dec 1893-1 Jun 1966. [Son of Jim and Sally (Rigsby) Atnip, husband of Nannie Crim.]

ATNIP, Nannie Crim. 8 Jun 1894-22 Oct 1970. [Daughter of Frank and _____ (_____) Crim, wife of Herman Tanley Atnip.]

JONES, Bryon. 21 Sep 1897-26 Apr 1974. [Son of Jim and Ellen (Capshaw) Jones, husband of Susie Fisher.]

JONES, Susie. 19 Aug 1908-15 Nov 1987. [Daughter of Enoch Lloyd and Georgia Winnie (Raymond) Fisher, wife of Bryon Jones.]

WOLF, Joseph Laban. 15 Apr 1901-19 Nov 1971. [Son of Caleb Alvin and Ida (DeMoss) Wolf, husband of Mary Kathleen McCord.]

WOLF, Mary Kathleen McCord. 30 Jan 1906-17 Dec 1975. [Wife of Joseph Laban Wolfe.]

WOLF, Leslie Albert. 2 Sep 1927-20 Nov 1983. [Son of Joseph Laban and Mary Kathleen (McCord) Wolf, husband of Doretta _____.]

WALKER, Silas Richard. 1917-7 Nov 1980. [Son of C. Dottie and Sarah (Mooneyham) Walker, husband of Margaret Wolf.]

BROWN, Edgar Alfred. 9 Jan 1894-6 May 1967. WWI. [Son of Harvey Lincoln and Mary Ester (Richards) Brown, husband of Jesse Pepper.]

JONES, Linda D. 12 Sep 1958-   . [Linda Doris Hamilton, wife of Jerald Randall Jones.]

JONES, Jerald Randall. 28 May 1940-26 Sep 1991. US Air Force. [Son of Charlie and Zula (Warren) Jones, husband of Linda D. Hamilton]

JONES, Zula. 1909 -   . [Zula Warren, wife of Charlie Jones.]

JONES, Charlie. 23 Jun 1904-25 Aug 1978. US Army. [Son of Joe and Bitty (Knight) Jones, Husband of Zula Warren, married 2 Jul 1926.]

Gardens of Memory, cont.

CATHEY, Mattie Lou. 18 Jan 1904-1 Apr 1979. [Daughter of James and Audie (Burkes) Harrell, wife of Samuel Wade Cathey.]

CATHEY, Samuel Wade. 17 May 1901-31 Aug 1964. [Son of John Newton and Maggie Linda (Bowlin) Cathey, husband of Mattie Lou Harrell.]

MARCOM, Jack Malcolm. 1934-12 Jul 1966. [Husband of Geneva J. Sherrell.]

SHERRELL, Geneva Joyce. No dates. [Wife of 1) Malcolm Marcom and 2) Earl Bailey.]

DAVIS, Deloris Mae. 23 May 1925-26 Oct 1975. [Daughter of Alton W. and Elizabeth (Minnick) Haas, wife of Roy A. Davis.]

DAVIS, Roy A. Sr. 21 Aug 1912-19 Oct 1977. [Son of Grover C. and Sadie (Sweet) Davis, husband of Deloris Mae Haas.]

MARCOM, Robert. 1930 - Jan 1992.

SMOOT, Veva Marcom. 1901-25 Dec 1969. [Mary Veva, daughter of Butler and Sarah (Davis) Brown, wife of 1) _____ Marcom and 2) M.S. "Dock" Smoot.]

DEROUIN, Olive. 11 Aug 1904-9 Dec 1973. [Daughter of David and Dorina (Renauld) Rochon, wife of Mose Derouin.]

DEROUIN, Mose. 8 Jun 1893-2 Sep 1968. WWI. [Son of Mose and Malvine (_____) Derouin, husband of Olive Rodhon.]

DAVIS, Audrey M. 1928 only date on stone.

BOYD, Paul H. 1921 - 31 Jan 1994. [Son of Bud and Fannie (Bouldin) Boyd, husband of 1) Alice Roberta Christian and 2) Joyce Dodson.]

BOYD, Alice Roberta. 13 Sep 1923-14 Apr 1973. [Daughter of Willie and Ona (Hitchcock) Christian, wife of Paul Henry Boyd, married 21 Feb 1943.]

CLARK, Ronnie N. 11 Sep 1946-22 Jan 1972.

SMITH, Velda L. 1935 - . [Velda Lee Curtis, wife of Ernest Carl Smith.]

SMITH, Ernest C. 14 May 1932-15 Jul 1978. [Ernest Carl, son of Virgil and Ocie Pearl (Bell) Smith, husband of Velda Lee Curtis.]

SMEAD, Gordon Allen. 17 Oct 1924-17 Mar 1989. WWI, KOREA, VIETNAM. [Son of Carl and Jenny (Hitchcock) Smead, husband of Carol A. Christensen.]

LANCE, Winfield S. Jr. 30 Jan 1928-8 Sep 1980. [Winfield Scott, "Buster", son of Winfield Scott and Hallie (Griffith) Lance, husband of Barbara Jean Welch.]

LANCE, Barbara Jean W. 1943 - . [Barbara Jean Welch, wife of Winfield S. "Buster" Lance, Jr.]

WELCH, Willie. 1 Aug 1901-29 Oct 1967. WWI. [William B., son of Lee and Bell (Dawton) Welch, husband of Minnie Bennett.]

Gardens of Memory, cont.

WELCH, Minnie G. 2 Mar 1914-   . [Minnie G. Bennett, wife of
        William B. Welch.]

DICKSON, Thomas Edward. 27 Mar 1941-27 Nov 1989. [Son of Dillard Thomas
        and Katherine (Davis) Dickson, husband of Nedra Ann Stanley.]

DICKSON, Nedra Ann. 25 Feb 1941-   . [Nedra Ann Stanley, wife of
        Thomas Edward Dickson, married 16 Jul 1960.]

CASEY, Billy J. 1919 -   .

CASEY, Mary S. 1922 -   .

PALMER, Hazel S. 11 Aug 1939-   . [Hazel S. Lance, wife of Hollis
        Paul Palmer.]

PALMER, Hollis Paul. 24 Aug 1931-26 Mar 1977. KOREA. [Son of William
        Arnold and Pauline (Sadler) Palmer, husband of Hazel S. Lance.]

PALMER, Pauline. 1907-7 Jan 1978. [Zeedler Pauline, daughter of Matthew
        and Valley (Spivey) Sadler, wife of William Arnold Palmer.]

PALMER, William A. 1904 - 27 Dec 1980. [William Arnold, son of Monroe and
        Mary (Wydell) Palmer, husband of Zeedler Pauline Sadler.]

SHARPE, Billy Allen. [Son of Clifton B. and Effie Mai (Stewart) Sharpe,
        husband of Bobbie Jean Walker.]

SHARPE, Bobbie Jean Walker. No dates. [Wife of Billy Allen Sharpe.]

HUTCHINGS, Myrtle M. 1932 -   .

HUTCHINGS, James T. 1929 -   .

FRISBY, Leonard Allen. 2 Oct 1973-19 Aug 1983. [Son of Larry and Laurie
        (Smead) Frisby, grandson of Gordon A. Smead and grandson of
        Charlie Frisby.]

RAMSEY, Kenneth E. 9 Jan 1958-23 May 1992. [Son of Joe Edward and Mary
        A.(Savage) Ramsey, husband of 1) Betty Jean Locke and 2)
        Fonella Barnes.]

RAMSEY, Betty Jean. 12 Oct 1959-3 Nov 1985. [Daughter of Fred and Maggie
        Mae (Wood) Locke, wife of Kenneth Edward Ramsey, married 4 Mar
        1978.]

UNDERWOOD, Rufus Y. 27 Aug 1895-8 Sep 1975. WWI. [Son of James and
        Della (Good) Underwood, husband of Vernie Lena Pennington,
        married 6 May 1921.]

UNDERWOOD, Vernie L. 2 Mar 1904-8 Apr 1908. [Vernie Lena, daughter of
        William Iron and Nora (Hennessee) Pennington, wife of Rufus
        Youree Underwood.]

UNDERWOOD, Winfred Y. 14 Nov 1922-14 Oct 1986. WWII. [Son of Rufus Y.
        and Vernie Lena (Pennington) Underwood. Single.]

LINK, Charles A. 1923 -   . [Husband of Emma Boyd.]

LINK, Emma Lou. 1925 -   . [Emma Boyd, wife of Charles A. Link.]

LINK, Donnie Allen. 24 Mar 1958-19 Feb 1983. [Son of Charles and Emma (Boyd) Link.]

KENNER, Mary E. 1903 - 16 Mat 1980. [Mary Elizabeth, daughter of Alfred and Susie (Roberts) Taylor, wife of Benjamin Franklin Keener, married 16 Dec 1922.]

KEENER, William M. 15 Jul 1928-24 Jul 1991. [William Monroe, son of Benjamin Franklin and Mary Elizabeth (Taylor) Keener, husband of Mary Jo Mills, married 19 Nov 1949.]

KEENER, Mary Jo. 16 May 1930 -   . [Daughter of Cantrell and Mattie Ruth (Norris) Mills, wife of William Monroe Keener.]

BILES, Josephine B. 16 Jun 1911-20 Sep 1968.. [Daisy Josephine, daughter of Jim and Leoma (Farliss) Butcher, wife of _____ Biles.]

BUTCHER, Jean. Died 14 May 1993, age 60 years. [Jean Evelyn, daughter of Isaac and Frances (Smartt) Rhea, wife of Billy Butcher.]

CLAMPITT, Mary Green. Died 10 Jul 1993, age 87 years. [Daughter of Jake and Annie Laurie (_____) Green, married 1) Vincent Walsh and 2) David Paul Clampitt.]

CLAMPITT, David Paul. 1906 - 18 Jan 1974. [Second husband of Mary (Green) Walsh.]

DELONG, Lillie J. 21 Apr 1933 -   . [Lillie Elvira, daughter of Goebel and Ethel May (Hillis) Jennings, wife of 1) David Eugene Delong and 2) K.L. Travis.]

DELONG, David Eugene. 5 Sep 1929-30 Nov 1976. KOREA. [Son of A.F. "Tip" and Effie (_____) Delong, husband of Lillie Elvira Jennings, married 5 Oct 1951.]

DELONG, William Joseph. 18 Feb 1987-18 Feb 1987. [Infant son of Billy Wayne and Susan Laverne (Lyle) DeLong.]

TEMPLETON, Pleas C. Jr. 2 Jul 1937-23 Oct 1970. Air Force. [Son of Pleas and Dimple J. (Murdock) Allen Templeton, husband of Billie Lois Brady.]

TEMPLETON, Mark Deran. 29 Oct 1963-16 Dec 1968. [Son of Pleas C. Jr. and Billie Lois (Brady) Templeton, Jr.]

PRATER, Ronald Lynn. 25 Sep 1968-12 Nov 1968. [Son of Oliver and _____ (Hobbs) Prater.]

TAYLOR, Frances Evelyn. 28 Jul 1919-25 Feb 1988. [Daughter of William M. and Leona (Smith) Taylor. Single.]

TAYLOR, William M. 6 Mar 1896-27 Jul 1988. [William Melton, son of William Lewis and Nancy Ellen (Pollard) Taylor, husband of Leona Smith.]

TAYLOR, Leona S. 25 Dec 1883-8 Apr 1973. [Leona Smith, wife of William Melton Taylor.]

PRATER, Russell Irwin. 13 Oct 1970-28 Oct 1970. [Infant son of Leonard and Faye (Stubblefield) Prater.]

CROUCH, Owen M. 16 Feb 1897-2 Oct 1974.   US Army. [Owen Marshall, son
        of Edward and Harriett (Burch) Crouch, husband of 1) Cora Laura
        Rogers and 2) Alta (Schoenfield) Costa.]

COPE, Marvin. 1923 -   .

COPE, Mildred M. 1923 -   .

WALKER, James O. 11 Jun 1931 -   .

WALKER, Thelma L. 16 Jan 1938 -   .

FITTS, Dorothy T. 1923 -   .

FITTS, Roy W. 1921 -   .

HILLIS, Sam W. 1897 - 29 Jan 1982. [Son of Jim and Mary (Martin) Hillis,
        husband of Dora Grace Simons.]

HILLIS, Grace D. Nov 1895 - 17 Jul 1987. [Dora Grace, daughter of Andrew
        Jackson "Jack" and Adelaide (Yager) Simons, wife of Sam W.
        Hillis.]

SIMONS, Harold R. 10 May 1909-3 Jan 1987. [Harold Raymond, son of
        Benjamin Claude and Ellen (Butcher) Simons, husband of Mary
        Alvesta Jordan, married 19 Jan 1935.]

SIMONS, Mary A. 25 Jul 1912-18 Jun 1990. [Daughter of David Miller and
        Josephine (Simpson) Jordan, wife of Harold Raymond Simons.]

STEWART, Philip R. 5 Sep 1933-19 May 1991. KOREA. [Son of Himey Robert
        and Annie Frances (Robinson) Stewart.]

STEWART, Frances R. 1912 -   . [Frances Robinson, wife fo Himey
        Robert Stewart.]

STEWART, Himey R. 1906 - 12 Sep 1974. [Himey Robert, son of George and
        Kate (Williams) Stewart, husband of Frances Robinson.]

JARRELL, Frances M. 1919 -   .

JARRELL, J. Willard. 1915 -   .

CROUCH, Edward I. 22 Jun 1895 - 29 Dec 1979. [Edward Iowa, son of Edward
        and Harriet (Burch) Crouch, husband of 1) Bettie Florence Sisk
        and 2) Dovie Marie Wilson.]

CROUCH, William Lee "W.L." 27 Jun 1901-21 Oct 1986. [Son of Edd and
        Harriet (Burch) Crouch, husband of 1) _____ Redmon (div.), 2)
        Virgie Robinson Davis (div.), and 3) Della (_____) Chandler
        (div.)]

PENDERGRAPH, Mazel G. 1930 -   .

PENDERGRAPH, Harold U. 1921 -   .

CAMPBELL, Opal S. 21 May 1916 - 27 Jan 1975. [Daughter of James Holiday
        and Parlee (Bailey) Underhill, wife of Claude M. Campbell.]

Gardens of Memory, cont.

CAMPBELL, Claude M. 20 Feb 1912-23 Dec 1979. [Son of Charlie and Maggie (Boles) Campbell, married Opal Underhill on 29 Aug 1936.]

WILLIAMS, Margaret W. 14 May 1916- .

WILLIAMS, Wesley B. 16 Jul 1917 - .

VANDAGRIFF, Maude A. 1898 - Mar 1983.

VANDAGRIFF, Roy J. 1899 - Jul 1979.

HAYES, Woodrow. 1 Nov 1912-18 Jul 1990. [Son of Jasper Columbus and Mandy (Wilkerson) Hayes, husband of Leona Edwards.]

HAYES, Leona. 1914 - [Leona Edwards, wife of Vallas Woodrow Hayes.]

HAYES, Ira. 28 Mar 1904-30 Mar 1978. [Ira Aaron, son of Columbus and Manda (Wilkerson) Hayes, wife of Christine West.]

HAYES, Christine. 1924 - . [Christine West, wife of Ira Aaron Hayes.]

YOUNG, Robert F. 1910 - . [Husband of 1) Ruby Vaughn and 2) Pauline _____.]

YOUNG, Ruby L. 1918-13 Aug 1975. [Daughter of Floyd and Della (Adcock) Vaughn, wife of Robert F. Young.]

YOUNG, Mary Hilda. 1938 - Jun 1981. [Daughter of Robert F. and Ruby (Vaughn) Young, wife of Billy Jack Shelby.]

HOOD, Athron T. 1908 - .

HOOD, Margie P. 1926 - .

FERGASON, Preston Irvin. 24 Feb 1917-30 Apr 1986. WWII. [Son of Ervin and Nora Marie (_____) Fergason, husband of Mollie Louveda Knowles.]

FERGASON, Mollie Louveda. 13 Feb 1931 - . [Daughter of Homer Douglas and Myrtle (Turner) Knowles, wife of Preston Irvin Fergason.]

KNOWLES, Homer. 1902 - 10 Jan 1978. [Homer Douglas, son of Pierce and Lou Ann (Young) Knowles, husband of Minnie Myrtle Turner.]

KNOWLES, Myrtle. 1908 - 31 Dec 1991. [Minnie Myrtle, daughter of John and Mary Martella (_____) Turner, wife of Homer Douglas Knowles.]

LAWSON, Charles Gary. 20 Dec 1954-5 Sep 1976. [Son of Charles M. and Peggy (Martin) Lawson. Single.]

JACO, Elizabeth K. 1934 - . [Elizabeth Knowles, wife of James Hubert Jaco.]

JACO, J. Hubert. 1925 - 24 Sep 1991. [James Hubert, son of Solon and Tina (Luna) Jaco, husband of Elizabeth Knowles.]

TITTSWORTH, Nancy A.   1911-13 Feb 1986.   [Nancy Audrey, daughter of Charlie Whitt and Kizzie (Johnson) Robinson, wife of James N. Tittsworth.]

TITTSWORTH, James N.   1911-30 Jun 1988.   [Son of James W. and Nancy (Ferrell) Tittsworth, husband of Nancy Audrey Robinson.]

DAVENPORT, Novella B.   1903 - 15 Aug 1986.   [Rachel Novella, daughter of Silas and Martha Ethel (Parsley) Bain, wife of Clyde Fisher Davenport, married 17 Dec 1922.]

DAVENPORT, Clyde Fisher Sr.   1 Jun 1903-16 Nov 1980.   [Son of William Newton and Early (Reed) Davenport, husband of Rachel Novella Bain.]

DAVENPORT, Lois Grove.   12 Sep 1933 -   .   [Wife of Clyde F. Davenport, Jr.]

DAVENPORT, Clyde F., Jr.   17 May 1931-27 Oct 1985.   [Son of Clyde Fisher Sr. and Rachel Novella (Bain) Davenport, husband of Lois Grove.]

PRATER, Pauline N. 1922 -   .

PRATER, Charles L.   1916 -   .

HENEGAR, James Milton. 29 Apr 1904-26 Feb 1970.   [Son of James T. and Ada Alice (Garner) Henegar, husband of Annie Gladys Woods.]

HENEGAR, Annie G. 5 Nov 1905-27 Mar 1980.   [Annie Gladys, daughter of Robert L. and Ambie (Hart) Wood, wife of James Milton Henegar.]

MORRISON, Carl S., Sr.   1932 -   . [Son of Joseph Sutton and Thelma (Hickerson) Morrison, husband of 1) Jo Ellen Prater, married 25 Jan 1950 (div) and 2) Mae Nell Bounds.]

MORRISON, Nell.   30 Sep 1930 -   .   [Mae Nell, daughter of Charles I. and Annie (Adcock) Bounds, wife of 1) Joe Blair (div) and 2) Carl S. Morrison.]

CROUCH, William E.   1928 - 2 Mar 1985. [Son of Marshall and Cora Laura (Rogers) Crouch, husband of 1) Evelyn Young and 2) Doris Bradshaw.]

CROUCH, Doris L. 1935 -   .   [Doris Bradshaw, wife of William E. Crouch.]

PONDER, Delton T.   1934 - Jul 1991.

PONDER, Sarah A.   1945 -   .

TERRY, Nathaniel. 31 Oct 1925-9 Mar 1980.   WWII.   [Son of Walter Joe and Cindy Bell (Spurlock) Terry, husband of Gladys Brown.]

TERRY, Priscilla.   20 Aug 1921-16 Nov 1979.   [Daughter of Hardy Sr. and Jesse (Mazey) Cope, wife of John Walter Terry, Sr., married 12 Jul 1942.]

TERRY, John Walter, Sr.   No dates.   [Husband of Priscilla Cope.]

Gardens of Memory, cont.

DENTON, William J.B. 8 Jun 1896 - 28 May 1993. WWI and WWII. [Son of
        Greenville and Della (Fuston) Denton, husband of Mary D.
        Walden.]

HALEY, Charles Michael. 8 May 1957-17 Jan 1976. [Son of Dean and Doris
        (Denton) Haley. Single.]

HENEGAR, Shelia Jane. 30 Mar 1959-17 Jan 1976. [Daughter of Ernest and
        Doris (Link) Henegar. Single.]

GRIBBLE, George S. 30 Apr 1894-15 Jul 1989. [George Sutton, son of
        George Washington and Martha (Bounds) Gribble, husband of Rilla
        Dell Pistole, married 22 Dec 1924.]

GRIBBLE, Rilla Dell. 1908 - 7 Apr 1979. [Rilla Dell Pistole, wife of
        George Sutton Gribble.]

McCORMACK, Charles E. 24 Dec 1908 -   . [Charles Edward, son of
        Jasper H. and Nettie (Guy) McCormick, husband of Hazel Irene
        Hodge, married 24 Dec 1945.]

McCORMACK, Hazel I. 19 Sep 1912-29 Apr 1993. [Daughter of Ernest and
        Julia Mae (Martin) Hodges, wife of Charles Edward McCormick.]

HITTSON, Hershel B. 6 Nov 1909-30 Sep 1993. [Hershel Bob, son of William
        M. and Willie (Bryan) Hittson, husband of Ollie P. Oakley.]

HITTSON, Ollie P. 1909-17 Apr 1994. [Daughter of Isaac and Mary (Green)
        Coakley, wife of Hershel Bob Hittson.]

GILLETTE, Willie Dudley. 1904-13 Dec 1992. [Son of Henry and Alice
        (Knowles) Gillette, husband of Mabel Irene McCormick.]

GILLETTE, Mabel Irene. 1906 -   . [Mabel Irene McCormick, wife of
        Willie Dudley Gillette.]

SNIDER, Smith L. 1929 -   .

SNIDER, Willie G. 1921 -   .

SMITH, Kathleen. 13 Dec 1929-16 Apr 1990. [Daughter of Phillip Sr. and
        Ruby (Spurlock) Smith. Single.]

SMITH, Phillip Sr. 17 Aug 1896-17 Apr 1988. [Son of Button and Betty
        (Spurlock) Smith, husband of Ruby Spurlock.]

SMITH, Ruby. 30 Sep 1897-8 May 1989. [Daughter of Billy and Mary
        (Snelling) Spurlock, wife of Phillip Smith Sr.]

MATHEWS, Margaret J. Spurlock. 16 Jun 1918-21 Oct 1980. [Daughter of
        William and Mary (Snelling) Spurlock.]

TURMAN, Jessie S. 1912 -   .

SPENCER, Edna R. 19 Nov 1914-5 Jan 1984. [Daughter of Rase Stone and
        Will Miller, wife of Thomas Timothy Spencer.]

SPENCER, Thomas T. 15 Oct 1900-4 Aug 1987. [Thomas Timothy, son of
        Thomas Harrison and Lou Rhena (Patterson) Spencer.]

Gardens of Memory, cont.

SPENCER, Mildred G. 20 Feb 1917-26 Dec 1981. [Daughter of John and Eula (Pope) Gordon, wife of Roy Smith Spencer.]

SPENCER, Roy Smith. 29 Jul 1913-27 May 1988. WWII. [Son of Thomas Harrison and Rhena (Patterson) Spencer, husband of Mildred Gordon, married 21 Dec 1935.]

REAGAN, Fannie E. 19 Jun 1917 -   . [Fannie Ogletree, wife of 1) William G. Reagan, Sr, and 2) _____ _____.]

REAGAN, William G. Sr. 17 Jul 1918-25 Feb 1981. [Son of William Porter and Grace (Glidewell) Reagan, husband of Fannie Ogletree.]

WANAMAKER, Hazel Annette. 8 Jun 1937-   . [Daughter of John Franklin and Beulah (Pearson) Phillips, wife of Carl Cantrell Wanamaker.]

WANAMAKER, Carl. 28 Jul 1936 -   . [Carl Cantrell, son of Sidney Jacob and Zoda Bell (Coppinger) Wanamaker, husband of Hazel Annette Phillips.]

SEVERT, Bland B. 8 Apr 1923-27 Feb 1988. WWII.

SEVERT, Helen. 20 Sep 1924 -   .

GWYN, Leonard. 17 Jul 1931-21 Dec 1989. [Son of Leonard Sr. and Vera (Willis) Gwyn, husband of Thelma Winton.]

GWYN, Thelma. 20 Nov 1933 -   . [Thelma Winton, wife of Leonard Gwyn, Jr.]

PARRISH, Beatrice Ann. 28 Nov 1940-6 Jun 1980. [Daughter of Richard Monroe and Ottis (Hood) Grannam, wife of Andrew Parrish, Jr.]

HENEGAR, Alton, Jr. 23 Apr 1916-21 Dec 1984. WWII, KOREA, VIETNAM. [Son of Alton and Lydia (Spurlock) Henegar, husband of Doranella Conger, married 8 Mar 1955.]

HOBBS, Millard. 31 May 1908-15 Aug 1982. [Millard Clark, son of Lawrence and Dessie (Tipton) Hobbs, husband of Georgia Whitwell.]

TRAVIS, Jessie Mai. 16 Apr 1900-1 Sep 1983. [Daughter of Robert and Hattie (VanHoosier) Gilley, wife of Bert Finis Travis who died 12 Oct 1980.]

PHIFER, Shannon "Briana". 1 Feb 1977-4 Feb 1983. [Daughter of Albert and Susan (Oliver) Phifer.]

HOWARD, Asa T. 1 Aug 1910-3 Sep 1983. [Asa Thornton, son of James Franklin and Lou Dora (Cunningham) Howard, husband of Ola Mai Wilson.]

HOWARD, Ola Mai. 28 Jun 1914-   . [Daughter of Joseph Firm and Mattie Ann (Pennington) Wilson, wife of Asa Thornton Howard, married 20 Oct 1932.]

PEDIGO, E. Frances. 1936 -   .

PEDIGO, Thurman L. 1935-   .

BENDZOLOWICZ, Darlene. 1941 -   . [Darlene Robinson, wife of
            Francis Joseph Bendzolwicz.]

BENDZOLOWICZ, Francis J.   1913 - 9 Aug 1977. [Francis Joseph, son of
            Frank and Gladys (_____) Bendzlowicz, native of Brooklyn, NY,
            husband of Darlene Robinson.]

BILLINGS, Avo Pelham. 9 Jun 1924-   . [Daughter of A.C. and
            Lillie (Hillis) Hennessee, married 1) to Dewey Pelham on 10 Aug
            1946 and 2) to Artis Lee Billings.]

BILLINGS, Artis Lee. 21 Nov 1927-27 Mar 1984. KOREA. [Son of Pete and
            Hallie (Adcock) Billings, married 1) _____ _____ and 2) To
            Avo (Hennessee) Pelham.]

ADAMS, Lonnie. 31 Aug 1913-6 Apg 1992. [Son of Bob and Maude (Elkins)
            Adams, husband of Lillian Ozell McCormick.]

ADAMS, Lillian O. 1923 -   . [Lillian Ozelle McCormick, wife of
            Lonnie Adams.]

BRADY, John Todd. 5 Dec 1914-24 Oct 1991. [Son of John Patrick and Eliza
            Jane (Pope) Brady, husband of Rebecca Prker.]

BRADY, Rebecca L.   27 Mar 1912-25 Mar 1977. [Daughter of Alfred and
            Maggie Dalena (Doyle) Parker, wife of John Todd Brady.]

PRESTON, Hervey. 18 Sep 1883-30 Sep 1979. [Son of Gentry and Elizabeth
            (Jones) Preston, husband of Verna Griffith.]

PRESTON, Verna. 9 May 1898-14 Apr 1976. [Daughter of Ephram and Fronia
            (Ward) Griffith, wife of Hervey Preston.]

PRESTON, Harry M. 1930 -   . [Son of Hervey and Verna (Griffith)
            Preston.]

PRESTON, Betty S. 1934 -   .

PEDIGO, Mable. 1917-1 Apr 1987. [Daughter of William Riley and Allie
            (Maxwell) Gambrell, wife of Toy Ralph Pedigo.]

PEDIGO, Toy Ralph. 1913 - 20 Sep 1987. [Son of Pleasant M. and Lillian
            (Reeder) Pedigo, husband of Mable Gambrell.]

GAY, Glennie E. 14 Jul 1907-6 Feb 1993. [Glennie Edward, son of George
            Washington and Nancy Jane (Vickers) Gay, husband of Mattie
            Pauline Sauls.]

GAY, M. Pauline. 23 Mar 1913 -   . [Mattie Pauline, daughter of
            Samuel Jackson and Mandy (Hall) Sauls, wife of Glennie Edward
            Gay, married 29 Oct 1929 in DeKalb County, TN.]

GAY, Ernest Edward. 2 Apr 1931-2 May 1994. [Son of Glennie Edward and
            Mattie Pauline (Sauls) Gay, husband of Ruth Blevins.]

GAY, Ruth Blevins.   . [Wife of Ernest Edward Gay.]

HOBBS, Jason Blaine. 3 Nov 1971-4 Aug 1975.

BROWN, Richard H.   11 Oct 1915-28 Aug 1989. WWII. [Son of Hervie and

Allie (Savage) Brown. Single.]

MARTIN, Eulous. 1907 - 25 Dec 1991. [Son of Theodore and Martha E.
(_____) Martin, husband of Juanita R. Stubblefield.]

MARTIN, Juanita R. 1912 - 14 May 1987. [Daughter of Charlie and Janie
(_____) Stubblefield, wife of Eulous Martin.]

HENDRICKS, Rosa B. 5 Nov 1887-22 Dec 1983. [Daughter of Billy and Martha
Jane (Mason) Perkins, wife of Jonathan Hendricks.]

BLAIR, Virgil, Jr. 25 May 1933-17 Nov 1993. [Son of Virgil Sr. and
Beulah (Brady) Blair, husband of Ann McCormick (div).]

HAYES, Morgan C. 14 Jan 1935 -   . [Morgan Cecil Hayes, husband of
Bonnie Sue Phillips, married 2 May _____.]

HAYES, Bonnie Sue. 4 Sep 1937-   . [Daughter of Earl D. and
Virginia Ruth (Page) Phillips, wife of Morgan Cecil Hayes.]

SLUSHER, Marguerite G. 3 Dec 1919-15 Oct 1980. [Daughter of Joseph
Daniel and Marguerite (Hargroves) Gregory, wife of William S.
Slusher, Sr.]

SLUSHER, William S. Sr. 5 Mar 1920-12 Jul 1992. WWII. [Son of Peter B.
Sr. and Pearl Susan (Lawrence) Slusher, husband of 1)
Marguerite Gregory, married 30 Aug 1943, and 2) Mary Frances
(Harbin) Scott.]

WOOD, Willie. 1926 - 9 Feb 1979. [Charlotte Willie, daughter of Tom and
Ada (Grimes) Grimes, wife of Walter Allan Wood.]

WOOD, Walter A. 1925 -   . [Walter Allan Wood, husband of
Charlotte Willie Grimes.]

GREEN, Betty J. 8 Apr 1941 -   [Betty Jean, daughter of Joe and Mary
Elizabeth (Hillis) Patrick, wife of 1) Walter L. Green and 2)
_____ _____.]

GREEN, Walter L. 15 Jul 1936-21 Sep 1979. [Son of Elam A. and Amanda
(Green) Green, husband of Betty Jean Patrick.]

LAKE, Dallas L. 1909 - 13 Sep 1989. [Son of Thaxton B. and Mary
(Bennett) Lake, husband of Eleanor Z. _____.]

LAKE, Eleanor Z. 1915 -   . [Wife of Dallas L. Lake.]

ROMANS, Lillie E. 1907 - 7 Oct 1988. [Lillie Ella _____, wife of Elish
Paul Romans.]

ROMANS, E. Paul. 1908-1 Dec 1975. [Elish Paul, son of Horace Greely and
Ada (Murphy) Romans, husband of Lillie E. _____.]

COWANS, William George. 20 Nov 1923-8 Jun 1983. WWII. [Son of George
Cummings and Maggie (Crowell) Cowans of England. Husband of
Mary Schilz.]

COWANS, Mary S. 5 Aug 1921-3 Feb 1979. [Daughter of Herman and Bertha
(Donegan) Schilz, wife of William George Cowans.]

RAINS, Sam Ross. 8 Nov 1908-4 Aug 1980. WWII. [Son of Newton and Prudie (Swope) Rains, husband of Lorene Talbert.]

RAINS, Lorene Talbert. 22 Apr 1919-24 Mar 1991. [Dorothy Lorene, daughter of Leroy and Octa (Moore) Talbert, wife of Sam Ross Rains.]

JACOBS, Jack B. 30 Dec 1925-29 Mar 1990. WWII. [Son of Frank and Cheslie (Wilson) Jacobs, wife of Juanita Fisher.]

JACOBS, Juanita F. 1930 - . [Juanita Fisher, wife of Jack B. Jacobs.]

TALLEY, Marvin H. 1903 - . [Husband of Jeannette Roach.]

TALLEY, Jeannette R. 1902 - 4 Nov 1990. [Daughter of Elisha and Carrie (Myers) Roach.]

ROBINSON, Charlie H. 1915 - Apr 1977.

ROBINSON, Thelma A. 1924 - . [Wife of 1) Charlie H. Robinson and 2) George Jones.]

DEBERRY, Homer Lee. 1924 - 29 Apr 1990.

DEBERRY, Mary Clela. 1930 - .

McCLINTOCK, Margaret Ann. 1943 - 8 Jun 1982. [Daughter of Dallas and Eleanor (Zikefoose) Lake, wife of Lewis McClintock.]

TODD, Thomas J. 1920 - . [Husband of 1) Dorothy Evelyn Barnes and 2) Pauline Ferguson.]

TODD, Dorothy E. 9 Mar 1923-8 Dec 1980. [Daughter of Robert Roy and Elizabeth (Hayes) Barnes, wife of Thomas J. Todd.]

SIMONS, Aubrey W. 26 Oct 1913-11 Jan 1986. [Aubrey Walling, son of Taylor and Susan (Keener) Simons, husband of Anna Bell Todd.]

SIMONS, Anna Belle. 24 Jul 1911-24 May 1989. [Daughter of Jack Leonard and Martha Elizabeth (_____) Todd, wife of Aubrey Walling Simons.]

SIMONS, Walling T. 21 Jun 1937-15 Nov 1993. [Walling Todd, son of Aubrey Walling and Anna Bell (Todd) Simons, husband of Tessa _____.]

McCORMICK, David Clayton. 2 Dec 1921-23 Nov 1985. WWII. [Son of Lee and Dovie (Guy) McCormick, husband of Rebecca Adams.]

CHAFFIN, H.C. 1916-5 Jan 1982. [Son of Robert and Dora (White) Chaffin, husband of Geraldine Gillespie.]

CHAFFIN, Geraldine. 1915 - . [Geraldine Gillespie, wife of H.C. Chaffin.]

LYTLE, Beecher Jewel. 30 Jun 1923-16 Jan 1993. WWII. [Son of James Jefferson and Margaret Pearl (Clendenon) Lytle, husband of Mary Elizabeth Frazier.]

LYTLE, Mary Elizabeth. 23 Jan 1931- . [Daughter of William

Gardens of Memory, cont.

Marion and Ollie Mai (York) Frazier, wife of Beecher Jewel Lytle, married 2 May 1950.]

SWAN, H. Evelyn. 1919-12 Dec 1992. [Daughter of Wade and Jimmie (Bryan) Sanders, wife of Vernon Steve Swan, Sr.]

SWAN, Vernon S. 3 Apr 1908-17 Nov 1982. [Son of Sam and Ida Josephine (Smithson) Swan, husband of 1) Mennie Belle Usselton and 2) Evelyn Sanders.]

KNUDSON, Jean Ann. 1942 -   .

KNUDSON, Clifford, 17 Jan 1940 -   .

JONES, Alta J. 1899-17 Mar 1993. [Alta Jane, daughter of Perry Green and Callie (Pinegar) Judkins, wife of Sam Mason Jones.]

JONES, Sam M. 28 Sep 1899-4 Aug 1980. [Son of Frank and Elizabeth (Ray) Jones, husband of Alta Jane Judkins.]

SHERRELL, Roy C. 1913-16 Dec 1986. [Roy Clarence, son of Roscoe and Flora (Howell) Sherrell, husband of Dorothy Mansell.]

SHERRELL, Dorothy M. 1927 -   . [Dorothy Mansell, wife of Roy Clarence Sherrell.]

HALE, James Ronald. 28 May 1951-16 Apr 1982. VIETNAM. [Son of Harvel and Frances (Hennessee) Hale.]

HAYES, James A. "Jim" 1927 - 4 Mar 1990. [Son of James Roy and Mozelle (Anderson) Hayes.]

HAYES, James Roy. 1897 - 20 Jul 1991. WWI. [Son of William Haywood and Ludie (Baker) Hayes, husband of Mozelle Anderson, married 26 Jan 1919.]

HAYES, Mozelle A. 1901-22 Jun 1980. [Daughter of John and Sarah (Cope) Anderson, wife of James Roy Hayes.]

JOHNSON, Leonard C. 1928 -   .

JOHNSON, Thelma B. 1934 -   .

CAVASHERE, James Burt. 29 Nov 1917-26 Nov 1985. [Son of Willie and Rosie (Tidus) Cavashere, husband of Elsie Smith.]

CAVASHERE, Elsie M. 1918 -   . [Elsie Smith, wife of James Burt Cavashere.]

HUDSON, Austin P. "Jack" 16 Feb 1924-   . [Austin Peay, son of Charlie Carrick and Alma Lee (Anderson) Hudson, husband of Berchie Mozell (Billings] Hudson.]

HUDSON, Berchie M. 2 Jun 1924 -   . [Daughter of John Morgan and Susie Emma (Hayes) Billings, wife of Austin Peay Hudson, married 25 Apr 1942.]

HUDSON, Johannas A. 18 Apr 1948-15 May 1976. [Joe, son of Austin Peay and Berchie Mozell (Billings) Hudson, husband of Kay Fambroch, married June 1967.]

70

MORTON, William L. 11 Dec 1927-4 Mar 1993. [Son of Lycurgus and Mattie
        Bell (Tanner) Morton, husband of Geraldine Davenport.]

MORTON, Geraldine. 23 Dec 1943 -   . [Geraldine Davenport, wife of
        William L. Morton.]

TOBITT, Linda Rose. 1957 - 5 Apr 1984. [Daughter of John H. and Estelle
        (Judkins) Redman, wife of Cyril Edgar Tobitt.]

TOBITT, Cyril Edgar. 1957 -   . [Husband of Linda Rose Redmon.]

SHOEMAKE, Richard Lynn 1945 -   . [Husband of Robbie Lynn
        Redmon, married 1 Sep 1967.]

SHOEMAKE, Robbie Jane. 5 Mar 1947 -   . [Daughter of John H. and
        Estelle (Judkins) Redmon, wife of Richard Lynn Shoemake.]

REDMON, John H. 1903-27 Aug 1986. [Son of Felix Terry and Ella Mae
        (Williams) Redmon, husband of Era Estelle Judkins.]

REDMON, Estelle E. 4 Feb 1909-27 Jun 1994. [Era Estelle, daughter of
        Perry Green and Callie (Pinegar) Judkins, wife of John H.
        Redmon.]

KING, Hannah Brooke. 8 Mar 1989-21 Jan 1990. [Daughter of Timothy Mark
        and Kathy Annette (Hale) King.]

FOX, James E. 1926 -   .

FOX, Anna M. 1925 - 30 Jan 1991. [Daughter of Levi and Bessie (_____)
        Teague, wife of James E. Fox.]

ASTA, Edward L. 21 Dec 1908-11 Feb 1984. [Son of Augustin and Illumine
        (Perleri) Asta, husband of Mamie L. McGee.]

ASTA, Mamie M. 1915 -   . [Mamie L. McGee, wife of Edward L.
        Asta.]

REYNOLDS, Thomas LeRoy. 10 Oct 1921-13 Jun 1983. WWII. [Son of Thomas
        and Belle (Lowe) Reynolds.]

BROWN, Hugh. 27 Jun 1915-19 Oct 1991. [Husband of Margaret A. Rion.]

BROWN, Margaret A. 3 Aug 1923-   . [Margaret A. Rion, wife of
        Hugh Brown.]

ADAMS, Mercer L. 1910-10 Jun 1994. [Son of Bob and Maude Lee (Elkins)
        Adams, husband of Edna Myrtle Turner.]

ADAMS, Edna M. 7 Jan 1908-5 Oct 1990. [Edna Myrtle, daughter of Jim and
        Melvina (Reeder) Turner, wife of Mercer L. Adams, Sr.]

HENNY, Howard. 9 Feb 1920-20 Jul 1985. WWII. [Son of Edward and
        Celestine (Genzia) Henny, husband of Alice Mae Scott.]

HENNY, Michael Corey. 23 Feb 1969-2 Aug 1989. [Son of Howard Jr. and
        Peggy Corinne (Smith) Henny. Single.]

REDMON, Amanda Leann. 18 Sep 1978-2 Oct 1981. [Daughter of Leroy and
        Brenda (Stembridge) Redmon.]

Gardens of Memory, cont.

PERKINS, Harold. 1922-22 Mar 1991. [Son of James C. and Lillie (_____) Perkins, husband of Bertha Mae Parker.]

PERKINS, Bertha. 1927-24 Jan 1990. [Bertha Mae, daughter of Aubrey and Etta May (_____) Parker, wife of Harold J. Perkins.]

NORRIS, James Robert. 6 Jun 1932 -   . Son of Elbert Lee and Mollie (Roberts) Norris, husband of Minnie Gertrude Manus.]

NORRIS, Minnie Gertrude. 25 Dec 1936-26 Jan 1990. [Daughter of Steve and Willie Mae (Smith) Manus, wife of James Robert Norris, married 11 Sep 1954.]

NEWBY, Tabitha Ann. 13 Dec 1976-6 Jul 1978. [Daughter of Charles P. and Patricia (Redmon) Newby.]

GREEN, J.D. 26 Oct 1915-5 Oct 1989. WWII. [Son of Thomas D. and Hettie (Barrett) Green, husband of Mozell Judkins, married 23 Jun 1934.]

GREEN, Mozell. 11 Nov 1918-   . [Mozell Judkins, wife of Rev. J.D. Green.]

YOUNGLOVE, Robert S. 8 Jan 1921-24 Sep 1971. WWII. [Son of Robert D. and Wave (Cate) Younglove, husband of Muriel Nadine Hope.]

YOUNGLOVE, Muriel N. 11 Apr 1921-   . [Muriel Nadine Hope, wife of Robert S. Younglove.]

HAMRICK, Imogene. 1936 only date on stone.

ELROD, Sammy D. 4 Dec 1937-29 Nov 1991. [Sammy David, son of Jim Douglas and Myrtle Opal (Bogle) Elrod, husband of Carolyn Davis.]

ELROD, Carolyn D. 1940 -   . [Carolyn Davis, wife of Sammy David Elrod.]

DODD, William Billy David. 1954 - 28 Sep 1993. [Son of Brown and Dorothy (_____) Dodd.]

STANLEY, Gentry L. 1929 -   . [Son of Henry J. and Sarah (Walker) Stanley, husband of Dorothy E. _____.]

STANLEY, Dorothy E. 1934 -   . [Wife of 1) Brown Dodd (div.) and 2) Gentry L. Stanley.]

ELROD, W. Eugene. 21 Sep 1936-1 May 1975. US Army. [William Eugene, son of Jim and Opal (Bogle) Elrod, husband of Carolyn Shaffer.]

ELROD, Opal B. 15 Jun 1915-1 Jul 1986. [Daughter of Moscow and Azzielene (Thompson) Bogle, wife of James Douglas "Jim" Elrod.]

ELROD, Jim D. 2 Mar 1907-   . [Son of Charley Celmer and Bertha Almeta (Watson) Elrod, husband of Opal Bogle.]

PATTERSON, Jonah. 1923 -   . [Husband of Thelma Henny.]

PATTERSON, Thelma H. 25 Jul 1923-26 Aug 1982. [Daughter of Edward and Celestine (Genzia) Henny, wife of Jonah Patterson, married 31 Jul 1971.]

72

TRIVETT, Ada Bain. 21 Jan 1909-9 Oct 1980. [Ada Edwina, daughter of
        Edward Monroe and Ethel (Green) Bain, wife of Andrew Franklin
        Trivett.]

HOLLAND, Lois. 1927 -   .

HOLLAND, Jimmie L. 1936 -   .

MILLER, C.C. "Red". 6 Oct 1899-1 Sep 1978. [Claude Chester, son of Eli
        and Dora (Hunter) Miller, husband of Mary Elizabeth Moore.]

MILLER, Mary E. 1911 -6 May 1986. [Mary Elizabeth, daughter of Silas
        David and Annie Mae (Durham) Moore, wife of 1) Denton Barnes
        who died in 1974 and 2) Claude Chester "Red" Miller.]

GRISSOM, Juanita M. 12 Oct 1927-18 May 1990. [Daughter of Walter Lee and
        Thedra Ann (Jones) Black, wife of Allen K. Grissom.]

GRISSOM, Allen K. 2 Mar 1924-   . [Husband of Juanita M. Black,
        married 28 Jan 1945.]

ALLEN, Bonnie Lee. 30 Jul 1912-17 Aug 1971. [Daughter of Perry and
        Elizabeth (_____) Hillis, wife of 1) Frank Allen and 2) Richard
        Dodd (div.)]

NORMAN, Lyndsey Marie. 9 Sep 1985 only date on stone. [Infant daughter
        of Dave and Lynn (_____) Norman.]

DELOACH, Anne J. 27 Jan 1916-9 Sep 1981. [Daughter of Robert Corker and
        Ruth (Ligon) Jackson, wife of Tom Madden Deloach.]

DELOACH, Thomas M. Sr. 2 Apr 1911-29 Dec 1989. WWII. [Thomas Madden,
        son of Thomas M. and Elise (Moore) Deloach, husband of Anne
        Jackson.]

McDOWELL, Thomas A. 1 Sep 1912-24 May 1972. WWII. [Thomas Arnold, son
        of Mason Bryan and Mary Alice (Richey) McDowell, husband of 1)
        Magnolia Fults, married 6 Jun 1936 and 2) Martha Lee Roberts,
        married 17 Sep 1949.]

ALLEN, Hoyt G. 1906 - 18 Sep 1988.

REDMON, Donna K. 1951 -   .

REDMON, Keith. 1949 -   .

HENNESSEE, Albert A. 16 Feb 1899 - 7 Dec 1987. [Son of Jim and Nancy
        (Wright) Hennessee. Single.]

BEECHUM, Benton. 1912 - 19 Jan 1988. [Son of John and Della (Thomason)
        Beechum, husband of Manie R. _____.]

BEECHUM, Manie R. 1919 -   . [Wife of Benton Beechum.]

McCORD, Ralph W. 5 Nov 1917-11 Nov 1982. WWII. [Son of Horace and
        Willie Mae (Overton) McCord, husband of Odell Parsley, married
        18 Mar 1943.]

McCORD, Odell Parsley. 4 Apr 1919-   . [Daughter of Jewell and
        Estie (Dodd) Parsley, wife of Ralph W. McCord.]

Gardens of Memory, cont.

RAINS, Macon O.   1928 -   .

RAINS, Virgil V.   1923 -   .

HALLUM, Wanda C.   1941 -   .

HALLUM, Gerald G.   1934 -   .

HALLUM, Edna B.   1909 -   .

HALLUM, Harry Gordon.   1905 - 19 Oct 1978.

TANNER, Mary Lee.   1910 -   .

TANNER, Harvey Lee.   1903 -   .

FOSTER, Margie N.   1920 -   .

FOSTER, Harold G.   1910 -   .

MELTON, Ethel.   1892 - 25 Dec 1981. [Emma Ethel, daughter of Ben Lewis
          and Melissa (Wafer) Taylor.]

CATEN, Thelma M.   1 Dec 1918-17 Apr 1990.   [Thelma Mae, daughter of
          Hampton Denny and Pheba Mae (Reynolds) Caten.   Single.]

CATEN, William Lloyd.   20 Feb 1925-30 Oct 1979.   KOREA. [Son of Hampton
          and Pheba Mae (Reynolds) Caten, husband of Bessie Johnson.]

JORDAN, Harold L.   1921 - 1992.

JORDAN, Edna S.   1921 -   .

BRIGGS, Robert C.,Jr.   8 Sep 1915-   .

BRIGGS, Elizabeth F.   10 Jan 1916-   .

WHITAKER, Robert Aaron.   1931 -   .

WHITAKER, Jimmie L.   1907 -   .

WHITAKER, Richard E.   1905 - 24 Jul 1989. [Son of Aaron and Celia (_____)
          Whitaker.]

WARD, James A.   1926 -   .

WARD, Grace A.   1929 -   .

SEALS, Mack.   10 Apr 1898-24 Jun 1981. [Son of Solomon and Josephine
          (Ramsey) Seals, husband of Pearl Kinser.]

SEALS, Pearl K. 26 Aug 1897-7 Sep 1990. [Daughter of Jacob and Isabella
          (Toppens) Kinser, wife of Mack Seals.]

McBRIDE, Willie M.   21 Dec 1920-22 Apr 1993. [Willie Marie, daughter of
          Isaac and Mary Ann (Green) Coakley, wife of Willard McBride who
          died 13 Apr 1980.]

SANDERS, Cleveland S.   16 May 1919-6 Sep 1981. WWII. [Son of Robert and
          Estell (Robinson) Sanders, husband of Emogene Vaughn.]

Gardens of Memory, cont.

SANDERS, Emogene.   12 Apr 1929-   . [Emogene Vaughn, wife of
            Cleveland S. Sanders.]

HONEYCUTT, Robert Dale.   1966-1990.

DAVIS, Don M.   1957 -   .

DAVIS, Carolyn S.   1954 -   .

HONEYCUTT, Elmer R.   1936 -   . [Son of William and Sallie
            (Harvey) Honeycutt.]

HONEYCUTT, Linda L. 1942 -   .

SCOTT, Maude M.   15 May 1924 -   . [Wife of Erby Sedberry Scott.]

SCOTT, Erby Sedberry. 11 Sep 1918-3 Feb 1992. WWII. [Son of Alex and
            Ella (King) Scott, husband of Maude M. _____.]

FULTS, Charlie Clency.   12 Jun 1908-24 Jun 1991. [Son of Dave and Julie
            (McCormick) Fults, husband of Ollie Mae Sanders.]

FULTS, Ollie Mae.   19 Apr 1909-7 Aug 1986. [Daughter of Jim and Britan
            (_____) Sanders, wife of Charlie Clency Fults.]

TATE, Gertrude Fults. 17 Feb 1932-15 Jul 1983. [Daughter of Charlie Clency
            and Ollie Mae (Sanders) Fults, wife of William B. Tate.]

RAMSEY, Clyde William.   15 Dec 1924-31 Jul 1989. WWII. [Son of Ivy Joe
            and Allie (Spurlock) Ramsey, husband of Sarah J. _____.]

RAMSEY, Sarah J. 1927 -   . [Wife of Clyde William Ramsey.]

CHAPMAN, Ralph L.   31 Jul 1938-6 Sep 1992. [Son of Lee and Sylvia Mae
            (Moore) Chapman, husband of Myrtis June Starnes.]

CHAPMAN, M. June. 1938 -   . [Myrtis June Starnes, wife of Ralph
            L. Chapman.]

BROWN, Annie R. 1916 -   .

STARNES, William L.   3 Jul 1905-11 Feb 1985. [Son of E.C. and Addie
            (Wright) Starnes, husband of Mattie Lou Brazelton.]

STARNES, Mattie L.   1908 -   . [Mattie Lou Brazelton, wife of
            William Lawrence Starnes, married 18 Jul 1925.]

DILLARD, Jep.   1936 -   . [Husband of Mary Elizabeth Brown.]

DILLARD, Mary E. Brown.   17 Jan 1936-23 Aug 1989. [Daughter of Alvin H.
            and Florine (Locke) Brown, wife of Jep Dillard.]

BROWN, Florine Locke.   14 Jan 1920-27 Feb 1982. [Daughter of Harry and
            Hattie Mae (King) Locke, wife of Alvin H. Brown, married on 4
            Oct 1934]

BROWN, Alvin H.   9 Oct 1905-2 Jun 1984. [Son of Columbus and Lena
            (Mitchell) Brown, husband of Florine Locke.]

BROWN, Sarah Helen.   9 Oct 1934-7 Apr 1987. [Daughter of Alvin H. and

Gardens of Memory, cont.

Florine (Locke) Brown.]

BROWN, Annie Ruth. 1944 -   . [Daughter of Alvin H. and Florine
        (Locke) Brown.]

DAVENPORT, I.E. 1905 -   .

DAVENPORT, Annie Lula. 1909 -   .

HUTCHINS, Peggy E. 21 May 1929-   .

HOLTZCLAW, Martin E. 18 Nov 1920-3 Apr 1980. WWII. [Son of William
        Martin and Sarah Anne Geneva (Hampton) Holtzclaw, husband of
        Mildred Green.]

HOLTZCLAW, Mildred G. 5 Oct 1920-   . [Daughter of Wiley and Maude
        (_____) Green, wife of Martin Edward Holtzclaw.]

RAMBO, Murphy. 1905 -   .

RAMBY, Annie D. 1907 -   .

DILLARD, William K. 1938 -   .

DILLARD, Sarah L. 1939 -   .

WRIGHT, Hattie Elizabeth. 1919 -   . [Hattie Elizabeth Battles,
        wife of Wilson Wright.]

BATTLES, William Louis. 1943 -   .

BATTLES, Carolyn S. 1948 -   .

McCORMICK, Lila Jo. 4 Sep 1929-2 Feb 1993. [Daughter of Jess and Effie
        (Gilbert) Jones, wife of Glendull McCormick.]

FERRELL, Richard U. 1918 -   . [Husband of Joyce E. Trent.]

FERRELL, Joyce E. 1923 - 31 Jul 1982. [Daughter of Coley and Jennie
        (Scarberry) Trent, wife of Richard Ferrell.]

*DEWITT, Eugene Knapp. Born 6 May 1887 in Steuben, NY. Died 9 Jan 1963.

*BENNETT, Elmer Forrest. Born 28 Jul 1897 in Coffee County, TN, died 4
        Apr 1966. Son of Walter and Nora (Lovell) Bennett, husband of
        Velma McAfee.

GARMON CEMETERY

Location: On hill to right after crossing Charles Creek bridge on Francis Ferry Road.

GARMON, Will. Died 13 Aug 1963, age 85 years. [Son of Samuel and Ruth C. (Blanton) Garmon. Single]

GARMON, Rausa. Died 14 Feb 1966, age 66. [Daughter of Samuel and Ruth C. (Blanton) Garmon. Single.]

GARMON, Samuel. 15 May 1837-12 Jun 1918. [Husband of Ruth C. Blanton, married 22 Dec 1877 in Cannon County, TN.]

GARMON, Malissa. 28 Jan 1884-5 Oct 1902. [Daughter of Samuel and Ruth C. (Blanton) Garmon. Single.]

GARMON, Mary B. 17 Dec 1880-8 Feb 1899. [Daughter of Samuel and Ruth C. (Blanton) Garmon. Single.]

GARMON, Ruth Caroline. 1850-13 Jan 1924. [Daughter of Vincent and Mattie (_____) Blanton, wife of Sam Garmon.]

GARMON, Mattie B. 13 Jun 1879-26 Feb 1950. [Daughter of Samuel and Ruth Caroline (Blanton) Garmon. Single.]

GATH CEMETERY

Location: On Hwy 56 at Gath Baptist Church.

DODD, Stella Jennings. 22 Mar 1885-26 Sep 1986. [Daughter of James and Tennie (Keaton) Jennings, raised by Wm. Jordan and Cynthis (Fuston) King, wife of Charles Harrison Dodd.]

DODD, Charles Harrison. 25 Nov 1879-20 Nov 1962. [Son of John R. and Sarah Elizabeth (Mathis) Dodd, husband of Stella Jennings.]

DODD, John R. 9 Mar 1855-19 Feb 1938. [Husband of Sarah Mathis.]

DODD, Sarah. 7 Feb 1859-5 Mar 1922. [Sarah Elizabeth Mathis, wife of John R. Dodd.]

KING, C.J. 31 Dec 1840-3 Apr 1912. [Cynthia J. Fuston, wife of 1) James Allen, married 18 Oct 1866 in Dekalb County, Tn and 2) W.J. King.]

KING, W.J. 27 Dec 1842-2 Jan 1911. [William Jordan, son of James and Agnes (Strickland) King, husband of 1) Martha E. Bogle, married 1 Nov 1866 in Cannon County, TN 2) Martha C. Bailey, married 27 Sep 1878 and 3) Cynthia (Fuston) Allen.]

KING, Newell James. 21 Oct 1911-5 Oct 1914. [Son of W.S. and N.B.

(_____) King.]

HALE, Frank E.   26 Mar 1890-24 Jan 1962.   [Husband of Nancy L. _____.]

HALE, Nancy L.   19 Nov 1890-8 Aug 1974.   [Wife of Frank E. Hale.]

HERNDON, J.B.   20 Jan 1864-14 Jul 1918.   [Joe B., husband of Della Jane
        Keaton.

HERNDON, D.J.   10 Nov 1870-28 Sep 1932.   [Della Jane, daughter of Peter
        N.J. and Nancy T. A. (McGee) Keaton, wife of 1) Joe B. Herndon,
        married 10 Dec 1885 in Cannon County, TN, 2) Thomas H. "Tucker"
        Grissom, married 27 Sep 1919 and 3) John W. Akeman, married 11
        Nov 1929.]

LYLES, J.T.   2 Sep 1856-20 Mar 1914.   [James Thomas, husband of Mourning
        B. _____.]

LYLES, Mourning B.   16 Feb 1863-   . [Wife of James Thomas Lyles.]

KEATON, Peter N.J.   22 May 1850-23 Aug 1921.   {Peter N. James, son of
        Peter and Mollie J. (_____) Keaton, husband of Nancy Tennessee
        Ann McGee.]

KEATON, T.A. 11 May 1853-23 Jul 1924.   [Nancy Tennessee Ann McGee, wife of
        Peter N. James Keaton, married 10 Oct 1869 in Cannon County, TN.

BOGLE, Sarah.   26 Jul 1844-24 Feb 1946.   [Daughter of Neal and Betty
        (Davenport) Smith, wife of Tom Bogle.]

ANDERSON, William Horace.   6 Dec 1874-8 Jan 1952.   [Son of John and
        Rebecca (Spurlock) Anderson, Husband of Frances Elizabeth
        Bryson.]

ANDERSON, Infant of W.H. Anderson and wife.   Born and died 4 Sep 1928.

ANDERSON, Frances.   22 Mar 1888-29 Dec 1967.   [Frances Elizabeth,
        daughter of Tom and Sarah (Bogle) Bryson, wife of 1) William H.
        Anderson and 2) Noah Bost.]

GREEN, Ella Rosie.   4 Feb 1891-17 Jan 1979.   [Daughter of Tom and Sarah
        (_____) Smith, wife of Thomas Green.]

LYLE, Janie G.   16 Nov 1910-16 Mar 1924.   [Daughter of W.F. and Maude
        (Wilson) Lyle.]

KEITH, J.C.   17 Aug 1917-20 Mar 1936.   [Robert J.C., son of Robert and
        Lissie (Adamson) Keith.]

KEITH, Lissie. 22 Jan 1896-23 Nov 1958.   [Lissie Adamson, wife of Robert
        Keith.]

KEITH, Robert.   30 Jan 1892-19 Mar 1917.   [Husband of Lissie Adamson.]

KEITH, Wilbert.   19 Dec 1934-20 Jul 1987.   [Son of Robert and Lissie
        (Adamson) Keith.   Single.]

BOWMAN, Edward I.   17 Sep 1899-24 Mar 1970.   [Son of David Lee and Alice
        (DeHaven) Bowman, husband of Johnnie T. King.]

BOWMAN, Johnnie T.   18 Nov 1904-   . [Daughter of Adum and Jennie
        (Hale) King, wife of Edward T. Bowman.]

KING, Adum U. 2 Jul 1877-4 Jan 1953. [Son of John M. and Lucy (Barrett)
        King, husband of Jennie Hale.]

KING, Jennie H. 1 Apr 1876-13 May 1955. [Daughter of Tommie and Mary
        (Dodd) Hale, wife of Adum U. King.]

HALE, T.G. 15 Mar 1849-19 Aug 1926. [Thomas G., son of John and Julia
        (_____) Hale, husband of Mary E. _____.]

HALE, Mary E. 13 Feb 1851-3 Oct 1914. [Wife of Thomas G. Hale.]

HALE, Alberta. 3 Jun 1906-28 May 1912. [Daughter of P.L. and Willie
        (_____) Hale.]

KING, Thelma. 1907-1929.

KING, Selma. 1907-1931. [Husband of Lois _____.]

KING, Lois. 1907-19__. [Wife of Selma King.]

HALE, Clyde E. 3 Apr 1919-5 Jan 1920. [Son of F.E. and Nancy L. (_____)
        Hale.]

HALE, Dorothy Lee. 8 Apr 1929-3 Jun 1931. [Daughter of F.E. and Nancy L.
        (_____) Hale.]

BULLARD, Benjamin. 6 Feb 1836-16 Oct 1928. [Husband of Annie (_____)
        Crawford.]

BULLARD, Annie C. 1843-23 Sep 1928. (Wife of 1) _____ Crawford and 2)
        Benjamin Bullard.]

SPARKMAN, Irvin. 7 Feb 1870-21 Jan 1923. [Son of Elvin and Permelia
        (Russell) Sparkman, husband of Sarah Crawford.]

SPARKMAN, Sarah. 27 Dec 1869-16 Aug 1962. [Daughter of William Calloway
        and Julia (Roberts) Crawford, wife of Irvin Sparkman.]

MITCHELL, G.W. 28 Jun 1857-12 Feb 1927. [George Washington, son of John
        Wesley and Hixie (McGregor) Mitchell, husband of Mary Evaline
        Webb, married 2 Mar 1882.]

MITCHELL, M.E. 22 Apr 1867-1 Sep 1951. [Mary Evaline, daughter of Riley
        and Rutha (Denton) Webb, wife of George Washington Mitchell.]

SUMMERS, Octa M. 26 Dec 1890-24 Mar 1974. [Daughter of George Washington
        and Mary Evaline (Webb) Mitchell, wife of Hershell Summers.]

TOLBERT, Ruby Louise. 18 Mar 1928-28 Aug 1931. [Daughter of Toy F. and
        Leona (Anderson) Tolbert.]

RASCOE, S.D.R. 6 Jan 1869-11 Mar 1936. [Stokley D.R. Rascoe, husband of
        Blanche Reeves, married 9 Dec 1894.]

RASCOE, Blanche. 7 Sep 1869-7 Jan 1951. [Blanche Evelyn, daughter of
        Thomas and Sallie (Hancock) Reeves, wife of Stokley D.R. Rascoe.]

CRIPPS, C.C.   22 May 1885-28 Mar 1941.   [Charlie C., son of H.R. and
        Margaret Frances (Dodd) Cripps, husband of Mattie _____.

CRIPPS, M.F.   22 Nov 1852-2 Apr 1935.   [Margaret Frances, daughter of
        Hiram and Gensey (Adamson) Dodd, wife of H.R. Cripps.]

CRIPPS, H.R.   16 Aug 1854-17 Mar 1932.   [Son of Pete and _____ (Bain)
        Cripps, husband of Margaret Frances Dodd.]

CRIPPS, M.C.   1882-19__.   [Daughter of H.R. and Margaret Frances (Dodd)
        Cripps.]

COPE, Aubrey Ray.   28 Aug 1934-20 Dec 1934.   [Son of Tolbert M. and Ruby
        (Denton) Cope.]

COPE, Tolbert M.   25 Dec 1910-19 Feb 1967.   [Husband of Ruby Denton.]

COPE, Rubie G.   26 Aug 1915-   .   [Rubie G. Denton, wife of Tolbert
        M. Cope.]

KEITH, Nancy Missoura.   1 Jun 1894-7 Jan 1950.   [Daughter of R.W.and Lucy
        (Biggs) Raymond, wife of Isaac Lee Keith.]

KEITH, Isaac Lee.   26 Aug 1892-2 Apr 1976.   [Son of Thomas Philmore and
        Lucy Jane (Braswell) Keith, husband of 1) Nancy Missoura Raymond
        and 2) Lela Ferrell.]

TAYLOR, George W.   30 Nov 1907-31 May 1951.

CRAWFORD, Eugene.   7 Nov 1882-8 Dec 1951.   [Son of _____ and Annie C.
        (_____) Crawford, husband of Bessie Kelley.]

CRAWFORD, Bessie.   30 May 1894-7 Oct 1979.   [Bessie Louisa, daughter of
        Bethel and Lucy (Ward) Kelly, wife of Eugene Crawford.]

DODD, Shug.   9 Aug 1878-27 Aug 1956.   [Shug H., son of Milton and Rebecca
        (Turney) Dodd, husband of Della Hale.]

DODD, Della H.   1877 - 1948.   [Della Hale, wife of Shug H. Dodd.]

DODD, James M.   9 Jun 1903-14 Jun 1973.   [Husband of Della Griffin,
        married 28 Jul 1944.]

DODD, Della G.   1 Sep 1911-   .   [Della Griffin, wife of James
        Dodd.]

DIXON, Brenda Kay.   4 Nov 1948 only date on stone.

WALKER, Earl.   5 Dec 1897-19 Sep 1961.

NEAL, Ray A.   16 Jun 1902-14 Jun 1964. WWII. [Ray Ambers, son of Clayton
        Melvin and Charlie (Bennett) Neal, husband of Mary Winnie
        Raymond.]

NEAL, Mary W.   23 Nov 1902-17 Nov 1974.   [Mary Winnie, daughter of Robert
        and Lucy (Biggs) Raymond, wife of Ray Ambers Neal.]

NEELY, Louvernia.   6 Oct 1903-21 Jan 1987.   [Daughter of Charlie and
        Claudia (Blankenship) Jones, wife of Fuller Neely.]

Gath Cemetery, Cont.

NEELY, Fuller. 6 Nov 1897-6 Sep 1963. [Husband of Louvernia Jones.]

HALE, Sallie M. 10 Apr 1894-13 Mar 1971. [Daughter of W.G. and Edna (King) Moss, wife of Charlie T. Hale.]

HALE, Charlie T. 30 Jul 1881-9 Apr 1962. [Husband of Sallie Moss.]

MOSS, Edna E. 27 Apr 1865-19 Jan 1935. [Edna E. King, wife of W.F. Moss.]

MOSS, W.F. 10 Sep 1836-14 Jul 1936. [Husband of Edna E. King.]

*DENTON, Van Lee. Died 25 Jun 1913, age 11 months.

DENTON, Mettie. 8 Jan 1882- 1964. [Mettie Kelley, second wife of Grover Cleveland Denton.]

DENTON, G.C. 19 Oct 1885-3 Aug 1942. [Grover Cleveland, son of Isaac and Samantha (Trapp) Denton, grandson of Joseph and Mary (McGinniss) Trapp and of Rev. Isaac and Rutha (Walling) Denton, husband of 1)_____ _____ and 2) Mettie Kelley.]

VANATTA, Margie. 5 Feb 1928 only date on stone.

VANATTA, W.J. 24 Jan 1872-2 Jul 1935. [Son of James and Sarah T. (Pugh) Vanatta, husband of Zora Myrtle Keith.]

VANATTA, Zora Keith. 30 Dec 1888-8 May 1959. [Zora Myrtle, daughter of Thomas and Jane (Vanatta) Keith, wife of 1) W.J. Vanatta and 2) Bethel Mullican.

VANATTA, Charles A. 1 Jul 1930-17 Oct 1964. US Army.

SCOTT, Thomas L. 2 Oct 1894-24 Aug 1931. [Thomas Luther, son of J.M. and Mary (Delong) Scott.]

KING, A.D. 8 Mar 1913-15 Jul 1934. [Son of T. Hatton and Kinnie (Keaton) King. Single.]

KING, Dovie. 13 Feb 1926-22 May 1930. [Daughter of T. Hatton and Kinnie (Keaton) King.]

KING, W.H. 20 Jul 1938-6 Sep 1938. [Wm. H., son of T. Hatton and Kinnie (Keaton) King.]

KING, Kinnie. 27 Sep 1895-25 Mar 1945. [Daughter of Billy and Fannie (Rigsby) Keaton, wife of T. Hatton King.]

KING, T.H. 12 Oct 1887-9 Feb 1972. [T. Hatton King, husband of Kinnie Keaton.]

CLARK, Ruby Pauline. 17 Aug 1911-15 Dec 1915. [Daughter of William and Alice (Jones) Clark.]

CATEN, Hampton D. 19 Oct 1898-5 Sep 1954. [Hampton Denny, son of William and Mary Lou (Thomison) Caten, husband of Mae Reynolds.]

CATEN, Mae. 30 Dec 1896-6 Jul 1940. [Daughter of James and Mollie (Keaton) Reynolds, wife of Hampton Denny Caten.]

CATEN, Jewell June. 25 Jun 1935-14 Mar 1940. [Daughter of Hampton Denny and Mae (Reynolds) Caten.]

CATEN, Margarett F. 14 Aug 1923-17 Oct 1923. [Margaret Frances, daughter of Hampton Denny and Mae (Reynolds) Caten.]

GOGGINS, J.J. 23 Jul 1849-2 Nov 1914. [John Jordon, husband of Martha C. Vandagriff.]

GOGGINS, Martha. 11 Apr 1850-15 Jan 1928. [Martha C. Vandagriff, wife of John Jordon Goggins.]

DODD, H.M. 16 May 1857-9 Sep 1942.

MATHIS, Nadean R. 12 Sep 1948-   .

MATHIS, Robert Tullis. 28 Oct 1904-11 Dec 1987. [Son of John Horace and Connie Josephine (Arnette) Mathis. Single.]

MATHIS, Morris Ray. 6 Jan 1934-   .

MATHIS, Dewey S. 2 Jul 1909-   . [Husband of Velma Mai Roller, married 27 Sep 1930.]

MATHIS, Velma L. 25 Jul 1912-   . [Velma Mai Roller, wife of Dewey S. Mathis.]

MATHIS, J.H. 22 Jun 1857-3 May 1932. [John Horace Mathis, husband of Connie Arnett.]

MATHIS, M.J. 1871-1915.

MATHIS, Ollie May. 1 Jul 1897-10 Jan 1916. [Daughter of John Horace and Connie (Arnett) Mathis.]

MATHIS, F.M. 1895-1916.
MATHIS, I.L. 1902-1916.
MATHIS, S.M. 1892-1917.
        Children of John Horace and Connie (Arnett) Mathis.

MATHIS, E.C. 30 May 1893-3 May 1916. [E. Carl, son of John Horace and Connie (Arnett) Mathis.]

MATHIS, Hiram W. 1 Apr 1907-13 Jun 1959. [Son of John Horace and Connie (Arnett) Mathis.]

WOMACK, Mary Bass. 28 Jun 1833-20 Jan 1922. [Mary Ann, daughter of Archibald and _____ (Phillips) Bass, wife of James J. Womack.]

HALEY, Lela Mary. 13 Feb 1920-29 Jun 1924. [Daughter of Sampson and Helen (Spurlock) Haley.]

DENTON, Georgia Edward. 1928 - 1931.

KING, John Miller. 3 Apr 1856-3 Dec 1933. [Husband of Sarah Lucinda Barrett, married 1 Oct 1876 in Cannon County, TN.]

KING, Sarah Lucinda. 2 Apr 1857-23 Jan 1937. [Sarah Lucinda Barnett, wife of John Miller King.]

Gath Cemetery, Cont.

WOODWARD, Herman Lee. Born and died 14 Feb 1946.

ROSS, Charlie A. 7 Jul 1910-4 May 1981. [Charlie Austin, son of Robert
        and Martha (Bullard) Ross, husband of Ophia Lee Crawford.]

ROSS, Ophia L. 6 Jun 1911-20 Feb 1988. [Ophia Lee, daughter of Eugene
        and Bessie (Kelley) Crawford, wife of 1) Charlie A. Ross and 2)
        Tom Graham.]

ROSS, Nelda Juanita. 18 Aug 1938-19 Aug 1938. [Daughter of Charlie A.
        and Ophia Lee (Crawford) Ross.]

LYLE, Robert Lee. 27 Nov 1882-30 Sep 1940. [Husband of Vera Pearl Hale.]

LYLE, Vera Pearl. 4 Nov 1881-18 Aug 1964. [Daughter of Hiram and Helen
        (Sellars) Hale, wife of Robert Lee Lyle.]

VANDAGRIFF, James L. 13 Jul 1923-10 Apr 1992. WWII, KOREA, VIETNAM.
        [James Lafayette, son of William Troy and Nettie Elizabeth
        (Mullican) Vandagriff, husband of Christine Williams.]

VANDAGRIFF, Robert Frank. 29 Oct 1914-25 Sep 1981. WWII. [Son of
        William T. and Elizabeth (Mullican) Vandagriff. Single.]

VANDAGRIFF, Nettie E. 18 Sep 1894-24 Dec 1972. [Nettie Elizabeth
        Mullican, wife of William T. Vandagriff.]

VANDAGRIFF, William T. 16 Feb 1894-29 Oct 1979. [William Troy, son of
        _____ and Susie (Farmer) Vandagriff, husband of Nettie Elizabeth
        Mullican.]

YORK, Alice Mitchell. 10 Oct 1900-   . [Wife of Venus Christopher
        York.]

YORK, Venus C. 18 Oct 1892-3 Feb 1965. [Son of E.B. "Burr" and Louise
        (Jaco) York, husband of Alice Mitchell.]

WOMACK, Betty Frances. 17 May 1947-17 Jun 1947. [Daughter of John Calvin
        and Edith Virginia (Ward) Womack.]

WOMACK, Addie. 22 Nov 1887-31 Jan 1961. [Martha Adaline, daughter of
        Calvin and Mary (Cantrell) Loring, wife of Joe Lee Womack.]

WOMACK, Joe L. 28 Jan 1870-19 Apr 1950. [Joe Lee, son of Abner Monroe
        and Mary Ann (Cantrell) Womack, husband of Martha Adaline
        Loring.]

WOMACK, John C. 30 Dec 1913-   .

HALE, Mary Pauline. 19 Dec 1907-7 Mar 1973.

HALE, Fred Louis. 14 Jan 1942-5 Dec 1952. [Son of _____ and Mary Pauline
        (_____) Hale.]

RICH, Bethel A.D. 27 Aug 1922-12 Mar 1945. Killed in WWII. [Son of
        Marcus G. and Motie Gertrude (Kelley) Rich. Single.]

RICH, Motie Gertrude. 10 Sep 1879-24 Jan 1957. [Daughter of Bethel and
        Lucy (Ward) Kelley, wife of Marcus G. Rich, married Sep 1897 in
        Cannon County, TN.]

Gath Cemetery, Cont.

RICH, Marcus G.   27 Feb 1878-26 Oct 1955. [Son of James Obey and Frances
        Elvira (Hale) Rich, husband of Motie Gertrude Kelley.]

MITCHELL, Hallie Ethel.   26 Nov 1887-4 May 1959. [Hallie Ethel Foster,
        wife of Oliver L. Mitchell.]

MITCHELL, Oliver.   16 Apr 1884-10 Oct 1976. [Son of George Washington and
        Mary Evaline (Webb) Mitchell, husband of Hallie Ethel Foster,
        married 23 Jul 1907.]

CANTRELL, Clara B.   6 Apr 1915-   . [Clara Bell, daughter of
        Oliver and Hallie Ethel (Foster) Mitchell, wife of Shelton E.
        Cantrell.]

CANTRELL, Shelton E.   24 Apr 1906-12 Feb 1947. [Son of Ransom and Lillian
        (_____) Cantrell, husband of Clara Belle Mitchell.]

CANTRELL, W. Carson.   28 Sep 1916-   . [Husband of Mary Lee Hale,
        married 2 Dec 1939.]

CANTRELL, Mary Lee Hale.   31 Oct 1921-   . [Wife of W. Carson
        Cantrell.]

CANTRELL, Selma Eugene.   6 July 1944 only date on stone.

CANTRELL, Lenice Hale.   Born and died 27 Apr 1941.

RICH, Flora E.   1909 - 1970. [Flora Dugan, wife of Johnnie F. Rich.]

RICH, Johnnie F.   1906-   . [Husband of 1) Flora E. Dugan, 2) _____
        _____ and 3) _____ _____.]

RICH, Bobby.   28 Feb 1929-3 Mar 1929. [Son of Johnnie F. and Flora E.
        (Dugan) Rich.]

HALE, Mrs. Nancy.   Died 3 Aug 1974, aged 83 years, 8 months and 19 days.

YOUNG, Esther Marshall.   5 Jan 1909-7 May 1929. [Wife of H.L. Young.]

YOUNG, Julia.   6 Feb 1904-10 Aug 1915. [Daughter of H. Lester and Matilda
        E. (King) Young.]

*YOUNG, Asa Overton.   Died 16 Mar 1920, age 19, son of H. Lester and
        Matilda E. (King) Young.

BROWN, E.C.   23 Feb 1900-30 Dec 1972.

BROWN, J.E.   29 May 1898-18 Apr 1960.

KEATON, Willie K.   11 Nov 1905-10 Jul 1925. [Son of Monroe and Mary
        Elizabeth (Green) Keaton.]

KEATON, Mary E.   13 Jan 1880-16 Apr 1948. [Mary Elizabeth, daughter of
        Lewis Napoleon Bonaparte "Poley" and Nancy (Mullican) Green, wife
        of Monroe Keaton, married 12 Mar 1905.]

KEATON, Monroe.   9 Nov 1871-5 Jul 1953. [Son of James and Martha (Hayes)
        Keaton, husband of 1) Mary E. Green and 2) Fannie Davenport.]

KEATON, Quixie Lucille.   7 Dec 1908-9 Dec 1908. [Daughter of Wm. Lawrence and Minnie Belle (Little) Keaton.]

KEATON, Rev. W.L. 25 Apr 1880-21 Sep 1966. [William Lawrence, husband of
    Minnie Belle Little.]

KEATON, Minnie Belle. 21 Jul 1882-22 Feb 1949. [Minnie Belle Little,
    wife of Rev. William Lawrence Keaton.]

HILL, Ollie Mary Jane. 10 Feb 1913-10 June 1990. [Daughter of Rev. Wm.
    Lawrence and Minnie Belle (Little) Keaton, wife of James Polk
    Hill.]

HILL, James Polk. 18 Nov 1907-26 Mar 1982. [Son of Sidney Albert and
    Emma Euphemia (Lynch) Hill, husband of Ollie Mary Jane Keaton,
    married 9 Feb 1937.]

CURTIS, Troy Lee. 1 Jun 1915-   . Son of Roscoe and Anna (Hayes)
    Curtis.]

BURGESS, Monika Lynn. 23 Dec 1964-22 Jul 1965. [Daughter of Harlen and
    Nina (Raymond) Burgess.]

RAYMOND, Jerry W. 19 Nov 1944-7 Sep 1976. [Son of Walter and Agnes
    (_____) Raymond, husband of Kathy Buterbaugh.]

HICKS, Dorothy F. 17 Jun 1932-   . [Wife of Toye W. Hicks.]

HICKS, Toye W. 10 Feb 1917-12 Mar 1988. [Son of Willie Thomas and Fannie
    (Mullican) Hicks, husband of Dorothy F. _____.]

CURTIS, Roscoe C. 13 Feb 1885-29 Jun 1956. [Husband of Anna Hayes.]

CURTIS, Anna Hayes. 17 Jul 1891-9 Oct 1973. [Wife of Roscoe C. Curtis.]

CRAIN, James P. 1890-29 Mar 1982. [James Parker, son of Eugene Clay and
    Mary Josie (_____) Crain, husband of Vera M. _____.]

CRAIN, Vera M. 1893 - 1955. [Wife of James P. Crain.]

FRANKS, J.B. 14 Sep 1892-26 Nov 1968. [James B., son of Spencer and
    Alton (Dillon) Franks, husband of Ila Rascoe.]

FRANKS, Ila Rascoe. 4 Nov 1895-   . [Daughter of Stokley D.R. and
    Blanche Evelyn (Reeves) Rascoe, wife of 1) James B. Franks and
    2) _____ _____.]

YORK, U.J. 29 Apr 1883-11 Oct 1955. [Uriah Jaco, son of Elihue Burr and
    Louise (Jaco) York, husband of Lela Bond.]

YORK, Lela. 11 Jul 1884-24 Nov 1959. [Lela Bond, wife of Uriah Jaco
    York.]

YORK, Jesse Lee. 26 Jul 1913-18 Jul 1988. [Son of Uriah Jaco and Lela
    (Bond) York, husband of Ethel Perry.]

YORK, Ethel Perry. 12 Aug 1912-   . [Wife of Jesse Lee York.]

FOSTER, Howard. 20 Oct 1913-   . [Husband of 1) Evaline Patton
    and 2) _____ _____.]

FOSTER, Evaline. 7 Oct 1917-12 May 1957. [Daughter of J.B. and Mamie
        (Beckwith) Patton, wife of Howard Foster.]

BEAR_ID, Hallie Mai. 2 Jun 1922-27 May 1974.

GRIFFIN, Junnie Alberta. 16 Jul 1912-   . [Wife of Ernest Alton
        Griffith.]

GRIFFIN, Ernest Alton. 3 Aug 1896-28 Jun 1966. [Husband of Junnie
        Alberta _____.]

ENGLISH, Lalah Egner. 30 Sep 1905-   . [Wife of Amos A. English.]

ENGLISH, Amos A. 28 Aug 1902-28 Jan 1979. [Husband of Lalah Egner,
        married 17 Dec 1921.]

HALE, Axie C. 17 Aug 1899-16 May 1974. [Daughter of Rev. John William
        and Hallie (Campbell) Cooley, wife of William G. Hale.]

HALE, William G. 10 Oct 1893-22 Jul 1979. [Son of T.G. and Mary (Dodd)
        Hale, husband of Axie Cooley.]

HALE, Robert H. 18 Jan 1888-11 Feb 1974. [Robert Harrison, son of Thomas
        and Mary Elizabeth (Dodd) Hale, husband of Flara Kelly.]

HALE, Flara K. 11 Oct 1891-9 Dec 1973. [Flara Kelly, wife of Robert H.
        Hale.]

HALE, Janie C. 30 Oct 1916-   . [Janie Cantrell, wife of Grady H.
        Hale.]

HALE, Grady H. 7 Jan 1916-30 Nov 1987. [Son of Robert H. and Flora
        (Kelly) Hale, husband of Janie Cantrell, married 20 Oct 1935.]

HALE, Bea. No dates or other information.

HALE, Harding. No dates or other information.

COOLEY, George Edward. 16 Aug 1913-21 Jan 1972. [Son of Rev. John W. and
        Hallie (Campbell) Cooley, husband of Ruth Martin, married 10 Nov
        1935.]

MEEHAN, Ruth Cooley. 8 Feb 1917-30 Oct 1986. [Ruth Martin, wife of 1)
        George Edward Cooley and 2) _____ Meehan.]

MITCHELL, Eliza Rape. 30 Mar 1905-28 Jan 1985. [Eliza Mae Rape, wife of
        James T. Mitchell.]

MITCHELL, James T. 23 Dec 1897-1 Apr 1971. [James Tillman, son of George
        Washington and Mary Evaline (Webb) Mitchell, husband of Eliza Mae
        Rape.]

SWANN, Stephanie J. "Joanie". 22 Jun 1967-11 Jul 1985.

CANTRELL, John C. 19 Apr 1924-6 Feb 1981. [John Curtis, son of Charles
        Hershell and Daisy (Turner) Cantrell, husband of Alma L. Womack,
        married 24 Apr 1943.]

CANTRELL, Alma L. 14 Oct 1925-   . [Alma Womack, wife of John
        Curtis Cantrell.]

BURBAGE, Ralph B. 30 Jul 1921-2 Jan 1979. WWII. [Son of Wilburn Clifton and Delma (Boyd) Burbage, husband of Alton Smith.]

BURBAGE, Alton. 1920 only date on stone. [Wife of Ralph B. Burbage.]

GRISSOM, Luther S. 14 Aug 1907-   .   [Husband of Hilda Mae Ginn.]

GRISSOM, Hilda M. 8 Nov 1913-2 Mar 1983. [Hilda Mae, daughter of A.L. and Emma Lee (Green) Ginn, wife of Luther S. Grissom.]

JONES, Emily T. 13 Aug 1915-   .   [Emily Tittsworth, wife of Russell Jones.]

JONES, Russell. 24 Dec 1913-21 Mar 1989. [Son of Bob and Lillie (_____) Jones, husband of Emily Tittsworth.]

MITCHELL, Flora Bell Dodd. 20 Aug 1905-   .   [Wife of George W. Mitchell.]

MITCHELL, George W. 14 Feb 1904-30 Mar 1993. [George Washington, son of George Washington Sr. and Evaline (Webb) Mitchell, husband of Flora Belle Dodd.]

*SPURLOCK, Mary, died 18 Oct 1917, age 78 years, wife of Abram Spurlock, maiden name Newby.

*BRAGG, Thomas Jefferson. Died 28 Aug 1924, age 28 years, 10 months and 6 days. Son of T.P. and Emma (Groom) Bragg.

*REED, Gladys May. 23 Nov 1917-27 Aug 1924. Daughter of Ervin and Stacy (Griffin) Reed.

*OAKLEY, Edman. 8 Oct 1851-23 Mar 1936. Son of Sam and Minerva (_____) Oakley.

*WOMACK, Shirley Jean. 10 Dec 1954-6 Jan 1955. Daughter of Calvin and Eva (Wood) Womack.

*BROOM, Grover Cleveland. 11 May 1888- 26 Jan 1931. Son of James and Lou (Murphy) Broom.

*YOUNG, Lotie Melton. 11 Apr 1898-30 Sep 1963. Son of Henry Lester and Sarah (_____) Young, husband of Freda Mitchell.

*KEATON, Sam. 2 Mar 1851-16 Oct 1941. Son of John and Annie (Fuston) Keaton, married first to Cynthia King on 1 Oct 1874 and second on 3 Jan 1897 to Nancy E. Jane King who was born 11 Dec 1840 and died Jul 1927, sister of Cynthia King. Both marriages are in Cannon County, TN.

*KEATON, Cynthia. 13 May 1851-11 Oct 1892. Daughter of James and Agnes (Strickland) King, wife of Sam Keaton.

*VANATTA, Thomas Filmore. 6 Oct 1920-11 Aug 1951. Son of W.J. and Zora Myrtle (Keith) Vanatta. Single.

*VANATTA, William Jr. 12 Jun 1935-20 May 1936. Son of William J. and Zora Myrtle (Keith) Vanatta.

*VANATTA, Dorothy Harris. 20 Dec 1932-27 Jan 1933. Daughter of William

Gath Cemetery, Cont.

J. and Zora Myrtle (Keith) Vanatta.

*KEATON, Maudie Agnes. 14 Feb 1882-25 Apr 1946. Daughter of Sam and Cynthia (King) Keaton, single.

*KEATON, Delilia. 22 May 1878-15 Dec 1946. Daughter of James and Martha (Hayes) Keaton, single.

*ANDERSON, Dixie Oleen, died 23 Feb 1922, age 3 months.

*MULLICAN, Aubrey Pascal. 14 Dec 1915-2 Feb 1916. Son of Lonnie and Helen (Manford) Mullican.

GOODSON/MULLICAN CEMETERY

Location: On the launching ramp road at Rock Island, TN.

McWHIRTER, R.T. 11 May 1848-21 Apr 1870.

GOODSON, Memphis. 11 Oct 1848-11 Jan 1865.

GOODSON, Tansy E.A. 17 Mar 1824-24 Jan 1879. [Wife of A.J. Goodson.]

GOODSON, Andrew. 15 Feb 1814-10 Feb 1892. [A.J., husband of 1) Tansy E.A. _____, 2) _____ _____.]

GOODSON, Martha B. 28 Jan 1855-17 Jan 1885. [Daughter of A.J. and Tansy E.A. (_____) Goodson.]

GOODSON, Elisie. 12 Sep 1874-18 Jan 1907. [Elisie L. Goodson, wife of S.D. Goodson, married 25 Jul 1899.]

MOONEYHAM, Anna. 24 Feb 1847-9 Oct 1924. [Daughter of William and Lucinda (Womack) Mullican, second wife of Charles W. Mooneyham who was buried in Caney Fork Cemetery.]

MULLICAN, W.W. 12 Mar 1820-29 Aug 1912. [William W., son of William and Wilmoth (Bruce) Mullican, husband of Lucinda Womack.]

MULLICAN, Lucinda. 21 Sep 1818-20 Apr 1891. [Daughter of William and Anna (Goodson) Womack, wife of William W. Mullican, married 22 Mar 1842.]

MULLICAN, Sallie. 5 Jul 1844-11 Oct 1882. [Daughter of William W. and Lucinda (Womack) Mullican. Single.]

MULLICAN, Elizabeth. 8 Apr 1853-14 Jul 1875. [Daughter of William W. and Lucinda (Womack) Mullican.]

MULLICAN, William. 13 Mar 1843-Apr 1843. [Son of William W. and Lucinda (Womack) Mullican.]

Fifteen to twenty graves marked with fieldstones.

GRANGE HALL CEMETERY

Location: Beside Grange Hall Church of Christ off Crisp Springs Road.

MITCHELL, Odra. 11 Nov 1904-6 Aug 1988. [Villa Odra, son of Kelly
O'Neal and Melinda Josephine (Sparkman) Mitchell, husband of Nina
Turner, married 9 Nov 1932.]

MITCHELL, Nina. 16 Sep 1910-   . [Nina Mae, daughter of H. Cleve
and Myrtle (Dodd) Turner, wife of 1) Charlie Cunningham, married
11 Jul 1924 and 2) Villa Odra Mitchell.]

MITCHELL, Amanda M. 22 Apr 1884-12 Feb 1955. [Amanda Malvina, "Mollie",
daughter of James Monroe and Belle (Walker) Gann, married 1) Heck
Hurst and 2) Kelly O'Neal Mitchell.]

MITCHELL, Kelly O'Neal. 21 Jan 1879-28 Oct 1953. [Son of Harmon T. and
Martha "Mattie" (Young) Mitchell, husband of 1) Malinda Josephine
Sparkman and 2) Amanda Malvina Gann, married 6 Feb 1913.]

MITCHELL, Martha. Sep 1857-28 Feb 1913. [Martha E., daughter of Joseph
and _____ (_____) Young, wife of Harmon T. Mitchell.]

MITCHELL, Harmon T. Jul 1845-1918. [Son of Arthur and Malinda (Haston)
Mitchell, wife of Martha "Mattie" Young.]

BOLEY, William T. 28 Sep 1872-1 Aug 1910. [William Thomas Boley, husband
of Georgia Anna Mitchell, married 11 Nov 1897.]

BOLEY, Georgia Anna. 21 Dec 1873-1 Aug 1929. [Daughter of Harmon T. and
Martha E. (Young) Mitchell, wife of William Thomas Boley.]

WHEELER, Joseph Edward. 1 Nov 1913-2 Mar 1914. [Son of Nathan R. and
Holly (Young) Wheeler.]

YOUNG, Joseph. 1 Aug 1826-11 Nov 1910. [Husband of Emily Sneed, married
22 Nov 1860 in Wilson County, TN.]

YOUNG, Emily. 30 Dec 1839-3 Oct 1909. [Emily Sneed, wife of Joseph
Young.]

SMOOT, Infant. 22 Feb 1902-23 Feb 1902. [Daughter of John Calhoun
Breckenridge and Myra Octavia (Darnell) Smoot.]

MATTHEWS, Mary Jane Todd. 2 Jan 1845-26 Jul 1920. [Wife of Thomas
Matthews.]

MATTHEWS, Thomas. 5 Jan 1827-23 Mar 1912. [Son of Lemuel and Hannah
(_____) Matthews, husband of Mary Jane Todd.]

MATTHEWS, Lena P. 18 Mar 1878-26 Apr 1901. [Daughter of Thomas and Mary
Jane (Todd) Matthews, single.]

LANNOM, Rankin R. 19 Sep 1824-19 Oct 1913.

HAGEWOOD, James C. [3 Sep] 1855-[20 Nov] 1923. [Husband of Sarah H.
Carroll.]

HAGEWOOD, Sarah H. Carroll. 1850-[31 Dec] 1928. [Daughter of Carroll L. and Sarah (Daniel) Carroll, wife of James C. Hagewood.]

BROWN, Frank. 25 Sep 1863-7 Mar 1913. [Son of William Isaac and Sallie (Bishop) Brown, husband of Sarah Jane Bryan, married 4 Feb 1884.]

BROWN, Sallie. 11 Dec 1868-12 Aug 1942. [Sarah Jane, daughter of William and Mary (Hammons) Bryan, granddaughter of Joseph Wilson and Rebecca (Hawks) Bryan, wife of Frank Brown.]

BROWN, Walter C. [20 Feb] 1888-[18 Feb] 1976. [Walter Cleveland, son of Frank and Sarah Jane (Bryan) Brown, husband of Lottie Eva Crouch, married 8 Aug 1912.]

BROWN, Lottie Eva. [9 May] 1890-[30 Jun] 1956. [Daughter of Loss H. and Lucy J. (Herndon) Crouch, wife of Walter Cleveland Brown.]

TODD, Ruth Brown. 17 Apr 1891-13 Jun 1985. [Daughter of Frank and Sarah Jane "Sallie" (Bryan) Brown, wife of Jake Todd.]

LOWERY, Olin O. 28 May 1921-5 Feb 1991. WWII. [Husband of Albert Grace Todd.]

LOWERY, Albert Grace Todd. 18 Apr 1916-   . [Daughter of Jake and Ruthie May (Brown) Todd, wife of Olin O. Lowery.]

WOMACK, Zettie Fordyge. 16 Oct 1885-21 Jul 1909. [Daughter of J.H. and _____ (_____) Fordyge, wife of Frank Womack, married 27 Aug 1904.]

CANTRELL, Martha Victoria. 28 Aug 1865-6 Feb 1940.

MATTESON, Andrew J. 2 Oct 1844-7 Aug 1909. [Husband of Mattie _____.]

OVERALL, Infant. 8 Oct 1913-9 Oct 1913. [Infant of Lebious B. and Rose Ada (Rich) Overall.]

DODD, Horace B. 26 Jan 1883-Jun 1946. [Son of James Hiram and Abbigail (Starkey) Dodd, husband of Louisa Gamble, married 5 Jul 1914.]

DODD, Louise G. 26 Jan 1883-Aug 1972. [Louise Gamble, wife of Horace B. Dodd.]

McBROOM, Adam. [16 Jun] 1875-[22 Oct] 1929. [Son of Alexander and Mary (Hoover) McBroom, husband of Willie Cassandra Dodd, married 15 Oct 1902.]

McBROOM, Willie. [6 Jan] 1879- [24 Oct] 1938. [Willie Cassandra, daughter of James Hiram and Abbigail (Starkey) Dodd, wife of 1) Adam McBroom and 2) W.K. Elder.]

DODD, Mary Bessie. 13 Oct 1892-5 Dec 1907. [Daughter of James Hiram and Abbigail "Abbie" (Starkey) Dodd.]

DODD, Bertha. 10 Sep 1885-26 Jul 1905. [Lillie Bertha, daughter of James Hiram and Abbigail (Starkey) Dodd.]

DODD, J.H. 24 May 1848-14 Oct 1919. [James Hiram, son of Hiram N. and Rachel Ginsey (Adamson) Dodd, husband of Abbigail Starkey.]

DODD, Abbigail. 4 Mar 1857-7 Dec 1930. [Daughter of Isaiah and Cassandra
        (_____) Starkey, wife of James Hiram Dodd.]

MELTON, Infant. Born and died 4 Dec 1916. [Daughter of P.E. and Ethel
        (Kirkpatrick) Melton.]

MELTON, Thomas Calvin. 22 May 1853-2 Nov 1934. [Son of Joseph and Sarah
        (_____) Melton, husband of Sarah Catherine Paris.]

MELTON, Sarah Catherine. 16 Sep 1851-9 Jun 1903. [Sarah Catherine Paris,
        wife of Thomas Calvin Melton, married 24 Aug 1879.]

SMITH, Mary Irene. 18 Jul 1864-14 Jan 1910. [Wife of Lem Smith.]

SMITH, Lem. 5 Mar 1868-31 Aug 1907. [Son of Azel and Elmina P. (Wolcott)
        Smith, husband of Mary Irene _____.]

SMITH, Lemuel. Died 11 Jun 1902, aged 95 years, 15 days.

SWEET, E.M. [No dates.] CSA.

HALE, Adelbert, Jr. 7 Nov 1883-21 Jan 1907.

SMITH, Elmina P. 14 Apr 1834-7 Mar 1916. [Daughter of William and _____
        (Brown) Wolcott), wife of Azel Smith.]

SMITH, Azel. 4 May 1835-18 Apr 1915. [Son of Lemuel and _____ (_____)
        Smith, husband of Elmina P. Wolcott.]

ELAM, Sallie J. 8 Oct 1860-22 Feb 1898. [First wife of N.B. Elam.]

ELAM, N.B. 19 Sep 1856-31 Oct 1928. [Son of Henry L. and Nancy (Young)
        Elam, husband of 1) Sallie J. _____ and 2) Betty Snipes.]

ELAM, Lillie May. 28 Feb 1907-12 May 1907. [Daughter of H.L. and Lizzie
        (_____) Elam.]

ELAM, Lizzie. 25 Sep 1882-4 Apr 1907. [Wife of H.L. Elam.]

TRUITT, Turney. 10 Apr 1914-20 Apr 1914. [Son of John and Mary (_____)
        Truitt.]

COLE, Walter M. 12 Sep 1904-8 Jun 1982. [Walter Monroe, son of Joseph
        Ray and Matilda Victoria (Howell) Cole, husband of Ruby Maynard,
        married 21 Mar 1926.]

COLE, Ruby M. 4 May 1908-   . [Daughter of William Lawson "Loss"
        and Betty Ann (Allison) Maynard, wife of Walter Monroe Cole.]

CRISP, Columbus. 27 Sep 1885-22 Jul 1919. [Son of Yearby A. and Serena
        (Masey) Crisp, husband of Ina Brainard, married 22 Mar 1877.]

CRISP, Ina. 10 Oct 1859-23 Aug 1936. [Daughter of S.R. and Emily P.
        (Doty) Brainard, wife of Columbus Crisp. Her name given as Inez
        in her obituary.]

FULTS, Alice Crisp. 22 Dec 1881-23 May 1908. [Daughter of Columbus and
        Ina (Brainard) Crisp, wife of William A. Fults.]

DOTY, Susan. 18 Jul 1797-29 Sep 1877. [Wife of Jerry Doty.]

BRAINARD, S.R. 4 Jun 1813-5 Feb 1888. [Husband of Emily P. Doty.]

BRAINARD, Emily. 6 Jan 1817-4 Jul 1895. [Daughter of Jerry and Susan
        (_____) Doty, wife of S.R. Brainard.]

KIRBY, John. 2 Jun 1862-29 Apr 1915. [Husband of Millie Wood, married 25
        Feb 1897.]

KIRBY, Millie. 28 Jul 1885-4 Aug 1903. [Millie Wood, wife of John Kirby.
        Census gives date of birth as 1875.]

KIRBY, M. [Fieldstone, no dates.]

MELTON, MacClin Petway. 1856 - 1893. "Father of Minnie Melton Safley".
        [Son of Joseph and Elizabeth (_____) Melton, husband of Mary
        "Mollie" Hoodenpyle.]

TALLEY, Josie Summers. [13 Mar] 1870-[21 Mar] 1940. [Josephine, daughter
        of George William and Susan Paralee (Brewer) Summers, wife of
        William Frank Talley, married 23 Dec 1894.]

SUMMERS, Susan Paralee. [Dec] 1851-[16 Jul] 1904. [Susan Paralee Brewer,
        wife of George William Summers.]

SUMMERS, George. [Dec] 1838- 1917. [George William Summers, husband of
        Susan Paralee Brewer, married 1 Mar 1868.]

WOOTEN, Richard Franklin. 17 Jun 1933-14 Feb 1934. [Son of G.J. and
        Mable (Brewer) Wooten.]

WOOTEN, Mary Sue. Born and died 17 Jun 1933. [Daughter of G.J. and Mable
        (Brewer) Wooten.]

WOOTEN, Mable B. 15 May 1898-21 May 1990. [Daughter of Oliver Franklin
        and Bellzora (Henegar) Brewer, wife of Garvis Wooten.]

MALONE, Roy L. 2 Dec 1895-11 Jul 1979. [Ray Leon, son of Samuel Hayes
        and Mattie (Jenkins) Malone, husband of Mary Brewer.]

MALONE, May B. 22 Oct 1895-   . [Frances May, daughter of Oliver
        Franklin and Belle (Henegar) Brewer, wife of Roy Leon Malone.]

BREWER, Thomas Hayes. 15 Nov 1919-8 Dec 1919. [Son of Clarence and Verna
        (Malone) Brewer.]

ANDERSON, Henry G. 4 Jan 1891-29 Jun 1945. [Henry Grant, son of Isaac
        Alexander and Sarah Jane (Darnell) Anderson, grandson of Elijah
        and Elizabeth (Crisp) Anderson, husband of Margaret Smoot,
        married 6 Sep 1914.]

ANDERSON, Margaret S. 22 Jul 1896-7 Dec 1981. ["Maggie", daughter of
        James Madison "Matt" and Jennie May (Darnell) Smoot, wife of 1)
        Henry Grant Anderson and 2) Ernest McCamy.]

ANDERSON, Betty Jane. 17 Feb 1934-18 Feb 1934. [Daughter of Henry Grant
        and Margaret (Smoot) Anderson.]

SMOOT, Matt. 18 May 1868-17 Jan 1940. [James Madison, son of William
        and Matilda (Anderson) Smoot, husband of Jennie May Darnell,
        married 2 Feb 1890.]

SMOOT, May. 6 May 1872-14 Sep 1941. [Jennie May, daughter of James Thomas
        and Ann Elizabeth (Darnell) Darnell, wife of James Madison Smoot]

SMOOT, Willie Matt. 30 Oct 1897-1 Dec 1912. [Daughter of James Madison
        and Jennie May (Darnell) Smoot.
        Single.]

BREWER, Thomas Atlas. 17 May 1885-28 Jul 1915. [Son of Oliver Franklin
        and Bellzora (Henegar) Brewer, husband of Bessie Darnell.]

BREWER, Royce Lee.   12 Apr 1914-11 Aug 1914.
BREWER, Infant son.   3 Nov 1911-12 Nov 1911.
        Children of Thomas Atlas and Bessie (Darnell) Brewer.

PARIS, Joe R. 7 Feb 1843-29 Apr 1930. [Joseph R., son of John B. and
        Elizabeth (Elledge) Paris, husband of Bettie Logan, married 25
        Jul 1866 in Cannon County, TN.]

PARIS, Bettie Logan. 1 Aug 1845-13 May 1923. [Daughter of ____ and
        Elizabeth (Long) Logan, wife of Joseph R. Paris.]

PARIS, Maysle. 23 Jul 1888-6 Aug 1911. [Daughter of Joseph R. and Bettie
        (Logan) Paris. Single.]

JONES, Infant daughter. Born and died 7 May 1878.
JONES, Infant son.   29 Jun 1868-6 Sep 1868.
        Children of J.E. and Elizabeth T. (Henegar) Jones.

MELTON, Alfred Foster. 1871 - 1893. [Husband of Amanda Endora Simpson,
        married 25 Dec 1892.]

LAROSCHE, P.A. 29 Mar 1859-2 Sep 1902.

BAILEY, Abbie B. 25 Jul 1877-3 Oct 1923. [Mary Abbie, daughter of Richard
        D. and Mary (Blair) Belcher, wife of Tolbert B. Bailey.]

BAILEY, Tolbert B.   11 Jul 1871-18 Jan 1939. [Son of William J. and
        Martha (Melton) Bailey, husband of Mary Abbie Belcher, married
        14 Nov 1897.]

BELCHER, R.D. 8 Dec 1837-10 Apr 1881. [Richard D. Belcher, husband of
        Mary Blair.]

CRISP, Solomon. 13 Dec 1857-21 Oct 1861. [Son of Yearby A. and Serena
        (Masey) Crisp.]

CRISP, Serena Masey. 8 Oct 1835-17 Sep 1895. [Daughter of Solomon and
        Sarah A. (_____) Masey, wife of Yearby A. Crisp.]

CRISP, Y.A. 15 May 1832-3 Jul 1911. [Yearby A., son of Chesley and Sarah
        (Burch) Crisp, husband of Serena Masey, married 27 Sep 1853.]

SNIPES, Lonzy Polk. Died 26 Aug 1902, aged about 63 years.

CRISP, Albert Walter. 1 Apr 1883-12 Mar 1965. [Son of James Polk and
        Pharibe Angeline (Jones) Crisp, husband of Laura Argo.]

CRISP, W.F. 7 Jul 1886-20 Jul 1949. [William Frank, son of James Polk
        and Pharibe Angeline (Jones) Crisp, husband of Ethel Williams
        (div.).]

Grange Hall Cemetery, cont.

CRISP, Bessie Mae. 27 Jan 1891-13 Dec 1936. [Daughter of James Polk and
          Pharibe Angeline (Jones) Crisp.]

CRISP, James P. 13 Oct 1845-3 Oct 1898. [James Polk, son of Chesley and
          Sarah (Burch) Crisp, husband of Pharibe Angeline Jones, married
          2 Mar 1859.]

CRISP, Pharibe Angeline. 2 Feb 1848-23 Sep 1923. [Daughter of Zachariah
          B. and Eliza Jane (Biles) Jones, wife of James Polk Crisp.]

CRISP, Georgia.   22 Jun 1881-10 Apr 1882.
CRISP, Zachariah C.   18 Sep 1873-8 Oct 1876.
          Children of James Polk and Parabee Angeline (Jones) Crisp.

JONES, J.L. 1840 - 31 Jan 1909. [Joseph L., son of Zachariah B. and
          Eliza Jane (Biles) Jones, husband of Fannie B. Wilson, married
          1 Aug 1860.]

JONES, Z.B. [12 Apr] 1812 - 1878. [Zachariah B. Jones, husband of Eliza
          Jane Biles.]

JONES, Eliza Jane. 1818 - 1909. [Eliza Janes Biles, wife of Zachariah B.
          Jones.]

CRAWLEY, Lafayette. 22 Aug 1827-14 Sep 1910. [Son of Lemuel and Martha
          (Neville) Crawley, husband of 1) Luzena Emuline Jones, married
          6 Mar 1872 and 2) Mrs. Lula J. Brixey, married 31 Oct 1893.]

CRAWLEY, Emuline. 12 Mar 1841-27 Jan 1890. [Luzena Emuline, daughter of
          Zachariah B. and Eliza Jane (Biles) Jones, first wife of
          Lafayette Crawley.]

HENEGAR, J.C. 20 Feb 1834-25 Sep 1895. [John C., son of George
          Washington and Martha Elizabeth (Freeman) Henegar, husband of
          Nancy Paulina York, married 15 Nov 1853.]

HENEGAR, Nancy Paulina. 28 May 1830-19 Feb 1914. [Daughter of William
          and Temperance (_____) York, wife of John C. Henegar.]

GILLEY, Isaac I.A. 6 Apr 1856-30 Jun 1914. [Son of Acton Young and
          Rebecca (Wilson) Gilley, husband of 1) Mary Elizabeth Anderson,
          married 11 Feb 1877 and 2) Minnie Mae Thomas, married 24 Feb
          1907.]

GILLEY, Mary Elizabeth. 14 Jul 1858-31 Jan 1904. [Daughter of Isaac and
          Nancy A. (Henegar) Anderson, first wife of Isaac A. Gilley,
          married 11 Feb 1877.]

ANDERSON, Nancy A. 30 Mar 1868-19 Nov 1873. [Daughter of Isaac and Nancy
          (Henegar) Anderson.]

HENEGAR, George W. 27 Jul 1807-27 Jul 1870. [Husband of Martha Elizabeth
          Freeman.]

HENEGAR, Elizabeth Freeman. 28 Oct 1809-1 Dec 1872. [Martha Elizabeth
          Freeman, wife of George W. Henegar.]

JONES, Bell. 7 Jun 1855-5 Aug 1876. [Bellzora, daughter of George W. and
          Martha E. (Freeman) Henegar, first wife of Philander D. Jones,
          married 30 Oct 1872.]

Grange Hall Cemetery, cont.

JONES, Martha L. 14 Feb 1858-16 Nov 1881. [Daughter of John C. and Nancy Paulina (York) Henegar, second wife of Philander D. Jones, married 24 Jan 1878.]

ANDERSON, Nancy A. 12 Oct 1830-2 Nov 1906. [Daughter of George W. and Elizabeth (Freeman) Henegar, wife of 1) Patrick H. Bragg (divorced on 28 Sep 1852) and 2) Isaac Anderson.]

ANDERSON, Isaac. 28 Apr 1833-24 Nov 1909. [Husband of Nancy A. Henegar, married 7 Aug 1856.]

JONES, P.D.   20 Feb 1845-16 Feb 1913. [Philander D., son of Zachariah B. and Eliza Jane (Biles) Jones, husband of 1) Bellzora Henegar and 2) Martha L. Henegar.]

CROUCH, Infant daughter.   Born and died 11 Dec 1897.
CROUCH, Ruby Belle.   14 Oct 1900-24 Jan 1903.
CROUCH, Infant son.   Died 7 Dec 1907.
        Children of H.N. and Gertie (Gilley) Crouch.

CUNNINGHAM, Jesse Adam. 30 Oct 1914-28 May 1959. [Son of Jesse and Bertha (Underwood) Cunningham, husband of Della Mae Denton.]

CUNNINGHAM, Della Mae. 23 Feb 1918-19 Oct 1980. [Daughter of Isaac and Matilda Ann (Smoot) Denton, wife of Jesse Adam Cunningham.]

DENTON, Isaac. 30 Aug 1892-12 Nov 1918. [Son of Green V. and Adella (Fuston) Denton, husband of Matilda Ann Smoot, married 6 Jun 1915.]

DENTON, Matilda. 4 Feb 1892-26 Sep 1973. [Matilda Ann, daughter of James Madison and Jennie May (Darnell) Smoot, wife of 1) Isaac Denton and 2) Jesse Burks.]

BREWER, Essie Dean. 15 Jul 1932-1 Mar 1934. [Daughter of Arnold Matt and Frances (Scott) Brewer.]

BREWER, Arnold M. 3 Mar 1901-11 Jul 1966. [Arnold Matt, son of Oliver Franklin and Bellzora (Henegar) Brewer, husband of Frances Scott.]

BREWER, Frances M. 9 Jul 1906-   . [Daughter of William and Adeline (Fults) Scott, wife of Arnold Matt Brewer.]

BREWER, Arnold Matt, Jr. 12 May 1930-28 Feb 1979. [Son of Arnold Matt and Frances M. (Scott) Brewer, husband of June Lance.]

BREWER, June Lance. 22 Jun 1932-13 Oct 1988. [Daughter of Jewel and Annabelle (Griffith) Lance, wife of Arnold Matt Brewer, Jr.]

SMITH, Roy T. 5 Jun 1890-2 May 1961. [Son of William Butler and Charlotte (Frazier) Smith, husband of Belle Crouch.]

SMITH, Belle C. 15 Dec 1892-11 Nov 1974. [Daughter of Loss H. and Lucy J. (Herndon) Crouch, wife of Roy T. Smith.]

SMITH, William Butler. 2 Jun 1863-29 Jul 1940. [Son of Turner B. and Mary (Stone) Smith, husband of Charlotte Frazier, married 17 Dec 1882.]

SMITH, Charlotte. 31 Jul 1855-25 Jan 1937. [Daughter of Travis Marion and Sarah (Lionberry) Frazier, wife of William Butler Smith.]

BREWER, O.F. 22 Apr 1859-10 Jan 1948. [Oliver Franklin, son of Oliver Franklin and Pheobe (Melton) Brewer, husband of Bellzora "Belle" Henegar.]

BREWER, Belle. 23 Jan 1867-8 Apr 1946. [Bellzora, daughter of Thomas J. and Mary Elizabeth (Smoot) Henegar, wife of Oliver Franklin Brewer.]

BREWER, Cibbie. 24 Jan 1889-28 Oct 1944. [Daughter of Oliver Franklin and Bellzora (Henegar) Brewer, wife of Colonel W. Frazier.]

KITSOS, Minnie Smoot. 12 Oct 1896-18 Feb 1980. [Daughter of William H. and Elizabeth (Gilley) Smoot, wife of 1) W. Tom Outlaw, married 15 Mar 1911 and 2) John D. Kitsos.]

SMOOT, William H. 19 Feb 1847-3 Oct 1903. [William Henley, son of William and Matilda (Anderson) Smoot, husband of Elizabeth Frances Isabel Gilley.]

SMOOT, Elizabeth F. 3 Sep 1852-   . [Elizabeth Frances Isabel, daughter of Acton Y. and Rebecca (Wilson) Gilley, wife of William Henley Smoot.]

HENEGAR, James T. 10 Mar 1867-25 Apr 1929. [Son of Samuel Clay and Tira Ann (Crisp) Henegar, husband of Ada Alice Garner.]

HENEGAR, Ada A. 13 Mar 1875-27 Sep 1953. [Ada Alice, daughter of Reuben Comer and Nancy Frances (Bryan) Garner, wife of James T. Henegar.]

HENEGAR, Infant Son.   1 Feb 1898-7 Feb 1898.
HENEGAR, Minnie L.   23 Dec 1900-5 Jul 1901.
          Children of Samuel Clay and Eliza (Phillips) Henegar.

HENEGAR, Octa Bell. 2 Aug 1877-11 Jul 1898. [Daughter of Samuel Clay and Tira Ann (Crisp) Henegar. Single.]

HENEGAR, S.C. 13 Aug 1843-29 Nov 1926. [Samuel Clay, son of George Washington and Elizabeth (Freeman) Henegar, husband of 1) Tira Ann Crisp and 2) Eliza (Phillips) Spears, married 25 Nov 1896.]

HENEGAR, Tira Ann. 1 Oct 1843-8 Oct 1891. [Daughter of Chesley and Sarah (Burch) Crisp, first wife of Samuel Clay Henegar, marriage lic. 2 Oct 1861.]

HENEGAR, Mary A. 20 Jun 1881-4 Nov 1883. [Mary Ann, daughter of Samuel Clay and Tira Ann (Crisp) Henegar.]

HENEGAR, Thomas J., Sr. 31 Aug 1840-3 May 1918. [Thomas Jefferson, son of George Washington and Elizabeth (Freeman) Henegar, husband of 1) Mary Elizabeth Smoot, married 12 Sep 1858 and 2) Susan Sophia Smoot.]

HENEGAR, Mary E. 6 Apr 1843-9 May 1883. [Mary Elizabeth, daughter of William and Matilda (Anderson) Smoot, wife of Thomas J. Henegar.]

HENEGAR, Infant son. 9 May 1883-23 Nov 1883. [Son of Thomas Jefferson and Mary Elizabeth (Smoot) Henegar.]

*HENEGAR, Thomas Jefferson, Jr. Born 28 Mar 1889, died 8 Oct 1918. Son of Thomas Jefferson and Susan Sophia (Smoot) Henegar.

OUTLAW, Lizzie May. 1 May 1874-23 Oct 1907. [Daughter of Thomas J. and Mary Elizabeth (Smoot) Henegar, wife of Glen Thomas Outlaw, married 29 Nov 1893.]

MARTIN, Robert M. Died 2 Aug 1891, aged 32 years, 7 months, 1 day. [Husband of Bettie Henegar, married 13 Nov 1884. She is buried at Mt View Cemetery.]

RHEAY, Horace H. 11 Nov 1898-23 Mar 1901. [Son of Isaac L. and Bettie (Henegar) Martin Rheay.]

ANDERSON, Infant daughter.   29 Oct 1881-11 Nov 1881.
ANDERSON, John L.   11 Oct 1887-14 Apr 1888.
ANDERSON, Mary Cleo.   26 Sep 1882-26 Oct 1889.
          Children of James C. and Sarah C. (Jones) Anderson.

ANDERSON, J.C. 26 Nov 1849-9 Aug 1910. [James C., son of Elijah and Elizabeth (Crisp) Anderson, husband of Sarah C. Jones.]

ANDERSON, S.C. 16 Jan 1851-10 Dec 1923. [Sarah C., daughter of Zachariah B. and Eliza Jane (Biles) Jones, wife of James C. Anderson, married 14 Oct 1877.]

ANDERSON, Albert R. 28 Feb 1885-22 Apr 1914. [Son of James C. and Sarah C. (Jones) Anderson.]

HENEGAR, Charlie Ramsey. 1 Sep 1901-5 Nov 1901. [Son of John Bell and Rhoda L. (Collier) Henegar.]

HENEGAR, Sarah May. 12 Aug 1862-4 Jun 1890. [Sarah May Bowie, daughter of ____ and Mary F.(____) Bowie, first wife of John Bell Henegar, married 18 Dec 1883.]

LONG, Mary F. 3 Oct 1851-10 Jan 1888. [Wife of 1) _____ Bowie and 2) Samuel Long.]

HAMMER, Eva W. Bowie. 26 Aug 1860-14 Jun 1884. [Wife of E.B. Hammer, married 8 Jan 1877.]

ROACH, Pearl.   11 May 1887-13 Sep 1903.
ROACH, Dovie.   27 Feb 1882-27 Feb 1900.
          Daughters of John Eugene and Nancy (Smoot) Roach.

ROACH, Nancy P. 12 Mar 1858-20 Jun 1897. [Daughter of William and Matilda (Anderson) Smoot, first wife of John Eugene Roach, married 12 May 1878.]

CROWLEY, G.W. 15 Dec 1827-29 Nov 1911. [George Washington, son of Lemuel and Martha (Neville) Crawley, husband of 1) Lou Jones and 2) Roxie Edwards.]

CROWLEY, Lou Jones. Died 15 Oct 1886. [Wife of George Washington Crowley, married 30 Jan 1872.]

HENEGAR, Eliza. [11 Aug] 1863-[23 Mar] 1933. [Eliza Phillips, wife of 1)

Grange Hall Cemetery, cont.

Frank Spears and 2) Samuel Clay Henegar.]

GILLEY, Katherine. 20 Jun 1910-11 Mar 1911. [Daughter of W.M. and Willie
(_____) Gilley.]

GILLEY, Lou Etta. 26 Jul 1880-29 Apr 1913. [Lou Etta Jacobs, wife of
Colonel C. Gilley, married 4 Jul 1899.]

JACOBS, Allie. 6 Mar 1874-11 Oct 1918. [Husband of Lena Gilley, married
25 Jun 1899.]

JACOBS, Lena. 18 May 1881-9 Mar 1967. [Lena Gilley, wife of Allie
Jacobs.]

JACOBS, Minnie Lee.   11 Sep 1907-29 Jul 1934.
JACOBS, Mattie.   2 Jul 1901-1 Sep 1940.
     Daughters of Allie and Lena (Gilley) Jacobs, single.

SMITH, Nancy May. 25 Feb 1923-2 Jan 1927. [Daughter of William Joseph
and Thula (Hennessee) Smith.]

SMITH, William Joseph. 15 Sep 1885-26 Feb 1956. [Son of William Butler
and Charlotte (Frazier) Smith, husband of Darthula Hennessee.]

SMITH, Dar. Thula. 27 Dec 1891-22 Jul 1978. [Darthula, daughter of James
and Nancy (Wright) Hennessee, wife of 1) Levi Rutledge and 2)
William Joseph Smith.]

SMITH, Richard J. 5 Mar 1897-23 Jul 1961. [Richard John, son of William
Butler and Charlotte (Frazier) Smith, husband of Mary Ann
Holland, married 24 Apr 1926.]

SMITH, Mary Ann. 28 Mar 1907-   . [Daughter of Arrick Casswell
and Bettie (Dodd) Holland, wife of Richard John Smith.]

KIRBY, Lena.   19 Apr 1892-23 May 1915.
KIRBY, Susie.   9 Mar 1899-8 Jun 1919.
KIRBY, Octa.   8 Oct 1894-9 May 1927.
     Daughters of Abner B. and Hila Elizabeth (Morrow) Kirby. Single.

KIRBY, A.B.   13 Feb 1866-13 Nov 1936. [Abner B., husband of Hila
Elizabeth Morrow, married 30 Sep 1886.]

KIRBY, Bettie. 5 Jun 1866-21 Apr 1957. [Hila Elizabeth, daughter of
William Robert and Mary (Cope) Morrow, wife of Abner B. Kirby.]

WOOD, H.G. "Hillie". 6 Oct 1885-28 Mar 1930. [Son of Andrew Jackson and
Saphronia A. (Wilson) Wood, husband of Arzona "Zonie" Burch,
married 21 Jul 1907.]

WOOD, Arzona. 6 Sep 1889-29 Mar 1912. [Daughter of _____ and Josephine
(_____) Burch, wife of Hillie G. Wood.]

ROACH, J.E. 12 May 1854-15 Feb 1918. [John Eugene, son of William and
Sarah (Elrod) Roach, husband of 1) Nancy P. Smoot, married 12 May
1878 and 2) Sarah Elizabeth Anderson, married 22 Aug 1897.]

ROACH, S.E. Anderson. 24 Apr 1860-18 Mar 1922. [Sarah Elizabeth,
daughter of Elijah and Elizabeth (Crisp) Anderson, wife of John
Eugene Roach.]

ROACH, Anna L.   1 Nov 1899-18 Oct 1906.
ROACH, William B.   11 Jun 1901-1 Sep 1901.
ROACH, Alvin Carter.   22 Apr 1890-15 Feb 1914.
        Children of William F. and Martha "Mattie" (Anderson) Roach.

ROACH, W.F. June 1862-1935. [William F. Roach, husband of Martha Anderson]

ROACH, Martha.   11 Mar 1872-17 Feb 1948.   [Daughter of Elijah and
        Elizabeth (Crisp) Anderson, wife of William F. Roach, married 24
        Dec 1889.]

SHIELDS, Rhodman Kinner.   10 Aug 1894-14 Jun 1963.   [Son of Robert Bruce
        and Lucy Virginia (Temples) Shields, husband of Hassie Ciller
        Gilbert, married 22 Aug 1915.]

SHIELDS, Hassie Ciller.   31 Aug 1894-8 Feb 1980.   [Daughter of Joseph
        Edmund and Martha Reams (Rutledge) Gilbert, wife of Rhodman
        Kinner Shields.]

SHIELDS, Robert B.   23 Feb 1833-26 May 1902.   [Robert Bruce, son of
        Alexander and Matilda (_____) Shields, husband of Lucy Virginia
        Temples, married 31 Jul 1878.]

SHIELDS, L. Virginia. 22 May 1858-23 Oct 1918. [Lucy Virginia Temples,
        wife of Robert Bruce Shields.]

SMITH, J.J.   15 Jun 1858-15 Feb 1913.   [John J. Smith, husband of Anna
        Eliza Nurney.]

SMITH, Ann.   19 Apr 1857-17 Feb 1955.   [Anna Eliza, daughter of Hiram and
        Eliza (_____) Nurney, wife of John J. Smith.]

BAITS, Cora Bell. 22 Nov 1885-29 Nov 1895. Daughter of _____ and
        Queen Baits.

SINGLETON, Harriett A.E.   24 Aug 1831-25 Jan 1909.

SMITH, Carl.   23 Oct 1926-27 Sep 1967.   [Carl Brown, son of George Otto
        and Collie Belle (Walker) Smith, husband of Betty Passons,
        married 14 Jul 1950.]

SMITH, Betty.   10 Apr 1932-24 Feb 1991.   [Daughter of Dallas and Lola
        Belle (Wilson) Passons, wife of 1) Carl Smith, and 2) Robert Lee,
        married 18 Nov 1978.]

SMITH, Otto.   23 Mar 1884-30 Jul 1963.   [George Otto, son of John J. and
        Anna Eliza (Nurney) Smith, husband of Clara Belle Walker, married
        29 Sep 1919.]

SMITH, Collie. [29 Mar] 1900-7 Apr 1976. [Collie Belle, daughter of John
        and Mattie (Wilson) Walker, wife of 1) George Otto Smith, and 2)
        Chester Cooley.]

*COOLEY, Chester Francis. Died 8 May 1976, son of Charles and Lillie Mae
        (_____) Cooley, husband of 1) _____ _____, and 2) to Collie
        Belle (Walker) Smith.

BURCH, George W. 1836 - 1900. CSA. [Husband of Margaret Wilson, married
        25 Jul 1883.]

Grange Hall Cemetery, cont.

BURCH, Melvin. 9 Mar 1886-9 Mar 1908. [James Melvin, son of _____ and
    Josephine (_____) Burch, married Sophronia Elizabeth Wood on 11
    Jun 1906.]

ORRICK, Luna Burch. 1883 - 1911. [Wife of _____ Orrick.]

CRAWLEY, Sam L. 19 Apr 1903-6 Feb 1904. [Son of D.B. and Pheobe (_____)
    Crawley.]

CRAWLEY, Sam J. 27 Aug 1873-28 Oct 1906. [Son of Lafayette and Luzena
    Emaline (Jones) Crawley.]

RIGSBY, Jennie H. 7 Aug 1857-7 Jan 1923. [Mary Jane, daughter of James
    H. and _____ (_____) Herndon, wife of Nelson C. Rigsby.]

RIGSBY, Nelse C. 28 Jul 1850-26 Aug 1910. [Nelson C. Rigsby, husband of
    Mary Jane "Jennie" Herndon, married 2 Jan 1873, Cannon County,
    TN.]

BLANKS, Alice. 1911 - 18 Dec 1993. [Daughter of William Horace and
    Charlotte Elizabeth (Nokes) Dutton, wife of Clarence Blanks.]

WOODEN, C. R. "Clint". 13 Feb 1908-20 May 1988. [Son of Fate and Nan
    (_____) Wooden, husband of 1) Viola West and 2) Edna Mae
    Sanders.]

WOODEN, Viola. 31 Mar 1904-11 Feb 1946. [Daughter of James and Nancy
    (Summers) West, first wife of Clint Wooden.]

SANDERS, Harlan Roy. 14 Mar 1926-8 Sep 1940. [Son of Clint and Viola
    (West) Wooden.]

DUTTON, Horace. 13 Nov 1874-9 Sep 1947. [William Horace, son of James
    Allen and Alcey Elizabeth (Allison) Dutton, husband of Elizabeth
    Nokes.]

DUTTON, Lizzie. 24 Dec 1877-18 Jul 1961. [Elizabeth, daughter of Sam and
    Paralee (Davis) Nokes, wife of William Horace Dutton.]

NOKES, Parilee. Died 2 May 1925 age about 72 years. [Parilee Davis, wife
    of Samuel L. Nokes.]

NOKES, S.L. 16 Jul 1857-14 Mar 1921. [Sam L., son of Jonas and Sabrina
    (_____) Nokes, husband of Parilee Davis.]

DUTTON, Ann Elizabeth. Born and died 24 Dec 1930. [Daughter of John and
    Lesta (Craven) Dutton.]

DUTTON, Cornie Lee. 10 Oct 1901-8 Sep 1964. WWII. [Son of William
    Horace and Elizabeth (Nokes) Dutton, husband of Julia Burch,
    married 22 Feb 1927, divorced.]

DAVIS, Asa. 2 Nov 1882-12 Sep 1968. [Asa P., son of Anderson and Mary
    (_____) Davis, husband of Hassie Bular Smith.]

DAVIS, Hassie B. 26 Jul 1893-12 Jun 1962. [Hassie Bular, daughter of
    William Butler and Charlotte (Frazier) Smith, wife of Asa P.
    Davis.]

ROACH, Rema. 30 May 1917-19 Jun 1917.

ROACH, Ramah.   30 Mar 1917-20 Jun 1917.
          Twin children of Colonel E. and Ellen (Anderson) Roach.

SMITHSON, E.W. 22 May 1854-1 Nov 1940. [Son of Calvin and Luann (Kersey)
          Smithson, husband of Mollie Reed.]

SMITHSON, Mollie. 16 Dec 1866-15 Mar 1918. [Daughter of Lee and Malinda
          (White) Reed, wife of E.W. Smithson.]

SMITHSON, William Calvin. 13 Jul 1900-12 Sep 1969. WWII. [Son of E.W.
          and Mollie (Read) Smithson, husband of Luann Kersey.]

KILMER, Hulda. 29 Oct 1840-15 Jul 1918. [Wife of Van R. Kilmer.]

KILMER, V.R. 29 Apr 1837-8 May 1914. [Husband of Hulda _____.]

SMITH, George W.   15 Jul 1892-18 Jul 1916.   [Son of Will and Lottie
          (Kilmer) Smith, husband of Phronia Elizabeth Campbell.]

FREED, J.M.   16 Nov 1841-4 Dec 1917.   [Joseph M., son of Joseph and Mary
          (Webb) Freed, husband of Matilda _____.]

FREED, Matilda C. 27 Jun 1865-19 Sep 1912. [wife of Joseph M. Freed.]

MEDLEY, Hazel Marie. 2 Jan 1906-28 Jan 1911. Daughter of G.T. and S.J.
          Medley.

CROUCH, Dillard.   15 Nov 1859-15 Oct 1908.   [Son of Edward and Pelina
          (Adams) Crouch.]

CROUCH, Loss H. 15 Oct 1862-26 Jun 1919. [Loss Hill, son of Edward and
          Pelina (Adams) Crouch, husband of Lucy J. Herndon, married 4 Oct
          1885.]

CROUCH, Lucy J.   7 Jan 1866-26 Mar 1936.   [Lucy Josephine, daughter of
          Jacob and Charlotte "Lottie" (Brown) Herndon, wife of Loss Hill
          Crouch.]

SMITH, Florence Louise.   13 May 1916-11 Jul 1931.   [Daughter of James
          Marion and Golda (Crouch) Smith.]

SMITH, Golda Crouch. 22 Jun 1888-19 Jul 1926. [Daughter of Loss Hill and
          Lucy Josephine (Herndon) Crouch, wife of James Marion Smith.]

GANN, Bobby Joe. [Homemade tombstone, no other information.]

GANN, Roof Harp. [Homemade tombstone, no other information.]

DAVIS, Claude Monroe. 27 Dec 1882-10 Apr 1909. [Son of John and Jane
          (_____) Davis.]

PENNINGTON, Bobbie Lucille. 14 Dec 1919-9 Feb 1920.
PENNINGTON, Margrit Azline. 18 Nov 1920-14 Mar 1922.
          Daughters of Calvin T. and Clio Annie (Cantrell) Pennington.

CULLEN, Ellen F. 13 Dec 1915-5 Sep 1917.   Daughter of J.R. and Rillie
          Cullen.

CUNNINGHAM, Charlie Richard. 26 Apr 1900-18 May 1954. [Son of Fate and
          Dora (Good) Cunningham, husband of 1) Nina May Turner, married

Grange Hall Cemetery, cont.

11 Jul 1924, and 2) Maggie Earl. Divorced from both wives.]

YORK, Henry. [Fieldstone. Born 12 May 1855, died 15 May 1935, son of Nathaniel and Cora K.A. (Arledge) York.]

GREEN, Dora Good Cunningham. [Fieldstone, no dates. Dora Good, wife of 1) Fate Cunningham and 2) _____ Green.]

CUNNINGHAM, William.   1 Jul 1917-16 Sep 1918.
CUNNINGHAM, Cecil Mason.   1 Jul 1919-17 May 1972.
        Sons of Jesse Calvin and Bertha (Underwood) Cunningham.

CUNNINGHAM, Jess C. 30 Apr 1896-30 Dec 1959. [Jesse Calvin, son of Fate and Dora (Good) Cunningham, husband of 1) Bertha Underwood and 2) Bessie Tenpenny.]

CUNNINGHAM, Bertha. 12 Nov 1892-21 Jan 1933. [Daughter of Jim and Della (Goode) Underwood, wife of James Calvin Cunningham.]

HOWARD, Robert Lee. 24 Nov 1913-5 Oct 1918.
HOWARD, Infant.   Born 31 Mar 1918.

LAWS, S.E. 20 Apr 1857-4 May 1921. [Saphronia, daughter of Hugh and Elva (_____) Agers, wife of M.C. Laws.]

*LAWS, M.C. Born 6 May 1857, Died 20 Mar 1932. Son of Joel and Millie (Edwards) Laws, husband of Saphronia Agers.

*POTTER, Ethel. Died 5 Jun 1920, age 37 years, daughter of M.C. and Saphornia (Agers) Laws, wife of Dan S. Potter.

STROUD, Edna Alene. 30 Apr 1881-2 Nov 1939. [Wife of James T. Stroud.]

CROUCH, Brown Loss, Jr. 3 Dec 1905-3 Jan 1969. [Son of Loss Hill and Charlotte Josephine (Herndon) Crouch, husband of Jimmie Lee Prater, married 3 Aug 1928.]

CROUCH, Jimmie Lee. 15 Aug 1912-   . [Daughter of James and _____ (_____) Prater, wife of Brown Loss Crouch, Jr.]

HOLT, Jesse. 14 Nov 1879-20 Jul 1957. [Jesse Fielding, son of Henderson and Martha C. (Williams) Holt, husband of 1) Jane Hennessee and 2) Myrtle Page, married 1912.]

HOLT, Myrtle. 11 Jan 1896-8 Mar 1986. [Myrtle Gertrude, daughter of Andrew and Eliza Louise (Neil) Page, second wife of Jesse Fielding Holt.]

HOLT, Herbert Lee. 28 Jan 1914-22 Nov 1980. [Son of Jesse Fielding and Myrtle (Page) Holt, husband of Mary Elizabeth Brown.]

HOLT, Mary Elizabeth. 8 Jun 1923-   . [Daughter of Walter C. and Lottie Eva (Crouch) Brown, wife of Herbert Lee Holt.]

HOLT, Orville Lee. 27 May 1920-19 Nov 1982. WWII. [Son of Walter Willard and Mary Bell (Gann) Holt. Single.]

HOLT, Walter Clifton. 3 May 1922-26 Dec 1951. WWII. [Son of Walter Willard and Mary Belle (Gann) Holt, husband of Gwyendelene Pennington.]

HOLT, Raymond Edward. 20 Apr 1917-25 Aug 1944. WWII. [Son of Walter Willard and Mary Belle (Gann) Holt, husband of Annie Brown.]

HOLT, Walter W. 22 Jun 1882-14 Mar 1940. [Walter Willard, son of Henderson and Martha C. (Williams) Holt, husband of Mary Belle Gann.]

HOLT, Mary B. 20 Oct 1897-21 Oct 1973. [Mary Belle, daughter of James Monroe and Catherine Belle (Walker) Gann, wife of Walter Willard Holt. They were parents of 18 children, 10 boys and 8 girls.]

HOLT, Mary. Born and died 16 Jan 1912. [First child]
HOLT, Gracie Mae. 28 Dec 1914-27 Sept 1936. [Third child]
HOLT, Beulah Mae. 13 Mar 1919-15 Aug 1919. [Sixth child]
HOLT, Moral Lester. 18 Apr 1924-8 Apr 1925. [Ninth child]
HOLT, Hoyt Oliver. 28 Jun 1925-16 Jul 1933. [Tenth child]
HOLT, Jewel. 3 Jun 1932-18 Feb 1933. [Fourteenth child]
HOLT, Infant son. Born and died 18 Aug 1933. [Fifteenth child]
        Children of Walter Willard and Mary Belle (Gann) Holt.

PENNINGTON, Calvin T. 29 Nov 1895-31 Mar 1963. [Son of William R. and Eliza Nora (Hennessee) Pennington, husband of Clio Annie Cantrell.]

PENNINGTON, Annie C. 17 Aug 1903-12 Nov 1960. [Clio Annie, daughter of Fred J. and Clio (Head) Cantrell, wife of Calvin T. Pennington.]

PENNINGTON, William R. 4 Apr 1873-28 Nov 1923. [Son of Aaron "Iron" and Emaline (Smith) Pennington, husband of Nora Hennessee.]

PENNINGTON, Nora H. 13 Jun 1872-5 Apr 1940. [Daughter of William and Martha (Lance) Hennessee, granddaughter of Alexander and Tabitha (Smith) Hennessee, wife of William R. Pennington.]

GANN, Florence Elizabeth. 23 June 1934-21 Sep 1934. [Daughter of Harrison and Amanda (Parsley) Gann.]

PENNINGTON, Winton Aubrey. 12 Oct 1934-10 Jan 1935. [Son of Calvin T. and Clio Annie (Cantrell) Pennington.]

TURNER, Maudie Mae. 1908 - 15 Nov 1986. [Daughter of William R. and Nora (Hennessee) Pennington, wife of Alvin Aubrey Turner, married 9 Jul 1924.]

TURNER, James Gordon. 1927 - 1989. [Son of Alvin Aubrey and Maudie Mae (Pennington) Turner. Single.]

WINFIELD, Burton James. 22 May 1925-13 Dec 1991. [Stone here, but buried out of state.]

WINFIELD, Rose Geraldine. 18 Feb 1928-15 Mar 1988. [Daughter of Calvin T. and Clio Annie (Cantrell) Pennington, wife of _____ McGee.]

GANN, Monroe. 15 Mar 1859-15 Oct 1936. [Son of Nathan and Parthena (Harris) Gann, husband of Catherine Belle Walker, married 10 Dec 1879 in Cannon County, TN.]

GANN, Catherine Belle. 2 Dec 1861-2 Apr 1937. [Daughter of John and Melvina (_____) Walker, wife of James Monroe Gann.]

GANN, William "Bill" Nathan. 13 Dec 1892-28 Jul 1941. [Son of James Monroe and Catherine Belle (Walker) Gann, husband of Fannie Martin.]

GANN, Brenda Gale. 10 Jan 1950-11 Jan 1950. [Daughter of Ben and Lois (Parker) Gann.]

GANN, James Howard. 23 Mar 1914-9 Apr 1980. WWII. [Son of Benjamin Harrison and Amanda (Parsley) Gann, husband of Willie Maude King.]

GANN, Willie Maude. 15 Mar 1908- . [Willie Maude King, wife of 1) Clarence Tenpenny, married 1 Jul 1925, and 2) James Howard Gann.]

MILLER, Rosie M. 8 Mar 1925- . [Daughter of Benjamin Harrison and Amanda (Parsley) Gann, wife of Jessie B. Miller (divorced).]

MILLER, Jessie B. 6 Jul 1923 - . [Husband of Rosie M. Gann.]

HEARN, Elizabeth F. [No other information]

MILLER, Lonnie M. 18 Nov 1947-30 Aug 1973. [Lonnie Mason, son of Jesse B. and Rosie Mildred (Gann) Miller.]

MILLER, Ronnie, Jr. 25 Oct 1948-18 Jul 1950. [Son of Jesse B. and Rosie Mildred (Gann) Miller.]

GANN, Infant. Born and died 13 Dec 1919. [Infant of Harrison and Amanda (Parsley) Gann.]

GANN, Benjamin Harrison. 14 Feb 1886-24 Oct 1960. [Son of James Monroe and Catherine Belle (Walker) Gann, husband of Amanda Parsley.]

GANN, Amanda P. 6 May 1891-31 Jan 1969. [Daughter of Thomas P. and Calidonia (Foster) Parsley, wife of Benjamin Harrison Gann.]

KING, David R. 18 Nov 1948- . [Son of Jessie H. and Lillian Virginia (Hines) King, husband of 1) Linda E. Miller (div.) and 2) Jackie D. Bain.]

KING, Linda E. 16 Oct 1949- . [Daughter of Jesse B. and Rosie Mildred (Gann) Miller, wife of 1) David R. King (div.) and 2)_____ _____.]

ROGERS, Sidney Robert. 3 Apr 1913-17 Nov 1984. [Son of Oscar and Hattie (Northcutt) Rogers, husband of Nannie Belle Gann, married 2 Feb 1942.]

ROGERS, Nannie Bell Gann. 26 Mar 1918- . [Daughter of Benjamin Harrison and Amanda (Parsley) Gann, wife of Sidney Robert Rogers.]

HOLLAND, Elizabeth. 15 Mar 1847-2 Sep 1935.

SHIELDS, Lewis F. 4 Sep 1921-12 Sep 1986. WWII. [Son of Rhodman Kinner and Hassie Cillar (Gilbert) Shileds, husband of Helen McLaughlin.]

SHIELDS, Everett Leon. 14 Sep 1928-24 Jul 1979. [Son of Rhodman Kinner

and Hassie Cillar (Gilbert) Shields, husband of Mary Melissa
_____.]

SHIELDS, Mary Melissa. 7 Feb 1926-   . [Wife of Everett Leon
     Shields, marriage date on stone 30 Apr 1947.]

HARRIS, Billie Wayne. 20 Dec 1946-23 Dec 1946. [Son of Bill and Lula
     (Allison) Harris.]

TUBB, Dewey Howard. Born and died 29 Oct 1971.

WOODEN, Auvil. 25 Jan 1905-13 Mar 1965. [Son of Fate and Nan (_____)
     Wooden, husband of 1) Cleo Holland and 2) Gertrude (Holt)
     Taylor.]

WOODEN, Gertrude. 10 Jun 1916-23 Apr 1992. [Daughter of Jesse Fielding
     and Myrtle Gertrude (Page) Holt, wife of 1) Sam Taylor (div.) and
     2) Auvil Wooden.]

SMITH, Martha N. 11 Feb 1934-6 Mar 1991. [Martha Nell, wife of Myrl T.
     Smith.]

SMITH, Myrl T. 13 Nov 1929-   . [Son of George Otto and Clara Bell
     "Collie" (Walker) Smith, husband of Martha Nell _____,]

SMITH, Lori Jean. 6 Feb 1972-12 Feb 1972.

MASON, Kenneth E. 18 Dec 1930-   . [Kenneth Elton, son of Linsey
     Elton and Anna Belle (Tamner) Mason, husband of Evelyn Carrie
     Wilson.]

MASON, Evelyn Wilson. 1 May 1932-   . [Evelyn Carrie, daughter of
     Willard Robe and Ellen Cecil (Hickman) Wilson, wife of Kenneth
     Elton Mason.]

SMITH, David Cordell. 9 Oct 1963-21 Jan 1964. [Son of Wallace and Mary
     Ellen (Whittman) Smith.]

HOLT, James Willard. 10 Nov 1918-18 Jun 1982. [Son of Jesse Fielding and
     Myrtle Gertrude (Page) Holt, husband of Margie I. Gann.]

HOLT, Margie I. Gann. 15 Mar 1923-13 Dec 1983. [Margie Irene, daughter
     of William Nathan and Fannie Maude (Martin) Gann, wife of 1)
     _____ _____ and 2) James Willard Holt.]

HOLT, Billy Ray. Born and died 6 Jun 1952. [Son of James Willard and
     Margie I. (Gann) Holt.]

HAGEWOOD, George. 16 Feb 1922-10 Dec 1981. [Son of Thomas and Effie
     (Murphy) Hagewood. Single.]

COSTELLO, Elmus. 1 May 1905-18 May 1977. [Daughter of Thomas and Effie
     (Murphy) Hagewood, wife of _____ Costello.]

HAGEWOOD, Thomas R. 1878 - 24 Apr 1940. [Son of James C. and Sarah H.
     (Carroll) Hagewood, husband of Effie Murphy.]

HAGEWOOD, Effie L. 1880 - 1960. [Effie L. Murphy, wife of Thomas R.
     Hagewood.]

MEDLEY, Jessica Rae "Jessie". 30 Oct 1987-18 May 1990. [Daughter of Larry Hugh and Gina (_____) Medley.]

MEDLEY, Larry Hugh. 26 Mar 1947 - 7 Sep 1989. VIETNAM. [Son of Royce and Mildred (Pennington) Medley, husband of 1) Carolyn Farless and 2) Gina _____.]

TURLEY, J.C. 7 Feb 1931-   .

TURLEY, J.C., Jr. 2 Oct 1961-18 Feb 1981.

*SANDERS, Eugene. Born 22 Dec 1858, died 19 Feb 1931. Son of W.M. and _____ (_____) Sanders.

*MULLICAN, Pearl. Born 28 May 1896, died 23 Feb 1913. Daughter of Dr. J.A. and Minnie B. (Anderson) Clark, wife of Willie T. Mullican, married 25 Dec 1912.

VAUGHN, Infant. Born and died 27 Mar 1940. [Son of G.B. and Gertrude (Simmons) Vaughn.]

DODD, Franki Nicole 1993-1993.

GRIFFITH, Kenneth N. 30 Jul 1953-7 Feb 1992. [Son of Billy and Ann (Crouch) Griffith, husband of 1) Marie Jaco (div) and 2) _____ _____.]

GRIFFITH, Ann L. 1 Jun 1934 -   . [Daughter of Brown and Jimmie Lee (Prater) Crouch, wife of Billy N. Griffith.]

GRIFFITH, Billy N. 27 Jun 1930-   . [Husband of Ann Louise Crouch, married 19 May 1951.]

*LAWS, Roy Franklin, died 14 Jun 1922, aged 2 months and 14 days.

*McGEE, Rose Gereldine, died 15 Mar 1988, age 60 years, daughter of Calvin Thomas and Annie (Cantrell) Pennington, wife of _____ McGee.

*BAILY, Mary Susan. Born 29 Oct 1842, died 11 May 1928. Daughter of Sandy and Emily (Talley) Blair, wife of _____ Baily.

*CROUCH, Harriet Burch. Born 2 Oct 1864, Cherokee Indian, second wife of Ed Crouch, married 9 Aug 1894.

*CLARK, Sallie M. Born 11 Oct 1834, died 6 Jun 1915. Bill rendered to C.S. Clark.

*FIELD, Vera. Died 18 Mar 1916, age 16 years. Daughter of Jordan and Maggie (Laws) Field.

*PIKE, H.P. Died 28 Sep 1916, age 81 years. Hugh P., husband of Mary Emmaline (Snipes) Garth Cawthorn, married 10 Jan 1911.

*PIKE, Emmaline. Born 23 Jan 1839, died 23 Oct 1921. Mary Emmaline Snipes, wife of 1) Jesse T. Garth, married 4 Nov 1852, 2) Isaac Cawthorn, married 18 Dec 1879, and 3) Hugh P. Pike, married 10 Jan 1911.

*YORK, Henry. Born 12 May 1855, died 15 May 1935, son of Nathaniel and

Grange Hall Cemetery, cont.

Cora K. (Arledge) York, husband of Bertha Mai McGowan.

*HENEGAR, Dorothy Joyce. Born 26 Nov 1932, died 16 Dec 1932, daughter of Milton and Gladys (Woods) Henegar.

*CROUCH, Hattie Pearl. Born and died 29 Oct 1926, daughter of O.M. and Laura (Rogers) Crouch.

*CROUCH, Edward. Born and died 10 Sep 1927, son of O.M. and Laura (Rogers) Crouch.

*WOOTEN, Richard. Born 17 Jun 1933, died 17 Feb 1934, son of G.F. and Mabel (Brewer) Wooten.

*TURNER, Donnie Gene. Born 13 Apr 1949, died 30 Oct 1949, son of Alvin and Maudie Mae (Pennington) Turner.

*MULLICAN, Robert. Died 26 Dec 1921, age 7 months, 7 days. Bill rendered to Tom Mullican.

GREEN CEMETERY

Location: On Francis Ferry Road.

GREEN, Infant. 10 Dec 1899-16 Dec 1899. [Infant daughter of Mathew Compton and Eliza E. (Kirby) Green.]

GREEN, Thomas M. 8 Dec 1884-29 Jun 1894. [Son of Mathew Compton and Eliza E. (Kirby) Green.]

GREEN, Sarah N.L. 18 Dec 1882-26 Apr 1894. [Daughter of Mathew Compton and Eliza E. (Kirby) Green.]

COPE, Plinea E. Green. 16 Nov 1876-22 May 1894. [Plinea Green, wife of Tom Cope, married 2 Oct 1892.]

GREEN, Mary A. 27 May 1821-12 May 1903. [Mary Ann, daughter of Mathew and Nancy (_____) Compton, wife of Shadrack Green.]

GREEN, Elder Shadrack. 12 May 1820-8 Nov 1881. [Son of Joseph and Sarah (Mooney) Green, husband of Mary Ann Compton. On his headstone is written: "Why did the Old Baptist call for my credentials for preaching the Resurrection?"]

GREEN, Napoleon Boneparte. 1859-   . [Son of Shadrack and Mary Ann (Compton) Green, husband of Nancy Mullican, married 31 Oct 1878.]

9 unmarked graves.

GUEST HOLLOW CONFEDERATE CEMETERY

Location: 1 Mile south of Morrison near Hwy 55.

HOUSTON, Capt. William Y.   Co. G, 8th Texas Cavalry.
BUTLER, Lt. William W.   Co. A, 8th Texas Cavalry.
PETTUS, Sgt. J.T.   8th Texas Cavalry.
KENNEDY, Pvt. G.B.   Co. C, 8th Texas Cavalry.
PETTY, Pvt. James   Co. F, 8th Texas Cavalry.
BELL, Pvt. John   Co. C, 8th Tennessee Cavalry.
CROCKETT, Pvt. F.M.   Co. A, 8th Tennessee Cavalry.
CURRAN, Pvt. James   Co. A, 8th Tennessee Cavalry.
ELLISON, Pvt. J.H.   Co. A, 8th Tennessee Cavalry.
FARROW, Pvt. Sam   Co. A, 8th Tennessee Cavalry.
GREEN, Pvt. James   Co. C, 8th Tennessee Cavalry.
McDOWELL, Pvt. Jack   Co. K, 8th Tennessee Cavalry.
NEIL, Pvt. W.J.   Co. A, 8th Tennessee Cavalry.
NEWSOM, Pvt. Joe   Co. K, 8th Tennessee Cavalry.

The above Conferedate soldiers were killed on 29 Aug 1862 in their attack on the Morrison Station Stockade. They were buried in a mass grave in a field just north and east of the railroad trestle (exact location unknown at this time). After the Federal forces withdrew to Nashville, a Morrison family removed the bodies and reburied them in individual caskets made from walnut lumber.

GWYN CEMETERY

Location: On Hwy 108 in Viola.

GWYN, Hugh. 1 Sep 1818-18 Aug 1873. [Son of Ransom and Elizabeth
      (Sheppard) Gwyn, husband of 1)_____ _____ and 2) Mary Evans.]

PEAY, Mary Gwyn. 4 Apr 1828-22 Aug 1913. [Mary Evans, wife of Hugh Gwyn,
      married secondly {as his third wife} Thomas Terrell Peay on 21
      Aug 1889.]

GWYN, Milton H. 4 Sep 1826-4 Jun 1902. [Son of Ransom and Elizabeth
      (Sheppard) Gwyn, husband of Nannie Wood.]

GWYN, Nannie M. 23 Dec 1836-2 May 1935. [Nannie M. Wood, wife of Milton
      H. Gwyn.]

WOOTEN, Anna Amelia, died 1 Sep 1891, age 2 years.
WOOTEN, Myrtle Elizabeth, died July 1863, age 8 years.
      [Daughters of David Hampton and Martha Jane (Gwyn) Wooten.]

WOOTEN, D.H. 22 Jul 1830-5 May 1900. [David Hampton, son of Jonathan and
      Nancy (Hampton) Wooten, husband of Martha Jane Gwyn, married 6

Dec 1853.]

WOOTEN, Martha J. 10 Dec 1834-19 Jun 1894. [Martha Jane, daughter of Ransom and Margaret McConnell (Davidson) Gwyn, wife of David Hampton Wooten.]

GWYN, Remus. Died 19 Jul 1841, age 3 years. [Son of Ransom and Margaret McConnell (Davidson) Gwyn.]

GWYN, Sarah, died 1835. [Daughter of Joshua and Susanna (_____) Hickerson, wife of James Gwyn.]

GWYN, James. Died 1835. [Son of James and Sarah (Hickerson) Gwyn.]

COULSON, Amelia. 1820-1 Jul 1844. [Daughter of Ransom and Elizabeth (Sheppard) Gwyn, wife of David Coulson.]

GWYN, Richard. 19 Jun 186_-26 Aug 186_. [Son of Hugh and Mary (Evans) Gwyn.]

MABRY, Thomas Elliott. 5 Jan 1828-11 Oct 1911. [Son of Nathaniel and Martha (Elliott) Mabry, husband of Julia Gwyn, married 24 Nov 1859.]

MABRY, Julia. 25 Jan 1843-1922. [Daughter of Ransom and Margaret McConnell (Davidson) Gwyn, wife of Thomas Elliott Mabry.]

SMITH, Mary Brown. 30 Apr 1863-7 Oct 1908. [Daughter of Thomas Elliott and Julia (Gwyn) Mabry, wife of J. Harris Smith.]

MABRY, John D. Aug 1873-26 Nov 1875. [John Davidson, son of Thomas Elliott and Julia (Gwyn) Mabry.]

GWYN, Romulus. 1838-12 Apr 1862. [Son of Ransom and Margaret McConnell (Davidson) Gwyn. Romulus Gwyn died of wounds received in the Battle of Murfreesboro. Family history says that he is buried there, but has a stone in the Gwyn Cemetery.]

GWYN, Ransom. 1790-8 Feb 1872. [Son of James and Amelia (Lenior) Gwyn, married 1) Elizabeth Shepard, 2) Margaret McConnell Davidson and 3) Margarite McLean on 21 Nov 1871 when he was 81.]

GWYN, Elizabeth. 1796-19 Jul 1831. [Daughter of James and Pheobe (Maston) Shepherd, first wife of Ransom Gwyn.]

GWYN, Margaret M. 1802-21 Apr 1868. [Margaret McConnell, daughter of Hugh and Jane (Vance) Davidson, second wife of Ransom Gwyn.]

HASH CEMETERY

Location: at Rock Island, Tn on Ed Sparkman-Roy Kuhn farms

*JONES, Thomas A. Born ca 1812, married 1 May 1861 to Tabitha Hash.

*JONES, Tabitha Hash. Born ca 1828, daughter of Thomas and Drucilla
    (Howell) Hash.

Two children of the above couple.

*HASH, Drucilla "Drucy" Howell. Born 1794 in Grayson County, VA, died in
    Warren County, TN, consort of Thomas Hash.

*HASH, Thomas, born 2 Apr 1792 in NC, died 1864 in TN, came to Warren
    County about 1810. Husband of Drucilla Howell.

*HASH, Adaline E. Born 1820, died 1832, daughter of Thomas and Drucilla
    (Howell) Hash.

Other unmarked graves.

HAYES CEMETERY

Location: Irving College area.

HAYES, William.   26 Sep 1780-24 Jan 1857. [William M., husband of 1)
    _____ _____ and 2) Tempie McDaniel.]

HAYES, Tempie. 16 Mar 1815-25 Jan 1893. [Tempie McDaniel, second wife of
    William M. Hayes.]

CUNNINGHAM, Matilda. 22 Oct 1802-25 May 1836. [Matilda Hayes, daughter
    of William Hayes and his first wife. First wife of Thomas
    Cunningham.]

SEITZ, Nellie. 22 Jul 1824-24 Jun 1903. [Daughter of William M. Hayes
    and his first wife. Married 1) to Phillip McGregor, 2) to
    William Lynch Dearing on 26 Feb 1868 and 3) to Logan Seitz on
    15 Dec 1883.]

CUNNINGHAM, Mary. 25 Aug 1813-17 Sep 1864. [Daughter of Jesse and Phatha
    (Stiles) Safley, second wife of Thomas Cunningham.]

CUNNINGHAM, M.A. 6 Oct 1837-23 Jul 1862. [Mary Ann, daughter of Thomas
    and Mary (Safley) Cunningham.]

STUBBLEFIELD, William. 28 Oct 1871-13 Sep 1873. [Son of Napoleon
    Boneparte and Nancy Jane (Hayes) Stubblefield.]

*HAYES, Samuel David. Inscription on stone "Samuel David.. House...of
    FL". Hayes family information says that Samuel David was a
    student at Benitt College when he became ill and died.

HEBRON CEMETERY

Location: One mile west of Irving College.

BARNES, Misty Cinitha. Born and died 14 Feb 1975. [Daughter of Roger
        Eugene and Rhonda (Hickey) Barnes, granddaughter of Wallace
        Barnes and of Bill Hickey.]

MILSTEAD, Thomas E. 30 Nov 1929-   . [Thomas Earl, son of Claud
        and Lena (Cunningham) Milstead, husband of 1) Eona York, married
        18 Nov 1950, and 2) Edna Sullivan.]

MILSTEAD, Eona York. 11 Oct 1931-23 Sep 1980. [Daughter of Henry and
        Bertha (McGowan) York, wife of Thomas Earle Milstead.]

RHEA, Russ. 1911-17 Aug 1983. [Son of Bill and Laura (Smartt) Rhea,
        husband of Mae Elizabeth Byrd.]

RHEA, Mae. 1918-21 Jun 1979. [Mae Elizabeth Byrd, daughter of George and
        Mary (Madison) Byrd, wife of Russ Rhea.]

GINN, Wavie F. 1925-19 Feb 1989. [Daughter of Arcey and Lillie (Fults)
        Rhea, wife of Garvin Ginn.]

HILLIS, Beatrice Wanamaker. 20 Dec 1918-   . [Daughter of Beecher
        and Ollie (Coppinger) Wanamaker, wife of Arlin Hillis.]

RHEA, Fred. 19 Jul 1914-8 Apr 1985. [Son of Robert and Carlee (Smartt)
        Rhea, husband of Leaoma Fults, married 6 Jun 1937.]

RHEA, Leaoma. 22 Mar 1915-28 Aug 1993. [Daughter of France and Nannie
        (Rhea) Fults, wife of Fred Rhea.]

WALKER, Alvin J. 18 Mar 1919-31 Mar 1989. [Son of John and Zettie
        (Prater) Walker, husband of Dovie Mooneyham.]

WALKER, Dovie M. 2 Mar 1919-   . [Daughter of John and Minnie
        (Dodson) Mooneyham.]

WARE, Thurman. 26 Oct 1916-22 Aug 1984. [Son of Isham W. and Ethel
        (Muncey) Ware, husband of Gilberta Woodlee.]

WARE, Gilberta Woodlee. 20 Jul 1922-   . [Daughter of Claud and
        Oshia (Hughes) Woodlee, wife of Thurman Ware.]

CAGLE, Waymon McCoy. 15 Sep 1911-31 Jul 1991. [Son of Harvey and Martha
        Emma (Hobbs) Cagle, husband of Clemma Iola Killian.]

CAGLE, Clemma Iola. 1 May 1920-   . [Daughter of Henry M. and
        Savannah (Smartt) Killian, wife of Waymon McCoy Cagle.]

THROWER, Gregory L. Born and died 24 Nov 1985
THROWER, Jeffery G. Born and died 24 Nov 1985
        [Twin sons of James and Lou Ann (Nunley) Thrower.]

RUSSELL, Ora Nelson Sr. 27 Nov 1925-8 Oct 1988. WWII-KOREA. [Son of
        Elihue and Bessie (Jones) Russell, married, as his fifth wife
        Bertha Lee (Fults) Hodges.]

111

FULTS, Charles Odell. 29 Aug 1934-15 Mar 1989. [Son of Russell and Georgia (Fults) Fults, husband of 1) Elma Jean Johnson and 2) Glenda Faye Masters.]

NORTHCUTT, John Lawson Sr. 18 Nov 1910-23 Mar 1991. [Son of Jonathan D. and Minnie Nye (Simpson) Northcutt, husband of Lucy Catherine Rust, married 18 Apr 1931.]

NORTHCUTT, Lucy Catherine Rust. 20 Dec 1911-21 Jun 1985. [Daughter of Arthur and Rosa (Lampley) Rust, wife of John Lawson Northcutt Sr.]

MARSINI, John A. 17 Feb 1939-   . [Son of Augustus and Mary (_____) Marsini, husband of Billie Sue Sullivan.]

MARSINI, Billie Sue. 17 Jul 1940-2 Jun 1981. [Daughter of William Alton and Wilma Lou (Hobbs) Sullivan, wife of John A. Marsini.

BLANKENSHIP, Donald F. "Don". 27 Apr 1932-15 Dec 1980. [Son of Miller R. and Lorene (Farless) Blankenship, husband of Ruth Doak, married 23 Nov 1950.]

BLANKENSHIP, Ruth D. 3 Feb 1933-   . [Daughter of Brown and Wilma Lou (Hobbs) Doak, wife of 1) Donald F. Blankenship and 2) Loe Waddell.]

CAGLE, Theodore L. 7 Jul 1918-31 Dec 1990. WWII. [Theodore Lester, son of Harve and Lemma (Hobbs) Cagle, husband of Ruby Perry, married 12 May 1951. On the back of his stone is written "Parents of Wanda, Rhodessa, Theodore Jr."]

CAGLE, Ruby C. 27 Dec 1932-   . [Daughter of Robert and Bertha (Cobb) Perry from KY, wife of Theodore Lester Cagle. On the back of her stone is written "Parents of Deborah, Michael and Ouida."]

KELLEY, Charles David. 9 Nov 1927-22 May 1973. WWII. [Son of Bedford Forest and Susie (Barnes) Kelley, husband of Sylvia Lina Myrick Argo.]

KELLEY, Sylvia. 30 Aug 1927-   . [Sylvia Lina Myrick, daughter of Murray Bedford and Mary Maude (Hobbs) Argo, wife of Charles David Kelley.]

SULLIVAN, William Alton. 1913-1993. [Son of William Abraham and Sophia J. (Anderson) Sullivan, husband of Wilma Hobbs.]

PANTER, Charles Arthur. 16 Oct 1892-7 Jul 1982. [Son of James and Sarah Jane (Clendenon) Panter, husband of Alma Lois Clendenon, married 8 Aug 1919.]

PANTER, Alma Lois. 3 Aug 1898-1 Oct 1974. [Daughter of William and Lucy (Barnes) Clendenon, wife of Charles Arthur Panter.]

JENNINGS, Emma. 6 Dec 1905-11 Jun 1988. [Emma Irene, daughter of Lloyd and Nannie Frances (Hobbs) Cagle, wife of 1) Cheatum Nunley and 2) Clabe Jennings.]

JENNINGS, Clabe. 12 Jun 1902-30 Jan 1993. [Son of Jessie and Belzora (Roberts) Jennings, husband of Emma Irene Cagle, married 15 Oct

1932.]

NUNLEY, Raymon E. 23 Apr 1946-3 Nov 1988. [Raymon Edward, son of Alvin
          and Eva Jean (Roberts) Nunley, husband of 1) Wilma G. Tate,
          married 11 Aug 1964, and 2) Mary J. Turner, married 28 Dec
          1979.]

NUNLEY, Mary J. 2 Jan 1957-   . [Daughter of Bill and Laura
          (Roberts) Turner, wife of Raymon Edward Nunley.]

ARGO, Fred Wayne. 12 Dec 1944-31 Aug 1992. [Son of Jesse Clyde and
          Gladys Gertrude (Bouldin) Argo, husband of Phyllis Terryl
          Campbell, married 24 Oct 1964.]

ARGO, Phyllis Terryl. 28 Nov 1946-   . [Daughter of Vernon and
          Pauline (Wanamaker) Campbell, wife of Fred Wayne Argo.]

CUNNINGHAM, Anthony D. 10 Jan 1955-14 Oct 1976. [Anthony Darrell, son of
          Fred and Lucy E. (Roberts) Cunningham. Single.]

CUNNINGHAM, Fred. 28 Jan 1933-14 Aug 1993. [Son of Claud and Hollie
          (Rogers) Cunningham, husband of Lucy E. Roberts.]

CUNNINGHAM, Lucy E. 21 Jun 1934-   . [Daughter of Dread and
          Beulah (Madewell) Roberts, wife of Fred Cunningham.]

CUNNINGHAM, Roy. 19 May 1927-18 Dec 1981. [Roy Clinton, son of Claud and
          Hollie (Rogers) Cunningham, husband of Clair Lee Numcey, married
          16 Jul 1947.]

CUNNINGHAM, Clair. 7 May 1925-26 Dec 1984. [Clair Lee, daughter of James
          L. and Eva Smith (McBride) Muncey, wife of Roy Clinton
          Cunningham.]

HOBBS, Kathy Barnes. 12 Aug 1954-17 Dec 1989. [Kathy Jean, daughter of
          L.H. "Bud" and Irene (Milstead) Barnes, wife of 1) Steve Wade,
          married 12 Aug 1971 and 2) Houston Randy Hobbs.]

TUCKER, Wm. Bearl. 15 Feb 1924-   . [Son of Charlie and Ida
          Louise (Roberts) Tucker, husband of 1) Audrey Lee Cunningham,
          married 31 Jan 1942, and 2) Charlene Panter Coppinger, married
          1 Sep 1982.]

TUCKER, Audrey L. 29 Jun 1922-25 Jul 1982. [Audrey Lee, daughter of
          James Claud and Hollie Claire (Rogers) Cunningham, wife of
          William Bearl Tucker.]

RHEA, Eugene. 6 Jul 1908-13 May 1983. [Son of Robert and Ruth (Fults)
          Rhea, husband of Lenzie Rhea.]

RHEA, Lenzie. 18 Sep 1903-29 Aug 1981. [Daughter of Lyman and Nellie
          (Countiss) Rhea, wife of Eugene Rhea.]

HOBBS, Emma K. 17 Jan 1908-3 Sep 1983. [Daughter of Bucker and Opal
          (_____) Keathley, wife of John Hobbs.]

HOBBS, John. 14 Aug 1914-10 Aug 1983. [Son of James and Lula (Woodlee)
          Hobbs, husband of Emma Keathley.]

SMARTT, Leonard Bill. 28 Mar 1925-18 Feb 1990. WWII-KOREA. [Son of

Rushie and Letta (Scott) Smartt.]

RHEA, Finis "Buttermilk". Died 9 Mar 1977. [Son of Robert and Carlee (Smartt) Rhea.]

SMARTT, Jessie E. 10 Jul 1929- . [Son of Marcus and Lillie (Smartt) Smartt.]

SMARTT, Lillie. 26 Jan 1905-30 Mar 1993. [Daughter of Harris and Mary (Nunley) Smartt, wife of Marcus Smartt. "Mrs. Lillie Lewis" on foot stone.]

SMARTT, Marcus. 18 Oct 1902-18 Jul 1957. [Son of Benjamin Franklin and Lucy (Hobbs) Smartt, husband of Lillie Smartt.]

SMARTT, Frank. 1878-1940. [Benjamin Franklin, son of Reuben and Sarah (Nunley) Smartt, husband of Lucy (Hobbs) Northcutt.]

SMARTT, Lucy. 15 Sep 1871-22 Dec 1944. [Daughter of Christopher C. and Elizabeth (Smith) Hobbs, wife of 1) Frank Cheatum Northuctt and 2) Benjamin Franklin Smartt.]

GROSS, Adam D. 30 Nov 1867-27 Jul 1951. [Adam Daniel, son of Asa and Sarah (Bost) Gross, husband of Elizabeth Mansfield.]

GROSS, Elizabeth Mansfield. 5 Nov 1869-16 Jan 1948. [Daughter of Thomas Jefferson and Sarah Elizabeth (Barnes) Mansfield, wife of Adam Daniel Gross.]

GROSS, Audrey Lee. 14 Apr 1889-3 Aug 1975. [Daughter of Adam Daniel and Elizabeth (Mansfield) Gross. Single.]

WILLIAMS, John Marion. 28 Dec 1906-23 Mar 1979. US Army. [Son of Tom and Ida (Whitaker) Williams, husband of Wallie Gross, married 6 Mar 1937.]

WILLIAMS, Wallie Gross. 15 May 1908- . [Daughter of Adam Daniel and Elizabeth (Mansfield) Gross, wife of John Marion Williams.]

CURTIS, Aaron Edward. 21 Apr 1941-25 Apr 1941. [Son of Aaron Lowell and Mary Lou (Barnes) Curtis.]

CURTIS, Aaron Lowell. 13 May 1915-1 Mar 1969. [Son of Aaron Escal and Queen Vickie (Bales) Curtis, husband of Mary Lou Barnes.]

CURTIS, Mary Lou Barnes. 11 Jun 1917- . [Daughter of Ed V. and Lula (Nunley) Barnes, wife of Aaron Lowell Curtis.]

CURTIS, Aaron Escal. 19 Nov 1889-4 Apr 1971. [Son of Lewis Elmore and Carrie (Bess) Curtis, husband of Queen Vickie Bales.]

CURTIS, Queen Vickie. 8 Mar 1894-8 Dec 1988. [Daughter of William and Alice (Palmer) Bales, wife of Aaron Escal Curtis.]

MILSTEAD, George E. 21 Aug 1912-15 Oct 1979. [George Eugene, son of Samuel Claud and Lena May (Cunningham) Milstead, husband of Mary Edith Curtis.]

MILSTEAD, Mary Edith Curtis. 15 Sep 1917- . [Daughter of Aaron

Escal and Queen Vickie (Bales) Curtis, wife of 1) George Eugene Milstead and 2) D.V. Northcutt.]

MILSTEAD,Waymon Gary, I. 20 Jan 1939-21 Dec 1979. [Son of George Eugene and Mary Edith (Curtis) Milstead, husband of Carrie Jane Pyburn.]

MILSTEAD, Carrie Jane. 1 Nov 1942-   . [Carrie Jane Pyburn, wife of 1) Waymon Gary Milstead, I, and 2) Arnold Wilson.]

BARNES, Ruby W. 21 Apr 1902-15 Dec 1976. [Daughter of Isham and Tim (Myers) Ware, wife of B. Wince Barnes.]

BARNES, B. Wince. 23 Feb 1896-30 Nov 1976. [Son of Charles Irving Lafayette and Lucy (Nunley) Barnes, husband of Ruby Ware, married 14 May 1919.]

CLENDENON, Erma P. 8 Oct 1909-   . [Daughter of Lafayette F. and Mary (Scott) Panter, wife of Loften Clendenon.]

CLENDENON, Loften. 26 Jul 1903-24 Apr 1981. [Son of William Washington and Lucy Emma (Barnes) Clendenon, husband of Erma Panter, married 24 Dec 1929.]

CLENDENON, Lucy E. 8 Sep 1878-21 Jan 1958. [Lucy Emma, daughter of Campbell and Catherine (Bess) Barnes, wife of William Washington Clendenon.]

CLENDENON, William W. 7 Dec 1868-19 Dec 1949. [William Washington, son of James Newton and Mary Catherine (Stubblefield) Clendenon, husband of Lucy Emma Barnes, married 30 Jan 1895.]

BARNES, L.H. "Bud". 21 Apr 1915-18 Jun 1993. [Lonnie Haskell, son of Edward and Lula (Nunley) Barnes, husband of Irene Milstead.]

BARNES, Irene. 4 May 1918-   . [Janie Irene Milstead, wife of Lonnie Haskell "Bud" Barnes, married 3 Jun 1937.]

BARNES, Susan. Born and died 29 Oct 1947. [Daughter of Lonnie Haskell "Bud" and Janie Irene (Milstead) Barnes.]

SMITH, Claude Ray. 17 Mar 1919-23 Nov 1984. WWII. [Son of Hence and Ollie (Wheeler) Smith, husband of Edna L. Wagner, married 10 Jul 1942.]

SMITH, Edna L. Wagner. 6 Apr 1922-   . [Daughter of William Jacob and Minnie (Whittenburg) Wagoner, wife of Claude Ray Smith.]

WAGNER, Minnie. 10 Nov 1893-16 Aug 1968. [Minnie Eugene, daughter of John and Alice (Wheeler) Whittenburg, wife of William Jacob Wagner, married 10 Nov 1916.]

WAGNER, W. J. 3 Aug 1890-17 Oct 1939. [William Jacob, son of George and Mary (Cardwell) Wagner, husband of Minnie Eugene Whittenburg.]

MOFFITT, Haskel Jerome. 11 Nov 1919-20 Jun 1957. [Son of Haskel Bouldin and Sarah Janie (Meadows) Moffitt.]

MOFFITT, Sarah Janie. 5 Jun 1889-25 Aug 1955. [Daughter of Jerome J. and Emma I. (Etter) Meadows, wife of Haskel Bouldin Moffitt.]

115

MOFFITT, Haskel Bouldin. 1 Apr 1890-10 Dec 1948. [Son of Elijah Lewis and Maggie Queen (Bouldin) Moffitt, husband of Sarah Janie Meadows, married 27 Dec 1911.]

SMARTT, Emma Queen. 3 Aug 1917-   . [Daughter of Haskel Bouldin and Sarah Janie (Meadows) Moffitt, wife of Paul Smartt.]

SMARTT, Paul. 15 Jun 1903-9 Mar 1984. [Son of Marion and Myrick (Nunley) Smartt, husband of Emma Queen Moffitt, married 2 Jan 1935.]

WOODLEE, Lemma L. 7 May 1907-13 Jun 1976. [Lemma Lee, daughter of Frank and Lucy (Hobbs) Smartt, wife of Henry Clay Woodlee.]

WOODLEE, Henry C. 8 Jul 1902-   . [Henry Clay, son of Andrew Beecher and Fannie Harrison (Nunley) Woodlee, husband of Lemma Lee Smartt, married 4 Nov 1928.]

BAKER, Edgar Hal. 7 Sep 1918-   . [Husband of Imogene Gross, married 5 Oct 1940.]

BAKER, Imogene Gross. 15 Nov 1922-   . [Wife of Edgar Hal Baker.]

ARNOLD, J.T. 9 Feb 1908-13 Jul 1991. [Son of Tom and Ollie (Wiser) Arnold, husband of Alda Hobbs, married 28 Mar 1934.]

ARNOLD, Alda Hobbs. 6 Aug 1911-   . [Daughter of Robert and Maude (Nunley) Hobbs, wife of J.T. Arnold.]

ARNOLD, Infant. Born and died 4 Dec 1935. [Son of J.T. and Alda (Hobbs) Arnold.]

BARNES, Chester W. 18 Feb 1894-10 Aug 1970. [Chester Wallace, son of Charles Irving Lafayette and Lucy (Nunley) Barnes, husband of Francis Lee Hill.]

BARNES, Francis L. 19 Aug 1896-3 Apr 1975. [Francis Lee, daughter of Sidney and Emma (Lynch) Hill, wife of Chester Wallace Barnes.]

BAKER, Everett E. 14 May 1948-22 May 1969. Military Marker. [Son of Charles and Evelyn (Sullivan) Baker, husband of Lillian Elaine Brady.]

BRADY, Tony Eric. 29 Dec 1957-22 May 1969. [Son of Marcus and Lucy Emma (Barnes) Brady.]

BRADY, Charles W. Born and died 26 Jun 1940. [Son of Marcus and Lucy Emma (Barnes) Brady.]

HILL, Phillis A. Born and died 26 Nov 1942. [Phillis Agnes, daughter of J. Polk and Ollie (Keaton) Hill.]

ARGO, Murray Bedford. 10 Apr 1884-25 Aug 1949. [Son of Josiah Joseph and Lina (Hobbs) Argo, husband of Mary Maude Hobbs.]

ARGO, Mary Maude. 15 Dec 1890-13 Aug 1971. [Daughter of Thomas Marion and Myrick (Miller) Hobbs, wife of Murray Bedford Argo, married 9 May 1908.]

BARNES, Addie M. 15 Jun 1920-9 Oct 1949. [Addie Marie, daughter of Richard and Clemmie (Estes) Madewell, wife of Lowell Barnes.]

BARNES, Lowell. 22 Sep 1919-22 Nov 1911. [Son of Wendell and Athelia M. (Boyd) Barnes, husband of 1) Addie M. Madewell and 2) Mildred J. Roberts.]

BARNES, Mildred J. 28 Jun 1931-   . [Daughter of Dread and Beulah (Madewell) Roberts, second wife of Lowell Barnes.]

HILLIS, Clinton P. 7 May 1919-28 Sep 1992. [Clinton Pierce, son of Frank Pierce and Amanda Jane (Wanamaker) Hillis, husband of Melba Barnes.]

BARNES, Melba. 13 Nov 1922-   . [Wife of Clinton Pierce Hillis.]

CUNNINGHAM, Hollie. 21 Sep 1899-20 Apr 1989. [Hollie Claire, daughter of Harrison McKinley and Mary Wilsie (Hennessee) Rogers, wife of James Claud Cunningham, married 10 Sep 1920.]

CUNNINGHAM, Claud. 22 Aug 1898-9 Sep 1970. [James Claud, son of Jess and Ellen (Mayo) Cunningham, husband of Hollie Claire Rogers.]

FORD, E. Price. 8 Jul 1864-11 Mar 1938. [Son of William and Elvira (Myers) Ford, husband of Hester Lock.]

FORD, Hester Lock. 29 Oct 1885-29 May 1970. [Daughter of Hugh A. and Parthena (Hamilton) Lock, wife of 1) Edward Price Ford and 2) J.E. Witt, married 28 Feb 1940.]

HILL, Evanell. 23 Jun 1930-20 Jul 1935. [Daughter of James Clifford and Mary Magdalene (Stotts) Hill.]

HILL, Lena. 13 Dec 1903-21 Jul 1961. [Mary Magdalene, daughter of James and Henrietta (Barnes) Stotts, wife of James Clifford Hill.]

HILL, Clifford. 23 Mar 1901-31 Mar 1970. [James Clifford, son of Sidney Albert and Emma Euphemia (Lynch) Hill, husband of 1) Mary Magdalene Stotts and 2) Alia C. Davis, married 23 Oct 1962.]

MOFFITT, Eva Haas. 11 Nov 1898-28 Jul 1978. [Eva McCrary, daughter of Phillip and Ella Louise (Kay) Haas, wife of Guy Robert Moffitt, Sr.]

MOFFITT, Guy Robert, Sr. 2 Aug 1896-26 Apr 1973. WWI. [Son of Venus and Maggie (Bouldin) Moffitt, husband of Eva McCrary Haas.]

MOFFITT, Infants. Born and died 17 Jul 1942. [Infant son and daughter of Mr. and Mrs Guy R. Moffitt, Jr.]

MARTIN, Lou. 27 Apr 1880-14 Feb 1959. [Lou Cindy, daughter of Charles Irving Lafayette and Lucy (Nunley) Barnes, wife of Eugene Robert Martin, married 8 Jun 1899.]

MARTIN, Eugene. 16 Apr 1877-10 May 1949. [Eugene Robert, son of Elijah and Harriet (Etter) Martin, husband of Lou Cindy Barnes.]

BARNES, H. Marcus. 26 Jan 1901-11 Jan 1972. [Son of Charles Irving Lafayette and Lucy (Nunley) Barnes.]

BARNES, Lucy Nunley. 1 Nov 1860-1 Dec 1950. [Daughter of Jess and Deida (Hobbs) Nunley, wife of Charles Irving Lafayette Barnes.]

BARNES, C. Irving L. 9 May 1856-20 Oct 1935. [Charles Irving Lafayette, son of Isaac and Susan E. (Hill) Barnes, husband of Lucy Nunley.]

HOBBS, Sarah Elizabeth "Betha". 21 May 1906-10 Apr 1977. [Daughter of George amd Minerva (Mansfield) Perry, wife of Marcus Lafayette Hobbs.]

HOBBS, Marcus L. 18 Jan 1906-   . [Marcus Lafayette, son of Thomas Marion and Myrick (Miller) Hobbs, husband of 1) Sarah Elizabeth Perry and 2) Lillie (Woodlee) Hobbs.]

WILLIS, Venie. 5 Feb 1880-2 Jan 1882. [Daughter of George T. and Gracy A. (Smith) Willis.]

GROSS, Rosa Lee. 27 Mar 1900-9 Dec 1959. [Daughter of James and Janie (Fults) Hobbs, wife of Willie W. Gross.]

GROSS, Willie W. 16 Feb 1896-10 Mar 1935. [Son of Adam Daniel and Elizabeth (Mansfield) Gross, husband of Rosa Lee Hobbs.]

PERRY, Houston. 5 Apr 1910-2 Jul 1928. [John Houston, son of George Washington and Minerva Jane (Mansfield) Perry, single.]

PERRY, Minerva. 12 Jul 1867-7 Apr 1958. [Minerva Jane, daughter of Thomas Jefferson and Sarah Elizabeth (Barnes) Mansfield, wife of George Washington Perry.]

PERRY, George W. 8 Feb 1868-21 May 1956. [George Washington, son of John Houston and Frances Elizabeth (King) Perry, husband of Minerva Janes Mansfield, married 4 Nov 1896.]

MEADOWS, Infant. 13 Apr 1885-8 Oct 1885. [Son of Jerome J. and Emma I. (Etter) Meadows.]

MEADOWS, Jerome J. 11 Dec 1852-21 Nov 1944. [Son of William Morris and Sarah Jane (Moffitt) Meadows, husband of Emma I. Etter.]

MEADOWS, Emma I. 28 Feb 1851-6 Jan 1924. [Daughter of Henry and Elizabeth Jane (Morrison) Etter, wife of Jerome J. Meadows, married 26 Jun 1879.]

MEADOWS, W.M. 28 Aug 1821-23 Jun 1900. "Veteran of Mexican War". [William Morris, son of Vincent and E. (Lawrence) Meadows, husband of Sarah Jane Moffitt.]

MEADOWS, Sarah J. 15 Jan 1831-20 Sep 1887. [Sarah Jane, daughter of Aaron and Harriet (Hill) Moffitt, wife of William Morris Meadows, married 2 Jan 1850.]

MOFFITT, Patrick Narve. 25 Mar 1882-28 Nov 1961. [Son of Venus C. and Maggie Lou (Bouldin) Moffitt, husband of Margie Lee Meadows.]

MOFFITT, Margie Lee. 2 Sep 1886-29 Apr 1990. [Daughter of Jerome J. and Emma I. (Etter) Meadows, wife of Patrick Narve Moffitt.

MOFFITT, Hon. F.M. 16 Jan 1835-18 Aug 1900. "Member of the House of Representatives 1873-1874". [Francis Marion, son of Aaron and Harriet (Hill) Moffitt, husband of 1) Elizabeth Martin, married 24 Oct 1865, 2) Mary Worthington, 3) Mollie Amont and 4) Tennie

Crain.]

MOFFITT, Tennie. 21 Apr (1871)-(11 Jan 1913). [Tennie Crain, fourth wife of F.M. Moffitt. Her name is on one side of his stone, although she is actually buried at Shellsford Cemetery by her second husband Romulus C. Dodson whom she married on 17 Aug 1905.]

MOFFITT, Wallace H. 2 Nov 1923-20 Jul 1934. [Wallace Herman, Son of Haskel Bouldin and Sarah Janie (Meadows) Moffitt.]

MOFFITT, Geraldine. 25 Nov 1912-1 Sep 1936. [Daughter of Haskel Bouldin and Sarah Janie (Meadows) Moffitt.]

BARNES, Infant. Born and died 12 Nov 1912. [Infant son of Harris Bradford and Lucille (McGregor) Barnes.]

BARNES, Lucille McGregor. 10 Jan 1893-5 Jun 1966. [Virginia Lucille, daughter of Bruce and Mollie (Phelps) McGregor, wife of Harris Bradford Barnes, Sr.]

BARNES, Harris Bradford, Sr. 11 Apr 1890-13 Sep 1984. [Son of Charles Irving Lafayette and Lucy (Nunley) Barnes, husband of Virginia Lucille McGregor.]

FORD, James S. Oct 1847-7 Oct 1917. [Son of William W. and Elvira (Myers) Ford, husband of Ida Elizabeth Meadows, married 13 Apr 1894.]

PUTTY, George E. 6 Sep 1900-7 Jul 1915. [Son of William E. and Florence (Ford) Putty.]

PUTTY, Florence P. 28 Nov 1862-25 Oct 1928. [Daughter of William W. and Elvira (Myers) Ford, wife of William E. Putty, married 18 Jun 1894.]

WIGINGTON, J.G. Mar 1847-22 Mar 1918. [John Griffin, son of James and Drucilla (Spain) Wigington, husband of Elizabeth Ford, married 6 Jun 1889.]

WIGINGTON, Elizabeth. 5 Oct 1868-11 May 1928. [Daughter of William W. and Elvira (Myers) Ford, wife of John Griffin Wigington.]

NORTHCUTT, Cathy Rose. Born and died 30 Dec 1950. [Daughter of John and Jo Ruth (Gross) Northcutt.]

NORTHCUTT, Deborah Ann. Born and died 26 Nov 1951. [Daughter of John and Jo Ruth (Gross) Northcutt.]

CLENDENON, Sallie. 17 Mar 1909-24 Oct 1984. [Daughter of George and Nancy (McCorkle) Pearson, wife of Roy Clendenon.]

CLENDENON, Roy. 13 Feb 1899-9 Jun 1982. [Son of James and Martha (Patrick) Clendenon, husband of Sallie Pearson, married 22 May 1933.]

CLENDENON, Alace. 23 Dec 1883-30 Jun 1964. [Daughter of Jesse Dodson "Doc" and Jane Vickers (Maxwell) Jennings, wife of Harmon Venus Clendenon.]

CLENDENON, Harmon. 4 Sep 1881-28 Oct 1969. [Harmon Venus, son of James

Newton and Mary Catherine (Stubblefield) Clendenon, husband of Alace Jennings.]

BARNES, Jessie E. Born 1924-   . [Jessie E. Thompson, wife of 1) Harris Bradford Barnes, Jr. and 2) Earl M. Smith.]

BARNES, Harris B., Jr. 6 Apr 1916-12 Jul 1965. WWII. [Harris Bradford, son of Harris Bradford and Lucille (McGregor) Barnes, husband of Jessie Thompson.]

BARNES, Infant. Born and died 7 Sep 1952. [Infant son of Harris Bradford Jr. and Jessie (Thompson) Barnes.]

WHITTENBURG, Willie C. 25 Mar 1891-24 Dec 1964. [William Charles, son of John and Alice (Wheeler) Whittenbury, husband of Mary Ruth Davidson, married 16 Sep 1916. She is buried at Dechard, Tn with her people.]

WALLING, Laura. 10 Dec 1888-27 Mar 1969. [Daughter of John and Alice (Wheeler) Whittenburg, wife of James Harve Walling.]

WALLING, Harve. 3 Nov 1881-24 Jan 1969. [James Harve, son of Monroe Cason and Violet Ann (Myers) Walling, husband of Laura Whittneburg.]

WARE, Tim. 24 Sep 1872-11 Nov 1913. [Daughter of James Calvin and Louisa Scott (Northcutt) Myers, wife of Isham Wash Ware.]

WARE, Isham W. 19 Mar 1868-5 Aug 1928. [Isham Wash, son of Isham Wash and Katherine (Argo) Ware, husband of 1) Tim Myers and 2) Ethel Muncey, married 2 Jul 1916.]

*WARE, Ethel Muncey. Died 17 Apr 1946, daughter of Thomas Jasper and Elizabeth (Lytle) Muncey, second wife of Isham W. Ware.

MAXWELL, Maggie E. 4 May 1867-26 Dec 1936. [Daughter of George W. and Sarah (Pursley) Mayo, wife of William M. Maxwell, married 14 Mar 1886.]

BOYD, Roberta. 22 Apr 1919-25 Jan 1920. [Margurite Roberta, daughter of Fernando Campbell and Sarah Jane (Maxwell) Boyd.]

BOYD, Lorena May. 22 May 1907-7 Mar 1910. [Daughter of Fernando Campbell and Sarah Jane (Maxwell) Boyd.]

BARNES, Athelia M. 15 Oct 1896-26 Aug 1967. [Daughter of John Henry Harrison and Susan Edna (Tate) Boyd, wife of Wendell Barnes (div.).]

BOYD, Ollie Mae. 1 Nov 1899-1 May 1917. [Daughter of John Henry Harrison and Susan Edna (Tate) Boyd.]

BOYD, John H.H. 11 Feb 1861-21 Feb 1924. [John Henry Harrison, son of Fernando Campbell and Elizabeth Jane (Winchester) Boyd, husband of 1) Ersey Johnson who died 15 Nov 1892, and 2) Susan Edna Tate.]

BOYD, Edna. 3 Dec 1877-29 Dec 1958. [Susan Edna, daughter of D.M. "Doc" and Adelaide (Dearing) Tate, second wife of John Henry Harrison Boyd.]

STUBBLEFIELD, Opal Lee Boyd. 16 Jul 1906-23 Apr 1988. [Daughter of John Henry Harrison and Susan Edna (Tate) Boyd, first wife of Hiram B. Stubblefield (div.).]

ETTER, Roscoe, Jr. Born and died 18 Apr 1915. [Son of Dr. Roscoe and Frances (Duggan) Etter.]

ETTER, E. Bruce. 7 Oct 1868-23 Feb 1897. [Son of William G. and Electra Charlotte (Hill) Etter.]

ROACH, Jane Parks. 3 Jul 1856-28 Feb 1922. [Daughter of Carroll and Hixey (Bullen) Parks, wife of J. Wilburn Roach.]

ROACH, J. Wilburn. 23 May 1861-10 Jun 1910. [Son of William Marion and Elmira (McBride) Roach, husband of Jane Parks.]

PERRY, Charles T. 10 Mar 1898-17 Oct 1972. [Son of George Washington and Minerva Jane (Mansfield) Perry, husband of Grace Moore.]

PERRY, Grace Moore. 5 Feb 1913-13 Mar 1991. [Daughter of Silas D. and Annie (Durham) Moore, wife of Charles T. Perry.]

PARKS, J.E. 5 Jan 1871-15 Oct 1874. [Son of George W. and Eulitia H. (Cunningham) Parks.]

PARKS, Eulitia H. 16 Feb 1843-7 Dec 1875. [Daughter of Thomas and Mary "Polly" (Safley) Cunningham, first wife of George W. Parks, married 2 Dec 1869.]

PARKS, George W. 1 Sep 1842-13 Jul 1923. [Son of Carroll and Hixey (Bullen) Parks, husband of 1) Eulitia H. Cunningham and 2) Ella M. Hill.]

PARKS, Ella M. 3 Mar 1857-5 Jan 1935. [Daughter of Israel and Katherine (Daniels) Hill, second wife of George W. Parks, married 22 Oct 1889.]

CAGLE, Harvey M. 12 Jun 1892-8 Apr 1953. [Harvey McCoy, son of Preston Alexander and Sarah (Nunley) Cagle, husband of Lemma M. Hobbs.]

CAGLE, Lemma M. 2 Dec 1893-13 Mar 1954. [Daughter of Thomas Marion and Myrick (Miller) Hobbs, wife of Harvey McCoy Cagle, married 15 Dce 1910.]

CAGLE, Leola. 27 Nov 1913-6 Jun 1933. [Leola Cagle Scott, but Scott not written on her stone. Daughter of Harvey McCoy and Lemma M. (Hobbs) Cagle, wife of R. S. Scott, married 12 May 1933.]

PARKS, James M. 20 Feb 1840-21 Sep 1863. [Son of Carroll and Hixey (Bullen) Parks.]

PARKS, Carroll. 22 Apr 1818-9 Jan 1892. [Husband of Hixey Bullen, married 25 Sep 1838.]

PARKS, Hixey. 16 Nov 1820-10 Aug 1899. [Hixey Bullen, wife of Carroll Parks.]

PARKS, Mackey T. 16 Aug 1881-1 Jul 1883. [Son of John M. and Loucretta (Stubblefield) Parks.]

PARKS, John M.   2 Apr 1848-28 Dec 1886.   [Son of Carroll and Hixey (Bullen) Parks, husband of Loucretta Stubblefield.]

PARKS, Lou.   8 Jan 1849-2 Dec 1928.   [Loucretta, daughter of William Jeffery and Rebecca (Garner) Reynolds Stubblefield, wife of John M. Parks.]

CARDWELL, Martha.   16 Jan 1851-28 Sep 1893.   [Daughter of Carroll and Hixey (Bullen) Parks, wife of James Cardwell, married 11 Aug 1870.]

GARNER, Martha J.   10 Oct 1843-27 Mar 1889.   [Daughter of John E. and Jane (Parker) Clark, first wife of William Euclid Garner.]

GARDNER, Mary.   14 Apr 1875-7 Jun 1900.   [Daughter of John M. and Loucretta (Stubblefield) Parks, wife of James R. Gardner, Sr.]

*GARDNER, James R., Sr.   20 Oct 1848-3 Jan 1935.   [Son of William Hunter and Sarah (Hoodenphyl) Gardner, husband of Mary Parks.]

GARDNER, William Ira.   11 Nov 1896-21 Oct 1903.   [Son of James R. and Mary (Parks) Gardner.]

HOBBS, Martealia.   5 May 1857-21 May 1945.   [Sarah Martealia, daughter of Christopher H. and Elizabeth (Smith) Hobbs, wife of Gilbert Fults (div.).]

HOBBS, Christopher H.   22 Nov 1834-31 Aug 1910.   [Son of Richard and Ester (Smartt) Hobbs, husband of Elizabeth Smith, married 5 Feb 1855 in Grundy County, TN.]

HOBBS, Elizabeth.   28 Apr 1836-26 Jul 1905.   [Daughter of _____ and Nancy (_____) Smith, wife of Christopher H. Hobbs.]

HOBBS, Dick.   17 Jan 1874-9 Mar 1902.   [Richard H., son of Christopher H. and Elizabeth (Smith) Hobbs, first husband of Ella Fults.]

ARGO, Frank (Boss).   22 Nov 1887-11 Oct 1961.   [Son of Josiah Joseph and Lina (Hobbs) Argo.   Single.]

ARGO, Fred.   14 Jul 1889-9 Feb 1953.   [Son of Josiah Joseph and Lina (Hobbs) Argo.   Single.]

ARGO, Joseph.   25 Feb 1851-8 May 1902.   [Josiah Joseph, son of George and Mary (Nunley) Argo, husband of Lina Hobbs, married 17 Dec 1883.]

ARGO, Lina.   12 Dec 1863-15 Oct 1912.   [Daughter of Christopher H. and Elizabeth (Smith) Hobbs, wife of Josiah Joseph Argo.]

WHITTENBURG, John.   1862-1940.   [Husband of Alice Wheeler.]

WHITTENBURG, Alice.   22 Apr 1864-4 Apr 1930.   [Daughter of K.T. and Sarah (Craig) Wheeler, wife of John Whittenburg.]

HILL, Lennie Pearl.   6 Jan 1896-17 Mar 1945.   [Daughter of John and Alice (Wheeler) Whittenburg, wife of Mark Erwart Hill, married 18 Mar 1918.]

HILL, Erwart.   25 Apr 1898-   .   [Mark Erwart, son of A. Putnam and Mollie (Woodlee) Hill, husband of 1) Lennie Pearl

Whittenburg, married 18 Mar 1918 and 2) Virla Viands, married 2 Aug 1950.]

PANTER, Maggie. 9 May 1884-31 Mar 1959. [Daughter of John and Alice (Wheeler) Whittenburg, wife of Lafayette F. Panter.]

BARNES, Jesse L., Sr. 12 Feb 1884-27 Apr 1955. [Jesse Lafayette, son of Charles Irving Lafayette and Lucy (Nunley) Barnes, husband of Mary Hill.]

BARNES, Mary H. 16 Feb 1889-20 Nov 1957. [Daughter of Sidney Albert and Nancy (Bouldin) Hill, wife of Jesse Lafayette Barnes, Sr.]

BOTTOMS, Quim C. Barnes 21 Oct 1914-20 Jan 1970. [Quim Cantrell, daughter of Jesse Lafayette and Mary (Hill) Barnes, wife of Clarence C. Bottoms, married 19 Oct 1945.]

BOTTOMS, Clarence C. 10 Mar 1918-   . [Son of Joe and Wavie (Crain) Bottoms, married 1) to Quim Cantrell Barnes and 2) to _____ Myers.]

BARNES, Sidney Wayne. 27 Dec 1943-12 Nov 1964. [Son of Jesse Lafayette Jr. and Jackoleen (Rosenbaum) Barnes, husband of Sandra Ware.]

BARNES, J.L., Jr. 9 Jun 1918-19 Jun 1993. [Jesse Lafayette, son of Jesse Lafayette "Fate" and Mary (Hill) Barnes, husband of Jackoleen Rosenbaum.]

BARNES, Jackloeen R. 11 Aug 1924-   . [Daughter of Jake and Gloria (Blevins) Rosenbaum, wife of Jesse Lafayette Barnes, Jr.]

MUNCEY, Allie Mai. 27 Oct 1924-22 Dec 1966. [Daughter of James Claud and Hollie (Rogers) Cunningham, first wife of George Muncey, married May 1946.]

MUNCEY, Denise. Born and died 27 Mar 1957. [Daughter of George and Allie Mai (Cunningham) Muncey.]

MUNCEY, Lou Ethel. 1 Sep 1930-6 Jan 1958. [Daughter of Rushie and Lettie (Scott) Smartt, wife of Walter Muncey.]

MUNCEY, Eva. 13 Apr 1889-15 Feb 1973. [Daughter of _____ and Lithia Kiami Smith, wife of James L. Muncey.]

MUNCEY, James L. 18 May 1884-30 Mar 1960. [Son of Jasper and Elizabeth (Lytle) Muncey, husband of Eva Smith, married 30 Apr 1905.]

ROGERS, Wilma J. 21 Aug 1947-   . [Wilma June, daughter of Saint Elmo and Maggie Lou (Muncey) Rogers.]

ROGERS, Maggie M. 17 May 1916-   . [Maggie Lou, daughter of James L. and Eva (Smith) Muncey, wife of Saint Elmo Rogers.]

ROGERS, Saint E. 1 May 1907-25 May 1981. [Saint Elmo, son of Harrison McKinley and Mary Wilsie (Hennessee) Rogers, husband of Maggie Lou Muncey, married 17 Jul 1937.]

PEPPER, Wilma L. 12 Sep 1916-   . [Wilma Louise, daughter of Martin Tipton and Mary Edna (Maxwell) Wiseman, wife of James Eston Pepper.]

PEPPER, James E. 14 Mar 1916-12 May 1993. [James Eston, son of Aaron A. and Lillie Bell (Roach) Pepper, husband of Wilma Louise Wiseman.]

CAGLE, Claudis Rickey. Born and died 1 Jul 1955. [Son of Claudis Brown and Lois (Hackett) Cagle.]

HOBBS, Refus. 16 Nov 1884-15 Sep 1908. [Son of Stephen and Jane (Campbell) Hobbs.]

HOBBS, Rufes. 22 Nov 1883-28 Jun 1906. [Son of Stephen and Jane (Campbell) Hobbs.]

HOBBS, Emma E. 13 Apr 1904-24 Aug 1921. [Emma Elizabeth, daughter of James and Janie (Fults) Hobbs.]

HOBBS, Janie. 29 Nov 1865-17 Nov 1940. [Daughter of David and Amanda (Fitch) Fults, wife of 1) James Hobbs, married 18 Mar 1886 and 2) Frank Smith Woodlee, married 19 Apr 1938.]

HOBBS, James. 15 Aug 1866-18 May 1937. [Son of Christopher H. and Elizabeth (Smith) Hobbs, husband of Janie Fults, married 18 Mar 1886.]

ROBERTS, Jesse Douglas. 6 June 1897-6 Aug 1988. WWI. [Son of John and Lucy (_____) Roberts, husband of Grover Lee Woodlee, married 24 Jan 1920.]

ROBERTS, Grover Lee Woodlee. 24 Nov 1892-23 Dec 1943. [Daughter of Frank Smith and Myrtle (Hobbs) Woodlee, wife of Jesse Douglas Roberts.]

WOODLEE, Charity Lee. 24 Feb 1891-17 Apr 1928. [Daughter of Frank Smith and Myrtle (Hobbs) Woodlee. Single.]

WOODLEE, Lemma May. 22 Feb 1905-2 Apr 1905. [Daughter of Frank Smith and Myrtle (Hobbs) Woodlee.]

WOODLEE, Myrtle Hobbs. 28 Mar 1869-14 May 1936. [Daughter of Christopher H. and Elizabeth (Smith) Hobbs, wife of Frank Smith Woodlee, married 27 Mar 1890.]

WOODLEE, Frank Smith. 15 Nov 1866-26 Dec 1952. [Son of William A. and Mary Ann (Smith) Woodlee, husband of 1) Myrtle Hobbs married 27 Mar 1890, and 2) Janie (Fults) Hobbs, married 19 Apr 1938.]

WOODLEE, Lemma May. 22 Feb 1905-2 Apr 1905. [Daughter of Frank Smith and Myrtle (Hobbs) Woodlee.]

WOMACK, Infant. Born and died 11 Oct 1896. [Infant of Dr. Arsey and Ella (Hayes) Womack.]

BOYD, Charlotte Gross. 10 Feb 1899-26 Mar 1986. [Daughter of Adam Daniel and Elizabeth (Mansfield) Gross, wife of Marshall L. Boyd.]

BOYD, Marshall L. 1 Mar 1899-1 Jun 1965. [Son of Samuel and Sallie Marshall (McGregor) Boyd, husband of Charlotte Gross.]

BOYD, Samuel L. 19 Jul 1857-23 May 1927. [Son of Jasper and Margaret (Turner) Boyd, husband of 1) Sally Marshall McGregor, married

Hebron Cemetery, cont.

13 Jun 1893 and 2) Frances (McGregor) Hayes.]

BOYD, Frances M. 26 Nov 1869-9 Feb 1942. [Daughter of Jason and Tressa (Sims) McGregor, wife of 1) James Hayes, married 22 May 1889, and 2) to Samuel L. Boyd.]

HAYES, J.R. 22 Apr 1867-17 Jun 1896. [James R., son of Martin Patrick and Mary L. (Parks) Hayes, first husband of Frances McGregor, married 22 May 1889.]

HAYES, Sallie. 14 Dec 1895-19 Dec 1914. [Daughter of James R. and Frances (McGregor) Hayes, single.]

STUBBLEFIELD, Rebecca. 27 Sep 1874-17 Jan 1889. [Daughter of Napoleon Bonaparte and Nancy Jane (Hayes) Stubblefield. Single.]

STUBBLEFIELD, Nancy J. 9 Feb 1844-18 May 1936. [Nancy Jane, daughter of William and Tempie (McDaniel) Hayes, wife of Napoleon Bonaparte Stubblefield.]

STUBBLEFIELD, N.B. 30 Jan 1844-19 Mar 1916. CSA. [Napoleon Bonaparte, son of William Jeffery and Rebecca (Garner) Reynolds Stubblefield, husband of Nancy Jane Hayes.]

HAYES, Mary L. 11 Jul 1845-25 Oct 1872. [Daughter of Carroll and Hixey (Bullen) Parks, wife of Martin Patrick Hayes.]

HAYES, M.P. 27 Nov 1838-23 Feb 1884. [Martin Patrick, son of William M. and Temperance (McDaniel) Hayes, husband of Mary L. Parks, married 15 Nov 1865.]

CLENDENON, Alice Ruth. 8 Jan 1933-2 Dec 1934. [Daughter of Charles Clayton and Minerva Louise (Rhea) Clendenon.]

CLENDENON, Elsie Marie. 14 Jun 1935-24 Nov 1941. [Daughter of Charles Clayton and Minerva Louise (Rhea) Clendenon.]

CLENDENON, Charles Clayton. 22 Mar 1903-2 May 1968. [Son of Harmon Venus and Alice (Jennings) Clendenon, husband of 1) Minerva Louise Rhea and 2) Etta Nunley Panter.]

CLENDENON, Minerva Louise. 10 Nov 1902-29 Jul 1957. [Daughter of Robert and Ruth (Fults) Rhea, first wife of Charles Clayton Clendenon.]

CUNNINGHAM, Matilda. 1845-2 Aug 1918. [Daughter of Jesse R. and Mary Jane (Miller) Cunningham, single.]

CUNNINGHAM, W. C. 4 Mar 1847-14 Sep 1878. [William C., son of Thomas and Mary "Polly" (Safley) Cunningham, husband of Lucy E. Logue, married 24 Aug 1869.]

CUNNINGHAM, Lucy E. 20 Sep 1852-6 Nov 1876. [Lucy E. Logue, wife of William C. Cunningham.]

CUNNINGHAM, Jess. 10 Sep 1868-19 Jun 1933. [Jesse Russell, son of Tom and Mary (Lowe) Cunningham, husband of Ellen Mayo.]

CUNNINGHAM, Ellen. 27 Jul 1869-19 Mar 1949. [Daughter of George W. and Sarah (Pursley) Mayo, wife of Jesse Russell Cunningham.]

MAYO, Sarah Purlsey. 1841-1916. [Wife of George W. Mayo, married 15 May 1858. George W. is buried at Increase.]

GROSS, Gladys Woodlee. 21 Jul 1901-   . [Daughter of Levi and Betty (Willis) Woodlee, wife of 1) William Sutton Myers and 2) Arsey M. Gross. William Myers is buried at Armstrong.]

GROSS, Arsey M. 1 Mar 1891-22 Sep 1966. [Son of Adam Daniel and Elizabeth (Mansfield) Gross, husband of 1) Wallie May Bales and 2) Gladys (Woodlee) Myers.]

GROSS, Wallie. 2 May 1891-16 Apr 1954. [Wallie May, daughter of William Anderson and Alice (Palmer) Bales, wife of Arsey M. Gross.]

GROSS, Infant. Born and died 4 Aug 1917. [Infant of Arsey M. and Wallie May (Bales) Gross.]

BOULDIN, Mary. 27 Jul 1860-16 Oct 1943. [Daughter of Narve and Nancy (Grove) Bouldin, granddaughter of Noble Bouldin and of Lewis and Susannah (Knight) Bouldin, wife of Thomas Bouldin, married 6 Oct 1887.]

BOULDIN, Tom. 4 Jun 1851-25 Apr 1924. [Thomas, son of Noble and Elizabeth (Grissom) Bouldin, grandson of Gidean and Mary (Hill) Bouldin and great grandson of Noble Bouldin, husband of 1) Eliza Bouldin Argo and 2) to Mary "Shug" Bouldin.]

BOULDIN, Bettie. 23 Feb 1894-4 Jan 1919. [Elizabeth, daughter of Thomas and Mary (Bouldin) Bouldin. Single.]

SIMONS, Willard. 16 Feb 1922-9 Jul 1981. WWII. [Son of John William and Luella (Mayo) Simons, husband of Naomi Hill.]

RHEA, Ivory. 26 Dec 1911-   . [Son of Robert and Ruth (Fults) Rhea, husband of 1) Mary E. Smartt and 2) Willie Hobbs Dodson, married 18 Jan 1975.]

RHEA, Mary E. Smartt. 23 Jul 1916-17 Apr 1973. [Daughter of Rushie and Letta (Scott) Smartt, wife of Ivory Rhea.]

SMARTT, Rushie. 27 May 1885-17 Mar 1963. [Son of Milton and Mary "Polly" (Fults) Smartt, husband of Letta Scott.]

SMARTT, Letta Scott. 22 Apr 1894-31 Oct 1958. [Daughter of William and Caldonia (Smartt) Scott, wife of Rushie Smartt.]

HALE, Debra Ellen. 19 May 1959-10 Oct 1959. [Daughter of James W. and Ethel Ollene (Cunningham) Hale.]

HALE, James W. 1 May 1939-23 Jun 1966. [Son of Thurman H. and Verna Beatrice (Davis) Hale, husband of Ethel Ollene Cunningham.]

HALE, Ollene Cunningham. 13 Feb 1939-   . [Ethel Ollene, daughter of James Claud and Hollie Claire (Rogers) Cunningham, wife of James W. Hale.]

HALE, Christopher C. "Chris". 12 Jun 1961-31 Aug 1985. [Son of James W. and Ollene (Cunningham) Hale.]

HOBBS, Larry Eugene. 14 Feb 1947-19 Jan 1993. VIETNAM. [Son of Ira

Hartley and Lurline (Sharp) Hobbs, husband of Janice _____.]

HOBBS, Ira Hartley. 3 Jun 1920-19 Apr 1959. [Son of Frank and Vivian (Smartt) Hobbs, husband of Lurline Sharp.]

WOODLEE, Marguerite. 8 Jun 1922-   . [Daughter of James and Oshia H. (Stoner) Wanamaker Woodlee, wife of Ozra Ellis Woodlee.]

WOODLEE, O.E. (Ozra Ellis). 19 Dec 1910-9 May 1962. [Son of Frank Smith and Myrtle (Hobbs) Woodlee, husband of Marguerite Woodlee.]

WOODLEE, Oshia H. 27 Aug 1898-7 May 1989. [Daughter of _____ and Maggie Stoner, wife of 1) _____ Wanamaker and 2) James W. Woodlee.]

WOODLEE, James W. 15 Dec 1895-4 May 1971. [Son of Jim and Mary (Hobbs) Woodlee, husband of Oshia H. (Stoner) Wanamaker, married 4 Jan 1920.]

ARGO, Jennie. 19 Feb 1903-6 Feb 1983. [Daughter of Harris and Mary (Nunley) Smartt, wife of Howary Argo, married 17 Jun 1923.]

ARGO, Howary. 14 Mar 1893-1 Jan 1979. [Son of Josiah Joseph and Lina (Hobbs) Argo, husband of Jennie Smartt.]

WISEMAN, Wayman T. 19 Oct 1925-29 Aug 1989. [Wayman Tipton, son of Martin Tipton and Mary Edna (Maxwell) Wiseman.]

WISEMAN, Mary Edna. 28 Apr 1890-3 Apr 1962. [Daughter of William M. and Margaret Elizabeth (Mayo) Maxwell, wife of Martin Tipton Wiseman.]

WISEMAN, Martin T. 12 Jan 1890-20 Sep 1975. [Martin Tipton, son of George, Sr. and Mary (Gillentine) Wiseman, husband of Mary Edna Maxwell.]

WISEMAN, Mary Helen. Born and died 13 Oct 1915. [Daughter of Martin Tipton and Mary Edna (Maxwell) Wiseman.]

WISEMAN, Jewel Dee. 13 Aug 1918-2 Oct 1923. [Son of Martin Tipton and Mary Edna (Maxwell) Wiseman.]

WISEMAN, Earl Willis. 20 Jul 1934-21 Jul 1945. [Son of Martin Tipton and Mary Edna (Maxwell) Wiseman.]

PANTER, Charles Arthur. 19 May 1933-12 Feb 1934. [Son of Charles Arthur and Alma Lois (Clendenon) Panter.]

CUNNINGHAM, Thomas. 25 Oct 1799-23 Mar 1886. [Son of John and Nancy (Dodson) Cunningham, husband of 1) Matilda Hayes and 2) Mary "Polly" Safley.]

CUNNINGHAM, G.H. 25 Aug 1831-27 Sep 1878. [Greenberry H., son of Thomas and Matilda (Hayes) Cunningham, husband of Martha Gipson Miller, married 7 Nov 1853.]

CUNNINGHAM, John M. 10 Mar 1845-21 May 1885. [Son of Thomas and Mary (Safley) Cunningham. Single.]

CUNNINGHAM, James W. 2 Feb 1853-12 Jan 1889. [Son of Thomas and Mary

(Safley) Cunningham.]

COUCH, Cleo Cunningham. 31 Oct 1893-26 Dec 1972. [Cleo Modena, daughter of William Hayes and Mary Susan (Curtis) Cunningham, wife of _____ Couch.]

CUNNINGHAM, William Hayes. 30 May 1856-22 Dec 1929. [Son of Jesse R. and Mary (Miller) Cunningham, husband of Mary Susan Curtis, married 3 Feb 1886.]

CUNNINGHAM, Mary Susan. 17 Sep 1869-18 Feb 1904. [Daughter of William Washington and Letisha (Dodson) Curtis, wife of William Hayes Cunningham.]

CUNNINGHAM, J.W. 28 Dec 1887-11 Jul 1888. [Son of William Hayes and Mary Susan (Curtis) Cunningham.]

CUNNINGHAM, Willie Jane. 15 Dec 1898-2 Sep 1905. [Daughter of William Hayes and Mary Susan (Curtis) Cunningham.]

BARNES, Infant. 8 May 1903-16 May 1903. [Infant son of Dr. William C. and Hallie (Cagle) Barnes.]

BARNES, Benjamin Nelson. 14 Oct 1895-1 Sep 1896. [Son of Dr. William C. and Hallie (Cagle) Barnes.]

BARNES, Lela. 16 Dec 1900-   . [Daughter of Dr. William C. and Hallie (Cagle) Barnes.]

COPPINGER, Jennie. 30 Dec 1859-30 Oct 1902. [Virginia A., daughter of Dr. William C. and Bethia (Hill) Barnes, wife of James Levander Coppinger.]

COPPINGER, Jas. L. 17 Jun 1853-11 Jan 1937. [James Levander, son of David and Beersheba (Tipton) Coppinger, husband of Virginia A. "Jennie" Barnes.]

COPPINGER, William Herbert. 28 Jan 1887-5 Nov 1932. [Son of James Levander and Virginia A. (Barnes) Coppinger.]

BARNES, Bethia. 13 Jun 1842-14 Nov 1879. [Daughter of Hugh Lawson White and Virginia A. (Dearing) Hill, wife of Dr. William C. Barnes.]

BARNES, Dr. W. C. 16 Mar 1831-19 Dec 1917. [William Carroll, son of Charles and Susannah (Smith) Barnes, husband of 1) Bethia Hill, married 5 Feb 1859 and 2) Hallie Cagle, married 21 Nov 1894.]

BARNES, Hallie Cagle. 7 Jan 1873-6 Nov 1912. [Daughter of Benjamin Silas and Laura (Armstrong) Cagle, wife of Dr. William C. Barnes.]

HALL, Dan. 1892-1893. [Son of D.B. and Charity (Barnes) Hall.]

PATRICK, Jadie. 10 Feb 1912-27 Apr 1939. [Daughter of Lafayette F. and Amanda (Pearson) Patrick. Single.]

UNDERHILL, Amanda Patrick. 23 Jun 1892-14 Jan 1983. [Daughter of George and Nancy (McCorkle) Pearson, wife of 1) Lafayette Patrick, 2) William Patrick, and 3) Frank Underhill.]

PATRICK, L. F. 13 Feb 1864-17 Nov 1929. [Lafayette F., son of Houston and

Caroline (Nunley) Patrick, grandson of Moses Patrick, husband of 1) Susan E. Nunley, married 20 Jan 1887 and 2) Amanda Pearson, married 11 May 1911.]

PATRICK, Susan E. 12 Apr 1849-25 May 1907. [Daughter of Adam and Mary (Argo) Nunley, wife of Lafayette F. Patrick.]

FULTS, Georgia. 28 Jun 1901-25 May 1975. [Daughter of Ruben and Laura Louella (Hayes) Fults, wife of 1) Russell Fults and 2) Bill Harden.]

FULTS, Russell. 11 Aug 1884-8 May 1968. [Son of George and Mary (Smartt) Fults, husband of 1) Nancy Hillis who died 2 Jul 1917 and is buried at Smyrna Cemetery and 2) to Georgia Fults, his first cousin.]

HODGES, Walter E. 16 Sep 1948-19 Sep 1948. [Walter Eugene, son of Elmer Walter and Bertha Lee (Fults) Hodges.]

HODGES, Elmer Walter. 7 Jan 1916-31 Aug 1978. [Son of Frank and Della (Cantrell) Hodges, husband of Bertha Lee Fults.]

TORRES, Erica Ann. 6 Dec 1983-8 Dec 1983. [Daughter of Heriberto Eric and Barbara A. (Hodges) Torres.]

BARNES, Stanley E. 15 Jul 1938- . [Stanley Eugene, son of Lonnie Haskel and Irene (Milstead) Barnes, husband of Nadean Lytle, married 10 May 1956.]

BARNES, Nadean L. 16 Jan 1938- . [Daughter of Alley Walter Marcus Lafayette and Nettie Lee (Whitman) Lytle, wife of Stanley Eugene Barnes.]

ARGO, Joe Thomas. 19 May 1941-18 Oct 1993. [Son of Jesse Clyde and Gladys Gertrude (Bouldin) Argo, husband of Joyce Ann Bennett, married 27 Jul 1963.]

ARGO, Joyce Ann. 22 Dec 1942-27 Jul 1965. [Daughter of Elmer and Velma Grace (McAfee) Bennett, wife of Joe Thomas Argo.]

HOBBS, Vivian Equilla. 30 Jan 1899-17 Jun 1975. [Daughter of Wiley S. and Emma Maude (Tanner) Smartt, wife of Frank Hobbs.]

HOBBS, Frank. 31 Aug 1897-21 Aug 1985. [Son of Richard and Ella (Fults) Hobbs, husband of Vivian Equilla Smartt, married 30 Aug 1919.]

FULTS, Doshie. 29 Mar 1907-13 Jan 1992. [Daughter of Steve and Rosie Bell (Argo) Smartt, wife of Elzie Fults.]

FULTS, Elzie. Died 3 May 1982 at age 82. [Son of George and Mary (Smartt) Fults, husband of Doshie Smartt.]

FULTS, Emma Elizabeth. 16 May 1937-10 Feb 1940. [Daughter of Elzie and Doshie (Smartt) Fults.]

*FULTS, Infant. Born and died 2 Nov 1942. [Infant daughter of Elzie and Doshie (Smartt) Fults.]

ARGO, Gladys G. 15 Oct 1917- . [Gladys Gertrude, daughter of Jim Buck and Susie (Rogers) Bouldin, wife of Jesse Clyde Argo.]

Hebron Cemetery, cont.

ARGO, Jesse C.   29 Aug 1909-29 Nov 1979.   [Jesse Clyde, son of Murray Bedford and Mary Maude (Hobbs) Argo, husband of Gladys Gertrude Bouldin.]

FULTS, Floyd Harris.   18 Aug 1886-22 May 1937.   {Death records give dates as 19 Aug 1885-24 Feb 1938} [Son of George and Mary (Smartt) Fults, husband of Mary Lou Curtis.]

FULTS, Mary Lou Curtis.   9 Aug 1889-23 Sep 1953.   {Death records give dates as 9 Aug 1888-27 Sep 1953} [Daughter of Wiley and Mary Susan (Bouldin) Curtis, wife of 1) Willie Bess, 2) Floyd Harris Fults, 3) Charlie Barrett, and 4) _____ Cunningham.]

FULTS, H.T.   27 Aug 1925-20 Jul 1939.   [Son of Floyd Harris and Mary Lou (Curtis) Fults.]

FULTS, Mattie Lee.   16 Nov 1927-26 Dec 1928.   [Daughter of Floyd Harris and Mary Lou (Curtis) Fults.]

FULTS, Ralph Franklin.   10 May 1924-30 Nov 1928.   [Son of Floyd Harris and Mary Lou (Curtis) Fults.]

FULTS, William Clayton.   9 Oct 1919-6 Dec 1919.   [Son of Floyd Harris and Mary Lou (Curtis) Fults.]

FULTS, Roberta.   25 Jan 1921-11 Oct 1923.   [Daughter of Floyd Harris and Mary Lou (Curtis) Fults.]

CAGLE, Mary.   Born 1940-   [Mary Magdalene Ledbetter, second wife of Claudis Brown Cagle.]

CAGLE, Claudis Brown.   11 Jan 1916-6 Dec 1980.   WWII.   [Son of Harvey and Lemma (Hobbs) Cagle, husband of 1) Louise Reed, married 4 Dec 1937 (Div.) and 2) Mary Magdalene Ledbetter, married 4 Mar 1976.]

HENNESSEE, Nora Lee.   1 Jan 1923-14 Nov 1924.   [Daughter of George F. and Mollie (Green) Hennessee.]

HENNESSEE, Mary Bell.   22 Mar 1925-9 Apr 1925.   [Daughter of George F. and Mollie (Green) Hennessee.]

PEARSON, Nancy.   11 Dec 1871-19 Dec 1948.   [Daughter of Robert and Sallie (Brown) McCorkle, wife of George Pearson.]

PEARSON, George.   19 Jun 1872-20 Sep 1942.   [George Douglas, son of James and Deliah (Turner) Pearson, husband of Nancy McCorkle.]

PEARSON, Bertha.   11 Jun 1903-23 Feb 1920.   [Daughter of George Douglas and Nancy (McCorkle) Pearson.]

MILSTEAD, Lena.   9 Sep 1895-3 Nov 1985.   [Magdalene, daughter of Jess and Ellen (Mayo) Cunningham, wife of Samuel Claud Milstead.]

MILSTEAD, Claud.   18 May 1888-1 Oct 1961.   [Samuel Claud, son of William and Serena Janie (Rogers) Milstead, husband of Magdalene "Lena" Cunningham, married 28 Sep 1910.]

MILSTEAD, Lorene.   4 Mar 1918-13 Nov 1931.   [Ellen Lorene, daughter of Samuel Claud and Lena (Cunningham) Milstead.]

MILSTEAD, Alma. 1 Jun 1925-14 Nov 1926. [Daughter of Samuel Claud and Lena (Cunningham) Milstead.]

MILSTEAD, Lee. 24 Oct 1915-24 Oct 1917. [Son of Samuel Claud and Lena (Cunningham) Milstead.]

MILSTEAD, Bill. 1 Nov 1920-22 Jan 1959. [Jesse William, son of Samuel Claud and Lena (Cunningham) Milstead.]

CHRISTIAN, O.B. 25 Dec 1844-15 Jul 1914. CSA. [Orland Bradley, son of William Thorton and Mary Elizbeth (Lusk) Christian, husband of Mary Elizabeth Freeman.]

*CHRISTIAN, Mary Elizabeth Freeman. 31 Jul 1844-5 Feb 1929. [Daughter of _____ and Harriet (Christian) Freeman, wife of 1) William R. Martin, married 7 Oct 1860 and 2) Orland Bradley Christian, married 4 May 1871.]

SMITH, Flora W. 29 Jun 1903-   . [Flora Walker, wife of Luther M. Smith.]

SMITH, Luther M. 19 Sep 1900-4 May 1987. [Son of Marion and Lizzie (Roach) Smith, husband of Flora Walker.]

SAFLEY, Nannie A. Cardwell. 31 Oct 1852-12 Oct 1893. [Daughter of John and Sarah (Kell) Cardwell, wife of Leonidus Safley, married 18 Nov 1884.]

SAFLEY, Lon. 2 Jun 1845-24 Jun 1916. [Leonadis, son of David and Jane (Morrison) Safley, husband of 1) Lou Randolph, married 23 Nov 1869 and 2) Nancy A. "Nannie" Cardwell.]

SAFLEY, George L. Died 21 Jul 1886, aged 6 months, 9 days. [Son of Leonadis and Nancy (Cardwell) Safley, twin brother of John R. Safley.]

SAFLEY, Jane. 20 Apr 1807-23 Oct 1884. [Jane Morrison, wife of David Safley.]

SAFLEY, David. 24 Aug 1809-5 Oct 1893. [Son of Jesse and Phatha (Stiles) Safley, husband of Jane Morrison.]

SAFLEY, J.A. 24 Nov 1836-19 Jun 1884. [Jessee A., son of David and Jane (Morrison) Safley, husband of Sarah Ann Forrest, married 24 Sep 1860.]

PANTER, Sara Jane Clendenon. 14 Jan 1859-26 Feb 1949. [Daughter of Francis Marion and Mahala (Martin) Clendenon, second wife of James Panter.]

PANTER, Clyde. 6 Dec 1889-16 Jul 1934. [Son of James and Sarah Jane (Clendenon) Panter. Single.]

SOLOMON, Nancy. 2 Dec 1840-4 Feb 1920. [Daughter of Willis L. and Myrick (Safley) Solomon. Single.]

SOLOMON, Fatha. 5 Oct 1847-4 Feb 1917. [Daughter of Willis L. and Myrick (Safley) Solomon, wife of James E. Solomon, married 8 Feb 1883.]

SOLOMON, W.L. 25 Dec 1809-22 Jun 1877. [Willis L., son of Bennett and

Ava (McGregor) Solomon, husband of Myrick Safley.]

SOLOMON, Myrick Safley. 16 May 1815-22 Dec 1903. [Daughter of Jessee and Phatha (Stiles) Safley, granddaughter of William and Susan Rebecca (Edwards) Stiles, wife of Willis L. Solomon.]

SOLOMON, B.J. 14 Sep 1842-3 Feb 1863. "Killed at Fort Donalson 3 Feb 1863 In Defence of the South. His Remains still lie there. He was Faithful Till Death." [Bennett Jason, son of Willis L. and Myrick (Safley) Solomon.]

NUNLEY, Lillie. 9 Apr 1879-18 Nov 1880. [Daughter of John Wesley and Mary E. (Solomon) Nunley.]

NUNLEY, Mary E. 8 Apr 1887-15 Jul 1887. [Daughter of John Wesley and Mary E. (Solomon) Nunley.]

NUNLEY, John Wesley. 13 Mar 1851-10 Aug 1900. [Son of John "Jackie" and Margaret (Smith) Nunley, husband of Mary E. Solomon, married 20 Feb 1871.]

NUNLEY, Mary E. 25 Dec 1851-9 Sep 1887. [Daughter of Willis L. and Myrick (Safley) Solomon, wife of John Wesley Nunley.]

HOBBS, Marvin. 14 Aug 1881-16 Jan 1960. [Daughter of Fred and Martha (Smartt) Myers, second wife of Thomas H. Hobbs.]

HOBBS, Tom. 10 Jun 1872-17 Jun 1962. [Thomas H., son of Christopher H. and Elizabeth (Smith) Hobbs, husband of 1) Maggie Nunley and 2) Marvin Myers.]

HOBBS, Maggie. 20 Jun 1874-18 May 1901. [Daughter of John Wesley and Mary Elizabeth (Solomon) Nunley, first wife of Thomas H. Hobbs.]

HOBBS, Arnold. 2 Feb 1896-5 Jun 1898. [Son of Thomas H. and Maggie (Nunley) Hobbs.]

HOBBS, Emma. 7 Aug 1899-13 Aug 1899. [Daughter of Thomas H. and Maggie (Nunley) Hobbs.]

HOBBS, Lizzie. 8 May 1900-30 Jun 1900. [Daughter of Thomas H. and Maggie (Nunley) Hobbs.]

HOBBS, Birtha. 4 Aug 1903-8 Nov 1904. [Daughter of Thomas H. and Marvin (Myers) Hobbs.]

HOBBS, Florence. 8 Nov 1904-8 Dec 1909. [Daughter of Thomas H. and Marvin (Myers) Hobbs.]

HOBBS, Noble. 16 Jan 1913-25 Jun 1913. [Son of Thomas H. and Marvin (Myers) Hobbs.]

HOBBS, Hollie. 4 Feb 1911-17 Jan 1955. [Daughter of Thomas H. and Marvin (Myers) Hobbs. Single.]

HOBBS, Clifton. 14 Dec 1908-15 Oct 1961. [Son of Thomas H. and Marvin (Myers) Hobbs. Single.]

WARE, I.W., Jr. 4 Feb 1920- . [Isham Washington, son of Isham Washington, Sr. and Ethel (Muncey) Ware, husband of Mary Ellen

Cunningham.]

WARE, Mary Ellen. 3 Aug 1930-   [Daughter of James Claud and
        Hollie Claire (Rogers) Cunningham, wife of Isham Washington
        Ware, Jr.]

WARE, Stevie Lynn. 8 Dec 1951-3 Apr 1974. [Son of Isham Washington, Jr.
        and Mary Ellen (Cunningham) Ware. Single.]

FULTS, Amos. 8 Nov 1895-16 Apr 1973. [Son of George K. and Lee Annie
        (Hobbs) Fults, husband of Junnie Argo.]

FULTS, Junnie Argo. 12 Nov 1885-8 May 1969. [Daughter of Josiah Joseph
        and Lena (Hobbs) Argo, wife of Amos Fults.]

THAXTON, Susie B. 19 Apr 1888-5 May 1975. [Daughter of Charles Irvin
        Lafayette and Lucy (Nunley) Barnes, wife of 1) Lusk C.
        Stubblefield, married 5 Jan 1908, 2) Bedford Forest Kelley,
        married 12 Feb 1927, and 3) George Thaxton, married 9 Feb 1954.]

FULTS, Thomas Loyd "Tommy". 29 May 1954-12 Jul 1981. [Son of John Henry
        Russell and Annie Beatrice (Elkins) Fults, husband of 1) Lois
        C. Crawford, married 28 Apr 1972, 2) Louise _____, and 3) Katy
        Bain.]

FULTS, Annie B. 2 Aug 1931-   . [Annie Beatrice, daughter of
        James Franklin and Violet (Johnson) Elkins, wife of John Henry
        Russell Fults.]

FULTS, John Henry. 24 Dec 1924-8 Mar 1970. [John Henry Russell, son of
        Russell and Georgia (_____) Fults, husband of Annie Beatrice
        Elkins.]

ROBERTS, Elizabeth. 12 Sep 1920-   . [Elizabeth Lee, daughter of
        John and Hattie Jane (Green) Smartt, wife of James Walter
        Roberts, married 27 Aug 1940.]

ROBERTS, Walter. 4 Jul 1919-   . [James Walter, son of Bill and
        Margaret (Bouldin) Roberts, husband of Elizabeth Lee Smartt.]

ROBERTS, Rayburn. Born and died 2 May 1947. [Son of James Walter and
        Elizabeth Lee (Smartt) Roberts.]

ROBERTS, Infant. Born and died 1 Jul 1942. [Infant son of James Walter
        and Elizbeth Lee (Smartt) Roberts.]

SMARTT, Wesley. Died 11 Apr 1928, age 79 years. [Son of John and Rachel
        (Thompson) Smartt, husband of Easter Fults, married 5 Mar 1877
        in Grundy County, TN.]

SMARTT, Easter. Died 12 Jun 1926, age 62 years. [Daughter of Daniel and
        Sarah (Green) Fults, wife of Wesley Smartt.]

MASON, Molly Roberts. 24 Sep 1876-8 Jul 1911. [Daughter of Christopher
        Columbus and Emma (Hughes) Roberts, wife of Addison Eli Mason,
        married 15 Sep 1893. {He is buried in Miller Cemetery in
        Plevna, AL.}]

ROBERTS, C.C. 29 Nov 1851-14 May 1912. [Christopher Columbus Roberts,
        husband of Emma Hughes, married 27 Aug 1873.]

CARTER, Offie C. 11 May 1909-7 Sep 1916. [Son of A. Lexington and Amanda (Coppinger) Carter.]

CARTER, A.L. 28 Apr 1857-8 Apr 1927. [A. Lexington, son of George and _____ (_____) Carter, husband of Amanda Coppinger.]

CARTER, Amanda. Aug 1862-1932. [Daughter of Jess and Rachel (Nunley) Coppinger, wife of A. Lexington Carter.]

HOBBS, Maggie. 20 Jun 1874-18 May 1900. [Daughter of John Wesley and Mary E. (Solomon) Nunley, wife of Thomas H. Hobbs. {She has two stones.}]

JONES, Mary Ann. 2 Jun 1831-17 Nov 1903. [Daughter of Abraham and Ceallie (_____) Jones. Single.]

SMARTT, Myrick. 28 Nov 1876-29 Sep 1905. [Daughter of John Wesley and Mary Elizabeth (Solomon) Nunley, first wife of Francis Marion Smartt.]

SMARTT, Marion. 5 Mar 1875-22 May 1967. [Francis Marion, son of Ruben and Sarah Jane (Nunley) Smartt, husband of 1) Myrick Nunley and 2) Nancy Ellen Nunley {sisters}]

SMARTT, Ellen. 19 Apr 1882-26 Feb 1955. [Nancy Ellen, daughter of John Wesley and Mary Elizabeth (Solomon) Nunley, second wife of Francis Marion Smartt.]

SMARTT, Infant. 27 Dec 1915 only date on stone. [Son of Francis Marion and Nancy Ellen (Nunley) Smartt.]

SMITH, Arthur M. 18 Apr 1877-22 Jan 1879. [Son of Monroe Marion and Ava (Solomon) Smith.]

SMITH, Lissy. 27 Nov 1856-29 May 1926. [Sarah Elizabeth, daughter of Marion and Melvina (McBride) Roach, second wife of Monroe Marion Smith.]

SMITH, Marion. 10 Aug 1846-10 Sep 1928. [Monroe Marion, son of Thomas C. and Elizabeth (Miles) Smith, husband of 1) Ava Solomon and 2) Sarah Elizabeth Roach, married 5 Aug 1897. {Death record has death date as 11 Nov}]

SMITH, Infant. No dates. [Infant of Monroe Marion and Sarah Elizabeth (Roach) Smith.]

SMITH, Ava. 29 Nov 1844-12 Jun 1896. [Daughter of Willis L. and Myrick (Safley) Solomon, first wife of Monroe Marion Smith.]

SMITH, Jess. 7 Mar 1870-12 Sep 1949. [Son of Monroe Marion and Ava (Solomon) Smith. Single.]

RHEA, Ema Lee. 13 May 1907-18 Jul 1935. [Daughter of Lyman and Nellie (Countiss) Rhea.]

HILL, Lela. 30 Nov 1874-20 Apr 1954. [Daughter of John and Jane (Countiss) Hill. Single.]

JORDEN, Anderson. 28 Oct 1811-13 Aug 1889. [Husband of Darcas _____.]

JORDAN, Darcas.   6 Jan 1809-30 Jan 1891.   [Wife of Anderson Jorden.
        {Funeral home has date of death as 1892.}]

RHEA, Walter.   7 Mar 1904-30 Apr 1991.   [Son of Robert and Ruth (Fults)
        Rhea, husband of Ocie Mae Rhea, married 8 Jun 1928.]

RHEA, Ocie Mae.   27 Apr 1905-   .   [Daughter of Lymon and Nettie
        (Countiss) Rhea, wife of Walter Rhea.]

RHEA, Marley Jolene.   14 Oct 1942-25 Mar 1943.   [Daughter of Walter R. and
        Ocie Mae (Rhea) Rhea.]

COUNTISS, Mary.   8 Jan 1848-19 Jun 1925.   [Daughter of William and
        Prudence (Dykes) Countiss.   Single.]

COUNTISS, Prudie.   26 Jun 1827-6 Nov 1906.   [Prudence, daughter of Isham
        and Prudence (Choate) Dykes, wife of William M. Countiss.]

RHEA, Austin.   12 Jan 1936-23 Feb 1938.   [Son of Arsey W. and Lillie
        (Fults) Rhea.]

RHEA, Lillie F.   8 Feb 1898-3 Oct 1983.   [Daughter of George and Mary
        (Smartt) Fults, wife of Arsey Womack Rhea.]

RHEA, Arsey W.   26 Apr 1894-27 Aug 1959.   [Arsey Womack, son of Lyman and
        Nellie (Countiss) Rhea, husband of Lillie Fults.]

*FARLESS, Geneva Rhea.   Born 17 Sep 1915, died 4 Sep 1941, daughter of
        Robert and Carlie (Smartt) Rhea, wife of William Farless.

*FULTS, George.   Died 30 Jan 1938, age about 84 years.   Son of John and
        Jean (Hobbs) Fults, husband of Mary Smartt.

*HOBBS, Lydia Campbell.   Died 24 Aug 1927, age 68 years, daughter of B.E.
        and Bettie (_____) Campbell, second wife of John Hobbs.

*KEMP, R.C.   Died 27 Feb 1922, age 76 years.   No further information.

*KAHLER, Sophia, died 27 Feb 1920, age 80 years.   Death record has name
        spelled KOCHLER.

*MEADOWS, Infant, born and died 11 Feb 1921, child of C.H. and Josephine
        (Darnell) Meadows.

*ROBERTS, Alma Edna, born 22 Oct 1915, died 22 Dec 1915, daughter of Ike
        and Rachel (Smartt) Roberts.

*ROBERTS, Infant, born 8 Oct 1920, died 12 Oct 1920, child of Ike and
        Rachel (Smartt) Roberts.

*ROBERTS, Wilma Sue.   Born 27 May 1944, died 27 Sep 1945, daughter of
        Clara Roberts.

*TEMPLETON, Pina Jane Rogers, born 24 Apr 1905, died 14 May 1929, daughter
        of Harrison and Mary (Hennessee) Rogers, wife of William W.
        Templeton.

*SAIN, James Blanton, born and died 25 Sep 1946, son of James R. and Eva
        Mae (Roberts) Sain.

Hebron Cemetery, cont.

*SMITH, Orvell B., born 29 May 1881, died 10 Jun 1930, son of Monroe
         Marion and Ava (Solomon) Smith, husband of Vernie Hale, married
         28 Jan 1913.

*RHEA, Robert, died 15 Nov 1945, age 68 years, son of Ike and Nancy (Bess)
        Rhea, husband of 1) Ruth Fults and 2) Carlee Smartt.

*HOBBS, Harris Gorden. Born 4 Aug 1891, died 24 Jul 1963, son of James and
         Janie (Fults) Hobbs, husband of Bonnie Hall.

*FULTS, Francis. Died 26 Jan 1917, age about 30 years, son of George and
         Mary (Smartt) Fults.

HENNESSEE CEMETERY

Location: On Hwy 8, on first road to the right past Collins River
     Bridge.

BROWN, Rachel. 9 Mar 1872-18 Mar 1877.

HENNESSEE, William M. 6 Jan _____-20 Aug 1881.

HENNESSEE, Mary Jane. 11 Apr 1858-3 Nov 1876. [Daughter of James C. and
          Maxie (Dodson) Hennessee.]

HENNESSEE, Rachel. 1800-Dec 1881. [Rachel Wilcher, wife of Patrick S.
          Hennessee.]

HENNESSEE, Patrick S. 1791-Dec 1860. [Husband of Rachel Wilcher.]

HENNESSEE, James C. 15 Dec 1818-11 Mar 1862. [Son of Patrick S. and
          Rachel (Wilcher) Hennessee, husband of Maxie Dodson.]

HENNESSEE, Maxie. 18 Mar 1824-17 Sep 1899. [Daughter of Elijah and
          Sallie (McGregor) Dodson, wife of James C. Hennessee.]

HENNESSEE, Sarah J. 19 Jun 1870-29 Jun 1871.
HENNESSEE, Mary A. 23 Dec 1879- 3 Jan 1880.
          "Daughters of P. S. and M. S. Hennessee"

HENNESSEE, James Thomas. 23 Jan 1875-25 Jan 1875. [Son of James and
          Rachel Ann (Hennessee) Hennessee.]

HENNESSEE, Elza W. Born and Died Apr 1860. [Son of Samuel M. and Mahala
          (Harper) Hennessee.]

HENNESSEE, Thomas. Born ca 1832-   . CSA. [Son of Patrick S.
          and Rachel (Wilcher) Hennessee.]

HENNESSEE, Andy Franklin. 21 Aug 1878-4 May 1882. [Son of James and
          Rachel Ann (Hennessee) Hennessee.]

HENNESSEE, James. 3 Nov 1846-22 Feb 1927. [Son of Thomas and Sally (Jennings) Hennessee, husband of Rachel Ann Hennessee, married 18 Jul 1869.]

HENNESSEE, Rachel Ann. 11 Nov 1847-29 Apr 1883. [Daughter of James C. and Maxie (Dodson) Hennessee, wife of James Hennessee.]

HERNDON CEMETERY

Location: On Morrison/Centertown Road, near Centertown.

HERNDON, Eliza J. 9 Jun 1879-2 Nov 1879. Daughter J.M. and S.E. Herndon.

HERNDON, H.R. 9 Jun 1861-7 Mar 1886. Son of J.M. and S.A. Herndon.

CATHRAN, Mary. 20 Dec 1927-6 Jan 1899. [Mary Scroggins, wife of Henry D. Cathran.]

HALEY, Lizzie. 31 Dec 1893-25 Jun 1894.

HALEY, George Washington. 16 Sep 1884-13 Feb 1888.

HALEY, Sis. 18 Jul 1865-30 Jan 1919. [Narcissa, daughter of Henry and Mary (Scroggins) Cathran, married Alex Haley on 23 Dec 1884.]

HICKORY GROVE CEMETERY

Location: In the Earlyville Community.

ROBINSON, Jesse. 30 Jan 1827-1862. [Husband of Violet Jane _____.]

ROBINSON, Violet Jane. 12 Jan 1826-14 Nov 1903. [Wife of Jesse Robinson.]

KIRBY, Marshall F. 14 Jan 1850-12 Nov 1931. [Marshall Filmore, son of Alfred and Malissa (Campbell) Kirby, husband of Milly C. Phillips, married 28 Feb 1873.]

KIRBY, Millie C. 3 Mar 1858-3 Oct 1928. [Millie C. Phillips, wife of Marshall Filmore Kirby.]

KIRBY, Melissa. Died 6 Feb 1895, age about 80 years. [Melissa Campbell, wife of Alfred Kirby.]

KIRBY, Alfred. No Dates. [Born ca 1810 (1860 Census), died about age 75.

Son of William Kirby and his first wife _____, husband of Melissa Campbell.]

KIRBY, S.J. 15 Jan 1853-27 Jul 1873.

KIRBY, J. 10 Nov 1845-23 Oct 1864. [Jasper, son of John and Melinda (____) Kirby.]

OWEN, Nannie Wilson. 1851-28 Nov 1908. [Daughter of William and Emeline (Kirby) Wilson, second wife of Shelah H. Owen.]

OWEN, Shelah H. 28 Jun 1858-6 May 1948. [Shelah Hatton, "Bob", son of R.L. and Mary (Odom) Owen, husband of 1) Betty Wilson, married 14 Sep 1876 and 2) Nannie Wilson, married 11 Apr 1880.]

WILSON, Nancy P. 8 Dec 1856-31 Oct 1929. [Daughter of Joshua and Eliza J. (Couch) Pennington, wife of Ed Wilson, married 23 Feb 1877.]

WILSON, Ed. 4 Mar 1855-30 Jul 1923. [Edmond, son of William and Emeline (Kirby) Wilson, husband of Nancy Pennington.]

W.W. [Footmarker. Headstone broken and parts missing.]

WILSON, Clessie Thruman. 11 Aug 1901-23 Aug 1902.

WILSON, Willis Brown. 10 Oct 1899-25 Mar 1900.

PRESTON, Charley. 4 May 1866-4 Nov 1870. [Son of William C. and Mary Jane (Mitchell) Preston.]

OWEN, Betty Wilson. 1855-1878. [Daughter of William and Emeline (Kirby) Wilson, first wife of Shelah Hatton Owen, married 14 Sep 1876.]

WILSON, Willie. 7 May 1878-30 Jun 1878.

*BROWN, Susan L. 10 Aug 1846-13 May 1890. [Daughter of John O. and Louisa A. (_____) Pope, wife of Thomas Brown.]

SPURLOCK, Charles A. 27 Dec 1856-12 Nov 1938. [Husband of Parasada Dodd.]

SPURLOCK, Parasada. 14 Feb 1856-26 Aug 1924. [Daughter of William and Charlotta (Mathis) Dodd, wife of Charles A. Spurlock.]

SKELTON, John. Died 27 Apr 1893, age 87 years. [Husband of Mary _____.]

SKELTON, Mary. Died July 1886, age near 80 years. [Wife of John Skelton.]

*SKELTON, William J., born about 1860, died 10 Jun 1912, son of John and Mary (_____) Skelton.

*MITCHELL, Elizabeth, died in Jan 1904, daughter of John and Mary (_____) Skelton, wife of Dave Mitchell, married 29 Nov 1854.

HIGGINBOTHAM CEMETERY

Location: On Shellsford Road.

HIGGINBOTHAM, Sam. 1897-1944. [Mation Samuel Higginbotham, born 17 Sep
        1897, died 23 Sep 1944, married 8 May 1915 to Lettie Scott. He
        was son of James W. and Lucinda Ann (Rogers) Higginbotham.]

HIGGINBOTHAM, Lettie. 1899-   . [Daughter of William and Delia
        (Fults) Scott, wife of 1) Mation Samuel Higginbotham and 2)
        William T. Traughber. Although there is a tombstone for her
        here, she is buried at Shellsford Cemetery beside her second
        husband. Funeral home records give date of death as 19 Aug
        1970.]

HIGGINBOTHAM, Infant. Born and died 22 Jun 1919. [Infant son of Sam and
        Lettie (Scott) Higginbotham.]

BOST, America. 28 Apr 1866-4 Feb 1895. [Daughter of Aaron and Margaret
        L. (Collier) Higginbotham, wife of William Daniel "Dock" Bost,
        married 13 Dec 1885.]

HIGGINBOTHAM, Henry. 21 Dec 1824-10 Sep 1892. [Henry B., son of Aaron
        and Mary (Brooks) Allen Higginbotham, married 1) Mary
        Pennington, 2) Mary Jane McGregor on 9 Dec 1862, and 3) to
        Rebecca Atnip on 17 Oct 1880.]

HIGGINBOTHAM, Mary J. 9 Sep 1844-25 Jul 1879. [Mary Jane, daughter of
        Jason and Margaret (Pennington) McGregor, second wife of Henry
        B. Higginbotham.]

CHASTEEN, Infant. Born and died in Dec 1888. [Infant son of Charles
        Burlison and Maggie J. (Higginbotham) Chasteen.]

CHASTEEN, Emma. 6 Jul 1885-18 Sep 1885. [Daughter of Charles Burlison
        and Maggie J. (Higginbotham) Chasteen.]

CHASTEEN, C.B. 24 Nov 1846-24 Dec 1888. [Charles Burlison, son of Miles
        and Mariah (Burlison) Chasteen, husband of Maggie J.
        Higginbotham, married 14 Sep 1884.]

CHASTEEN, Maggie. 10 Dec 1851-8 Apr 1890. [Daughter of Henry B. and Mary
        Jane (McGregor) Higginbotham, wife of C.B. Chasteen. Birth date
        on this new tombstone is probably incorrect, as 1870-1880 census
        records for Warren County give her birth date as ca 1867.]

HIGGINBOTHAM, Samuel E. 23 Apr 1811-8 Mar 1886. Mexican War. [Son of
        Aaron and Elizabeth (Christian) Higginbotham, husband of
        Margaret Ferguson.]

HIGGINBOTHAM, Mary. 12 Oct 1838-11 Apr 1861. [Daughter of Henry and
        _____ (_____) Pennington, first wife of Henry B. Higginbotham,
        married 7 Jan 1856.]

HIGGINBOTHAM, William. 15 Jan 1861-7 Oct 1880. [Son of Aaron and Margaret
        L. (Collier) Higginbotham.]

HIGGINBOTHAM, Josie. 28 Apr 1866-31 Jul 1868. [Daughter of Aaron and
        Margaret L. (Collier) Higginbotham.]

HIGGINBOTHAM, Maggie. 24 Aug 1876-22 Dec 1881. [Daughter of Aaron and
        Margaret L. (Collier) Higginbotham.]

Higginbotham Cemetery, Cont.

ARLEDGE, Mary E.   16 Dec 1862-10 Dec 1900.   [Daughter of Aaron and
          Margaret L. (Collier) Higginbotham, wife of W.C. Arledge,
          married 8 Oct 1882.]

HIGGINBOTHAM, Aaron.   23 Jan 1839-12 Jul 1920.   [Son of Samuel E. and
          Margaret (Ferguson) Higginbotham, husband of Margaret L.
          Collier, married 11 Feb 1860.]

HIGGINBOTHAM, Margaret.   28 Nov 1840-20 Feb 1919.   [Daughter of James and
          Tamer (Grove) Collier, wife of Aaron Higginbotham.]

HIGGINBOTHAM, Frank.   12 Sep 1881-7 Sep 1919.   [Son of Aaron and Margaret
          L. (Collier) Higginbotham.]

HIGGINBOTHAM, Jess.   16 Sep 1895-6 Oct 1918.   WWI. .."Lost at Sea.." [Son
          of James W. and Lucinda Ann (Rogers) Higginbotham, husband of
          Eliza Scott.]

HIGGINBOTHAM, Sinda.   1867-1949.   [Lucinda Ann, 4 Oct 1867-30 Jun 1949,
          daughter of William and Tabitha (McGregor) Rogers, wife of James
          W. Higginbotham.]

HIGGINBOTHAM, James W.   1870-1955.   [2 Jul 1870-10 Nov 1955, son of Aaron
          and Margaret L. (Collier) Higginbotham, husband of Lucinda Ann
          Rogers, married 27 Dec 1888.]

HIGGINBOTHAM, Erford.   2 Dec 1899-16 Dec 1899.   [Son of James W. and
          Lucinda Ann (Rogers) Higginbotham.]

HIGGINBOTHAM, Mollie.   11 Jul 1892-19 Oct 1892.   [Daughter of James W. and
          Lucinda Ann (Rogers) Higginbotham.]

HIGGINBOTHAM, Frank.   1 Sep 1891-3 Sep 1891.   [Son of James W. and Lucinda
          Ann (Rogers) Higginbotham.]

JONES, Infants.   Born and died 15 Aug 1892.   [Infant daughters of J.M. and
          Nettie (_____) Jones.]

BOST, Roy.   30 Sep 1895-16 Dec 1973.   [Son of Jonathan J. "J.J." and Bell
          Zora (Higginbotham) Bost.]

McGREGOR, Fanny Ann.   23 Nov 1817-10 Aug 1865.   [Daughter of Aaron and
          Elizabeth (Christian) Higginbotham, wife of Alfred McGregor.]

*ARLEDGE, Fred.   1884-19 Feb 1902.   Son of William C. and Mary E.
          (Higginbotham) Arledge.

*ARLEDGE, Jesse. Died 12 Mar 1905, age 18 years, son of W.C. Arledge.

*EARLES, Hackett Ross.   Oct 1915-16 Jan 1917.   Son of H.R. and Maude
          (Higginbotham) Earles.

*HIGGINBOTHAM, Mary Brooks.   Born ca 1783, wife of 1) John Allen and 2)
          Aaron Higginbotham.   {At one time there was a stone for her
          which read "Mary Brooks, wife of William Aaron Higginbotham,
          Sr.}

*HIGGINBOTHAM, Aaron.   10 May 1778-13 Aug 1869.   Surveyor, turnpike
          builder and discoverer of Higginbotham Cave (Cumberland
          Caverns).   Son of Samuel and Jane (Satterwhite) Higginbotham,

140

grandson of Aaron and Clara (Graves) Higginbotham and great-
grandson of John and Frances (Riley) Higginbotham. He married
1) Elizabeth Christian and 2) to Mary (Brooks) Allen.

*HIGGINBOTHAM, Elizabeth. 4 May 1834-15 Oct 1917. Daughter of Richard
        and Mary (Freeman) England, wife of James Madison "J.M."
        Higginbotham.

*HIGGINBOTHAM, Florence, born ca 1856, died young. Daughter of H.B. and
        Mary (Pennington) Higginbotham.

*HIGGINBOTHAM, Jackson. No dates available but said to be the first
        person buried in Higginbotham Cemetery. Son of Aaron and Mary
        (Brooks) Higginbotham, died as a small boy.

*HIGGINBOTHAM, Margaret. 17 Jan 1817-14 Jul 1885. Margaret Ferguson,
        wife of Samuel E. Higginbotham.

*HIGGINBOTHAM, Margaret. 23 Dec 1907-1 Jun 1916. Daughter of Drury and
        Linnie (Akeman) Higginbotham.

*Tom, the slave of Aaron Higginbotham, who rescued Aaron after he was
trapped in Higginbotham Cave for three days and three nights.

*HIGGINBOTHAM, Victoria, born ca 1857, died young. Daughter of Henry B.
        and Mary (Pennington) Higginbotham.

*REEDY, Infant. Born and died 18 Apr 1928, child of Elmer and Bulah
        (Broyles) Reedy.

*GREEN, Blanch Allen. Born 28 Apr 1928, died 11 May 1928, daughter of
        L.C. and Etta (Boren) Green.

*HIGGINBOTHAM, Mrs J.H. From Warren County Times, 21 Jun 1907. "Mrs
        Higginbotham died Sunday (June 16). Buried at Family Cemetery."

HILL'S CREEK CEMETERY

Location: Hill's Creek area, near Center Hill Church.

PERRY, Homer O. 23 Oct 1895-12 Sep 1971. WWI. [Son of Taylor and
        Rebecca (Smith) Perry, husband of Louvisa (Christian) Turner.

PERRY, Louvisa. 15 Aug 1904-28 Dec 1987. [Daughter of John C. and Hassie
        (Cagle) Christian, wife of 1) Dick Turner and 2) Homer O.
        Perry.]

KING, Lela Ruth. 19 Sep 1881-9 Oct 1957. [Daughter of William Taylor and
        Rebecca Caroline (Smith) Perry, wife of William Decator King.]

KING, William Decator. 13 Sep 1883-10 Jan 1960. [Son of Jasper and
        Lucinda (Slaughter) King, husband of Lela Ruth Perry.]

Hill's Creek Cemetery, Cont.

BOULDIN, Ruth Perry. 28 Aug 1910-   . [Daughter of Horace Floyd
        and Annie Cordelia (Jordan) Perry, wife of Marion Andrew
        Bouldin.]

BOULDIN, Marion Andrew. 8 Jul 1911-10 Nov 1983. WWII. [Son of Henry and
        Florida (Richardson) Bouldin, husband of Ruth Perry.]

PERRY, Rebecca. 25 Apr 1850-31 Mar 1925. [Rebecca Caroline, daughter of
        Jake and Nancy (Hill) Smith, wife of William Taylor Perry,
        married 22 Jan 1873.]

PERRY, Taylor. 22 Feb 1851-27 Nov 1911. [William Taylor, son of John and
        Malinda (Dykes) Perry, husband of Rebecca Smith.]

PERRY, Cordelia. 8 Nov 1884-30 Jun 1975. [Anna Cordelia, daughter of
        Tom and Nancy Tabitha (Clark) Jordan, granddaughter of Isaac
        Newton and Martha (Roberts) Clark, great-granddaughter of
        William Bennett and Sarah (Martin) Roberts, wife of Horace Floyd
        Perry.]

PERRY, Horace Floyd. 28 Jan 1874-7 Oct 1943. [Son of Taylor and
        Rebecca (Smith) Perry, husband of Anna Cordelia Jordan, married
        1 Nov 1900.]

PERRY, Napoleon L. 1 Oct 1905-7 Jun 1960. [Napoleon Lonzo, son of Horace
        Floyd and Annie Cornelia (Jordan) Perry.]

PERRY, S.L. Lorenzo. 9 Feb 1903-11 Oct 1978. [Sherry Lorenzo, son of
        Horace Floyd and Anna Cordelia (Jordan) Perry.]

PERRY, Isiah. 13 Jan 1860-18 Mar 1946. [Son of John and Malinda (Dykes)
        Perry. Single.]

*PERRY, Charles Edward. 14 Oct 1918-2 Jan 1934. Son of Robert Lawson and
        Delia Clara (Lytle) Perry.

*PERRY, Robert L., Jr. Died 3 Jul 1965, age 32 years, 10 months and 10
        days, son of Robert Lawson and Delia Clara (Lytle) Perry.]

WEDDINGTON, Athelia P. 4 Feb 1922-7 Apr 1957. [Athelia Arlene, daughter
        of Robert Lawson and Delia Clara (Lytle) Perry, married 1) to
        Tommy Lee Pepper, married 13 May 1939 in Coffee County (div.)
        and 2) to William Weddington.]

JONES, Rhoda Delia Clara Lytle Perry. 28 Apr 1898 - 25 Jan 1981.
        [Daughter of George and Mina Jane (Mansfield) Lytle, married 1)
        Robert Lawson Perry in 1913 and 2) to Edd Jones.]

*PERRY, Floyd. Died 12 Aug 1917 at age 7 months, son of Lizzie Perry.

PERRY, Robert L. 1892-24 Mar 1969. [Robert Lawson, son of William
        Taylor and Rebecca Caroline (Smith) Perry, husband of Delia
        Clara Lytle.]

BESS, C.C. 11 Jul 1856-26 Oct 1932. [Chatam C., son of John and Linsey
        (Hill) Bess, husband of Rosia Hobbs.]

BESS, Rosia. 9 Oct 1861-8 Dec 1930. [Daughter of Archibald and Martha
        (Bond) Hobbs, wife of Chatam C. Bess.]

CHRISTIAN, Nettie. 19 May 1857-26 Apr 1936. [Perneta, daughter of Andrew and Mary "Polly" (Dodson) Martin, wife of James M. Christian.]

CHRISTIAN, James. 6 Dec 1845-12 Jan 1919. [James M., son of Peyton and Margaret (Pace) Christian, husband of Nettie Martin.]

CHRISTIAN, Thurman. 6 Apr 1928- . [Son of Oscar and Della (Taylor) Christian, husband of Alice M. Ward, married 2 Oct 1965.]

CHRISTIAN, Alice M. 26 Jul 1945- . [Alice M. Ward, wife of Thurman Christian.]

PANTER, John. 7 Nov 1857-29 Mar 1927. [Son of James and Sarah Jane (Clendenen) Panter, husband of Cora Christian.]

PANTER, Cora. 3 Dec 1890-18 Apr 1972. [Daughter of James and Perneta "Nettie" (Martin) Christian, wife of John Panter.]

CHRISTIAN, Evelyn. 28 Jul 1920-27 May 1921. [Daughter of Oscar and Della (Taylor) Christian.]

CHRISTIAN, Oscar. 19 Jun 1888-30 Jan 1931. [Son of James and Perneta "Nettie" (Martin) Christian, husband of Della Taylor.]

MADEWELL, Della Christian. 27 Mar 1898-19 Apr 1989. [Della Pearl, daughter of Andrew J. and Laura (Bess) Taylor, married 1) to Oscar Christian and 2) to Charlie B. Madewell.]

MADEWELL, Charlie B. 1 Oct 1910-5 Jul 1989. [Son of Sidney and Laura (King) Madewell, husband of Della Pearl Taylor.]

CHRISTIAN, Oma Lee. 7 Jul 1924-14 Aug 1924. [Daughter of Oscar and Della Pearl (Taylor) Christian.]

CATHCART, William Henry. 8 Oct 1921- . [Husband of Melba Christine Clendenon.]

CATHCART, Melba Christine Clendenon. 16 Oct 1926-23 Sep 1991. [Daughter of Livy and Emma Gladys (Turner) Clendenon, wife of William Henry Cathcart.]

CLENDENON, Livy. 6 Dec 1904-8 Nov 1982. [Son of Marion and Adell (Curtis) Clendenon, husband of Emma Gladys Turner.]

CLENDENON, Emma Gladys Turner. 2 Oct 1908-11 Aug 1983. [Daughter of Elliott and Bessie (Dick) Turner, wife of Livy Clendenon.]

TURNER, Bessie D. 14 May 1881-1 Sep 1971. [Daughter of Josh and Mary (Thurston) Dick, wife of Elliott Turner.]

TURNER, Elliott. 14 Aug 1875-14 Jun 1931. [Son of Ozias Denton and Martha (McCorkle) Turner, husband of Bessie Dick.]

TURNER, E. Wayne. 15 Apr 1903-2 Jun 1991. [Everett Wayne, son of Elliott and Bessie (Dick) Turner, husband of Annie Lee Panter.]

TURNER, Annie Panter. 8 Aug 1905-8 Feb 1984. [Annie Lee, daughter of Lafayette and Mary (Scott) Panter, wife of Everett Wayne Turner.]

BESS, Gertie Turner. 28 Apr 1889-1 Mar 1981. [Daughter of William W. and Martha Jane (Powell) Turner, wife of Grover Cleveland Bess.

BESS, Grover C. 7 Sep 1884-26 Mar 1964. [Grover Cleveland, son of John and Templa Ann (Williams) Bess, husband of Gertie Turner.]

POWERS, John Leonard. Born and died 5 Apr 1927. [Son of Hubert and _____ (_____) Powers.]

PANTER, John C. 27 Jun 1902-26 Dec 1949. [John Cooper, son of Lafayette and Mary (Scott) Panter, husband of 1) Cleo Kesey, married 12 Aug 1923, and 2) Lorena Curtis, married 5 Sep 1933.]

PANTER, Lorena. 9 Oct 1905- . [Daughter of Greenberry Martin and Martha (Tanner) Curtis, second wife of John Cooper Panter.]

BARNES, Lillian. 5 Aug 1877-16 Feb 1950. [Daughter of Elliott and Harriett (Bess) Boyd, wife of Mack Barnes.]

BARNES, Mack. 5 Jan 1878-13 Nov 1958. [Son of Elijah and Julia (Curtis) Barnes, husband of Lillian Boyd, married 1 Sep 1900.]

PANTER, Audley Burris. 26 Mar 1908-27 Oct 1985. [Son of Francis Marion and Myrtle Lula (Christian) Panter, husband of Lena Mai Roberts.]

PANTER, Lena Mai. 16 Feb 1924- . [Lena Mai Roberts, wife of Audley Burris Panter.]

PANTER, Leslie W. (Jack). 23 Mar 1921-29 Aug 1987. [Leslie Waymon, son of Marion and Myrtle (Christian) Panter, husband of Lena Estelle Stacy, married 27 July 1946.]

PANTER, Lena Estelle. 10 May 1926- . [Lena Estelle Stacy, wife of Leslie Waymon Panter.]

BARNES, Irene McGee. 9 Oct 1911- . [Daughter of Edd and Manerva (Douglas) McGee, wife of Alton Barnes.]

BARNES, Alton. 11 Dec 1904-27 Jan 1985. [Son of Mack and Lillie (Boyd) Barnes, husband of Irene McGee, married 31 Dec 1932.]

STACY, Lee Grover. 7 Dec 1885-3 Jan 1973. [Husband of Minnie _____.]

STACY, Wavie P. 27 Apr 1912- . [Wavie Lillian, daughter of Francis Marion and Myrtle Lula (Christian) Panter, wife of Richard Howard Stacy.]

STACY, Richard H. 12 Nov 1907-6 Jan 1984. [Richard Howard, son of Lee Grover and Minnie (_____) Stacy, husband of Wavie Lillian Panter, married 22 Jan 1931.]

STACY, Donnie Joe. 20 Aug 1941-27 Jul 1965. [Son of Richard H. and Wavie (Panter) Stacy, husband of Glenda Sue Stubblefield (div.)]

PANTER, Aubrey Maynard (Dub). 2 Apr 1910-23 Jun 1962. [Son of Francis Marion and Myrtle Lula (Christian) Panter, husband of Lila Mae Barnes, married 1 Nov 1932.]

PANTER, Lila Mai Barnes. 8 Jul 1915-31 Jul 1967. [Daughter of John H.

and Janie Lee (Bales) Barnes, wife of Aubrey Maynard Panter.]

PANTER, F.M. 9 Sep 1882-9 Jun 1949. [Francis Marion, son of James and Sarah (Clendenon) Panter, husband of Myrtle Lula Christian, married 27 Apr 1905.]

PANTER, Myrtle Lula. 26 Aug 1892-1 Feb 1968. [Daughter of Farzell G. and Josie (Barnes) Christian, wife of Francis Marion Panter.]

CLENDENON, Patsy Sue. 5 Aug 1940-22 Nov 1942. [Daughter of Lannie Villa and Jadie Pauline (Panter) Clendenon.]

CLENDENON, Jadie P. 23 Apr 1918-17 Mar 1982. [Jadie Pauline, daughter of Francis Marion and Myrtle Lula (Christian) Panter, wife of Lannie Villa Clendenon.]

CLENDENON, Lannie V. 22 Jun 1912-   . [Lannie Villa, son of James Newton and Nettie (Bouldin) Clendenon, husband of Jadie Pauline Panter, married 29 Jul 1938.]

NUNLEY, Minnie Williams. 23 Sep 1906-13 Sep 1976. [Daughter of Calvin and Mattie (_____) Bush, married 1) to Doc Williams and 2) to Herbert Andrew Nunley.]

NUNLEY, Herbert Andrew. 26 Feb 1902-13 Jun 1968. [Son of Jay and ____ (_____) Nunley, husband of 1) Bessie Caldonia Taylor and 2) Minnie (Bush) Williams.]

NUNLEY, Bessie Caldonia Taylor. 30 Nov 1901-12 Sep 1936. [First wife of Herbert Andrew Turner.]

BOULDIN, Daulton. 16 Jan 1881-23 Jul 1959. [Dalton William, son of Thomas and Ellie (Curtis) Bouldin, husband of Lela Pearl Christian, married 11 Jun 1906.]

BOULDIN, Pearl. 6 Jan 1890-26 Dec 1985. [Lela Pearl, daughter of Farzell G. and Josie (Barnes) Christian, wife of Daulton William Bouldin.]

CHRISTIAN, Jennie. 12 Oct 1892-8 May 1947. [Jennie Evelyn, daughter of Thomas E. and Sarah Elizabeth (Slaughter) Curtis, wife of Loyd Christian.]

CHRISTIAN, Loyd. 3 Oct 1888-1 Dec 1964. [Son of Farzell and Josie (Barnes) Christian, husband of Jennie Evelyn Curtis.]

CURTIS, Bruce C. 5 Apr 1895-13 Oct 1976. [Son of Lewis Elmore and Carrie (Bess) Curtis, husband of Bessie Gillentine.]

CURTIS, Bessie G. 21 Mar 1894-27 Mar 1976. [Daughter of Joe Arthur and Vida (Campen) Gillentine, wife of Bruce C. Curtis.]

CURTIS, Bruce C., Jr. 7 Apr 1924-3 Feb 1983. [Son of Bruce C., Sr. and Bessie (Gillentine) Curtis, husband of 1) Agnes Clendenon and 2) Linda Sue Rhea.]

CURTIS, Linda Sue Rhea. 19 May 1945-   . [Second wife of Bruce C. Curtis, Jr.]

BOULDIN, Florida. 1 May 1885-27 Jun 1950. [Mary Florida, daughter of

Robert and Isabel (Roberts) Richardson, wife of Hervy Bouldin.]

BOULDIN, Hervy E.   31 Jan 1886-25 Nov 1979. [Son of Andrew Jackson and
        Rachel (Nunley) Bouldin, husband of Mary Florida Richardson,
        married 11 Oct 1907.]

BOULDIN, Robert Kelton.   4 Nov 1908-23 May 1971. [Son of Hervy and Mary
        Florida (Richardson) Bouldin, husband of Leona Finchum, married
        16 Oct 1937.]

BOULDIN, Leona May.   10 May 1916-   . [Leona Finchum, wife of
        Robert Kelton Bouldin.]

RHEA, Harris. 2 May 1895-6 Dec 1981. WWI. [James Harris, son of Charlie
        and Vinnie (Madewell) Rhea, husband of Gladys Marie Bouldin,
        married 15 Jul 1944.]

RHEA, Gladys M.   13 Apr 1924-   . [Gladys Marie, daughter of Hervy
        E. and Mary Florida (Richardson) Bouldin, wife of James Harris
        Rhea.]

BOULDIN, John Herby.   10 Jul 1938-10 May 1976. [Son of Robert Kelton and
        Leona (Finchum) Bouldin.   Single.]

BOULDIN, Cassandra Lynne.   1 Jul 1962-29 Oct 1962.   [Daughter of Amasa
        Berne and Ramon (McGuire) Bouldin.]

CLENDENON, Charles W.   20 Mar 1902-20 Jul 1954. [Charles William, son of
        Marion and Adell (Curtis) Clendenon, husband of Cora Leoma
        Curtis.]

CLENDENON, Leoma.   5 Apr 1911-23 Jul 1991.   [Cora Leoma, daughter of
        Emmett and Marilda (Curtis) Curtis, wife of Charles William
        Clendenon.]

CURTIS, Emmitt.   28 Mar 1882-26 Apr 1965.   [Son of Irving and Mary
        (McCorkle) Curtis.]

CURTIS, Marilda.   11 Jul 1891-3 Jan 1965. [Daughter of Thomas Elkana and
        Sarah Elizabeth (Slaughter) Curtis.]

TAYLOR, Andrew.   20 Dec 1870-10 Jan 1954.   [Son of Andrew Jackson and
        Catherine (Dunlap) Taylor, husband of Laura Jane Bess.]

TAYLOR, Laura Jane Bess.   3 Dec 1873-20 Oct 1947. [Daughter of John and
        Tempy Ann (Williams) Bess, wife of Andrew Jackson Taylor,
        married 19 May 1895.]

LYTLE, K.M.   15 Sep 1925-9 Oct 1926.
LYTLE, Ralph Douglas.   26 Oct 1933-27 Oct 1933.
LYTLE, Glenn Arlis.   18 Jul 1935-28 Jul 1937.
        Sons of Mr. and Mrs. Marcus Lytle.

GROVE, Eloise.   28 Aug 1917-   . [Daughter of Emmitt and Marilda
        (Curtis) Curtis, wife of Clabe Grove.]

GROVE, Clabe.   7 Jun 1909-19 Oct 1991. [Son of Wyatt Lane and Arcola
        (Martin) Grove, husband of Eloise Curtis, married 2 Jun 1935.]

SLAUGHTER, James A.   19 Feb 1885-21 Jan 1948. [Son of Hughey J. and Cora

(Bess) Slaughter, husband of Hallie Barnes.]

SLAUGHTER, Hallie Barnes. 16 Apr 1888-7 Apr 1969. [Daughter of Addison and Mary (Panter) Barnes, wife of James A. Slaughter.]

SLAUGHTER, Charles Nolan. 1918-29 Aug 1986. [Son of James A. and Hallie (Barnes) Slaughter.]

CHRISTIAN, Herve Mabile. 8 Apr 1881-9 Oct 1959. [Son of Orland Bradley and Mary Elizabeth (Martin) Christian, husband of Vera Parks, married 27 Apr 1926.]

CHRISTIAN, Vera Parks. 1 Oct 1893-13 Oct 1967. [Daughter of George W. and Ella M. (Hill) Parks, wife of Herve Mabile Christian.]

BROWN, William Larry. 1 Feb 1953-24 Jul 1962. [Son of Howard and Georgie D. (Church) Brown.]

TAYLOR, Samuel N. 18 Feb 1869-30 Jul 1960. [Samuel Nelson, son of Andrew Jackson and Catherine (Dunlap) Taylor, husband of Suella Bess.]

TAYLOR, Suella B. 9 Jun 1878-   . [Daughter of John J. and Tempie (Williams) Bess, wife of Samuel Nelson Taylor.]

TAYLOR, Murdis Marie. 24 Mar 1928-   . [Murdis Marie Knowland, wife of Paul Taylor.]

TAYLOR, Paul. 18 Jun 1913-9 Nov 1991. [Son of Samuel N. and Suella (Bess) Taylor, husband of Murdis Marie Knowland.]

TAYLOR, Dannis Wayne. 8 Sep 1959-18 Sep 1959. [Son of Paul and Murdis Marie (Knowland) Taylor.]

McCLURE, Infant. [No dates]. "Infant son of the McClures, Born Dead."

McCLURE, Ronald D. "Hoppy". 29 Apr 1955-30 Aug 1984. [Son of Marlin and Ada (Church) Vaughn McClure, grandson of J.T. and Mattie Mae (Fults) Church, husband of Rita Elkins, married 6 Nov 1974.]

McCLURE, Reta F. 27 Feb 1957-   . [Wife of Ronald D. McClure.]

McCLURE, Bobby Jewell. Died 14 Mar 1960, aged 2 months.

YOUNGBLOOD, William Jason. 13 May 1971-7 Aug 1971. [Son of Jesse Lee and Billie Ruth (Brown) Youngblood.]

KING, Lillie Mabel. 5 Jul 1898-   . [Lillie Mabel Cooley, wife of Robert L. King.]

KING, Robert L. 14 Jul 1884-10 Oct 1958. [Robert Lee, son of John R. and Letha (Waters) King, husband of Lillie Mabel Cooley.]

KING, R. L., Jr. 5 Jul 1928-16 Dec 1934. [Robert Lee, Jr., son of Robert L. and Lillie Mabel (Cooley) King.]

CHURCH, Jewell Eugene. 19 Jan 1932-12 Oct 1957. ["Sonny", son of J.T. and Maggie Mae (Fults) Church.]

CHURCH, Vickie Joan. 10 Nov 1954-   . [Wife of Jimmy Joe Church.]

CHURCH, Jimmy Joe. 18 Apr 1950-   . [Son of J.T. and Mattie Mae
        (Fults) Church, husband of 1) _____ Delong, 2) Katherine Diane
        Hollandsworth, and 3) Vickie Joan _____.]

CHURCH, Jimmy Wayne "He-Man". 31 May 1981-29 Dec 1992. [Son of Jimmy Joe
        and Katherine Diane (Hollandsworth) Church.]

CHURCH, J.D. 23 Apr 1929-12 May 1929. [Son of J.T. and Mattie Mae
        (Fults) Church.]

CHURCH, Freddie. 19 May 1937-29 May 1937. [Son of J.T. and Mattie Mae
        (Fults) Church.]

CHURCH, Donna Lena. 5 Sep 1946-5 Sep 1946. [Daughter of J.T. and Mattie
        Mae (Fults) Church.]

SLAUGHTER, Jesse Eli. 26 Jul 1892-7 Aug 1960. [Son of Hughey J. and Cora
        (Bess) Slaughter, husband of Grace Lee Fults.]

SLAUGHTER, Grace Lee. 9 Nov 1898-5 Jan 1982. [Daughter of Reuben and
        Ella (Hayes) Fults, wife of Jesse Eli Slaughter.]

SLAUGHTER, Leon. 14 May 1922-28 Jan 1928. [Son of Jesse Eli and Grace
        Lee (Fults) Slaughter.]

SLAUGHTER, Lodema Lee. 7 May 1928-14 Jul 1975. [Daughter of Jesse Eli
        and Grace Lee (Fults) Slaughter.]

CHURCH, J.T. Sr. 24 Apr 1905-11 Jun 1976. [Son of Thomas and Epsie
        (_____) Church, husband of Mattie Mae Fults.]

CHURCH, Mattie M. 13 May 1913-   . [Mattie Mae, daughter of Reuben
        and Ella (Hayes) Fults, wife of J.T. Church.]

KING, Lethia. 22 Mar 1860-18 Dec 1935. [Lethia Waters, wife of John R.
        King.]

KING, John R. 11 Oct 1853-27 Nov 1914. [Son of John R., Sr. and Susan
        (Stokes) King, husband of Letha Waters.]

WATSON, Jerry Dale. 6 Mar 1950-3 Jun 1950. [Son of Joe L. and Jessie Mae
        (King) Watson.]

CROWE, Ernest C. 27 Feb 1905-29 Jan 1972. [Husband of Inis L. King.]

CROWE, Inis L. 7 May 1916-14 Dec 1984. [Inis Lee, daughter of Robert Lee
        and Lillie Mabel (Cooley) King, wife of Ernest C. Crowe.]

CROWE, James Douglas. 3 Nov 1956-4 Nov 1956. [Son of Ernest C. aand Inis
        Lee (King) Crowe.]

CROWE, Brenda Sue. 4 Nov 1951-19 Feb 1991. [Daughter of Ernest C. and
        Inis Lee (King) Crowe.]

KING, Osmond. 18 Apr 1921-12 Oct 1980. WWII. [Son of Robert Lee and
        Lillie Mabel (Cooley) King, husband of Betty June Teeters.]

KING, Betty June. 15 Feb 1933-14 Oct 1963. [Daughter of Gordon and
        Eugenia (Dykes) Teeters, wife of Osmond King.]

Hill's Creek Cemetery, Cont.

KING, Melinda Sue.   14 Dec 1959-20 Jan 1960.   [Daughter of Osmond and
           Betty June (Teeters) King.]

KING, Rhoda Gay. Died 31 May 1972, aged 5 days.

SCOTT, Candy Kay.   14 May 1965-20 Aug 1965.   [Daughter of Odus and Lottie
           (King) Scott, granddaughter of Newton King.]

[Two unreadable tombstones]

KING, Newton A.   31 May 1910-5 May 1973.   [Newton Alex, son of Jesse and
           Dora (Perry) King, husband of Rosa Lee King.]

MADEWELL, Shirley L.   20 Jun 1912-10 Nov 1981.   [Son of Sidney and Laura
           (King) Madewell, husband of Flora Golda Priest, married 29 Nov
           1947.]

MADEWELL, Goldie Priest. 1922 - 27 Nov 1982. [Daughter of Tim and Nettie
           (Grove) Priest, wife of Shirley L. Madewell.]

MADEWELL, Wilma Adean. Born and died 17 Oct 1937. [Daughter of Shirley
           and Flora Golda (Priest) Madewell.]

MADEWELL, Charles. Born and died 17 Oct 1937. [Son of Charles and Della
           (Taylor) Madewell.]

MADEWELL, Johnnie L. 1 Jun 1914-6 Jan 1983. [Son of Sidney Clayborn and
           Laura (King) Madewell, husband of Rilla A. Vaughn.]

MADEWELL, Rilla A.   17 Aug 1923-   .   [Rilla A. Vaughn, wife of
           Johnnie L. Madewell.]

PANTER, Alma.   13 Jan 1917-10 Sep 1978.   [Daughter of Dalton William and
           Lela Pearl (Christian) Bouldin, wife of Noland Lorn Panter.]

PANTER, Lorn.   28 Apr 1914-4 Dec 1958.   [Noland Lorn, son of John and Cora
           (Christian) Panter, husband of Alma Bouldin, married 23 Apr
           1938.]

WALKER, Maggie. 7 Jul 1909- 1981. [Maggie Marie, daughter of John and
           Cora (Christian) Panter, wife of Brintley Walker.]

WALKER, Brintley. 21 Sep 1904-6 Oct 1980. [Son of Isaac Clinton and Lula
           (Poore) Walker, husband of Maggie Panter, married 3 Apr 1927.]

BESS, Jonah Everett. 7 Dec 1906-27 Oct 1989.   [Husband of Gracie Velma
           Bouldin.]

BESS, Gracie Velma Bouldin. 19 Oct 1910-2 Dec 1986. [Daughter of Dalton
           William and Lela Pearl (Christian) Bouldin, wife of Jonah
           Everett Bess.]

BESS, Ralph Earl.   7 May 1935-4 Jan 1987.   [Son of Jonah Everett and
           Gracie Velma (Bouldin) Bess. Single.]

BROCK, Charles R.   7 Aug 1941-31 Oct 1992.   [Son of Odell and Emma
           (Dalberry) Brock, husband of Wilma L. Slaughter ,married 3 Jun
           1962.]

BROCK, Wilma L.   17 Jun 1940-   .   [Daughter of Jess Eli and Grace

Hill's Creek Cemetery, Cont.

Lee (Fults) Slaughter, wife of Charles R. Brock.]

PANTER, Erma E.   28 Oct 1914-   . [Erma Evelyn, daughter of Aaron and Catherine (Taylor) Curtis, wife of James Edward "Buddy" Panter.]

PANTER, James E.   16 Nov 1910-9 May 1985. [Son of John and Cora (Christian) Panter, husband of Erma E. Curtis, married 29 Dec 1931.]

CLENDENON, James N.   7 Jun 1879-18 Dec 1960.   [James Newton, son of Francis Marion and Sarah Catherine (Martin) Clendenon, husband of Marjorie Jennetta Bouldin.]

CLENDENON, Nettie B.   16 Jan 1888-17 Mar 1963.   [Marjorie Jennetta, daughter of Thomas and Ellie (Curtis) Bouldin, wife of James Newton Clendenon.]

CURTIS, Seawillow.   9 Jan 1912-   . [Daughter of Don and Mary (Christian) Hitchcock, wife of Clabern L. Curtis.]

CURTIS, Clabern L.   4 Dec 1904-   . [Son of Joseph Martin and Mary (King) Curtis, husband of Seawillow Hitchcock, married 2 Apr 1932.]

CURTIS, Virginia C.   31 Mar 1953-   . [Virginia Carol Judkins, wife of James Anthony "Tony" Curtis.]

CURTIS, James A.   27 Nov 1949-18 Jul 1983. [Son of Arthur Martin and Myrtle Avo (Dodson) Curtis, husband of Virginia Carol Judkins.]

PERRY, Johnnie W.   4 May 1916-20 Aug 1983. [Son of James T. and Mary (Smith) Perry, husband of Alvilda King.]

PERRY, Alvilda K.   10 May 1921-30 Mar 1990. [Daughter of Elijah and Susie (King) King, wife of Johnie W. Perry.]

VALIMONT, Lorene Sanders.   10 Apr 1918-3 Oct 1992.   [Daughter of George and Jenny (Hobbs) Sanders, married thirdly to Wendell Valimont.]

CURTIS, Arzie W.   5 Apr 1895-3 May 1971. [Son of Irvin and Betty Well (Bouldin) Curtis, husband of Alda L. Boyd, married 13 May 1917.]

CURTIS, Alda L.   8 Sep 1894-9 May 1973. [Alda L. Boyd, wife of Arzie W. Curtis.]

CURTIS, Arthur Martin.   10 Mar 1909-25 May 1966. [Son of Joseph Martin and Mary (King) Curtis, husband of Myrtle Avo Dodson, married 19 Apr 1930.]

CURTIS, Myrtle A. Dodson.   22 Mar 1909-5 Jul 1980. [Myrtle Avo, daughter of Alonzo and Bertie (Russell) Dodson, wife of Arthur Martin Curtis.]

PERRY, Charles E.   6 Nov 1944-25 Apr 1973. [Son of Isaac and Berthenia (King) Perry.]

PERRY, Berthenia K.   18 Feb 1918-22 Apr 1971. [Ollie Berthina, daughter of Elijah and Susie (King) King, wife of Isaac Perry.]

PERRY, Isaac. 15 May 1913-21 May 1974. [Son of James T. and Mary (Smith) Perry, husband of Ollie Berthina King.]

TAYLOR, Irene Curtis. 6 Feb 1912-   . [Daughter of Greenberry Martin and Martha (Tanner) Curtis, wife of Oliver C. Taylor.]

TAYLOR, Oliver C. 25 May 1904-29 Jul 1985. [Oliver Cleveland, son of Andrew J. and Laura Jane (Bess) Taylor, husband of Irene Curtis, married 24 Apr 1927.]

TAYLOR, Peggy Wimberly. 22 May 1930-   . [Daughter of Oscar and Clara (Coppinger) Wimberly, wife of Glynn Concord Taylor.]

TAYLOR, Glynn C. 13 Nov 1928-8 Jan 1972. KOREA. [Glynn Concord, son of Oliver Cleveland and Irene (Curtis) Taylor, husband of Peggy Wimberly.]

KOHLUS, Walter P. 16 Jul 1897-8 Jun 1969. [Walter Philip, son of Chris Edward and Ida Mae (Winfred) Kohlus, husband of Bonnie Lee Green.]

KOHLUS, Bonnie G. 29 Mar 1910-23 Aug 1985. [Daughter of Bill and Bertha Ann (Prater) Green, wife of Walter Phillip Kohlus.]

ROBERTS, Mardie E. 15 Sep 1862-28 May 1941. [Daughter of Andrew and Lucy (____) King.]

CURTIS, E.L. 17 Jan 1913-25 Apr 1968. [Elijah Lewis, son of Lewis Elmore and Alice (Walling) Grissom Curtis, husband of Menda Louise Howard. The stone lists his sons as Carl Lewis, Elijah Lewis II, and Michael Anthony and his daughters as Ida Jean, Virginia Mae and Edith Lotel.]

CURTIS, Finis. 20 Jun 1881-4 Sep 1956. [Son of William Elihue and Tennessee (Green) Curtis, single.]

*CURTIS, Etta Belle. 13 Nov 1917-3 Mar 1921.

CURTIS, Frank. 6 Apr 1888-11 Apr 1963. [Son of William Elihue and Tennessee (Green) Curtis, husband of Lillie Rhea.]

CURTIS, Lillie. 6 Sep 1893-30 Nov 1970. [Daughter of Charlie and Vinnie (Madewell) Rhea, wife of Frank Curtis.]

CURTIS, Tennessee. 13 Jul 1851-7 Nov 1913. [Daughter of John and Sarah (____) Green, wife of William Elihue Curtis, married 6 Jan 1876.]

CURTIS, Aura. 21 Oct 1876-12 Nov 1951. [Daughter of William Elihue and Tennessee (Green) Curtis. Single.]

CURTIS, Infant. Born and died 3 Jun 1923. [Son of Lewis Elmore and Alice (Walling) Grissom Curtis.]

CURTIS, Emmer. 11 Nov 1884-24 Jan 1898. [Daughter of Lewis Elmore and Carrie (Bess) Curtis.]

CURTIS, Lewis Elmore. 17 Sep 1856-13 Feb 1934. [Son of Aaron and Margaret (Bouldin) Curtis, husband of 1) Carrie Bess, married 3 Aug 1879 and 2) Alice (Walling) Grissom, married 3 Sep 1911 in Van Buren County, TN.]

CURTIS, Cary Bess. 26 May 1862-18 Jun 1896. [Daughter of John and Tempy
    Ann (Williams) Bess, first wife of Lewis Elmore Curtis.]

CLENDENEN, Adell. 5 Oct 1882-26 Jun 1906. [Daughter of Lewis Elmore and
    Carrie (Bess) Curtis, wife of Francis Marion Clendenen.]

CLENDENEN, Marion. 10 Mar 1875-16 Jul 1942. [Francis Marion, son of
    Charles W. and Elizabeth (Barnes) Clendenon, husband of 1) Adell
    Curtis, married 30 Dec 1899 and 2) Parriet Curtis.]

CLENDENEN, Callie. 8 Dec 1873-23 Aug 1939. [Daughter of Charles W. and
    Eliza (Barnes) Clendenen. Single.]

ROBIRDS, Mandy. 3 Sep 1906-2 Jan 1907. [Daughter of William Thomas and
    Margaret (Bouldin) Robirds.]

CURTIS, Henry. 30 May 1902-13 Oct 1957. [John Henry, son of William and
    Martha (Perry) Curtis, husband of Wavie Roberts.]

CURTIS, Wavie. 12 Oct 1906-   . [Daughter of George W. and Della
    (Jones) Roberts, wife of John Henry Curtis.]

CURTIS, William R. 14 Oct 1870-21 Dec 1967. [Son of Wiley and Mary Susan
    (Bouldin) Curtis, husband of 1) Martha Perry, 2) Bethia Ann
    Prater and 3) Mollie Meeks.]

LYTLE, Malundia. 1 Aug 1861-17 Feb 1919. [Sarah Malinda, daughter of
    William Washington and Letisha (Dodson) Curtis, first wife of
    James Jefferson Lytle.]

LYTLE, Pearl. 6 Jul 1893-27 Dec 1959. [Margaret Pearl, daughter of
    Francis Marion and Sarah Catherine (Martin) Clendenon, second
    wife of James Jefferson Lytle.]

LYTLE, James. 29 Oct 1872-24 Dec 1943. [James Jefferson, son of George
    and Mina Jane (Mansfield) Lytle, husband of 1) Malinda Curtis,
    and 2) Margaret Pearl Clendenon, married 5 May 1922.]

CLENDENON, Mose P. 11 Feb 1885-30 May 1968. [Son of Francis Marion and
    Sarah Catherine (Martin) Clendenon. Single.]

SLAUGHTER, Hugh. 10 Jan 1860-14 Nov 1923. [Husband of Cora J. Bess,
    married 3 Jan 1884.]

SLAUGHTER, Cora J. Died 14 Apr 1902, age about 42 years. [Daughter of
    Eli and Lear (Killian) Bess, wife of Hugh Slaughter.]

SLAUGHTER, Euphemia.   15 Apr 1894-25 Jan 1911.
SLAUGHTER, Anna.   25 Oct 1897-6 Jul 1902.
    [Daughters of Hugh and Cora J. (Bess) Slaughter.]

PERRY, John H. 8 Sep 1844-25 Apr 1900. [John Houston, son of John and
    Malinda "Linnie" (Dykes) Perry, married 1) Martha Green on 4 Feb
    1864, 2) to Mary E. King on 19 Sep 1865, and 3) to Margaret
    King.]

ROLLINS, James. 1 Jan 1836-8 Dec 1887.

BOULDIN, Thomas.   2 Feb 1854-10 Feb 1907. [Son of William and Jemima
          (Williams) Bouldin, husband of Elvana Curtis, married 12 Sep
          1875.]

BOULDIN, Ellie.   19 Dec 1858-13 Apr 1925.   [Elvana, daughter of William
          and Letisha (Dodson) Curtis, wife of Thomas Bouldin.]

BOLIN, Merica Allis.   29 Jun 1876-22 Sep 1885.   [Daughter of Thomas and
          Ellie (Curtis) Bouldin.]

HERRIN, Sidney. Died 16 May 1883, age about 100 years. [Wife of William
          Herrin.]

BESHERSE, William.   4 Aug 1803-15 Dec 1897. [Husband of 1) _____ _____
          and 2) Sally Herrin, married 3 Nov 1845 in Cannon County, TN.]

BESHERSE, Sally.   1831 - 7 Jun 1898.   [Daughter of William and Sidney
          (_____) Herrin, wife of William Besherse.]

MARTIN, Nannie. 18 Feb 1865-16 Mar 1886. [Daughter of Elijah and Adaline
          (Moffitt) Hillis, wife of Floyd Martin, married 21 Jun 1883.]

BOULDIN, Emma. 26 Dec 1859-8 Feb 1882. [Daughter of Jesse and Elizabeth
          (Hayes) Martin, wife of Joseph R. Bouldin, married 8 Sep 1881.]

BOULDIN, Infant Son.   Born and died 22 Jul 1927.
BOULDIN, Leola Mae.   17 Mar 1911-8 Jul 1916.
BOULDIN, Alverta.   22 Jun 1908-5 May 1909.
BOULDIN, Leon.   23 Jul 1917-28 Jul 1933.
     [Children of Andrew Arthur Haden and Josie (Curtis) Bouldin.]

BOULDIN, A.H.   13 Dec 1883-3 Jan 1950.   [Andrew Arthur Haden, son of
          Thomas and Ellie (Curtis) Bouldin, husband of Josie Curtis,
          married 16 Jul 1905 in Van Buren County, TN.]

BOULDIN, Josie.   11 Apr 1884-14 Mar 1966.   [Daughter of Henderson and
          Almeda (Hillis) Curtis, wife of Andrew Arthur Haden Bouldin.]

BOULDIN, Arzy Bryan. 29 Jan 1911-18 Jun 1993. [Son of Andrew Jackson and
          Rachel (Nunley) Bouldin, husband of Mary Ella Fults, married 26
          Sep 1936.]

BOULDIN, Mary Ella Fults.   10 Oct 1921-12 Oct 1972.   [Daughter of Russell
          and Georgia (_____) Fults, wife of Arzy Bryan Bouldin.]

BOULDIN, Earnest. Died 1901, age 2 years.

BOULDIN, Frank. 6 Apr 1892-3 Feb 1928. [Son of Andrew Jackson and Rachel
          (Nunley) Bouldin, married 1) Delia C. Bonner and 2) Emma Roberts
          on 3 Mar 1924.]

BOULDIN, Murphy Ancle, Sr.   17 Oct 1895-26 May 1979.   [Son of Andrew
          Jackson and Rachel (Nunley) Bouldin, husband of Ova Lee
          Hitchcock, married 11 Mar 1917 in Van Buren County, TN.]

BOULDIN, Andrew Jackson. Aug 1865-25 May 1928.   [Son of William and
          Jemima (Williams) Bouldin, husband of Rachel Nunley.]

BOULDIN, Rachel. Died 2 Apr 1942, age 73 years. [Daughter of Willis and
          Nancy (Brown) Nunley, wife of Andrew Jackson Bouldin.]

BOULDIN, Rachel B.   7 Jul 1937-14 Jul 1937.
BOULDIN, Harold D.   2 Jun 1963-2 Jun 1963.
          [Children of Arzy Bryan and Mary Ella (Fults) Bouldin.]

BESS, Emma E. 25 Sep 1854-4 May 1862.

BESS, John. 1826 - 1858. [Son of Bazel and Mary "Polly" (Johnson) Bess,
          husband of Brittania Barnes.]

BOYD, Lester. 8 Apr 1885-19 Jan 1888.

BOYD, Emma Eugenia. 20 Jun 1874-19 Jul 1874.

BOULDIN, G.W.   13 Nov 1857-8 Nov 1858.
BOULDIN, Cora.   9 Jun 1864-22 Jan 1965.
BOULDIN, Narvel.   12 Jan 1870-28 Oct 1885.
BOULDIN, W.J.   29 Jan 1862-26 Jan 1869.
          [Children of Elisha L. and Mary (Grove) Bouldin.]

BOULDIN, E.L.   12 Mar 1830-8 Jun 1876. [Elisha L., son of Lewis and
          Susanna "Suckey" (Knight) Bouldin, wife of Mary Grove, married
          13 Nov 1856.]

BOULDIN, Mary. 30 May 1834-14 Mar 1902. "Daughter of William Groves and
          Wife Elisha Bouldin." [Daughter of William and Margaret
          (Robertson) Grove, wife of Elisha L. Bouldin.]

BOULDIN, Ella. 8 Feb 1876-14 Nov 1879. [Daughter of Elisha L. and Mary
          (Grove) Bouldin.]

CURTIS, Elihu. 17 Oct 1852-16 Jun 1927. [William Elihu, son of Aaron and
          Margaret (Bouldin) Curtis, husband of Tennessee Green, married
          6 Jan 1876.]

CURTIS, Eugene. 14 Nov 1878-11 Dec 1878. [Son of William Elihu and
          Tennessee (Green) Curtis.]

*BOULDIN, Nancy. 3 Oct 1837-17 Mar 1915. [Daughter of William R. and
          Margaret (Robinson) Grove, wife of Narve Bouldin.]

BARNES, Arkie. "Daughter of Isaac ...." Broken stone, no dates.

BARNES, Cara. 30 May 1882-26 Nov 1887. [Daughter of Isaac and Mary A.
          (Bess) Barnes.]

BARNES, Susan. 25 Nov 1871-17 Nov 1875. [Daughter of Isaac and Susanna
          (Hill) Barnes.]

PERRY, John. 15 Feb 1816-14 Sep 1884. [Son of Alexander and Elizabeth
          (Woodlee) Perry, husband of Malinda "Linnie" Dykes.]

CHEEK, M.S. 18 Apr 1875-4 Dec 1877. [Son of William and Gemima (_____)
          Cheek.]

LYTLE, Johney.   10 Mar 1877-26 Jan 1892.
LYTLE, Robert D.{Broken}   -4 Aug 1897.
LYTLE, {broken}   29 Oct 1881-11 Aug 1901.
LYTLE, Julia Ida.   28 Jun 1885-18 Aug 1908.
          [Children of George Washington and Mina Jane (Mansfield) Lytle.]

Hill's Creek Cemetery, Cont.

LYTLE, George Washington. 1854 - 1926. [Husband of Mina Jane Mansfield, married 20 Aug 1871.]

LYTLE, Mina Jane Mansfield. 12 Apr 1855-27 Sep 1941. [Daughter of Jeff and _____ (_____) Mansfield, wife of George Washington Lytle.]

_____, Isabella. Wife of ..... {Broken rock, no dates or surname}

SLAUGHTER, Jesse. No dates. [Son of Jesse and Sarah (____) Slaughter, husband of Euphania Bess, married 20 Apr 1884.]

SLAUGHTER, Euphania Bess. Died 14 Jan 1916, age 56. [Daughter of Eli and Lear (Killian) Bess, wife of Jesse Slaughter.]

McCORMICK, Cora Lee Slaughter. 26 Aug 1896-28 Aug 1969. [Daughter of Jesse and Euphania (Bess) Slaughter, wife of Elijah McCormick.]

McCORMICK, Elijah W. 19 Nov 1890-25 Feb 1988. [Son of James Madison and Martha Ann (Mayes) McCormick, husband of Cora Lee Slaughter.]

BESS, Hervey. 12 Aug 1888-15 Aug 1888.

BESS, Robert B. 1842 - 1876. CSA. [Son of Eli and Lear (Killian) Bess, husband of Sarah "Sady" Morton, married 28 Aug 1867.]

PERRY, Isaac Floid. Born and died 12 Mar 1884. [Son of Isaac and Arkansas (Beshears) Perry.]

PERRY, Henry. 22 Sep 1842-18 Nov 1861. [Son of John and Malinda (Dykes) Perry.]

PERRY, Joe Wheeler, died 14 Dec 1971, age 69 years. [Son of Isaac and Martha (Hambrick) Perry, husband of Lela Brown.]

*PERRY, Jim. 6 Mar 1873-2 Nov 1939. Son of John and Betsy (King) Perry.

LYNCH, Euphemy. 23 Jul 1853-28 Apr 1874. [Daughter of Benjamin and Rebecca (Wallace) Hill, wife of William Lynch.]

HILL, Emma Cain. 18 Mar 1851-28 Feb 1933. [Rebecca Emma, daughter of George and Rebecca (Stone) Cain, wife of Virgil Hill.]

HILL, Virgil. 2 Mar 1851-15 Jan 1933. [Son of Hugh Lawson White and Virginia (Dearing) Hill, husband of Rebecca Emma Cain.]

HILL, Mary. 3 Nov 1883-10 Feb 1885. [Daughter of Virgil and Rebecca Emma (Cain) Hill.]

HILL, Hester V. 11 Jun 1887-12 Jan 1888. [Daughter of Virgil and Rebecca Emma (Cain) Hill.]

WILLIAMS, Mary. 8 May 1827-6 Jul 1863. [Mary Barnes, wife of William Williams.]

CATES, Mary Bess. 4 Jan 1875-20 Jul 1963. [Mary A., daughter of Israel Putnam and Balzora Ward (Dearing) Bess, third wife of James A. Cates, married 22 Sep 1895.]

CATES, Bessie. 17 Jul 1896-12 Sep 1896. [Daughter of James A. and Mary A. (Bess) Cates.]

Hill's Creek Cemetery, Cont.

BESS, Walter.   7 Oct 1869-20 Oct 1869.   [Son of Israel P. and Balzora
        (Dearing) Bess.]

BESS, Balsora.   10 Jun 1840-8 Feb 1892.   [Balzora Ward, daughter of
        William Lynch Smith and Mary Terry (Harrison) Dearing, wife of
        Israel Putnam Bess.]

BESS, Israel P.   29 Mar 1844-1 Oct 1910.   [Israel Putnam, son of John and
        Elenza Grundy (Hill) Bess, husband of 1) Balzora W. Dearing,
        married 2 Jan 1869 and 2) Maria Elizabeth (Robertson) Davenport,
        married 21 Nov 1892.]

CATES, Vernon.   31 Mar 1898-27 Oct 1911.   [Son of James A. and Mary A.
        (Bess) Cates.]

SLAUGHTER, Daisia.   7 Jun 1885-17 May 1886.

BESS, Tempa Ann.   7 Mar 1870-9 May 1899.   [Daughter of William and Jemima
        (Williams) Bouldin, second wife of Arwood Bess.]

BESS, Arwood.   2 Apr 1867-14 Dec 1897.   [Son of John and Elenza Grundy
        (Hill) Bess, husband of 1) Alice Grove, married 15 Jan 1889 and
        2) Temperance Ann Bouldin, married 8 Nov 1896.]

BESS, Alice.   21 May 1851-2 Apr 1890.   [Daughter of William and Margaret
        (Robertson) Grove(s), first wife of Arwood Bess.]

BESS, Infant.   Born and died 31 Jan 1890.   Infant of Arwood and Alice
        (Grove or Groves) Bess.]

*BESS, Nazarilla.   24 Sep 1897-26 Mar 1923. [Son of Arwood and Tempa Ann
        (Bouldin) Bess.]

BESS, John.   14 Mar 1815-21 Feb 1876.   [Husband of Elinza Grundy Hill.]

BESS, Elinzie.   1 Feb 1822-1 Nov 1901. [Elinza Grundy, daughter of Henry
        John Alexander and Polly (Johnson) Hill, wife of John Bess.]

HILL, Dearing.   28 Jan 1844-8 Jul 1844.
HILL, Livingston.   5 Oct 1845-1 Sep 1852.
        [Sons of Hugh Lawson White and Virginia (Dearing) Hill.]

HILL, Lovicy.   21 Nov 1822-27 Nov 1839.   [Daughter of Isaac and Eliza
        (Hill) Hill.]

HILL, Melchizedek.   12 Jul 1857-12 Dec 1857.

COOPWOOD, Harriet Dearing.   1829 - 1911.   [Harriet Smith, daughter of
        William Lynch Smith and Mary (Harrison) Dearing, wife of 1)
        _____ Campbell and 2) _____ Coopwood.]

HILL, Hugh L.W.   1 Mar 1810-18 Jan 1892.   [Hugh Lawson White, son of
        Henry John Alexander and Susannah (Swales) Savage Hill, husband
        of Virginia A. Dearing, married 14 May 1840.]

HILL, Virginia A.   3 Jul 1823-4 Dec 1908.   [Virginia Ann, daughter of Col.
        William Lynch Smith and Mary Terry (Harrison) Dearing, wife of
        Hugh Lawson White Hill.]

DEARING, William L.S.   7 Apr 1796-12 Jun 1876.   [William Lynch Smith

Dearing, born in Orange County, VA, husband of 1) Mary Terry
Harrison and 2) Nellie Hayes McGregor, married 26 Feb 1868.]

DEARING, Mary T.   18 Mar 1799-6 Sep 1864.   [Mary Terry, daughter of
Ainsworth and Dolly Coleman (Stone) Harrison, wife of William
Lynch Smith Dearing.]

HILL, Leonora Myers. 12 Aug 1856-19 Apr 1927. [Daughter of John R. and
Parneta (England) Myers, wife of Franklin Hill.]

HILL, Frank. 20 Jul 1855-20 May 1920.   [Franklin, son of Hugh Lawson
White and Virginia Ann (Dearing) Hill, husband of Leonora Myers,
married 24 Jun 1875.]

HILL, Infant Son.   11 Jul 1876-24 Jul 1876.
HILL, N. Virginia.   26 Jul 1883-30 Nov 1887.
       [Children of Franklin and Leonora (Myers) Hill.]

WHEELER, Maggie G. 5 Jul 1852-4 Jul 1896.

WHEELER, S.H. 23 Nov 1836-29 Oct 1896.

McLEAN, Mary E. 5 Nov 1833-30 Nov 1882.

NELSON, Elizabeth. 11 Apr 1811-25 May 1873.

HILL, Lillian Lee. 31 Jan 1865-17 May 1882. [Daughter of Israel P. and
Catherine N. (Daniels) Hill.]

HILL, Israel P. 19 Jan 1825-1 Jul 1909. [Israel Putnam, husband of
Catherine Daniels, married 19 Sep 1850.]

HILL, Catherine N. 8 Oct 1830-22 Nov 1911. [Catherine N. Daniels, wife
of Israel P. Hill.]

*HILL, Isaac. 15 Feb 1854-21 Nov 1931. Son of Israel P. and Catherine
(Daniels) Hill. Single.

HILL, Infant. Born and died 31 Oct 1922. [Infant of N.M. and Beatrice
(Green) Hill.]

HILL, William C. 21 Sep 1820-20 Aug 1901. [William Carroll, son of Henry
John Alexander and Polly (Johnson) Hill. Single. {Bible record
gives date of birth as 1 Apr 1818.}]

HILL, Isaac, Sr. 20 Dec 1797-16 Oct 1871. [Son of Henry John Alexander
and Susannah (Swales) Savage Hill, husband of 1) Eliza Hill,
married 25 Aug 1818, 2) Millie (Douglas) Harrison, widow of
George Harrison, married 7 Apr 1862, and 3) Margaret (Pace)
Christian, widow of Peyton Christian, married 23 Aug 1871.]

HILL, Eliza. 4 Feb 1800-8 Nov 1859. [Daughter of William and Lydia White
(Jones) Hill, first wife of Isaac Hill, Sr.]

MARTIN, Lydia S. 6 Mar 1828-27 May 1863. [Lydia S. Hill, wife of Elijah
Martin.]

CURTIS, Marthia Ann. 2 Oct 1875-3 Sep 1879. [Daughter of Jacob and Mirah
Elizabeth (Dodson) Curtis.]

157

CURTIS, Sarah Jane. 13 Jun 1878-15 Sep 1879. [Daughter of Jacob and Mirah Elizabeth (Dodson) Curtis.]

CURTIS, Octalee. 29 Oct 1881-7 Sep 1899. [Daughter of Jacob and Mirah Elizabeth (Dodson) Curtis.]

CURTIS, Mirah E. 3 Jan 1841-13 Dec 1909. [Mirah Elizabeth, daughter of Eli and Jansie (Ware) Dodson, wife of Jacob Curtis.]

CURTIS, Jacob. 9 Feb 1841-9 Jun 1915. [Son of Chelsey and Rebecca (Martin) Curtis, husband of Mirah Elizabeth Dodson.]

*CAGLE, Laura Matilda Curtis. No dates. Daughter of Jacob and Mirah Elizabeth (Dodson) Curtis, wife of Isaac Cagle, married 16 Apr 1888.

CURTIS, Lucy. 14 Feb 1903-19 Aug 1942. [Lucinda Ella, daughter of Thomas Elkonia and Sarah Elizabeth (Slaughter) Curtis.]

CURTIS, Sarah Elizabeth. 3 Oct 1866-23 Oct 1927. [Daughter of Jesse and Sarah (Blair) Slaughter, wife of Thomas Elkonia Curtis.]

CURTIS, Thomas E. 6 Sep 1863-6 Mar 1937. [Thomas Elkonia, son of Jacob and Mirah Elizabeth (Dodson) Curtis, husband of Sara Elizabeth Slaughter, married 18 Sep 1888.]

CURTIS, Richard Hurman. 15 Mar 1898-20 Mar 1903. [Son of Thomas Elkonia and Sara Elizabeth (Slaughter) Curtis.]

CURTIS, Infant daughter.   Born and died 11 Feb 1890.
CURTIS, Elige.   22 Sep 1895-28 Jan 1898.
  [Children of Thomas Elkonia and Sara Elizabeth (Slaughter) Curtis.]

CURTIS, Joseph Martin. 2 Jun 1873-12 Jul 1939. [Son of Jacob and Mirah Elizabeth (Dodson) Curtis, husband of Mary King.]

CURTIS, Mauda Eller. 13 Aug 1905-23 Dec 1906. [Daughter of Joseph and Mary (King) Curtis.]

CURTIS, Mary K. 19 Mar 1882-3 Dec 1957. [Daughter of John R. and Letha (Walters) King, wife of Joseph Martin Curtis.]

CURTIS, J.G. 19 Feb 1936-17 Mar 1939.

CURTIS, Haskell J. 24 Sep 1899-12 May 1991. [Haskell Jacob, son of Joseph Martin and Angie (Slaughter) Curtis, husband of Ethel Ella Green.]

CURTIS, Ethel E. 30 Mar 1905-15 Mar 1977. [Ethel Ella, daughter of Pat and Mary (Lytle) Green, wife of Haskell Jacob Curtis.]

CURTIS, William Jackson. 15 Mar 1860-23 Apr 1916. [Son of Jacob and Mirah Elizabeth (Dodson) Curtis, husband of Parriet Curtis, married 14 Jan 1893.]

SCOTT, Sala Ann. 15 Jul 1876-28 Oct 1876. [Daughter of Henry Samuel and Elizabeth J. (Boyd) Scott.]

CURTIS, Larence. 28 Oct 1910-16 Dec 1910. [Son of Emmitt and Marilda (Curtis) Curtis.]

CURTIS, Irving. 9 Sep 1854-7 May 1937. [Son of Aaron and Margaret (Bouldin) Curtis, husband of 1) Mary McCorkle, married 30 Oct 1879 and 2) Betty Bouldin, married 14 Feb 1888 in Van Buren County, TN.]

CURTIS, Betty Well. Died 1 Oct 1938, age 78 years. [Daughter of Noble and Elizabeth (Grissom) Bouldin, second wife of Irving Curtis.]

CURTIS, Leola. 23 Oct 1922-29 Jan 1940. [Daughter of Martin and Ethel (Curtis) Curtis.]

CURTIS, Martin. 21 Dec 1891-26 Mar 1956. [Son of Irving and Betty Well (Bouldin) Curtis, husband of Ethel Curtis.]

CURTIS, Ethel. 4 May 1894-23 Sep 1929. [Daughter of William Jackson and Parrott (Curtis) Curtis, wife of Martin Curtis.]

CURTIS, Martha. 10 Nov 1877-28 Feb 1941. [Daughter of Newton and Margaret (Curtis) Tanner, wife of Greenberry Martin Curtis.]

CURTIS, Greenberry Martin. 9 May 1873-11 Oct 1942. [Son of William and Letisha (Dodson) Curtis, husband of Martha Tanner, married 6 Feb 1901 in Van Buren County, Tn.]

*CURTIS, Etta Bell. Died 3 Mar 1921 age 34 years. Daughter of Malinda Curtis.

*CURTIS, Martha, died 7 Oct 1917, age 32 years, daughter of John and Malinda (Dykes) Perry, wife of _____ Curtis.

CAGLE, John Andrew. 4 Oct 1884-3 Nov 1884. [Son of Andrew Jackson and Martha (Goldston) Cagle.]

CURTIS, Aaron. 15 Sep 1893-14 Feb 1919. [Son of Irving and Betty Well (Bouldin) Curtis, husband of Cathren Taylor.]

CURTIS, Cathren. 9 Jun 1894-12 Jan 1942. [Cathren Taylor, wife of Aaron Curtis.]

CURTIS, Infant. 19 Jan 1919 only date on stone. [Son of Aaron and Cahtren (Taylor) Curtis.]

TAYLOR, Floid Ianthis. 29 Jun 1885-17 Mar 1887. [Son of Norman and Mary (Snellgroves) Taylor.]

CAGLE, John. 9 Apr 1842-1 Feb 1869. [John David, husband of Martha Alice Taylor, married 9 Sep 1863.]

TAYLOR, Sarah Leweller. 18 Sep 1882-31 Oct 1882. [Daughter of John A. and Sidney (Beshears) Taylor.]

TAYLOR, Joe R. 7 May 1893-8 Jun 1953. WWI. [Son of Norman and Mary (Snellgrove) Taylor, husband of Mary Thompson.]

TAYLOR, Willis. 23 Oct 1833-7 Sep 1884. [Son of Willis and Martha "Pattie" (Word) Taylor. Single.]

TAYLOR, Sam. No dates on stone. [Son of Norman and Mary Ann (Snellgrove) Taylor, twin to Joe R. Taylor, born 7 May 1893, married Lela Gertrude Holt on 10 Jun 1939 (div.)]

TAYLOR, Grady. No dates on stone. [26 Oct 1882-29 Apr 1914, son of Norman and Mary Ann (Snellgrove) Taylor, husband of Dorothy M. Tilley.]

TAYLOR, A.J. 3 May 1837-24 Nov 1901. [Andrew Jackson, son of Willis and Martha "Pattie" (Word) Taylor, husband of Chatran Dunlap.]

TAYLOR, Cathran. 11 Dec 1843-9 Jan 1941. {Funeral home record gives date of death as 1942.} [Daughter of John and Mary (Hendrix) Dunlap, wife of Andrew Jackson Taylor.]

TAYLOR, Margie Cleo Elliott. 27 Jan 1916-4 Aug 1935. [Wife of Paul Taylor, married 22 Sep 1934.]

TAYLOR, Arthur. 4 Jul 1827-6 Jun 1888. [William Arthur, son of Willis and Martha "Pattie" (Word) Taylor, husband of Nancy Vance.]

TAYLOR, Norman. No dates on stone. [7 May 1853-8 May 1950. Son of William Arthur and Nancy (Vance) Taylor, husband of Mary Snellgrove, married 29 Jan 1882.]

TAYLOR, Mary. No dates on stone. [Mary Snellgrove, born 1866, daughter of _____ and Nancy Adaline (Dunlap) Snellgrove.]

TAYLOR, Edith Hennessee. 8 Oct 1924- . [Wife of Lester Willard Taylor.]

TAYLOR, Lester Willard. 12 May 1919-12 Dec 1981. WWII. [Son of Andrew Jackson and Anna C. (Brown) Taylor, husband of Edith Hennessee.]

TAYLOR, Andrew Jackson. 12 Jul 1898-9 Jun 1974. [Son of Thomas and Marilda (Slaughter) Taylor, husband of Anna C. Brown.]

TAYLOR, Anna C. 8 Feb 1900-26 Oct 1984. [Daughter of Arthur and Mary (Bess) Brown, wife of 1) Andrew Jackson Taylor and 2) Robert Smith.]

McGEE, Nellie Taylor. 10 Dec 1925- . [Daughter of Andrew Jackson and Anna C. (Brown) Taylor, wife of Floyd L. McGee.]

McGEE, Floyd L. 18 Dec 1921-16 Jul 1988. [Son of Martin and Lela (Dixon) McGee, husband of Nellie Taylor.]

*TAYLOR, Mrs. Nancy, died 14 Sep 1908, age 78 years.

TAYLOR, Martha Allona. 13 Apr 1876-8 Sep 1879.

CLENDENON, Parrott. 7 Dec 1877-2 Jan 1954. [Daughter of William and Letisha (Dodson) Curtis, wife of 1) William J. Curtis and 2) Marion Clendenon.]

HILL, Jonathan P. 12 Jan 1833-8 Nov 1888. [Son of Irvin and Eleanor (Morgan) Hill, husband of Vesta Scott, married 12 Jul 1956.]

HILL, Vesta? (Broken stone). 8 Nov 1831-27 ___ 1878.

HILL, J.M. 29 Apr 1867-9 Oct 1867. [Son of Jonathan P. and Vesta (Scott) Hill.]

BARNES, Isaac. 22 Jun 1863-24 Jun 1864. [Son of Isaac and Susannah

Elinor (Hill) Barnes.]

HILL, Susan. 23 May 1825-30 Jun 1903. [Susan Brock, wife of Irving Lafayette Hill.]

BARNES, Susanna Elinor. 31 Jul 1834-11 Jul 1879. [Daughter of Irving & Eleanor (Morgan) Hill, wife of Isaac Barnes, married 21 May 1853. {He is buried at Big Sink Cemetery.}]

HILL, J.L. 1 Feb 1880-1 Jun 1880. [Son of J.A. and Jane (_____) Hill.]

HILL, John A. 11 Jun 1847-11 Aug 1881. [John Alexander, son of Irving Lafayette and Susanna (Brock) Hill, husband of Jane _____.]

HILL, H. No dates or other information.

BESS, Bazel. 1806 - 29 Apr 1881. [Son of Issie John and _____ (_____) Bess, husband of Polly Johnson.]

BESS, Polly Johnson. 19 Jan 1787-18 Apr 1870. [Wife of Bazel Bess.]

HILL, Henry A. 7 Feb 1775-1 Aug 1825. [Henry John Alexander, son of Isaac Sr. and Lucinda (Wallace) Hill, husband of Susannah Swales.]

HILL, Susanna Swales. 31 Dec 1767-23 Sep 1846. [Daughter of John and Eleanor (_____) Swales, wife of 1) Sterling Savage and 2) Henry John Alexander Hill.]

HILL, Elenor H. 7 Oct 1799-21 Jul 1860. [Daughter of David and Martha (Hill) Morgan, wife of Erven Hill.]

HILL, Erven. 17 Jul 1796-15 Apr 1836. [Son of John Alexander and Susan (Swales) Hill, husband of Elenor Hill, his first cousin.]

HILL, Jesse J. 22 Aug 1822-15 Oct 1846. Mexican War. [Son of Irvin and Eleanor (Morgan) Hill, buried in Gulf of Mexico returning from the Mexican War.]

HILL, John A. 14 Dec 1816-22 Sep 1846. Mexican War. [John Alexander, son of Irvin and Eleanor (Morgan) Hill, killed at the Battle of Monterey, Mexico.]

Hill, Carroll Hill. 1 Apr 1818-8 Sep 1870.

SMITH, Isaac. 2 Feb 1788- . "Mexican War 1855." [Husband of Brittania Savage, married 25 Dec 1811.]

SMITH, Brittania. 20 Jun 1793- . [Brittania Savage, wife of Isaac Smith.]

*BOULDIN, William. Oct 1824-ca 1907. Son of Lewis and Susannah (Knight) Bouldin, husband of Jemima Williams.

*BOULDIN, Jemima Williams. Born 1832, daughter of William Sr. and Elizabeth (McGregor) Williams, wife of William Bouldin.

BESHEARS, Eliddie Ann. 11 Jan 1864-6 Jul 1888. [Eliddie Ann Taylor, wife of Thomas Beshears.]

*BESHEARS, Thomas. ca 1857-31 May 1932. Son of William and Sally (Herrin) Beshears, husband of 1) Eliddie Ann Taylor, married 13 Nov 1884, 2) Nancy Adeline Snellgroves, married 11 Dec 1888, and 3) Nancy Johnson Clemens, married 11 Feb 1925.

BESHERSE, Arthur. 30 Jun 1888-12 Jul 1888. [Son of Thomas and Eliddia Ann (Taylor) Beshears.]

*BESHEARS, Nancy Adeline Snellgroves, died Sep 1924 at age 89 years, 9 months and 25 days. Daughter of John and Mary (Hendrix) Dunlap, married 1) to _____ Snellgroves, and 2) as his second wife to Thomas Bershears on 11 Dec 1888.

*TAYLOR, John H. {No Dates} Husband of Sidney Beshears, married 7 Dec 1881.

TAYLOR, Sidna. 1861-27 Nov 1938. [Sidney, daughter of William and Sallie (Herrin) Beshears, wife of John H. Taylor.]

HILL, Francis S. 15 Dec 1804-24 Dec 1834. [Frances Pickett, wife of Isaac Hill who was the son of Benjamin and Rebecca (Wallace) Hill.]

MOFFITT, Harriett. 22 Sep 1808-15 Aug 1886. [Daughter of Henry John Alexander Hill and Polly Johnson. Wife of Aaron Moffitt.]

MOFFITT, Aaron. 1 Aug 1802-about 15 Apr 1881. [Husband of Harriett Hill.

MEADOWS, Virginia A. 15 Dec 1850-23 Apr 1856.
MEADOWS, Augustus. 14 May 1859-27 Nov 1860.
MEADOWS, Deborah. 15 Jan 1863-10 Nov 1863.
      [Children of William Morris and Sarah Jane (Moffitt) Meadows.]

*HILL, Sallie. Died 5 Jun 1900, age 74 years.

*HILL, "Aunt Annie". From Warren County Times 8 May 1908. "Burned and died Saturday. Buried at Hill's Creek."

*COPPINGER, Gary Phillip. Born and died 9 Oct 1951. Son of Phillip and Daphine (Curtis) Coppinger.

*BARNES, Ezra. 29 Sep 1900-7 Dec 1923. Son of Andrew and Eliza (Clendenon) Barnes.

McGEE, Louisa. 29 Dec 1846-28 May 1893. [Daughter of John and Elenza Grundy (Hill) Bess, wife of Archibald C. McGee.]

McGEE, A.C. 26 Jul 1842-26 Oct 1885. [Archibald C., son of Clendenon and Martha (England) McGee, husband of Louisa Bess, married 29 Sep 1864.]

McGEE, Willie Eugenia. 26 Jul 1882-27 Jun 1885. [Daughter of Archibald C. and Louisa (Bess) McGee.]

McGEE, Johney. 25 Dec 1865-7 Aug 1867. [Son of Archibald C. and Louisa (Bess) McGee.]

McGEE, Mary Jane. 1 May 1869-8 Sep 1870. [Daughter of Archibald C. and Louisa (Bess) McGee.]

Hill's Creek Cemetery, Cont.

McGEE, James Morgan. 29 Jul 1884-25 Mar 1886. [Son of Archibald C. and
Louisa (Bess) McGee.]

BROWN, Ernest B. 7 Mar 1908-2 Nov 1993. [Son of Luther and Laura
(Slaughter) Brown, husband of Josephine Brown.]

BROWN, Josephine. 28 Dec 1909-31 Aug 1990. [Daughter of Arthur and Mary
(Bess) Brown, wife of Ernest B. Brown.]

BARNES, Wallene E. 26 Nov 1920-23 Jun 1987. [Daughter of Andrew and
Eliza Jane (Boyd) Barnes.]

BARNES, Harley B. 4 Aug 1919-21 Sep 1987. WWII. [Son of Andrew and
Eliza Jane (Boyd) Barnes.]

BARNES, Loy. 9 May 1922-23 Nov 1980. WWII. [Son of Andrew and Eliza
Jane (Boyd) Barnes.]

BARNES, Eliza J. 21 Dec 1887-23 Sep 1961. [Eliza Jane, daughter of
Elliott and Harriett (Bess) Boyd, wife of Andrew Barnes.]

BARNES, Andrew. 20 Jun 1869-10 Oct 1934. [Husband of Eliza Jane Boyd.]

BROWN, Beverly Carl. 28 Feb 1937-13 May 1983. KOREA. [Son of Ernest B.
and Josephine (Brown) Brown, husband of Melba Jean Rogers.]

BROWN, Willis Esten. 2 Aug 1918-25 Jan 1989. WWII. [Son of John William
and Nancy Ollie (Brown) Brown, husband of Annie Bell Savage.]

BROWN, Nancy Ollie. 1900-10 Feb 1988. [Daughter of William B. and Martha
(Scruggs) Brown, wife of John William Brown.]

BROWN, John W. Mar 1888-6 May 1975. [Son of Arthur and Mary Ann (Bess)
Brown, husband of Nancy Ollie Brown.]

BROWN, George C. 1 Feb 1907-25 Oct 1982. [Son of Arthur and Mary Ann
(Bess) Brown, married 1) Wavie Dill and 2) Rilda K. Myers.]

BROWN, Rilda K. 10 May 1921-27 Jul 1989. [Daughter of Elijah and Susie
(King) King, wife of 1) George C. Brown and 2) Cebert Myers.]

STEVENSON, Joe Wilson Jr. 16 Oct 1927- . [Husband of Mary Lou
Perry, married 23 Apr 1950.]

STEVENSON, Mary Lou Perry. 12 Mar 1926- . [Daughter of Joe
Wheeler and Lela (Brown) Perry, wife of Joe Wilson Stevenson,
Jr.]

BROWN, Arthur. 10 May 1861-9 Oct 1911. [Husband of Mary Ann Bess,
married 5 Jun 1887.]

BROWN, Mary. 1 May 1868-25 Apr 1956. [Mary Ann, daughter of John and
Tempy Ann (Williams) Bess, wife of Arthur Brown.]

BROWN, Thomas J. 27 Aug 1890-9 Apr 1968. [Thomas Jasper, son of Arthur
and Mary Ann (Bess) Brown, husband of 1) Rachel Ferguson, 2)
Pearl (Fults) Meadows and 3) Pearl Tanner.]

DRAKE, Annie. 19 Jun 1879-4 May 1916. [Daughter of Thomas and Eliza J.
(Bess) Panter, wife of C.D. Drake, married 1 Nov 1902.]

163

PANTER, Eliza. 18 Aug 1857-2 Apr 1921. [Eliza J, daughter of John and Brittannia (Barnes) Bess, wife of Thomas Panter, married 12 Jun 1878.]

PANTER, Lizzie. 22 Nov 1884-3 Jun 1966. [Elizabeth, daughter of James and Sarah Jane (Clendenon) Panter.]

BESS, Tommy B. 13 Dec 1892-29 Sep 1986. [Son of Allison and Martha Josephine (Boyd) Bess, husband of Halie Panter.]

BESS, Halie Panter. 3 Nov 1897-1 Jul 1990. [Daughter of James and Sarah Jane (Clendenon) Panter, wife of Tommy B. Bess.]

BESS, D.L. 4 Feb 1916-5 Oct 1949. [Marcus Dee Lafayette, son of Tommy B. and Halie (Panter) Bess. Single.]

BESS, Josephine. 26 Jul 1922-17 Apr 1941. [Martha Josephine, daughter of Tommy B. and Halie (Panter) Bess.]

BESS, Britanna. 18 Dec 1833-1 May 1921. [Daughter of Charles and Susannah "Susan" (Smith) Barnes, wife of John Bess.]

BESS, M.D.L. 8 Aug 1895-19 Jan 1915. [Marcus Dee Lafayette, son of Allison and Martha Josie (Boyd) Bess.]

BESS, Josie. 16 Aug 1871-29 Apr 1899. [Martha Josephine, daughter of Marcus Dee Lafayette and Martha E. (Akeman) Boyd, wife of Allison Bess.]

BESS, Allison. 29 Jun 1865-1 May 1962. [Son of John and Britanna (Barnes) Bess, husband of Martha Josephine Boyd, married in 1891.]

BESS, John. 8 May 1840-5 Aug 1893. [Son of Eli and Lear (Killian) Bess, husband of Tempiean Williams, married 9 Aug 1867.]

BESS, Tempiean. 5 Jun 1848-5 Dec 1933. [Daughter of William Jr. and Mary (Barnes) Williams, wife of John Bess.]

_____, Henry. {Unreadable Stone}

BESS, Florence L. 18 Sep 1885-2 Jun 1902. [Daughter of Andrew Jackson and Mary (Mayfield) Bess.]

BESS, Infant. Born and died 14 Jul 1900. [Son of Andrew Jackson and Mary (Mayfield) Bess.]

BOYD, William Anderson. 11 Dec 1881-28 Sep 1956. [Son of Elliott Hodge "Dock" and Harriet (Bess) Boyd. Single.]

BOYD, E.H. 26 Jun 1843-17 Feb 1918. [Elliott Hodge, son of Elliott and Drucilla (Moore) Boyd, husband of Harriet Bess, married 26 Jan 1872.]

BOYD, Harriet. 16 Nov 1852-17 Feb 1913. [Daughter of John and Brittanna (Barnes) Bess, wife of Elliott Hodge Boyd.]

BOYD, Charlie. 23 Jul 1875-7 Feb 1900. [Son of Elliott Hodge and Harriet (Bess) Boyd.]

BOYD, Private Harlie. 8 Mar 1889-17 Oct 1918. WWI. "Killed in Action".
[Son of Elliott Hodge and Harriet (Bess) Boyd.]

CLENDENON, Francis M. 1 Nov 1835-14 Nov 1919. [Son of James Marion and
Clarissa (Clark) Clendenon, husband of 1) Mahalia Martin,
married 27 Jan 1857 and 2) Sarah Catherine Martin.]

CLENDENON, Sarah Martin. 25 Jan 1853-1 Mar 1926. [Daughter of William
Andrew and Mary Ann "Polly" (Dodson) Martin, wife of Francis
Marion Clendenon.]

JENNINGS, Sarah Adeline. 19 Jun 1883-7 Aug 1917. [Daughter of Jake and
Cherlene (Dunlap) Taylor, wife of Thomas Jennings.]

JENNINGS, Tom. 2 Aug 1877-4 Aug 1956. [Son of Jessie Dodson "Dock" and
Jane (Vickers) Jennings, husband of Sarah Adeline Taylor,
married 17 Nov 1903.]

JENNINGS, Franklin H. 24 Nov 1904-17 Dec 1924. [Son of Tom and Sarah
Adeline (Taylor) Jennings.]

JENNINGS, Wilma Ruth. 9 Jun 1935-9 May 1936. [Daughter of George and
Alice (Picket) Jennings.]

*CURTIS, Infant. Born and died 20 Oct 1922. Child of _____ and Charline
(Taylor) Curtis.

TAYLOR, Frank. 9 Nov 1880-16 Nov 1975. [Son of Andrew J. and Sarah
(Dunlap) Taylor, husband of Bertha Taylor.]

TAYLOR, Bertha. 13 Feb 1893-10 Aug 1948. [Daughter of Tom and Marilda
(Slaughter) Taylor, wife of Frank Taylor.]

TAYLOR, Infant. 4 Feb 1916-5 Feb 1916. [Infant of Frank and Bertha
(Taylor) Taylor.]

TAYLOR, Infant. Born and died 8 Jun 1917. [Son of Livie Lonzo and
Beatrice (Lytle) Taylor.]

BARNES, Lena Mai. 4 Apr 1917-29 Apr 1918. [Daughter of John Albert
Sidney and Lillie Ann (Panter) Barnes.]

CLENDENEN, Jessie Dee. 14 Feb 1905-13 May 1921. [Son of William Rice and
Nancy Belle (Curtis) Clendenen.]

CLENDENEN, Ida Pearl. 28 Dec 1910-18 Oct 1924. [Daughter of William
Rice and Nancy Belle (Curtis) Clendenen.]

KEENER, Clarence Edward. 19 Jul 1930-2 Mar 1977. KOREA. [Son of Delbert
D. and Jewell (Langston) Keener.]

KEENER, Erlene Pickett. "Mother". {No further information}

BOYD, James Richard. 6 Oct 1927-23 Oct 1992. [Son of Darris Richard and
Evelyn Mae (Coppinger) Boyd.]

BOYD, Darris Richard. 19 Feb 1882-5 Jan 1944. [Son of Elliott Hodge and
Harriet (Bess) Boyd, husband of Evelyn Mae Coppinger.]

BOYD, Evelyn Mae. 1 May 1896-9 Jan 1956. [Daughter of Jefferson Davis

"Jeff" and Naomi "Ome" (Wanamaker) Coppinger, wife of Darris Richard Boyd.]

BOYD, Oscar. 8 May 1891-12 Apr 1947. [Son of Elliott "Dock" and Harriet (Bess) Boyd, husband of Mary Agness Lytle, married 26 Dec 1913.]

BOYD, Mary. 10 Mar 1893-30 Aug 1969. [Daughter of James Jefferson Lytle and his first wife Malinda Curtis. Wife of Oscar Boyd.]

*BOYD, Eunice Virginia. 13 Feb 1923-5 Dec 1923. [Daughter of Oscar and Mary (Lytle) Boyd.]

BOYD, James Duncan "J.D." 27 Aug 1926-9 Jul 1983. WWII. [Son of Oscar and Mary Agness (Lytle) Boyd, husband of Ada Linder.]

BOYD, Ada P. 11 Mar 1925-27 Dec 1985. [Ada P. Linder, wife of James Duncan Boyd.]

BOYD, Marshall W. 4 Jan 1915-3 Feb 1974. WWII. [Son of Oscar and Mary Agness (Lytle) Boyd.]

BOYD, Junior. 1944-1944. [Son of Clifton and Edith (Bennett) Boyd.]

BOYD, Mildrew. 1944-1946. [Funeral home record gives birth and death dates as 7 Sep 1944 and 9 Sep 1944. Son of Clifton Alex and Edith (Bennett) Boyd.]

*BOYD, Infant. Born and died 2 Jul 1941, son of Clifton and Edith (Bennett) Boyd.

BOYD, Clifton Alex. 28 Mar 1920-17 Dec 1987. WWII. [Son of Darris Richard and Evelyn Mae (Coppinger) Boyd.]

BOYD, Corbet G. 1923-13 Oct 1993. [Son of Daris and Evelyn (Coppinger) Boyd, husband of Irene Bost.]

BOYD, Clinton Lee. 21 May 1918-28 Jul 1993. [Son of Oscar and Mary Agness (Lytle) Boyd, husband of Selma Taylor.]

HILL BURYING GROUND

Location: 2-3 miles from Hills Creek Cemetery on top of mountain.

*HILL, Isaac. 22 Jul 1748-28 Jul 1925.

*Hill, Dr. Dick. 1804-1868.

*HILL, Lafayette. 1824-1869.

*HILL, Johnston. 1835-1888.

*Hill, Francis. 1804-1834.

*BARNES, Eliza, died 28 Nov 1900, age 25 years.

HOPEWELL CEMETERY

Location: Near the intersection of Old Shelbyville Road and Hwy 55 Bypass.

*SAVAGE, F.B. 8 Mar 1872-20 Feb 1928. Frank Savage.

BURKS, Leon. 28 Jan 1899-1 Apr 1928. Son of Howard and _____ (_____) Burks. Single.

SAVAGE, Will. Died 9 Nov 1953, age 78 years. Husband of Nora Martin, married 28 Oct 1894.

*SAVAGE, Nora Martin. 10 May 1874-7 Sep 1937. Wife of Will Savage.

SAVAGE, Lucion. Died 22 Aug 1932, age 37 years. Son of Will and Nora (Martin) Savage. Single.

*BONNER, Buford Franklin. Died 21 Aug 1975, age 33 years. Son of Harrison and Frances (Martin) Bonner.

*BONNER, Harrison. Died 5 Aug 1941, age 38 years. Husband of Frances Martin.

FAVORS, Betty. 1927-4 Jan 1983. [Daughter of Harrison and Frances (Martin) Bonner, wife of Carl L. Favors.]

*TANNER, Fleming. Died 24 Mar 1938, age 60 years. Son of John L. and Tilda (Tracy) Tanner, single.

TANNER, John L. 20 Jul 1830-30 Mar 1916. 4th TN Inf. [Husband of Tilda Tracy.]

TANNER, Tilda. Died 1912. [Tilda Tracy, wife of John L. Tanner.]

TANNER, Mary. Died 17 Feb 1915, age about 71 years.

HALE, John Alford. 1925-17 Feb 1926.

HALE, Bill. Born and died 9 Aug 1924. [Son of William and Bertha (Neal) Hale.]

MASSEY, Ann. 1796-7 May 1877. [In the J.S. Maddux household in the 1850-1870 Censuses of Warren County.]

GRAHAM, Jaine. [No further information.]

BURKS, Guy. 9 Nov 1888-10 Dec 1889.

*BURKS, Lula. Died 22 Jan 1919, age 25 years, daughter of Howard and Emma (Thomas) Burks.

*DUNCAN, Alfred H. Died 20 Nov 1912, age 85 years. Rev. A.H. Duncan, husband of Elizabeth Bishop, married 6 Jun 1880.

BURKS, Nannie P. 9 May 1845-24 Feb 1870. [Daughter of R.P. and Mary (_____) Burks.]

Hopewell Cemetery, Cont.

PARIS, Ritchard C. 29 Mar 1859-8 Apr 1859.

ROBERSON, Sarah I. 17 Jul 1831-21 Sep 1870. [Sarah Isbell Shockley, wife
        of Joseph H. Roberson.]

ROBERSON, Nathaniel. 3 May 1800-9 Jun 1854. [Husband of Wady Lindsey.]

ROBERSON, Laura Isbell. 16 Sep 1870-18 Sep 1871. [Daughter of Joseph H.
        and Sarah (Shockley) Roberson.]

ROBERSON, Mary Lee. 6 Jan 1869-10 Nov 1872. [Daughter of Joseph H. and
        Sarah I. (Shockley) Roberson.]

ROBERSON, J.H. 26 Jan 1835-16 Jul 1883. [Joseph H., son of Nathaniel and
        Wady (Lindsey) Roberson, husband of Sarah Isbell Shockley,
        married 17 Feb 1859.]

HENDRIX, J.P. 22 Feb 1824-10 Mar 1914. [James P., son of Campbell and
        Elizabeth (_____) Hendrix.]

HENDRIX, Nancy P. 2 Aug 1813-25 Oct 1888. [Daughter of Campbell and
        Elizabeth (_____) Hendrix.]

WOODLEE, S.J. 9 Oct 1820-19 Jun 1907. [Susan Ann, daughter of Campbell
        and Elizabeth (_____) Hendrix, wife of Levi Woodlee, married 1
        Oct 1873.]

HENDRIX, E.F. 6 Dec 1785-2 Apr 1862. [Elizabeth, wife of Campbell
        Hendrix.]

HENDRIX, C. 25 Oct 1785-11 Jun 1872. [Campbell Hendrix, husband of
        Elizabeth _____.]

RIGGS, Watson. 2 Feb 1777-26 Mar 1869. [Husband of Temperance _____.]

RIGGS, Temperance. 16 Apr 1780-30 Mar 1869. [Wife of Watson Riggs.]

HENDRIX, Presley J. 24 Nov 1818-10 Jun 1895. [Son of Campbell and
        Elizabeth (_____) Hendrix, husband of Bethiah Riggs.]

SMITH, Mary. 12 Jan 1808-22 Jan 1863. [Wife of Charles W. Smith.]

SMITH, Alexander S. 11 Nov 1832-29 Nov 1877. [Son of Charles W. and Mary
        (_____) Smith.]

BURKS, Susan. 26 Sep 1819-29 Mar 1883.

*YOUNG, John Marion "Jack", died 3 Apr 1953, age about 78 years. Son of
        Ace and _____ (Richards) Young, husband of Queenie Bynum Bates.

*TANNER, Luther. 16 Apr 1928-21 Apr 1928. Son of Albert and Alta (Jones)
        Tanner.

*STEPP, Jack. Died 25 Jul 1928, age 77 years. Son of Carrol and Eliza
        (_____) Stepp.

*BATEY, Miss _____, died 1 Sep 1928, age about 45 years.

*NUNLEY, Franzina. Died 16 Oct 1928, age about 75 years.

*FULLER, Daisy. Died 24 Oct 1928, age about 18 years.

*SMITH, Jess Phillip. Born and died 14 Jun 1920, son of Phillip and Ruby
        (Spurlock) Smith.

*SMITH, Louise. Died 27 Jul 1919, age 11 years, daughter of Frank and
        Addie (Settles) Smith.

*BILES, James. Died 15 Mar 1920, age 36 years. Son of Nick and Florence
        (Spurlock) Biles.

*SMITH, Hope. Died 13 Dec 1917, age about 50 years.

*HENNESSEE, Andrew. Died 18 Jan 1929, age 80 years.

*LOCKE, Hazel. Died 23 May 1920, age 22 years.

*SAVAGE, William. Died 25 Oct 1924, age 3 months.

*SAVAGE, Sam. Died 26 Oct 1924, age 36 years.

*HENEGAR, Frank. Died Nov 1913, age 65 years.

*McGREGOR, Sallie. Died 11 Mar 1916.

*SMITH, Frank. Died 15 Feb 1925, age 42 years.

*SETTLES, Joe. Died 18 Jun 1916.

*KING, Matt. Died 24 Feb 1917, age 45 years.

*MARTIN, Ernest. Born 6 Jan 1900, died 23 Nov 1938, son of Thomas and
        Lillie (Savage) Martin.

*MORTON, William Clayborn. Born 28 Nov 1917, died 20 Dec 1925. Son of
        L.P. and Betty (Green) Morton.

*BROYLES, Mattie. Born 14 Feb 1855, died 24 Dec 1925. Daughter of C.P.
        and Fannie (Mears) Herriman.

*HALE, Robert. Born 30 Jun 1926, died 31 Jul 1926.

*MARTIN, Thomas. Born 24 Sep 1893, died 5 Jul 1931. Son of Joe and
        Marjorie (Burks) Martin.

*MORFORD, Flora. Died 13 Mar 1930, age 70 years. Daughter of Abe and
        Mary (Blue) Northcutt.

*BROWN, Woodfin. Born 15 Jul 1938, died 22 Dec 1938. Son of _____ and
        Gladys (_____) Brown.

*MARTIN, John. Died 31 Dec 1936, age 89 years.

*ODELL, Vestie. Died 14 Sep 1937, age 23 years.

*KINDLEY, Mary L. Born 17 Jan 1919, died 29 Jan 1919. Daughter of Jack
        and Sallie (Gunn) Kindley.

*SAVAGE, Thedore. Died 15 Jan 1908, age 28 years.

Hopewell Cemetery, Cont.

*HOLLAND, Clara Belle. 20 Sep 1900-10 Mar 1930. Daughter of Alfred Grant and Rosalind (Odineal) Duncan, wife of Arrick Caswell Holland.

*LOCKE, Louis. Died 27 Feb 1928, age 78 years. Son of Harry and Frances (Reed) Locke, husband of _____ Farmer.

*DYE, Margaret Ann. Died 9 May 1908, age 74 years.

*BILES, Florence. Died 1907, age 39 years. Florence Spurlock, wife of Nick Biles, married 21 Dec 1882.

*WASHINGTON, Esau. Died 12 Feb 1913.

*BURKS, Willie. Died 17 Aug 1913, age 9 years.

*WHITE, Esther. Died 18 Apr 1928, age 78 years. Daughter of Alex and Maria (McClain) Smartt.

*BONNER, Harrison, Jr. Born 15 Sep 1928, died 27 Oct 1928. Son of Harrison and Frances (Martin) Bonner.

*BILES, Julia. Died 24 Feb 1912, age 30 years.

*PARKER, Hulon. Died 9 Apr 1912, age 65 years.

*SAVAGE, Ben. Born 17 Aug 1871, died 12 Feb 1919.

*SPURLOCK, John. Died 23 Feb 1919, age 60 years.

*MAXEY, Emma. Died 31 Dec 1926.

*BROWN, Allie. Died 18 May 1927, age 34 years. Daughter of Sam and Allie (Burks) Savage.

*QUALES, Bill. Died 30 Jul 1927, age 70 years.

*SAVAGE, Effa. Died 16 Aug 1918, age 20 years.

*McCORKLE, Jess. Died 4 Apr 1918, age about 76 years.

*SPURLOCK, Mary. Died 24 Mar 1918, age 56 years. Daughter of Dennis and Tamor (Smith) Rust.

*BUCK, Infant. Born 15 Mar 1916, died 6 Apr 1916. Son of Charlie and Laura (Martin) Buck.

*WEBB, Ambrose. Died 25 Nov 1918, age 30 years.

*BURKS, Mable. Died 28 Nov 1918, age 22 years.

*WOODLEE, Charlie. Died 21 Dec 1918, age abour 45 years.

*LOCKE, Lee. Died 14 May 1918.

*SPURLOCK, Robert. Died 21 Dec 1920, age 60 years. Son of Judy Spurlock.

*SAVAGE, William. Died 25 Jun 1915, age 80 years. Husband of Nora Martin, married on 28 Oct 1894.

*SAVAGE, Nora. Born 10 May 1874, died 7 Sep 1937, wife of William

Hopewell Cemetery, Cont.

Savage. Maiden name Nora Martin.

*BURKS, W.H. Died 18 Jul 1915.

*VICKERS, Milton. Died 24 Dec 1920, age 80 years. Husband of Ann Wooten, married on 5 Jan 1876.

*VICKERS, Annie. Died 20 Oct 1915, age 70 years. Wife of Milton Vickers.

*NEAL, Lane. Died 10 Apr 1914, age about 23 years.

*MADEWELL, Dicie. Born 1834, died 7 Jun 1914.

*CALDWELL, Susan. Born 1841, died 2 Jun 1914. Daughter of Jess and Ollie (Murphy) Caldwell.

*SMITH, James. Died 11 Aug 1914, age about 110 years.

*SMITH, Frank. Died 11 Dec 1914, age 50 years.

*BURKS, Richard P. Died 24 Jul 1889, age 73 years. Husband of E.T. Paris, married on 17 Feb 1857.

*TEMPLESS, Mable Lee. Died 21 Mar 1908 age 8 years, 3 months. Charge to J.S. Burroughs.

*MAHER, Carrie. Died 24 Apr 1903, age 48 years. Charge to George Maher.

*TANNER, Infant. Born and died 14 Sep 1904. Infant of Albert Tanner.

*TEMPLESS, Infant. Born and died 10 Oct 1903. Charge to Burroughs Ross Colville Co.

*HENESSEE, Sarah. Died 5 Nov 1903, age 58 years.

*TANNER, Infant. Died 2 Apr 1904, infant of William Tanner.

*WILSON, Charles. Died 25 May 1904, age 1 year, 9 months, and 25 days. Bill to Fate Wilson.

*BYNUM, Infant. Died 17 Jul 1904, age 2 years. Infant of William Bynum.

*SAVAGE, Eva. Died 19 Jan 1905, age 21 years. Bill to James Savage.

*BILES, Nick. Died 6 Jul 1905, age 60 years.

*SPURLOCK, Judy. Died 28 Dec 1905. Bill to John Spurlock.

*BILES, Wilford. Died 17 Sep 1909, age 1 year, 3 months. Bill to Jim Biles.

*BURKS, Henry. Died 20 May 1910, age 14 years. Bill to H.W. Burks.

*SWANGER, Sallie Evelyn. Born 28 Oct 1888, died 17 Sep 1955. Daughter of Ben F.L. and Sarah (Todd) Woods, wife of William A. Swanger.

*DUNCAN, Floyd. Died 28 Jan 1906, age 4 months. Bill to Tom C. Duncan.

*SAVAGE, Rufus. Died 29 Mar 1900, age 1 year, 2 months, 27 days. Bill to J.L. Dempsey.

Hopewell Cemetery, Cont.

*BYARS, Andrew. Died 4 Jul 1900, age 1 year 6 Months. Bill to J.L.
        Dempsey.

*MADDUX, Theodore. Died between 27 Jul and 4 Aug 1900, age 56 years.
        Bill to his father.

*BYARS, Florence. Died 14 Aug 1900, age 6 years. Bill to J.C. Biles.

*SPURLOCK, Maurice. Died 7 Mar 1901, age 20 years. Bill to Bob Spurlock.

*WHITE, John. Died 17 May 1924, age 45 years.

*SPURLOCK, Leara. Died 15 Apr 1924, age 80 years.

*HILL, Julia A. Died 30 Sep 1922, age 21 years. Daughter of John and
        Sindie (Cope) Spurlock.

*HILL, Martha Elizabeth. Born 25 Dec 1921, died 29 Jul 1922. Daughter of
        Obed and Julia A. (Spurlock) Hill.

*RAMSEY, William Hershal. Died 22 Aug 1922, age 23 years. Son of Dave
        Ramsey.

*TIDWELL, Rebecca. Died 22 Jun 1901, age 55 years. Bill to Mose Tidwell.

*TIDWELL, Sudie. Died 26 Jul 1901, age 16 years 5 months and 10 days.
        Bill to Henry Tidwell.

*TIDWELL, Henry. Died 3 Apr 1919, age 75 years. Husband of Bettie Smith.

*TIDWELL, Bettie. Died 19 Sep 1921, age 76 years. Daughter of Dennis and
        Tena (_____) Smith, wife of Henry Tidwell.

*TIDWELL, Alfred. Born 24 Aug 1889, died 8 Jul 1921. Son of Henry and
        Bettie (Smith) Tidwell.

HULETT CEMETERY

Location: Off Old Shelbyville Road past Jacksboro.

UMBARGER, N.J. 14 Feb 1872-4 May 1888. [Jane, daughter of Samuel and
        Rhoda Stincy (Green) Hunter Umbarger.]

STUBBLEFIELD, U.L. 3 Apr 1886-10 Feb 1888. [Daughter of Robert L. and
        Martha (Umbarger) Stubblefield.]

UMGARGER, L.B. 29 Apr 1870-3 Nov 1881. [Louisana "Todie", daughter of
        Samuel and Rhoda S. (Green) Hunter Umbarger.]

UMBARGER, Samuel. 28 Mar 1809-9 Jul 1879. [Son of John and Barbary

Hulett Cemetery, Cont.

(Bickle) Umbarger, husband of Rhoda S. (Green) Hunter, License dated 17 Apr 1868, solemnized 4 Nov 1870.]

UMBARGER, John. 14 May 1827-12 May 1905. [Son of John and Barbara (Bickle) Umbarger, husband of Barthenia _____.]

UMBARGER, Barbary. 4 Nov 1820-5 Jul 1886. [Daughter of John and Barbara (Bickle) Umbarger.]

WISER, Irva V.   17 Mar 1874-4 Apr 1900.
WISER, Anna A.   17 Mar 18_0-13 Mar 1900.
        [Children of William and Lovie (_____) Wiser.]

RAINS, William Presley. 1835-13 Apr 1913. [Son of Larkin and Elizabeth (Curtis) Rains, husband of Ruth Davis.]

RAINS, Rutha. 18 May 1874 only date on stone.

RAINS, N.B. {Dates unreadable}

DAVIS, Martha. 25 May 1868-25 Aug 1951. [Daughter of George W. and Elizabeth (Hawk) Davis. Single.]

DAVIS, Elizabeth. 4 Jun 1817-9 Oct 1915. [Daughter of Tom E. and Nancy (Street) Davis.]

*SHELTON, Prisie. 7 Oct 1863-20 Aug 1919. [Presley Ann, daughter of William Presley and Ruth (Davis) Rains, wife of _____ Shelton.]

*HULLETT, John. No other information.

*UMBARGER, Frances. No other information.

*FREEZE, Martha. Died 25 Aug _____, age 83 years, 3 months, 25 days.

IVY BLUFF CEMETERY

Location: Left of Hwy 70 at crossroads just before Cannon County line.

BOGLE, Carol and Harold. Born and died 14 April 1927. [Twins of Mr. and Mrs. Lonnie Bogle.]

CAMPBELL, C.S. 1 Sep 1851-19 Dec 1935. [Clayton Sevier, son of E.H. and Malinda (Lance) Campbell, husband of Annie E. Webb, married 21 Dec 1870.]

CAMPBELL, Annie E. 20 Jul 1852-26 Oct 1908. [Annie E. Webb, wife of C.S. Campbell.]

CAMPBELL, Eliza Edna. 1880 - 1970. [Eliza Edna Campbell, wife of Robert David Campbell, married 6 Nov 1910.]

CAMPBELL, Robert David. 27 Aug 1890-15 Aug 1945. [Son of Clayton Sevier and Annie (Webb) Campbell, husband of Eliza Edna Campbell.]

SMITHSON, Marion Jr. Born and died 10 Sep 1919. [Son of Marion A. and Effie (_____) Smithson.]

YOUNGBLOOD, Leslie. No dates or other information.

YOUNGBLOOD, Azlene. 9 Jan 1893-15 Jan 1926.

YOUNGBLOOD, J.O. 6 Dec 1879-25 Nov 1940. [James Otis, son of James A. and Martha E. (Prater) Youngblood, husband of Delia Ferrell.]

DAVIS, Deliah. 7 Mar 1870-4 Jan 1947. [Daughter of Wash and _____ (_____) Crook, wife of John Davis.]

YOUNGBLOOD, Carrie. Died 20 Apr 1971. [Carrie Ann, wife of James Robert Youngblood.]

YOUNGBLOOD, Dallas. 25 Jul 1885-8 May 1965. [Son of John Henry and Sarah (West) Youngblood. Single.]

MURPHY, Beecher B. 9 Oct 1899-23 Nov 1973. US Army.

MURPHY, Della W. Campbell. 10 Jun 1884-22 Oct 1964. [Daughter of George and Alice (Wheeler) Campbell, wife of John K. Murphy.]

MURPHY, John K. 8 Jan 1879-13 Apr 1948. [Son of Timothy T. and Caroline (Muncey) Murphy, husband of Della Campbell.]

MURPHY, Dorsie Guy. 4 Feb 1901-26 Feb 1905. [Son of John K. and Della W. (Campbell) Murphy.]

CARDER, Thomas F.M. 7 Jan 1838-9 Aug 1906. [Thomas Frank M., husband of Matilda Campbell.]

174

CARDER, Matilda P. 4 Jul 1849-14 Feb 1939. [Daughter of E.H. and Malinda (Lance) Campbell, wife of Thomas Frank M. Carder.]

MURPHY, Floyd. 30 Jun 1904-16 Mar 1987. [Son of John K. and Della (Campbell) Murphy, husband of Noma B. Powell, married 13 Jul 1930.]

MURPHY, Noma B. 5 Aug 1911-28 Feb 1981. [Daughter of John and Lettie (Grizzell) Powell, wife of Floyd Murphy.]

LOGAN, Violet Mai. 30 Apr 1922-17 Mar 1934.
LOGAN, Howard Earl. 23 Oct 1931-8 Jun 1932.
LOGAN, William Vernon. 1 Dec 1920-15 Jun 1922.

MUNCY, Mollie Hamilton. 21 Sep 1873-21 Sep 1932. [Mollie Frances, daughter of Harvy and Pince (Reed) Hamilton, wife of Hatton Muncy.]

MUNCY, Hatton. 18 Nov 1872-29 Apr 1945. [Son of Elie H. and Mary Catherine (Campbell) Muncy, husband of Mollie Frances Hamilton.]

MUNCY, Mary C. 23 Jun 1847-13 Mar 1919. [Mary Catherine, daughter of Eldridge Henderson and Hannah (Close) Campbell, wife of Elie Hamilton Muncy, married 4 Feb 1872.]

MUNCY, Elie H. 19 Jan 1833-20 Oct 1919. [Elie Hamilton, son of John and Elizabeth (Jarvis) Muncy, husband of Mary Catherine Campbell.]

MUNCY, Annie May. 4 Oct 1881-9 Nov 1909. [Annie May Logan, first wife of Tully Oscar Muncy.]

MUNCY, Catherine O. 19 Jan 1928-26 Jan 1928. [Catherine Olean, daughter of Tully Oscar and his second wife Hattie Ann (Vinson) Muncy.]

MUNCY, Raymond H. 16 May 1906-7 Jun 1929. [Son of Tully Oscar and Annie May (Logan) Muncy, husband of Hettie Youngblood.]

MUNCEY, Benton E. 27 Jan 1925-1 Mar 1941. [Benton Eldridge, son of Raymond H. and Hettie (Youngblood) Muncy.]

*ROJAS, Mrs. Hettie. No dates. Daughter of Joseph and Eva (Earls) Youngblood, wife of 1) Raymond H. Muncey, 2) _____ Hooker, and 3) Diero Rojas.]

HOOKER, James E. 28 Mar 1932-16 Jan 1943. [Son of _____ and Hettie (Youngblood) Hooker.]

DAVIS, John. 15 Jan 1842-15 Mar 1914. [Son of Thomas C. and _____ (_____) Davis, husband of Mary Lou Youngblood, married 30 Nov 1861.]

DAVIS, Mary Lou Youngblood. 3 Aug 1846-16 Dec 1921. [Daughter of Joe and _____ (Lance) Youngblood, wife of John C. Davis.]

TODD, John Rufus. 20 Sep 1921-4 Nov 1921. [Son of William Tom and Velier

(Davis) Todd.]

TODD, Vlier E. 29 Jul 1880-2 Dec 1940. [Velier Etter, daughter of John
        and Mary Lou (Youngblood) Davis, wife of William Tom Todd.]

TODD, William Tom. 31 May 1885-20 Feb 1955. [Son of Allen and Betty (St.
        John) Todd, husband of Vlier Etter Davis.]

R.D.T.   No name, dates or other information.

M.J.T.   No name, dates or other information.

HEGINBOTHAM, Pairsaid.   1848 - 1935. [Matilda Pairsaid, daughter of
        Willford   and   Mary   F.   (Melton)   Lutrell,   wife   of   Joseph
        Heginbotham.]

HEGINBOTHAM, Joseph.   1845 - 1934. [Son of Joe and _____ (_____)
        Higginbotham, husband of Matilda Parasaid Lutrell.]

LANCE, Hattie Lou. 23 Aug 1917-   . [Hattie Lou Todd, wife of
        Jessie Euberne Lance.]

LANCE, Jesse Euberne. 28 Apr 1901-29 Jul 1976. WWI. [Son of Henry
        Balem and America Isabell (Davenport) Lance, husband of Hattie
        Lou Todd, married 1 Oct 1951.]

TITTLE, John Roy. 23 Jul 1928-9 Sep 1931. [Son of Roy Delta and Malissa
        J. (Woods) Tittle.]

TITTLE, Malissie J. Wood. 26 Sep 1891-21 Sep 1955. [Daughter of Ben F.L.
        and Sarah (Todd) Woods, second wife of Roy D. Tittle, married 16
        Nov 1924.]

TITTLE, Roy D. 22 Jun 1883-8 Jun 1957. [Roy Delta, son of Sam and Sarah
        Ann (Lance) Tittle, husband of 1) Hassie Rigsby, 2) Malissie J.
        Woods, and 3) Susie Ferrell.]

TITTLE, Hassie Rigsby. 27 Mar 1887-3 Mar 1924. [First wife of Roy Delta
        Tittle.]

RIGSBY, Lucy Ann. 1852 - 8 Sep 1920. [Daughter of Cleve and _____
        (_____) Higdon, wife of John Rigsby.]

RIGSBY, _____ {Broken stone, name missing}. 29 Feb 1881-15 Aug 1899.

VINSON, Infant.   Born and died 12 Jan 1898.
VINSON, Shely.   15 Feb 1901-24 Nov 1904.
VINSON, Colonel, Jr. Born and died 1909.
VINSON, Leburn.   23 Jun 1911-23 Sep 1913.
        Children of Colonel C. and Hettie (_____) Vinson.

VINSON, Colonel C. Jul 1870-18 Oct 1932. [Husband of Hettie _____.]

VINSON, Hettie. 3 Apr 1877-2 Sep 1969. [Wife of Colonel C. Vinson.]

*VINSON, John Woodrow. 5 Aug 1916-20 Jun 1920. [Son of Ike and Letha (Cummings) Vinson.]

VINSON, Jodie L. 9 Nov 1906-4 Oct 1980. [Jodie Laymon, son of Colonel C. and Hettie (_____) Vinson, husband of Viola Cox.]

FERGUSON, Willard J. 19 Nov 1913-7 May 1985. [Husband of Ethel Vinson.]

FERGUSON, Ethel V. 9 Jun 1918-   . [Wife of Willard J. Ferguson.]

SMITH, Lucille Vinson. 28 Jan 1914-6 Jan 1993.

JENNINGS, Burley W. 28 Jan 1915-30 Jan 1979. [Husband of Macon Nichols Jennings, married 28 Nov 1938.]

JENNINGS, Macon N. 6 Dec 1921-   . [Wife of Burley W. Jennings.]

JENNINGS, Asilean Davis. 28 Jan 1890-28 Nov 1973. [Alice Asilean Davis, wife of Aubrey F. Jennings.]

JENNINGS, Aubrey F. 19 Jan 1891-4 May 1965. [Aubrey Francis, son of J.W. and Sylvia Ann (Barrett) Jennings, husband of Asilean Davis.]

JENNINGS, Vurner L. 31 Mar 1911-2 Jan 1915. [Daughter of Aubrey F. and Alice Asilean (Davis) Jennings.]

McNUTT, Annie C. Jennings. 4 Aug 1922-12 Mar 1972. [Daughter of Aubrey F. and Alice Asilean (Davis) Jennings, wife of _____ McNutt.]

LANCE, Virginia Ann Tenpenny. 21 Feb 1868-30 Dec 1906. [Wife of T.L. Lance.]

LANCE, T.L. 11 Apr 1867-17 Mar 1930. [Husband of Virginia Ann Tenpenny.]

PRATER, Lesley Hoover. 30 Dec 1909-7 Nov 1921. [Son of B.H. and Millie (Etter) Prater.]

PRATER, Millie Etter. 7 Nov 1887-20 Mar 1913. [Wife of B.H. Prater.]

TUCKER, Emma Novella. 26 Dec 1872-12 Nov 1934.

DAVIS, E.H. 20 Jun 1871-24 Dec 1898. [Eldridge Henderson Davis, husband of Lou Ella Campbell.]

DAVIS, Ella. 18 Apr 1877-24 Sep 1947. [Lou Ella, daughter of John and Mary (Taylor) Campbell, wife of Eldridge Henderson Davis.]

DAVIS, Leona. 21 Aug 1890-10 Dec 1932. [Daughter of R.M. and Dora (Patton) Mitchell, wife of Shelah H. Davis.]

DAVIS, Shelah H. 3 Sep 1897-3 Apr 1984. [Son of Eldridge H. and Lou Ella (Campbell) Davis, husband of Leona Mitchell.]

BARRETT, Hettie M. 1890 - 1977. [Wife of Ed Clark Barrett.]

BARRETT, Ed Clark. 1890 - 1965. [Husband of Hettie M. _____.]

BARRETT, Ray. 10 Apr 1928-15 Aug 1929. [Son of Ed Clark and Hettie M.
        (_____) Barrett.]

HIGGINS, Georgia Lee. 6 Aug 1906-23 Jun 1979. [Georgia Lee Melton, wife
        of Robert France Higgins.]

HIGGINS, Robert France. 21 Mar 1903-2 Nov 1967. [Son of Murf and Susan
        Ella (Milligan) Higgins, husband of Georgia Lee Melton.]

MATHIS, Ellis Homer. 12 Jan 1907-3 Oct 1967. [Son of W.B. and Nova
        (Barrett) Mathis, husband of Lela Frances Jennings.]

MATHIS, Lela Jennings. 22 May 1912-11 Nov 1984. [Lela Frances, daughter
        of Aubrey F. and Asilean (Davis) Jennings, husband of Ellis Homer
        Mathis.]

DAVIS, Betty B. Died 19 Oct 1974, aged 82 years, 8 months, and 20 days.
        [Daughter of James Sidney and Mary (Bray) Blanton, wife of Willie
        Ernest Davis.]

DAVIS, Willie Earnest. 4 Jan 1888-17 Mar 1940. [Son of Joe Ridley and
        Mary Frances (Whitlock) Davis, husband of Betty Blanton.]

GIBSON, Jimmie Brown. 29 Apr 1936-6 May 1936. [Son of John B. and Siby
        Lee (Davis) Gibson.]

HETRICK, Sylvia Davis. 19 Feb 1909-21 Sep 1983.

MAYO, Louisa Jane. 9 Oct 1903-23 Oct 1958. [Daughter of Joe Ridley and
        Mary Frances (Whitlock) Davis, wife of Ernest Mayo.]

DAVIS, J.R. 9 Jul 1863-29 Jan 1923. [Joe Ridley, son of John and Mary
        (Youngblood) Davis, husband of Mary Frances Whitlock, married 31
        Jan 1886.]

DAVIS, Mary Frances. 15 May 1866-10 Apr 1913. [Daughter of James and
        Sarah (_____) Whitlock, wife of Joe Ridley Davis.]

DAVIS, James Claudie. 9 Dec 1893-30 Apr 1900.
DAVIS, Joseph   27 Jul 1892-25 Aug 1892.
    Sons of Joe Ridley and Mary Frances (Whitlock) Davis

YOUNGBLOOD, Claudia. 26 Jul 1909-20 Dec 1929 . [Daughter of James A. and
        Martha E. (Prater) Youngblood.]

YOUNGBLOOD, Roy. 14 Jan 1894-22 Dec 1917, "Died at Camp Gordan in US
        Army." [Son of James A. and Martha E. (Prater) Youngblood.]

YOUNGBLOOD, Ottey Eldg. 21 Mar 1891- __ Jul ____ {Broken rock}. [Son of
        James A. and Martha E. (Prater) Youngblood.]

YOUNGBLOOD, J.A. 15 Oct 1850-6 Sep 1926. [James A. Youngblood, husband
        of Martha E. Prater, married 21 Aug 1870.]

Ivy Bluff Cemetery, Cont.

YOUNGBLOOD, Martha E. 13 Sep 1854-14 Jul 1918. [Martha E. Prater, wife
of James A. Youngblood.]

CAMPBELL, Annie L. 24 Dec 1900-4 Jan 1903. [Daughter of Charlie W. and
Maggie (Boles) Campbell.]

CAMPBELL, Charlie W. 2 Apr 1875-25 Feb 1934. [Son of Clayton Sevier and
Annie E. (Webb) Campbell, husband of Maggie Boles.]

CAMPBELL, Maggie Boles. 29 Jun 1880-15 Jul 1967. [Daughter of Henry and
Alice (Brown) Boles, Wife of 1) Charlie W. Campbell and 2) E.D.
Golden.]

TAYLOR, Roberta C. 6 Nov 1906-   . [Daughter of Charlie W. and
Maggie (Boles) Campbell, wife of Almer W. Taylor.]

TAYLOR, Almer W. 12 May 1907-   . [Husband of Roberta Campbell.]

LANCE, Infant. Born and died 19 Feb 1919. [Son of Mr. and Mrs. Albert
Lance.]

LANCE, Louise J. 1918-   . [Louise Jones, wife of Flavil Kermit
Lance.]

LANCE, Flavil K. 1909 - 1981. [Flavil Kermit, son of James Albert and
Betty Ann (Carr) Lance, husband of Louise Jones.]

TURNER, Toni C. Lance. 19 Jan 1943-30 Apr 1980. [Toni Carolyn, daughter
of Flavil K. and Louise (Jones) Lance, wife of Jesse F. Turner.]

TURNER, Jesse F. 17 Mar 1940-   . [Husband of Toni Carolyn Lance,
married 19 Jun 1960.]

LANCE, James A. 15 May 1842-18 Nov 1923. [Son of Henry and Eliza (Bates)
Lance, husband of Martha Jane Bates, married 18 Dec 1867.]

LANCE, Martha J. Bates. 29 Sep 1841-6 May 1926. [Martha Jane Bates,
wife of James A. Lance.]

LANCE, Ida. 17 Oct 1882-16 Aug 1883. [Daughter of James A and Martha
Jane (Bates) Lance.]

DAVENPORT, Lois Eron. 16 Nov 1901-30 Nov 1902. [Daughter of Maj. James
Simpson and Martha (Lance) Davenport.]

DUGGIN, Walter Emerson. 14 Jan 1918-27 Sep 1923. [Son of Fernando
Cortez, Sr. and Alice Matilda (Lance) Duggin.]

YOUNGBLOOD, Ruby Ventrice.   Age 5.
YOUNGBLOOD, Infant Son.   Born and died 1895.
   Children of Samuel B. and Tennie (Tucker) Youngblood.

POWELL, Magnolia. 1 Nov 1895-12 Apr 1989. [Daughter of Cain and Kizzie
(Green) Golden, wife of Charlie Powell.]

Ivy Bluff Cemetery, Cont.

POWELL, Charles T. 8 Jun 1892-20 Jun 1983. [Husband of Magnolia Golden.]

POWELL, Inez. 1923 - 1924. [Daughter of John F. and Essie (Lassater) Powell.]

POWELL, Essie. 22 Feb 1892-1 Dec 1942. [Daughter of Joe and _____ (_____) Lassater, wife of John F. Powell.]

POWELL, John F. 30 Nov 1883-22 Oct 1927. [Husband of Essie Lassater.]

MATHIS, Nora E. Barrett. 15 Jul 1886-15 Feb 1965. [Daughter of W.H. and Martha Ann (Gannon) Barrett, wife of Will B. Mathis.]

MATHIS, Will B. 6 Oct 1882-14 Jul 1973. [Husband of Nora Barrett.]

MATHIS, Bob C. 17 Mar 1921-4 Jul 1980. [Son of Will B. and Nora E. (Barrett) Mathis, husband of Grace Rains, married 14 Jun 1941.]

MATHIS, Grace Rains. 11 May 1920-   . [Wife of Bob C. Mathis.]

MATHIS, Mildred B. 20 Apr 1920-   . [Mildred Bailey, wife of Fred G. Mathis.]

MATHIS, Fred G. 30 Nov 1916-11 Sep 1977. [Fred Gray, son of Will B. and Nora (Barrett) Mathis, husband of Mildred Bailey, married 8 Sep 1936.]

MATHIS, Edd Clayton. 5 Mar 1909-22 Apr 1985. [Son of Will B. and Nora E. (Barrett) Mathis, husband of Tamar Agnes Certain.]

MATHIS, Tamar Agnes. 14 Sep 1918-30 Oct 1991. [Daughter of Green Fletcher and _____ (_____) Certain, wife of Ed Clayton Mathis.]

GAITHER, Ralph W. 1925 - 1928. [Son of Arthur and _____ (_____) Gaiter.]

DURHAM, William R. 5 Mar 1903-12 Aug 1967. [Son of Aaron and Lizzie (Driver) Durham, husband of Kittie Lorena Powell.]

DURHAM, Kittie L. 27 Aug 1899-30 Nov 1970. [Kittie Lorena, daughter of Thomas and Mary (Murphy) Powell, wife of William R. Durham.]

YOUNGBLOOD, Charley Tullie. 6 Apr 1895-12 Mar 1896. [Son of M.A. and W.J. (_____) Youngblood.]

MAYO, Paul. 30 Oct 1913-25 Jan 1983. WWII. [Husband of Grace Marie Ritchey.]

MAYO, Grace Ritchey. 4 Oct 1916-   . [Grace Marie Ritchey, wife of Paul Mayo.]

MAYO, H.L. 27 Mar 1866-6 Oct 1921. [Herc. Lee, son of Benjamin Franklin and Stacy (Melton) Mayo, husband of Zora Higgins.]

MAYO, Zora Higgins. 7 Jun 1876-6 Jun 1961. [Wife of Herc. Lee Mayo.]

LANCE, Margaret Youngblood. 20 Mar 1812-18 Jan 1888. [Second wife of James Jasper Lance.]

LANCE, James Jasper. 25 Oct 1791-16 Feb 1879. [Husband of 1) Mary Prater and 2) Margaret Youngblood.]

LANCE, Mary Prather. 10 Mar 1794-19 Mar 1831.

LANCE, Mary Gertrude. 24 Nov 1877-20 Aug 1906. [Daughter of James J. and Bettie V. (Ware) Lance.]

LANCE, James J. 11 Dec 1834-9 Jan 1920. [Son of James and Margaret (Youngblood) Lance, husband of Elizabeth V. "Bettie" Ware, married 8 May 1870.]

LANCE, Betty V. 14 Mar 1846-12 Apr 1907. [Elizabeth V. Ware, wife of James J. Lance.]

LANCE, Ellenalida. 8 Jan 1873-12 Apr 1917. [Daughter of James J. and Betty V. (Ware) Lance.]

TAYLOR, Margaret Novella. 2 Apr 1892-28 Jul 1967. [Daughter of Monroe and America Levina (Travis) Duke, wife of Vester E. Taylor.]

TAYLOR, Vester E. 15 Aug 1892-28 May 1975. WWI. [Husband of Margaret Novella Duke.]

DANIEL, Nancy. 4 May 1840-22 Jun 1884. [Nancy A. Lance, wife of John C. Daniel, married 29 Nov 1864.]

YOUNGBLOOD, Charlie Newton. 12 Dec 1905-3 Nov 1907.
YOUNGBLOOD, Myrtle Ruth. 26 Jan 1916-22 Jun 1916.
  Children of Joseph F. and Daisy (Gamble) Youngblood.

YOUNGBLOOD, Daisy L. 15 Oct 1880-18 Jun 1949. [Daisy L. Gamble, wife of Joseph F. Youngblood.]

YOUNGBLOOD, Joseph F. 7 Jan 1878-3 Jan 1957. [Husband of Daisy Gamble.]

TAYLOR, Adell. 10 Jun 1897-7 Feb 1922.

TAYLOR, Joseph L. 27 Feb 1895-16 Nov 1939. [Son of James A. and Minnie B. (Spradley) Taylor, husband of Maud Foster.]

TAYLOR, Minnie. 9 Jan 1871-9 Jun 1947. [Minnie Belle, daughter of William Bryant and Annie (Keith) Spradley, wife of James A. Taylor.]

TAYLOR, J.A. 23 Sep 1862-20 Apr 1934. [James A. Taylor, husband of Minnie Belle Spradley.]

SMITH, Paul E. 9 Dec 1931-24 Jan 1932. [Paul Edward, son of P.T. and Beula Mai (Scott) Smith.]

TAYLOR, Steven K. 26 Nov 1960-13 Oct 1974. [Son of Willie V. and

Ivy Bluff Cemetery, Cont.

        Cornelia (Chisam) Taylor.]

TAYLOR, Cornelia Chisam. 13 Nov 1918-   . [Wife of Willie V.
        Taylor.]

TAYLOR, Willie V. 6 Jul 1918-4 Jan 1991. [Husband of Cornelia Chisam.]

TAYLOR, Maude F. 26 Jul 1891-11 Dec 1977. [Maude Foster, wife of Joseph
        L. Taylor.]

GANN, Lula Scott. 5 Mar 1916-10 Jan 1993. [Daughter of Jim M. and Eva
        Mae (Young) Gann.]

STILES, Johnnie Sue. 11 Dec 1938 only date on stone. "Daughter".
        [Daughter of _____ and Pauline (_____) Stiles.]

STILES, Pauline. 11 Jun 1918 only date on stone. "Mother".

SCOTT, Chester Arthur. 20 Mar 1921-29 Oct 1954. WWII.

YOUNG, Mandy B. 10 Aug 1850-3 Dec 1934. [Amanda Bogle, wife of E.M.
        Young, married 14 Dec 1876 in Cannon County, TN.]

YOUNG, Alex. 28 Feb 1876-1 May 1934. [S.A., son of E.M. and Mandy
        (Bogle) Young, single.]

CAMPBELL, Herbert L. 2 Jul 1890-30 Jan 1970. [Son of John and Mary
        Elizabeth (Taylor) Campbell, husband of Gladys Campbell.]

CAMPBELL, Gladys L. 9 Jan 1893-30 Sep 1971. [Daughter of George and Mary
        (Warren) Campbell, wife of Herbert L. Campbell.]

CAMPBELL, Callie J. 5 Jul 1882-10 Jan 1950. [Callie Joanna, daughter of
        John and Mary Elizabeth (Taylor) Campbell, single.]

CAMPBELL, Beecher. 8 Apr 1888-9 Oct 1957. [Taylor Beecher, son of John
        and Mary Elizabeth (Taylor) Campbell, husband of 1) Luphema
        Tenpenny and 2) Martha Mathis Gann.]

CAMPBELL, Luphema. 8 Dec 1889-26 Apr 1943. [Daughter of Bob and Malissie
        (Woods) Tenpenny, first wife of Beecher Campbell.]

CAMPBELL, Alta Mae. 11 Jun 1908-18 Dec 1925. [Daughter of Beecher and
        Luphema (Tenpenny) Campbell, single.]

CAMPBELL, J.L. 1855 - 1920. [John L. Campbell, husband of Mary E.
        Taylor, married 19 Jan 1876.]

CAMPBELL, Mary. 1850 - 1925. [Mary Elizabeth Taylor, wife of John L.
        Campbell.]

J.C.C. No other data.

YOUNGBLOOD, Caldonia Ann. 1 Oct 1848-3 Feb 1878. [Caldonia Ann Taylor,
        wife of Benjamin F. Youngblood, married 19 Jan 1876.]

YOUNGBLOOD, Benj. F. 14 Sep 1834-8 Mar 1909. [Benjamin F., son of Allen
        and Verlinne (_____) Youngblood, husband of Caldonia Ann Taylor.]

LANCE, Callie T. 13 Feb 1869-13 Nov 1874. [Daughter of Joseph N. and
        Ellen V. (Taylor) Lance.]

LANCE, J. N. 6 Sep 1838-24 May 1917. {Funeral home record has date of
        death as 1914}. [Joseph N., son of James and Margaret
        (Youngblood) Lance, husband of Ellen V. Taylor, married 2 Sep
        1868.]

LANCE, Ellen V. 13 Feb 1843-27 Mar 1916. [Daughter of Anderson and Nancy
        (_____) Taylor, wife of Joseph N. Lance.]

TAYLOR, Margarett E. 15 Oct 1865-12 Mar 1893. [Daughter of Creed and
        Sarah (_____) Taylor.]

FLYNN, Jane. 28 Feb 1846-17 Jan 1923. [Malinda Jane, daughter of Hugh
        French and Lucinda (_____) Hopkins, wife of Dennes Flynn.]

FLYNN, Dennes. 22 Jun 1812-21 Jun 1896. [Husband of Melinda Jane
        Hopkins, married 18 Sep 1862.]

BOGLE, Jennie Ruth. 2 May 1949-10 May 1949. [Daughter of Floyd and
        Dorothy (McGee) Bogle.]

PRATER, Debra Faye. Born and died 23 Jan 1964. [Daughter of Wilmer
        Curtis and Deletta Faye (Tate) Prater.]

PRATER, Flora D. 2 Apr 1920-   . [Flora Dale, wife of Medford
        Prater.]

PRATER, Medford. 23 Jun 1908-29 Jan 1986. [Son of James Edward and Ibbie
        Jane (Youngblood) Prater, husband of Flora Dale, married 11 Dec
        1937.]

PRATER, Allen Sr. 16 Jan 1919-1 Apr 1993. [Son of James Edward and Ibie
        Jane (Youngblood) Prater, husband of Beatrice _____, married
        26 Apr 1942.]

PRATER, Beatrice. 24 Jul 1927-   . [Wife of Allen Prater.]

HALE, John M. 24 Jan 1927-17 Dec 1985. WWII.

THOMPSON, Ruben. Died 20 Sep 1959, age 87 years, 3 months, 8 days.
        [Husband of Maggie Arnetta Bogle.]

THOMPSON, Maggie Arnetta. 19 Dec 1880-22 Feb 1945. [Daughter of Neal and
        Mary (King) Bogle, wife of Ruben Thompson.]

THOMPSON, Willene. Born and died 18 Jul 1937. [Daughter of Willie Ruben
        and Georgia Azzeline (Morgan) Thompson.]

THOMPSON, Willie Reuben. 10 Dec 1917-4 Feb 1948. [Son of Ruben and
        Maggie Arnetta (Bogle) Thompson, husband of Georgia Azzeline

Morgan.]

HOLLANDSWORTH, Ezekiel J. 4 Nov 1884-2 Dec 1965. [Ezekiel Josire, son of
        John and Elizabeth (Watson) Hollandsworth, husband of Cleo B.
        Johnson.]

HOLLANDSWORTH, Cleo B. 1 Aug 1894-28 Sep 1963. [Daughter of Harrison and
        Julia (Pickett) Johnson, wife of Ezekiel Josire Hollandsworth.]

HOLLANDSWORTH, Leatha E. 1919 - 1940. [Leatha Elizabeth, daughter of
        Ezekiel J. and Cleo (Johnson) Hollandsworth, wife of Roman E.
        Walker.]

HOLLANDSWORTH, Frank B. Born and died 1924. [Son of Ezekiel Josire and
        Cleo B. (Johnson) Hollandsworth.]

STACY, Maria. 7 Dec 1854-13 Feb 1891. [Daughter of L.D. and Rosana
        (Bynum) Stacy. Single.]

STACY, Rosanah. 31 Dec 1828-30 May 1899. [Rosanah Bynum, wife of L.D.
        Stacy.]

STACY, L.D. 21 Feb 1828-14 Jun 1900. [Husband of Rosanah Bynum, married
        25 Nov 1848.]

TAYLOR, Mary E. Bezley. 31 Dec 1827-21 Oct 1901. [Wife of Creed
        Taylor.]

TAYLOR, Creed. 9 Feb 1833-12 Aug 1908. [Husband of Mary E. Bezley.]

OWEN, Mary J. 22 May 1900-1 Jan 1966. [Daughter of Wm. Frazier and
        Mary Dee (Woods) Todd, wife of John Balaam Owen.]

OWEN, Johnnie B. 20 Sep 1899-11 Jul 1971. [John Balaam, son of Jeremiah
        Jackson and Mary Jane (Lance) Owen, husband of Mary J. Todd.]

JONES, Mary Lou Campbell-Plourd. 27 Jan 1918-   . [Mary Lou
        Campbell, wife of 1) _____ Plourd and 2) David Franklin Jones.]

JONES, David Franklin. 20 Nov 1914-8 Sep 1968. [Husband of Mary Lou
        (Campbell) Plourd.]

JONES, Johnnie Mildred. 15 May 1913-   . [Wife of James Herbert
        Jones.]

JONES, James Herbert. 25 Dec 1910-14 Sep 1975. [Husband of Johnnie
        Mildred _____.]

MEADOWS, Evelyn Lois. 3 Aug 1925-30 Jul 1981. [Evelyn Jones, wife of
        _____ Meadows.]

REED, Frank Allen. 3 Dec 1902-12 Oct 1976.

OWEN, Dorsey Everett. 5 Sep 1925-21 Jun 1990. WWII. [Son of Johnny and
        Mary (Todd) Owen.]

SMITHSON, Florence. 10 Sep 1894-12 Oct 1898.

SMITHSON, Dellah. 2 May 1882-3 Jul 1892. [Daughter of T.G. and S.C. Smithson.]

SMITHSON, Isaac Fletcher. No dates.

PRESTON, Mae Bell. 6 May 1876-14 Aug 1945.

WILSON, A.F. 10 Oct 1843-3 Jan 1891.

SMITHSON, Eupha J. Died 1893. [Eupha Jennie Smith, wife of N.B. Smithson, married 23 Jan 1894.]

SMITHSON, D.C. 1854 - 1900. [Husband of Docia _____.]

SMITHSON, Docia. 1859 - 1928. [Wife of D.C. Smithson.]

SMITHSON, Mammie. No dates or other information.
SMITHSON, Edger. No dates or other information.
SMITHSON, Delter. No dates or other information.

MORGAN, Gladys Thompson. 10 Feb 1923-   . [Wife of Ernest Elmore Morgan.]

MORGAN, Ernest Elmore. 7 Jan 1919-   . [Husband of Gladys Thompson, married 26 Aug 1939.]

SMITHSON, Bessie May. 23 May 1920-23 Jun 1920.
SMITHSON, R.A.   4 Jul 1921-13 Aug 1921.
SMITHSON, J.B.   6 Oct 1923-26 Nov 1923.
    Children of J.L. and Media (_____) Smithson.

*SMITHSON, David Reese. 6 Oct 1923-26 Nov 1923. Son of Jess and _____ (Morgan) Smithson.

PRATER, Gearldean. 3 Aug 1940-   . [Wife of Arthur Huston Prater.]

PRATER, Arthur Huston. 16 Sep 1937-1 Dec 1990. [Son of Quince and Pearl (Youngblood) Prater, husband of Gearldean _____.]

PRATER, Quince. 5 Sep 1902-30 Mar 1986. [Son of Porter and Ona (Logan) Prater, husband of Pearl Youngblood.]

MYERS, Clementine. 31 Jul 1936-   . [Clementine Hobbs, wife of Millard Myers.]

MYERS, Millard. 27 Dec 1935-7 May 1993. [Son of Henry and Julia (Coppinger) Myers, husband of Clementine Hobbs.]

MYERS, Millard Wayne. 21 Jul 1970-   . [Son of Millard and Clementine (Hobbs) Myers.]

MORGAN, Infant Daughter. 22 Jun 1940-29 Jun 1940. [Mary Sandra, daughter of Ernest and Gladys (Thompson) Morgan.]

THOMPSON, John Calvin. 21 Jan 1896-24 Feb 1966. WWI. [Husband of Lillie Mae Bost.]

THOMPSON, Lillie Abel. 27 Apr 1899-4 Apr 1971. [Lillie Mae, daughter of Jonathan and Bellzora (_____) Bost, wife of John Calvin Thompson.]

NORTHCUTT, William A. 2 Sep 1855-2 Mar 1936. [Husband of Caroline Todd, married 25 Dec 1873 in Cannon County, TN.]

NORTHCUTT, Caroline. 3 Jun 1860-21 Nov 1905. [Caroline Todd, wife of William A. Northcutt.]

NORTHCUTT, Callie. Died 25 Nov 1905, age 45 years, 19 days.

NORTHCUTT, Adaline. Died 13 Jan _____, age 19 years.

NORTHCUTT, Tilda. 24 Sep 1902-25 May 1904. [Matilda Northcutt.]

NORTHCUTT, William N. 10 May 1900-5 Jul 1900. [Son of J.A. and Nannie (_____) Northcutt.]

BENNETT, Bill. 1861-27 May 1911. [Husband of Ida Rigsby.]

BENNETT, John K. 22 Jun 1908-2 Mar 1914. [Son of Bill and Ida (Rigsby) Bennett.]

HIGDON, James A. 25 Apr 1902-4 Jul 1903.

*VAUGHT, Alice, born 5 Apr 1852, died 2 May 1930, daughter of Calvin and Frances (Robinson) Higdon.

*COOPER, Nancy Jane, died 27 Feb 1923, age 29 years, 9 days, daughter of John M. and Martha Ann (Duke) Parker.

*OWEN, John William, born 20 Jun 1921, died 28 Feb 1941, son of John Balaam and Mary Jane (Todd) Owen. Single.

*PRATER, Martha Linda, born 12 Jun 1894, died 21 feb 1945, daughter of Alley and Bettie (St. John) Todd, wife of J. Newton Prater.

*FERRELL, Eliza, born 20 Jun 1868, died 12 Aug 1944, daughter of John and Mary (Youngblood) Davis, wife of John Ferrell.

*LANCE, Betty Ann, born 8 Sep 1880, died 22 Apr 1954, daughter of John S. and Margaret (Bennett) Carr, wife of James Albert Lance.

*RIGSBY, William, born 17 Aug 1876, died 27 Feb 1950, son of John K. and Lucy (Higdon) Rigsby, husband of Mattie Youngblood.

*RIGSBY, Mattie, born 17 Aug 1877, died 30 Mar 1950, daughter of John Henry and Sarah (West) Youngblood.

*BYARS, Walter Evans, born 8 Sep 1915, died 18 Dec 1963, son of Harold H.

and Hassie Lee (Glenn) Byars, husband of Lucille Swanger.

*HAMILTON, Margaret, died 29 Mar 1909, age 80 years.

*HOLLANDSWORTH, Infant, born 8 May 1924, died 18 Jul 1924, child of
    Ezekiel and Cleo (Johnson) Hollandsworth.

*PIRTLE, Hassie, born 27 Mar 1887, died 3 Mar 1924, daughter of John K.
    and Lucy (Higdon) Rigsby.

*BREWER, Laura Jane, born 16 Jan 1846, died 23 Dec 1923, daughter of
    George and Fannie (Lutrell) Lance.

*CARRICK, Lonnie, died 15 Aug 1914, age 25 years, son of Jim and Nancy
    (King) Carrick.

*PRATER, Ethel, born 11 Aug 1924, died 13 Mar 1925, daughter of Jim and
    Ibby (Youngblood) Prater.

MEARS, Lucille M. Dennis. 15 May 1925-13 Mar 1989. [Daughter of Addie
    and Emmie (_____) Dennis, wife of Carmon R. Mears, married 6 Dec
    1964.]

MEARS, Carmon R. 8 Mar 1924-   . [Husband of Lucille M. Dennis.]

HOLLANDSWORTH, Robert C. 16 Jan 1912-1 Oct 1991. [Son of E.J. and Cleo
    (Johnson) Hollandsworth.]

ARMSTRONG, Byron E. 24 Jul 1897-16 Apr 1984.

JACKSBORO/TROUSDALE CEMETERY

Location: Next to Trousdale Church of Christ, Jacksboro Community

MITCHELL, Hoyet Lee. 13 Dec 1908-17 Mar 1909.

SMOOT, Thomas C.   27 Oct 1898-19 Dec 1988.   [Son of Claude and Mary
        (Mitchell) Smoot, husband of 1) Rree Lassiter and 2) Coreba
        (Thomas) Huett.]

SMOOT, Rree.   19 Apr 1903-5 Jul 1962.   [Daughter of James Luke and
        Palemna (Allmon) Lassiter, wife of Thomas C. Smoot.]

GILLEY, J.W.   25 Apr 1866-8 Aug 1912.   [James W. Gilley, husband of
        Sarah E. Brown.]

GILLEY, Sarah E.   10 Nov 1865-7 Jun 1960.   [Daughter of A.J. and Nancy
        (Duke) Brown, wife of James W. Gilley.]

BREWER, J.H.   4 Oct 1871-26 Jun 1929.   [Jesse Hill, son of Joel and
        Mary Elizabeth (Spangler) Brewer, husband of Anna Crawley,
        married 12 Aug 1892.]

BREWER, Anna.   18 Oct 1872-28 Nov 1942.   [Sally Anna, daughter of George
        W. and Lou (Jones) Crawley, wife of Jesse Hill Brewer.]

ELAM, Marcella. 30 Aug 1924-3 Nov 1924.   [Daughter of George and Cora
        (Brewer) Elam.]

UNDERHILL, J.H.   2 Jan 1874-21 Jan 1947.   [James Holiday, son of George
        W. and Malissa (Rigsby) Underhill, husband of Paralee Bailey.]

UNDERHILL, Parilee.   4 Aug 1877-4 Oct 1952. [Daughter of William and
        Martha E. (Melton) Bailey, wife of James Holiday Underhill.]

AKERS, William "Bill".   9 Dec 1852-20 Jun 1906.   [William M., son of
        William Riley and _____ (McKnight) Akers, husband of Delphine
        Rains, married 31 Dec 1876.]

AKERS, Delphine Rains.   20 Jun 1849-20 Jun 1906.   [Daughter of Larkin
        and Elizabeth (Curtis) Rains, wife of William M. Akers.]

AKERS, Colonel.   16 Jul 1882-20 Jun 1906.   [Son of William M. and
        Delphine (Rains) Akers.]

AKERS, William.   13 Nov 1893-20 Jun 1906.   [Son of William M. and Delphine
        (Rains) Akers.]

WILSON, Roy J., Jr.   14 Mar 1926-22 Aug 1985.   WWII. [Roy Jackson, Jr.,
        son of Roy Jackson, Sr. and Eula Pearl (Shirley) Wilson, husband
        of Mary Elizabeth "Lizzie" Youngblood, married 13 May 1944.]

WILSON, Mary E.   11 May 1928-   . [Daughter of Robert and Sammie
        (Tittle) Youngblood, wife of Roy Jackson Wilson, Jr.]

WILSON, Connie Sue.   23 Jun 1954- 26 Jun 1954. [Daughter of Roy Jackson,
        Jr. and Mary Elizabeth (Youngblood) Wilson.]

WILSON, Roy J. 5 Aug 1902-8 Dec 1980. [Roy Jackson, Sr., son of Huey
        Jackson and Mary Elizabeth (Pennington) Wilson, husband of Eula

Pearl Shirley, married 23 Mar 1924.]

WILSON, Eula Pearl. 1 Dec 1906-16 Sep 1987. [Daughter of Joe and Harriett (Gannon) Shirley, wife of Roy Jackson Wilson.]

RAINS, E.L. 20 Dec 1923-   . [Son of General Crit and Annie (Martin) Rains, husband of Ora Higgins.]

RAINS, Willie T. 18 Feb 1922-3 Jun 1978. [Willie Thurman, son of General Critt and Annie (Martin) Rains, husband of Nellie Jo Whitman, married 13 Mar 1954.]

RAINS, Nellie Jo. 6 Dec 1930-   . [Nellie Jo Whitman, wife of Willie Thurman Rains.]

RAINS, Tommie McGuire. 19 Dec 1916-26 Jun 1990. [Son of General Crit and Mary Ann (Martin) Rains.]

RAINS, Enoch J. 4 Oct 1878-28 Oct 1954. [Son of R.K. and Susan (Akers) Rains. Single.]

BREWER, Russell. 28 Jan 1785-1 Sep 1858. [Husband of Nancy B. Tolliver.]

BREWER, Nancy. 9 Feb 1785-27 Feb 1969. [Nancy B. Tolliver, wife of Russell Brewer.]

BREWER, Icybely. 26 Jan 1812-27 Oct 1875. [Wife of John Brewer.]

BREWER, John. 13 Jun 1814-6 Jun 1894. [Son of Russell and Nancy B. (Tolliver) Brewer, husband of Icybely _____.]

ALLMON, Thelma. 12 Aug 1917-22 Jan 1919. [Daughter of C.H. and H.B. (_____) Allmon.]

OUTLAW, Leonard P.   Died at age 3 years and 6 months. No dates.
OUTLAW, Cleo Bell.   Died 2 Aug 1910, age 3 weeks.
     Children of W. Thomas and Cora (Smoot) Outlaw.

OUTLAW, Cora Smoot. 13 Jul 1888-16 Jul 1910. [Cora Bell, daughter of William Henley and Elizabeth Frances Isabel (Gilley) Smoot, second wife of W. Thomas Outlaw.]

OUTLAW, W. Thomas. Died Sep 1929. [William Thomas Outlaw, husband of 1)_____ _____, 2) Cora Bell Smoot, married 16 Jul 1910, and 3)Minerva Elizabeth "Minnie" Smoot, married 15 Mar 1911.]

ELKINS, Vicy J. 17 Nov 1859-9 Apr 1935. [Vicy Jane, daughter of James and Nancy (_____) Pittman, wife of J.Preston S. Elkins, married 7 Mar 1875 in Cannon County, TN.]

McMAHAN, Amanda. 10 Jun 1892-13 Mar 1913. [Wife of A.W. McMahan.]

ELKINS, G.W. 4 Dec 1854-2 Oct 1919. [George W., son of Gabriel and Mary L. (_____) Elkins, husband of Ruth Ann Melton, married 23 Dec 1877.]

ELKINS, Ruth Ann. 23 Oct 1859-29 Apr 1931. [Ruth Ann Melton, wife of George W. Elkins.]

ELKINS, Martha Ann. 21 Jun 1883-10 Apr 1931. [Daughter of George W. and

Ruth Ann (Melton) Elkins.]

STARKEY, Casandra. 1820-8 Aug 1905. [Wife of Isaiah Starkey.]

McFARLIN, A.P. 24 Aug 1813-18 Mar 1879. [Anger Price McFarlin, husband of Sarah Martha Brewer.]

McFARLIN, Sarah. 26 Dec 1812-5 Feb 1832. [Sarah Martha, daughter of Russell and Nancy B. (Toliver) Brewer, wife of Anger Price McFarlin.]

DAVIS, Sarah. 1789 - 1853.

DAVIS, Jonathan G. 1823 - 1904.

DAVIS, Elizabeth G. 1831 - 1877.

DAVIS, Christian M. 1834 - 1905.

MARTIN, Infant. 29 Jul 1908-1 Aug 1908. [Infant of Richard H. and Martha (_____) Martin.]

BREWER, Henry. 16 May 1807-25 Aug 1877. [Son of Russell and Nancy B. (Toliver) Brewer, husband of Matilda _____.]

BREWER, Matilda. 2 Jan 1811-11 Feb 1889. [Wife of Henry Brewer.]

BREWER, J.R. 11 Oct 1850-20 May 1902. [Son of Henry and Matilda (_____) Brewer, husband of Parrie _____.]

BREWER, Parrie. 1 Feb 1840-22 Feb 1920. [Wife of J.R. Brewer.]

MITCHELL, Nancy J. 7 Apr 1852-7 Jun 1911. [Nancy J. Crouch, married 1) G.W. Smith on 29 Dec 1878 and 2) C.R. Mitchell on 5 Mar 1898.]

MITCHELL, L.A. 1870 - 1932. [Leander A. Mitchell, husband of Blanche Smith, married 15 Jan 1905.]

MITCHELL, Blanche. 1884 - 14 Aug 1979. [Daughter of John W. and Tennessee Caroline (Fletcher) Smith, wife of Leander A. Mitchell.]

MITCHELL, Homer. 26 Jul 1909-30 May 1948.

MITCHELL, Martin C. 14 Nov 1901-12 Oct 1954. [Son of Robert A. and Ella (Smith) Mitchell, husband of Edith Pearson.]

SMITH, Mary. 5 Sep 1823-12 May 1912. [Mary Stone, wife of 1) John N. Bailey, married 3 Jun 1838 and 2) T.B. Smith, married 20 Jun 1860 in Cannon County, TN.]

MARKUM, Delia. 16 Aug 1869-   . [Delia Shirley, wife of Ike Marcum.]

MARKUM, Ike. 1 Aug 1869-26 Jul 1914. [Son of Charles and Sarah C.(Blair) Markum, husband of Delia Shirley, married 9 Mar 1890. Death Certificate gives name as J.M. Marcom, birth as 26 Aug 1869, death as 28 Jul 1914.]

BURKS, Jesse. 27 Apr 1870-20 Oct 1957. [Son of R.B. and Rachel (Wiser)

Burks, husband of 1) Annie Shirley, married 21 Dec 1892 and 2) Matilda Smoot, married 6 Sep 1922.]

BURKS, Annie. 5 May 1873-31 Jul 1920. [Daughter of John W. and Margaret (Bailey) Shirley, wife of Jesse Burks.]

SHIRLEY, M. E. 15 Jan 1845-22 Apr 1915. [Margaret E. Bailey, wife of John W. Shirley, marriage 28 Dec 1859, Cannon County, TN.]

SHIRLEY, J. W. 4 Jun 1840-17 Jan 1904. [John W., husband of Margaret E Bailey.]

SHIRLEY, R.H. 22 Oct 1877-12 Oct 1903. [Roland H., son of John W. and Margaret E. (Bailey) Shirley.]

REYNOLDS, Niner Myrtle. 6 May 1881-10 May 1903. [Daughter of John W. and Margaret (Bailey) Shirley, first wife of Alfred Reynolds.]

FRAZIER, Media. 20 May 1900-4 Jul 1918. [Daughter of R.M. and Melissa (Shirley) Temple, first wife of William Marion Frazier.]

FRAZIER, Emma Hobbs. 30 Aug 1901-14 Feb 1923. [Daughter of James Julius and Josie (Turner) Hobbs, second wife of Wm. Marion Frazier.]

FRAZIER, Ollie York. 24 May 1901-17 Oct 1935. [Ollie Mai York, third wife of William Marion Frazier.]

FRAZIER, William M. 25 Jan 1894-19 Dec 1966. [William Marion, son of Alfred and Martha (Bonner) Frazier, husband of 1) Media Temple, married 19 Dec 1915, 2) Emma Hobbs, married 2 Jan 1921, 3) Ollie Mai York, married 2 Nov 1924, and 4) Carrie J. (Austin) Mullins, married 12 Oct 1941.]

SAYERS, Orval L. 5 May 1928-6 Feb 1972. [Son of Grada and Nola (_____) Sayers, "Cpl, U.S. Air Force".]

SHIRLEY, J.N. 22 Mar 1865-29 Nov 1943. [Joe N., son of John W. and Margaret (Bailey) Shirley, husband of 1) Mary Ella Frazier, married 22 Feb 1883 and 2) Harriet Gannon, married 22 Dec 1897.]

SHIRLEY, Harriett. 16 Aug 1879-13 May 1969. [Daughter of Will H. and Mary Elizabeth (Faulkenberry) Gannon, wife of Joe N. Shirley.]

SHIRLEY, Willie A. 14 Mar 1894-8 Aug 1958. [Willie Alvin, son of John B. and Mollie (Wiser) Shirley, husband of Liza York.]

ELKINS, Frank. 25 Nov 1877-20 Mar 1935. [Funeral home records give date of death as 22 Mar 1936. James Franklin, son of Press and Vica Jane (Pittman) Elkins, husband of Violet Elkins.]

SWANN, Violet Elkins. 15 Jun 1893-10 Sep 1982. [Wife of 1) Frank Elkins and 2) _____ Swann.]

SHIRLEY, Infant Daughter. Born and died 1884.
SHIRLEY, Alfred D. 1886-1886.
    Children of John W. and Margaret (Bailey) Shirley.

McAFEE, Brown. 17 Sep 1892-18 Jun 1896. [Son of J.B. and M.E. (_____) McAfee.]

BAILEY, Hallie. 7 Nov 1863-8 Sep 1923. [Daughter of James Alfred "Tip" and Jennie Jane (St.John) Bailey. Single.]

BAILEY, J.A. 10 Sep 1839-5 Jul 1918. [James Alfred, husband of Margaret Jane St. John.]

BAILEY, Jennie. 31 Mar 1841- [died ca 1921]. [Margaret Jane, daughter of John and Margaret (Ford) St.John, wife of James Alfred Bailey.]

BURKS, Infant son. 21 Nov 1916 only date on stone. [William Young, son of Vernie and Mary Etta (Young) Burks.]

BURKS, Thurman. 12 Apr 1897-31 Jul 1905. [Son of Henry Thomas and Mary F. (_____) Burks.]

BURKS, Bonnie Lee. 11 May 1893-4 Jul 1907. [Daughter of Henry Thomas and Mary F. (_____) Burks.]

YOUNG, Phillip W. 17 Jul 1916-20 Jan 1919. [Son of Lear Young.]

BURKS, Henry Thomas. 13 Oct 1870-24 May 1923. [Husband of Mary F. _____.]

BURKS, Mary F. 9 Jul 1876-28 Sep 1971. [Wife of Henry Thomas Burks.]

FOX, Raymond Lee. 7 Sep 1938=19 Jan 1994. [Son of Jace Wesley and Berdie May (McDonald) Fox, husband of Robbie Lee Brown.]

FOX, Robbie Brown. 28 Mar 1939- . [Wife of Raymond Lee Fox.]

SWOAPE, S. Ross. 26 Jun 1870-6 May 1909. [Samuel Ross Swoape, husband of Annie Rains.]

SWOAPE, Annie R. 23 Apr 1854-18 Dec 1941. [Annie Birdine, daughter of Larkin and Elizabeth (Curtis) Rains, husband of Samuel Ross Swoape.]

SMOOT, William Clancy. 26 Oct 1906-23 Sep 1907.
SMOOT, Isaac N. 15 Jul 1908-21 Jan 1916.
    Children of Isaac Newton and Annie Marie (Clancy) Smoot.

SMOOT, Isaac Newton. 22 Feb 1881-14 Feb 1957. [Son of William Henley and Frances Elizabeth Isabel (Gilley) Smoot, husband of Annie Marie Clancy.]

SMOOT, Annie M. 13 Sep 1882-1 Sep 1951. [Annie Marie, daughter of John and Delia Christine (Golden) Clancy, wife of Isaac Newton Smoot, married 13 Feb 1906.]

SMOOT, Charlie P. 8 Dec 1918-12 Apr 1977. WWII. [Son of Isaac Newton and Annie Marie (Clancy) Smoot.]

SHIRLEY, Autie Frances Akers. 23 Jan 1889-29 May 1928. [Daughter of Isaac and Hannah (Brown) Akers, second wife of John B. Shirley.]

SHIRLEY, John B. 16 Nov 1868-21 Mar 1926. [Husband of 1) Mollie Wiser, married 18 Apr 1889 in Coffee County, TN, and 2) Autie Frances Akers, married 10 Apr 1909.]

SHIRLEY, Mollie. 8 Sep 1870-29 Mar 1901. [Daugher of Thomas and Rebecca

(_____) Wiser, first wife of John B. Shirley.]

MARKUM, Dalton.   16 Mar 1890-24 Mar 1890.
MARKUM, Alfred.   27 Nov 1892-17 Aug 1913.
        Sons of Isaac M. and Delia (Shirley) Markum.

MARTIN, Infant. 29 Jul 1908-1 Aug 1908.   [Son of Richard M. and Martha
        (Myers) Martin.]

MARTIN, Rachel. 17 Jan 1848-5 Jan 1913.   [Rachel Bouldin, wife of Jesse
        Martin.]

HILLIS, Orval. 29 Aug 1912-3 Jun 1913.   [Son of James W. and Mary
        (Martin) Hillis.]

MARTIN, Suella. 29 Nov 1883-12 Mar 1920. [Daughter of Andrew Jackson and
        Addie (Yager) Simons, wife of Marion Martin. Death Certificate
        gives name as Louella Martin, born 29 Nov 1884, died 11 Mar
        1920.]

RAINS, Annie Martin. 8 Jan 1888-20 Jun 1952. [Daughter of Jesse and
        Rachel (Bouldin) Martin, wife of General Crit Rains.]

RAINS, G.C. 2 Nov 1887-11 Sep 1956. [General Crit, son of Rufus K. and
        Susan (Akers) Rains, husband of Annie Martin.]

MARTIN, John E. May 1883-30 Jan 1939. [Son of Jesse and Rachel (Bouldin)
        Martin, husband of Eva Lark (div.)]

HOLLIS, Wavie L. 30 Jan 1915-   . Wavie Louise, daughter of
        General Crit and Annie (Martin) Rains, wife of William Howard
        Hollis.]

HOLLIS, William Howard. 18 Nov 1910-6 Apr 1981. [Son of George D. and
        Ethel (Byford) Hollis, husband of Wavie Louise Rains, married 20
        Dec 1944.]

MITCHELL, C.R. 11 Nov 1854-25 Jul 1914.   [C. Robert, son of Greenberry
        and Cynthia (Brewer) Mitchell, husband of 1) Martha A. Davenport,
        married 8 May 1873 and 2) Nancy J. Smith, married 5 Mar 1899.]

MITCHELL, Martha Davenport. 9 Sep 1852-16 Aug 1889. [Wife of C. Robert
        Mitchell.]

MITCHELL, Cynthia. 5 Sep 1831-3 May 1898.   [Daughter of Solomon and
        Elizabeth (_____) Brewer, wife of Greenberry B. Mitchell.]

MITCHELL, G.B. 23 May 1832-6 Apr 1899. [Greenberry B., son of Robert and
        Jane (_____) Mitchell, husband of Cynthia Brewer.]

MITCHELL, Infant. Born and died 25 Jul 1913. [Son of C.R. and Ella
        (_____) Mitchell.]

MITCHELL, John. 19 Aug 1887-17 Mar 1910. [Son of C.R. and _____ (_____)
        Mitchell.]

BROWN, Holder L. 6 Apr 1885-14 Aug 1936.

BROWN, Waymon. 3 Jul 1901-8 Sep 1927.

JAKES, Bettie Duke. 24 Mar 1875-16 Mar 1976. [Daughter of Alex and Ann
        (Almond) Duke, wife of Samuel Toney Jakes.]

JAKES, Samuel Toney. 25 Nov 1872-12 Oct 1943. [Son of John and Catherine
        (Sherrell) Jakes, husband of Bettie Duke.]

COLE, Infant son. Born and died 6 Feb 1946. [Russel George, son of
        Melville Raymond and Vaudrene (Elam) Cole.]

BYFORD, George Ware. 6 Sep 1848-16 Jun 1916. [Husband of Eugenia Ann
        Foster.]

BYFORD, Eugenia Ann. 9 Sep 1853-12 Jun 1941. [Daughter of Robert and
        Zenohia Finley (Soape) Foster, wife of George W. Byford.]

BYFORD, William Robert. 5 Apr 1880-6 Jan 1957. [Son of George Ware and
        Eugenia Ann (Foster) Byford, husband of Idella Emaline Sissom.]

BYFORD, Idella Emaline. 3 Oct 1878-6 Jul 1951. [Daughter of A.J. and
        Elizabeth (Cooper) Sissom, wife of William Robert Byford.]

SHIRLEY, Hatten Roland. 6 Jun 1901-25 Mar 1985. [Son of Joe and Harriett
        (Gann) Shirley, husband of 1) Ruby May Wilson and 2) Rita
        Chambers Clendenon.]

SHIRLEY, Ruby May. 23 May 1904-22 Sep 1944. [Daughter of Huey Jackson
        and Mary Elizabeth (Pennington) Wilson, first wife of Hatton
        Roland Shirley.]

SMOOT, Mary J. 11 Apr 1876-9 Mar 1966. [Mary Jane, daughter of C. Robert
        and Martha (Davenport) Mitchell, wife of Claud Martin Smoot.]

SMOOT, Claud M. 2 Jun 1878-3 Aug 1936. [Claud Martin, son of William
        Henley and Elizabeth Frances Isabel (Gilley) Smoot, husband of
        Mary Jane Mitchell, married 19 Dec 1897.]

ROGERS, Travis Jr. 1 Dec 1924-25 Dec 1924. [Son of H. Travis and B.M.
        (_____) Rogers.

SMOOT, Della Lorene. 12 Jan 1905-15 Jan 1910. [Daughter of Claud Martin
        and Mary Jane (Mitchell) Smoot.]

MITCHELL, D.W.A. 18 Nov 1860-13 Feb 1929. [First husband of Louella
        Pennington, married 26 Feb 1899.]

MITCHELL, Louella. 23 Dec 1874-11 Oct 1952. [Daughter of Clayburn and
        Delila C. (Lutrell) Pennington, wife of 1) D.W.A. Mitchell, 2)
        Ephriam Bobbitt, married 17 Apr 1930, 3) _____ Haley, and 4)
        Milie C. Bell, married 26 Mar 1944.]

PENNINGTON, Charley C. 24 Nov 1876-23 Dec 1936. [Son of Clayborn and
        Delila Caroline (Lutrell) Pennington, husband of Jossie Wood,
        married 25 Jan 1907.]

PENNINGTON, Jossie D. 6 Aug 1886-20 Mar 1926. [Jossie D. Wood, wife of
        Charley Clayburn Pennington.]

PENNINGTON, Iron Howard. 26 Jun 1897-15 Aug 1965. WWI. [Son of Clayburn
        and Delila Caroline (Lutrell) Pennington, husband of Cleo Good,
        married 26 Oct 1920.]

PENNINGTON, Cleo. 10 Jul 1904-20 Jun 1984. [Daughter of Robert Hershel
    and Bertha L. (Zadie) Good, wife of Iron Howard Pennington.]

PENNINGTON, Millard J. 11 Aug 1921-29 Jan 1973. WWII and Korea. [Son of
    Iron Howard and Cleo (Good) Pennington.]

SWAN, Mennie B. 23 Dec 1908-28 Jan 1941. [Mennie Bell, daughter of Joe
    and Phronia (Bryant) Usselton, first wife of Vernon Steve Swan.]

SWAN, Vernon S. 3 Apr 1908-17 Nov 1982. [Stone here but he is buried at
    Gardens of Memory. Vernon Steve, Sr., son of Sam and Ida
    Josephine (Smithson) Swan, husband of 1) Mennie Bell Usselton and
    2) H. Evelyn _____.]

CROUCH, Media S. 8 May 1905-10 Sep 1967. [Daughter of Sam and Ida
    Josephine (Smithson) Swann, wife of Ernest Crouch.]

CROUCH, Ernest. 22 Jul 1900-6 Jul 1933. [Son of John W. and Eliza
    (Messick) Crouch, husband of Media Swann.]

*CROUCH, Harry Clinton. 22 Oct 1925-23 Mar 1927. [Son of Ernest and
    Media (Swann) Crouch.]

SWAN, Ida. 26 Dec 1876-31 Jan 1947. [Ida Josephine, daughter of Riston
    and Hester Lucy (Muncey) Smithson, wife of Sam Swan.]

SWAN, Sam. 25 Jun 1877-23 Mar 1929. [Husband of Ida Josephine Smithson.]

RAINS, Dovie Young. 15 Sep 1896-12 Mar 1986. [Daughter of William Calvin
    and Ann (Teal) Young, wife of Rufus J. Rains.]

RAINS, Rufus J. 24 Aug 1891-18 Oct 1974. [Son of Rufus K. and Susan C.
    (Akers) Rains,husband of Dovie Young, married 1 Jan 1913.]

FOUTCH, J.E. 3 Mar 1840-   . [J. Emeline, wife of John C.Foutch.]

FOUTCH, J.C. 14 Oct 1834-15 Sep 1915. [John C. Foutch, husband of J.
    Emeline _____.]

JAMES, Bessie Lero. 29 Apr 1902-15 Sep 1903. [Daughter of H.F. and L.M.
    (_____) James.]

ALLMON, E.H. 18 Jul 1845-11 Feb 1921. [Ephram H., husband of P.T.
    "Tenny" McGill, married 13 Jul 1864 in Cannon County, TN.]

ALLMON, P.T. 22 Jun 1846-9 Nov 1919. [P. T. "Tenny" McGill, wife of
    Ephriam H. Allmon.]

LASSITER, James L. 30 Aug 1874-26 Aug 1949. [James Luke, son of Joseph
    and Mattie (Williams) Lassiter, husband of Polemna Tennessee
    Allmon.]

LASSITER, Polemna T. 8 Sep 1877-1 Sep 1962. [Polemna Tennessee, daughter
    of Ephriam and P.T. "Tenny" (McGill) Allmon, wife of James Luke
    Lassiter.]

LASSITER, Veva Wilola. 19 Aug 1920-2 Apr 1979. [Daughter of James Luke
    and Polemna T. (Allmon) Lassiter. Single.]

*ELKINS, Infant. Born and died 27 Dec 1919, daughter of George T. and Mary

Ann (McGuire) Elkins.

ELKINS, Mary McGuire. 6 Jun 1888-20 Feb 1920. [Daughter of Harry Lee and Anna (Heady) McGuire, wife of George T. Elkins.]

McGUIRE, Dr. Harry Lee. 1862 - 3 May 1939. [Husband of Anna Heady.]

McGUIRE, Anna Heady. 1862 - 1946. [Wife of Dr. Harry Lee McGuire.]

SIMON, Windonia. 11 Feb 1920-26 Jan 1927. [Daughter of Herbert D. and Hester A. (Swann) Simon.]

SIMON, H.D. 6 Jan 1891-24 Jan 1981. [Herbert D. Simon, husband of Hester A. Swann.]

SIMON, Hester A. 18 Mar 1900-3 Mar 1982. [Daughter of Sam and Ida Josephine (Smithson) Swan, wife of Herbert D. Simon.]

CUNNINGHAM, Paul James. 15 Aug 1934-8 Aug 1992. [Son of Paul and Mildred Kathleen (Clary) Cunningham. Single.]

CUNNINGHAM, Bee Irving. 6 Aug 1942-15 Jan 1957. [Son of Paul and Mildred Kathleen (Clary) Cunningham.]

LASSITER, Joe H. 22 Sep 1846-9 Dec 1921. [Husband of Mattie A. Saffle, married 11 Mar 1869 in Cannon County, Tn.]

LASSITER, Mattie. 16 Jan 1854-11 Jan 1923. [Mattie A. Saffle, wife of Joe H. Lassiter.]

HENNESSEE, Mary Ann. 1 Jun 1862-19 Aug 1924. [Daughter of Peyton and Margaret (Pace) Christian, wife of James Thomas Hennessee, married 8 Nov 1883.]

HENNESSEE, J.T. 11 Oct 1855-13 Aug 1943. [James Thomas, son of James C. and Maxie (Dodson) Hennessee, husband of 1) Mary Ann Christian and 2) Nora Campbell.]

ELAM, Cora Swoape. 12 Jul 1894-11 Jul 1976. [Daughter of Samuel Ross and Annie (Rains) Swoape, wife of Henry L. Elam.]

ELAM, Henry L. 3 Apr 1884-26 Apr 1968. [Son of James Buchanan and Rachel Ann (Shelton) Elam, husband of Cora Swoape.]

ELAM, J.B. 21 Nov 1858-24 Jul 1927. [James Buchanan, son of Henry L. and Nancy (Young) Elam, husband of Rachel Ann Shelton.]

ELAM, Rachel. 31 May 1863-13 Sep 1946. [Rachel Ann, daughter of James and Polly Ann (Hoover) Shelton, wife of James B. Elam.]

WILSON, Mary E. 4 Mar 1885-31 Jan 1920. [Mary Elizabeth, daughter of Clayborn and Caroline (Lutrell) Pennington, wife of Hugh Jackson Wilson.]

WILSON, H.J. 10 Nov 1870 - 15 Jun 1944. [Hughie Jackson, son of Hugh J. and Phronia (Braken) Wilson, husband of 1) Mary Ann Pennington and 2) Eva Lemons.]

WILSON, Brown Ramsey. 4 Oct 1911-21 Mar 1990. [Son of Hugh Jackson Jr. and Mary Elizabeth (Pennington) Wilson.]

WILLIAMS, Hoyt S. 23 Aug 1905-15 Mar 1920. [Hoyt Smoot, son of Calvin H. and Daisy Lee (Coffey) Williams.]

WILSON, Wauline. 22 May 1928-30 Oct 1929. [Daughter of Roy Jackson, Sr., and Eula Pearl (Shirley) Wilson.]

WILLIAMS, Calvin H. 14 Oct 1869-20 Apr 1950. [Calvin Henderson, son of Joe and Tennessee (Webster) Williams, husband of Daisy Lee Coffey, married 25 Feb 1894 in Cannon County, TN.]

WILLIAMS, Daisy Lee. 18 Feb 1879-28 Oct 1950. [Daughter of James F. and Sarah (Reed) Coffey, wife of Calvin Henderson Williams.]

WILLIAMS, Curtis H. 14 Oct 1912-12 Jun 1946. [Son of Calvin Henderson and Daisy Lee (Coffey) Williams, husband of Maymie McMahan.]

BARNES, Arlie Weymon. 1922 - 1924. [Son of R. Hough and Rebecca (Richie) Barnes. Death record gives birth date as 5 Feb 1923 and death as 3 Feb 1924.]

BARNES, R. Hough. 1882 - 1948.

BARNES, Rebecca R. 1891 - 1966. [Rebecca Richie, wife of R. Hough Barnes.]

CUNNINGHAM. B. 8 Jan 1878-21 Nov 1940. [Zora Bee, husband of Sarah Hannah Parker, married 4 Jul 1897.]

CUNNINGHAM, Hannah. 4 Apr 1879-26 Mar 1964. [Sarah Hannah, daughter of James Richard and Hannah S. (McAfee) Parker, wife of Zora Bee Cunningham.]

TITTSWORTH, Lillie Bell. 5 Dec 1929-5 Dec 1929.

BISHOP, Myrtle. 14 Dec 1901-14 Aug 1956. [Daughter of Charles and Lizzie (Jones) Jarrell, wife of Jesse Bishop.]

BARNES, James P. 24 Jan 1872-16 Jun 1942. [James Porter, son of John and Malinda (Whittimore) Barnes, husband of Mary Jane Espy, married 25 Dec 1894 in Cannon County, Tn.]

BARNES, Mary J. 3 Dec 1881-30 Jan 1953. [Mary Jane, daughter of George and Ella (McCullough) Espy, wife of James Porter Barnes.]

BARNES, Elsie. 10 Jan 1910-22 Feb 1968. [Daughter of James Porter and Mary Jane (Espy) Barnes, single.]

BARNES, Raymond N. 19 Jul 1925-   . [Son of James Porter and Mary Jane (Espy) Barnes, husband of Uva Jean Lewis, married 22 Oct 1942.]

BARNES, Uva Jean Lewis. 5 Mar 1925-   . [Wife of Raymond N. Barnes.]

SHERRELL, Infant. Born and died 9 Aug 1930. Son of Alton and Grace (Hollis) Sherrell.]

SHERRELL, Grace Hollis. 29 Jun 1908-   . [Daughter of George David and Ethel (Byford) Hollis, husband of Alton Sherrell.]

HOLLIS, Ethel B.   29 Mar 1887-29 Sep 1975. [Minnie Ethel, daughter of
        John and Cynthia (Wilson) Byford, wife of Goerge D. Hollis,
        married 10 Sep 1905.]

HOLLIS, George D.   26 Feb 1880-29 Apr 1957. [Son of John H. and Jo Ann
        (Simpson) Hollis, husband of Minnie Ethel Byford.]

TODD, Fronie B.   29 May 1890-23 Oct 1973. [Wife of Joe Todd, married 25
        Dec 1921.]

TODD, Joe. 8 Mar 1895-20 Feb 1970. [Husband of Fronie B. _____.]

HIGGINS, George C.   2 Nov 1923-27 May 1926.
HIGGINS, Estell.   17 Oct 1925-24 Oct 1925.

HALL, Billy Wayne. 6 Oct 1931-2 Jun 1933. [Son of Vester and Ollie Mai
        (Rains) Hall.]

HALL, Ollie R.   13 Aug 1911-18 May 1981. [Daughter of General Crit and
        Annie (Martin) Rains, wife of Vester Homer Hall.]

HALL, Vester H.   7 Jan 1907-11 Aug 1978. [Vester Homer, son of James A.
        and Martha (Haley) Hall, husband of Ollie Rains, married 23 Feb
        1930.]

TODD, Wilson. 3 Jan 1842-30 Sep 1925. [Son of Hiram and Henrietta (Espy)
        Todd, husband of Mary Jane Barnes, married 20 Oct 1860 in Cannon
        County, Tn.]

TODD, Mary Jane.   1 Jan 1843-17 Jun 1920. [Mary Jane Barnes, wife of
        Wilson Todd. Funeral home records give date of birth as 1 Jan
        1844 and death as 16 Jun 1920.]

CARRICK, Cecil. 10 May 1920-22 Aug 1921. [Son of W.J. and L.H. (_____)
        Carrick.]

ESPY, G. W.   21 Jan 1859-19 Mar 1938.   [George W., husband of Ellen
        McCullough, married 3 Jun 1877 in Cannon County, TN.]

ESPY, Ellen.   10 Oct 1861-17 Apr 1950.   [Daughter of John and Elvira
        (Spry) McCullough, wife of George W. Espy.]

MILLS, Leona. 16 Dec 1911-16 Jan 1926. [Daughter of Newton Calvin and
        Dollie (Espy) Mills.]

MILLS, Newton C.   26 Apr 1876-24 Feb 1960. [Newton Calvin, son of John
        and Lou Cindy (Whittimore) Mills, husband of Dollie Espy, married
        24 Feb 1906.]

MILLS, Dollie Espy. 28 Oct 1889-2 Aug 1977. [Daughter of George W. and
        Ellen (McCullough) Espy, wife of Newton Calvin Mills.]

HALL, James A. 18 Feb 1878-6 Jul 1939. [James Alexander, son of John and
        Mollie (Williams) Hall, husband of Martha Rebecca Haley.]

HALL, Martha R.   9 Dec 1883-10 Sep 1949. [Martha Rebecca, daughter of
        George J. and Elizabeth (Mears) Haley, wife of James Alexander
        Hall.]

SUMMERS, Lewis Clark. 30 Jun 1937-22 Apr 1941. [Son of Gwyn and Joelene (Shirley) Summers.]

SUMMERS, Anna. 29 Nov 1887-10 Dec 1967. [Daughter of John and Elizabeth (Sparks) Heatherly, second wife of George W. Summers.]

SUMMERS, George W. 18 Jun 1878-7 Aug 1935. [Son of John and Mary (_____) Summers, husband of 1) Hannah Heatherly and 2) Anna Heatherly.]

SUMMERS, Hannah. 29 Nov 1887-27 Apr 1905. [Daughter of John and Elizabeth (Sparks) Heatherly, first wife of George W. Summers.]

SUMMERS, Gwyn. 1909 - 1987. [Son of George W. and Anna (Heatherly) Summers, husband of Jolene Shirley.]

SUMMERS, Jolene. 1915 - . [Daughter of Joe N. and Harriett Tennessee (Gannon) Shirley, wife of Gwyn Summers.]

BAILEY, Melton, Jr. 24 Apr 1939-5 Jul 1933. [Son of Melton and Hannah Mai (Summers) Bailey.]

SCOTT, Jesse C. 1 Nov 1904-20 Jan 1983. [Son of William Martin and Eliza A. (Deberry) Scott, husband of Bertha Cecil Mills.]

SCOTT, Bertha C. 1 Feb 1905-4 May 1979. [Bertha Cecil, daughter of James William and Julia (Espy) Mills, wife of Jesse C. Scott.]

CUNNINGHAM, Irvin H. 21 Dec 1900-5 Jul 1982. [Irvin Hugh, son of Zora Bee and Hannah (Parker) Cunningham, husband of Lela Lucille Sherrell.]

CUNNINGHAM, Lela L. 31 Aug 1902-3 Oct 1970. [Lela Lucille Sherrell, wife of Irvin H. Cunningham.]

CUNNINGHAM, Hannah Louise. No dates. [Daughter of Irvin Hugh and Lela Lucille (Sherrell) Cunningham. Single.]

MILLS, Julia Espy. 23 Feb 1879-1 Jul 1957. [Daughter of George W. and Ellen (McCullough) Espy, wife of James William Mills.]

MILLS, James W. 3 Apr 1871-15 Nov 1928. [Husband of Julia E. Espy.]

MILLS, Fowler Elizabeth. 1910 - 15 Apr 1988. [Daughter of Will D. and Elizabeth (Good) Cates, wife of James Herschell Mills.]

MILLS, James Herschell. 1907 - 2 Jun 1990. [Son of James William and Julia (Espy) Mills, husband of Fowler Elizabeth Cates.]

GILLEY, Lula C. 7 May 1874-4 Nov 1933. [Daughter of John and Lucindy (Whittimore) Barnes, wife of Caleb C. Gilley.]

GILLEY, Caleb C. 15 Aug 1869-15 Jul 1945. [Son of Simm and Clementine (Kirby) Gilley, husband of Lula Lucille Barnes, married 17 Aug 1892, Cannon County, TN.]

BARNES, Robert. 29 Jul 1926-29 Jul 1939. [Son of John and Izzie (Gilley) Barnes.]

BARNES, Izzie Gilley. 7 Oct 1895-24 Oct 1967. [Daughter of John Caleb and Lula (Barnes) Gilley, wife of John Barnes.]

GRANDSTAFF, Vurna L. 15 Jul 1907-16 Aug 1936. [Son of Oscar L. and Laura A. (Elam) Grandstaff. Single.]

GRANDSTAFF, Oscar L. 11 Oct 1878-18 May 1960. [Husband of Laura Ann Elam.]

GRANDSTAFF, Laura A. 10 Dec 1881-14 May 1969. [Laura Ann Elam, wife of Oscar L. Grandstaff.]

GRANDSTAFF, Cecil Burger. 28 Jul 1913-16 Nov 1992. [Son of Oscar L. and Laura Ann (Elam) Grandstaff, husband of Audry Gay White.]

GRANDSTAFF, Audry Gay. 1 Aug 1920-3 Nov 1981. [Wife of Cecil Burger Grandstaff.]

SIMMONS, Rebecca M. 11 May 1922-12 Aug 1939. [Daughter of Genoia N. and Hattie B. (Melton) Milligan, wife of Rufus Elmo Simmons.]

MILLIGAN, Genoia N. 29 Oct 1885-23 May 1954. [Son of Alex and Rebecca (Jones) Milligan, husband of Hattie B. Melton.]

MILLIGAN, Hattie B. 26 Nov 1885-21 Feb 1948. [Daughter of John R. and Liza Parasada (Preston) Melton, wife of Genoia N. Milligan.]

NORTHCUTT, Thurman L. 24 May 1903-27 Mar 1979. [Thurman Lee, son of Anderson and Ida (Worley) Northcutt, husband of Georgia Mae Reynolds, married 1 Oct 1926.]

NORTHCUTT, Georgia M. 15 Aug 1909-31 Aug 1982. [Georgia Mae, daughter of Alfred and Mary Jane (Shirley) Reynolds, wife of Thurman Lee Northcutt.]

SMOOT, Brenda Faye Northcutt. 1948 - 22 Jan 1994. [Daughter of Thurman Lee and Georgia Mae (Reynolds) Northcutt, wife of John Isaac Smoot, married 12 Nov 1967.]

SMOOT, John Isaac. No dates. ["Jackie", son of Johnny Golden and _____ (_____) Smoot, husband of Brenda Faye Northcutt.]

ROSS, Mary Wilma. 21 Jan 1912-8 Nov 1977. [Daughter of James Wayne and Zora Ethel (Shook) Young, wife of Harry Hugh Ross.]

ROSS, Harry Hugh. 27 May 1905-27 Sep 1975. [Son of William Michael and Minnie Mae (Davis) Ross, husband of Mary Wilma Young.]

BARNES, John R. 24 Jan 1898-7 Feb 1957. [Son of James and Mary Jane (Espy) Barnes, husband of 1) Izzie Gilley (div) and 2) Mary Florence _____.]

*ARGO, Thomas. Born 20 Aug 1844, died June 1910, son of Robert M. and Eliza (Vickers) Argo, husband of Laura Mitchell.

*ARGO, Laura. Born ca 1859, died 23 Jul 1917, daughter of G.B. and _____ (Brewer) Mitchell, wife of Thomas Argo.

*REYNOLDS, G. Alfred, "Alf". No birth or death dates found. Husband of 1) Niner Myrtle Shirley, 2) Mary Jane Shirley and 3) Myrtle Jarrell, married 19 Apr 1925.

*REYNOLDS, Mary Jane Shirley. Born 14 Jul 1885, died 23 Feb 1922.

Daughter of Joe and Mary E. (Frazier) Shirley, second wife of Alfred Reynolds, married 18 Mar 1906.

*BURKS, Emily Shirley. No birth or death dates found. Daughter of John W. and Margaret (Bailey) Shirley, wife of Pet Burks.

*JUDKINS, Bessie Jane, died 26 Nov 1966, age about 74 years, daughter of John and _____ (_____) Ashworth, wife of Tom Judkins.

*YOUNGBLOOD, J.C., Jr. Born and died 5 Jun 1941, son of Clifford and Illileen (Smoot) Youngblood.

*SWAN, Electie. Born 19 Jul 1904, died 26 Dec 1932, daughter of W.C. and Annie (Teal) Young, wife of Barney Swan.

*ELKINS, Newton Columbus, born 8 Oct 1876, died 23 Dec 1962, son of Preston and Vicie Jane (Pittman) Elkins, husband of Bessie Jane Spencer.

*TEMPLES, Mrs. Will. Born Jan 1866, died 3 Mar 1916.

*MARBERRY, Isaac, born 26 Feb 1915, died 6 Mar 1915, son of Aaron and Ella (Gardner) Marberry.

*SCOTT, Gary Dale. 2 Aug 1962-3 Aug 1962. [Son of Bobby Joe and Norma Jo (Wolfe) Scott.]

JACO CEMETERY

Location: On crossroad to Highland Road near Remus McCormick's.

COPE, Susannah Jones. 1 May 1836-18 Jan 1916.

JONES, Daniel. Born in 1812-7 Sep 1879. [Husband of Susan Jones.]

*JONES, Susan. 1807-1916. [Wife of Daniel Jones.]

JACO, Osker. 18 Feb 1902-15 Apr 1904. Son of E.L. Jaco.

SMITH, Mary Sanders. 6 Jan 1859-28 Aug 1906. [Wife of Elzy Jaco.]

JACO, Elzy. 18__ - 195_. [Husband of Mary Sanders Smith.]

JOHNSON CEMETERY

Location: About 1/2 mile off Hwy 30 near Eureka Church of Christ.

HALE, Betty E. 1876-1901. [Betty Elizabeth, daughter of William C. and Frances Cordelia (Dorsey) Sullivan, wife of Jefferson Hale.]

HALE, Rayburn. Born and died 1901. [Son of Jefferson and Betty Elizabeth (Sullivan) Hale.]

JOHNSON, Elizabeth. 25 Sep 1832-17 Feb 1917. [Daughter of Matthew and Mary Elizabeth (_____) Dyer, wife of 1) Michael Rhodes, married 18 Feb 1847, 2) Joe Dorsey and 3) James Calvin Johnson, married 7 Sep 1857.]

JOHNSON, J.C. 7 May 1821-30 Oct 1881. [James Calvin Johnson, husband of 1) Sarah Neal, married 5 Jan 1842, 2) Ella Rhodes, married 4 Jul 1850 and 3) Elizabeth Dyer.]

WITT, Charlie. Dec 1890-7 Mar 1891. [Son of William and Mary (Johnson) Witt.]

#McCLURE, Sarah Johnson, born 18 Nov 1857, death date unknown, daughter of James Calvin and Elizabeth (Dyer) Johnson, wife of James McClure, married 19 Jan 1878.

#SULLIVAN, William C., born 1854, died 1897, son of James and Lucinda (Black) Sullivan, husband of Frances Cordelia Dorsey, married 19 Jul 1872.

#SULLIVAN, Frances Cordelia, born 1856, died 1897, daughter of Joe and Elizabeth Dyer (Rhodes) Dorsey, wife of William C. Sullivan.

*JOHNSON, Russell, born 1863, died 26 Jun 1911, bill rendered to Andy Johnson.

#HALE, Dan, born 1898, died 1898, aged 4 months, son of Isom and Daisy (Sullivan) Hale.

\#   Information from Landon Hale, Van Buren County Historian

JONES CEMETERY

Location: Lucky Community

JONES, Mary. 22 May 1816-10 Feb 1907. [Wife of William Jones.]

EARLS, Samantha Paralee. 11 Jan 1849-1 Mar 1880 [Samantha Paralee Jones, wife of William Earls, married 28 Jan 1877.]

Jones Cemetery, Cont.

JONES, Furm Washington. 10 Jun 1885-30 Oct 1886.

HOOSER, Louise Jane. 21 Jun 1844-6 Sep 1868.

Three field stones with the following dates but with unreadable names:
        1861-Mar 1869
        8 ___ 1818-3 Mar 1867
        and "died Mar 1859".

Several other unreadable field stones.

JONES CEMETERY

Location: Near Oak Grove Church of Christ on J.P. Stanley farm.

STEMBRIDGE, Horace Jones. 19 Aug 1905-7 Mar 1914. [Son of Tom and Minnie
        Delilah (Jones) Stembridge.]

STEMBRIDGE, Jules. 2 Jan 1893-6 Jan 1896. [Son of William Roland and
        Sarah A. (Phillips) Stembridge.]

STEMBRIDGE, Johney. 25 Sep 1881-11 Jul 1890. [Son of William Roland and
        Sarah A. (Phillips) Stembridge.]

MILLER, Pollie. 25 Dec 1832-7 Jul 1888. [Mary "Polly" Webb, wife of 1)
        James Stembridge, 2) David Forrester, married 11 Oct 1867 and 3)
        E. Miller, married 5 Jan 1881.]

STEMBRIDGE, T.W. 22 Dec 1851-2 Jul 1914. [Thomas Webb, son of James and
        Mary "Polly" (Webb) Stembridge, husband of Rutha Rigsby.]

STEMBRIDGE, Jennie. 22 Dec 1879-2 Jun 1888. [Daughter of Thomas Webb and
        Ruth (Rigsby) Stembridge.]

STEMBRIDGE, Bertie Lee. 10 Jul 1919-6 Sep 1919. [Daughter of James
        Houston and Lida Myrtle (Gannon) Stembridge.]

STEMBRIDGE, Thomas Fisher. 9 Jan 1923-6 Sep 1923. [Son of James Houston
        and Lida Myrtle (Gannon) Stembridge.]

MARCUM, S.B. 30 Nov 1834-Sep 1863.

JONES, Alsey. Died 14 Oct 1879, age 72 years. [Son of James and Charity
        (_____) Jones, husband of Melvinna Moore.]

JONES, Vinnie. Died 13 Jul 1889, age 86 years. [Melvinna Moore, wife of
        Alsey Jones.]

MURPHY, Doctor Franklin. 6 Sep 1830-6 Sep 1907. [Husband of Eliz. _____]

MURPHY, Eliz. 6 Jun 1832-6 Jun 1907. [Wife of Doctor Franklin Murphy.]

JONES, Minnie A. 22 Aug 1874-10 Oct 1940. [Minnie Adeline, daughter of

Abner Monroe and Mary Ann (Cantrell) Womack, wife of Jesse London Jones.]

JONES, Jesse L. 26 Sep 1871-28 Mar 1918. [Son of Matthew Jenkins and Nancy Jane (Mullican) Jones, husband of Minnie Adeline Womack, married 25 Dec 1895.]

JONES, George Leland. 15 Jun 1899-21 Feb 1914. [Son of Jesse London and Minnie Adeline (Womack) Jones.]

JONES, Jesse Noel. Born and died 11 May 1912. [Son of Jesse London and Minnie Adeline (Womack) Jones.]

JONES, Mary Belle. 31 Jan 1911-21 May 1911. [Daughter of Jesse London and Minnie Adeline (Womack) Jones.]

WHEELER, Dosia. 13 Nov 1865-22 Dec 1905. [Theodocia, daughter of Matthew Jenkins and Nancy Jane (Mullican) Jones, wife of William F. Wheeler, married 2 Jun 1886.]

STROUD, Sussie E. Noc 1845-6 Mar 1910. [Daughter of Alsey and Melvina (Moore) Jones, wife of Bryant Stroud.]

NELSON, Tennie. 31 Mar 1867-16 Oct 1898.

HOLCOMB, J. R. Feb 1789-21 Mar 1866. [Jeptha R. Holcomb, husband of Martha _____.]

HOLCOMB, Melvina. 23 Sep 1828-13 Nov 1888. [Daughter of Jeptha R. and Martha (_____) Holcomb.]

PHILLIPS, Lizzie Ella. 9 Nov 1892-11 Nov 1892. [Daughter of William Thomas and Mary (Holcomb) Phillips.]

PHILLIPS, Flora Catherine. 22 Jun 1897-9 Jul 1898. [Daughter of William Thomas and Mary (Holcomb) Phillips.]

NEWBY, Synthia. 14 Jul 1810-21 Jul 1877. [Wife of William B.R. Newby.]

NEWBY, Adah Bell. Died 21 Oct 1887, aged 1 year, 10 months and 18 days. [Daughter of General N. and Sarah E. (Marcum) Newby.]

NEWBY, General. 23 Dec 1863-19 Aug 1889. [Son of General N.M. and Sarah (Wheeler) Newby, grandson of William B.R. and Synthia (_____) Newby, husband of Sarah E. Marcum, married 5 Nov 1882.]

*NEWBY, Sarah Elizabeth Marcum. No dates. Daughter of Leander and Rosanna (Lewis) Marcum, granddaughter of Rulless and Delilah (Moore) Lewis.]

GASAWAY, H.G. 2 Jan 1890-29 Jun 1891. [Child of C.H. and Susan C. (Dobbs) Gasaway.]

DOBBS, Eliza. 20 Mar 1815-20 Aug 1892.

MARLER, James A. 5 Aug 1833-4 Oct 1906. [James Alexander, husband of Susan Jones, married 13 Mar 1856.]

MARLER, Susan. 26 Jan 1838-5 Oct 1900. [Daughter of Isaac and Alcinda (_____) Jones, wife of James Alexander Marler.]

Jones Cemetery, Cont.

BAKER, Mariah C. 28 May 1828-22 Oct 1900.

MARLER, Joseph L. 25 Nov 1867-8 Aug 1904. [Son of James Alexander and Susan (Jones) Marler.]

EDGE, Z. 10 Feb 1826-18 Jul 1890. [Zebedee, son of Levi and Mary (Stockstill) Edge, husband of Mary Ann VanHooser, married 7 Mar 1850.]

*EDGE, Mary Ann. 22 Jan 1826-1899. [Daughter of Isaac and Jeston (Pigg) VanHooser, wife of Zebedee Edge.]

HALE, Rebecka Mary. 13 Dec 1845-14 Mar 1913. [Daughter of John C. and Hannah (_____) Jones, wife of Albert Hale.]

NEWBY, W.H. 30 Sep 1849-19 Apr 1909. [William H., son of William B.R. and Synthia (_____) Newby, husband of Martha Paralee Womack, married 12 Apr 1891. Martha is buried at Oak Grove Cemetery near Dibrell.]

NEWBY, Martha E. 23 Jun 1874-18 Aug 1907. [Daughter of William H. and Martha "Mattie" (Womack) Newby.]

CHRISTIAN, Tennessee H. 6 Mar 1845-6 Jun 1908. [Daughter of William B.R. and Synthia (_____) Newby, wife of Hiram J. Christian, married 30 Aug 1891.]

NEWBY, Elizabeth A. 26 Aug 1836-28 Aug 1902. [Daughter of William B.R. and Synthia (_____) Newby.]

NEWBY, Mary. 16 Oct 1847-12 Jun 1883. [Mary Pickett, first wife of William H. Newby, married 3 Oct 1871.]

NEWBY, Mary F. 16 Jan 1882-12 Aug 1883. [Daughter of J.A. and M.L. (Crane) Newby.]

*JONES, Aunt Polly. Died 10 Feb 1907, aged 92 years, 9 months and 18 days.

*HALE, Jennie. Died 5 Jun 1905, age 5 years, daughter of William Harvey and Martha J. (Marler) Hale.

KELL CEMETERY

__Location: Leesburg Community south of McMinnville.

KELL, Thomas.   16 May 1791-18 Sep 1877.   [Son of William and _____
          (_____) Kell, husband of Lydia Lakey.]

KELL, Lydia Lakey. 16 Sep 1793-17 Oct 1877. [Daughter of Thomas and Anna
          (Hadley) Lakey, wife of Thomas Kell.]

LAKEY, Anna. Mar 1758-6 Oct 1841. [Daughter of Simon and _____ (_____)
          Hadley, wife of Thomas Lakey, married Jan 1777. Thomas Lakey
          was born in 1751.]

KELL, Isabella. 24 Feb 1824-9 Dec 1879. [Daughter of Thomas and Lydia
          (Lakey) Kell.]

KELL, Nimrod. 13 Feb 1839-28 Nov 1877. [Son of Thomas and Lydia (Lakey)
          Kell, husband of 1) Angeline Higginbotham, married 1 Nov 1860
          and 2) Jane Christian, married 11 Jun 1876.]

KELL, Angeline. 9 Jan 1840-17 Apr 1874. [Angeline Higginbotham, wife of
          Nimrod Kell.]

KELL, Mary. 11 Mar 1867-19 Dec 1882. [Daughter of Nimrod and Angeline
          (Higginbotham) Kell.]

KELL, L.E. 12 Jan 1870-20 Jan 1890. [Lydia E., daughter of Nimrod and
          Angeline (Higginbotham) Kell.]

KING CEMETERY

   Location: On Viola road one and a half miles south of Brookside
      Community Club Building. This cemetery was nearly destroyed.

KING, John H. 3 Feb 1837-30 Jan 1928. [Son of Wilson and Elizabeth
          (Sellars) King, husband of Amanda Malvina Higginbotham, married
          3 Feb 1867.]

Several fieldstones and unmarked graves.

The following are new markers:

KING, Phillip. 1760-1836. REVOLUTIONARY WAR.   [Husband of Nancy
          Woodson.]

KING, Nancy. Died 27 Oct 1840. [Nancy Woodson, wife of Phillip King.]

KING, Wilson Cleary Nelson. 1802-1877. [Son of Phillip and Nancy
          (Woodson) King, married 1) Elizabeth Sellars and 2) Elizabeth
          (Reynolds) Colville, married 5 Mar 1874.]

KING, Elizabeth. 1810-1872. [First wife of Wilson Cleary Nelson King.]

KIRBY CEMETERY

Location: In Earlyville community.

HARDING, Tommie J.   6 Sep 1893-12 Sep 1967.   [Tommie Jane, daughter of Robert and Ida (Summers) Thomas, wife of James Lewis Harding.]

HARDING, James L.   1 May 1875-31 Jul 1961.   [James Lewis, son of Dr. C.C. and Narcisus (Spurlock) Harding, husband of Tommie Jane Thomas.]

HARDING, Mary.   2 Dec 1926-17 Nov 1928.   [Daughter of James Lewis and Tommie Jane (Thomas) Harding.]

HARDING, Murray S.   Born and died Sep 1950.   [Murray Stephenson, son of Murray and Vivian May (Rutledge) Harding.]

HOLDER, M. Bell.   26 Jul 1880-19 Oct 1947.   [Amanda Belle, daughter of John and Mary (Stewart) Wilson, wife of John H. Holder, married 10 Dec 1895.]

HOLDER, John H.   24 Oct 1874-18 Jul 1941.   [John Henry, son of Louis and Pattie (Paris) Holder, husband of Amanda Belle Wilson, married 10 Dec 1895.]

HOLDER, Roy H.   30 May 1906-12 May 1928.   [Son of John and Amanda Bell (Wilson) Holder, single.]

MASEY, Frank.   27 Nov 1900-26 Jan 1920.   [Son of James M. and Lillie B. (Wilson) Masey.]

MASEY, Nellie E.   1 Oct 1898-30 May 1919.   [Daughter of James M. and Lillie B. (Wilson) Masey.]

MASEY, Margaret V.   26 May 1892-12 Feb 1915.   [Daughter of James M. and Lillie B. (Wilson) Masey.]

MASEY, Lillie B.   26 May 1871-27 Jan 1919.   [Lillie Brown, daughter of John and Mary (Stewart) Wilson, wife of James M. Masey.]

MASEY, James M.   6 May 1872-21 Oct 1942.   [Husband of Lillie Brown Wilson, died in Monticello, IL.]

MASEY, Ellis.   1 Apr 1903-4 Apr 1930.   [Son of James M. and Lillie Brown (Wilson) Masey.]

MASEY, James O.   28 Aug 1910-27 Mar 1957.   WWII.   [James Odis, son of James M. and Lillie B. (Wilson) Masey, husband of Thiren Mae Dennis.]

MASEY, Thiren Mae.   2 Jun 1917-1983.   [Thiren Mae Dennis, wife of James Odis Masey.]

MASEY, Ruff L.   5 Jun 1872-8 Sep 1943.   [Rufus Lewis, son of W.W. "Buck" and Margaret J. (Young) Mazey of Cannon County, husband of Elizabeth Jane Wilson.]

MASEY, Jinnie. 22 Apr 1873-7 Oct 1940.   [Elizabeth Jane, daughter of John B. and Mary (Stewart) Wilson, wife of Rufus Lewis Masey.]

TUBB, C.L.   11 Sep 1871-7 Oct 1940.   [Calvin Leland, son of Jack and

Lottie (Parton) Tubb, husband of 1) Nellie Wilson, and 2) Allie Hughes.]

TUBB, Nellie. 12 Jul 1884-14 Feb 1920. [Nellie Wilson, first wife of Calvin Leland Tubb, married 2 Oct 1901.]

WILSON, John B. 17 Jul 1845-30 Sep 1918. [Son of William and Emeline (Kirby) Wilson, married Mary C. Stewart on 31 Oct 1867.]

WILSON, Mary C. 19 Jul 1852-26 Mar 1911. [Mary C. Stewart, wife of John B. Wilson.]

WILSON, William. Died 28 Feb 1899, age 80 years. [Husband of Emeline Kirby.]

WILSON, Emeline. 1821- . [Daughter of William and _____ (_____) Kirby, wife of William Wilson.]

WILSON, Joe Firm. 3 Apr 1861-14 Feb 1924. [Husband of Mattie Ann Pennington, married 20 Dec 1886.]

WILSON, Mattie Ann Pennington. 1 Apr 1871-29 Mar 1942. [Wife of Joe Firm Wilson.]

BOGLE, Ernest Thomas. 1904-23 Jan 1934. [Son of James and Mattie (Brown) Bogle.]

HARDING, N.G. 1846-7 Jun 1930. [Narcisus Geneva, daughter of Joe Frank and Elmira (Howard) Spurlock, wife of Dr. Carpenter C. Harding.]

HARDING, Oscar. 10 May 1881-6 Mar 1917. [Son of Dr. C.C. and Narcisus Geneva (Spurlock) Harding, husband of Nettie Spurlock.]

JONES, Nettie Harding. 23 May 1885-27 Mar 1949. [Daughter of Charles and Perseda (Dodd) Spurlock, wife of 1) Oscar Harding and 2) Hugh L. Jones, married 29 Jan 1949.]

KIRBY, R.S. 9 Mar 1849-15 Mar 1927. [Robert Shelley, son of James and Rosanna (Smith) Kirby, husband of Sarah D. Smithson.]

KIRBY, Sarah J. 29 Dec 1856-1 Jun 1890. [Sarah Jackaline Smithson, wife of Robert Shelley Kirby, married 4 Oct 1871 in Cannon Co., TN.]

KIRBY, J.S. 21 Dec 1881-23 Mar 1950. [John Sampson, son of Robert Shelley and Sarah (Smithson) Kirby, husband of Martha Thompson.]

THURMAN, Margaret Elizabeth. 6 Dec 1851-31 Aug 1935. [Margaret Elizabeth McDaniel, wife of Charlie Thurman.]

WILSON, Phebie Jane Ford. 1 Sep 1852-7 Aug 1916. [Daughter of _____ and _____ (Green) Ford, wife of James C. Wilson.]

WILSON, J.C. 3 Jan 1844-21 May 1929. [James C., son of William and Emeline (Kirby) Wilson, husband of Phebie Jane Ford.]

HAWKINS, Offie L. 11 Sep 1889-14 Aug 1971. [Offie Lillian, daughter of James C. and Phebie Jane (Ford) Wilson, wife of Willis Hawkins.]

HAWKINS, Willis. 12 Nov 1888-27 Dec 1962. [John Willis, son of John and Amanda (Jones) Hawkins, husband of 1) Offie Lillian Wilson and

2) Mae Dodd.]

HAMMER, R.C. 1851-1897. [Robert C. Hammer, son of R. B. and Lucinda
(_____) Hammer, husband of Jennie Jones, married 8 Mar 1873.]

HAMMER, Jennie. 1857-Mar 1895. [Virginia, daughter of Eli and Ruth Ann
(Herndon) Jones, wife of Robert C. Hammer.]

HAMMER, Lura.   1872-1891
HAMMER, Willie.   1880-1899
HAMMER, Victor V.   18 Aug 1882-6 Jun 1899
HAMMER, Edith A.   13 Jul 1898-7 Oct 1898

HAMMER, William H. 17 Jul 1861-27 Feb 1946. [William Henry, son of Berry
and Lucinda (Bratcher) Hammer, husband of Amanda Elizabeth
Jones, married 29 Apr 1888.]

HAMMER, Amanda E. 18 Mar 1868-9 Jan 1942. [Amanda Elizabeth, daughter of
Eli and Ruth Ann (Herndon) Jones, wife of William H. Hammer.]

HAMMER, Bertha V. 30 Jan 1897-5 Feb 1917. [Daughter of William H. and
Amanda Elizabeth (Jones) Hammer.]

JONES, J. Claude. 31 Jul 1880-12 Apr 1906. [Son of Eli and Ruth Ann
(Herndon) Jones.]

BAILEY, Lucinda F. 13 Nov 1860-14 Jan 1928. [Lucinda Frances, daughter
of Eli and Ruth Ann (Herndon) Jones.]

*BAILEY, John D. 29 Feb 1860-27 Feb 1929. Son of W.J. and Martha E.
(Melton) Bailey, husband of Lucinda Frances Jones.

JONES, J.W.   6 Jun 1874-23 Nov 1906   [John]
JONES, Mattie   1862-1926 [Martha]
JONES, J.F.   1867-1900 [Joseph]

JONES, Eli. 25 Mar 1927-29 Nov 1903. [Son of Matthew and Mary (_____)
Jones, husband of Ruth Ann Herndon, married 15 Dec 1853.]

JONES, Ruth A. 30 Aug 1835-5 Dec 1914. [Ruth Ann, daughter of Jacob and
Jane (West) Herndon, wife of Eli Jones.]

KIRBY, W.T. 17 Jun 1849-5 Sep 1927. [William Taylor, son of William and
Malinda (Hammerstein) Kirby, husband of Mary Caroline Campbell,
married 12 May 1892.]

HAWKINS, Mabel Clair. 4 Dec 1905-9 Oct 1907. [Daughter of William and
_____ (_____) Hawkins.]

WILSON, Ethel M. 5 Jul 1894-22 Jan 1895. [Daughter of James C. and
Phebie Jane (Ford) Wilson.]

BELL, Artie E. 22 May 1872-20 Jan 1894. [Daughter of James C. and Phebie
Jane (Ford) Wilson, wife of T.C. Bell, married 14 Oct 1893.]

*BELL, T.C. "Dock" died Jul 1894, husband of Artie E. Wilson.

WILSON, Charlie E. 2 Aug 1870-22 Mar 1887.

WILSON, Jessie J. 8 Jan 1887-27 Feb 1887.

Kirby Cemetery, Cont.

DULEU, Samuel Z.   2 Jul 1886-2 May 1887.   [Son of John B. and Mary A.
      (_____) Duleu.]

DULEU, John B.   21 Sep 1832-7 Mar 1890.

DULEU, Mary A.   26 Aug 1884-19 May 1907.   [Wife of John B. Duleu.]

WORLEY, Lorin A.   28 May 1840-10 Jan 1923.   Union Army.   [Lorin Anderson
      Worley, husband of Harriet Orrick, married 30 Jul 1899.]

KIRBY, William J.   29 Jan 1894-11 Jan 1976.   [Son of William Taylor and
      Mary Caroline (Campbell) Kirby, single.]

KIRBY, Mary.   10 Jan 1875-3 Mar 1960.   [Mary Caroline Campbell, wife of
      William Taylor "Ruff" Kirby.]

KIRBY, Charlie.   9 Jan 1904-12 Mar 1920.   [Son of William Taylor "Ruff"
      and Mary Caroline (Campbell) Kirby.   Single.]

STEMBRIDGE, Martha.   28 Oct 1896-30 Jun 1961.   [Martha Frances, daughter
      of William Taylor and Mary Caroline (Campbell) Kirby, wife of
      John Henry Stembridge.]

STEMBRIDGE, Henry.   27 Nov 1894-1971.   [John Henry, son of William Nelson
      and Hattie (Jones) Stembridge, husband of 1) Martha Kirby and
      2) Fannie Hobbs.]

JONES, Jennie F.   6 Feb 1891-8 Apr 1977.   [Jennie Ferrell, wife of Jewell
      H. Jones.]

JONES, Jewell H.   20 Jun 1899-7 Sep 1924.   [Son of John P. and Allie M.
      (Jones) Jones, husband of Jennie Ferrell.]

JONES, John P.   19 Jan 1869-Dec 1922.   [Son of Noah B. and Mary Adaline
      (Countiss) Jones, husband of Allie Mintie Jones, married 17 Feb
      1889.]

McGEE, Allie Mintie.   20 May 1871-11 Jun 1949.   [Alminta, daughter of Eli
      and Ruth Ann (Herndon) Jones, wife of 1) John P. Jones, married
      17 Feb 1889, and 2) Elijah McGee, married 18 Aug 1926.]

SIMPSON, Ernest W.   16 Jun 1922-20 Jun 1989.   WWII.   [Husband of Irene K.
      (_____) married 29 Nov 1946.]

SIMPSON, Irene K.   15 Sep 1928-   .   [Wife of Ernest W. Simpson.]

SIMPSON, Annie L.   7 Jul 1895-15 Nov 1967.   [Annie Luther, daughter of
      George and Callie (Pylent) Lindsey, wife of Herman R. Simpson.]

SIMPSON, Herman R.   4 Sep 1892-9 Feb 1967.   [Herman Robert, son of Andrew
      Jackson and Linnie (Bailey) Simpson, husband of Annie Luther
      Lindsey.]

NUNLEY, James William.   5 Jul 1947-11 Jan 1970.   Vietnam.

NUNLEY, Charity Hope Knight.   Born and died 15 Mar 1976.

STEMBRIDGE, John Marshall.   25 Sep 1933-19 Jul 1986.   [Husband of Dorothy
      Ann McGowan, married 1 Feb 1964.]

STEMBRIDGE, Dorothy Ann M. 27 Jun 1940-   . [Dorothy Ann McGowan, wife of John Marshall Stembridge.]

KIRBY, Henry Clay. 17 Oct 1892-19 Jul 1910. [Son of James and Melvina (Pennington) Kirby.]

KIRBY, Ada Magaline. 11 Apr 1890-2 Sep 1891. [Daughter of James and Melvina (Pennington) Kirby.]

KIRBY, Laura Louise. 30 Jun 1878-7 Jul 1879. [Daughter of James and Melvina (Pennington) Kirby.]

KIRBY, James. 30 Nov 1816-22 Apr 1883. [Husband of Rosanna Smith.]

KIRBY, Rosanna. 23 May 1818-1 Dec 1892. [Rosanna Smith, wife of James Kirby.]

SMITH, Eward C. 1 Jan 1818-   .

ALLEN, Virginia A. 12 Sep 1870-20 Apr 1875. [Daughter of T.P. and Harriett (_____) Allen.]

ALLEN, Colonel Andrew. 17 May 1877-31 Oct 1884.
ALLEN, Edna Isabell.   7 Aug 1883-11 Nov 1892.
  [Children of William Worth and Sarah Abigail (Whitlock) Allen.]

ALLEN, Abbigail. 10 Jul 1858-11 Aug 1929. [Sarah Abbigail, daughter of J.K.P. and Lucy (Orrick) Whitlock, Wife of William Worth Allen.]

ALLEN, W.W. 28 Oct 1849-17 Dec 1927. [William Worth, son of Thomas and Mary (_____) Allen, husband of Sarah Abbigail Whitlock.]

STEMBRIDGE, Sharah Melinda. 17 Apr 1905-16 Sep 1982. ["Linnie", daughter of Wm. James and Mary (Campbell) Kirby, wife of Alfred Joe Stembridge. New stone has "Linnie Kirby Stembridge".]

STEMBRIDGE, Alfred Joe. 17 May 1902-17 Oct 1989. [Son of William Nelson and Hattie (Jones) Stembridge, husband of Sarah Melinda Kirby.]

STEMBRIDGE, Charles Henry. 22 Apr 1928-26 May 1928. [Son of John Henry and Martha (Kirby) Stembridge.]

*CAMPBELL, Lucy. Died 23 Sep 1914, daughter of William and Emaline (Kirby) Wilson, married H. Greenley Campbell on 1 Jul 1894.

*STEMBRIDGE, Gladys Louise, born 4 Apr 1926, died 17 Apr 1926, daughter of John Henry and Martha (Kirby) Stembridge.

*HAMMER, Charlie B. Died 31 Aug 1952, son of Robert and Jennie (Jones) Hammer, husband of Zonie _____.

*KIRBY, Susanna, born 1 Mar 1824, died 2 Mar 1919, daughter of John and Sarah (Pigg) Pace, wife of Benjamin L. Kirby.

*THRUMAN, Elisha Martin, born 1 May 1886, died 2 Feb 1914, son of Charlie A. and Margaret Elizabeth (McDaniel) Thurman.

*KIRBY, Benjamin L. Died 1895, son of William and _____ (_____) Kirby, husband of Susanna Pace. Civil War veteran.

LANCE CEMETERY

Location: Four miles south of Centertown.

LANCE, Sarah A. 1 Jan 1842-19 Jul 1910. [Daughter of Joseph and Susan (_____) Waggoner, wife of Ervin C. Lance.]

LANCE, Ervin C. 1839-1916. [Son of Henry and Eliza (_____) Lance, husband of Sarah Wagoner.]

ROBERSON, John A.C. 14 Dec 1859-11 Aug 1860. [Son of Joseph Hyder and his first wife Sarah (Shockley) Roberson.]

SHOCKLEY, James P. 27 Aug 1834-17 Jul 1871.

LANCE, Haner. 11 Jun 1872 only date on old fieldstone.

LANCE, Hannah. 1855-1872. [Probably same as above.]

LANCE, Henry. 1816-1896. [Husband of Eliza _____.]

LANCE, Eliza. 1820-1911. [Wife of Henry Lance.]

FUSTON, Eliza. 1 Dec 1894-2 Aug 1896. [Hannah Elizabeth, daughter of Nicholas Tilmon and Martha Tennessee (Lance) Fuston.]

FUSTON, James. 8 Jan 1891-4 sep 1913. [Son of Nicholas Tilmon and Martha Tennessee (Lance) Fuston.]

FUSTON, Tilmon. 14 Jan 1861-10 Dec 1896. [Nicholas Tilmon, son of William Jefferson and Mary (Byars) Fuston, husband of Martha Tennessee "Tennie" Lance, grandson of Andy and Eliza (Jones) Fuston.]

FUSTON, Tennie. 15 Jul 1859-12 Feb 1939. [Martha Tennessee, daughter of Henry and Eliza (Bates) Lance, wife of Nicholas Tilmon Fuston.]

FUSTON, Henry O. 26 Jan 1890-6 Jun 1948. WWI. [Son of Nicholas Tilmon and Martha Tennessee (Lance) Fuston. Single.]

About 15 more fieldstones marking graves.

LEESBURG CEMETERY

Location: Off Hwy 56 south of McMinnville, in Leesburg Community. Ask for exact location from a Leesburg resident.

GRAYSON, Gilbert. 21 Dec 1857-15 Mar 1953. [Husband of Lillian Patterson, married 28 Dec 1882.]

GRAYSON, Lillian. 6 May 1865-30 Nov 1944. [Daughter of Isaac and Sarah
        (Marbury) Patterson, wife of Gilbert Grayson.]

CUMMINGS, Beulah Grayson. 1 Dec 1899-16 Oct 1942. [Daughter of Gilbert
        and Lillian (Patterson) Grayson, wife of Will Cummings.]

GRAYSON, Ruby. 30 Apr 1896-31 May 1929. [Daughter of Gilbert and Lillian
        (Patterson) Grayson. Single.]

PATTERSON, Henry. 1869 - 1939. [Son of Isaac and Sarah (_____)
        Patterson.]

GRAYSON, Hugh. 26 Sep 1894-5 Sep 1953. WWI. [Son of Gilbert and Lillian
        (Patterson) Grayson, husband of Katherine Marbury.]

COPE, Hardy, Jr. 7 Mar 1923-12 Oct 1980. WWII. [Son of Hardy, Sr. and
        Jessie Mazy (_____) Cope, husband of Ruth Grayson.]

COPE, Ruth Grayson. 12 Jul 1927-17 Jun 1962. [Daughter of Alex and Ethel
        (Buchannan) Grayson, wife of Hardy Cope, Jr.]

MARBURY, Ivy Willis. 18 Oct 1922-11 Feb 1965. WWII. [Son of Simon and
        Mary Ann (Rion) Marbury, husband of Isabell Walker.]

MARBURY, Simon Pope. 10 Nov 1900-31 Oct 1937. [Son of John and Elizabeth
        (Grayson) Marbury, husband of Tootsie Smith (div)]

MARBURY, Kent Labell. 9 Aug 1960-31 Jan 1961.

MARBURY, Ivy Lynn. 11 Oct 1958-20 Oct 1960.

MARBURY, James Bostick. 19 Aug 1917-15 Jan 1918. [Son of John and
        Elizabeth (Grayson) Marbury.]

MARBURY, Elizabeth G. 10 Jul 1883-3 Feb 1979. [Daughter of Gilbert and
        Lillian (Patterson) Grayson, wife of John Marbury, married 10
        Feb 1900.]

MARBURY, John. 7 Feb 1881-Jan 1981. [Husband of Elizabeth Grayson.]

WORTHINGTON, Annie Edna. 14 Jan 1914-   . [Annie Edna Walling,
        wife of Clarence B. Worthington.]

WORTHINGTON, Clarence B. 12 Sep 1911-9 Jul 1987. [Son of Buford and Etta
        (Lusk) Worthington, husband of Annie Edna Walling, married 25
        Dec 1937.]

HUDDLESTON, Asberry. 1 Dec 1893-22 Jul 1918. [Son of Isham and Emma
        (Bates) Huddleston, husband of Sue Foster, married 6 Oct 1917.]

WALLING, Joe. 3 Mar 1870-26 Jun 1954. [Son of Alfred "Alf" and Elizabeth
        "Bettie" (Patterson) Walling, husband of Oshia Coppinger.]

WALLING, Oshia. Nov 1883-19 Feb 1911. [Daughter of Thomas and Tilla
        (Marbury) Coppinger, wife of Joe Walling.]

WALLING, Raymond H. 6 Sep 1927-5 Nov 1965. WWII. [Son of Smith and
        Josephine (McKinley) Walling, husband of Leatrice Noble.]

WALLING, Josephine, died 27 Apr 1976, age 65 years. [Daughter of Jack and

Leesburg Cemetery, Cont.

Sally (Gwynn) McKinley, wife of Smith Walling.]

*WALLING, Smith. Died 5 Apr 1970, son of Joe and Oshia (Coppinger) Walling, husband of Josephine McKinley.

*WALLING, Betty Lou. Born 7 Jan 1933, died 23 Jan 1959. Single.

*GRAYSON, Viola, died 24 Jun 1935, daughter of Alex and Ethel (Buchannon) Grayson.

GRAYSON, A.A. 6 Jun 1892-4 Aug 1964. [Alexander A., son of Gilbert and Lillian (Patterson) Grayson, husband of Ethel Buchanan.]

WILLIAMS, Elizabeth. 3 Sep 1897-24 May 1926.

FORD, Frank. 21 Apr 1900-9 Jan 1971. WWI. [Son of Tom and Jeanette (_____) Ford, husband of Mable Louise Patterson.]

*FORD, Mable Louise. Born 12 Nov 1905, died 17 Aug 1965, daughter of Jones and Canzada (Coppinger) Patterson, wife of Frank Ford.

*FORD, Louise. Born 28 Jan 1934, died 9 Feb 1934, daughter of Frank and Mabel (Patterson) Ford.

OFFICER, Pauline. 24 Oct 1898-19 Mar 1976. [Daughter of Jones Patterson and Hattie (Parker) Patterson.]

McREYNOLDS, George A. Died 31 Aug 1935. WWI. [George Augusta, son of Martin and _____ (_____) McReynolds.]

PATTERSON, Mrs. G.A. 4 Nov 1858-18 Apr 1900. [Wife of G.A. Patterson.]

GRAYSON, Elnora. 10 Apr 1905-10 May 1936. [Daughter of Aaron and Ethel (Gardner) Marbury, wife of Gilbert Grayson.]

BROWN, Herbert. 13 Apr 1889-27 Feb 1961. [Son of George and Florence (Gardner) Brown, husband of Ammie French.]

BROWN, Ammie E. 3 Nov 1888-17 Sep 1973. [Ammie E. French, wife of Herbert Brown.]

BROWN, James Leeper. 29 May 1927- 4 Jul 1928. [Son of Herbert and Ammie E. (French) Brown.]

BROWN, Florence. 23 Apr 1870-4 May 1903. [Daughter of Madison and Mary (_____) Gardner, wife of George W. Brown, married 10 May 1893.]

*BROWN, George W. Born 29 Nov 1866, died 5 Jun 1930, son of Wesley R. and Sarah (Gardner) Brown, husband of Florence Gardner.

BROWN, Annie. 14 Jan 1871-10 Oct 1945.

OAKLEY, Addie. 22 May 1864-10 Jul 1945. [Adalade, daughter of Madison "Matt" and Mary (_____) Gardner, wife of Will Oakley.]

LEE, Joe B. 14 Aug 1902-19 May 1990. [Son of John and Jennie (Donahue) Lee, husband of Marietta Marbury.]

LEE, Marietta. 27 May 1916-   . [Daughter of Aaron and Ethel (Gardner) Marbury, wife of Joe B. Lee.]

*McKINLEY, Louis. Born 1916, died 30 May 1988, son of Jack and Sally
          (Gwynn) McKinley, husband of Clara Frances Grayson.

*WINTON, Clara P. Born 1925, died 12 Mar 1987. Clara Frances, daughter
          of Willie Lee and Rebecca Sue (Foster) Grayson, wife of 1) _____
          McKinley and 2) Hollis Winton.

PATTERSON, Hattie. Nov 1875-5 Oct 1906. [Daughter of Preston and Ritter
          (Mason) Parker, wife of Jones Patterson, married 30 Dec 1895.]

WOODS, Eden. 30 Apr 1891-31 Dec 1946. WWI.

McCLARTY, Reathy. 1882-11 Feb 1981. [Daughter of Minor and Lucy
          (Patterson) Gardner, wife of Comer McClarty.]

BREWINGTON, Pearl. 1894-25 Oct 1978. [Daughter of Sam and Lucy (Marbury)
          Foster, wife of Joe Brewington.]

GRAYSON, Sussie. 1895-10 Nov 1977. [Rebecca Susie, daughter of Sam and
          Lucy (Marbury) Foster, wife of Willie Lee Grayson.]

RAMSEY, Annie Mae. 1900 - 4 May 1993. [Daughter of William and Phronie
          (Gardner) Ramsey.]

GRAYSON, George L. 23 Aug 1919-10 Jul 1991. WWII. [Son of Annie Mae
          Ramsey and George Grayson.]

McREYNOLDS, Willie. 7 Jul 1896-19 Sep 1974. [Son of John and Saphronia
          (Gardner) McReynolds, husband of Alvilda Brown.]

RAMSEY, Lucy D. 31 Dec 1916-4 Aug 1970. [Lucy Dean, daughter of Will and
          Saphronia (Gardner) Ramsey.]

McREYNOLDS, Nathan. 11 Jan 1895-31 May 1956. WWI. [Son of John and
          Saphronia (Gardner) McReynolds, husband of Odell Huddleston.]

McREYNOLDS, Wallace. 11 Aug 1897-3 Feb 1977. WWII. [Son of John and
          Saphronia (Gardner) McReynolds, husband of Rhoda Grayson.]

McREYNOLDS, Rhodie. 31 Mar 1910-27 Mar 1945. [Daughter of Mack and Susie
          (Ramsey) Grayson, married Wallace McReynolds on 13 Nov 1927.]

GRAYSON, Sylva. [July 1864-16 Dec 1935]. [Daughter of Isaac and Sarah
          (Marbury) Patterson, wife of Alexander Grayson, married 11 Mar
          1888.]

GRAYSON, Alexander. [Dec 1859-28 Apr 1932.] [Son of Simon Poke and
          Simpie (_____) Grayson, husband of Sylva Patterson.]

FOSTER, Sam. [Aug 1846]-11 Feb 1930. [Son of _____ and Mary (_____)
          Foster, husband of Lucy Marbury, married 5 Oct 1872.]

FOSTER, Lucy. Died 22 Nov 1929. [Daughter of Jack and Lucinda (Black)
          Marbury, wife of Sam Foster. Born about 1855. Funeral home has
          date of death as 1928.]

PRATER, Benjamin. Died 25 Sep 1936.

McREYNOLDS, Percilla. 25 Oct 1844-21 Aug 1907. [Percilla Lamb, wife of
          Anderson McReynolds.]

McREYNOLDS, Anderson. 15 Mar 1835-4 Mar 1912. [Husband of Percilla Lamb.]

WALDERN, Hallie. 14 Sep 1881-21 Mar 1931. [Daughter of Anderson and Percilla (Lamb) McReynolds. Funeral home records give year of death as 1934.]

CUMMINGS, Mary Elizabeth. 29 Jul 1866-30 May 1945. [Daughter of Anderson and Percilla (Lamb) McReynolds, wife of Jarrett Cummings.]

GARDNER, Sallie A. 5 Feb 1846-1 May 1914. [Sarah Ann, daughter of Sid and Lucy (Moore) Crowder, wife of Matt Gardner, married 7 Sep 1885.]

GARDNER, Matt B. Dec 1816-28 Dec 1917. [Husband of Sarah A. Gardner.]

BREWINGTON, Bettie E. Brown. 16 May 1870-8 Oct 1915. [Bettie E. Brown, wife of William Brewington]

BREWINGTON, William. 16 Apr 1862-14 Sep 1938. [Husband of Bettie E. Brown.]

McKINLEY, Jack. 10 Jun 1882-27 Dec 1981. [Husband of Sallie Gwyn.]

McKINLEY, Sallie. [11 Sep] 1888-[3 Feb] 1959. [Daughter of George and _____ (_____) Gwynn, wife of Jack McKinley.]

ROBERTSON, Donald. 1937 - 27 Jan 1994. [Son of Lee and Lillie (Patterson) Robertson.]

BILES, Dorothy. 1929 - 9 Nov 1974. [Daughter of Harrison and Frances (_____) Bonner, wife of Fred Biles.]

BILES, Fred. 1932 - 26 Jun 1980. WWII. [Son of Eural and Leola (Ramsey) Biles, husband of Dorothy Bonner.]

*McREYNOLDS, Martin. 1845 - 9 Sep 1914.

*GRAYSON, Infant. Born and died 6 Apr 1952, son of Magnolia Grayson.

*MARBURY, Aaron. born 14 Feb 1886, died 10 Apr 1952, son of Cy and Jane (Side) Marbury, husband of Ethel Gardner.

*PATTERSON, Jones. Born 15 Nov 1872, died 29 Jul 1952, son of Isaac and Sarah (Marbury) Patterson, husband of 1) Hattie Parker and 2) Canzada Coppinger.

*MARKS, Lula. Died 6 Jun 1910, age 46.

*HILL, Johnnie. Died 28 May 1911, age 10 months.

*McREYNOLDS, Elizabeth. Died 27 Jun 1911.

*WOODLEY, Ely. Died 7 Sep 1912, age 83 years.

*PATTERSON, Amos. Died 7 Jul 1920, age 16 years.

*YORK, Infant. Born and died 18 Oct 1920.

*McREYNOLDS, Mary. Died 15 Feb 1919, age 26 years.

Leesburg Cemetery, Cont.

*MARBURY, Cora. Died 6 Jan 1913, wife of Cyrus (Cy) Marbury.

*BROWN, George. Died 17 Apr 1918.

*GRAYSON, J.D. Died 27 Oct 1924, age 2 months.

*BROWN, George W. Born 29 Nov 1866, died 5 Jun 1930, son of Wesley R. and
      Sarah (Gardner) Brown.

*GRAYSON, Evelyn. Born 9 Nov 1928, died 4 Jan 1929, daughter of W.L. and
      Susie (Foster) Grayson.

*RAMSEY, Phronie (Sophrona). Born 11 May 1876, died 22 Dec 1938, daughter
      of Mat and Mary (_____) Gardner, wife of 1) John McReynolds,
      married 21 Jan 1893 and 2) Bill Ramsey, married 4 Sep 1905.

*GRAYSON, Mary Alexander. Died 20 Sep 1923, age 18 days.

*PARKER, Nelson Masy. Born 24 Oct 1893, died 6 Jun 1914, son of William
      Preston and Emily (Stevenson) Parker.

*MARBURY, Isaac. Born 26 Feb 1915, died 6 Mar 1915. Son of Aaron and
      Ella (Gardner) Marbury.

*GRAYSON, John. Born 1908, died 7 Apr 1915, son of Mack and Susie
      (Ramsey) Grayson.

*PARKER, Jannie. Born 8 Jun 1887, died 30 Jan 1916, daughter of Preston
      and _____ (_____) Parker.

*GRAYSON, Goldie May. Born 20 Aug 1917, died 2 Aug 1941, daughter of Will
      and Beulah (Lusk) Carr, wife of Gilbert Grayson.

*GRAYSON, Gell Berta. Born 19 Oct 1938, died 29 Jul 1941, daughter of
      Gilbert and Goldie May (Carr) Grayson.

*ROBERTS, Infant. Born and died 25 Jan 1950, child of Cowan and Arizona
      (Grayson) Roberts.

HOLLAND, Lucy Marbury. Born Jul 1878, died 12 Jul 1906, wife of Walter
      Holland, married 4 Jun 1898.

McREYNOLDS, William "Will". Born Jan 1872, died 28 Apr 1931, son of
      Anderson and Priscilla (Lamb) McReynolds.

JONES, Ermon. Died 5 Mar 1991, age 79 years, daughter of Ollies and Mary
      (Rines) Hunter, wife of Willie Jones.

*RAMSEY, Donnie. Born and died 7 Nov 1961, infant of Hubert and Roberta
      (Winton) Ramsey.

*HILL, Theadoshia. Born 10 Aug 1855, died 30 Nov 1934, daughter of George
      and Mary (Lamb) Grayson, wife of Gwyn Hill.

*BAKER, Infant. Born and died 12 Jan 1916, infant of Herbert and Sarah
      (Terry) Baker.

*GRAYSON, Lizzie. Born 29 Dec 1917, died 9 Apr 1918, daughter of Mack and
      Susie (Ramsey) Grayson.

Leesburg Cemetery, Cont.

*GRAYSON, Gilberta. Born 12 Sep 1920, died 30 Sep 1920, daughter of Alex
        and Ethel (Buchanan) Grayson.

*MARBURY, Ethel. Born Oct 1887, died 25 Dec 1920, daughter of Minor and
        Lucy (Patterson) Gardner, wife of Aaron Marbury.

*McKINLEY, Infant. Born and died 23 May 1923, infant of Jack and Sallie
        (Gwyn) McKinley.

*RAMSEY, William "Bill Tate". Born 1 Jan 1862, died 6 Aug 1953, son of
        Emily Ramsey, husband of Sophrona (Gardner) McReynolds, married
        4 Sep 1905.

*COPPINGER, Thomas B. Died 20 Oct 1939, husband of Tiller Marbury,
        married 14 Jul 1878.

*COPPINGER, Tiller. Born Oct 1857, died 23 Feb 1942, daughter of Jack and
        Lucinda (Smith) Marbury, wife of Tom Coppinger.

*GRAYSON, Ike Henry. Born 3 Nov 1883, died 2 Feb 1949, son of Gilbert and
        Lillian (Patterson) Grayson, husband of Emma Linsey.

*McKINLEY, Clara Elora. Born 2 Jan 1906, died 15 Jan 1965, daughter of
        Lewis and Matilda (Willis) Vonnoy, wife of Raymond McKinley.

*GRAYSON, James William. Born 8 Sep 1905, died 10 Jun 1955, son of Mack
        and Susie (Ramsey) Grayson, husband of Virginia Marbury.

*JOHNSON, Dianne Faye. Born and died 15 Jun 1956, daughter of James
        Edward and Ellen Lucille (Wade) Johnson.

*GRAYSON, Infant. Born and died 15 Jun 1956. Infant of James and Shirley
        Jean (Ramsey) Grayson.

*MARBURY, Infants. Born and died 19 Feb 1936. Twins of Mary Marbury.

*SHOCKLEY, Infant. Born and died 26 Feb 1936. Infant of Herman and
        Bertha (_____) Shockley.

*BROWN, Infant. Born and died 12 Apr 1936. Infant of Lawrence and
        Margaret (Grayson) Brown.

*WOODS, Jane Tryn. Died 13 Nov 1970, aged 3 months, daughter of Thomas
        Fred and Josephine (McKinley) Woods.

*WOODS, Pamela Lynn. Died 10 Dec 1970, age 2 1/2 years, daughter of
        Thomas Fred and Josephine (McKinley) Woods.

LIBERTY CEMETERY

Location: Off Hwy 55W, 1/4 mile outside Liberty city limits.

FULTS, Ophia Locke. 1 Feb 1893-25 Jan 1942. [Elizabeth Ophelia, daughter
    of Wm. Wallace and Mary Frances (Estes) Locke, wife of James
    Ethan Fults, married 9 Dec 1919.]

LOCKE, Beatrice. 13 Dec 1917-17 Mar 1939. [Daughter of John Thomas and
    May Belle (Merriman) Locke. Single.]

LOCKE, Belle Merriman. 16 Jul 1888-9 Aug 1988. [May Belle, daughter of
    Isaac Mack and Martha Selina (Cass) Merriman, wife of John
    Thomas Locke.]

LOCKE, John Thomas. 13 Nov 1883-27 Feb 1970. [Son of William Wallace and
    Mary F. (Estes) Locke, husband of May Belle Merriman, married
    3 Jul 1910.]

NEAL, Calvin A. 26 Jan 1905-18 Jul 1935. [Calvin Anderson, son of Melvin
    Russell and Charlie (Bennett) Neal, husband of Madge Riggs,
    married 12 Apr 1924.]

NEAL, Madge R. 10 Dec 1900-19 Dec 1985. [Daughter of Clyde and Elva
    (Hinkley) Riggs, wife of Calvin Anderson Neal.]

NEAL, Melvin R. 18 Jun 1881-26 Jul 1943. [Melvin Russell, son of David
    and Susan Frankie (Arnold) Neal, husband of Charlie Bennett.]

RIGGS, Elva Mai. 23 Feb 1875-16 May 1940. [Daughter of Orin and Martha
    (Huskin) Hinkley, wife of Clyde Benny Riggs.]

RIGGS, Clyde B. 6 Nov 1874-17 Feb 1949. [Clyde Benny, son of John and
    Margaret (Thomas) Riggs, husband of Elva Mai Hinkley, married
    25 Aug 1897.]

CANTRELL, Toy P. 20 Jun 1900-23 Apr 1957. [Toy Preston, son of Sam and
    Malissa (Cantrell) Cantrell, husband of Virginia Riggs.]

CANTRELL, Virginia R. 1907 -25 Oct 1989. [Virginia Gladys "Ted" ,
    daughter of Clyde and Elva (Hinkley) Riggs, wife of 1) Toy
    Preston Cantrell and 2) Joe S. Bell.]

LAWSON, Fred. 8 Feb 1873-9 Dec 1965. [Son of Peter and Jennie (Lane)
    Lawson, husband of Betty Lowe.]

LAWSON, Betty. 22 Jan 1876-5 Apr 1957. [Daughter of Charles and Sarah
    (Moon) Lowe, wife of Fred Lawson.]

McBRIDE, Emma Luella. 9 Dec 1890-1 Jul 1936. [Emma Luella Bolt, wife of
    Fulton McBride.]

McBRIDE, Fulton. 23 May 1887-10 Mar 1937. [Husband of Emma Luella Bolt,
    married 28 Feb 1915.]

McBRIDE, S/Sgt Johnny F. 23 Oct 1929-20 Dec 1952. WWII. [Johnny Fulton,
    son of Fulton and Emma Luella (Bolt) McBride. Single.]

MUNCEY, Charlie M. 28 Feb 1891-8 Feb 1955. [Charles Morgan, son of
    Matthew and Clarissa (Shrader) Muncey, husband of 1) Mary

Liberty Cemetery, Cont.

Bershie Newby and 2) Earline Reno, married in 1949.]

MUNCEY, Earline Reno. 3 Jun 1918-   . [Wife of Charles M. Muncey.]

KEEL, Howrie Louis. 18 Jun 1918-24 Jun 1987. WWII. [Son of Bryon and
        Rona Catherine (Jarrell) Keel, husband of Gladys Beatrice
        McBride.]

KEEL, Gladys B. 22 Apr 1916-24 Feb 1983. [Gladys Beatrice, daughter of
        Fulton and Emma Luella (Holt) McBride, wife of Howrie Louis
        Keel.]

BUTCHER, Vester E. Jr. Born and died 3 Nov 1945. [Son of Vester and
        Dorothy (Lawson) Butcher.]

BUTCHER, Mary Linda.   Born and died 29 Aug 1948.
BUTCHER, Joyce Euline. 5 Sep 1950-9 Oct 1950.
BUTCHER, Melbalene.   Born and died 1952.
        Children of Valter and Elsie Mae (Lawson) Butcher.

BUTCHER, Valter M.   1906-1954. [Valter Mason, husband of Elsie Mae
        Lawson.]

BUTCHER, Elsie M.   1910-7 Aug 1987. [Elsie Mae, daughter of Fred and
        Betty (Lowe) Lawson, husband of Valter M. Butcher.]

TILLETT, Lillian G. 16 Feb 1909-17 Mar 1993. [Lillian Gladious, daughter
        of Hezekiah and Delia (_____) Turner, wife of C.H. Tillett.]

TILLETT, C.H.   30 Apr 1905-10 Mar 1986.   [Son of Fred F. and Eva
        (Northcutt) Tillett, husband of Lillian G. Turner.]

TILLETT, C.H., Jr. 20 Nov 1927 only date on stone. [Son of C. H. and
        Lillian G. (Turner) Tillett.]

TILLETT, L.M.   1902 - 1937.   [Son of Fred F. and Eva (Northcutt)
        Tillett.]

TILLETT, Fred F. 30 Nov 1879-30 Oct 1944. [Fred Fuston, son of George
        and Jennie (Atnip) Tillett, husband of Eva Northcutt.]

TILLETT, Eva. 13 Mar 1882-1 Jun 1942. [Daughter of Elijah and Sarah
        (Evans) Northcutt, wife of Fred Fuston Tillett.]

DAVIS, Jane. 17 Jun 1851-14 Oct 1938. [Mary Jane, daughter of Wm. R. and
        Nancy Jane (Dyer) Bennett, wife of John Davis.]

DAVIS, John. 15 May 1849-12 Nov 1944. [Son of Amos and _____ (Bishop)
        Davis, husband of Jane Bennett, married 6 Jul 1876.]

BARRETT, Hiram. 4 Feb 1888-11 May 1973. [Hiram H., husband of Callie
        Nancy Davis.]

*BARRETT, Callie Nancy. 17 Jul 1888-30 Jan 1957. [Daughter of John and
        Mary Jane (Bennett) Davis, wife of Hiram H. Barrett.]

THAXTON, Will Annen. 8 Jan 1893-21 Feb 1947. [Son of Ira Thomas and
        Minnie Flora (Locke) Thaxton, husband of Nannie Lee Bell.]

THAXTON, Nannie Lee.   30 Jan 1892-22 Jul 1964.   [Date of death from funeral home records is 22 Jul 1956. Daughter of W.A. and Nancy (Gibbs) Bell.]

*THAXTON, Ada Eugina. Died 22 Nov 1906, age 1 year.

THAXTON, William Annen, Jr. 15 Sep 1915-2 May 1964. [Son of William Annen and Nannie Lee (Bell) Thaxton, husband of Dovie Clading Lawrence.]

THAXTON, Dovie Clading. 1916 - 1981. [Daughter of James and Sarah Catherine (Luna) Lawrence, wife of William A. Thaxton, Jr.]

WOOD, R.L. 20 Aug 1879-31 Dec 1961. [Robert L., son of Alexander Hamilton and Annie (St. John) Wood, husband of 1) Amby Hart and 2) Myrtle Wilson.]

WOOD, Amby. 30 Dec 1880-6 Feb 1919. [Funeral home record gives date of birth as 31 Dec 1874. Daughter of Buck and Mary (Wood) Hart, wife of Robert L. Wood.]

WOODS, Cleveland. 10 Sep 1884-14 Jul 1934. [Grover Cleveland, son of Alexander Hamilton and Annie (St. John) Wood.]

EARLE, Mabel N. 17 Jul 1891-27 Dec 1967. [Mable Claricy, daughter of John Andrew and Ann (Bragg) Newman, wife of Claude Earls.]

NEWMAN, John Andrew. 26 Apr 1857-27 Feb 1918. [Son of Andrew Jackson and Elizabeth (Kimbro) Newman, husband of Ann Bragg, married 6 Jan 1885.]

NEWMAN, Ann Bragg. 6 Aug 1865-28 Dec 1932. [Wife of John Andrew Newman.]

ROGERS, Leona Z. 24 Oct 1917-21 Jun 1973. [Daughter of Oscar and Hattie (Northcutt) Rogers. Single.]

ROGERS, Hattie. 26 Jan 1890-6 Jan 1952. [Hattie Almeda, daughter of J.R. and Ora (Mann) Northcutt, wife of Oscar Rogers.]

ROGERS, Oscar. 28 May 1885-5 Jul 1948. [Oscar Sidney, son of James R., Sr. and Florence (Schrader) Rogers, husband of Hattie Almeda Northcutt.]

ROGERS, Infant. Born and died 8 Sep 1915. [Infant of Oscar Sidney and Hattie (Northcutt) Rogers.]

CRAVEN, Johnnie. 1861 - 1927. [Margareth Edith, daughter, only child, of John O. and Elizabeth (Gibbs) Pepper, wife of Solomon Craven, married 28 Jul 1879.]

CRAVEN, Solomon. 28 Jun 1854- 1931. [Son of Charles and Phebe (_____) Craven, husband of Margaret Edith "Johnnie" Pepper.]

ROGERS, Velma Moore. 1 Oct 1878-16 May 1959. [Daughter of David and Ida (Garretson) Moore, wife of Jeff Rogers.]

ROGERS, Jeff. 9 Oct 1872-27 Jan 1930. [Son of James R., Sr. and Florence (Shrader) Rogers, husband of Velma Moore.]

ROGERS, Thomas Estes. Born and died 10 Aug 1920. [Son of Jeff and Velma (Moore) Rogers.]

SMARTT, Charles Hinkley. 11 Aug 1906-31 Mar 1992. [Son of Daniel Thomas
and Myrtle (Hinkley) Smartt, husband of Beulah Vista Perryman,
married 26 Aug 1941.]

SMARTT, Vista Perryman. 20 Jun 1908-18 Sep 1991. [Beulah Vista, daughter
of Henry E. and Alice (Smith) Perryman, wife of Charles Hinkley
Smartt.]

SMARTT, Dan T. 15 Jan 1873-1 May 1949. [Daniel Thomas, son of Wm. Thomas
and Rachel Hampton (Thomas) Smartt, husband of Myrtle Hinkley,
married 28 Oct 1903.]

SMARTT, Myrtle H. 23 Apr 1888-5 Feb 1983. [Daughter of Orion and Martha
(Huskin) Hinkley, wife of Daniel Thomas Smartt.]

SMARTT, Lela. 28 Aug 1908-7 May 1954. [Daughter of Daniel Thomas and
Myrtle (Hinkley) Smartt. Single.]

ROGERS, Jeames Bell. 1 Jan 1900-20 May 1941. [Son of Jeff and Velma
(Moore) Rogers.]

NEWMAN, Infant son. No dates. [Son of Andrew J. and Elizabeth (Kimbro)
Newman.]

SMARTT, Mary Esther. 22 Dec 1860-12 May 1869.
SMARTT, Claud Calhoun. 1 Sep 1869-31 Oct 1893.
    Children of William Thomas and Rachel Hampton (Thomas) Smartt.

SMARTT, William Hampton. 4 Jan 1875-5 Nov 1951. [Son of William Thomas
and Rachel Hampton (Thomas) Smartt.]

NEWMAN, Sallie S. 23 Mar 1877-22 Aug 1965. [Daughter of William Thomas
and Rachel Hampton (Thomas) Smartt, wife of Emmett Lee Newman.]

NEWMAN, Emmett Lee. 30 Sep 1870-10 Feb 1943. [Son of Andrew Jackson and
Elizabeth (Kimbro) Newman, husband of Sallie Smartt, married 28
Jun 1903.]

SMARTT, Samuel T. 3 Dec 1857-14 Jul 1921. [Samuel Thomas, son of Wm.
Thomas and Rachel Hampton (Thomas) Smartt, husband of Jay Hayes,
married 26 Nov 1905.]

SMARTT, Jay Hayes. 15 Jul 1867-19 Oct 1946. [Daughter of Henry L. and
Nancy (Etter) Hayes, wife of Samuel Thomas Smartt.]

SMARTT, Lena B. 21 Dec 1902-10 Jul 1978. [Lena Frances, daughter of M.H.
and _____ (_____) Bell, wife of William Hackett Smartt, II.]

SMARTT, William H., II. 20 Mar 1875-22 Jul 1945. [William Hackett, son
of William Hackett and Mary Jane (Bell) Smartt, husband of Lena
Frances Bell, married 13 Feb 1924.]

SMARTT, W.H., Sr. 15 Feb 1832-30 Aug 1911. William Hackett, son of
William Cheek and Elizabeth Hackett (Waterhouse) Smartt, husband
of Mary Jane Bell, married 15 Sep 1859.]

SMARTT, Mary J. 1 Apr 1839-12 Jan 1924. [Mary Jane, daughter of Nathan
and _____ (Bragg) Bell, wife of William Hackett Smartt, Sr.]

EDWARDS, Sydney S. 5 Nov 1872-12 Aug 1966. [Sydney Aileen, daughter of William Hackett and Mary Jane (Bell) Smartt, wife of Joseph Clarence Edwards.]

EDWARDS, Joe C. 20 Dec 1880-11 Nov 1944. [Joseph Clarence, son of James and _____ (Fletcher) Edwards, husband of Sydney Aileen Smartt, married 20 Aug 1919.]

N.H.S. [No other information]

RANKIN, Louisa D. 1846 - 18 Mar 1914. [Daughter of John W. and Zelphia (Lance) Dickey, second wife of John C. Rankin.]

RANKIN, John C. 11 Jun 1853-13 Jan 1937. [John Calvin, son of Jim and Amanda (_____) Rankin, husband of 1) Texann Pepper, 2) Louisa Dickey, married 2 Dec 1883, and 3) Melissa Hutchins, married 12 May 1915.]

RANKIN, Texann P. 1854 - 1881. [Daughter of Joseph Butcher and Eleanor (_____) Pepper. First wife of John C. Rankin, married 18 Aug 1875.]

RANKIN, Annie C. 20 Jun 1886-2 Feb 1969. [Annie Clarissy, daughter of Isaac Mack and Martha Celina (Cass) Merriman, wife of James Andrew Rankin.]

RANKIN, James A. 11 Jun 1880-11 Mar 1978. James Andrew, son of John C. and Texann (Pepper) Rankin, husband of Annie Clarissy Merriman, married 9 Nov 1904.]

CARR, E.O. [No other information.]

BELL, Joseph S. 9 Oct 1905-3 May 1985. [Son of William and Elizabeth (White) Bell, husband of Virginia Riggs.]

STEPP, Francis M. 19 Nov 1867-17 Dec 1950. [Francis Marion, son of William Carroll and Nancy (McGee) Stepp, husband of Emma Jane Gibbs, married 17 Mar 1888.]

STEPP, Emma Gibbs. 12 Jun 1867-24 May 1952. [Emma Jane, daughter of Samuel and Nancy Clementine (Crouch) Gibbs, wife of Francis Marion Stepp.]

GIBBS, Samuel J. 14 Mar 1838-11 Nov 1892. [Son of Edy and _____ (_____) Gibbs, husband of Nancy Clementine Crouch.]

GIBBS, Nancy C. 9 Apr 1840-19 Dec 1883. Nancy Clementine, daughter of Thomas and Alicy (_____) Crouch, wife of Samuel J. Gibbs.]

FANN, Virginia H. 2 Aug 1919, only date on stone. [No other information]

GIBBS, Maggie. 16 Oct 1872-24 Oct 1872. [Daughter of Samuel and Nancy Clementine (Crouch) Gibbs.]

McBRIDE, Sarah E. 1841-13 Jun 1971. [Sarah Elizabeth, daughter of Sanford J. and Lila Ann (Jordon) McBride.]

McBRIDE, George. 11 Jul 1850-5 Sep 1924. [Son of William and Adeline (Gibbs) McBride, husband of Mary E. Smith, married 29 May 1879.]

Liberty Cemetery, Cont.

McBRIDE, Lila Ann Jordon.   27 Mar 1908-17 Jul 1957.   [Wife of Sanford McBride.]

McBRIDE, Santford J.   15 Apr 1902-27 Jul 1968.   [Son of Thomas and Belle (Turner) McBride, husband of Lila Ann Jordon.]

*McBRIDE, Jackie Wayne.   Born 15 Dec 1942, died 8 Jul 1943. Son of Sanford J. and Lila Ann (Jordon) McBride.

*McBRIDE, Tom.   Born 15 Feb 1872, died 30 Nov 1941. Son of William and Adaline (Gibbs) McBride, husband of Mary Bell Turner.

McBRIDE, Clyde F.   9 Dec 1907-10 Jul 1939.   [Son of Thomas and Belle (Turner) McBride, husband of Faye _____.]

McBRIDE, Faye.   12 May 1907-   .   [Wife of Clyde F. McBride.]

McBRIDE, Mary Belle. 8 Aug 1875-29 Jul 1955. [Daughter of Bill and Mary (Campbell) Turner, wife of Thomas McBride, married 23 Dec 1895.]

CARTER, Nancy C. 24 Apr 1880-2 May 1880. [Daughter of Sam T. and Maggie T. (Pepper) Carter.]

PEPPER, Eleanor E.   11 Aug 1825-12 Feb 1873.   [Eleanor Gibbs, wife of Joseph B. Pepper.]

PEPPER, Joseph B. 2 Jul 1807-23 Jan 1875. [Joseph Butcher, son of Elisha II and Margaret (Morrow) Pepper, husband of Eleanor E. Gibbs.]

CRAVEN, Victoria.   12 Jan 1852-25 Aug 1877.   [Daughter of Joseph B. and Eleanor (Gibbs) Pepper, wife of Peter Craven, married 3 Dec 1873.]

SMARTT, Lizzie H. 8 May 1870-26 Feb 1871. [Lizzie Hackett, daughter of Wm. Hackett and Mary Jane (Bell) Smartt.]

BARRY, Mary Frances Smartt. 7 May 1925-27 Apr 1985. [Daughter of William Hackett II and Lena Frances (Bell) Smartt, wife of Robert H. Barry, married 27 Dec 1947.]

BRAGG, Richard M.   14 Jun 1833-11 Dec 1858.   [Son of Joseph M. and Clarissa T. (_____) Bragg. Single.]

BRAGG, Joseph M. 25 May 1798-9 Jul 1879. [Husband of Clarissa _____.]

BRAGG, Clarissa T. 25 Sep 1806-16 Aug 1851. [Wife of Joseph M. Bragg.]

BRAGG, Hugh T. 25 Nov 1831-22 Dec 1845.

BRAGG, Martha. 8 Feb 1845-Jun 1845.

RIGGS, Wiley. 9 Jan 1810-10 Mar 1899. [Husband of Nancy D. _____.]

RIGGS, Nancy D. 9 Jan 1810-6 Feb 1888. [Wife of Wiley Riggs.]

SMARTT, Martha. 6 Jul 1809-8 Oct 1809. [Death records give 1 Aug 1908. Daughter of William Cheek and Peggy (Colville) Smartt.]

SMARTT, Infant son. 25 May 1840-20 Oct 1840. [Son of Samuel Galiten and Mary Ann (Kennedy) Smartt.]

SMARTT, Mary A. 1 Apr 1819-1 Sep 1840. [Mary Ann Kennedy, wife of Samuel Galiten Smartt, married 20 Nov 1837.]

SMARTT, Infant Daughter. 25 Nov 1838-28 Nov 1838. [Daughter of Samuel Galiten and Mary Ann (Kennedy) Smartt.]

SMARTT, Cleopater. 10 Aug 1820-10 Jul 1939. [Daughter of William Cheek and Peggy (Colville) Smartt.]

SMARTT, William. Died 19 Nov 1826, age 2.
SMARTT, Panthia. Died 7 Nov 1826, age 8.
    Children of William Cheek and Peggy (Colville) Smartt.

RAMSEY, S. Mc. 13 Jan 1831-3 Dec 1897. [Sam McCaslin, son of David and Lucy (Dodson) Ramsey, husband of 1) Octavia Smartt, married 23 Jun 1853 and 2) Martha E. Smartt, married 22 Feb 1858.]

RAMSEY, Octavia. 20 Oct 1828-12 Mar 1857. [Daughter of Wm. Cheek and Elizabeth Hackett (Waterhouse) Smartt, first wife of Sam McCaslin Ramsey.]

RAMSEY, Martha E. 13 Feb 1838-19 Jun 1880. [Daughter of William Cheek and Elizabeth Hackett (Waterhouse) Smartt, second wife of Sam McCaslin Ramsey.]

SMARTT, Peggy. 25 Mar 1787-22 Feb 1827. [Margaret, daughter of Major Joseph, III and Sarah (Lusk) Colville, first wife of General William Cheek Smartt.]

SMARTT, Gen. W.C. 12 Nov 1785-18 Jun 1863. War of 1812. [William Cheek Smartt, husband of 1) Margaret Colville, married 13 Sep 1804 and 2) Elizabeth Waterhouse, married ca 1828.]

SMARTT, Elizabeth. 22 Feb 1791-1 May 1864. [Elizabeth Hackett Waterhouse, second wife of William Cheek Smartt.]

MOORE, Margaret. 29 Dec 1828-31 May 1845. [Daughter of Frank and Margaret M. (Davidson) Smartt, wife of John Moore, married 21 Jan 1845.]

HARMON, Eula Mai Taylor. 6 Mar 1923-28 Aug 1981. [Daughter of Jake and Gertrude Bernice (Gribble) Taylor, married 1) _____ Farless and 2) _____ Harmon.]

SMARTT, Frank. 8 Aug 1805-17 Mar 1843. [Francis Burwell, son of William Cheek and Peggy (Colville) Smartt, first husband of Margaret McConnell Davidson.]

McLEAN, Margaret M. 26 Dec 1807-14 May 1881. [Margaret McConnell Davidson, married 1) to Frank Smartt, married 8 Sep 1825, 2) to David Vance McLean on 4 Apr 1844, and 3) to Ransom Gwyn on 21 Nov 1871.]

McLEAN, D.V. 28 Nov 1801-29 Apr 1871. [David Vance McLean, second husband of Margaret McConnell (Davidson) Smartt.]

HOPKINS, Thomas. 13 May 1761-26 Mar 1836. "Born in Goochland County, Va." [Letter from descendent states that one of his wives was Mary Vaughn Campbell.]

Liberty Cemetery, Cont.

COLVILLE, Martha. No dates on stone. [Death date from family Bible 25
        Jan 1830. Martha Cheek, wife of 1) Francis Burwell Smartt II,
        married 29 Dec 1784 and 2) to Joseph Colville III, married 21
        Dec 1802.]

SMARTT, Mary Esta. 22 Dec 1860-12 May 1869. [Daughter of William Thomas
        and Rachel Hampton (Thomas) Smartt.]

COLVILLE, Major Lusk. 27 May 1791-5 Jul 1865. [Son of Joseph Colville,
        III and his first wife Sarah Lusk. Husband of 1) Cynthia
        Hackett and 2) Elizabeth Reynolds, married 28 Jan 1860.]

COLVILLE, Cynthia Hackett. 14 Dec 1792-26 Sep 1842. [First wife of Major
        Lusk Colville.]

COLVILLE, James F.   22 Jan 1822-18 Aug 1859.
COLVILLE, Ann Caroline.   11 Feb 1824-1 Dec 1843.
    Children of Lusk and Cynthia (Hackett) Colville.

DICKEY, Octavia L. 27 Oct 1859-11 May 1886. [Octavia Laughlin, daughter
        of Dr. T.C. and Sally (Laughlin) Smartt, wife of Hiram Lafayette
        Dickey, married 11 Nov 1880.]

SMARTT, D.C. 29 Sep 1859-24 Jul 1886. [Dewey C., son of Dr. Thomas
        Calhoun and Sally (Laughlin) Smartt.]

SMARTT, Temothy Kezer. Born 1843, died young.
SMARTT, Willie C.   Born 5 May 1845, died young.
SMARTT, Thomas C.   Born Oct 1853, died young.
    Sons of Dr. T.C. and Sally (Laughlin) Smartt.

SMARTT, Sally L. 3 Apr 1819-11 Feb 1872. [Daughter of Col. S.H. and Mary
        C. (_____) Laughlin, wife of Dr. Thomas Calhoun Smartt.]

SMARTT, Dr. T.C. 8 Nov 1811-24 Dec 1891. [Thomas Calhoun, son of William
        Cheek and Peggy (Colville) Smartt, husband of Sally Laughlin.]

*LAUGHLIN, John. 4 Nov 1766- 1813. Husband of Sarah Duncan.

*LAUGHLIN, Sarah. 3 Sep 1773-5 Nov 1843. Sarah Duncan, wife of John
        Laughlin.

*LAUGHLIN, Samuel Hervey. Died 5 May 1850 in Washington, D.C. [Son of
        John and Sarah (Duncan) Laughlin, husband of Mary Clarke. He
        died in Washington D.C. while serving as recorded in land grants
        office for President James K. Polk.]

LAUGHLIN, Mary Clarke. 11 Jun 1801-11 Nov 1840. [Mary Clarke, wife of
        Samuel Hervey Laughlin.]

LANCASTER, J.Hughes. 3 Oct 1912-13 May 1988. [Son of James Richard and
        Cora (_____) Lancaster, husband of Naomi Hughes.]

LANCASTER, Naomi Hughes. 11 Dec 1927-

MOORE, James H. 17 Jul 1927-19 Jan 1987. [James Haskel, son of B.J. and
        Ada (Blanks) Moore, husband of Evelyn Chilton, married 22 Jul
        1953.]

MOORE, Evelyn C. 22 Apr 1931-4 Nov 1991. [Daughter of Robert Kellum and

Lula Ann (Hussey) Chilton, wife of James Haskel Moore.]

HAMMER, Mary Johnson. 16 Feb 1909-4 Mar 1985. [Mary Katherine, daughter of John Franklin and Mary (Crocker) Johnson, married 1) to David C. Patterson and 2) to William Theodore Hammer.]

HAMMER, William Theodore. 17 Dec 1901-16 Mar 1991. [Son of W.H. and Amanda Elizabeth Hammer, husband of 1) Elizabeth Newman and 2) Mary Katherine (Johnson) Patterson.]

HAMMER, Elizabeth Newman. 4 May 1903-26 Aug 1953. [Daughter of George Edley and Elsie Flora Beatrice (Lane) Newman, first wife of William Theodore Hammer.]

ROGERS, Quim Northcutt. 5 Jun 1920-6 Nov 1984. WWII. [Son of Oscar and Mattie (Northcutt) Rogers, husband of Avis A. Gann, married 26 Nov 1943.]

ROGERS, Avis A. Gann. 23 May 1923- . [Daughter of Benjamin Harrison and Amanda (Parsley) Gann, wife of Quim Northcutt Rogers.]

MUNCEY, Frank Albert. 19 Feb 1920-8 Dec 1986. [Son of Jack and Bonnie Jean (McBride) Muncey, husband of Mary Elizabeth Turner, married 24 Nov 1940.]

MUNCEY, Elizabeth. 14 May 1925-16 Aug 1987. [Mary Elizabeth, daughter of Ruben and Katie (Hughes) Turner, wife of Frank Albert Muncey.]

GARRETSON, Nancy. 15 Nov 1793 "Stafford County, VA" - 20 Jul 1880. [Nancy Ross, daughter of William and _____ (_____) Ross, wife of William M. Garretson.]

GARRETSON, William M. 14 Oct 1774 "Baltimore, MD" - 15 Apr 1850. War of 1812. [Husband of Nancy Ross, married 1 Sep 1810 in VA.]

LANE, Alfred S. Died 4 Apr 1848. aged about 35 years. [Alfred Sidney, son of William, Jr. and Susanna Linton (Jennings) Lane, husband of Emily E. Garretson, married 19 Sep 1845.]

MASEY, Emily E. 1811-{unreadable}. [Daughter of William M. and Nancy (Ross) Garretson, wife of 1) Alfred Sidney Lane and 2) Solomon Masey.]

GROSS, Musadora S. 3 Jan 1851-24 Apr 1872. [Daughter of Martin and Ann (Garretson) Morrow, wife of Asa C. Gross, married 26 Jun 1871.]

MOORE, Ida J. 14 May 1860-29 Mar 1886. [Ida Jones, daughter of Thomas Marion and Jane Elizabeth (Garretson) Carter Estes, first wife of David E. Moore.]

MOORE, Ira J. 19 Mar 1886-18 Aug 1886. [Son of David E. and Ida Jones (Estes) Moore.]

MOORE, David E. 4 Dec 1849-28 Aug 1905. [Husband of 1) Ida Jones Estes, married 28 Dec 1876 and 2) Nannie Roach, married 7 Dec 1887.]

MOORE, Nannie A. 4 May 1859-10 Jul 1931. [Daughter of William Marion and Elmira (McBride) Roach, second wife of David E. Moore.]

Liberty Cemetery, Cont.

MOORE, Grace Riggs. 8 Aug 1898-5 Oct 1969. [Margarett Grace, daughter of
        Clyde D. and Elva (Hinkley) Riggs, wife of David Frank Moore,
        married 4 Jul 1917.]

MOORE, David Frank. 31 Jan 1896-5 Sep 1974. [Son of Albert P. and Martha
        (_____) Moore, husband of Grace Riggs.]

MOORE, J.C. 22 Dec 1936-   . [Husband of Barbara Bailey.]

MOORE, Barbara Bailey. 24 Feb 1939-21 May 1984. Daughter of Lewis and
        Edith (Jones) Bailey, wife of J.C. Moore.]

PERRY, Hosmer. 4 Aug 1896-25 Dec 1945. [Edward Hosmer, son of Frank and
        Betty (Hill) Perry.]

PERRY, Frank. 18 Apr 1873-8 Feb 1951. [Marion Franklin, son of John H.
        and Frances E. (King) Perry, husband of Mary Rebecca
        Kirkpatrick.]

PERRY, Mary Rebecca. 30 May 1869-20 May 1950. [Mary Rebecca Kirkpatrick,
        wife of Marion Franklin Perry.]

GILBERT, Harrison Joseph. 14 Feb 1892-30 Oct 1963.

PEPPER, Ann P. 5 Jan 1830-1 Apr 1893. [Ann Payne, daughter of Elisha and
        Margaret (Morrow) Pepper.]

ALLISON, John. Died 18 Dec 1852, aged 82 years, 3 months. [Husband of
        Mary Thaxton.]

*ALLISON, Mary. No dates. Wife of John Allison.

ROACH, Eliga B. 14 Feb 1856-27 Aug 1925. [Eliga Benton, son of Isham C.
        and Margaret (Pepper) Roach, husband of Nettie Jane Myers,
        married 20 Dec 1881.]

ROACH, Nettie J. 21 Sep 1860-5 Mar 1955. [Daughter of Miles and Sarah
        (Biles) Myers, married 1) to Eliga B. Roach and 2) to W.C. York
        on 26 Sep 1931. Funeral home records list her as Nettie York,
        giving her birth as 21 Sep 1859 and her death as 5 Mar 1955.]

ROACH, Daisy B. 19 Dec 1882-31 Aug 1899. [Daisy Beulah, daughter of
        Elijah Benton and Nettie Jane (Myers) Roach.]

ROACH, Sarah. 23 Aug 1884-21 Aug 1899. [Sarah Pinnie, daughter of Elijah
        Benton and Nettie Jane (Myers) Roach.]

ROACH, Isham C. 28 Sep 1820-11 Dec 1907. [Husband of Margaret P. Pepper,
        married 22 Feb 1849.]

ROACH, Margaret P. Pepper. 22 Jan 1822-22 Nov 1887. [Daughter of Elisha
        II and Margaret (Morrow) Pepper, wife of Isham Clark Roach.]

TAYLOR, Mary Ann. 6 Apr 1902-15 Feb 1945. [Daughter of J.E. and Martha
        (Rutledge) Gilbert, wife of James O. Taylor.]

TAYLOR, Jim O. 1886 - 7 Mar 1963. [James O Taylor, husband of Mary Ann
        Gilbert.]

FENNELL, Ralph N. 8 Nov 1926-28 Sep 1990. Korea. [Ralph Nolan, son of

Harmon M. and Myrtle Belle (Roach) Fennell.]

FENNELL, Myrtle Bell Roach. 5 Sep 1891-20 Jan 1991. [Daughter of Elijah
Benton and Nettie Jane (Myers) Roach, wife of Harmon Manford
Fennell.]

FENNELL, Harmon M. 1 May 1884-5 Oct 1945. [Harmon Manford, son of
Bartlett and Octa (Pennington) Fennell, husband of Myrtle Belle
Roach, married 28 Jun 1913.]

MORRISON, J.A. 9 Apr 1880-26 Aug 1948.

WOODS, Ulysses. 10 Jan 1894-12 Oct 1972. WWI. [Son of Alexander
Hamilton and Annie (St.John) Woods, husband of Ruby Hartt,
married 1 Jun 1935.]

WOODS, Ruby Hartt. 25 Mar 1896-21 May 1994. [Daughter of James Marion
and Eliza (Jaco) Hartt, wife of 1) Levi Rutledge, married 15 Sep
1915 and 2) Ulysses Woods, married 1 Jun 1935.]

JORDAN, James Henry. 19 Sep 1876-11 Mar 1963. [Son of Thomas and Lou
(Hines) Jordan, husband of Ollie Hickey.]

JORDAN, Ollie S. Hickey. 13 Nov 1876-   . [Wife of James Henry
Jordan.]

TENPENNY, Lannis L. 18 Sep 1892-17 Nov 1980. [Lannis Lester, son of
Robert H. and Melissa (Woods) Tenpenny, husband of Hattie Belle
Woods, married 9 Apr 1911.]

TENPENNY, Hattie B. Woods. 27 Jan 1892-17 May 1980. Hattie Belle,
daughter of Alexander Hamilton and Eliza Ann (St. John) Woods,
wife of Lannis Lester Tenpenny.]

LAWSON, Eugene. 14 Nov 1895-22 Jun 1964. WWI. [Son of Fred and Betty
(Lowe) Lawson, husband of Violet Elkins.]

ROGERS, Almond S. 16 Oct 1896-6 Mar 1966. [Almond Sage, son of Locke and
Mollie (Bolt) Rogers, husband of Lettie Arvilla Cates.]

ROGERS, Villa C. 22 Feb 1900-6 Jan 1967. Lettie Arvilla, daughter of
Meredith P. and Elizabeth P. (_____) Cates, wife of Almond Sage
Rogers.]

ROGERS, Arthur Lee. 4 May 1902-6 Dec 1957. [Son of Locke and Mollie
(Bolt) Rogers.]

ROGERS, Mollie. 29 Apr 1876-2 Jul 1944. [Daughter of James and Sarah
(Gray) Bolt, wife of Lock Rogers.]

ROGERS, Lock. 25 May 1876-13 Jun 1943. [Son of James and Florence
(Schrader) Rogers, husband of Mollie Bolt, married 2 Nov 1895.]

YOUNG, Luther H. 19 Jun 1920-6 Apr 1944. WWII. [Luther Harlon, son of
T.M. and Ann Clara (Winnard) Young, husband of Pauline Boren.]

YOUNG, Barbara Joan. 5 Feb 1944-1 May 1944. [Daughter of Luther Harlen
and Pauline (Boren) Young.]

SCHRAGEL, Willie Pearl. 31 May 1915-20 May 1980. [Daughter of Angalo and

Emma Lee (Green) Ginn, wife of 1) _____ Rose and 2) Alexander Schragel.]

GINN, Angalo L. 6 Jan 1882-29 Dec 1971. [Husband of Emma Lee Green.]

GINN, Emma Lee. 8 Jun 1892-16 Feb 1976. [Daughter of Frank J. and Letisha (Daugherty) Green, wife of Angalo Ginn.]

TENPENNY, Louise. 16 Aug 1929-5 Sep 1971. [Daughter of Ernest L. and Bessie (Pittard) Tenpenny.]

TENPENNY, Ernest L. 4 Feb 1902-11 May 1946. [Ernest Lemuel, son of Robert Brook and _____ (_____) Tenpenny, husband of Bessie Pittard.]

TENPENNY, Bessie. 14 Jun 1902-29 Apr 1967. [Daughter of William and Susie (Gannon) Pittard, wife of 1) Ernest L. Tenpenny and 2) Jesse Cunningham who is buried at Grange Hall.]

TENPENNY, James R. 1 Jan 1860-11 Sep 1946. [Son of _____ and Mary (_____) Tenpenny, husband of Roxie A. Peeler.]

TENPENNY, Roxie A. 23 Jan 1878-17 Aug 1956. [Daughter of Jesse and Sarah Elizabeth (Moore) Peeler, wife of 1) James R. Tenpenny and 2) Columbus Talley, married 23 Feb 1949.]

LUTRELL, William D. 21 Dec 1896-29 Jun 1953. WWI. [William Dorsey, son of John William and Frances Lula (Clark) Lutrell, husband of 1) Beulah Warren, married 14 May 1927 and 2) Martha Storms.]

HARPER, Anna Lee McBride. 12 Oct 1912-16 Aug 1977. [Daughter of Sam and Birdie (Muncey) McBride.]

GEBHARDT, Ethelda Grace. 10 Dec 1873-16 Jan 1964.

WILLIAMS, Stanley. 18 Apr 1891-28 Feb 1978. [Son of Sidney S. and Olive Alice (Williams) Williams, husband of 1) Jessie Lee Patton and 2) Lillian Hawkins.]

WILLIAMS, Jessie Lee. 11 May 1896-14 Aug 1960. [Daughter of Thomas and Marietta (Bratcher) Patton, wife of Stanley Williams.]

YOUNG, Raymond Eugene. 12 Apr 1906-16 Feb 1990. WWII. [Son of William Hill and Mattie Louise (Harris) Young, husband of 1) _____ _____ and 2) Barbara Louise Holt.]

YOUNG, Louise Holt. 27 Feb 1916-   . [Barbara Louise, daughter of Walter W. and Mary B. (Gann) Holt, second wife of Raymond Eugene Young.]

LJUBICH, Ivan B. 26 Feb 1917-   . "Born in Orme". [Ivan G. Ginn, wife of Dragoljub G. Ljubich.]

LJUBICH, Dragoljub G. 10 Oct 1912-5 Oct 1990. "Born in Yugoslovia." [Husband of Ivan G. Ginn.]

WILLIAMS, Aubrey E. 26 Nov 1875-5 Apr 1944.

BENNETT, Della M. 19 Oct 1877-18 Dec 1955. [Della Mildred, daughter of Sidney S. and Olive Alice (Williams) Williams, wife of Alonzo

Liberty Cemetery, Cont.

Bennett.]

*McBRIDE, Sam. Died 1 Nov 1921, age 57 years. Son of William and Adaline
    (Gibbs) McBride, husband of Birdie Cleoven Muncey.

McBRIDE, Birdie Cleoven. 21 Feb 1893-1 Mar 1946. [Daughter of Jasper and
    Lillian (Patterson) Muncey, wife of Sam McBride.]

McBRIDE, Oshie Mae. 18 Dec 1902-6 Nov 1992. [Daughter of Isaac and
    Mylanda (_____) Nunley, wife of Charlie Brown McBride.]

McBRIDE, Charlie Brown. 1 Dec 1896-21 Dec 1976. [Son of Sam and Jeannie
    (Cothan) McBride, husband of Oshie Mae Nunley, married 26 Nov
    1922.]

McBRIDE, Grady Clifton. 22 Aug 1919-   . [Son of Charlie Brown
    and Oshie Mae (Nunley) McBride.]

VANATTA, Grady A. 28 Dec 1922-24 Aug 1962. [Son of John and Lillian
    (Hale) Vanatta.]

TENPENNY, Lillian. 2 Sep 1907-21 Jan 1973. [Lillian Hale, wife of 1)
    John Vanatta and 2) Clarence N. Tenpenny.]

TENPENNY, Clarence N. 7 Mar 1905-31 Jan 1977. [Son of James R. and Roxie
    Ann (Talley) Tenpenny, married 1) to Maude King and 2) to
    Lillian Hale.]

TENPENNY, Clarence N. 17 Jun 1929-3 Jan 1984. [Son of Clarence N. and
    Maude (King) Tenpenny, husband of Juanita _____.]

HALE, John M. 28 Apr 1907-20 Feb 1951. [John Monroe, son of Joe and Mary
    Belle (Page) Hale, husband of Pauline Campbell.]

NORTHCUTT, Sam Dwayne. 11 Aug 1950-14 Aug 1950. [Son of Waymon and
    Genevieve (Harper) Northcutt.]

LUTTRELL, Frances Lula. 9 Aug 1868-1 Jan 1951. [Daughter of Thomas G.
    and Elizabeth (Smith) Clark, wife of John W. Luttrell, married
    16 Jul 1886.]

LUTTRELL, John William. 11 Dec 1868-25 May 1946. [Son of Crockett and
    Rosa Jane (Shrader) Luttrell, husband of Frances Lula Clark.]

*LUTTRELL, Rosa. Died 30 Aug 1911, age 79 years. [Daughter of John
    Daniel and Nancy (Smartt) Shrader, wife of David Crockett
    Luttrell, married 16 Oct 1858.]

BELL, Carl A. Born and died 22 Feb 1949. [Carl Anthony, son of Fred
    Brown and Edna Marie (Lawrence) Bell.]

DONEY, Randolph. 3 Feb 1921-29 Sep 1922. [Son of Sol and Sallie (Brady)
    Doney.]

CARTER, William. 14 Feb 1817-17 Sep 1863. [Husband of Nancy _____.]

CARTER, Nancy. 16 Feb 1817-19 Apr 1862. [Wife of William Carter.]

*HENDERSON, James Thomas, died 11 Jan 1982, age 49 years. Son of Henry
    Paul and Hallie (Tally) Henderson.

HENDERSON, Hal Thomas. 13 Jan 1961-26 Dec 1976. [Son of James Thomas and
          Eva Lois (Cantrell) Henderson.]

HENDERSON, Hallie T. 27 Aug 1902-21 Sep 1990. [Daughter of John Lucas
          and Elva (Wallace) Talley, wife of Henry Paul Henderson.]

HENDERSON, Henry. 23 Dec 1902-4 Jan 1968. [Henry Paul, son of Dan and
          Annie (_____) Henderson, husband of Hallie Talley.]

MUNCEY, Miles Isaac. 6 May 1880-12 Mar 1947. [Son of Thomas Jasper and
          Elizabeth (Lytle) Muncey, husband of 1) Lithia Kiami Smith,
          married 18 Sep 1898, 2) Martha Green and 3) Lillie Candas
          Luttrell, married 7 Dec 1922.]

MUNCEY, Lillie Candas. 7 Apr 1890-3 Feb 1982. [Daughter of John William
          and Frances (Clark) Luttrell, wife of Miles Isaac Muncey.]

MUNCEY, Lillard M. 10 Feb 1901-22 Jan 1977. [Son of Miles Isaac and
          Lithia Kiami (Smith) Muncey, husband of Margie Stroud.]

*MUNCEY, Margie Lee. 21 Jul 1914-   . [Daughter of Harry Brown
          Stroud and Lillie Candas Luttrell, wife of Lillard M. Muncey.]

LOGUE, Verna E. 13 Oct 1888-30 Oct 1963. [Verna Ellen, daughter of John
          and Mary Alice (Howell) Mullinax, wife of William Martin Logue.]

LOGUE, William M. 23 Aug 1883-18 Nov 1963. [William Martin, son of David
          Ramsey and Mary Ann (Martin) Logue, husband of Verna Ellen
          Mullinax.]

BELL, J. Manson. 5 Apr 1879-23 Sep 1954. Spanish American War. [Son of
          Joe and Becky (_____) Bell, husband of 1) Mary Jordon, married
          10 Nov 1901, 2) Clara Simpson and 3) Mattie Turner.]

BELL, Mattie E. 24 Jan 1904-7 Apr 1989. [Daughter of William H. and Sue
          (Jones) Turner, third wife of Manson Bell.]

JOHNSON, Willie Joe Peppers. 6 Jul 1919-1 Oct 1990. [Daughter of Charlie
          William and Phebia Elizabeth (Earls) Pepper, wife of Garner
          Cleveland Johnson.]

JOHNSON, Garner Cleveland. 29 Nov 1914-5 Mar 1975. WWII. [Husband of
          Willie Joe Peppers.]

JOHNSON, Roy Eugene. 16 Mar 1944-21 Dec 1948. [Son of Garner Cleveland
          and Willie Joe (Pepper) Johnson.]

BURCH, Bob J. 1912 - 1975. [Husband of Flora Lee Lawrence.]

BURCH, Flora Lee. 1914 -   . [Daughter of James and Sarah C. (Luna)
          Lawrence, wife of Bob Burch.]

LOCKE, Martha. 20 Nov 1833-21 Aug 1894. [Daughter of Sidney and Drucilla
          C. (_____) Ross, wife of John R. Locke.]

ROSS, Drucilla C. 20 Jun 1808-30 Oct 1893. [Wife of Sidney Ross.]

ROSS, Sidney. 1796 - 16 Aug 1880. [Husband of Drucilla _____.]

ROSS, Elizabeth J. 22 Aug 1842-6 Jul 1964. [Daughter of Sidney and

Drucilla C. (_____) Ross.]

LOCKE, Jones W. 30 Jun 1819-19 Aug 1965. [Son of Jesse P. and Clarissa (Bonner) Locke, husband of Mary E. Ross, married 25 Jan 1848.]

LOCKE, Mary E. 29 Jun 1828-5 Oct 1877. [Daughter of Sidney and Drucilla C. (_____) Ross, wife of Jones W. Locke.]

LOCKE, Sidney J. 21 Dec 1879-2 Aug 1881. [Sidney Jones, son of William Wallace and Mary Frances (Estes) Locke. Single.]

LOCKE, J.E. 24 Jun 1857-28 Nov 1920. [James Edgar, son of Jones W. and Mary E. (Ross) Locke. Single.]

LOCKE, W.W. 23 Nov 1853-7 Oct 1923. [William Wallace, son of Jones W. and Mary E. (Ross) Locke, husband of Mary Frances Estes, amrried 2 Oct 1876.]

LOCKE, Mary F. 15 Oct 1855-11 Jul 1934. [Mary Frances, daughter of Thomas and Jane E. (Garretson) Estes, wife of William Wallace Locke.]

HERSTINE, George R.C. 29 Jun 1898-10 Aug 1975. [Son of George and Amelia (Santee) Herstine, husband of Hazel Thomas.]

MALONEY, Pearl Locke. 28 Feb 1887-3 Feb 1977. [Daughter of William Wallace and Mary Frances (Estes) Locke, wife of W.M. Maloney.]

MOFFITT, May Locke. 7 Sep 1881-24 Feb 1975. [Ida May, daughter of William Wallace and Mary Jane (Estes) Locke, wife of Lester Bouldin Moffitt.]

MOFFITT, Lester B. 15 Jul 1886-17 Jan 1966. [Lester Bouldin, son of Elijah L. and Queen (Bouldin) Moffitt, husband of Ida May Locke.]

VAUGHN, Ruth Earls. 30 May 1920-6 Jan 1952. [Ruth Bell, daughter of Joe and Ivy (_____) Earls, husband of George David Vaughn.]

VAUGHN, Helen Marie. 13 Nov 1944-6 Mar 1962. [Daughter of George David and Ruth Belle (Earls) Vaughn. Single.]

WEST, Ricky Darnell. Born and died 10 Apr 1955.

POTTER, Betty. 9 Oct 1866-14 Dec 1933. [Mary Elizabeth, daughter of John and Martha (Ross) Locke, wife of John Houston Potter.]

POTTER, John. 12 Nov 1864-13 Dec 1940. [John Houston, son of Jackson and Martha (Youngblood) Potter, husband of Bettie Locke, married 4 May 1899.]

MOFFITT, M. Louise. 11 Mar 1910-30 Sep 1983. [Mary Louise, daughter of Lester Bouldin and Ida May (Locke) Moffitt. Single.]

MOFFITT, Gentry W. 24 Jul 1911-   . [Gentry Ward, son of Lester Bouldin and Ida May (Locke) Moffitt.]

COPELAND, Evelyn Moffitt. 7 Feb 1915-26 Sep 1986. [Ophia Evelyn, daughter of Lester Bouldin and Ida May (Locke) Moffitt, wife of Mayo Copeland, married 16 Apr 1938.]

Liberty Cemetery, Cont.

HUMBLE, Zachary T. 26 Jan 1847-8 May 1863.

CANTRELL, Charles James. 21 Jan 1919-9 May 1990. [Son of William and
        Cleo (Ward) Cantrell, husband of M. Alline McCormick, married
        20 Mar 1943.]

CANTRELL, M. Alline McCormick. 2 Dec 1922-   . [Wife of Charles
        James Cantrell.]

McCORMICK, Ophia P. 7 Jun 1900-3 Jan 1952. [Eliza Ophia P., daughter of
        Parker and Mary (Mullican) Womack, wife of Tommie Leander
        McCormick.]

McCORMICK, Tommie L. 1 Feb 1895-10 Jan 1957. WWI. [Tommie Leander, son
        of Clayton and Maggie (Templeton) McCormick, husband of 1) Eliza
        Ophia P. Womack, married 4 Sep 1919, and 2) Delta Reed.]

HOLDEN, R.W. 7 May 1879-9 Feb 1952. [Robert Wellington, son of Jesse and
        Cordelia (Greene) Holden, husband of Pearl Horne.]

BOLT, Sarah. Died 17 Feb 1960. [Wife of Cicero L. Bolt.]

BOLT, C.L. 1871 - 1952. [Husband of Sarah _____.]

BOLT, James R. Died 18 Apr 1902, age 73 years.

WHITTENBURG, Susie McBride. 22 Apr 1910-21 Feb 1971. [Daughter of Sam
        and Birdie (Muncey) McBride, wife of Jim Whittenburg, married
        20 Sep 1930.]

MUNCEY, J.C. 1931 - 1 Mar 1991. [Son of Jack and Bonnie (McBride)
        Muncey.]

VAUGHN, Phyllis A. 7 Feb 1927-   . [Phyllis A. Kirschbaum, wife
        of Thomas Woodrow Vaughn.]

VAUGHN, Thomas W. 4 Jan 1913-4 Jan 1971. [Thomas Woodrow, son of James
        Francis and Martha (Hargis) Vaughn, husband of Phyllis A.
        Kirschbaum.]

CRAVEN, Floyd. Jun 1906-May 1964.

BURCH, Maggie Z. 2 May 1904-30 Jul 1986. [Daughter of Alex and Anna
        Belle (Turner) Earles, wife of Robert D. Burch.]

BURCH, Robert D. 19 Nov 1896-10 Feb 1964. WWI. Robert Dudley, son of
        Robert Washington and America (Reed) Burch, husband of Maggie
        Earles.]

STEPP, James Errett. 25 Jan 1891-28 Mar 1966. WWI. [Son of Francis M.
        and Emma (Gibbs) Stepp.]

COLLINS, James Edward. 1946-16 Feb 1994. [Son of J.R. and Margaret
        (Muncey) Collins.]

STEPP, Melba Orndorff. 20 Dec 1896-17 May 1969. [Daughter of Eli
        Christian and Grace (Sinsabaugh) Orndorff, wife of Howry Orville
        Stepp.]

STEPP, Howry Orville. 21 Dec 1889-8 Sep 1973. [Son of Francis M. and

Emma (Gibbs) Stepp, husband of Melba Orndorff.]

STEPP, Francis Earl. 17 Feb 1905-23 Jan 1964. [Son of Francis M. and Emma (Gibbs) Stepp, husband of Mary Louise Briggs.]

STEPP, Louise Briggs. 13 Oct 1904-29 Feb 1984. [Daughter of Jahugh and Lila (Hovis) Briggs, wife of Francis Earl Stepp.]

LAWSON, Elmer Ray. 26 Apr 1899-10 May 1976. [Son of Fred and Betty (Lowe) Lawson, husband of Vertice Holloway.]

STEVENS, Aubrey E. 1905 - 14 Mar 1980. [Aubrey Eston, son of Nicholas Wellington and Bertie (Griffith) Stevens, husband of 1) Mazel Lawson and 2) Bertha Fann.]

STEVENS, Mazel L. 10 Sep 1903-27 Jan 1956. [Mazel Leona, daughter of Fred and Betty (Lowe) Lawson, wife of Aubrey Eston Stevens.]

CANTRELL, James Daniel "Danny". 16 Sep 1958-24 Dec 1989. [Son of Jim and Gladys (Smith) Cantrell, husband of Debbie Green.]

CANTRELL, James A. 28 Aug 1912-   . [Husband of Georgia Hazel Hallum]

CANTRELL, Georgia Hazel. 13 Dec 1915-13 Nov 1983. [Daughter of George W. and Betty (Presley) Hallum, wife of James A. Cantrell.]

CANTRELL, Glen Alden. 6 Jul 1939-3 Oct 1983. Vietnam. [Son of James A. and Georgia Hazel (Hallum) Cantrell, husband of Dorothy Melton.]

HALLUM, Betty Presley. 25 Sep 1888-12 Mar 1955. [Wife of George W. Hallum.]

CHILTON, Randal Neil. Born and died 19 Sep 1959. [Son of William C. and Nelma (Woodlee) Chilton.]

STARKEY, Minnie Davis. 7 Aug 1878-24 Nov 1952. [Daughter of Bluford and Henrietta (Cantrell) Davis, wife of Andy Starkey.]

CHILTON, Icie. 5 Oct 1901-26 Nov 1984. [Daughter of Andrew and Minnie (Davis) Starkey, wife of Will J. Chilton.]

CHILTON, Bill. 6 Apr 1900-2 Dec 1979. [Will J., son of W.A. and Sarah Jane (Martin) Chilton, husband of Icie Starkey, married 2 Feb 1935.]

CHILTON, Margaret Ann. 22 Nov 1937-18 Oct 1980. [Daughter of Will J. and Icie (Starkey) Chilton. Single.]

MUNCEY, Naomie Y. 10 May 1908-26 Feb 1988. [Daughter of Tom and Lena (Banks) Young, wife of Radion Seals Muncey.]

MUNCEY, Radion S. 19 Feb 1911-   . [Radion Seals, son of George Washington, Sr. and Margaret (Pepper) Muncey, husband of Naomie Young, married 7 Dec 1934.]

HUMBLE, Margaret W. 23 Oct 1796-22 Apr 1881. [Daughter of Mordecai and _____ (_____) Bean, wife of Isaac Humble.]

HUMBLE, Isaac. 10 Sep 1795-24 Nov 1882. [Husband of Margaret W. Bean.]

235

PEPPER, Phebia Earls. 8 Jul 1901-22 Dec 1989. [Phebia Elizabeth, daughter of Alexander and Anna Belle (Turner) Earls, wife of Charlie W. Pepper.]

PEPPER, Charlie W. 23 Dec 1899-9 Aug 1980. [Charles William, son of William J. and Nerva Elizabeth (Rogers) Pepper, husband of Phebia Elizabeth Earls.]

PEPPER, Charles O. 28 Aug 1929-28 Dec 1974. [Charles Otis, son of Charles William and Phebia Elizabeth (Earls) Pepper.]

CANTRELL, Malissie. 5 Oct 1879-13 May 1955. [Daughter of Ed and Fannie (Mason) Cantrell, wife of Samuel M. Cantrell.

CANTRELL, Samuel M. 9 Sep 1870-23 Mar 1964. [Son of Pleas and Lucy (Elkins) Cantrell, husband of Malissie Cantrell.]

WATSON, Benjamin Logan. 17 Feb 1977019 Feb 1977.

JUDKINS, Callie Young. 9 May 1893-25 Mar 1962. [Daughter of Isaac and Ellenora (Petty) Young, wife of Henry Thomas Judkins.]

JUDKINS, Henry Thomas. 14 Jan 1889-14 Nov 1973. WWI. [Husband of Callie Young.]

JUDKINS, Shirley Ann. 23 Sep 1945-7 Dec 1955. [Daughter of Dillard Edward and Georgia (Rogers) Judkins.

JUDKINS, Dillard Edward. 9 Aug 1908-12 Aug 1960. [Son of Henry Thomas and Callie (Young) Judkins, husband of Georgia Rogers.]

JUDKINS, Georgia Rogers. 14 Dec 1915-   . [Wife of Dillard Edward Judkins.]

NASH, Infant son. Born and died 21 Mar 1973. [Infant of Carl Jr. and Jennifer (Laxson) Nash.]

SCOTT, Glenn Clemmon. 31 Aug 1933-10 Jun 1992. Korea and Vietnam. [Son of Howard and Villa (McBride) Scott.]

BONNER, Robert Carl. 7 Sep 1955-30 Mar 1963. [Son of Clifton and Edna Lois (Vanatta) Bonner.]

BONNER, Clifton Sutton. 11 May 1922-18 Sep 1991. WWII. [Husband of Edna Lois Vanatta, married 1 Feb 1946.]

BONNER, Edna L. 3 Jun 1928-   . Edna Lois, wife of Clifton Sutton Bonner.]

JORDON, Alvin T. 6 Apr 1901-13 Nov 1961. [Alvin Thomas, son of Wm. Perry and Linnie Frances (Williams) Jordon, husband of Edith Jane Walker.]

JORDON, Edith J. 14 Oct 1903-29 Jul 1990. [Edith Jane, daughter of John Thomas and Mattie (Wilson) Walker, wife of 1) Alvin Thomas Jordon and 2) Walter Cantrell.]

JORDON, Molly Evon. 1909 - 24 Jan 1988. [Daughter of John and _____ (_____) Brock, wife of 1) Henry Jordon and 2) Henry Barrett.]

JORDON, Norma Tracy. 17 Jun 1930-1 Mar 1933. [Daughter of Henry and Molly Evon (Brock) Jordon.]

CRAVEN, Lula Mae. 17 May 1896-9 Jul 1969. [Daughter of Jim and Minnie Mae (Johnson) Smith, wife of Owen W. Craven.]

CRAVEN, Owen W. 9 Mar 1892-5 Apr 1981. [Son of Benjamin Thomas and Anna Bell (Morrison) Craven, husband of Lula Mae Smith.]

HOLMES, Aline Craven. 2 Feb 1920-10 Oct 1988. [Daughter of Owen W. and Lula Mae (Smith) Craven, wife of Robert Holmes.]

CRAVEN, Oliver Bethel. 26 Nov 1936-22 Apr 1984. [Son of Owen W. and Lula Mae (Smith) Craven.]

WOMACK, O. P. 20 May 1904-4 May 1968. [Orah P., son of Parker and Mary (Mullinax) Womack, husband of Dora V. Masters, married 2 Oct 1927.]

WOMACK, Dora V. 11 Feb 1903-31 Oct 1982. [Dora V. Masters, wife of 1) Orah P. Womack, and 2) Clarence Morgan, married 4 Oct 1969.]

BONNER, Cynthia Jewell. Born and died 12 Apr 1969.

CANTRELL, Laura. 18 Jul 1890-30 Sep 1978. [Laura Elizabeth, daughter of Arthur and Emma (Binkley) Stewart, wife of Walter Cantrell.]

CANTRELL, Walter. 1 Jul 1886-19 Apr 1961. [Son of John and Sarah (Redmon) Cantrell, husband of Laura Elizabeth Stewart.]

PEPPER, Mary K. 12 Jul 1938-   . [Mary Katherine Brown, wife of Austin C. Pepper.]

PEPPER, Austin C. 29 Nov 1936-21 Apr 1992. [Son of Charlie William and Phebia (Earls) Pepper, married 1) to Joyce Marie Roberts and 2) to Mary Katherine Brown.]

PEPPER, Cindy R. 24 Jul 1960-18 Sep 1960. [Cindy Rene, daughter of Austin Clark and Mary Katherine (Brown) Pepper.]

POTTER, Anna P. 4 Mar 1936 only date on stone. [Daughter of John Hackett and Jennie M. (_____) Potter.]

POTTER, Jennie M. 1 May 1904-17 Jan 1993. [Jennie Mae, daughter of William and Eanore (_____) Barrett, wife of John Hacket Potter.]

POTTER, John Hackett. 4 Sep 1896-17 Dec 1974. [Son of John Huston and Mary Elizabeth (Locke) Potter, husband of Jennie M. Barrett.]

MASTERS, Jesse. 12 Apr 1886-20 Jan 1965. WWI. [Jesse Newton, son of James B. and Elizabeth Ann (Freeze) Masters, husband of 1) Ada Cox, married 6 Mar 1917 and 2) Myrtle Hussey, married 15 Jan 1939.]

MASTERS, Myrtle. Died 12 Nov 1968, age 67 years. [Myrtle Inex, daughter of Terry H. and Mary J. (Hibdon) Hussey, wife of Jesse Newton Masters.]

DULANEY, Herman Avery. Born and died 29 May 1935. [Son of Jenry Avery and Ruth Magoline (Muncey) Dulaney.]

MUNCEY, Clarissa. 15 Dec 1850-24 Dec 1904. [Daughter of John D. and Nancy (Smith) Schrader, wife of Madison Matthew Mucey.]

MUNCEY, Madison Matthew. 1845 - 18 Jan 1925. [Son of John Harve and Mattie (Bailey) Muncey, husband of Clarissa Schrader, married 17 Apr 1870.]

MUNCEY, George W. 17 Oct 1877-20 May 1955. [George Washington, son of Madison Matthew and Clarissa (Schrader) Muncey, husband of Margaret Pepper, married 8 Oct 1900 in Coffee County, TN.]

MUNCEY, Maggie. 27 Apr 1886-22 Feb 1962. [Margaret, daughter of William J. and Manerva Elizabeth (Rogers) Pepper, wife of George Washington Muncey.]

*MUNCEY, Ruby. Born 7 Mar 1904, died 17 Aug 1918, daughter of George Washington and Margaret (Pepper) Muncey.

*MUNCEY, Clercy May. Born 9 Jun 1909, died 24 Jun 1901, daughter of George Washington and Margaret (Pepper) Muncey.

*MUNCEY, Hattie Bell. Born 27 Apr 1902, died 6 Oct 1904, daughter of George Washington and Margaret (Pepper) Muncey.

*MUNCEY, Clarissa Mary. Born 3 Nov 1903, died 8 Oct 1904, daughter of George Washington and Margaret (Pepper) Muncey.

*MUNCEY, James Andrew. Born 30 Dec 1907, died 25 Aug 1908, son of George Washington and Margaret (Pepper) Muncey.

*MUNCEY, Mattie Lou. Born 1917, died 14 Jul 1919, daughter of William Asa and Pearl (Hennessee) Muncey.

*MUNCEY, Irene. Died 11 May 1920, age 21 days, daughter of Charlie Morgan and Mary Bershie (Nunley) Muncey.

*SCHRADER, Mary Ann. Died 26 Jul 1910, age 65 years, daughter of John D. and Nancy (Smith) Schrader. Single.

MASEY, L.R. 28 Sep 1846-13 Aug 1916. [L. Randolph, son of Randolph and Lucinda (Carson) Masey, husband of Margaret McBride.]

MASEY, M.E. 4 Nov 1854-23 Oct 1913. [Margaret E. McBride, wife of L. Randolph Masey.]

LEE, Alonson H. 6 Mar 1878-29 Jan 1898. [Son of T.J. and L.C. (_____) Lee.]

CLOUGH, Edwin C. 28 Apr 1858-9 Aug 1897.

HINKLEY, Martha B. 1847 - 1905. [Wife of Orion D. Hinkley.]

HINKLEY, O.D. 1838 - 10 May 1906. [Orion D., husband of Martha B. _____.]

KING, Wm. White. 5 Oct 1841-20 May 1924. [Son of Thomas Jefferson and Frances (Ramsey) King, husband of Mary Lou Thomas, married 24 Nov 1872.]

KING, Mary Lou. 1845-21 Mar 1911. [Daughter of Benjamin C. and Mary

(Robinson) Thomas, wife of William White King.]

THOMAS, Pamela E. 1833-5 Apr 1905. [Pamela Elizabeth "Betty", daughter of Benjamin C. and Mary (Robinson) Thomas. Single.]

THOMAS, B.C. 4 Jul 1807-25 Nov 1888. [Benjamin C. Thomas, husband of Mary Robinson.]

THOMAS, Mary Robinson. 31 Mar 1806-26 Apr 1880. [Wife of Benjamin C. Thomas.]

RIGGS, J.R. 1837 - 26 Dec 1919. [John R., son of Hardy and Mary (_____) Riggs, husband of Margaret D. Thomas.]

RIGGS, Margaret D. Thomas. 26 Apr 1840-6 Nov 1876. [Daughter of Benjamin and Mary (Robinson) Thomas, wife of John R. Riggs.]

RIGGS, Virginia Caroline. 7 Feb 1832-30 Dec 1912.

RIGGS, Martha W.   17 Oct 1853-17 Feb 1916.
RIGGS, Mary B.   23 Jun 1855-19 Feb 1916.
RIGGS, Margaret F.   4 Sep 1852-9 Apr 1927.
     Daughters of Hardy and Mary (_____) Riggs.

SMARTT, William T. 17 Feb 1826-25 Jun 1900. [William Thomas, son of Bennett White and Esther (Edmondson) Smartt, husband of Rachel Hampton Thomas, married 21 Jan 1858.]

SMARTT, Hampton. 31 Mar 1837-27 Jan 1903. [Rachel Hampton, daughter of Benjamin C. and Mary (Robinson) Thomas, wife of William Thomas Smartt.]

SMARTT, Claude. C. 1 Sep 1869-31 Oct 1893. [Claude Calhoun, son of Bennett White and Rachel Hampton (Thomas) Smartt.]

BLAIR, Willie Bryant. 4 Dec 1869-28 may 1900. [First wife of James P. Blair.]

BLAIR, James P. 23 Dec 1870-24 Feb 1940. [Husband of 1) Willie Bryant, married 5 May 1892 and 2) Willie Singleton, married 30 Jun 1900.]

BLAIR, Willie Singleton. 6 Mar 1879-18 Jul 1915. [Second wife of James P. Blair.]

BLAIR, William W. 1886 - 28 Aug 1961. [Son of C.F. and Della (Gouger) Blair, husband of Myrtle Paris.]

BLAIR, Myrtle. 2 May 1880-15 May 1914. [Daughter of Frank and Georgia (Tompkins) Paris, wife of William W. Blair.]

BLAIR, Edgar. 25 Apr 1880-27 Mar 1963. [Son of John B. and Cornelia (Paris) Blair. Single.]

BLAIR, Capt J.B. 20 Sep 1827-7 Jan 1911. CSA. [John B., son of Andrew J. and Nelly (_____) Blair, husband of 1) Sarah Paris, married 2 Oct 1859, and 2) Cornelia Paris, married 15 Jul 1865.]

NEWMAN, Andrew. 30 Sep 1830-4 Aug 1900. [Andrew Jackson, son of G.S. and Jemima (_____) Newman, husband of Elizabeth P. Kimbro, married

15 Jan 1854.]

NEWMAN, Elizabeth P.   4 Aug 1837-28 Sep 1914.   [Daughter of John and
    Prudence (_____) Kimbro, wife of Andrew Jackson Newman.]

BLAIR, C.F.   19 Jan 1925-22 Jan 1925.   [Son of William W. and Myrtle
    (Paris) Blair.]

BLAIR, Alton O. 5 Oct 1891-15 Nov 1940. WWI. [Alton Otto. Son of Carol
    F. and Della (Gouger) Blair, husband of Florence Davis.]

MAYFIELD, Florence Blair.   27 Mar 1901-29 Oct 1983.   [Clata Florence,
    daughter of Logan and Hattie (Martin) Davis, wife of 1) Alton
    O. Blair and 2) Waymon Mayfield.]

EDGE, Bettie Craven.   17 Oct 1881-6 Feb 1939. [Daughter of Peter and Dora
    (Gibbs) Craven, wife of Zeb Edge.]

CRAVEN, Peter. 1 Oct 1850-11 Mar 1936. [Son of Charles and Pheobe (Coe)
    Craven, husband of 1) Victoria Pepper, married 3 Dec 1893 and
    2) Dora Frances Gibbs, married 28 Aug 1878.]

CRAVEN, Dora.   23 Jan 1854-10 Dec 1939.   [Dora Frances, daughter of Sam
    and Elizabeth (_____) Gibbs, second wife of Peter Craven.]

CRAVEN, Thomas S. 7 Sep 1879-28 Oct 1966. [Son of Peter and Dora (Gibbs)
    Wilcher Craven, husband of Maggie Mai Cooper.]

CRAVEN, Maggie Mai.   10 Jul 1881-27 Jan 1944. [Daughter of H.G. and Jane
    (Anderson) Cooper, wife of Thomas S. Craven.]

CRAVEN, Maggie Pearl. No dates. [Daughter of Thomas and Maggie Mai
    (Cooper) Craven.]

CRAVEN, O.W. 1 Jan 1940-11 Nov 1943.

CRAVEN, Clara Pearl. 6 Sep 1896-7 Mar 1903. [Daughter of John H. and
    Hattie (Thatch) Craven.]

CRAVEN, Mamie Edith. 3 Oct 1898-27 Feb 1903. [Daughter of John H. and
    Hattie (Thatch) Craven.]

CRAVEN, Charles. 31 Jan 1822-9 May 1899. [Husband of Phebe _____.]

CRAVEN, Phebe. 7 Sep 1821-25 Jan 1892. [Wife of Charles Craven.]

CRAVEN, Oliver B. 26 Nov 1895-15 Feb 1956. [Oliver Bethel, son of Thomas
    and Angeline (Morrison) Craven, husband of Ora Boyd.]

CRAVEN, Ben. 27 Apr 1884-6 Jan 1954. [Benjamin Franklin, son of Peter
    and Dora (Gibbs) Craven. Single.]

SUMMERHILL, George W. 22 Feb 1898-5 Oct 1899. [Son of George W. and Annie
    (Pearsall) Summerhill.]

BLAIR, C.F. 27 Jan 1861-19 Oct 1921. [Carroll F., son of John B. and
    Sarah (Paris) Blair, husband of Della Gouger, married 3 Dec
    1884.]

BLAIR, Della Gouger. 28 Feb 1862-21 Feb 1926. [Wife of Carroll F. Blair.]

Liberty Cemetery, Cont.

PISTOLE, Charles Hershel. 23 Mar 1932-24 Mar 1932. [Son of Charles and
        Catherine (Blanks) Pistole.]

PISTOLE, Charlie E. 17 Oct 1904-   . [Husband of Catherine Blanks,
        married 1 Jun 1929.]

PISTOLE, Catherine B. 25 Aug 1905-4 Dec 1982. [Daughter of John Wilburn
        and Ada Louella (Merriman) Blanks, wife of Charlie Pistole.]

WOODS, Martha Amelia. 6 Aug 1902-   . [Wife ot Tom Robert Woods.]

WOODS, Tom Robert. 8 Sep 1901-24 Aug 1992. [Husband of Martha Amelia
        _____.]

BLANKS, John Wilburn. 20 Mar 1870-9 Nov 1956. [Son of John S. B. and
        Permelia (Duncan) Blanks, husband of Ada Merriman, married 6 Oct
        1895.]

BLANKS, Ada Luella. 1877 - 1968. [Ada Luella Merriman, wife of John
        Wilburn Blanks.]

BLANKS, Infant. Born and died 17 Mar 1898. [Daughter of John Wilburn and
        Ann (Merriman) Blanks.]

WOODS, Evelyn Marie. 1 Sep 1924-28 Nov 1927.

ROGERS, James R., Sr. 1850-30 May 1919. [Son of ____ and Martha R.
        (____) Rogers, husband of Florence Schrader, married 5 May
        1869.]

ROGERS, Florence S. 1856 - 1897. [Florence Schrader, wife of James R.
        Rogers, Sr.]

ROGERS, Martha R. 1827 - 1895.

ROGERS, James. 14 Oct 1877-8 Jul 1910. [Son of James Sr. and Florence
        (Schrader) Rogers.]

JOHNSON, Infant. Born and died 29 Oct 1954. [Daughter of James T. and
        Louise (____) Johnson.]

ROWAN, Jennie H. 16 Sep 1881-13 May 1958. [Daughter of Henry B. and
        Rebecca (Atnip) Higginbotham, wife of Stokley D. Rowan, married
        1 Jun 1900.]

ATNIP, Mary Fuston. 20 Apr 1821-4 Sep 1903. [Daughter of Jonathan Rufus
        and Rebecca (Stanley) Fuston, wife of Stephen Atnip, married 24
        Dec 1841 in DeKalb County, TN.]

ATNIP, Stephen. 1822 - 29 Mar 1866. [Son of Benjamin and _____ (____)
        Atnip, husband of Mary Fuston.]

HIGGINBOTHAM, Rebecca Atnip. 2 Mar 1844-19 Jan 1916. [Daughter of
        Stephen and Mary (Fuston) Atnip, third wife of Henry B.
        Higginbotham.]

FANSHIER, Rev. John. 25 Nov 1815-12 May 1886. [Husband of Ann Lewis,
        married 22 Mar 1837.]

[Unmarked fieldstone.]

FANSHIER, Hester Cass. Nov 1851-15 Feb 1921. [Daughter of Richard and Louise (McCorkle) Cass, wife of James W. Fanshier.]

FANSHIER, James W. 7 Mar 1853-25 May 1914. [Son of John and Ann (Lewis) Fanshier, husband of Hester Cass, married 23 Sep 1888.]

FANSHIER, Charles S. 31 Aug 1849-10 Sep 1916. [Son of John and Ann (Lewis) Fanshier.]

PEPPER, William C. 27 Oct 1820-23 Jun 1896. [William C. Smartt Pepper, son of Elisha II and Margaret (Morrow) Pepper, husband of Cynthia Allison.]

PEPPER, Cynthia. 9 May 1843-24 Jun 1918. [Daughter of James Sr. and Cynthia Caroline (Thaxton) Allison, wife of William C. Pepper.]

RICHARDSON, William Allen. 30 Jul 1878-19 May 1961. [Husband of Margaret Frances Pepper.]

RICHARDSON, Margaret Pepper. 20 Jul 1883-1 Apr 1953. [Margaret Frances, daughter of William C. S. and Cynthia (Allison) Pepper, wife of William Allen Richardson.]

PEPPER, William T. 7 Aug 1869-20 Dec 1915. [William Thomas, son of William C. S. and Cynthia (Allison) Pepper.]

TALLEY, C.C. 15 Jul 1874-14 Aug 1952. [Columbus Caleb, son of James H. and Martha Ann (Powell) Talley, husband of 1) Martha Pearlee Green, married 39 Nov 1902 and 2) Roxie (Pealer) Tenpenny.]

GREEN, Lettisha. Apr 1862-5 Apr 1940. [Lettisha Daughtery, wife of Eli Green, married 18 Apr 1875.]

TALLEY, Martha P. 21 Feb 1878-27 Nov 1910. [Martha Pearlee, daughter of Frank Eli and Lettisha (Daughtery) Green, first wife of Columbus C. Talley.]

TALLEY, Frank P. 16 Nov 1903-9 Jan 1904. [Frank Parker, son of Columbus Caleb and Martha Pearlee (Green) Talley.]

*TALLEY, William Frank. Born 17 Oct 1866, died 20 Dec 1940, son of James and Martha (Powell) Talley.

SMARTT, Infant. 14 May 1854-15 May 1854. [Daughter of Samuel Galiten and Elizabeth (McGeehee) Smartt.]

SMARTT, Elizabeth. 15 Dec 1819-27 May 1854. [Elizabeth McGeehee, second wife of Samuel Galiten Smartt, married 30 Nov 1843.]

SMARTT, Martha R. 6 Jul 1826-15 Apr 1872. [Martha Robinson, married 1) to _____ Graham and 2) as his third wife Samuel Galiten Smartt on 3 Apr 1855.]

SMARTT, John Rose. 18 Mar 1864-26 Nov 1888. [Son of Samuel Galiten and Martha (Robinson) Smartt.]

SIPE, Bessie Marie. 14 Aug 1906-7 Jul 1913. [Daughter of O.H. and Mary (Sipe) Sipe.]

CARTER, W.B. 12 Sep 1833-30 Mar 1881. [William B., husband of Margaret

Morrison, married 15 Jul 1854.]

CARTER, H.C.   30 Apr 1873-30 Apr 1880.

CARTER, Lillie Ann. __ July ____-   .

NEWMAN, Clyve Haskell. 12 Jan 1908-6 Feb 1993. [Son of Emmett Lee and
    Sallie (Smartt) Newman, husband of Willa Mae Waid, married 17
    Aug 1941.]

NEWMAN, Willa Mae Waid. 16 Jul 1903-25 Nov 1976. [Wife of Clyve Haskell
    Newman.]

NEWMAN, Nancy Waid. Born and died 4 Jun 1942. [Daughter of Clyve H. and
    Willa Mae (Waid) Newman.]

TURNER, R.G.   30 Sep 1905-11 Oct 1967. [Raymond George, son of James
    Jackson and Hallie Florence (Whitman) Turner, husband of Mary
    Flora Turner.]

TURNER, Mary F.   20 Feb 1910-13 Dec 1989. [Mary Flora, daughter of
    Bernard and Evia Ann (Young) Turner, wife of Raymond George
    Turner.]

YOUNG, Martha M.   12 Aug 1872-20 Feb 1951. [Wife of Rev. Edd Young.]

CHILTON, R. Kellum.   16 Nov 1902-17 Aug 1968. [Robert Kellum Chilton,
    husband of Lula Ann Hussey.]

CHILTON, Lula A.   17 Oct 1906-21 Dec 1989. [Lula Ann, daughter of Terry
    Henry and Mary Jane (Hibdon) Hussey, wife of Robert Kellum
    Chilton.]

CAMPBELL, John Dee.   13 Jan 1872-18 Jan 1945. [Son of John Dillard and
    Elizabeth (Haley) Campbell, husband of Annie King.]

VINSON, Odis Lavor.   1926 - 1990.

VINSON, Gertrude.   14 Jun 1906-3 Sep 1993. [Daughter of John D. and Anna
    (King) Campbell, married 1) to Sterling Brown Vinson and 2) to
    _____ Davis.]

VINSON, Sterling B.   16 May 1900-4 Aug 1937. [Sterling Brown, son of
    _____ and Ella (_____) Vinson, husband of Gertrude Campbell.]

HUSSEY, Mary J. 7 Mar 1872-4 Dec 1936. [Mary Jane, daughter of Elias and
    Cellia (Stoner) Hibdon, wife of Terry Henry Hussey.]

HUSSEY, Terry H.   27 Sep 1881-26 Oct 1959. [Terry Henry, son of John
    Alfred and Martha Ann (Womack) Hussey, husband of 1) Mary Jane
    Hibdon and 2) Nettie Ray Dugan.]

HUSSEY, Child. Died 25 Sep 1909, age 6 years. [Child of Terry Henry and
    Mary Jane (Hibdon) Hussey.]

TURNER, Rebecca. 5 Aug 1932-21 May 1937. [Daughter of Thomas B. and Eva
    Ann (Young) Turner.]

TURNER, Eva Ann.   11 Feb 1892-20 Jul 1975. [Eva Ann Young, wife of Thomas
    Bernard Turner.]

TURNER, Thomas B. 8 Dec 1889-6 Dec 1968. [Thomas Bernard, son of John and
Mollie (Adcock) Turner, husband of Eva Ann Young.]

NEWMAN, Mary Frances Locke. 16 Sep 1911-   . [Daughter of William
Charles and Margaret Ella (Stubblefield) Locke, wife of George
Edley Newman, Jr.]

NEWMAN, George Edley, Jr. 10 Jul 1907-24 Aug 1978. [Son of George Edley
and Elsie Flora Beatrice (Lane) Newman, husband of Mary Frances
Locke, married 16 Sep 1932.]

NEWMAN, Charley Mae. 7 Oct 1902-8 Dec 1918. [Daughter of Andrew J. and
Elizabeth P. (Kimbro) Newman.]

NEWMAN, G.E. 30 Sep 1860-8 Jan 1925. [George Edley, son of Andrew J. and
Elizabeth P. (Kimbro) Newman, husband of Flora Lane, amrried 20
Dec 1893.]

NEWMAN, Flora Lane. 22 Apr 1868-5 Nov 1957. [Elsie Flora Beatrice,
daughter of James Jennings and Ann Elizabeth Frances (Lowery)
Lane, wife of George Edley Newman, Sr.]

PARIS, Lytle.   6 Aug 1908-13 May 1926.
PARIS, Rufus.   24 Jul 1903-14 Mar 1926.
    Sons of John R. and Mary Josephine (Smartt) Paris.

PARIS, John R. 12 Oct 1882-17 May 1966. [Son of Joe R. and Betty (Logan)
Paris, husband of Mary Josephine Smartt, married 22 May 1907.]

PARIS, Mary J. 11 Jul 1887-11 Nov 1981. [Mary Josephine, daughter of
Frank George and Anna Bell (Smartt) Smartt, wife of John R.
Paris.]

JORDAN, William P. 10 Feb 1879-17 Oct 1951. [William Perry, son of
Thomas and Louise (Hines) Jordan, husband of Lina Frances
Hobbs.]

JORDAN, Lina F. 28 Feb 1884-1 Apr 1942. [Lina Frances, daughter of ____
and Sallie (Williams) Hobbs, wife of William P. Jordan.]

WINTON, Horace Smartt. 25 Jan 1876-12 Nov 1880. [Son of Pleasant
Henderson and Lillian (Ramsey) Winton.]

WINTON, Lillian. 28 Apr 1854-17 Sep 1881. [Lula Lillian, daughter of
Samuel McCaslin and Octavia (Smartt) Ramsey, wife of Pleasant
Henderson Winton, married 10 Sep 1873.]

RHEA, Violet Zumbro. 30 Mar 1904-   [Wife of John Thomas Ray
(Rhea).]

RAY, John Thomas. 25 Aug 1890-11 Jun 1959. WWI. [Old stone has RAY, new
stone has RHEA.]

CHAMBERS, Katie. 10 Aug 1866-14 Aug 1886. [Daughter of William Davidson
and Josie (Savage) Smartt, wife of M. Chambers, married 3 Feb
1886.]

SMARTT, Josie C. 6 Oct 1834-6 Nov 1881. [Josephine Clark, daughter of
George and Elizabeth (Keener) Savage, first wife of Wm. Davidson
Smartt, married 5 May 1859.]

Liberty Cemetery, Cont.

SMARTT, W.G. 1872 - 1948.

SMARTT, Lucien S. 14 May 1869-30 Nov 1893. [Son of Wm. Davidson and
        Josie C. (Savage) Smartt.]

SMARTT, Josie. 27 Sep 1851-13 Dec 1890. [Josa Savage, second wife of Wm.
        Davidson Smartt, married 8 Nov 1882.]

SMARTT, W.D. 23 Jan 1832-13 Jan 1888. [William Davidson, son of Frank
        Burwell and Margaret (Davdison) Smartt, husband of 1) Josie C.
        Savage and 2) Josie Savage. Newspaper of 19 Jan 1889 gives his
        death date as 15 Jan 1889.]

PARIS, Clayton.   25 Jul 1908-12 Nov 1908.
PARIS, Clifford.   25 Jul 1908-10 Dec 1910.
    Twin sons of John R. and Mary Josephine (Smartt) Paris.

SMARTT, Aseneth.   Died 2 Jan 1889, aged 60 years, 5 months,14 days.
        [Daughter of Wm. Cheek and Elizabeth Hackett (Waterhouse)
        Smartt.]

SMARTT, G.M. 28 Feb 1814-22 Apr 1904. [George Madison, son of Wm. Cheek
        and Margaret (Colville) Smartt, married 1) 22 Dec 1840 to Ann
        Waterhouse and 2) to Cornelia Adalaide Smartt on 3 Sep 1872.]

SMARTT, Ann. 9 Feb 1821-2 Dec 1870. [Ann Waterhouse, first wife of
        George Madison Smartt.]

SMARTT, Cornelia A. 4 Jan 1842-8 May 1913. [Cornelia Adalaide, daughter
        of George White and Sarah Ann (Zachary) Smartt, second wife of
        George Madison Smartt.]

SMARTT, W. Dick. 1858 - 23 Aug 1913. [Son of George Madison and Ann
        (Waterhouse) Smartt.]

RAYBURN, Rev. James. 12 Dec 1868-30 Dec 1961. [Son of James G. and
        Margaret Elizabeth (McGill) Rayburn, husband of Annie George
        Smartt.]

RAYBURN, Annie Smartt. 31 Jan 1875-12 Mar 1954. [Annie George, daughter
        of George Madison and Cornelia Adalaide (Smartt) Smartt.]

MASTERS, Thelma Jean Rhea. 29 May 1922-27 Nov 1980. [Daughter of John
        Thomas and Violet (Zumbro) Rhea, first wife of Albert Leonard
        Masters.]

MERRIMAN, Lenora Tatum. 27 Mar 1913-4 Dec 1977. [Daughter of Clarence
        Bethel and Kelly (Stevens) Tatum, wife of Clyde E. Merriman.]

MERRIMAN, Clyde E. 8 Feb 1912-30 Jul 1977. WWII. [Son of Richard Allen
        and Nettie (Wood) Merriman, husband of Leonora Tatum.]

MERRIMAN, Ila Irene. 18 Mar 1911-25 Jun 1984. [Daughter of Jim and _____
        (_____) Hockman, wife of Harold Carr Merriman.]

MERRIMAN, Harold C. 21 Mar 1908-28 Jun 1986. WWII. [Harold Carr, son of
        Richard Allen and Nettie (Wood) Merriman, husband of Irene
        Hockman.]

**The following couple died in a house fire in Williamsburg, VA

and are buried there according to the Southern Standard, but have stones
here:
MERRIMAN, Richard Allen. 25 Jun 1949-26 Apr 1988. [Son of Clyde and
        Lenora (Tatum) Merriman, husband of Patricia Monahan.]

MERRIMAN, Patricia Monahan. 21 Sep 1948-26 Apr 1988. Daughter of _____
        and Mildred F. (_____) Monahan, wife of Richard Allen Merriman.

MERRIMAN, Martha Smith. 23 Feb 1918-29 Jun 1992. [Wife of Raymond
        Merriman.]

MERRIMAN, Raymond. 19 Jun 1910-3 Nov 1985. [Son of Richard A. and Nettie
        (Wood) Merriman, wife of Martha Smith.]

MERRIMAN, Estelle McCartney Evins. 3 Aug 1908-   . [Estelle
        McCartney wife of 1) William Jackson Evins and 2) Noel Bomar
        Merriman.]

MERRIMAN, Noel Bomar. 23 Aug 1906-15 Jan 1977. [Son of Richard Allen and
        Nettie (Wood) Merriman, second husband of Estelle McCartney.]

MERRIMAN, Richard A. 8 Aan 1880-29 May 1914. [Richard Allen, son of
        Isaac M. and Martha Celina (Cass) Merriman, husband of Nettie
        Wood.]

MERRIMAN, Nettie Wood. 29 Apr 1879-30 Nov 1930. [Daughter of Jack and
        Lizzie (Bomar) Wood, wife of Richard Allen Merriman.]

MERRIMAN, Richard Estil. 12 Feb 1914-23 Jun 1915. [Son of Richard Allen
        and Nettie (Wood) Merriman.]

BILES, Flora A. 24 Sep 1873-3 Aug 1960. [Daughter of James J. and Mary
        Josephine (Jones) Anderson, wife of Thomas Dowell Biles.]

BILES, Thomas D. 26 Sep 1861-5 Jan 1944. [Thomas Dowell, son of John
        Wesley and Agnes (Stanley) Biles, husband of Flora Anderson,
        married 21 May 1890.]

ANDERSON, Frank. 1878 - 1942.

HOPKINS, Bonnie A. 14 Mar 1886-11 Jul 1886. [Bonnie Anne, daughter of
        J.N. and Betty S. (Anderson) Hopkins.]

ANDERSON, James J. 1835 - 29 Dec 1916. [Son of James and _____ (_____)
        Anderson, husband of Mary Josephine Jones, married 29 Jul 1863.]

ANDERSON, Mary Josephine. 1844-10 Jul 1900. [Daughter of Andrew and
        Sarah (_____) Jones, wife of James J. Anderson.]

SMARTT, Ella. 9 Aug 1849-25 Apr 1889. [Ella Savage, wife of W.K. Smartt,
        married 26 Jan 1875.]

SMARTT, Erastus C. 1 Sep 1885-8 Jul 1887. [Son of W.K. and Ella (Savage)
        Smartt.]

REYNOLDS, Roy L. 8 Aug 1910-21 Sep 1974. WWII.

REYNOLDS, Janie Adelene M. 12 Nov 1918-20 Jul 1988. [Daughter of Harry
        L. and Birdie (Merriman) McClain, wife of Roy L. Reynolds.]

246

WILCHER, Elizabeth. Died Dec 1896 age 60 years. [Elizabeth Gibbs, married 1) to John O. Pepper on 24 Aug 1861 and 2) the A.P. Wilcher on 15 Nov 1868.]

WILCHER, A.P. No dates. [Archibald Price, son of Thomas Jr. and Pauline C. (Gordon) Wilcher, husband of Elizabeth (Gibbs) Pepper.]

WILCHER, Bonnie Lee.   No dates.
WILCHER, Lina.   No dates.
    Children of A.P. and Elizabeth (Gibbs) Wilcher.

CASS, Richard M.   22 Jan 1855-17 Sep 1943. [Richard Martin, son of Richard and Louisa (McConnell) Cass, husband of Lou Venia Hobbs.]

CASS, Lou Venia. 13 May 1870-6 Jan 1948. [Lou Venia Elizabeth, daughter of Ike and Rosie (Smith) Hobbs, wife of Richard Martin Cass.]

MERRIMAN, Lewis. 1906 - 15 Nov 1932. [Son of Elie H. Merriman. Single.]

MERRIMAN, Elie.   27 Jul 1884-12 Oct 1967.   [Daughter of Isaac M. and Martha (Cass) Merriamn.]

MERRIMAN, Matilda Jane. 15 Nov 1852-13 Sep 1920. [Daughter of Allen and Emmaline E. (_____) Merriman. Single.]

MERRIMAN, Isaac M. 10 May 1851-31 Dec 1910. [Son of Allen and Emmaline E. (_____) Merriman, husband of Martha Celina Cass, married 13 Dec 1874.]

MERRIMAN, Martha Cass. 22 Nov 1852-16 Mar 1930. [Martha Celina, daughter of Richard and Louisa (McConnell) Cass, wife of Isaac M. Merriman.]

MERRIMAN, Mary Matilda. 24 Apr 1882-23 Sep 1883. [Daughter of Isaac M. and Martha (Cass) Merriman.]

CRAVEN, Octa Magnolia. 31 Oct 1904-1 Sep 1923. [Daughter of Charles and Allison (Moore) Craven.]

CAGLE, Mary C. 1 Jun 1840-26 Jun 1913. [Mary Catherine, daughter of Bennett White and Esther (Edmonson) Smartt, third wife of Benjamin Stuart Cagle, married 12 Apr 1882.]

SMARTT, Martha E. 12 Jan 1823-1 Aug 1908. [Daughter of Bennett White and Esther (Edmonson) Smartt. Single.]

SMARTT, Jessie E. 16 Mar 1870-24 Jun 1894. [Jessie Elizabeth, daughter of James Preston and Mary A. (Smith) Smartt.]

SMARTT, Jennie R. 5 Feb 1872-18 Feb 1902. [Jennie Rebecca, daughter of James Preston and Mary A. (Smith) Smartt.]

SMARTT, J.P. 26 Sep 1827-6 Jul 1892. [James Preston, son of Bennett White and Esther (Edmonson) Smartt, husband of Mary A. Smith, married 30 Sep 1856.]

SMARTT, Mary A. 3 Sep 1834-18 Apr 1915. [Mary A. Smith, wife of James Preston Smartt.]

GRIZZELL, Ike. 27 Jan 1882-10 Aug 1969. [Son of Ervin and Tennie (Swan) Grizzell, husband of Fannie King, married 7 Feb 1912.]

GRIZZELL, Fannie King. 12 Jul 1883-24 Aug 1970. [Daughter of William White and Mary Lou (Thomas) King, wife of Ike Grizzell.]

KING, Maggie Hampton. 4 Feb 1877-2 Jan 1959. [Daughter of William White and Mary Lou (Thomas) King.]

WALLING, Ada. 28 Mar 1856-5 Feb 1892. [Lucy Ada, daughter of William C. and Sarah Anne (Bonner) Locke, first wife of Thomas Dillard Walling, married 5 Dec 1878.]

LOCKE, W.C. 12 Jan 1821-12 Dec 1906. [William C., son of Jesse P. and Clarcy (Bonner) Locke, husband of Sarah Ann Bonner.]

LOCKE, S.A. 6 Apr 1829-15 May 1913. [Sarah Ann Bonner, wife of William C. Locke.]

LOCKE, Hanna N. 1852-6 Sep 1921. [Hannah Narcissus, daughter of Green G. and Martha (Webb) Magness, wife of Jesse Burton Locke.]

LOCKE, Jesse B. 18 May 1848-11 Apr 1928. [Jesse Burton, son of William C. and Sarah Ann (Bonner) Locke, husband of Hannah Narcissus Magness.]

LOCKE, William Charles. 15 Jan 1877-27 Jul 1957. [Son of Jesse Burton and Hannah Narcissus (Magness) Locke, wife of Margaret Ella Stubblefield.]

LOCKE, Margaret Ella. 7 May 1876-20 Aug 1964. [Daughter of Elisha J. and Elizabeth (Martin) Stubblefield, wife of 1) David Foster Wagner, married 11 Dec 1892 and 2) William Charles Locke, married 24 Dec 1901.]

CRAVEN, Charles Floyd. 12 Mar 1874-6 Dec 1951. [Husband of Lenna Belle Allison.]

CRAVEN, Lenna Belle. 7 Sep 1882-24 Nov 1923. [Daughter of John and Lou (Cass) Allison, wife of Charles Floyd Craven.]

McGEE, Ella E. 2 Nov 1882-15 Jul 1956. [Ella Elizabeth, daughter of Abner D. and Louise (Morris) Womack, wife of Billy McGee.]

WOMACK, Louisa X. 17 May 1866-23 Feb 1923. [Daughter of Van Buren and Celina (Hampton) Morris, wife of Abner D. Womack. Death record gives her name as Louise Vantipp.]

WOMACK, Abner D. 28 Apr 1858-12 Jun 1914. [Abner Denton, son of Abner Monroe and Mary A. (Cantrell) Womack, husband of Louisa X. Morris, married 6 Oct 1881.]

WOMACK, F. Ethel. 21 Oct 1890-27 Mar 1892. [Daughter of Abner Denton and Louisa X. (Morris) Womack.]

MADDOX, Clarrisa Dru. 15 Jan 1850-6 Feb 1891. [Daughter of William C. and Sarah Ann (Bonner) Locke, wife of James W. Maddox, married 2 Nov 1873.]

WOOD, Bertha Pauline Roach. 13 Nov 1899-3 Aug 1922. [Daughter of Lee and

Callie (Allison) Roach, wife of Leslie P. Wood.]

CROUCH, Josephine. 3 May 1895-11 Mar 1904. [Daughter of W.L. and M. Josa (Blair) Crouch.]

FERRELL, Joseph E. 3 Jan 1877-21 Sep 1964. [Joseph Espy, son of Oscar and Martha (Cartwright) Ferrell, husband of 1) Emmie _____ and 2) Bessie Rogers.]

FERRELL, Emmie. 4 Apr 1883-7 Nov 1929. [First wife of Joseph E. Ferrell.]

ALTER, Mary. 1 Aug 1850-17 Apr 1899. [Wife of J.Q. Alter.]

DAVIS, Willie Evelyn. Born and died 1940.

HERRIMAN, Flaval E. 31 May 1928-8 Sep 1958. [Flaval Eugene, son of Columbus P. and Eppie Cordelia (Mullins) Herriman. Single.]

HERRIMAN, Eppie C. 16 Dec 1906-12 Mar 1957. [Eppie Cordelia, daughter of Edd and Frances (Gannon) Mullins, wife of Columbus P. Herriman.]

HERRIMAN, Columbus P. 5 Aug 1899-26 Jan 1940. [Son of Columbus P. and Mary Frances (Mears) Herriman, husband of Eppie Cordelia Mullins.]

DODSON, George Edward. 24 Jul 1928-14 Nov 1980. [Son of George Thurman and Jessie Emma (Farless) Dodson, husband of 1) Pauline Russell and 2) Dorothy Jo. Herriman.]

DODSON, Dorothy Herriman. No dates. [Daughter of Columbus P. and Eppie Cordelia (Mullins) Herriman, wife of George Edward Dodson, married 27 Mar 1959.]

HENCE, Chester J. 7 Apr 1882-15 Nov 1896.

LANE, Eden M. 20 Jun 1858-14 Mar 1942. [Eden Murphy, son of Charles Patrick and Caroline (Halteman) Lane, husband of Ethelda Williams.]

CAUTHORN, Mary. 18 Jun 1865-20 Jan 1920. [Daughter of J.C. and Furby (Melton) Griffin, wife of T.B. Caulthorn, married 12 Jul 1892.]

HENDERSON, Daniel. 2 Apr 1887-29 Apr 1944.]

*DAVIS, Ellen K. Died 13 Nov 1986, age 78 years. Daughter of Isaac and Mary Ann (Green) Coakley.]

COAKLEY, Fannie Mai. 3 Dec 1922-24 Jan 1943. [Daughter of Isaac Francis and Mary Ann (Green) Coakley.]

COAKLEY, Isaac F. 20 Sep 1878-24 Apr 1936. [Isaac Francis, son of Jim and Eliza (_____) Coakley, husband of Mary Ann Green.]

COAKLEY, Mary Green. 15 May 1882-12 May 1970. [Mary Ann, daughter of John and Lucinda (Baker) Green, wife of Isaac Francis Coakley.]

EVANS, Walter. 1 Feb 1921-4 Nov 1967. [Son of Charlie and Bessie Burch (Holland) Evans, husband of Ruby May Reed.]

Liberty Cemetery, Cont.

BARRETT, Henry T.   27 May 1892-7 Oct 1965.   [Son of John and Bell Zora
        (Deberry) Barrett, husband of 1) Lemma Ethel McCorkle and 2)
        Mollie Evon (Brock) Jordon.]

BARRETT, Lemma E. 18 May 1900-17 Feb 1942.   [Lemma Ethel, daughter of John
        Morgan and Harriett (Christian) McCorkle, first wife of Henry
        T. Barrett.]

EARLS, Raymond, Jr.   14 Jan 1933-6 Nov 1940.   [Raymond Eugene, Jr., son of
        Raymond Eugene and Myrtle (Rogers) Earls.]

EARLS, Mable L.   Died 2 Jan 1968, age 76 years.

EARLS, Myrtle E.   14 Sep 1910-10 Mar 1969.   [Myrtle Ellis, daughter of
        Lock and Mollie (Bolt) Rogers, wife of Raymond E. Earls.]

EARLS, Raymond E.   2 May 1910-   .   [Husband of Myrtle Ellis
        Rogers.]

TENPENNY, Flavil Hall.   20 Jan 1912-27 Feb 1968.   [Son of Lannie Lester
        and Hattie Belle (Woods) Tenpenny, husband of Mary Lee Logue,
        married 11 Jun 1932.]

TENPENNY, Mary Lee.   25 Nov 1913-15 Jun 1993.   [Daughter of William Martin
        and Vera Ellen (Mullinax) Logue, married 1) to Flavil Hall
        Tenpenny, and 2) to Willis Record.]

TENPENNY, Joe David.   12 Feb 1941-6 Aug 1941.
TENPENNY, Flavil Hall, Jr.   28 Jun 1933-4 Jun 1934.
        Sons of Flavil Hall and Mary Lee (Logue) Tenpenny.

BROWN, Dema.   29 Jun 1855-9 Jun 1937. [Daughter of _____ and Amy (_____)
        Green, wife of John H. Brown.]

BROWN, J.H. "Dump".   3 Feb 1845-12 May 1923.   [John H. Brown, husband of
        Dema C. Green, married 31 Dec 1872.]

HAMILTON, Henry Clay.   1908-1 Jul 1909.   Son of C.V. and M.V.
        Hamilton.

SEWELL, Sarah E.   17 Aug 1874-9 May 1959.   [Sarah Elizabeth, daughter of
        William H. and Almira Jane (Crawley) Thomas, wife of John T.
        Sewell, married 29 Dec 1904.]

THOMAS, Almira J.   10 Sep 1847-23 May 1934.   [Almira Jane, daughter of
        Joseph and Annie (Martin) Crawley, wife of William H. Thomas.]

THOMAS, William H.   5 Mar 1851-24 May 1937.   [Son of Joe and Betsy (Barr)
        Thomas, husband of Almira Jane Crawley.]

NICHOLS, Irma A.   22 Apr 1891-13 Mar 1948.   [Wife of Virgle Nichols.]

BURCH, James Edward.   9 Dec 1934-17 May 1935.   [Son of William Lee and
        Annie Parrott (Earls) Burch.]

BURCH, Wm. Lee.   10 Nov 1893-12 Oct 1970.   [William Lee, son of George
        Washington and America (Reed) Burch, husband of Annie Parrott
        Earls.]

BURCH, Annie P. Earls.   16 Mar 1906-   .   [Annie Parrott Earls, wife of William Lee Burch.

GREEN, Joyce Ann. Born and died 20 Mar 1947. [Daughter of W. Leo and Annie Pearl (Burch) Green.]

DUNLAP, Eddie E. 11 Dec 1918-27 Apr 1981. WWII. [Eddie Earl, son of R.L. and Zanie (Green) Dunlap, husband of 1) Idema Clark and 2) Beulah Hill.]

DUNLAP, Beulah. 10 Jul 1921-   . [Beulah Hill, wife of Eddie Earl Dunlap.]

BOLT, N.A. 6 Dec 1866-12 Feb 1943. [Noah Alexander, son of James R. and Sarah (Gray) Bolt, husband of Nancy Starkey, married 19 Aug 1894.]

BOLT, Nancy Starkey. 2 Jan 1852-12 Jan 1944. [Daughter of Jarvis and Martha [Deberry/Derryberry] Starkey, wife of Noah Alexander Bolt.]

HANKINS, Ernest Parks. Died 9 Sep 1971, age 83 years, __ months and 21 days. [Son of John William and Nora Alice (Gribble) Hankins, husband of 1) Mary Cotton, married 22 Oct 1911 and 2) to Anna Louise Hill on 2 May 1933.]

HANKINS, Anna Louise. 1912-18 Oct 1993. [Daughter of Joe and Minerva Elizabeth (Parsley) Hill, second wife of Ernest Parks Hankins.]

HANKINS, Ernest Hayden. 12 Oct 1935-15 Sep 1978. Korea. [Son of Ernest Parks and Louise (Hill) Hankins. Single.]

MILLS, Theodore. 18 Feb 1919-17 May 1982. WWII. [Son of Newton and Dolly (Espy) Mills, husband of Jodie Elizabeth Hill.]

MILLS, Jodie Hill. 27 Aug 1924-26 Nov 1984. [Daughter of Joe and Minerva Elizabeth (Parsley) Hill, wife of Theodore Mills.]

HILL, Charlie D. 3 Feb 1917-7 Jan 1983. WWII. [Son of Joe and Minerva Elizabeth (Parsley) Hill.]

HILL, Elizabeth. 13 Dec 1879-2 Dec 1945. [Minerva Elizabeth, daughter of James Alfred and Mary F. (McClellan) Parsley, wife of Joe Hill.]

HILL, Joe. 12 Jul 1879-18 Sep 1936. [Husband of Minerva Elizabeth Parsley, married 16 Oct 1896 in DeKalb County, TN.]

OGLES, Louise. 22 Jun 1909-20 Dec 1913. [Daughter of A.J. and Ollie (Pepper) Ogles.]

*OGLES, Andrew Johnson. 6 Feb 1865-8 Nov 1934. Son of Wight and Rebecca (Birdwell) Ogles, husband of Ollie Pepper.

*OGLES, Andrew G. 22 May 1917-2 Jul 1917. Son of Andrew Johnson and Elizabeth (Pepper) Ogles.

DUNHAM, Georgia Velma. 18 Sep 1908-15 Dec 1908. [Daughter of George W. and C.P. (_____) Durham.]

DUNEM, I. C. 2 Sep 1882-27 Oct 1901. [I. Clinton, son of G.W. and C.P. (_____) Dunham.]

Liberty Cemetery, Cont.

BURCH, George W. 1903-26 Nov 1979. [Son of George Washington and America (Reed) Burch, husband of Hallie Mae Ferrell.]

*BURCH, Johnny Alton. 4 Apr 1937-11 Jul 1955. Son of George W. and Hallie Mae (Ferrell) Burch.

*BURCH, Hallie Mae Ferrell. Died in 1953. Wife of George W. Burch.

BURCH, George Allen. Born and died 16 Oct 1933. [Son of George W. and Hallie Mae (Ferrell) Burch.

LEWIS, Ernest and Eugene. Only date 1 Sep 1912.

PALMER, T.H. 1874 - 5 Jan 1940. [Thomas Hamilton, son of Monroe and Jane (Edwards) Palmer, husband of Tennie Jane Higdon.]

PALMER, Tennie J. 1 Jun 1897-18 Jun 1933. [Tennie Jane, daughter of Lee and Sarah (Jordan) Higdon, wife of Thomas Hamilton Palmer.]

PALMER, W. Eston. 1897 - 1913. [Son of Thomas Hamilton and Tennie Jane (Higdon) Palmer.]

CANTRELL, Robert C. 7 May 1870-23 Mar 1889. [Son of Leonard and Mary (_____) Cantrell.

FRALEY, Jefferson Davis. 7 Mar 1874-9 Jan 1940. [Son of ____ and Martha (Arnold) Fraley, husband of Samantha Walker.]

FRALEY, Mary Ann. 1854 - 1926.

FRALEY, Doyle. 22 May 1912-15 Dec 1912. [Son of Jefferson Davis and Samantha (Walker) Fraley.]

*WALKER, J.R. 21 Jun 1870-13 Feb 1927. Son of Tom and _____ (_____) Walker, husband of Martha Eveline Wilson.

*WALKER, Martha Eveline. 25 Jan 1877-6 Feb 1930. Daughter of James and Phebie Jane (Ford) Wilson, wife of J.R. Walker.

*McBRIDE, John McEwell. 6 Sep 1857-25 May 1927. Son of William A. and Nancy Adelyne (Gibbs) McBride. Single.

*DAVIS, Hershell. Died 5 Oct 1984, age 91 years, son of Logan and Hattie (Martin) Davis, husband of Grace Barksdale.

*HOBBS, Frank Madison. Born 2 Dec 1858, died 27 Aug 1928, son of Ike and Rosie (Smith) Hobbs.

*HIGGINBOTHAM, Rebecca. Born 2 Mar 1844, died 18 Jan 1916, daughter of Stephen and Mary (Fuson) Atnip, wife of Henry B. Higginbotham.

*MORRISON, E.J. Died 21 Jun 1918, age 75 years.

*THOMAS, Robbie Lee. Born 8 Feb 1906, died 25 Apr 1925, daughter of J.S. and Lizzie (_____) Hill, wife of D.L. Thomas.

*HUSSEY, Martha. Martha Wilmont, died 13 Nov 1920, age 68 years, wife of John Alford Hussey.

*HUSSEY, John Alford. Born 28 Sep 1856, died 4 May 1942. Son of Henry and Martha Jane (Ferguson) Hussey, husband of Martha Wilmont.

*DUKE, Colonel. Born 1 Aug 1882, died 21 Jan 1955, son of Alex and Abb (Almond) Duke, husband of Ruby _____.

*BURCH, Clarence Edward. Born 7 Jan 1934, died 15 Jan 1934, son of Robert Dudley and Maggie (Earles) Burch.

*RANDOLPH, Anderson. Born 24 Feb 1826, died 11 Jan 1889, son of Henry and Sarah Jane (Pogue) Randolph, husband of Mary Ann Stiles who was buried in Bell County, TX.

*RANDOLPH, Martha Josephine. Born 14 May 1859, died 11 Jan 1889, daughter of Anderson and Mary Ann (Stiles) Randolph.

*RANDOLPH, James Martin. Born 16 Sep 1860, died 24 Jan 1862, son of Anderson and Mary Ann (Stiles) Randolph.

*MOORE, James H. Born 1927, died 19 Jan 1987, son of B.G. and Ada (Blanks) Moore, husband of Evelyn Chilton.

*EARLS, Jeffery Charles. Born 21 Mar 1967, died 22 Mar 1967, son of _____ and Christine (_____) Earls.

*SMITH, Gladys Beatrice. Born 10 Mar 1932, died 17 Mar 1932, daughter of Otto and Collie (Waller) Smith.

*PISTOLE, Charles Herschel. Born 23 Mar 1932, died 24 Mar 1932, son of Charles and Catherine (Blanks) Pistole.

*HICKEY, Claude. Born and died 15 Oct 1932, son of Claude and Catherine (Lutrell) Hickey.

*NUNNELLY, Joe Edward. Born and died 26 Apr 1931, son of Charles and Eunice (Brady) Nunnelly.

*LAWSON, Vester Eugene, Jr. Born 3 Nov 1945, died 3 Dec 1945, son of Vester Eugene and Dorothy (Fleming) Lawson.

*TALLEY, J.B. Born 9 Mar 1921, died 9 Mar 1944, son of Jerry and Lela (Bell) Talley.

*THAXTON, Infant son of Wm. A. and Claudine (Lawrence) Thaxton, born 4 Nov 1944, died 5 Nov 1944.

*THAXTON, Infant daughter of Wm. A. and Claudine (Lawrence) Thaxton, born 4 Nov 1944, died 4 Nov 1944.

THAXTON, James Earl. 31 Jul 1941-1 Aug 1941. [Son of William A. and Claudine (Lawrence) Thaxton.]

*RAINS, Elvira R. Died 29 Dec 1907, age 63 years.

*MUNCEY, Jasper D. "Jack". Born ca 1880, died 4 Aug 1952, son of Jasper and Elizabeth (Lytle) Muncey, husband of 1) Mary Rigsby, married 7 Jan 1903, 2) Rosa Jane Myers, married 28 Sep 1907, and 3) Bernice J. McBride, married 23 Dec 1924.

*MUNCEY, Myrtle Frances. Born 25 Apr 1927, died 18 Jan 1935, daughter of Jack and Bernice (McBride) Muncey.

Liberty Cemetery, Cont.

*OAKLEY, Lucy. Born 20 Aug 1880, died 21 Feb 1951, daughter of Richard
        and Elizabeth (Davis) Bailey, wife of W.H. Oakley.

*ROGERS, Infant. Born and died 7 Mar 1936.
*ROGERS, Infant. Born and died 22 Feb 1947.
*ROGERS, Louise Ray. Born and died 3 Jan 1937.
*ROGERS, Lawrence Roy. Born 21 Nov 1945, died 20 Jan 1946.
    Children of Rufe A. and Louise (Watley) Rogers.

*FULTS, Carson Oliver. Born 20 Nov 1944, died 10 Feb 1946, son of Oliver
        and Myrtle Aline (_____) Fults.

*MORTON, Infant. Born and died 6 Mar 1941, son of Edward Jr. and Bessie
        (Burch) Morton.

*HINDS, Oscar Ray. Born 21 Oct 1960, died 29 Oct 1960, son of Oscar Aaron
        and Georgia Frances (Muncey) Hinds.

*BURCH, America Lee. Born 1865, died 5 Feb 1935, daughter of Bill and
        Hannah (Fern) Reed, wife of Washington Burch.

*BURCH, R. Washington. Born 10 Jun 1861, died 12 Jun 1952, son of George
        and Mary Ann (_____) Burch, husband of America Lee Reed, married
        28 Sep 1884.

*PINEGAR, Willie. Born 16 Aug 1932, died 14 Feb 1933, son of B. and Alice
        (Young) Pinegar.

*EVANS, Bessie. Born and died 28 Aug 1942.
*EVANS, John.   Born and died 14 Nov 1951.
    Children of Walter and Ruby (Reed) Evans.

*HALLUM, Kathy Corlette. Born and died 16 Feb 1950, daughter of Woodrow
        and Kathleen (West) Hallum.

*PENDLETON, Judy Sharon. Born 7 Mar 1947, died 11 Oct 1947, daughter of
        Charles and Lillian (Muncey) Pendleton.

*EARLS, Mae Brister. Died 24 Nov 1912, age 9 years.

*LOWE, Charlie. Died 27 Feb 1913, age 86 years.

*HENNESSEE, Loyd. Died 9 Jul 1913, age 1 year.

*PALMER, William Eaton. Died 7 Jul 1913, age 14 years.

*CROUCH, J.B. Died 8 Feb 1907, age 60 years.

*STILES, Mrs E.J. DIed 7 Apr 1907, age 76 years.

*LOWE, Mrs Sallie. Died 9 Dec 1907, age 70 years.

*HOODENPYL, Phoebe. Born 1 Apr 1810, died 2 Oct 1834, daughter of Ericus
        and Rosanna (Pucket) Smith, wife of Phillip Gysberti Hoodenpyl,
        married 13 Oct 1829.

*SISK, Emma. Born 29 Apr 1859, died 22 Nov 1930, daughter of Willis and
        Ollie (Southern) Ashly, wife of Lot Sisk.

*CANTRELL, Cleo A. Born 23 Dec 1865, died 26 Jan 1929, daughter of John and Margaret (Payne) Head, wife of_____ Cantrell.

*WILSON, Mattie, died Dec 1896.

*HENDERSON, Joseph S. Died 27 Aug 1918, age 69 years, 9 months and 12 days.

*QUALES, Infant. Died 6 Jan 1919, age 5 years.

*BLACK, J.L., Jr. Born 2 Apr 1921, died 16 Apr 1921, son of J.L. and Annie V. (_____) Black.

*CANTRELL, Infant. Born and died 9 Jun 1919.
*CANTRELL, Infant. Born and died 14 Jul 1931.
     Infants of F. Rudie and Ola (Pinegar) Cnatrell.

*JONES, Samantha Jane. Born 9 Jan 1845, died 16 Apr 1914.

*ROGERS, Cecil Albert. Died 27 Apr 1927, age 17 years.

*ALLISON, Mary E. Died 7 Jan 1918, age 70 years.

*LOCKE, Nannie. Born 17 Jun 1867, died 28 Jan 1916, daughter of John and Martha (Ross) Locke.

*DUNHAM, Bertha Mae. Born 25 Aug 1916, died 12 Sep 1916, daughter of Paul and Willie (Jordon) Dunham.

*BASHAM, Tennie. Died 24 Jul 1917, age 33 years, daughter of Joe and Fannie (_____) Lowe, wife of Noah Basham, married 5 Aug 1908.

*BROWN, _____. Born Oct 1834, died 29 Feb 1908, daughter of Will and Daisy (Dunham) Brown.

*HODGE, Adrian. Died 28 Feb 1923, age 50 years.

*RAINS, Josiah, born Oct 1834, died 29 Feb 1908.

*DRAKE, _____. Died 2 Feb 1908, age 80 years.

*DAVIS, Mrs Joe. Died 26 Feb 1908.

*PARRIS, Clayton. Died 6 Nov 1908, age 3 months.

*SMITH, Sallie. Died 2 Jun 1912.

*TALLEY, Alma. Died 6 May 1920, age 33 years. She was Alma Hawthorn.

*TURNER, Annie Jane, died 2 Oct 1914, age 23 days.

*HOLLIS, Infant. Died 5 Nov 1914, infant of Jim Hillis.

*HUDDLESTON, Henry Clay. Died 1 Jul 1909, age 11.

*ETTER, G.L. Died 1917, age 1 day. (Twin)

*BARRETT, Ellen Canzada. Died 29 Dec 1925.

*ROGERS, Ricky Lee. Born 12 Nov 1963, died 15 Nov 1963, son of Thomas and Helen (Davidson) Rogers.

Liberty Cemetery, Cont.

*HOOSIER, Henry. Born 31 Oct 1873, died 31 May 1958, son of George W. and
        Sarah (Pelham) Hoosier, husband of Nannie _____.

*WILLIAMS, Georgia. Born 21 Jul 1898, died 8 Aug 1935, daughter of Jerry
        and Sallie (_____) Williams.

*CANTRELL, Fredrick James. Born 12 Nov 1862, died 10 Apr 1931, son of
        Cappy and _____ (Tittsworth) Cantrell.

*HINES, Urby. Born and died 4 Mar 1934, infant of Urby and Lemma (Perry)
        Hines.

*BROWN, John H. Died 12 May 1923, age 78 years.

*SMITHSON, J.A. Born 30 Sep 1878, died 8 Jun 1940, son of Bill and
        Elizabeth (_____) Smithson.

*FULTS, Charles Lewis. Born 6 Aug 1941, died 11 Nov 1941, son of Charles
        M. and Irene (Muncey) Fults.

*DUKE, Rebecca. Born 17 Mar 1858, died 23 Jan 1940, daughter of Wesley
        and Nancy (McFarlen) McMahan, wife of Calvin Duke.

*GANN, Infant. Born 9 Dec 1947, died 10 Dec 1947, Infant of Robert and
        Clara Belle (Harlow) Gann.

*PINEGAR, J.C. Born 1 Oct 1925, died 3 Jan 1961, son of B. and Alice
        (Young) Pinegar, husband of Beatrice May _____.

LUSK CEMETERY

Location: off Frances Ferry Road

LUSK, Sgt. John D. 2 Jun 1842-15 Aug 1892. [Son of William L. and
        Pamelia (_____) Lusk, husband of Louvisa Clark.]

LUSK, Louvisa. 18 Jan 1839-4 Mar 1889. [Daughter of Absolem and Mary
        (_____) Clark, wife of John D. Lusk, married 18 Dec 1866.]

Four graves marked with fieldstones.

LYTLE CEMETERY
This Cemetery has been destroyed.

Location: On old Lytle property on the mountain off Viola Road.

MUNCY, Thomas Jasper "Jack".   11 Jun 1848-8 Apr 1905. [Son of John C.
        and Perlina (Adams) Muncy, husband of Elizabeth Lytle, married
        7 Jan 1875.]

MUNCY, Elizabeth. 1853 - 28 Jan 1912. [Daughter of James and Elizabeth
        (Schrader) Lytle, wife of Thomas Jasper Muncey.]

NUNLEY, John. Died 9 Jul 1905.

NUNLEY, Lawson. Died 21 Mar 1907.

MUNCEY, Florence. 1890 - 15 Apr 1912. [Daughter of Thomas Jasper and
        Elizabeth (Lytle) Muncey.]

MUNCEY, Will. Died 26 Jul 1940. [Husband of Laura Nunley, married 15 Jun
        1904.]

MUNCIE, Myrtle. Died 11 Feb 1935.

Possibly other Lytle and Muncey family members buried here.

Name	Page	Name	Page	Name	Page	Name	Page
ABSTON, Enzena	57	. Hoyt G.	73	. Isaac Alexander	92	ARLEDGE, Cora K.A.	102
Mary Jane	57	. James	77	. James C.	97	. Fred	140
ADAMS, Bob	67,71	. John	140	. James J.	246	. Jesse	140
. Edna Myrtle	71	. Mary	139,141,211	. Jane	240	. Mary E.	140
. Jewel	19	. Nora Jane	46	. John	70,78	. William C.	140
. Lillian O.	67	. Parlina	3	. John L.	97	ARMES, Marie Lashie	37
. Lonnie	67	. Samuel N.	3	. Katherine	53	Wayne K.	37
. Mary	13	. Sarah Abigail	211	. Leona	79	ARMSTRONG, Byron E.	187
. Maude	67	. Shirley Ann	36	. Lois	46	Laura	128
. Maude Lee	71	. T.P.	211	. Margaret	92	ARNETTE,	
. Mercer L.	71	. Thomas	211	. Martha	99	Connie Josephine	82
. Pelina	101	. Virginia A.	211	. Mary Cleo	97	ARNOLD, Alda	116
. Perlina	257	. William Worth	211	. Mary Elizabeth	94	. Dela	1
. Rebecca	69	ALLEY, Mattie	26	. Mary Josephine	246	. Hattie	41
ADAMSON, Bethel Allen	18	. Mattie Bell	26	. Matilda	92,96-97	. Hazel	20
. Ewell Estelle	17	. Verhaden	26	. Minnie B.	106	. J.T.	116
. Gensey	80	ALLISON, Albert A.	21	. Mozelle	70	. Jackie A.	1
. Jesse W.	18	. Alcey Elizabeth	100	. Nancy A.	94-95	. Martha	252
. Jesse Walling	17	. Betty Ann	91	. Rebecca	78	. Ollie	116
. Lissie	78	. Callie	249	. Sarah	70	. Richard	1
. Norman W.	18	. Cynthia	242	. Sarah C.	97	. Rom	116
. Peggy A.	18	. Cynthia Caroline	242	. Sarah Elizabeth	98	. Susan Frankie	219
. Rachel Ginsey	90	. James Dow	19,21	. Sarah Jane	92	ASHLY, Emma	254
. Zadie	18	. James Sr.	242	. Sophia J.	112	. Ollie	254
ADCOCK, Annie	48,64	. John	228,248	. William Horace	78	. Willis	254
. Betty	44	. Lenna Belle	248	ARGO, Eliza	126,200	ASHWORTH, Bessie Jane	201
. Della	63	. Lou	21,248	. Emma Lou	38	John	201
. Elizabeth	41	. Lula	105	. Fannie	43	ASKEW, Elizabeth	44
. James	48	. Lula Allison	21	. Frank	122	ASTA, Augustin	71
. Mary Hannah	44	. Margie Lou	19	. Fred	122	. Edward L.	71
. Mollie	224	. Marjorie	19	. Fred Wayne	113	. Illumine	71
. Nancy Ann	53,55	. Mary	228	. George	122	. Mamie	71
. Norman	44	. Mary E.	255	. George Sanders	38	ATEY, Miss.	168
. Sarah	48	. Virgie Caline	19,21	. Gladys Gertrude	113	ATNIP, Benjamin	241
. Thelma Norene	44	. William Carter	21	.	129	. Billie A.	9
AGERS, Elva	102	ALLMON, C.H.	189	. Howary	127	. Herman Tanley	58
. Hugh	102	. Ephram H.	195	. James Corbly	43	. James Carl	10
. Saphronia E.	102	. H.B.	189	. Jennie	127	. Jennie	220
AKEMAN, Linnie	141	. P.T.	195	. Jennie B.	3	. Jim	58
Martha E.	164	. Palemna	188	. Jesse Clyde	113	. Mary	241,252
AKERMAN, John W.	78	. Polemna T.	195	.	129-130	. Nannie	58
AKERS, Autie Frances	192	. Tenny	195	. Jessie Ruth	43	. Rebecca	139,241,252
. Colene	51	. Thelma	189	. Jim D.	43	. Sally	58
. Colonet	188	ALMOND, Abb	253	. Joe Thomas	129	. Stephen	241,252
. Delphine	188	Ann	194	. Joseph	3	AUSTIN, Albert	21
. Hannah	192	ALREDGE, Cora K.	107	. Josiah Joseph	116,122	. Avo	21
. Isaac	192	ALTER, J.O.	249	.	127,133	. Carrie J.	191
. Susan	189,193	Mary	249	. Junie	133	. Dillard C.	53
. Susan C.	195	AMONT, Mollie	118	. Katherine	120	. Frances	53
. Susie	30	ANDERSON, Albert R.	97	. Laura	93,200	. Joseph Edward	19,31,53
. William M.	188	. Alma Lee	70	. Lena	116,133	. Josie	42
. William Riley	188	. Bertha	46	. Lillian	38	. Lawrence William	36
AKINS, Helen	10	. Betty Jane	92	. Lillie	43	. Louise C.	36
James F.	10	. Betty S.	246	. Lina	3,122,127	. Mary E.	19
ALDRIDGE, Lura	37	. Claude	46	. Mary	122,129	. Melvina	19
ALLEN, Bonnie Lee	73	. Claude Elson	46	. Mary Maude	112,130	. Ora Mae	31
. Chloe	5	. Dixie Oleen	88	. Murray Bedford	112,116	. Orville	31
. Colonel Andrew	211	. Elijah	92,97-99	.	130	. Rachel Evelee	19,31,53
. Edna Isabell	211	. Elizabeth	92,97-99	. Robert M.	200	. Thomas	19
. Elijah	3	. Ellen	101	. Rosie Bell	129	. Virgie Caline	19,21
. Fannie	10	. Flora	246	. Sylvia Lina Myrick	112	. William Orville	31
. Fannie Myrtle	3	. Frances Elizabeth	78	. Thomas	200	BAGWELL, Annie Lee	31
. Frank	73	. Frank	246	. Tom	3	BAILEY, Abbie	3
. Hanna	51	. Henry Grant	92	. Vick	38	. Anna	9
. Harriett	211	. Isaac	94-95	. William	43	. Barbara	228

BAILEY,(cont)
. Barry Lynn   2
. Billy E.   2-3
. Earl   59
. Edith   228
. Elizabeth   254
. Geneva Joyce   59
. Hallie   192
. Hannah Mai   199
. Hugh Edward   7
. James Alfred   192
. Jennie Jane   192
. John D.   209
. John N.   190
. Lewis   228
. Linnie   210
. Lois M.   2
. Louis Arnold   7
. Lucinda Frances   209
. Lucy   254
. Margaret   201
. Margaret E.   191
. Martha   93
. Martha C.   77
. Martha E. 54,188,209
. Mary   190
. Mary Abbie   93
. Mattie   238
. Melton Jr.   199
. Mildred   7,180
. Ora Lee   9
. Pairlee   2
. Paralee   188
. Parlee   54,62
. Richard   254
. Robert   9
. Stella   3
. Tolbert B.   3,93
. W.J.   209
. W.S.   3
. William   54,188
. William J.   93
. William Schuyler   3
BAILY,Mary Susan   106
BAIN,Ada Edwina   73
. Edward Monroe   73
. Ethel   73
. Jackie D.   48
. Julia Lee   7
. Julie Lee   8
. Katy   133
. Martha Ethel   64
. Rachel Novella   64
. Silas   64
BAKER,Charles   116
. Edgar Hal   116
. Evelyn   116
. Everett E.   116
. Helen Marie   1
. Herbert   217
. Imogene   116
. James Austin   1
. Jane   21
. John W.   1
. Lola Ather   1

. Lucinda   249
. Ludie   70
. Malchus Clinton   1
. Mariah C.   205
. Millie   7
. Sarah   217
. Vera M.   1
BALDWIN,Cecil C.   40
   Mary Catherine   40
BALES,Alice   114,126
. Janie Lee   145
. Queen Vickie   114
. Wallie May   126
. William   114
. William Anderson   126
BALEY,Emma   22
   Essie   1
BALLARD,Amanda   17
BARBEE,Ellen   56
. Gladys   56
. John   56
BARKER,Edna   2
. Florine   2
. Henry Clay Jr.   2
. Henry Clay Sr.   2
. Ruth   2,4
BARKLEY,Catherine   22
BARLOW,Johnnie W.   13
. Mamie   19
. Rachel   39
. Wilma Sue   13
BARNES,Addie Marie   116
. Addison   147
. Alton   144
. Andrew   162-163
. Annie   8
. Arkie   154
. Arlie Weymon   197
. Athelia M.   117,120
. B.Wince   115
. Benjamin Nelson   128
. Bethia   128
. Brittania   154
. Brittannia   164
. Bud   113,115
. Campbell   115
. Catherine   115
. Charity   128
. Charles   128,164
. Charles I.L.   115
. Charles Irvin L.   133
. Charles Irving L. 116
.   117-119,123
. Chester Wallace   116
. Cora   154
. Denton   73
. Dorothy Evelyn   69
. Ed.V.   114
. Edward   115
. Elijah   144
. Eliza   162,166
. Eliza Jane   163
. Elizabeth   69,152
. Elsie   197
. Ernest Lee   8

. Ezra   162
. Fonella   60
. Frances Lee   116
. G.W.   8
. H.Marcus   117
. Hallie   128,147
. Harley B.   163
. Harris Bradford   119
.   120
. Henrietta   117
. Hersie   6
. Irene   113,115,129,144
. Isaac 118,154,160-161
. Izzie   199
. Jack   8
. Jackoleen   123
. James   200
. James Porter   6,8,197
. Janie Lee   145
. Jennie   128
. Jesse L. Jr.   123
. Jesse L. Sr.   123
. Jessie E.   120
. John   144,197,199
. John Albert S.   165
. John R.   200
. Josie   145
. Julia   144
. Kathy Hean   113
. L.H.   113
. Lela   128
. Lela Mai   165
. Lila Mae   144
. Lillian   144
. Lillie   144
. Lillie Ann   165
. Lonnie Haskel   129
. Lonnie Haskell   115
. Lou Cindy   117
. Lowell   117
. Loy   163
. Lucille   119-120
. Lucindy   199
. Lucy   112,115-117,119
.   123,133
. Lucy Emma   115-116
. Lula   114-115
. Lula C.   199
. Mack   144
. Malinda   197
. Mary   123,147,155,164
. Mary A.   154
. Mary Florence   200
. Mary Jane 6,8,197-198
.   200
. Mary Lou   114
. Melba   117
. Mildred J.   117
. Misty Cinitha   111
. Nadean   129
. Nellie   8
. Quim Cantrell   123
. R.Hough   197
. Raymond N.   197
. Rebecca   197

. Rhonda   111
. Rilla Ozelle   8
. Robert   199
. Robert Roy   69
. Roger Eugene   111
. Ruby   115
. Sarah Elizabeth   114
.   118
. Sidney Wayne   123
. Stanley Eugene   129
. Susan   115,154
. Susan E.   118
. Susanna   154
. Susanna Elinor   161
. Susannah   128,160,164
. Susie   112,133
. Tempie Ann   164
. Uva Jean   197
. Virginia   119
. Virginia A.   128
. Wallace   111
. Wallene E.   163
. Wendell   117,120
. William Carroll   128
BARNHILL,Frances   25
   Georgia   41
BARODY,Donald Ernest 41
. Joseph   41
. Maude Mae   41
BARR,Betsy   250
BARRETT,Bell Zora   250
. Callie Nancy   220
. Eanore   237
. Ed Clark   177-178
. Ella   2
. Ellen Canzada   255
. Henry   236
. Henry T.   250
. Hettie   72
. Hettie M.   177-178
. Hiram H.   220
. James   2
. Jennie   52
. Jennie Mae   237
. John   250
. Lemma Ethel   250
. Lillian   2
. Lucy   79
. Martha Ann   180
. Nora E.   180
. Nova   178
. Ray   178
. Sarah Lucinda   82
. Sylvia Ann   177
. W.H.   180
. William   237
BARRY,Mary Frances   224
   Robert H.   224
BASHAM,Billy Ray   35
. Kenneth Ray   35
. Mattie Helen   35
. Melvena   36
. Noah   255
. Tennie   255
BASS,Archibald   82

===

BASS,(cont)		. Minnie B.	9	. Eliza J.	163-164	. Julia	170

BASS,(cont)
Mary Ann 82
BATES,Eliza 179
. Emma 213
. Martha Jane 179
. Minnie 51
. Queenie Byrum 168
. Susan 41
BATTLES,Carolyn S. 76
. Hattie Elizabeth 76
. William Louis 76
BAUER,Rosemary 15
BAYLESS,Betty 14
BEAN,Margaret W. 235
Mordecai 235
BEARID,Hallie Mai 86
BECK,Charles Robert 20
. Della Mae 20
. Gardo 20
. William Bedford 20
BECKWITH,Mamie 25
Patton 86
BEECHUM,Benton 73
. Della 73
. John 73
. Manie R. 73
BELCHER,Abbie 3
. Mary 93
. Mary Abbie 93
. Richard D. 93
BELECKI,Adam 6
. Anastasia 6
. Leo J. 6
. Ruby Etta 6
BELL,Artie 209
. Audrene 25
. Becky 232
. Belle 25
. Carl Anthony 231
. Clara Juanita 9
. Edna Marie 231
. Elizabeth 24,223
. Elsie 26
. Fred Brown 231
. Gladys 41
. Hattie 41
. Henry J. 41
. J.Manson 232
. Janet Kay 54
. Joe 232
. Joe S. 219
. John 22,108
. John J. 9
. Joseph S. 223
. Kenneth Francis 41
. Leighmon M. 26
. Lela 253
. Lena Frances 222
. Louella 194
. M.H. 222
. Mark Edwin Sr. 25
. Mary Jane 222-224
. Michael David 54
. Miles C. 194
. Minnie 22

. Minnie B. 9
. Nancy 221
. Nannie Lee 220-221
. Nathan 222
. Ocie Pearl 59
. Sandra Kay 54
. Sara Elizabeth 18
. Sarah Frances 22
. T.C. 209
. Thomas 54
. W.A. 221
. Walter Robertson 25
. William 223
. William Carl 22
BENDZOLOWICZ,Darlene 67
. Francis Joseph 67
. Frank 67
. Gladys 67
BENNETT,Alonzo 230
. Bill 186
. Charlie 80,219
. Charlie Florence 15
. Della Mildred 230
. Edith 166
. Elmer 129
. Elmer F. 33
. Elmer Forrest 76
. Ida 186
. John K. 186
. Joyce Ann 129
. Margaret 186
. Mary 68
. Mary Jane 220
. Minnie 59
. Minnie G. 60
. Nancy Jane 220
. Nora 33,76
. Velma 76
. Velma Grace 33,129
. Walter 33,76
. William R. 220
BESHEARS,Arkansas 155
. Arthur 162
. Eliddie Ann 161
. Nancy Adeline 162
. Sally 162
. Sidney 159,162
. Thomas 161-162
. William 162
BESHERSE,Sally 153
William 153
BESS,Allison 164
. Andrew Jackson 164
. Arwood 156
. Balzora 156
. Balzora Ward 155
. Bazel 154,161
. Brittannia 164
. Carrie 114,145,151-152
. Chatam C. 142
. Cora 148
. Cora J. 152
. Elenza 162
. Elenza Grundy 156
. Eli 152,155,164

. Eliza J. 163-164
. Emma 154
. Euphania 155
. Florence L. 164
. Gertie 144
. Gracie Velma 149
. Grover C. 144
. Halie 164
. Harriet 163-166
. Hervey 155
. Israel Putnam 155-156
. Issie John 161
. John 142,144,146,152
. 154,156,162,164
. John J. 147
. Jonah Everett 149
. Laura 143
. Laura Jane 146
. Lear 152,155,164
. Linsey 142
. Louisa 162-163
. M.D.L. 164
. Madie 58
. Marcus Dee L. 164
. Martha Ella 58
. Martha Josephine 164
. Mary 154,160,164
. Mary A. 154-155
. Mary Ann 163
. Nancy 136
. Nazarella 156
. Ralph Earl 149
. Robert B. 155
. Rosia 142
. Suella B. 147
. Tammy B. 164
. Tempa Ann 156
. Tempie 147
. Tempiean 164
. Templa Ann 144
. Tempy 152
. Tempy Ann 146
. Walter 156
. William John 58
BEZLEY,Mary E. 184
BICKLE,Barbara 173
Barbary 172
BIGBEE,Ilalie 37
. Wallace 36
. Wallace B. 37
BIGGS,Lucy 80
Lucy Ann 49
BILES,Agnes 246
. Bobbie Inez 41
. Dorothy 216
. Eliza Jane 94-95,97
. Eural 216
. Flora 246
. Florence 169-170
. Fred 216
. Harrison E. Sr. 41
. James 169
. Jim 171
. John Wesley 246
. Josephine 61

. Julia 170
. Leonia 216
. Nick 169-171
. Sarah 228
. Sarah E. 35
. Thomas D. 246
. Wilford 171
BILLINGS,Artis Lee 67
. Avo 67
. Berchie Mozell 40,70
. Hallie 67
. John Morgan 70
. Pete 67
. Susie Emma 70
BIRDWELL,Ova 12-13
Rebecca 251
BISHOP,Elizabeth 167
. Jesse 197
. Louise 57
. Myrtle 197
. Sallie 90
BLACK,Annie V. 255
. Gladys 3
. Gladys Loree 3
. J.L. 255
. Juanita M. 73
. Lucinda 202
. Marcus L. 3
. Margaret 3
. Thedra Ann 73
. Thomas Jefferson 3
. Walter Lee 73
BLACKBURN,Carletta 47
. James Cleveland 47
. Sarah Elizabeth 47
BLAIR,Alton Otto 240
. Andrew J. 239
. Beulah 30,68
. C.F. 239-240
. Carol F. 240
. Carroll F. 240
. Clata Florence 240
. Cornelia 239
. Della 239-240
. Edgar 239
. Emily 106
. James P. 239
. Joe 64
. John B. 239-240
. M.Josa 249
. Mary 93
. Mary Susan 106
. Myrtle 239-240
. Nellie 239
. Sandy 106
. Sarah 158,240
. Sarah C. 190
. Vesta L. 30
. Virgil Jr. 68
. Virgil Sr. 68
. Virgle 30
. William W. 239-240
. Willie Bryant 239
BLANKENSHIP,Beulah 20
. Claudia 80

===

BLANKENSHIP,(cont)
. Donald F.   112
. Lorene   112
. Miller R.   112
BLANKS,Ada   27,226,253
. Ada Louella   241
. Alice   100
. Catherine   241,253
. Clarence   100
. Edward A.   15
. Elsie   46
. James Martin   46
. John S.B.   241
. John Wilburn   241
. Lizzie Mae   15
. Martha Ella   15
. Ollie   46
. Permelia   241
BLANTON,Mattie   77
. Ruth Caroline   77
. Vincent   77
BLEVINS,Gloria   123
  Ruth   67
BLUE,Mary   169
BLUHM,Clara   30
BOBBITT,Ephriam   194
  Louella   194
BOGLE,Amanda   182
. Azzielene   72
. Carol   174
. Doris Elizabeh   15
. Dorothy   183
. Dorothy Lee   23
. Ernest Thomas   208
. Floyd   183
. Harold   174
. James   208
. Jennie Ruth   183
. Lonnie   174
. Lula Azzaline   15
. Maggie Arnetta   183
. Martha E.   77
. Mary   183
. Mattie   208
. Moscow   15,72
. Myrtle Opal   72
. Neal   183
. Opal   72
. Sarah   78
. Tom   78
. Virginia   36
BOHANNON,Sallie   46
BOLES,Alice   179
. Henry   179
. Maggie   63,179
BOLEY,Georgia Anna   89
  William Thomas   89
BOLIN,Merica Allis   153
BOLT,Cicero L.   234
. Emma Luella   219
. James   229
. James R.   234,251
. Mollie   229,250
. Nancy   251
. Noah Alexander   251

. Sarah   229,234,251
BOMAR,Lizzie   246
BOND,Anna E.   28
. Fannie   28
. Lela   85
. Martha   142
. Tennie   29
. William Henry H.   28
. William Jennings   28
BONEY,Jesse Smartt   33
  Robert Madison   33
BONNER,Betty   167
. Buford Franklin   167
. Clarcy   248
. Clarissa   233
. Clifton Sulton   236
. Cynthia Jewell   237
. Delia C.   153
. Dorothy   216
. Edna Lois   236
. Eliza Irene   43
. Frances   167,170,216
. Harrison   167,170,216
. Martha   191
. Mary Ann   43
. Pat   36
. Robert Carl   236
. Sarah Ann   248
. William Carroll   43
BOREN,Dolly   42
. Elba L.   26,46-47
. Etta   141
. Gilbert   42
. Jane   42
. Johnnie   6
. Lucinda   51
. Nelson   42
. Pauline   229
BORY,Dorotha   11
BOST,America   139
. Bell Zora   140
. Bellzora   186
. Charles Franklin   47
. Elba L.   26,46-47
. Frank Luther   26,46-47
. Hazel   46
. Irene   166
. Jeff   25
. Jonathan   186
. Jonathan J.   140
. Lillie Mae   186
. Lizzie Abigail   25
. Matilda Frances   25
. Noah   78
. Nola Bell   26
. Pauline   47
. Roy   140
. Sarah   114
. William Daniel   139
BOTTOMS,Clarence C. 123
. Jane   6
. Joe   123
. Quim Cantrell   123
. Wavie   123
BOULDIN,A.A.H.   153

. Alma   149
. Alverta   153
. Amasa Berne   146
. Andrew Arthur H.   153
. Andrew Jackson 29,146
.   153
. Arzy Bryan   153-154
. Bettie   126
. Betty Well   150,159
. Cassandra Lynn   146
. Clyde   29
. Cora   154
. Dalton William   149
. Dautlon William   145
. Elbert Floyd   29-30
. Elisha L.   154
. Eliza   126
. Elizabeth   126,159
. Ella   154
. Ellie   145,150,153
. Elvana   2
. Emma   153
. Ernest   153
. Florida   142
. Frank   153
. G.W.   154
. Gidean   126
. Gladys Gertrude   113
.   129-130
. Gladys Marie   146
. Gracie Velma   149
. Hallie   48
. Harold D.   154
. Harve   154
. Henry   142
. Hervy E.   146
. Jemima 2,153,156,161
. Jim Buck   129
. John Herby   146
. Joseph R.   153
. Josie   153
. Lela Pearl   149
. Leola Mae   153
. Leon   153
. Leona May   146
. Lewis   126,154,161
. Maggie   117
. Maggie Lou   118
. Maggie Queen   116
. Margaret   133,151-152
.   154,159
. Marion Andrew   142
. Marjorie Jenetta   150
. Mary   126,154
. Mary Ella   153-154
. Mary Florida   145
. Mary Susan   152
. Minnie   2,42
. Minnie Novella   1
. Murphy Ancle   153
. Nancy   123,126,154
. Narve   126
. Narvel   154
. Nellie   14
. Nettie   49

. Nobel   159
. Noble   126
. Ova Lee   153
. Queen   233
. Rachel   29,146,153,193
. Rachel B.   154
. Ramon   146
. Robert Kelton   146
. Ruth   142
. Susanna   154
. Susannah   126,161
. Susie   129
. Temperance Ann   156
. Thomas   2,126,145,150
.   153
. Velma Ida   29
. Vera Maxine   29-30
. W.J.   154
. William   2,153,156,161
BOUNDS,Annie   48,64
. Charles I.   64
. Charles Isham   53,55
. Charlie I.   48
. Lee Austin   53
. Mae Nell   64
. Malcolm Franklin   48
. Martha   65
. Mary Lynn   55
. Mary Novella   53
. Nancy Ann   53,55
. Olla   48
. Talitha H.   48
. William C.   48
BOWIE,Eva W.   97
. Mary F.   97
. Sarah May   97
BOWLIN,Maggie Linda 59
BOWMAN,Alice   78
. David Lee   78
. Edward I.   78
. Edward T.   79
. Johnnie T.   78-79
. Peggy J.   41
BOYD,Ada P.   166
. Alda L.   150
. Alf   16
. Alice Roberts   59
. Athelia M.   117
. Bud   59
. Charlie   164
. Charlotte   124
. Cleo Beatrice   18
. Clifton Alex   166
. Clinton Lee   166
. Cobet G.   166
. Delma   87
. Dorris Richard 165-166
. Edith   166
. Eliza Jane   163
. Elizabeth J.   158
. Elizabeth Jane   120
. Elliott   163,166
. Elliott Hodge 164-165
. Emma   61
. Emma Eugenia   154

==

BOYD,(cont)		. Lucy Emma	116	. Laura Jane	187	. Beverly Carl	163
. Emma Lou	60	. Marcus	116	. Mabel	107	. Billie Ruth	147
. Eunice Virginia	166	. Mary Ethel	13	. Mable	92	. Butler	59
. Evelyn Mae	165-166	. Rebecca L.	67	. Mary Elizabeth	188	. Cleo	23
. Fannie	59	. Sallie	231	. Matilda	190	. Columbus	75
. Fernando C.	27	. Tony Eric	116	. Nancy B.	189-190	. Cora	46
. Fernando Campbell	120	. Walter T.	13	. Oliver Franklin	92-93	. Daisy	255
. Harlie	165	BRAGG,Ann	221	.	95-96	. Dema	250
. Harriet	163-166	. Clarissa T.	224	. Parrie	190	. E.C.	84
. Irene	166	. Emma	87	. Pheobe	96	. Edgar Alfred	58
. James Duncan	166	. Hugh T.	224	. Royce Lee	93	. Emma	42
. James Richard	165	. Joseph M.	224	. Russell	189-190	. Ernest B.	163
. Jasper	124	. Martha	224	. Sarah Martha	190	. Ethel	58
. John Henry H.	120-121	. Patrick H.	95	. Solomon	193	. Eva	4,52
. Joseph Tallman	27	. Richard M.	224	. Susan Paralee	92	. Florence	214
. Joyce	59	. T.P.	87	. Thomas Atlas	93	. Florie	76
. Junior	166	. Thomas Jefferson	87	. Thomas Hayes	92	. Florine	75
. Lester	154	BRAINARD,Alice	91	. Verna	92	. Frances	33
. Lillie	144	. Emily	92	BREWINGTON,Bettie E.	216	. Frank	90
. Lorena May	120	. Emily P.	91	. Joe	215	. George	217
. Louise	16	. Ina	91	. Pearl	215	. George C.	163
. Malvina A.	34	. S.R.	92	. William	216	. George L.	42
. Marcus Dee L.	164	BRALEY,		BRIDGES,Ella	51	. George W.	214
. Margaret	124	Sarah Ann Isabel	21	Minnie	12	. Georgie D.	147
. Margurite	120	BRASWELL,Lucy Jane	80	BRIGGS,Elizabeth F.	74	. Gladys	64,169
. Marshall L.	124	BRATCHER,Abbie Coleen	14	. Jahugh	235	. Grace B.	16-17
. Marshall W.	166	. Hannah	14	. Lila	235	. Hannah	192
. Martha E.	164	. Jennie M.	14	. May Louise	235	. Harvey L.	16
. Martha Josephine	164	. John E. Sr.	14	. Robert C. Jr.	74	. Harvey Lincoln	58
. Mary Agnes	166	. Lillie	3	BRINKLEY,Emma	237	. Herbert	214
. Mildrew	166	. Lucinda	209	BRIXEY,Lula J.	94	. Hervie	67
. Nancy	34	. Marietta	230	BROCK,Billie G.	33	. Holder L.	193
. Opal Lee	121	. Nannie Lee	14	. Charles R.	149-150	. Howard	147
. Ora	240	. Noravella	56	. Emma	149	. Hugh	71
. Oscar	166	. Samuel Forrest	3	. Eola	33	. J.B.	58
. Paul Henry	59	. Stella	3	. John	236	. J.E.	84
. Robert	34	. Thomas W.	14	. John C.	33	. James Leeper	214
. Roberta	120	BRATTEN,Emma	42	. John Lafayette	33	. John	163
. Sallie Marshall	124	Minnie	11	. Mollie Evon	236	. John H.	250,256
. Samuel L.	124-125	BRAXTON,Herman	25	. Molly Evon	237	. John L.	16-17
. Sara	27	. Jennie	3	. Odell	149	. John Shelby	32
. Sara Jane	27	. Joe Thomas	25	. S.G.	33	. John William	163
. Sara R.	27	. M.Elizabeth	25	. Susan	161	. Josephine	163
. Sarah Jane	120	BRAZELTON,Mattie Lou	75	. Wilma L.	149	. Laura	163
. Selma	166	BRAZIER,Annie	14	BROOKS,Albert Milton	50	. Lawrence	218
. Susan Edna	120-121	BRENER,Mildred	7	. Annie Elizabeth	50	. Lena	75
. Thomas Ramsey	27	BREWER,Anna	188	. Ethel Morgan	50	. Lila	155
. William Anderson	164	. Arnold Matt	95	. Mary	139,141	. Lottie Eva	90,102
BOYLES,Bulah	141	. Arnold Matt Jr.	95	. Walter S. Sr.	50	. Luther	163
BRADLEY,Bessie	16	. Belle	96	BROOM,		. Margaret	9,218
. Clarence	16	. Bellzora	92-93,95-96	. Grover Cleveland	87	. Margaret A.	71
. Clarie	16	. Cibbie	96	. James	87	. Martha	163
. Lourene	16	. Clarence	92	. Lou	87	. Mary	160
. Margaret J.	16	. Cynthia	193	BROWN,A.J.	188	. Mary Ann	163
. Woodrow Wilson	16	. Elizabeth	193	. Alice	179	. Mary E.	16
BRADSHAW,Doris L.	64	. Essie Dean	95	. Allie	68,170	. Mary Elizabeth	75,102
BRADY,Belle	22	. Frances	95	. Alvin H.	75-76	. Mary Ester	58
. Beulah	30,68	. Frances May	92	. Ammie E.	214	. Mary Helen	52
. Billie Lois	61	. Henry	190	. Anna	41	. Mary Katherine	237
. Eliza Jane	67	. Icybely	189	. Anna C.	160	. Mary Sharon	42
. Eunice	253	. J.R.	190	. Annie	214	. Mary Vera	59
. John Patrick	67	. Jesse Hill	188	. Annie R.	75	. Mattie	208
. John Todd	67	. Joel	188	. Annie Ruth	76	. Nancy	153,188
. Lavern	13	. John	189	. Arthur	160,163	. Nancy Ollie	163
. Lillian Elaine	116	. June	95	. Bettie E.	216	. Onman L.	33

===

BROWN,(cont)		. Sarah Ann	44	. W.H.	171	. Edmond	46
. Onmon L.	32	. Wilma E.	48	. William Young	192	. Emma	111
. Paul Wayne	17	BURBAGE,Alton	87	. Willie	170	. Emma Irene	112
. Rachel	136	. Delma	87	BURLISON,Mariah	139	. Hallie	128
. Richard H.	67	. Ralph B.	87	BURNETT,Hennie	12	. Harve	112
. Robbie	192	. Wilburn Clifton	87	BURRIS,Virginia	43	. Harvey	111,130
. Ruth Mae	90	BURCH,America	234,250	BURROUGHS,J.S.	171	. Harvey McCoy	121
. Sallie	90	.	252	BURTON,Ben Hooper	43	. Hassie	141
. Sally	32	. America Lee	254	. Byrd	43	. Hugh	46
. Sarah	5,59,214,217	. Annie Parrott	250	. Lena	43	. Isaac	158
. Sarah E.	188	. Annie Pearl	251	. Mildred	43	. John David	159
. Sarah Helen	75	. Arzona	98	BUSH,Calvin	145	. Laura	128
. Shelby Edward	33	. Bob J.	232	. Mattie	145	. Laura Matilda	158
. Susan L.	138	. Clarence Edward	253	. Minnie	145	. Lemma	121,130
. Tempy Ann	163	. Flora Lee	232	BUTCHER,Bill F.	57	. Leola	121
. Thomas	138	. George	99,254	. Billy	61	. Lillie	43
. Tony Costella	52	. George Allen	252	. Daisy Josephine	61	. Lloyd	112
. Walter C.	102	. George W.	100,252	. Dorothy	220	. Lois	124
. Walter Cleveland	90	. Hallie Mae	252	. Ellen	62	. Martha	111
. Waymon	193	. Harriet	106	. Grace Katherine	21	. Mary	130
. Wesley R.	214,217	. James Edward	250	. Jean E.	57	. Mary C.	247
. Will	255	. Johnny Alton	252	. Jena Evelyn	61	. Michael	112
. William B.	163	. Josephine	98,100	. Jim	61	. Mollie	46
. William Isaac	90	. Julia	100	. Joyce Euline	220	. Nannie Frances	112
. William Larry	147	. Luna	100	. Leoma	61	. Ouida	112
. Willie Esten	163	. Maggie	253	. Mary Linda	220	. Preston Alexander	121
. Woodfin	169	. Maggie Z.	234	. Melbalene	220	. Rhodessa	112
BROYLES,Mattie	169	. Margaret	99-100	. Valter Mason	220	. Ruby	112
BRUCE,Wilmoth	88	. Mary Ann	254	. Vester E.	220	. Ruby E.	46
BRYAN,Ella Lee	4	. Melvin	100	BUTERBAUGH,Kathy	85	. Sarah	121
. Jessee Petway	4	. Robert Dudley	234,253	BUTLER,Josephine	38	. Theodore Lester	112
. Jimmie	70	. Robert Washington	234	William W.	108	. Wanda	112
. Joseph Wilson	90	. Sara	93	BYARS,Andrew	172	. Waymon McCoy	111
. Mary	90	. Sarah	94,96	. Florence	172	CAIN,Emma	155
. Mary Lorene	4	. Washington	254	. George Smith	43	. George	155
. Nancy Frances	96	. William Lee	250-251	. Harold H.	186	. Rebecca	155
. Rebecca	90	BURGESS,Harlen	85	. Hassie Lee	187	CALDWELL,Jane	50
. Sarah Jane	90	. Monika	85	. James H.	43	. Jess	171
. William	90	. Nina	85	. Leona	56	. Lizzie	13
. Willie	65	BURKES,Audie	59	. Martha Willie	43	. Ollie	171
BRYANT,John	58	BURKS,Adeline	11	. Melissa	43	. Susan	171
. Lucille A.	58	. Allie	170	. Walter Evans	186	CALLAHAN,Sarah Ann	32
. Mollie	58	. Bonnie Lee	192	BYFORD,Cynthia	198	CAMBELL,Annie	22
. Phronia	195	. Emily	201	. Ethel	193,197	. John D.	22
. Willie	239	. Emma	167	. Eugenia Ann	194	. Mazel Louise	22
BRYON,Dessie Jane	21	. Guy	167	. George Ware	194	. Willie Selmer	22
. George Abner	21	. Henry	171	. Idella Emaline	194	CAMPBELL, Claude M.	63
. Sarah Ann Isabel	21	. Henry Thomas	192	. John	198	. Alice	174
BRYSON,		. Howard	167	. Minnie Ethel	198	. Alta Mae	182
. Frances Elizabeth	78	. Jesse	95,190	. William Robert	194	. Anna	243
. Sarah	78	. Lean	167	BYNUM,Rosanah	184	. Annie E.	174,179
. Tom	78	. Lula	167	William	171	. B.E.	135
BUCHANAN,Dora	58	. Mable	170	BYRD,		. Beecher	15,43,182
. Ethel	213-214,218	. Marjorie	169	. Benjamin Franklin	39	. Bernice	43
. Henry	58	. Mary	167	. Clara	39	. Bertha Savanah	21
. Mary Ethel	58	. Mary Etta	192	. George	111	. Bettie	135
BUCK,Charlie	170	. Mary F.	192	. Mary	111	. Callie J.	182
Laura	170	. Mary Lou	11	. May Elizabeth	111	. Charlie	63
BUIE,Sara	34	. Nannie P.	167	. Raymond	39	. Charlie W.	179
BULLARD,Annie	79	. R.B.	190	CAGLE,Annie	4	. Claude M.	62
. Benjamin	79	. R.P.	167	. Benjamin Silas	128	. Clayton Sevier	174,179
. Martha	83	. Rachel	190	. Claudis Brown	124,130	. Della	175
BULLEN,Hixey	121-122,125	. Richard P.	171	. Claudis RIckey	124	. Della W.	174
BUMBALOUGH,		. Thurman	192	. Clemma Iola	111	. E.H.	174-175
. Near Frances	44	. Vernie	192	. Deborah	112	. Elbert Cleveland	43

==

===

CLENDENON,(cont)
. Nancy Belle   165
. Nettie   14,49
. Nettie B.   150
. Newton   120
. Oshia   24
. Patsy Sue   145
. Paul Eston   49
. Rita Chambers   194
. Roy   119
. Ruby Jean   49
. Sallie   119
. Sarah   145
. Sarah Catherine   150
.   152
. Sarah Jane 131,143,164
. William   112
. William J.   160
. William Rice   165
. William W.   115
CLINTON,Lula Ann   227
CLOSE,Hannah   175
     Josephine   24
CLOUGH,Edwin C.   238
CLOUSE,Newt   51
. Thelma   51
. Willie Reed   51
COAKLEY,Eliza   249
. Fannie Mai   249
. Isaac   74
. Isaac Francis   249
. Jim   249
. Mary Ann   74,249
. Willie Marie   74
COATS,Eola   33
COBB,Bertha   112
COE,Pheobe   240
COFFEY,Daisy Lee   197
. James F.   197
. Sarah   197
COLE,Joseph Ray   91
. Matilda Victoria   91
. Melville Raymond   194
. Ruby   91
. Russel George   194
. Vaudrene   194
. Walter Monroe   91
COLEMAN,Almer   41
. Beulah   41
. Rex A.   41
. Sandra   41
COLLIER,James   140
. Margaret L.   139-140
. Rhoda L.   97
. Tamer   140
COLLINGSWORTH,
     Margaret   32
COLLINS,Belle   53
. J.R.   234
. James Edward   234
. Margaret   234
. Tennessee   12
COLVILLE,Ann Carolyn   226
. Cynthia   226
. Elizabeth   206

. James F.   226
. JosephIII   226
. Lusk   226
. Major Joseph III   225
. Margaret   245
. Martha   226
. Peggy   225-226
. Sarah   225-226
COMPTON,Mary Ann   39,107
. Mathew   107
. Nancy   107
CONGER,Doranella   66
COOK,Clayton   49
. Dicy Elva   49
. L.A.   49
. Mary Ellen   49
. Sarah Ann   31
COOLEY,Axie   86
. Charles   99
. Chester Frances   99
. George Edward   86
. Hallie   86
. John William   86
. Lillie Mabel   148
. Lillie Mable   147
. Lillie Mae   99
. Ruth   86
COOPER,Edwin Woodrow   45
. Elizabeth   194
. H.G.   240
. J.W.   7
. James T.   7
. Jane   240
. Maggie Mai   240
. Minnie L   45
. Nancy Jane   186
. Ortie   45
. Theonia   7
. Thomas L.   45
. Wilda Ruby   7
COPE,Abner Lee   43
. Aubrey Ray   80
. Auston   42
. Charlie D.   5
. Hardy Jr.   213
. Hardy Sr.   64,213
. Jessie   64
. Jessie Mazy   213
. Marie   42
. Martha Willie   43
. Marvin   62
. Mary   98
. Mildred M.   62
. Plinea E.   107
. Priscilla   64
. Ruby G.   80
. Ruth   213
. Sarah   70
. Sindie   172
. Susannah   201
. Tolbert M.   80
. Tom   107
. Zora Belle   43
COPELAND,Clara Juanita   9
. Ethel   18

. Ethel Roxie   9
. Evelyn   233
. Marshall Lee   9
. Mattie Elizabeth   9
. Mayo   233
. Mayo Clayton   9
. Roscoe   18
. Roscoe Talmadge   9
. Thomas Carr   9
. Velma R.   18
COPENHAVER,Bell M.   13
. Bess M.   13
. Harry Valentine   13
. Mollie Eliza   13
COPPINGER,Amanda   134
. Amy Lee   13
. Beersheba   128
. Canzada   214,216
. Charlene   5
. Clara   151
. Daphine   162
. David   128
. Evelyn Mae   165-166
. Gary Phillip   162
. Gilbert   13
. James Lavander   128
. Jefferson   165
. Jefferson Davis   166
. Jennie   128
. Jess   134
. Jesse Willie   13
. Julia   185
. Lavern   13
. Lucy   5
. Martha   13
. Martha Abigail   13,52
. Marvin   5
. Naomi   166
. Oshia   213-214
. Patricia M.   52
. Phillip   162
. Rachel   134
. Thomas   213
. Thomas B.   218
. Tilla   213
. Tiller   218
. Virginia A.   128
. Wiley   5
. William A.   13
. William Herbert   128
. Willie A.   13
CORBETT,Hannah   53
. James Earl   53
. James Roy   53
COSTA,Alta   62
COSTELLO,Elmus   105
COTHAN,Jennie   231
COTTON,Mary   251
COUCH,Charlie C.   11
. Cleo Modena   128
. Lou Ann   11
. Pauline   11
COULSON,Amelia   109
     David   109
COUNTISS,Jane   134

. Mary   135
. Mary Adaline   210
. Nellie   113,134
. Nettie   135
. Prudence   135
. William M.   135
COVILLE,Peggy   224
COWAN,Margaret   24
COWANS,
. George Cummings   68
. Maggie   68
. Mary   68
. William George   68
COWART,Benjamin F.   40
     Lois Emma Jean   40
COX,Ada   237
     Viola   177
CRABTREE,Ethel   18
. Ethel Roxie   9
. Floyd   9
. Lucinda   9
CRADDOCK,June H.   9
     Robert C.   9
CRAIG,Sarah   122
CRAIN,Eugene Clay   85
. James Parker   85
. Mary Josie   85
. Tennie   119
. Vera M.   85
. Wavie   123
CRANE,M.L.   205
CRAVEN,Aline   237
. Allison   247
. Angeline   240
. Anna Bell   237
. Benjamin Franklin   240
. Benjamin Thomas   237
. Bettie   240
. Charles   221,240,247
. Charles Floyd   248
. Clara Pearl   240
. Dora   240
. Floyd   234
. Hattie   240
. John H.   240
. John William   21
. Johnnie   221
. Lenna Belle   248
. Lestor   100
. Lula Mae   237
. Maggie Mai   240
. Magie Pearl   240
. Mamie Edith   240
. Margaret Edith   221
. O.W.   240
. Octa Magnolia   247
. Oliver Bethel   237,240
. Owen W.   237
. Peter   224,240
. Phebe   221,240
. Pheobe   240
. Sarah Frances   22
. Sarah Mai   21
. Solomon   221
. Thomas   240

CRAVEN,(cont)
. Thomas S. 240
. Tracy Louise 21
. Victoria 224
CRAWFORD,Annie C. 80
. Bessie 83
. Bessie Louise 80
. Eugene 80,83
. Julia 79
. Lois C. 133
. Maude 49
. Ophia L. 83
. Ophie 4
. Sarah 79
. William Calloway 79
CRAWLEY,Almira Jane 250
. Annie 250
. Audrene 25
. D.B. 100
. George W. 188
. Joseph 250
. Lafayette 94,100
. Lemuel 94,97
. Lou 97,188
. Luzena Emaline 100
. Luzena Emuline 94
. Martha 94,97
. Pheobe 100
. Roberta 19
. Roxie 97
. Sally Anna 188
. Sam J. 100
. Sam L. 100
CRIM,Armela 9
. Frank 58
. Hallie Belle 5
. John 5
. Nannie 58
. Nannie Lou 5
CRIPPS,Charlie C. 80
. H.R. 80
. M.C. 80
. Margaret Frances 80
. Pete 80
CRISP,Albert Walter 93
. Alice 91
. Bessie Mae 94
. Chesley 93-94,96
. Columbus 91
. Elizabeth 92,97-99
. Ina 91
. James Polk 93-94
. Pharibe Angeline 93-94
. Sarah 93-94,96
. Serena 91,93
. Solomon 93
. Tira Ann 96
. William Frank 93
. Yearby A. 91,93
CROCKER,Mary 227
CROCKETT,F.M. 108
CRONIN,Doris 39
. Eva 39
. Frank 39
CROOK,Deliah 174

Wash 174
CROSSLIN,Charles Lee 16
. Lourine 16
. William Justin 16
CROTHERS,Kayla M. 52
CROUCH,Alicy 223
. Aline Stone 16
. Alta 62
. Ann Louise 106
. Annie 8
. Belle 95
. Betty Florence 62
. Brown 106
. Brown Loss 102
. Charles 16
. Charlotte -
. Josephine 102
. Cora Laura 62,64
. Della 62
. Dillard 101
. Doris L. 64
. Dovie Marie 62
. Ed 106
. Edward 62,101,107
. Edward Iowa 62
. Eliza 195
. Ernest 195
. Eva 39
. Gertie 95
. Golda 101
. H.N. 95
. Harriet 106
. Harriett 62
. Harry Clinton 195
. Hattie Pearl 107
. J.B. 254
. Jimmie Lee 102,106
. John W. 195
. Josephine 249
. Laura 107
. Loss H. 90,95
. Loss Hill 101-102
. Lottie Eva 90,102
. Lucy J. 90,95
. Lucy Josephine 101
. M.Josa 249
. Marshall 64
. Mary Eunice 16
. Media S. 195
. Nancy Clementine 223
. O.M. 107
. Owen Marshall 62
. Pelina 101
. Ruby Belle 95
. Samuel Mack 16
. Thomas 223
. Virgie 62
. W.L. 249
. William E. 64
. William Lee 62
CROWE,Brenda Sue 148
. Ernest C. 148
. Inis L. 148
. James Douglas 148
CROWELL,Maggie 68

CROWLEY,George W. 97
. Lou 97
CULLEN,Ellen F. 101
. J.R. 101
. Rillie 101
CULLEY,Roxie 32
CUMMINGHAM,
. Bee Irving 196
. Mildred Kathleen 196
. Paul 196
. Paul James 196
CUMMINGS,Beulah 213
. Dallas 28
. Jarrett 216
. Josie 28
. Letha 177
. Mary Elizabeth 216
. Ola Mae 28
. Sallie 28
. Warren 28
. Will 213
CUNNINGHAM,Allie Mai 123
. Anchony Darrell 113
. Annie 6
. Audrey Lee 113
. Bertha 95,102
. Cecil Mason 102
. Charlie Richard 101
. Clair Lee 113
. Claud 113
. Cleo Modena 128
. Cora 101
. Della Mae 95
. Dora 58,102
. Ellen 117,125,130
. Ethel Ollene 126
. Eulitia 121
. Ewell E. 18
. Fate 101-102
. Fletcher 6
. Fred 113
. Greenberry H. 127
. Hallie 113
. Hallie Claire 133
. Hannah 199
. Hannah Louise 199
. Hollie 123
. Hollie Claire 117,126
. Ida 54
. Irvin Hugh 199
. J.W. 128
. James Claud 113,117
. 123,126,133
. James W. 127
. Jane 6
. Jess 117,130
. Jesse 95,230
. Jesse Adam 95
. Jesse Calvin 102
. Jesse R. 128
. Jesse Russell 125
. John 127
. John M. 127
. Lela Lucille 199
. Lena 130-131

. Lena May 114
. Leon 23
. Lou Dora 34,66
. Lucy E. 113,125
. Mabel 46
. Magdalene 130
. Mary 110,121,125,128
. Mary Ann 110
. Mary Ellen 132-133
. Mary Jane 125
. Mary Susan 128
. Matilda 110,125,127
. Nancy 127
. Roy Clinton 113
. Sallie Ann 6
. Sarah Hannah 197
. Thomas 110,121,125,127
. Tom 125
. William 102
. William C. 125
. William Hayes 128
. Willie Jane 128
. Zora Bee 197,199
CUPP,Marie 52
CURRAN,James 108
CURTIS,Aaron 150-151,154
. 159
. Aaron Edward 114
. Aaron Escal 114-115
. Aaron Lowell 114
. Adel 42
. Adell 143,146,152
. Agnes 145
. Alda L. 150
. Alice Walling 151
. Almeda 153
. Angie 158
. Anna 85
. Arthur Martin 150
. Arzie W. 150
. Aura 151
. Bessie G. 145
. Betty Well 150,159
. Bruce C. 145
. Carl Lewis 151
. Carrie 114,145,151
. Cary 152
. Catherine 150
. Cathren 159
. Charline 165
. Chelsey 158
. Clabern L. 150
. Daphine 162
. Edith Lotel 151
. Elige 158
. Elihu 154
. Elijah Lewis 151
. Elijah Lewis II 151
. Elizabeth 173,192
. Ellie 145,150,153
. Eloise 146
. Elvana 2,153
. Emmer 151
. Emmett 146,158
. Erma Evelyn 150

CURTIS,(cont)
. Ethel   159
. Ethel Ella   158
. Etta Bell   151,159
. Eugene   154
. Finis   151
. Frank   151
. Greenberry M.   144,151
.   159
. Haskell Jacob   158
. Henderson   153
. Ida Jean   151
. Irene   151
. Irvin   150
. Irving   146,159
. J.G.   158
. Jacob   157-158
. James A.   150
. Jennie Evelyn   145
. John   44
. John Henry   152
. Joseph Martin   150,158
. Josie   153
. Julia   144
. Latisha   2
. Laura Matilda   158
. Lela A.   44
. Leola   159
. Letisha   128,152-153
.   159-160
. Lewis Elmore   114,145
.   151-152
. Linda Sue   145
. Lorene   144
. Lottie Geneva   56
. Lucinda Ella   158
. Malinda   152,166
. Malissie   44
. Margaret   154,159
. Margaret Malinda   6
. Marilda   146,158
. Martha 144,151-152,159
. Martha Ann   157
. Martin   159
. Mary   146,150
. Mary Edith   114-115
. Mary Lou   114,130
. Mary Susan   128,152
. Mauda Ellen   158
. Michael Anthony   151
. Minda Louise   151
. Mirah Elizabeth   157
.   158
. Myrtle Avo   150
. Nancy Bell   165
. Octalee   158
. Parriet   152,158
. Parrott   159-160
. Queen Vickie   114-115
. Rebecca   158
. Richard Hurman   158
. Roscoe C.   85
. Sarah Elizabeth   146
.   158
. Sarah Elizbeth   145

. Sarah Jane   158
. Sarah Malinda   152
. Seawillow   150
. Tennessee   151,154
. Thomas E.   145
. Thomas Elkana   146
. Thomas Elkona   158
. Troy Lee   85
. Velda Lee   59
. Virginia Carol   150
. Virginia Mae   151
. Wavie   152
. Wiley   152
. William   152-153,160
. William Elihu   154
. William Elihue   151
. William J.   160
. William Jackson   158
.   159
. William Washington   2
.   128,152
CUTTS,Herman   13
. Lizzie   13
. Wilma S.   13
DALBERRY,Emma   149
DAMRON,Mary M.   40
    Ronald E.   40
DANIEL,John C.   181
. Nancy A.   181
. Sarah   90
DANIELS,Catherine   157
    Katherine   121
DANY,Clara   41
. Joseph   41
. Margaret Dorothy   41
DARDEN,Grovene   54
    Ottie Louis   54
DARNELL,Ann Elizabeth   93
. Bessie   47
. Frank   45
. James Thomas   93
. Jennie May   92-93,95
. Josephine   135
. Leah   45
. Leoma   40
. Leoma Frances   45
. Myra Octavia   89
. Sarah Jane   92
DAUGHERTY,Letisha   230
DAUGHTERY,Lettisha   242
DAVENPORT,
. Alice Arlelia   46
. America I.   176
. Annie Lula   76
. Arthur   11
. Betty   11,78
. Clyde Fisher Jr.   64
. Clyde Fisher Sr.   64
. Doran E.   35
. Early   64
. Elsie   46
. Fannie   84
. Geraldine   71
. Hilda Cloise   28
. I.E.   76

. Isaac Perry   28
. Jennie Ruth   35
. Joseph Isaac   46
. Lois   64
. Maria Elizabeth   156
. Martha   193-194
. Mary C.   35
. Michael Lee   35
. Novella   64
. Ollie   46
. Patsy Dee   35
. Pauline   11
. Raydon Coleman   46
. Richard   11
. Susie   28
. William Newton   64
DAVESPORT,
. James Simpson   179
. Lois E.   179
. Martha   179
DAVEY,Allie   18
DAVIDSON,Helen   255
. Hugh   109
. Jane   109
. Margaret   245
. Margaret M.   109,225
. Mary Ruth   120
DAVIS,Alia C.   117
. Alice Aselean   177
. Amos   220
. Anderson   100
. Asa P.   100
. Asilean   178
. Aubrey   30
. Audrey M.   59
. Avo   21
. Bertie M.   37,39
. Betty B.   178
. Beulah   30
. Bluford   235
. Callie Nancy   220
. Carolyn   72
. Carolyn S.   75
. Christian M.   190
. Claude Monroe   101
. Cleo Beatrice   18
. Deliah   174
. Deloris Mae   59
. Don M.   75
. Edith   39
. Edward Thomas   40
. Eliza   186
. Elizabeth   173,254
. Elizabeth G.   190
. Ellen K.   249
. Elridge Henderson   177
. Emma Louvina   18
. Emma Nevado   14
. Felix Butler   30
. Florence   240
. Frances Ruth   49
. George S.   48
. George Smith Sr.   49
. George W.   173
. Gilbert W.   40

. Gladys   40
. Gladys Loree   3
. Grover C.   59
. Hassie Bular   100
. Hattie   240,252
. Henrietta   235
. Hershell   252
. I.M.   41
. Isaac   249
. Jane   101
. Jmaes Claudie   178
. Joe   255
. Joe Riley   178
. John   101,174,176,178
.   186,220
. John C.   175
. Jonathan G.   190
. Joseph   178
. Josie   40
. Katherine   60
. Leona   177
. Logan   240
. Logon   252
. Lola   13
. Loree   3
. Lou Ella   177
. Lucy Emma   18
. Mack Millian   3
. Madison Scott   3
. Martha   173
. Mary   100,178,186
. Mary Ann   249
. Mary Frances   178
. Mary Jane   220
. Mary Lou   175-176
. Mattie Ruth   14
. Minnie   235
. Minnie Mae   200
. Myrtle Troy   41
. Nancy   173
. Octa May   49
. Organ B.   18
. Parilee   100
. Reuben L.   15
. Roy A. Sr.   59
. Ruby   47
. Ruth   173
. Sadie   59
. Sally   41
. Sarah   59,190
. Shelah H.   177
. Siby Lee   178
. Sidney   14
. Sylvia   178
. Thomas C.   175
. Tinia Marie   54
. Tom E.   173
. Velier Etter   176
. Virgie Robinson   62
. Wandalee   15
. Willie Ernest   178
. Willie Evelyn   249
DAVY,Allie   26
DAWSON,Lela   8
DAWTON,Bell   59

Name	Page	Name	Page	Name	Page	Name	Page
DAY,Georgia Illa	30	. Van Lee	81	. John R.	77	. Laura B.	12
. Lori Ann	30	. William J.B.	65	. Louise G.	90	DOYLE,Maggie Dalena	67
. Roger Owen	30	DEROUIN,Malvine	59	. Mae	209	DRAKE,Annie	163
DEARING,Balzora Ward	155	. Mose	59	. Margaret Frances	80	. C.D.	163
.	156	. Olive	59	. Martha Sue	16	DREWER,Linda	24
. Mary A.	156	DETZEL,Catherine	14	. Mary	79	DRIVER,Effie	34
. Mary Terry	156-157	DEWITT,Eugene Knapp	76	. Mary Bessie	90	. Effie L.	20,23
. Virginia	155	DICK,Bessie D.	143	. Mary Elizabeth	86	. Garlin Elwood	20
. Virginia A.	128	. Josh	143	. Myrtle	89	. Hanry P.	20
. Virginia Ann	156-157	. Mary	143	. Parasada	138	. Henry P.	23,33
. William Lynch	110	DICKEY,		. Perseda	208	. Kizzie M.	33
. William Lynch S.	156	. Hiram Lafayette	226	. Rachel Ginsey	90	. Milas W.	23
.	157	. John W.	223	. Richard	73	. Sally	23
DEBERRY,Artie	18	. Louise	223	. Sarah Elizabeth	77	. Troy Houston	33
. Bell Zora	250	. Octavia Laughlin	226	. Shug	80	. Vada Lorene	20
. Eliza A.	199	. Zelphia	223	. Stella	77	DUDNEY,Joan	33
. Homer Lee	69	DICKSON,		. William	138	DUGAN,Charlie Grady	26
. Martha	251	. Dillard Thomas	60	. William David	72	. Flora E.	84
. Mary Clela	69	. Katherine	60	. Willie Cassandra	90	. Jesse Alvin	26
DEHAVEN,Alice	78	. Nedra Ann	60	DODSON,		. Nettie	26
DELOACH,Annie	73	. Thomas Edward	60	. Charles Clinton	12	. Violet	26
. Elise	73	DILL,Leona	24	. Dorothy J.	249	DUGGAN,Frances	121
. Thomas Madden	73	. Wavie	163	. Eli	158	DUGGIN,Alice Matilda	179
DELONG,A.F.	61	DILLARD,Jep	75	. Elijah	136	. Ferando Cortez	179
. Davie Eugene	61	. Mary Elizabeth	75	. George Edward	249	. Walter Emerson	179
. Effie	61	. Sarah L.	76	. George Thurman	249	DUKE,Abb	253
. Lillie Elvira	61	. William K.	76	. James Campbell	12	. Alex	194,253
. Mary	81	DILLON,Alton	85	. Jansie	158	. America Lovina	181
. Susan Laverene	61	. James Aud Sr.	39	. Jessie Emma	249	. Ann	194
. Wayne	61	. James Edward	39	. Joyce	59	. Bettie	194
. William Joseph	61	. Mary Ann	39	. Latisha	2	. Calvin	256
DEMPSEY,J.L.	171-172	. Mary Catherine	40	. Letisha	128,153,159	. Colonel	253
. Lula Bell	48	. Sarah Elizabeth	39	. Lucy	225	. Josephine	44
DENBY,Callie	34	DIRTING,Mary	43	. Martha	12	. Margaret Novella	181
DENNIS,Addie	187	DIXON,Brenda Kay	80	. Mary	19,143	. Martha Ann	186
. Emmie	187	. Dora E.	52	. Mary Ann	165	. Monroe	181
. Lillian	2	. Harry Lee	52	. Maxie	136-137,196	. Nancy	188
. Lucille M.	187	. Helen R.	52	. Mirah Elizabeth	157	. Ortie	45
. Sam	2	. John W.	52	.	158	. Rebecca	256
. Thiren Mae	207	. Lela	160	. Myrtle Avo	150	. Ruby	253
DENNO,Maude Mae	41	DOAK,Brown	112	. Sallie	136	DULANEY,Ernest Shelton	7
DENTON,Adella	95	. Ruth	112	. Sue	12	.	8
. American	22	. Wilma Lou	112	DONAHUE,Jennie	214	. Harriet	7
. Bessie	47	DOBBS,Bertha	27	DONEGAN,Bertha	68	. Herman Avery	237
. Bitha Marie	44	. Eliza	204	DONEY,Randolph	231	. James Warren	7
. Della	65	. Susan C.	204	. Sallie	231	. Jenry	237
. Della Mae	95	DODD,Abbigail	90-91	. Sol	231	. Julia Lee	7
. Doris	65	. Bertha	90	DORRIS,Decia	37	. Julie Lee	8
. Flora Ann	21	. Bettie	98	. Irene Lee	37	. Mary Harriet	8
. Georgia Edward	82	. Brown	72	. James J.	37	. Ruth Magaline	237
. Grace Katherine	21	. Charles Harrison	77	. James W.	37	DULEU,John B.	210
. Green V.	47,95	. Charlotta	138	DORSEY,Elizabeth	202	. Mary A.	210
. Greenville	65	. Della G.	80	. Frances Cordelia	202	. Samuel Z.	210
. Grover Cleveland	81	. Della H.	80	. Joe	202	DUNCAN,Alfred Grant	170
. Isaac	81,95	. Dorothy	72	DOTSON,Grover	45	. Alfred H.	167
. James William	21	. Estie	73	. Mattie Gertrude	45	. Clara Belle	170
. Lorene	45	. Flora Bell	87	. Mollie Fay	45	. Elizabeth	167
. Mary D.	65	. Franki Nicole	106	. Vernice	45	. Floyd	171
. Matilda Ann	95	. Gensey	80	DOTY,Emily P.	91-92	. Martha Eleanor	55
. Mattie	81	. H.M.	82	. Jerry	91-92	. Mollie Eliza	13
. Ray Overton	21	. Hiram	80	. Susan	91-92	. Nettie Ray	243
. Ruby G.	80	. Hiram N.	90	DOUGLAS,Millie	157	. Rosalind	170
. Ruth	47	. Horace B.	90	DOWNS,Alice	12	. Sarah	226
. Rutha	79,81	. James Hiram	90-91	. Bill Morris	12	. Tom C.	171
. Samantha	81	. James M.	80	. J.W.	12	DUNEM,C.P.	251

===

Name	Page	Name	Page	Name	Page	Name	Page
DUNEM,(cont)		. Prudence	135	. N.B.	91	. George W.	198-199
. George W.	251	EARL,Maggie	102	. Nancy	91	. Henrietta	198
. I.Clinton	251	EARLE,Annie	4	. Rachel Ann	6,30,196	. Julia	199
DUNHAM,Bertha Mae	255	. James Patterson	4	. Sallie Ann	6	. Mary Jane	8,197,200
. C.P.	251	. Jeff	4	. Sallie J.	91	ESTER,Ida Jones	227
. Daisy	255	. Mabel Claricy	221	. Scovie L.	6	. June Elizabeth	227
. George W.	251	EARLES,Alex	234	. Sharon Grace	8	. Thomas Marion	227
. Georgia Velma	251	. Anna Belle	234	. Vaudrene	194	ESTES,Clemmie	116
. Paul	255	. Donna	57	ELDER,W.K.	90	. Jane E.	233
. Willie	255	. Maggie Z.	234	ELKINS,		. Julia	9
DUNLAP,Beulah	251	EARLS,Alexander	236	. Annie Beatrice	133	. Mary Frances	219,233
. Catherine	146-147	. Anna Bell	236	. Dellie W.	2	. Thomas	233
. Cherlene	165	. Annie Parrot	250	. Frank	191	ETTER,E.Bruce	121
. Eddie Earl	251	. Beulah	30	. Gabriel	189	. Electra Charlotte	121
. John	162	. Christine	253	. George T.	195	. Elizabeth Jane	118
. Mary	162	. Claude	221	. George W.	189	. Emma I.	115,118
. Nancy Adaline	160	. Eva	175	. J.Preston	189	. Frances	121
. Nancy Adeline	162	. Ivy	233	. James Franklin	133,191	. G.W.	255
. R.L.	251	. Jeffery Charles	253	. Lucy	236	. Harriet	117
. Sarah	165	. Joe	233	. Martha Ann	189	. Henry	118
. Zanie	251	. Mable	250	. Mary	195	. Millie	177
DUNN,Annie Lowe	17	. Mae Brister	254	. Mary Ann	196	. Nancy	222
Nancy Clice	39	. Maggie	253	. Mary L.	189	. Poscoe	121
DURHAM,Aaron	180	. Myrtle	250	. Maude	67	. William G.	121
. Andrew Jack	40	. Phebia	237	. Maude Lee	71	EUBANKS,Christbelle	56
. Annie	121	. Phebia Elizabeth	236	. Newton Columbus	201	. Herman	56
. Annie Mae	73	. Raymond Eugene Jr.	250	. Press	191	. Liza	18
. Arnold B.	23	. Ruth Bell	233	. Preston	201	. Mildred	56
. Cleo	23	. Sally	44	. Rita	147	. Sarah	28
. Ella Mae	40	. Samantha Paralee	202	. Ruth Ann	189-190	EVANS,Bessie	254
. Etheline Grace	40	. William	202	. Vica Jane	191	. Bessie Burch	249
. George W.	23	EDGE,Bettie	240	. Vicie Jane	201	. Betty	55
. James Clifton	40	. Levi	205	. Vicy Jane	189	. Beulah	55
. Kitty Lorena	180	. Mary	205	. Violet	133,191,229	. Charlie	249
. Lizzie	180	. Zeb	240	ELLEDGE,Elizabeth	93	. Ira Ronald	55
. Nannie Lou	5	. Zebedee	205	Martha	109	. John	254
. Rufene	23	EDMONDSON,Esther	239	ELLIOTT,Margie Cleo	160	. Mary	108
. William R.	180	EDMONSON,Esther	247	Martha	109	. Nolan	55
DUTTON,		EDWARDS,Earl C.	38	ELLISON,J.H.	108	. Ronnie	55
. Alcey Elizabeth	100	. James	223	ELROD,Bertha	40	. Ruby	254
. Alice	100	. Jane	252	. Bertha A.	72	. Sarah	220
. Ann Elizabeth	100	. Jennie	38	. Carolyn	72	. Walter	249,254
. Charlotte	-	. John	38	. Charley C.	72	EVINS,Estelle	246
. Elizabeth	100	. Joseph Clarence	223	. Jim Douglas	72	William Jackson	246
. Cornie Lee	100	. Leona	63	. Madie B.	58	EWING,Dave	32
. James Allen	100	. Margaret	38	. Myrtle Opal	72	. Margaret	32
. John	100	. Millie	102	. Opal E.	72	. Mildred Culley	32
. Lesta	100	. Roxie	97	. Sammy David	72	. William Warren	32
. Mary	43	. Sidney Aileen	223	. Sarah	98	FAGAN,Ann	37
. William Horace	100	ELAM,Annie	6	. William Davis	58	FAMBROCH,Kay	70
DYE,Margaret Ann	170	. Bettie	91	. William Eugene	72	FANCHER,Susan Annie	33
DYER,Elizabeth	202	. Cora	196	EMERY,Lillie	3	FANN,Bertha	235
. Ethel Morgan	8	. H.L.	91	ENGLAND,Elizabeth	141	FANNING,Edora	49
. Florence M.	13	. Henry L.	91,196	. Martha	162	FANSHIER,Ann	242
. Hazel	20	. Hersie	6	. Mary	141	. Charles S.	242
. Jeff	20	. J.B.	30	. Parneta	157	. Hester Cass	242
. Maud	8,13	. James Buchanan	6,196	. Richard	141	. James W.	242
. Maude	20	. Jennie	38	ENGLISH,Amos A.	86	. John	241-242
. Nancy Jane	220	. Jessie Lilburn	6	. Lalah Egner	86	FARLESS,Carolyn	106
. William Jefferson	8,13	. Laura A.	200	. Mary E.	28	. Eula Mai	225
. William Ross	8	. Lillie May	91	EPSY,Mary Jane	6	. Geneva	135
DYKES,Eugenia	148	. Lizzie	91	ESPY,Dollie	198	. Hassie	15
. Isham	135	. Mary	31	. Dolly	251	. Ida	54
. Malinda	142,152	. Mary Emma	30	. Ella	197	. Jessie Emma	249
.	154-155,159	. Michael R.	8	. Ellen	198-199	. Leoma	61
				. George	197		

==

FARLESS,(cont)		. FISHER,Carrie	54	. Lucy	215	. Mark	4
. Lorene	112	. Enoch Lloyd	58	. Margie N.	74	. Mary Ruth	4
. Obie	54	. Georgia Winnie	58	. Mary	215	FREEMAN,Harriet	131
. Rachel	54	. Irene	38	. Maude	182	. Martha Elizabeth	94
. William	135	. Irvin	36	. Rebecca Sue	215	. Mary	141
FARLEY,Lucy	17	. Juanita	69	. Robert	194	. Mary Elizabeth	131
FARMER,Susie	83	. Laura M.	36	. Sam	215	FREEZE,Clarence E.	52
FARRELL,Emmaline	10	. Lawson	48	. Sue	213	. Elijah Lankford	43
. Helen	10	. Mary E.	48	. Susie	217	. Elizabeth Ann	237
. J.E.	10	. Mary Leona	36	. Zenohia Finley	194	. Eula	43
. Mattie Eunice	10	. Orville Stewart	36	FOUTCH,J.Emeline	195	. Jessie Ruth	43
FARRIS,Dexter	38	. Roy	54	John C.	195	. Martha	173
. Jewel B.	38	. Sallie Belle	48	FOX,Anna M.	71	. Minnie Pearl	52
. Josephine	38	. Susie	58	. Berdie May	192	. Pauline Edna	52
FARROW,Sam	108	FITTS,Dorothy T.	62	. Birdie Mae	45	FRENCH,Ammie E.	214
FAULKNER,Viola	33	Roy W.	62	. Catherine Mae	45	FRISBY,Charlie	60
FAVORS,Betty	167	FLATT,Catherine	12	. Jace Wesley	192	. Gordon A.	60
Carl L.	167	. Hulon D.	13	. James E.	71	. Larry	60
FELTS,Georgia	5	. Jefferson Douglas	13	. John Wesley	45	. Laurie	60
FENNELL,Bartlett	229	. Jefferson Douglass	12	. O.Richard	45	. Leonard Allen	60
. Harmon Manford	229	. Lee William	12	. Raymond	45	FULLER,Daisy	169
. Myrtle Belle	229	. Lola D.	13	. Raymond Lee	192	FULTS,Adeline	95
. Octa	229	. Ova	12-13	. Robbie	192	. Agnes	36
. Ralph Nolan	228	FLEMMING,Dorothy	253	FRALEY,Doyle	252	. Alice	91
FERGASON,Ervin	63	FLETCHER,Allie	28	. Jefferson Davis	252	. Amanda	124
. Mollie Louveda	63	FLORA,Bruce	4	. Martha	252	. Amos	133
. Nora Marie	63	Faye E.	4	. Mary Ann	252	. Annie Beatrice	133
. Preston Irvin	63	FLOYD,Emma Aleve	55	. Samantha	252	. Bertha Lee	111,129
FERGUSON,Catherine	5	. Lucille	55	FRANKLIN,Della	7	. Carson Oliver	254
. Ethel	177	. William H.	55	FRANKS,Alton	85	. Charles Lewis	256
. John A.	5	FLYNN,Dennes	183	. Carrie	38	. Charles M.	256
. Margaret	140-141	Jane	183	. Christopher Lee	38	. Charles Odell	112
. Martha Jane	253	FOLEY,Mary Ruth	4	. Clara	38	. Charlie Clency	75
. Mary Elizabeth	19	FORD,Charles	47	. Ila	85	. Daniel	133
. Mattie Ruth	5	. Edward Price	117	. James B.	85	. Dave	75
. Pauline	69	. Elizabeth	119	. James Marvin	38	. David	124
. Peter	5	. Elvira	117,119	. Jewel B.	38	. Doshie	129
. Rachel	163	. Florence	119	. Leborn	38	. Ella	122,148
. Willard J.	177	. Frank	214	. Letrell L.	38	. Elzie	129
FERN,Hannan	254	. Hester	117	. Spencer	85	. Emma Louise	129
FERRELL,Delia	174	. Ida Elizabeth	119	FRAZIER,Alfred	191	. Fannie	43
. Eliza	186	. James S.	119	. Charlotte	95,98,100	. Floyd Harris	130
. Emma Pearl	40	. Jane	47	. Ella	2	. France	111
. Emmie	249	. Jeanette	214	. Emma	191	. Francis	136
. Hallie Mae	252	. Louise	214	. Faye	4	. George	129-130,135-136
. J.B.	16	. Mable Louise	214	. Margie Lou	19	. George K.	133
. Jennie	210	. Margaret	192	. Marion	70	. Georgia	112,129,133
. Jennie Mai	16	. Phebie Jane	208-209	. Martha	19,191	.	153
. John	186	.	252	. Mary E.	201	. Gertrude	75
. Joseph Espy	249	. Steve	47	. Mary Elizabeth	69	. Gilbert	122
. Joyce E.	76	. Tom	214	. Media	191	. Grace Lee	148,150
. Lela	80	. William	117	. Ollie Mai	70,191	. H.T.	130
. Martha	249	. William W.	119	. Richard	4	. Irene	256
. Martha Sue	16	FORDYGE,J.H.	90	. Richard T.	2	. James Ethan	219
. Nancy	64	Zettie	90	. Robert	2,19	. Jane	124
. Oscar	249	FORREST,Sarah Ann	131	. Ruth	4	. Janie	136
. Richard U.	76	FORRESTER,David	203	. Ruth B.	2	. Jean	135
. Susie	176	Mary	203	. Spencer Otis	19	. John	135
FIELD,Jordan	106	FOSTER,Calidonia	104	. William	69	. John Henry R.	133
. Maggie	106	. Eugenia Ann	194	. William Marion	191	. Julie	75
. Vera	106	. Evaline	85-86	FREED,Joseph	101	. Junie	133
FINCHUM,Leona	146	. Hallie Ethel	84	. Joseph M.	101	. Laura Louella	129
FINLEY,Nell	12	. Harold G.	74	. Mary	101	. Leaoma	111
FISH,Cora Lillian	49	. Howard	85-86	FREEDLE,Annie B.	4	. Lee Annie	133
John Wiley	49	. Jewell	5	. Luther Mark	4	. Lillie	135

===

FULTS,(cont)
. Maggie Mae   147
. Magnolia   42,73
. Mary   126,129-130
.   135-136
. Mary Ella   153
. Mary Lou   130
. Mattie Lee   130
. Mattie Mae   148
. Myrtle Aline   254
. Nannie   111
. Oliver   254
. Ollie Mae   75
. Ophia   219
. Pearl   163
. Ralph Franklin   130
. Reuben   129,148
. Roberta   130
. Russell   112,129,133
.   153
. Ruth   113,125-126
. Sarah   133
. Thomas Loyd   133
. William A.   91
. William Clayton   130
FUQUA,Albert   58
. Charles   58
. Ferbie   58
. Fred A.   58
. Kaytella A.   58
. Lucille   58
FUSON,Cumella   25
. Mary   252
. Nancy   12
FUSTON,Andy   212
. Annie   87
. Bettie   3
. Cumilla   26
. Cynthia   77
. Della   65
. Eliza   212
. Hannah Elizabeth   212
. Henry O.   212
. James   212
. Jonathan Rufus   241
. Martha Tennessee   212
. Mary   212,241
. Nicholas Tilmon   212
. Rebeca   241
. William Jefferson   212
GAITHER,Arthur   180
  Ralph W.   180
GAMBLE,Daisy   181
  Louise   90
GAMBRELL,Allie   67
. Mable   67
. William Riley   67
GANN,Amanda   12,103-104
.   227
. Amanda Malvina   89
. Avis A.   227
. Belle   89
. Ben   104
. Benjamin Harrison   104
.   227

. Bobby Joe   101
. Brenda Gale   104
. Catherine Bell   103-104
. Clara Belle   256
. Cora Estelle   12
. Eva Mae   182
. Fannie Maude   105
. Florence Elizabeth   103
. Harrison   12,103
. James Howard   104
. James Monroe   89
.   103-104
. Jim M.   182
. Lois   104
. Lula Scott   182
. Margie Irene   105
. Martha   182
. Mary B.   230
. Mary Bell   102-103
. Monroe   103
. Nannie Bell   104
. Nathan   103
. Parthena   103
. Robert   256
. Roof Harp   101
. Rosie Mildred   104
. William Hoyt   12
. William Nathan   104-105
. Willie Maude   104
GANNON,Frances   249
. Harriett   189
. Harriett T.   199
. Lida Myrtle   203
. Martha   180
. Susie   230
GARDNER,Addie   214
. Ella   201,217
. Ethel   214,216,218
. Florence   214
. James R. Sr.   122
. Lucy   215,218
. Madison   214
. Mary   214,217
. Mat   217
. Matt S.   216
. Minas   218
. Minor   215
. Phronie   215
. Reathy   215
. Sallie A.   216
. Saphrona   217
. Saphronia   215
. Sarah   122,214,217
. Sophrona   218
. William Hunter   122
. William Ira   122
GARMON,Malissa   77
. Mary B.   77
. Mattie B.   77
. Rausa   77
. Ruth caroline   77
. Samuel   77
. Will   77
GARNER,Ada   1
. Ada Alice   6,64,96

. Martha J.   122
. Nancy Frances   96
. Rebecca   122
. Reuben Comer   96
. William E.   122
GARRETSON,Ann   227
. E.   233
. Emily E.   227
. Jane   233
. Jane Elizabeth   227
. Nancy   227
. William M.   227
GARRETT,Mary   13
. Nellie   13
. Oren R.   9
. Virgil   13
. William Thomas   13
GARTH,Jesse T.   106
  Mary Emmaline   106
GASAWAY,C.H.   204
. H.G.   204
. Susan C.   204
GAY,Ernset Edward   67
. Gennie Edward   67
. George W.   67
. Mattie Pauline   67
. Nancy Jane   67
. Ruth   67
GEBHARDT,
  Ethelda Grace   230
GENZIA,Celestine   71-72
GEORGE,Josephine   22
GEORGI,Clara   41
GIBBS,Adaline   224,231
. Adeline   223
. Dora Frances   240
. Eleanor   224
. Elizabeth   221,240,247
. Emma   234-235
. Emma Jane   223
. Maggie   223
. Nancy Adelyne   252
. Nancy Clementine   223
. Sam   240
. Samuel   223
GIBSON,Jimmie Brown   178
. John B.   178
. Siby Lee   178
GILBERT,Beulah   55
. Della Elizabeth   22,25
. Effie   76
. Georgia Elizabeth   25
. Harrison   25
. Harrison Joseph   22,228
. Hassie Cillar   104
. Hassie Ciller   99
. Hassie Eillar   105
. J.E.   228
. Joseph Edmund   99
. Martha   228
. Martha Reams   99
. Mary Ann   228
. Mazel Louise   22
. Verna Mae   25
GILISPIE,Adolphus D.   17

. Levi   17
. Lucy   17
. Mary K.   17
GILLEN,Bertha   2
. John   2
. Lillian   2
. William   2
GILLENTINE,Bessie   145
. Cora Halbert   24
. George Frank   24
. Grover   24
. Joe Arthur   145
. Joseph   24
. Mary   127
. Mary Vida   24
. Sally Ruth   24
. Vida   145
GILLESPIE,Chole   33
. David D.   33
. Geraldine   69
. John   33
. Mattie   33
. Soledad   33
GILLETTE,Alice   65
. Edith   10
. Henry   65
. Mabel Irene   65
. Willie Dudley   65
GILLEY,Acton Y.   96
. Acton Young   94
. Caleb C.   199
. Clementine   199
. Elizabeth F.I.   189
. Elizabeth Frances   -
.   I. 96
. Frances E.I.   192
. Gertie   95
. Hattie   66
. Isaac I.A.   94
. Izzie   199-200
. James W.   188
. Jessie Mai   66
. John Caleb   199
. Katherine   98
. Lena   98
. Leona   5
. Lou Etta   98
. Lula   199
. Lula C.   199
. Mary Elizabeth   94
. Rebecca   94,96
. Robert   66
. Sarah E.   188
. Simon   199
. W.M.   98
. Willie   98
GINN,A.L.   87
. Angalo   229
. Angalo L.   230
. Emma Lee   87,230
. Hilda Mae   87
. Ivan G.   230
GIPSON,Amanda Renee   18
. Clara   18
. Jane Drake   18

GIPSON,(cont)	GORDON,Eula 66	. Sylva 215	. Nannie Lee 43-44
. Jim 18	. John 66	. Theadoshia 217	. Naomi 57
. Mattie Gertrude 45	. Mildred 66	. Viola 214	. Napoleon Boneparte 107
GIVENS,Maggie 55	. Pauline C. 247	. W.L. 217	. Novella 4
Palmer 53	GORDY,Hassie Loring 48	. Willie Lee 215	. Pat 158
GLENN,Arthur O. 43	. James E. 48	GREEN,Amanda 68	. Plinea 107
. Arthur Odis 44	. James Taylor 48	. Amy 250	. Rhoda Stincy 172
. Betty Ruth 44	. Lula Bell 48	. Annie Lourie 61	. Samantha 34
. Bitha Marie 44	. Maxine 48	. Annie Pearl 251	. Sarah 107,133,151
. Hassie Lee 187	GOUGER,Della 239-240	. Beatrice 157	. Sarah N.L. 107
. John 44	GRACEY,Lou 21	. Bertha Ann 151	. Shadrack 107
. John Arthur 43	GRAELL,Julius 33	. Betty 169	. Tennessee 151,154
. Nannie Lee 43-44	Ruth 33	. Betty Jean 68	. Thomas 78
. Virginia 43	GRAHAM,Emily 18	. Bill 151	. Thomas D. 72
GLIDEWELL,Grace 66	. Janie 167	. Blanch Allen 141	. Thomas M. 107
GOGGINS,John Jordon 82	. Martha 242	. Bonnie 151	. W.Leo 251
Martha C. 82	. Mary 37	. Cora 12	. Walter L. 68
GOLDEN,Alaska Eleana 25	. Tom 83	. Cordelia 234	. Wiley 4,76
. Allen Ward 57	GRANDSTAFF,Audry Gay 200	. Debbie 235	. Zanie 251
. Cain 179	. Cecil Burger 200	. Dema C. 250	GREENE,
. Charles Compton 56	. Laura L. 200	. Dolly 42	. Mildred Lucille 19
. Delia Christine 192	. Oscar L. 200	. Dora 102	. Nancy L. 19
. Dicy Elva 49	. Vurna L. 200	. Elam A. 68	. Sammie A. 19
. Elkanah D. 56-57	GRANNOM,Beatrice Ann 66	. Eliza E. 107	GREER,Robbie 25
. Eula 51	. Ottis 66	. Eliza Elliott 57	Violet Lillian 14
. Flora Jane 57	. Richard Monroe 66	. Elizabeth 29	GREGORY,George D. 45
. Gladys 56	GRAVES,Clara 141	. Ella Rosie 78	. Georgia 45
. Henrietta 25	GRAY,Sarah 229,251	. Emma Lee 87,230	. Joseph Daniel 68
. John Rolfe 56	GRAYSON,Alex 213,218	. Ethel 73	. Lorene 45
. Josie Estella 25	. Alexander 58,215	. Ethel Ella 158	. Luke 45
. Kezzie 179	. Alexander A. 214	. Etta 141	. Marguerite 68
. Kissie 56	. Arizona 217	. Flaura 57	GRETZINGER,Benita 38
. Kissimoer 57	. Beulah 213	. Flora Belle 20	. Benjamin I. 38
. Lottie Geneva 56	. Clara Frances 215	. Florence 4	. Mary M. 38
. Lourene 56	. Elizabeth 213	. Frank Eli 242	GRIBBLE,Annie Marie 51
. Lucy Jane 51	. Elnora 214	. Frank J. 230	. Callie Lee 55
. Magnolia 179-180	. Ethel 58,213-214,218	. Hallie Belle 5	. Dee Ida 31
. Nicholas Charles 51	. Evelyn 217	. Harriet 7	. Dock Jackson 51
. Susie Mai 56	. Gell Berta 217	. Hettie 72	. George Sutton 65
GOLDTRAP,Corn 48	. George 217	. J.D. 72	. George Washington 65
GOOD,Bertha L. 195	. George L. 215	. Jake 61	. Gertrude Bernice 225
. Cleo 194-195	. Gilbert 212-214	. James 108	. James Alexander 31
. Della 60,102	. 217-218	. John 151,249	. Jennie 55
. Dora 101-102	. Gilberta 218	. Joseph 107	. Joe Butler 51
. Elizabeth 199	. Goldie May 217	. Joseph Samuel 57	. Julia 51
. Robert Hershel 195	. Hugh 213	. Joyce Ann 251	. Larry Q. 55
GOODLETT,Cliffard 11	. Ike Henry 218	. Kezzie 179	. Maggie B. 55
. Marjorie 11	. James 218	. Kissimoer 57	. Martha 65
. Sharon 11	. James William 218	. L.C. 141	. Nora Alice 251
GOODMAN,George 50	. John 217	. Letisha 230	. Oscar Newell 31
. John Walker 50	. Lillian 212-214,218	. Lettisha 242	. Rella Dell 65
. Mary 50	. Lizzie 217	. Lewis Napoleon B. 84	. Sarah Ann 31
. Rozelle 50	. Mack 215,217-218	. Lonnie 4	. Talitha 48
GOODSON,Andrew J. 88	. Magnolia 216	. Lucinda 249	GRIFFIN,Carl Elmo 22
. Anna 88	. Margaret 218	. Martha 152,232	. Della 80
. E.A. 88	. Mary 217	. Martha Pearlee 242	. Ernest Alton 86
. Elsie L. 88	. Mary Alexander 217	. Mary 61,65,158	. Furby 249
. Martha B. 88	. Rebecca Sue 215	. Mary Ann 74,107,249	. J.C. 249
. Memphis 88	. Rhodie 215	. Mary Elizabeth 84	. Junnie Alberta 86
. S.D. 88	. Ruby 213	. Mathew Compton 57,107	. Llewllyn 22
. Tansy E.A. 88	. Ruth 213	. Maude 76	. Mary 249
GOOLSBY,	. Shirley Jean 218	. Mildred 76	GRIFFITH,Ada 24
Sarah Katherine 34	. Simon Pike 215	. Mollie 130	. Anna Louise 106
GOOSBY,Sally 28	. Simpie 215	. Mozell 72	. Annabell 95
GOOSTREE,Lillie 34	. Susie 215,217-218	. Nancy 84	. Bertie 235

==

GRIFFITH,(cont)
. Billy N.   106
. Dolly   49
. Ephram   67
. Ernest T.   23
. Fate   24
. Fronia   67
. Hallie   59
. Hanna   23
. Kenneth N.   106
. Lillie Gertrude   24
. Media V.   23
. Paten   23
. Verna   67
GRIMES,Ada   68
. Charlotte Willie   68
. Tom   68
GRIMMETT,Betty   14
. Charles Edwin   14
. George Bayless   14
. Nancy Viola   14
. Thomas   14
GRISSOM,Alice   151
. Allen K.   73
. Betty Jo   26
. Elizabeth   159
. Hilda Mae   87
. Joe   12
. Juanita M.   73
. Luther S.   87
. Sally   12
. Sue   12
. Thomas H.   78
GRISWOLD,Gussie   39
. Norma Jean   38-39
. Walter H.   38-39
. William Houston   39
GRIZZELL,Ervin   248
. Flora Jane   57
. Ike   248
. Isaac John   57
. Julie Ann   57
. Lettie   175
. Tennie   248
GROOM,Emma   87
GROSS,Adam Daniel   114
                  118,124,126
. Arsey M.   126
. Asa   114
. Asa C.   227
. Audrey Lee   114
. Charlotte   124
. Elizabeth   114,118,124
                          126
. Ettie   48
. Gladys   126
. Imogene   116
. Jo Ruth   119
. Musadora   227
. Rosa Lee   118
. Sarah   114
. Wallie   114
. Wallie May   126
. Willie W.   118
GROVE,Alice   156

. Arcola   146
. Betty Sue   29
. Clabe   146
. Elmer   56
. Eloise   146
. Jennifer Caral   29
. John W.   29
. Lois   64
. Margaret   154,156
. Mary   154
. Mildred   56
. Nancy   126
. Nellie   42
. Nettie   149
. Tamer   140
. William   154,156
. Wyatt Lane   146
GROW,Mary Elizabeth   25
GUDGER,Harry G.   39
. Laura   39
. Margaret   39
. William H. Sr.   39
GULLEY,Carl   15
GUNN,Sallie   169
GUNTER,Caldean D.   28
. Edgar   39
. Joseph Fisher   39
. Mary   39
. Mary E.   28
. Ruby Mae   39
. Sallie   28
GUY,Dovie   69
    Nettie   65
GWYN,Amelia   109
. Elizabeth   108-109
. Hugh   108-109
. James   109
. Julia   109
. Leonard   66
. Leonard Sr.   66
. Margaret McConnell   109
. Martha Jane   108-109
. Mary   108-109
. Milton H.   108
. Nannie M.   108
. Ransom   108-109,225
. Remus   109
. Richard   109
. Romulus   109
. Sallie   218
. Sarah   109
. Thelma   66
. Vera   66
GWYNN,George   216
. Sallie   216
. Sally   215
HAAS,Alton W.   59
. Deloris Mae   59
. Elizabeth   59
. Ella Louise   117
. Eva McCrary   117
. Phillip   117
HACKETT,Cynthia   226
    Lois   124
HADLEY,Anna   206

HAGEWOOD,Effie L.   105
. Elmus   105
. George   105
. James C.   89-90,105
. Sarah H.   89-90,105
. Thomas R.   105
HALE,Adelbert   91
. Albert   205
. Alberta   79
. Axie   86
. Bea   86
. Bertha   167
. Betty Elizabeth   202
. Bill   167
. Charlie T.   81
. Christopher C.   126
. Clyde E.   79
. Daisy   202
. Dan   202
. Debra Ellen   126
. Della   80
. Dorothy Lee   79
. Ethel Ollene   126
. F.E.   79
. Flora   86
. Frances   70
. Frances Elvira   84
. Frank E.   78
. Fred Louis   83
. Grady H.   86
. Harding   86
. Harvel   70
. Helen   83
. Hiram   83
. Isom   202
. James Ronald   70
. James W.   126
. Janie   86
. Jefferson   202
. Jennie   79,205
. Joe   231
. John   79
. John Alford   167
. John M.   183
. John Monroe   231
. Julia   79
. Kathy Annette   71
. Landon   202
. Lillian   231
. Martha Ella   58
. Martha J.   205
. Mary   79
. Mary Belle   231
. Mary E.   79
. Mary Elizabeth   86
. Mary Lee   84
. Mary Pauline   83
. Nancy   84
. Nancy L.   78-79
. P.L.   79
. Rayburn   202
. Rebecka Mary   205
. Robert   169
. Robert Harrison   86
. Sallie   81

. Thomas G.   79,86
. Tommie   79
. Vera Pearl   83
. Vernie   136
. William   167
. William G.   86
. William Harvey   205
. Willie   79
HALEY,Alex   137
. Charles Michael   65
. Dean   65
. Doris   65
. Elizabeth   198,243
. Emma   21
. Eva   48
. George J.   198
. George W.   137
. Helen   82
. Lela Mary   82
. Leth   52
. Lizzie   137
. Louella   194
. Martha   52,198
. Martha Rebecca   18
. Narcissa   137
. Sampson   82
HALL,Anna   14
. Artie Deberry   18
. Billy Wayne   198
. Charity   128
. D.B.   128
. Don   128
. Henry   8
. Irvin Q.   14
. Irvin Quincy   14
. James A.   52,198
. James Alexander   18,198
. John   198
. Johnnie Jackson   18
. M.Ruth   14
. Mamie   8
. Mandy   67
. Martha   52,198
. Martha Rebecca   18,198
. Mollie   198
. Ollie Mai   198
. Paul Richard   8
. Pauline E.   52
. Rilla Ozelle   8
. Thurman Alvin   52
. Vester Homer   198
. Willard   14
HALLETT,Livina   30
HALLEY,Fannie   16
HALLUM,Betty   235
. Edna B.   74
. George W.   235
. Georgia Hazel   235
. Gerald G.   74
. Harry Gordon   74
. James A.   235
. Kathleen   254
. Kathy Corlette   254
. Wanda C.   74
. Woodrow   254

Name	Page	Name	Page	Name	Page	Name	Page
HALTEMAN,Caroline	249	. Narcisus	207	. Edgar L.	24	HEAD,Clio	103
HAMBRICK,Martha	155	. Narcisus Geneva	208	. Edgar Lee	20	. John	255
HAMILTON,C.V.	250	. Oscar	208	. Edward James	20	. Margaret	255
. Harvy	175	. Shelah Robert	26	. Kathleen	7	HEADY,Anna	196
. Henry Clay	250	. Tommie	37	. Linda Sue	3	HEARN,Elizabeth F.	104
. Linda D.	58	. Tommie Jane	207	. Lodema	42	HEATHERLY,Anna	199
. M.V.	250	. Vivian May	207	. Lola Mae	20	. Elizabeth	199
. Margaret	187	HARDISON,Clyde Baxter	37	. Lola Mai	24	. Hanna	199
. Mollie Frances	175	. Frances	37	. Malinda	89	. John	199
. Parthena	117	. Guy	37	. Rector L.	7,43	HEGINBOTHAM,Joe	176
. Pence	175	. Lura	37	. Rector Lesley	42	. Joseph	176
HAMLEY,Ada	29	HARDY,Ruby	40	. Rosemary	20	. Matilda Pairsaid	176
HAMMER,		HARGIS,Martha	234	. Ruth	44	HELSTROM,Ida	24
. Amanda Elizabeth	209	HARGROVES,Marguerite	68	. Violet	7,43	HELTON,Mamie	8
.	227	HARLOW,Clara Belle	256	. Violet H.	42	HENCE,Chester J.	249
. Berry	209	HARMON,Andrew	42	HATTON,Sarah	5	HENDERIXON,Mary	26
. E.B.	97	. Eula Mai	225	HAWK,Elizbeth	173	HENDERSON,Annie	232
. Edith A.	209	. Jenny Sue	42	HAWKINS,Amanda	208	. Daniel	249
. Eva W.	97	. William Claud	42	. John	208	. Don	232
. Jennie	209	. Wylene	42	. Lillian	230	. Eva Lois	232
. Lucinda	209	HARPER,Anna Lee	230	. Mabel Clair	209	. Hal Thomas	232
. Lura	209	. Genevieve	231	. Mary	39	. Hallie	231-232
. Mary Katherine	227	. Mahala	136	. Offie Lillian	208	. Henry Paul	231-232
. R.B.	209	HARRELL,Audie	59	. William	209	. James Thomas	231-232
. Robert C.	209	. James	59	. Willis	208	. Joseph S.	255
. Victor V.	209	. Mattie Lou	59	HAWKS,Rebecca	90	HENDRICKS,Jonathan	68
. W.N.	227	HARRIS,Angel D.	49	HAWTHORN,Alma	255	Rosa B.	68
. William Henry	209	. Bill	21,105	HAYES,Anna	85	HENDRIX,Campbell	168
. William Theodore	227	. Billie Wayne	105	. Bonnie Sue	68	. Elizabeth	168
. Willie	209	. Charles T.	49	. Christine	63	. Frankie	55
HAMMERSTEIN,Malinda	209	. Clarence L.	37	. Elizabeth	69,153	. James P.	168
HAMMONS,Mary	90	. Della	37	. Ella	124,148	. Jonathan	55
HAMPTON,Celina	248	. Irene	34	. Frances	125	. Joseph Jonathan	55
. Nancy	108	. James	33	. Georgia Meade	20	. Maggie	26
. Sarah Ann Geneva	76	. James Tyra	37	. Henry L.	222	. Nancy P.	168
HAMRICK,Imogene	72	. Lula	105	. Ira Aaron	63	. Presley	168
HANCOCK,Sallie	79	. Lula Allison	21	. James A.	70	. Rosa	55
HANES,James Everett	41	. Novella	44	. James R.	125	. Susan Ann	168
. James M.	41	. Reba Jo	37	. James Roy	70	HENDRIXSON,Celia Mae	30
. Virgie May	41	. Ruby	10	. Jasper Columbus	63	. Mattie J.	38
HANFORD,Naomi	57	. Ruth	33	. Jay	222	. William B.	38
HANKINS,		. Viola	33	. Johnny W.	42	HENEGAR,Ada	1
. Ernest Hayden	251	HARRISON,Ainsworth	157	. Leona	63	. Ada Alice	6,64,96
. Ernest Parks	251	. Dolly Coleman	157	. Ludie	70	. Alton Jr.	66
. John William	251	. George	157	. Mandy	63	. Alton Sr.	66
. Nora Alice	251	. Mary	156	. Martha	84,88	. Annie Gladys	64
HANNEN,Dorothee L.	29	. Mary Terry	156-157	. Martin Patrick	125	. Bellzora	92-94,96
HANNER,Charles B.	211	. Millie	157	. Mary L.	125	. Belzora	95
. Jennie	211	HART,Ambie	64	. Mary Sharon	42	. Bettie	97
. Robert	211	. Amby	221	. Matilda	110,127	. Charlie Ramsey	97
HARBIN,Mary Frances	68	. Buck	221	. Morgan Cecil	68	. Doranella	66
HARDCASTLE,Joie Ann	15	. Mary	221	. Mozelle	70	. Doris	65
. Josie	1	HARTT,Eliza	229	. Nancy	222	. Dorothy Joyce	107
. Mary Ella	52	. James Marion	229	. Nancy Jane	110,125	. Eliza	96-97
HARDEN,Bell	129	. Ruby	229	. Nellie	110	. Elizabeth	93,95-96
HARDING,Betty Jo	26	HARVEY,		. Sallie	125	. Ernest	65
. C.C.	207	. Frances Lorraine	24	. Samuel David	110	. George W.	94-96
. Carpenter C.	208	. Frank D.	24	. Susie Emma	70	. Georgia	7
. Cleva Dell	37	. Sallie	21	. Temperance	125	. Georgia L.	6
. Douglas Burke	26	HASH,Adaline E.	110	. Tempie	110	. Gladys	107
. James Earl	37	. Drucilla	110	. Vallas Woodrow	63	. H.Lucille	1
. James Lewis	37,207	. Tabitha	110	. William Haywood	70	. James Milton	64
. Mary	207	. Thomas	110	. William M.	110,125	. James T.	1,6,64,96
. Murray	207	HASTING,Mamie Ruth	17	. Woodrow	63	. John Bell	97
. Murray Stephenson	207	HASTON,Cyrus Edward	42	HAYNES,Beulah	41	. John C.	94-95

==

HENEGAR,(cont)		. Sarah	171	. Claude	253	HIGGINBOTTOM,	
. Lizzie May	97	. Sarah J.	136	. Ollie S.	229	. Flossye E.	17
. Lydia	66	. Tabitha	103	. Rhonda	111	. John Wesley	17
. Martha Elizabeth	94	. Thomas	136-137	HICKMAN,Ellen Cecil	105	. Norie Bell	17
. Martha L.	95	. Thula	98	HICKS,Bob P.	37	HIGGINS,Estelle	198
. Mary Ann	96	. William	103	. Dorothy F.	85	. George C.	198
. Mary Elizabeth	96-97	. William H.	136	. Fannie	85	. Georgia Lee	178
. Milton	107	HENNY,Celestine	71-72	. Mary Lou	37	. Mollie	36
. Minnie L.	96	. Edward	71-72	. Ronnie P.	37	. Murf	178
. Nancy A.	94	. Howard	71	. Toye W.	85	. Robert France	178
. Nancy Paulina	94-95	. Michael Carey	71	. William Thomas	85	. Susan Ella	178
. Octa Bell	96	. Peggy Corinne	71	HIGDON,Calvin	186	. Zora	180
. Perry Corder	1	. Thelma	72	. Cleve	176	HILDRETH,Zadie	18
. Rhoda L.	97	HERNDON,Charlotte	101	. Elsie May	40	HILL,A.Putnam	122
. Ruby Etta	6	. Charlotte	-	. Frances	186	. Anna Louise	251
. Samuel Clay	96,98	. Josephine	102	. James A.	186	. Annie	162
. Sarah May	97	. Della Jane	78	. James Wayne	40	. Barbara	44
. Shelia Jane	65	. Eliza J.	137	. John C.	40	. Beatrice	157
. Susan Sophia	97	. H.R.	137	. Lee	252	. Benjamin	155,162
. Thomas	96	. J.M.	137	. Lucy	187	. Bethia	128
. Thomas J. Jr.	97	. Jacob	101,209	. Lucy Ann	176	. Betty	6,228
. Thomas Jefferson	97	. James H.	100	. Sarah	252	. Beulah	251
. Thomas Jefferson	-	. Jane	209	. Tennie Jane	252	. Carroll	161
.	Sr. 96	. Joe B.	78	. Wilma J.	40	. Catherine N.	157
. Tira Ann	96	. Lucy H.	95	HIGGINBOTHAM,Aaron	139	. Charlie D.	251
HENESEE,Loyd	254	. Lucy J.	90	.	140-141	. Clarence Benjamin	44
HENNESSEE,A.C.	67	. Lucy Josephine	101	. Amanda Malvina	206	. Clay Brown	25
. Albert A.	73	. Mary Jane	100	. Angeline	206	. Dearing	156
. Alexander	103	. Ruth Ann	209-210	. Bell Zora	140	. Demps	25
. Andrew	169	. S.E.	137	. Clara	141	. Dick	166
. Andy Franklin	136	HERRIMAN,C.P.	169	. Drury	141	. Eleanor	160-161
. Arcie Womack	18	. Columbus P.	249	. Elizabeth	139-141	. Eleanor H.	161
. Avo	67	. Dorothy Jo	249	. Erford	140	. Electra Charlotte	121
. Darthula	98	. Eppie Cordelia	249	. Florence	141	. Elenza Grundy	156,162
. Edith	160	. Fannie	169	. Frances	141	. Eliza	156-157
. Eliza Nora	103	. Flavil Eugene	249	. Frank	140	. Elizabeth	17
. Eliza W.	136	. Mary Frances	249	. Henry B.	139,141,241	. Ella M.	121,147
. Frances	70	. Mattie	169	.	252	. Emma	116,155
. George F.	130	HERRIN,Sally	153,162	. Jackson	141	. Emma Euphemia	85,117
. Icie Lavone	18	. Sidney	153	. James Madison	141	. Ervin	161
. James	98,137	. William	153	. James W.	139-140	. Euphemy	155
. James C.	136-137,196	HERRING,Annie Mae	18	. Jane	140	. Evanell	117
. James Thomas	136,196	HERSTINE,Amelia	233	. Jennie	241	. Frances Lee	116
. Jane	102	. George R.	233	. Jess	140	. Francis	162,166
. Jim	73	HESTER,Bertie M.	39	. John	141	. Franklin	157
. Lillie	67	HETRICK,Sylvia	178	. Josie	139	. Fred Clay	48
. Mahala	136	HEWBY,Adah Bell	204	. Lettie	139	. Fred Leslie	48
. Martha	103	. General N.	204	. Linnie	141	. Gwyn	217
. Mary	135	. General N.M.	204	. Lucinda Ann	139-140	. H.	161
. Mary A.	136	. Sarah Elizabeth	204	. Maggie J.	139	. Harriet	118
. Mary Ann	196	. Synthia	204	. Margaret	140-141	. Hattie Mae	48
. Mary Bell	130	. William B.R.	204	. Margaret L.	139-140	. Henry John A.	156-157
. Mary Jane	136	HIBDON,Calvin C.	56	. Martha L.	139	.	161-162
. Mary Wilsie	117,123	. Cellia	243	. Mary	141	. Hester V.	155
. Maxie	136-137,196	. Elias	243	. Mary Brooks	140	. Hugh Lawson White	128
. Mollie	130	. Mary J.	237	. Mary E.	140	.	155-157
. Nancy	73,98	. Mary Jane	243	. Mary Jane	139	. Ida Mae	44
. Nora	60	. Novavella	56	. Mation S.	139	. Irvin	160
. Nora Lee	130	. Reba Wiona	56	. Mollie	140	. Irving Lafayette	161
. Patrick S.	136	. W.B.	56	. Rebecca	241,252	. Isaac	156-157,162,166
. Pearl	238	HICKERSON,David	30	. Samuel	140	. Isaac Sr.	161
. Rachel	136	. Emma	30	. Samuel E.	139-141	. Israel	121
. Rachel Ann	136-137	. Thelma	30,64	. Tom	141	. Israel Putnam	157
. Sally	137	HICKEY,Bill	111	. Victoria	141	. J.A.	161
. Samuel M.	136	. Catherine	253	. William	139	. J.L.	161

==

HILL,(cont)				. Orin	219	. Larry Eugene	126
. J.M.	160	. Virginia	155-156	. Orion	222	. Lawrence	66
. J.Polk	116	. Virginia A.	128	. Orion D.	238	. Lee Annie	133
. J.S.	252	. Virginia Ann	157	HITCHCOCK,Don	150	. Lemma	112,121
. James Clifford	117	. William	157	. Frances	43	. Lena	116,122,133
. James Polk	85	. William Carroll	157	. Georgia	3	. Lenna	130
. Jane	134,161	. Wilma E.	48	. Horace Edward	41	. Lillie	118
. Jesse J.	161	HILLIS,Adaline	153	. Houston Horace	41	. Lina	3,127
. Jodie Elizabeth	251	. Alice L.	14-15	. Ivena B.	41	. Lina Frances	224
. Joe	251	. Almeda	153	. Jenny	59	. Lizzie	132
. John	134	. Amanda Jane	117	. Loranzo Dow	43	. Lou Venia E.	247
. John A.	161	. Arch Edley	21	. Lottie Geneva	56	. Louvenne Elizabeth	49
. John Alexander	156,161	. Bettie	16	. Mary	150	. Lucy	114
. Johnnie	216	. Bonnie Lee	73	. Ona	59	. Lula	113
. Johnson	166	. Cara	38	. Ova Lee	153	. Lurline	127
. Jonathan P.	160	. Clara Edna	21	. Seawillow	150	. Lydia	135
. Joseph Lee	57	. Clinton Pierce	117	. Sophia Electra	41	. Maggie	132,134
. Julia A.	172	. Connie Avo	35	. Violet	7,43	. Marcus Lafayette	118
. Katherina	121	. Elijah	153	. Violet H.	42	. Martealie	122
. Lafayette	166	. Elizabeth	73	HITTSON,Hershel Bob	65	. Martha	13,132,142
. Lela	134	. Ethel May	61	. William M.	65	. Marvin	132
. Lena	117	. Frank Pierce	117	. Willie	65	. Mary	28,127
. Lennie Pearl	122	. Garmon	13	HIX,Mary Ellen	50	. Mary Maude	112,116,130
. Leonora	157	. Grace D.	62	HOBBS,Alda	116	. Maude	116
. Lillian Lee	157	. James W.	193	. Archibald	142	. Millard Clark	66
. Linsey	142	. Jim	62,255	. Arnold	132	. Myrick	116,118,121
. Livingston	156	. Laura Ann	13-14	. Birtha	132	. Myrtle	124,127
. Lizzie	252	. Lillie	67	. Christopher C.	114	. Nannie Frances	112
. Lizzie Abigail	25	. Lizzie	38	. Christopher H.	122,124	. Noble	132
. Lovicy	156	. Lois Pauline	46	.	132	. Refus	124
. Lucinda	161	. Lucy	21	. Clementine	185	. Richard	122
. Lydia S.	157	. Mary	62,193	. Clifton	132	. Robert	116
. Mark Erwart	122	. Mary Elizabeth	68	. Deida	117	. Rosa Lee	118
. Martha	161	. Mary Etta	7	. Dessie	66	. Rosia	142
. Martha Elizabeth	172	. Melba	117	. Elizabeth	114,122,124	. Rosie	247,252
. Mary	123,126,155	. Melvin	13-14	.	132	. Rufus	124
. Mary Magdalene	117	. Mildred	14	. Emma	111,132,191	. Sallie	224
. Melchizedek	156	. Minnie Louella	29	. Emma Elizabeth	124	. Sarah Elizabeth	118
. Minerva Elizabeth	251	. Nancy	129	. Ester	122	. Stephen	124
. Mollie	122	. Nancy Lodema	31	. Fannie	210	. Tennie P.	30
. N.M.	157	. Nannie	153	. Florence	132	. Thomas H.	132,134
. N.Virginia	157	. Nannie Lou	15	. Flossie Mae	28	. Thomas Marion	116,118
. Nancy	123,142	. Orval	193	. Frank	127	.	121
. Nola	25	. Perry	73	. Frank Madison	252	. Vivian	127
. Obed	172	. Sam W.	62	. Fred	132	. Wilma Lou	112
. Ollie	116	. Solomon	15	. Georgia	66	HOCKETT,Emma Pearl	40
. Ollie Mary Jane	85	HINDS,		. Grover L.	28	. Euless	40
. Phyllis Agnes	116	. Georgia Frances	254	. Harris Gorden	136	. Lois Emma Jean	40
. Polly	156-157	. Oscar Aaron	254	. Hervie	30	HOCKMAN,Ila Irene	245
. Rebecca	155,162	. Oscar Ray	254	. Hollis	132	. Jim	245
. Robbie Lee	252	HINES,Blanche Lemmer	6-7	. Idk	252	HODGE,Adrian	255
. Robert	44	. Franklin	7	. Ike	247	. Ernest	65
. Sallie	162	. Lemma	256	. Ira	126	. Hazel Irene	65
. Sally	44	. Lemmer	6	. Ira Hartley	127	. Julia Mae	65
. Sidney	116	. Lillian Virginia	104	. James	113,118,124,136	HODGES,Barbara A.	129
. Sidney Albert	85,117	. Louise	224	. James Julius	191	. Bertha Lee	111,129
.	123	. Mary Etta	7	. Jane	124	. Della	129
. Susan	161	. Mollie	6	. Janice	127	. Elmer Walter	129
. Susan E.	118	. Urby	7,256	. Janie	118,124,136	. Flossie	49
. Susanna	161	. Urby U.	6	. Jason Blaine	67	. Frank	129
. Susanna Elinor	161	. William	6	. Jean	135	. Hattie	49
. Susannah	156	HINKLEY,Elva	228	. Jim	28	. Ira	49
. Theadoshia	217	. Elva Mai	219	. John	135	. John W.	49
. Vesta	160	. Martha	219,222	. Josie	191	. Walter Eugene	129
. Virgil	155	. Martha B.	238	. Kathy Jean	113	HOGAN,Horace C.	17
		. Myrtle	222				

HOLCOMB,Dan	9	. Monroe	60	HOOPER,Howard	30	. Charles Carrick	70
. H.J.	9	. Paul	60	. Rhoda Kaye	30	. Etta Elaine	40
. Jeptha R.	204	. Peggy Jo	41	. Ruth	30	. Joe	70
. Martha	204	. Wavie Louise	193	HOOSER,Louise Jane	203	. Johnnas A.	70
. Mary	204	. William Arnold	60	HOOSIER,George W.	256	HUETT,Coreba	188
. Mattie	9	. William Howard	193	. Henry	256	HUFFMAN,Stella	43
. Melvina	204	. Zeedler Pauline	60	. Nannie	256	HUGHES Allie	208
HOLDEN,Cordelia	234	HOLLOWAY,Vertice	235	. Sarah	256	HUGHES,Angie	6
. Jesse	234	HOLMAN,Catherine	14	HOOVER,Dalton L	45	. Angie V.	5
. Robert Wellington	234	. George	14	. Dalton L.	40	. Calvin	6
HOLDER,Abbie Coleen	14	. Mildred Elizabeth	14	. Ella Elaine	40	. Daphne Geneva	27
. Amanda Belle	207	HOLMES,Aline	237	. Ila Mai	45	. Donnie	6
. John Henry	207	Robert	237	. Lawrence R.	45	. Emma	133
. Liza	54	HOLT,Barbara Louise	230	. Leoma Frances	45	. Geneva	28
. Louis	207	. Beulah Mae	103	. Leona	40	. Johnnie	6
. Pattie	207	. Billie Ray	105	. Mary	90	. Johnnie N.	6,36
. Roy H.	207	. Elsie	31	. Ronnie Lanier	40	. Katie	227
. Sally	12	. Emma Louella	220	HOPE,Muriel Nadien	72	. Nannie Lou	5
HOLLADNSWORTH,		. Gertrude	105	HOPKINS,Betty S.	246	. Naomi	226
Katherine	148	. Gracie Mae	103	. Bonnie Ann	246	. Nellie H.	5
HOLLAND,Allen	56	. Henderson	102-103	. Charlene	35	. Ocie	6,36
. Arrick Casswell	98	. Herbert Lee	102	. Charles E.	35	. Oshia	111
. Arrick Caswell	170	. Hoyt Oliver	103	. Hugh French	183	. W.C.	5
. BesseiBurch	249	. James Hillard	105	. J.N.	246	. William Calvin	6
. Bettie	98	. Jess	31	. Lucinda	183	. William Calvin Sr.	5
. Clara Belle	170	. Jesse	30	. Malinda Jane	183	HULLETT,John	173
. Cleo	105	. Jesse Fielding	102,105	. Thomas	225	HUMBLE,Isaac	235
. Elizabeth	104	. Jewel	103	HORN,Pearl	234	. Margaret W.	235
. Ellen	56	. Lela Gertrude	159	HORTHCUTT,Elijah	220	. Zachary T.	234
. James William	56	. Margie Irene	105	. Eva	220	HUNNICUTT,Anna Lee	31
. Jimmie L.	73	. Martha C.	102-103	. Mattie	227	. Chester A.	31
. Katrina	57	. Martha Ellen	31	. Sarah	220	. George	31
. Lamb	217	. Mary	103	HOSKINS,Nola	25	. Thelma J.	31
. Lillie	56	. Mary B.	230	HOUSTON,Emma	113	HUNT,Charles	37
. Lois	73	. Mary Bell	102	. John	113	. Daisy	47
. Mary	217	. Mary Belle	103	. Randy	113	. Daisy Susan	46
. Mary Ann	98	. Mary Elizabeth	102	. William	108	. Marie	37
. Priscilla	217	. Moral Lester	103	HOVIS,Lila	235	. Maude	37
. Walter	217	. Myrtie	30	HOWARD,Asa Thornten	66	. Sallie	46
HOLLANDSWORTH,		. Myrtle	31,102	. Evan L.	54-55	. William	46
. Bonnie L.	39	. Myrtle Gertrude	105	. Evelyn	55	HUNTER,Cora	48
. Cleo	187	. Orville Lee	102	. Grovene	54	. Dora	73
. Cleo B.	184	. Raymond Edward	103	. James Franklin	34,66	. Ermon	217
. Elizabeth	184	. Walter Clifton	102	. Lou Dora	34,66	. James C.	48
. Ella	2	. Walter W.	230	. Martha Alice	54-55	. John W.	48
. Elmer L.	39	. Walter Willard	102-103	. Menda Louise	151	. Leona	48
. Ezekiel	187	HOLTZCLAW,Martin E.	76	. Ola Mai	66	. Maggie Ruth	48
. Ezekiel J.	184	. Mildred	76	. Randa Gustava	34	. Mary	217
. Frank B.	184	. Sara Ann Geneva	76	. Robert Lee	102	. Ollie	217
. John	184	. William Martin	76	HOWELL,Drucilla	110	. Rhoda Stincy	172
. Leatha E.	184	HONEYCUTT,Elmer R.	75	. Emmaline	10	HUNTLEY,Ballard	38
. Robert C.	187	. Emma Lorine	21	. Flora	70	. Cora	38
HOLLINGSWORTH,Hattie	14	. George Larry	21	. James Otto	38	. Mildred Lee	38
HOLLINS,Louise	34	. Linda L.	75	. Victoria	91	HURST,Heck	89
Ted Eldred	34	. Robert Dale	75	HOWSER,Elaine	29	HURT,Willie	25
HOLLIS,Aldena	41	. Sallie	21,75	HUDDLESON,Odell	215	HUSKIN,Martha	219,222
. Arthur	41	. William	75	HUDDLESTON,Asberry	213	HUSSEY,Henry	252
. Dewey Franklin	41	. William Luther	21	. Emma	213	. John Alford	252
. Ethel	193,197-198	HOOD,Athron T.	63	. Henry Clay	255	. John Alfred	243
. George D.	193,198	Margie P.	63	. Isham	213	. Lila Ann	227
. George David	197	HOODENPYL,Phillip G.	254	HUDGENS,Sally	32	. Lula Ann	243
. Grace	197	Phoebe	254	HUDSON,Alma Lee	70	. Martha	252
. Jo Ann	198	HOODENPYLE,Mary	92	. Austin Pea	40	. Martha Ann	243
. John H.	198	Sarah	122	. Austin Peay	70	. Martha Jane	253
. Mary	60	HOOKER,James E.	175	. Berchie Mozell	40,70	. Mary J.	237

Name	Page	Name	Page	Name	Page	Name	Page
HUSSEY,(cont)		JARRELL,Charles	197	. Elma Jean	112	. Claudia	80
. Mary Jane	243	. Frances M.	62	. Ersey	120	. Daniel	201
. Myrtle Inex	237	. J.Willard	62	. Eva	55	. David Franklin	184
. Nettie	26	. Lizzie	197	. Firm Thomas	31	. Delilah	203
. Terry H.	237	. Myrtle	197,200	. Garner Cleveland	232	. Della	152
. Terry Henry	243	. Patricia Ann	32	. Harrison	184	. Donald Lynn	28
HUTCHINGS,Amon	22	. Rena	16	. James	202	. Dosia	204
. Catherine	22	. Rona Catherine	220	. James E.	47	. Edith	228
. Curry Sylvanus	22	JENKINS,Mattie	92	. James Edward	218	. Effie	76
. James T.	60	Thelma	31	. James Louis	47	. Eli	209-210
. Mary Ann	22	JENNINGS,Alace	119	. James T.	241	. Eliza	212
. Mildred Annie	47	. Alade	120	. John Franklin	227	. Eliza Jane	94-95,97
. Myrtle	60	. Alice	125,165	. Julia	184	. Elizabeth	70,93
HUTCHINS,Claiborne W.	32	. Annie C.	177	. Kizzie	64	. Elizbeth	67
. Liza	48	. Aselean	177	. Leonard C.	70	. Ellen	58
. Louise T.	32	. Asilean	178	. Lodema	42	. Emily T.	87
. Melissa	223	. Aubrey F.	178	. Louise	241	. Ermon	217
. Olla Belle	48	. Aubrey Frances	177	. Lucinda	3	. Eula Vic	14
. Peggy E.	76	. Beatrice	43	. Mary	154,202,227	. Evelyn Lois	184
. Sallie Belle	48	. Belzora	112	. Mary Katherine	227	. Francis Marion	28
. Webb	48	. Burley W.	177	. Mildred L.	47	. Frank	70
. Webster P.	48	. Clabe	112	. Minnie Mae	237	. Furm Washington	203
HUTSON,Mary	27	. Emma Irene	112	. Nancy	162	. George	16,69
HYATT,Clara Edna	21	. Ethel May	61	. Nancy Elizabeth	20	. George Leland	204
Lawrence E.	21	. Franklin H.	165	. Nancy Lodema	31	. Grace B.	16
Harris,Haley	51	. George	165	. Novella	44	. Hannah	205
IRBY,Mary Ruth	14	. Goebel	61	. Polly	157,161-162	. Harry Lee	20
Unice	14	. J.W.	177	. Rachel	28	. Hattie	210-211
IVEY,Ruby	35	. James	77	. Roy Eugene	232	. Hazel	20
JACKSON,Annie	73	. Jane	165	. Russell	202	. Hilda	28
. Emma	30	. Jane Vickers	119	. Sally	23	. Hugh L.	208
. Robert Corker	73	. Jess	43	. Sarah	202	. Ida	16
. Ruth	73	. Jesse Dodson	119	. Silas Oziar	44	. Isaac	204
JACO,Asker	201	. Jessie	112	. Thelma B.	70	. J.Claude	209
. E.L.	201	. Jessie Dodson	165	. Victor	17	. J.E.	93
. Eliza	229	. Lena Frances	178	. Violet	133	. J.F.	209
. Elizabeth K.	63	. Lillie	43	. Willie Joe	232	. J.M.	140
. Elzy	201	. Lillie Elvira	61	. Wilma	44	. J.W.	209
. J.Hubert	63	. Macon Nicholas	177	JOINES,Dellie W.	2	. James	203
. Louise	83	. Nettie	28	. John Harrison	2	. James D.	32
. Marie	106	. Sally	137	. Orvel Clayton	2	. James Herbert	184
. Maude	45	. Sarah Adeline	165	. Tennec Indiana	2	. Janice L.	20
. Solon	63	. Stella	77	JONES,Abraham	134	. Jennie	209-211
. Tabitha	10	. Susanna Linton	227	. Albert	28	. Jerald Randall	58
. Tina	63	. Sylvia Ann	177	. Alcinda	204	. Jess	76
JACOBS,Allie	98	. Tennie	77	. Alice	81	. Jesse London	204
. Charles A.	39	. Thomas	165	. Allie Mintie	210	. Jesse Noel	204
. Cheslie	69	. Vurner L.	177	. Alminta	210	. Jewell H.	210
. Dorothy Mae	39	. Wilma Ruth	165	. Alsey	203-204	. Jim	58
. Ella Lee	4	JENT,Catherine	31	. Alta	168	. Joe	58
. Frank	69	JOHNSON,Albert James	3	. Alta Jane	70	. John C.	205
. Jack B.	69	. Alice	47	. Amanda	208	. John P.	210
. Juanita	69	. Alma E.	31	. Amanda Elizabeth	209	. Johnnie Mildred	184
. Lena	98	. Andy	202	. Andrew	246	. Joseph L.	56,94
. Lou Etta	98	. Audrey Aileen	17	. Bellzora	94	. Josephine	246
. Mattie	98	. Bessie	74	. Bessie	111	. Lavern	28
. Minnie Lee	98	. Bill	3	. Bettie	56	. Lela Jo	76
JAKES,Bettie	194	. Calvin	202	. Bitty	58	. Lela Mai	7
. Catherine	194	. Cecil	44	. Bob	87	. Lillie	87
. John	194	. Cleo	187	. Bryan	58	. Linda D.	58
. Samuel Toney	194	. Cleo B.	184	. Ceallie	134	. Linda Doris	58
JAMES,Bessie Lero	195	. Daisy	17	. Charity	203	. Lizzie	197
. Grace G.	16	. Dianne Faye	218	. Charlie	58,80	. Lodie	39
. H.F.	195	. Elizabeth	202	. Chester E.	55-56	. Lou	97,188
. L.M.	195	. Ellen Lucille	218	. Clara	53	. Louise	32,179

==

JONES, (cont)		JORDAN, Anderson	135	. Ruby	40	. Nancy	29
. Louvernia	80-81	. Annie Cordelea	142	. Sam Cordell	40	. Nancy Missoura	80
. Lucille	55	. Claude	27	. Shirley Ann	236	. Robert	78
. Lucinda Frances	209	. David Miller	62	. Thomas Henry	40	. Robert J.C.	78
. Luzena Emaline	100	. Deborah	28	. Tom	201	. Ruth T.	29
. Luzena Emuline	94	. Dora Bell	27	. Virginia Carol	150	. Thomas	81
. Lydia White	157	. Dorcas	135	JULIAN, Florence M.	13	. Thomas Philmore	80
. Martha L.	95	. Edna S.	74	. Lloyd	13	. Wilbert	78
. Mary	202,209	. Elizabeth	7-8	. Mary	13	. Zora	81
. Mary Adaline	210	. Florence	7	. Will	13	. Zora Myrtle	87-88
. Mary Ann	134	. Frances W.	10	KAHLER, Sophia	135	KELL, Angeline	206
. Mary Bell	204	. Geneva	28	KAY, Ella Louise	117	. Claude	27
. Mary Lou	184	. Georgia	27	KEATHLEY, Emma	113	. Isabella	206
. Matthew	209	. Gladys Elizabeth	51	KEATON, Annie	87	. Le Roy	27
. Matthew Jenkins	204	. Gladys M.	26	. Billy	81	. Lydia	206
. Mattie	209	. Harold L.	74	. Cynthia	87-88	. Lydia E.	206
. Melvina	204	. James Henry	229	. Delilia	88	. Mary	206
. Mildred Lavoun	28	. Jesse	27	. Della Jane	78	. Nimrod	206
. Minnie Adeline	203-204	. Josephine	62	. James	84,88	. Sarah	131
. Nancy Jane	204	. Lila Ann	223	. John	87	. Sarah Ellen	27
. Nettie	140,208	. Lina Frances	224	. Kennie	81	. Sarah Othala	27
. Noah B.	210	. Lou	229	. Martha	84,88	. Thomas	206
. Nonnie Ethel	28	. Louise	224	. Mary Elizabeth	84	. William	206
. Ollie	9	. Magness	27-28	. Maudie Agnes	88	KELLEY, B.F.	30
. Orville Lee	39	. Martha Lee	51	. Minnie Belle	85	. Bedford Forest	112,133
. Ova	9	. Mary Alvesta	62	. Mollie	81	. Bessie	83
. Pharibe Angeline	93-94	. Mary Harriet	8	. Mollie J.	78	. Bethel	83
. Philander D.	94-95	. Melissa	229	. Monroe	84	. Carden Hubert	30
. Polly	205	. Mike	28	. Nancy E. Jane	87	. Charles David	112
. Rachel	28	. Nancy Tabitha	142	. Nancy T. Ann	78	. Clara	30
. Rebecca	200	. Ollie S.	229	. Ollie	116	. Lucy	83
. Rebecka Mary	205	. Robert Kelton Sr.	8	. Ollie Mary Jane	85	. Mary Wilma	30
. Rochel	53	. Robert L.	51	. Peter	78	. Mattie	81
. Ruby	52	. Robert Lee	7-8	. Peter N. James	78	. Motie Gertrude	83
. Ruby Mae	39	. Sandra Kay	54	. Quixie Lucille	84	. Susie	112
. Russell	87	. Sarah	252	. Sam	87-88	. Sylvia	112
. Ruth Ann	209-210	. Thomas	224,229	. Tennie	77	KELLIAN, Lear	164
. S.R.	9	. Tom	142	. Vannie	81	KELLY, Bessie Louisa	80
. Sam M.	70	. W. Albert	7	. William Laurence	84	. Bethel	80
. Samantha Jane	255	. William Perry	224	. William Lawrence	85	. Flora	86
. Samantha Paralee	202	JORDEN, Anderson	134	. Willie K.	84	. Lucy	80
. Sarah	246	Dorcus	134	KEEL, Byron	16,220	. Motie Gertrude	84
. Sarah Ann	32	JORDON, Alvin Thomas	236	. Charles Edward	16	KELSEY, Christine	19
. Sarah C.	97	. Edith Jane	236	. Gladys Beatrice	220	. Nancy L.	19
. Sarah Janes	55	. Henry	236-237	. Hawrie Louis	220	. Roberta	19
. Stella	43	. Lila Ann	224	. Louise	16	. Stanley T.	19
. Sue	232	. Linnie Frances	236	. Rena	16	. Vester B.	19
. Susah	201	. Mary	232	. Rona Catherine	220	KELTON, Florence	7
. Susan	204-205	. Molly Evon	236-237	KEENER, Brady	24	KEMP, R.C.	135
. Susie	58	. Norma Tracy	237	. Clarence Edward	165	KENDRICK, Mattie	34
. Sussie E.	204	. William Perry	236	. Delbert D.	165	KENNAMER, Abe	51
. Tabitha	110	. Willie	255	. Erlene	165	. Ella	51
. Taylor	55	JUDKINS, Alta Jane	70	. Jewell	165	. J.Harvey	51
. Terry Chester	55	. Bessie Jane	201	. Landon Brady	24	. Jewell	51
. Thelma	32	. Callie	70-71,236	. Leona	24	. Maggie	51
. Thelma A.	69	. Callie Ann	40	KEILBERG, Laura	39	. Patsy	51
. Thomas A.	110	. Dillard Edward	236	KEITH, Annie	181	KENNEDY, G.B.	108
. Vinnie	203	. Estelle	71	. Helen	19	Mary Ann	224-225
. Virgie Mae	42	. Georgie	236	. Isaac	29	KENNER,	
. Virginia R.	55	. Henry Thomas	236	. Isaac Lee	80	. Benjamin Franklin	61
. Virginia Ruth	56	. Howard R.	40	. J.B.	29	. Elizabeth	224
. William	41,202	. Lillian	50	. Jane	81	. Mary Elizabeth	61
. Willie	217	. Mozell	72	. Lela	80	. Mary Jo	61
. Zachariah B.	94-95,97	. Nancy L.	40	. Lissie	78	. William Monroe	61
. Zula	58	. Perry Green	70-71	. Lucy Jane	80	KERSEY, Luann	101

Name	Page	Name	Page	Name	Page	Name	Page
KESEY,Cleo	5,144	. Letha	147,158	. Emeline	138,208	. Walter Philip	151
Lizzie	43	. Lethia	148	. Henry Clay	211	KRAMER,Ida	33
KIDD,Dora Alice	49	. Lillian Virginia	48	. Hila Elizabeth	98	LACRONE,Edna Mae	57
. Jane	27	.	104	. James	211	LAFEVER,Arthur J.	57
. Joe	22	. Lillie Mabel	147-148	. Jasper	138	. Atlas	50
. Tennessee W.	22	. Linda E.	104	. Jim H.	4	. Lena	43
. Velma	22	. Lois	79	. John	92,138	. Maudie Mae	42
KILGORE,Malissie	44	. Lottie	149	. John Sampson	208	LAKE,Dallas	69
KILLIAN,Clemma Iola	111	. Lucinda	141	. Johnny Ray	50	. Dallas L.	68
. Henry M.	111	. Lucy	79,151	. Junior Floyd	50	. Eleanor	69
. Lear	152,155	. Maggie Hampton	248	. Kiyomi	50	. Eleanor Z.	68
. Savannah	111	. Mardie E.	151	. Lassie M.	4	. Eva	193
KILMER,Hulda	101	. Margaret	152	. Laura Louise	211	. Margaret Ann	69
. Lottie	101	. Martha	77	. Lena	98	. Mary	68
. Van R.	101	. Mary	158,183	. M.	92	. Thaxton B.	68
KIMBRO,Elizabeth	221-222	. Mary E.	152	. Malinda	209	LAKEY,Anna	206
. Elizabeth P.	224	. Mary Lou	238,248	. Malissa	137	. Lydia	206
.	239-240	. Matilda E.	84	. Marshall Filmore	137	. Simon	206
. John	240	. Matt	169	. Martha	211	. Thomas	206
. Prudence	240	. Maude	231	. Mary	211	LAMB,Percilla	215-216
KINDLEY,Jack	169	. Melinda Sue	149	. Mary Caroline	209-210	LAMBERT,Ferbie	58
. Mary L.	169	. N.B.	77	. Mattie	4	LAMY,Alcide Joseph	26
. Sallie	169	. Nancy	206	. Melinda	138	LANCASTER,Cora	226
KING,A.D.	81	. Nancy E. Jane	87	. Melvina	211	. J.Hughes	226
. Adam U.	79	. Newell James	77	. Millie C.	137	. James Richard	226
. Agnes	77,87	. Newton Alex	149	. Minnie	92	. Naomi	226
. Andrew	151	. Ollie	150	. Robert Shelley	208	LANCE,Ada	3
. Anna	243	. Osmond	148-149	. Rosanna	208,211	. Agnes U.	56
. Berthenia	150	. Phillip	206	. S.J.	138	. Albert	179
. Betsy	155	. R.L. Jr.	147	. Sarah Jackaline	208	. Aldena	41
. Betty June	148-149	. Rhoda Gay	149	. Susanna	211	. Alice Matilda	179
. Cynthia	87-88	. Robert Lee	147-148	. Susie Octa	98	. America Isabell	176
. Cynthia J.	77	. Rosa Lee	149	. T.G.	50	. Annabell	95
. David R.	48,104	. Sarah Lucinda	82	. Thurman G.	1	. Annie B.	4
. Dora	149	. Selma	79	. William	138,208-209	. Barbara Jean	59
. Dovie	81	. Sharon	23	.	211	. Bettie V.	181
. Edna E.	81	. Susan	148	. William J.	210	. Betty Ann	179,186
. Elijah	150	. Susie	150	. William James	211	. Bill	3
. Elizabeth	206	. T.Hatton	81	. William Taylor	209-210	. Billy E.	3
. Ella	75	. Thelma	79	KIRKLEY,Christbelle	56	. Buster	59
. Fannie	248	. Thomas Jefferson	238	KIRKPATRICK,		. Clowdy Hebron	11
. Frances	238	. Timothy Mark	71	Mary Rebecca	228	. Eliza	179,212
. Frances E.	228	. W.J.	77	KIRSCHBAUM,		. Ellen V.	183
. Frances Elizabeth	118	. William Decator	141	Phyllis A.	234	. Ellenalida	181
. Hannah Brooke	71	. William H.	81	KITSOS,John D.	96	. Ervin C.	212
. Hattie Mae	75	. William Jordan	77	Minnie	96	. Fannie	187
. Inis L.	148	. William White	238-239	KNIGHT,Bitty	58	. Flavil Kermit	179
. Jackie D.	48	.	248	. Cinda Down	28	. George	187
. Jacob Troy	48	. Wilson Cleary N.	206	. Paul D.	28	. Hallie	59
. James	77,87	KINNEY,Bruce	30	. Susannah	126,161	. Haner	212
. Jasper	141	. Elmer R.	30	KNOWLAND,		. Hannah	212
. Jennie	79	. Livina	30	Murdis Marie	147	. Hattie Lou	176
. Jesse	149	. Vesta L.	30	KNOWLES,Alice	65	. Helen H.	3
. Jessie H.	48,104	KINSER,Isabella	74	. Elizabeth	63	. Henry	179,212
. Jessie M.	48	. Jacob	74	. Homer Douglas	63	. Henry Balem	176
. Jessie Mae	148	. Pearl	74	. Lou Ann	63	. Henry D.	56
. John H.	206	KIRBY,Abner B.	98	. Minnie Myrtle	63	. Ida	179
. John M.	79	. Ada Magaline	211	. Mollie Louveda	63	. James	183
. John Miller	82	. Alfred	137	. Myrtle	63	. James Albert	179,186
. John R.	147-148,158	. Benjamin L.	211	. Pierce	63	. James Jasper	181
. Johnnie T.	78-79	. Charlie	210	KNUDSON,Clifford	70	. Jesse Euberne	176
. Kathy Annette	71	. Clementine	199	Jean Ann	70	. Jewel	95
. Kinnie	81	. Eliza E.	107	KOCHLER,Sophia	135	. Joseph N.	183
. Laura	143,149	. Eliza Elliott	57	KOHLUS,Chris Edward	151	. June	95
. Lela Ruth	141	. Emaline	211	. Ida Mae	151	. Kenneth	3

===

LORING,(cont)		. William L.	256	MADEWELL,Addie M.	117	. Samuet Houston	34

LORING,(cont)
. Mary 83
LOUGE,David Ramsey 232
. Mary Ann 232
. Verna Ellen 232
. William Martin 232
LOVE,Effie 34
. Effie L. 20
. Hattie 23
. James Landon 23
. Josie M. 23
. Katherine 53
. Martin Luther 53
. Mildred 23
. Sarah 23
. Shirley 23,54
. Shirlie 53
. Sylvapia 23
. Thomas Riley 23
. Tommy 23
. Willie Robert 23
LOVELL,Nora 33,76
LOWE,Belle 71
. Betty 219-220,229,235
. Charles 219
. Charlie 254
. Fannie 255
. Hennie 12
. Joe 255
. John 12
. Mary 125
. Mary Ellen 12
. Sallie 254
. Sarah 219
. Tennie 255
LOWERY,Albert Grace 90
. Ann Elizabeth F. 224
. Maggie Rruth 48
. Nettie Mae 55
. Olen O. 90
LOWRY,Frank 47
. Jane 47
. Mildred Annie 47
. Nolia 47
. Randolph Taylor 47
LUKENBAUGH,Patricia 42
. Paul 42
. Velma 42
LUNA,Burgess Wayne 52
. Jamie Jenell 52
. Liza 48
. Mary 5
. Nancy Kay 52
. Sarah C. 232
. Sarah Catherine 221
. Tina 63
LUSK,Beulah 217
. Ella Mai 6
. Etta 213
. Harriet 131
. John D. 256
. Louvisa 256
. Mary Elizabeth 131
. Pamelia 256
. Sarah 225-226

. William L. 256
LUTRELL,Caroline 196
. Catherine 253
. Fannie 187
. Frances Lula 230
. John William 230
. Lillie Candas 232
. Mary F. 176
. Matilda P. 176
. Willford 176
. William Dorsey 230
LUTTRELL,Crockett 231
. Frances Lula 231
. John William 231
. Rosa Jane 231
LYLE,Elizabeth 232
. Janie G. 78
. Maude 78
. Robert Lee 83
. Susan Laverne 61
. Vera Pearl 83
. W.F. 78
LYLES,Mourning B. 78
  james Thomas 78
LYNCH,Emma Euphemea 117
. Emma Euphemia 85
. Euphemy 155
. William 155
LYNN,Martha 10
  William 10
LYTLE,
. Alley Walter M.L. 129
. Beatrice 165
. Beecher Jewel 69-70
. Elizabeth 120,123,253
. 257
. George 152
. George W. 154-155
. Glenn Arlis 146
. James 257
. James Jefferson 69,152
. 166
. Johney 154
. Julia Ida 154
. K.M. 146
. Malinda 166
. Marcus 146
. Margaret Pearl 69,152
. Mary 158,166
. Mary Elizabeth 69
. Mina Jane 152,154
. Nadean 129
. Nettie Lee 129
. Pearl 152
. Ralph Douglas 146
. Robert D. 154
MABRY,John Davidson 109
. Julia 109
. Martha 109
. Mary Brown 109
. Nathaniel 109
. Thomas Elliott 109
MADDOX,Clarrisa 248
  James W. 248
MADDUX,Theodore 172

MADEWELL,Addie M. 117
. Addie Marie 116
. Arthur 14-15,50
. Beulah 117
. Charles 149
. Charles B. 143
. Clemmie 116
. Della 143,149
. Dicie 171
. Elizabeth 15
. Ethel 14-15,50
. Flora Golda 149
. Goldie 149
. James Willard 14
. Johnnie L. 149
. Juanita 57
. Laura 143,149
. Mildred E. 14
. Naomi 50
. Odie Avin 50
. Richard 116
. Rilla A. 149
. Shirley L. 149
. Sidney 143
. Sidney Clayborn 149
. Vinnie 146,151
. Wilma Adean 149
MADISON,Addison Eli 133
. Mary 111
. Molly 133
MAEBURY,Aaron 216
. Cyrus 216
. Jane 216
. Sarah 216
MAGNESS,Green G. 248
. Hanna Narcissus 248
. Martha 248
MAHAR,Pamela Jo 11
  Paul 11
MAHER,Carrie 171
  George 171
MALONE,Elizabeth E. 15
. Ellen 56
. Frances May 92
. Mable B. 92
. Mattie 92
. Roy Leon 92
. Samuel Hayes 92
MALONEY,Pearl 233
  W.M. 233
MANFORD,Helen 88
MANIS,Rosemary 20
MANN,Ora 221
MANSELL,Dorothy 70
MANSFIELD,Elizabeth 114
. 124
. Jeff 155
. Mina Jane 154-155
. Minerva Jane 121
. Sarah Elizabeth 114
. Thomas Jefferson 114
MANSVILLE,Elizabeth 118
  Minerva jane 118
MANTOOTH,Clyde C. 34
. Monnie C. 34

. Samuet Houston 34
MANUS,Minnie Gertrude 72
. Steve 72
. Willie Mae 72
MARBERRY,Aaron 201
. Ella 201
. Isaac 201
MARBURY,Aaron 214,218
. Cora 217
. Cyrus 217
. Elizabeth 213
. Elnora 214
. Ethel 214,218
. Ivy Lynn 213
. Ivy Willis 213
. Jack 215,218
. James Bostick 213
. John 213
. Katherine 213
. Kent Labell 213
. Lucinda 215,218
. Lucy 215,217
. Marietta 214
. Mary 218
. Mary Ann 213
. Sarah 215
. Simon 213
. Tilla 213
. Tiller 218
MARCOM,Geneva Joyce 59
. Jack Malcolm 59
. Robert 59
MARCUM,Leander 204
. Rosanna 204
. S.B. 203
. Sarah Elizabeth 204
MARKOWSKI,Edward C. 38
  Virginia Faye 38
MARKS,Lula 216
MARKUM,Alfred 193
. Charles 190
. Dalton 193
. Delia 190,193
. Ike 190
. Isaac M. 193
. J.M. 190
. Sarah 190
MARLER,
. James Alexander 204
. 205
. Joseph L. 205
. Martha J. 205
. Susan 204-205
MARSHALL,Carrie 44
MARSINI,Augustus 112
. Billie Sue 112
. John A. 112
. Mary 112
MARTIN,Andrew 143
. Annie 189,193,198,250
. Arcola 146
. Bettie 97
. Bradford A. Jr. 49
. Bradford Allen 49
. Cyrus Haston 22

==

MARTIN,(cont)
. Elijah   117
. Elijah Martin   157
. Elizabeth   118,153,248
. Ella Mae   27
. Elmer   54
. Elwood   22
. Emma   153
. Ernest   169
. Ester   22
. Eugene   117
. Eulous   68
. Eva   48
. Fannie   104
. Fannie Maude   105
. Floey   35
. Flossie Mae   28
. Floyd   153
. Frances   37,167,170
. George Alvin   48
. George Anderson   48
. Gwendolyn   49
. Harriet   27,117
. Hattie   240,252
. Henry   28
. Homer   12
. Howard   15
. Ida   49
. Jesse   153,193
. Joe   169
. John   169
. John E.   193
. Juanita R.   68
. Julia Mae   65
. Laura   170
. Lillie   169
. Lou Cindy   117
. Louella   193
. Lydia S.   157
. Mahala   131
. Mahalia   165
. Margorie   169
. Marion   193
. Marjorie A.   54
. Martha   190,193
. Martha E.   68
. Mary   62,143,193
. Mary Ann   165,232
. Mary Elizabeth   5
. Mary Elizabth   147
. Nancy Ann   189
. Nannie   153
. Nettie   28
. Nora   167,170-171
. Peggy   63
. Permeta   143
. Rachel   193
. Rance   27
. Rebecca   158
. Richard   193
. Richard H.   190
. Robert   117
. Robert M.   97
. Ruth   86
. Sallie Elizabeth   22

. Sam Sr.   27
. Sarah   142
. Sarah Catherine   150
.   152,165
. Sarah Jane   235
. Suella   193
. Theodore   68
. Thomas   169
. Tilly   12
. William Andrew   165
. William R.   131
. Wilsie Le   12
. Wilson   12
. Zora Belle   43
MASEY,Elizabeth Jane 207
. Ellis   207
. Frank   207
. James M.   207
. James Odis   207
. L.Randolph   238
. Lillie Brown   207
. Lucinda   238
. Margaret E.   238
. Margaret J.   207
. Margaret V.   207
. Nellie E.   207
. Randolph   238
. Rufus Lewis   207
. Sarah A.   93
. Serena   91,93
. Solomon   93,227
. Thiren Mae   207
. W.W.   207
MASON,Anna Belle   105
. Donald Richard   34-35
. Dorothy B.   57
. Ester Louise   34
. Evelyn Carrie   105
. Fannie   236
. George L.   34
. Kenneth Elton   105
. Linsey Elton   105
. Melba Jean   34
. Phillip   57
. Ritter   215
. Stephanie Renee   57
MASSEY,Ann   167
  Madeline   58
MASTERS,
. Albert Leonard   245
. Dora V.   237
. Elizabeth Ann   237
. Glenda Faye   112
. James B.   237
. Jesse Newton   237
. Margie   27
. Myrtle Inex   237
. Thelma Jean   245
MASTON,Pheobe   109
MATHEWS,Margaret J.   65
MATHIAS,Carl   34
. John Robert   34
. Lillie   34
. Sarah   34
. Terry Michael   34

MATHIS,Alta   43
. Bluford   43
. Bob C.   180
. Charlotta   138
. Connie Josephine   82
. Dewey S.   82
. E.Carl   82
. Edd Clayton   180
. Ellis Homer   178
. F.M.   82
. Fred Gray   180
. Grace   180
. Hassie Loring   48
. Hiram W.   82
. I.L.   82
. John Horace   82
. Lena Frances   178
. M.J.   82
. Marris Ray   82
. Mary   43
. Mildred   180
. Nadean R.   82
. Nora E.   180
. Nova   178
. Ollie May   82
. Robert Tullis   82
. S.M.   82
. Sarah Elizabeth   77
. Tamar Agnes   180
. Velma L.   82
. W.B.   178
. Will B.   180
MATTESON,Andrew J.   90
  Mattie   90
MATTHEWS,Hannah   89
. Lemuel   89
. Lena P.   89
. Mary Jane   89
. Thomas   89
MATTINGLY,Clarence   1
. Edith   1
. Edith Jenitta   1
. Treva Willodene   1
MATTOX,Anna   14
MAUGHAM,Irene   38
MAXEY,Emma   170
MAXWELL,Allie   36,67
. Atlas   50
. Grady M.   50
. Jane Vickers   119
. John   50
. Josie   50
. Maggie E.   120
. Margaret Elizabeth 127
. Mary Edna   123,127
. Sara Jane   27
. Sarah Jane   120
. William M.   120,127
MAYES,Charlene   32
MAYFIELD,
. Billy Marshall   44
. Carl J.   17
. Carrie   44
. Dessie B.   17
. Florence   240

. Joe   44
. Marie   44
. Mary   164
. Waymon   240
MAYNARD,Betty Ann   91
. Edna   18
. K.T.   18
. Kelly   18
. Liza   18
. Ruby   91
. William Lawson   91
. Wortie B.   18
MAYO,
. Benjamin Granklin 180
. Ellen   117,125,130
. Ernest   178
. George W.   120,125-126
. Grace Marie   180
. Herc Lee   180
. Louisa Jane   178
. Luella   126
. Maggie E.   120
. Margaret Elizabeth 127
. Paul   180
. Sarah   120,125-126
. Stacy   180
. Zora   180
MAZEY,Jesse   64
MEADOWS,Anna   9
. Augustus   162
. C.H.   135
. Deborah   162
. E.   118
. Emma I.   115,118
. Flossie   17
. Ida Elizabeth   119
. Jerome J.   115,118
. Josephine   135
. Margie Lee   118
. Mary Ethel   25
. Pearl   163
. Sarah Jane   118,162
. Sarah Janie   115-116
.   119
. Vincent   118
. Virginia A.   162
. William Morris 118,162
MEARS,Carmon R.   187
. Elizabeth   198
. Lucille M.   187
. Mary Frances   249
MEDLEY,Avo   23
. Carolyn   106
. Charlie C.   1
. Codie   55
. Dollie Bertha   55
. Essie   1
. G.T.   101
. George   55
. Gina   106
. Hazel   101
. Jessica Rae   106
. Katherine   55
. Larry Hugh   106
. Lucille   1

==

MEDLEY,(cont)	. Raymond 246	. John 198	. Kaytella A. 58
. Mary 19	. Richard A. 246	. Julia 199	. Kelly O'Neal 89
. Mildred 106	. Richard Allen 245-246	. Leona 198	. Laura 200
. Rachel Evalee 31	. Richard Estil 246	. Lou Cindy 198	. Leander A. 190
. Rachel Evelee 19,53	MESSICK,Brady 1	. Mary Jo 61	. Lena 75
. Royce 106	. Chrisley 1	. Mattie Ruth 61	. Leona 177
. S.J. 101	. Christine 1	. Newton 251	. Louella 194
. Verna Mae 23	. Clinton 1	. Newton Calvin 198	. Madeline 58
. William 19	. Eliza 195	. Theodore 251	. Malinda 89
MEEHAM,Ruth 86	. Ella 1	MILSTEAD,Allie 18	. Martha 89,193-194
MEEKS,Mollie 152	. Flowdy 1	. Alma 131	. Martin C. 190
MELTON,Alfred Foster 93	. Lida 1	. Carrie Jane 115	. Mary 188
. Amanda E. 93	MEURY,Bessie 19	. Claud 111	. Mary Evaline 79,84,86
. Bertha 20	. Frank 19	. Edna 111	. Mary Jane 138,194
. Dorothy 235	. Georgia Elizabeth 19	. Eona 111	. Melinda Josephine 89
. Elizabeth 92	MIDDLETON,Jeanette 1	. George Eugene 114-115	. Nancy J. 190
. Emma 21	MILES,Elizabeth 134	. Irene 113,115,129	. Nina Mae 89
. Ethel 74,91	MILLER,Arthur 36	. Janie Irene 115	. Octa M. 79
. Furby 249	. Bill 11	. Jesse 131	. Oliver 84
. Georgia Lee 178	. Charles Lee 36	. Lee 131	. R.M. 177
. Hattie B. 200	. Claude Chester 73	. Lena 111,130	. Robert 193
. John R. 200	. Dora 11,73	. Lena Mary 114	. Robert A. 190
. Joseph 91-92	. Dorotha 11	. Lizzie 11	. Villa Odra 89
. Liza Parasada 200	. E. 203	. Lorene 130	. Wylene 42
. MacClin Petway 92	. Edna 36	. Magdalene 130	MIXON,Georgia Illa 30
. Martha 93	. Eli 73	. Mary Edith 114-115	MOFFITT,Aaron 118,162
. Martha E. 54,188,209	. Howard P. 38	. Samuel Claud 114	. Adaline 153
. Mary 92	. Irene 38	. 130-131	. B.F. 22
. Mary F. 176	. Jane 42	. Serena Janie 130	. Elijah L. 233
. Minnie 92	. Jessie B. 104	. Thomas Earl 111	. Elijah Lewis 116
. P.E. 91	. Julia 51	. Waymon Gary 115	. Elizabeth 118
. Pheobe 96	. Leroy 11	. William 130-131	. Emma Queen 116
. Ruth Ann 189-190	. Linda E. 48	MINER,Laura Lee 37	. Eva McCrary 117
. Sara Mai 21	. Lonnie Mason 104	. Melissa Jane 37	. Evelyn 233
. Sarah 91	. Martha Gipson 127	. Tom 37	. F.M. 119
. Sarah Catherine 91	. Mary 56,128,203	MINNICK,Elizabeth 59	. Francis Marion 118
. Stacy 180	. Mary E. 19	MITCHELL,	. Gentry Ward 233
. Thomas Calvin 91	. Mary Elizabeth 73	. Amanda Malvina 89	. Guy Robert 117
. Willie 21	. Mary Hoida 5	. Arthur 89	. Harriet 27,118,162
MERRIMAN,Ada Louella 241	. Mary Jane 125	. Blanch 190	. Haskel Bouldin 115-116
. Allen 247	. Myrick 116,118,121	. C.Robert 193-194	. 119
. Annie Clarissy 223	. Norma J. 45	. Clara Bell 84	. Haskel Jerome 115
. Birdie 246	. Oscar L. 38	. Cynthia 193	. Herbert 22
. Clyde 246	. Pat 36	. D.W.A. 194	. Ira May 233
. Clyde E. 245	. Ronnie 104	. Dave 138	. Lester Bouldin 233
. Elie H. 247	. Rosie Mildred 104	. Dora 3,177	. Maggie 117
. Emmaline E. 247	. Shirley Ann 36	. Eliza Mae 86	. Maggie Lou 118
. Estelle McCartney 246	. Will 65	. Elizabeth 138	. Maggie Queen 116
. Harold Carr 245	. Worth 11	. Ella 190,193	. Mary 118
. Ila Irene 245	MILLIGAN,Alex 200	. Evaline 87	. Mary Louise 233
. Isaac M. 246-247	. Genora N. 200	. Flora Bell 87	. May 233
. Isaac Mack 219,223	. Hattie B. 200	. G.M. 200	. Mollie 118
. Lenora 245-246	. Rebecca 200	. George W. 79,84,86-87	. Ophia Evelyn 9,233
. Lewis 247	. Susan Ella 178	. Georgia Anna 89	. Patrick Narve 118
. Lida 1	MILLRANEY,Ella Mae 27	. Greenberry 193	. Pauline 21-22
. Martha 247	. Jane 27	. Guy 58	. Queen 233
. Martha Celina 223,246	. John 27	. Hallie Ethel 84	. Ruth 22
. Martha Selina 219	MILLS,Bertha Cecil 199	. Harmon T. 89	. Sarah Jane 118,162
. Martha Smith 246	. Cantrell 5,61	. Hixie 79	. Sarah Janie 115,119
. Mary Matilda 247	. Dollie 198	. Homer 190	. Tennie 118-119
. Matilda Jane 247	. Dollt 251	. Hoyte Lee 188	. Venus 117
. May Belle 219	. Fowler Elizabeth 199	. James Tillman 86	. Venus C. 118
. Nettie 245-246	. James Herschell 199	. Jane 193	. Wallace Hermon 119
. Noel Bomar 246	. James William 199	. John 193	MONAHAN,Mildred F. 246
. Particia 246	. Jodie 251	. John Wesley 79	. Patircia 246

===

MYERS,(cont)		. Oshie Mae	231	. David Clayton	69	. Mary Jane	162
. Clementine	185	. Sam	230-231,234	. Dovie	69	. Nancy	223
. Elvira	117,119	. Sanford J.	223-224	. Elijah	155	. Nancy T. Ann	78
. Henry	185	. Sarah Elizabeth	223	. Eliza Ophia P.	234	. Nellie	160
. James Calvin	120	. Susie	234	. Emmit	40	. Rose Gereldine	106
. James Monroe	18	. Thomas	224	. Gendull	76	. Willie Eugenia	162
. John R.	157	. Villa	236	. James Madison	155	McGEEHEE,Elizabeth	242
. Johnny Estell	18	. Willard	74	. Julie	75	McGIBONEY,Kathleen	7
. Julia	185	. William	223-224,231	. Lee	69	. Lola Ather	1
. Leonora	157	. William A.	252	. Lila Jo	76	. Millie	7
. Louisa Scott	120	. Willie Marie	74	. M.Allene	234	. Omar Cephas	7
. Martha	193	McBROOM,Adam	90	. Maggie	234	. Robert William	7
. Marvin	132	. Alexander	90	. Martha Ann	155	McGILL,	
. Miles	228	. Mary	90	. Mary	35	. Margaret Elizabeth	245
. Millard	185	. Willie Cassandra	90	. Ophia P.	234	. P.T.	195
. Millard Wayne	185	McCABE,Cornelia	7	. Rebecca	69	. Tenny	195
. Nettie Jane	228-229	McCAIG,Jessie Lee	27	. Tommie Leander	234	McGINNISS,Mary	81
. Parneta	157	McCAMY,Ernest	92	. Vera	1	McGOWAN,Bertha	111
. Rosa Jane	253	McCARTNEY,Estelle	246	. Virgie Elizabeth	40	. Bertha Mai	107
. Rutha	18	McCLAIN,Birdie	246	. Wilma	40	. Charlene	35
. Sarah	228	. Janie Adeline	246	McCOWAN,Jason Paul	35	. Dorothy Ann	210-211
. Theresa T.	18	. Juanita	38	McCULLOUGH,Ella	197	. Jimmy	35
. Tim	115,120	. Maria	170	. Ellen	198-199	McGREGOR,Alfred	140
. Violey Ann	120	. harry L.	246	. Elvira	198	. Ava	132
. William S.	126	McCLARTY,Comer	215	. John	198	. Bruce	119
McAFEE,Brown	191	Reathy	215	McDANIEL,		. Elizabeth	161
. Dovie	19	McCLARY,Homer	25	. Margaret Elizabeth	211	. Fanny Ann	140
. Hannah S.	197	McCLELLAN,Mary F.	251	. Martha Elizabeth	208	. Frances	125
. J.B.	191	McCLINTOCK,Lewis	69	. Temperance	125	. Hixie	79
. Jennie Bilbra	33	Margaret	69	. Tempie	110	. Jason	125,139
. M.E.	191	McCLURE,Ada	147	McDONALD,Berdie Mae	192	. Lucille	120
. Mary Emma	33	. Bobby Jewell	147	Birdie Mae	45	. Margaret	139
. Velma	76	. James	202	McDOWELL,		. Mary Jane	139
. Velma Grace	33,129	. Marlin	147	. Charley Tarlton	2	. Mollie	119
McBRIDE,Adaline	224,231	. Rita	147	. Jack	108	. Nellie Hayes	157
. Adeline	223	. Ronald D.	147	. Magnolia	73	. Phillip	110
. Anna Lee	230	. Sarah	202	. Manson Bryon	2	. Sallie	136,169
. Belle	224	McCONNELL,Louise	247	. Martha Lee	73	. Sally Marshall	124
. Bernice J.	253	McCORD,Horace	73	. Mary Alice	2,42,73	. Tabitha	140
. Birdie	230,234	. Lura	37	. Mason Bryan	42	. Tressa	125
. Birdie Cleoven	231	. Mary Kathleen	58	. Mason Bryon	73	. Vriginia Lucille	119
. Bonnie	234	. Odell	73	. Mildred C.	2	McGUIRE,Anna	196
. Bonnie Jean	227	. Ralph W.	73	. Thomas Arnold	42,73	. Harry Lee	196
. Charlie Brown	231	. Sandra	16	. Willie May	2	. Inez M.	42
. Clyde F.	224	. Willie Mae	73	McFARLEN,Nancy	256	. James Allen	42
. Elmira	121,227	McCORKLE,Harriet	32,250	McFARLIN,Anger Price	190	. Josie	42
. Elva	2	. J.M.	32	Sarah	190	. Mary Ann	196
. Emma Luella	219-220	. Jess	170	McGEE,Allie Mintie	210	. Ramon	146
. Ethel	14-15,50	. John Morgan	250	. Archibald	162	McKINLEY,Clara Elora	218
. Eva Smith	113	. Lemma Ethel	250	. Archibald C.	163	. Jack	213,215-216,218
. Faye	224	. Louise	242	. Billy	248	. Josephine	213-214,218
. Fulton	219-220	. Martha	143	. Clendenon	162	. Louis	215
. George	223	. Mary	159	. Dorothy	23,183	. Raymond	218
. Gladys Beatrice	220	. Nancy	119,128,130	. Elijah	210	. Sallie	214,216,218
. Grady Clifton	231	. Velma	32	. Ella Elizabeth	248	. Sally	215
. Jackie Wayne	224	McCORMACK,		. Emma Lou	38	McLEAN,David Vance	225
. Jennie	231	. Charles Edward	65	. Floyd L.	160	. Margaret McConnell	225
. John McEwell	252	. Hazel I.	65	. Irene	144	. Margarite	109
. Johnny Fulton	219	. Jasper H.	65	. James Morgon	163	. Mary E.	157
. Lila Ann	223-224	. Lillian Ozell	67	. Johney	162	McMAHAN,Maymie	197
. Malvina A.	34	. Mabel Irene	65	. Lela	160	. Nancy	256
. Margaret E.	238	. Nettie	65	. Louisa	162-163	. Rebecca	256
. Melvina	134	McCORMICK,Ann	68	. Mamie L.	71	. Wesley	256
. Nancy Adelyne	252	. Clayton	234	. Martha	162	McMAHON,A.W.	189
. Octa May	49	. Cora Lee	155	. Martin	160	Amanda	189

==

McMILLAN,Alice	45	NEVILLE,Martha	97	. Elizabeth	100	. Francene Catherine	15
. Claude Alton	41	NEWBY,Alice Lucille	14	. Jonas	100	. Frank	15
. Elizabeth	41	. Allie	45	. Parilee	100	. Nicholas Charles	15
. Listeth W.	41	. Andy Thomas	45	. Sabrina	100	. Rosemary	15
. Neal	45	. Bershie	220	. Sam L.	100	. Wilburn	15
. Stella T.	45	. Callie	34	NOLAN,Georgia	45	NUNLEY,Adam	129
. Susan	41	. Charles P.	72	NORMAN,Dove	73	. Allie	18
McMILLIAN,Estelle	44	. Della	37	. Lyndsey Marie	73	. Alpha	57
Stella	46	. Elizabeth	44	. Lynn	73	. Alvin	113
McNUTT,Annie C.	177	. Elizabeth A.	205	NORRIS,Elbert Lee	72	. Bessie	26
McREYNOLDS,Anderson	215	. Eula Vic	14	. Elva	10	. Bessie Caldonia	145
.	216-217	. G.C.	44	. James Robert	72	. Caroline	129
. Elizabeth	216	. George Carson	15	. Lola Mai	24	. Charity Hope	210
. George Augusta	214	. Hiram M.	51	. Mary Hoida	5	. Cheatum	112
. Hallie	216	. J.A.	205	. Mattie Ruth	5,61	. Commodore	57
. John	215	. James P.	44	. Minnie Gertrude	72	. Deida	117
. Martin	214,216	. Joe Sam	34	. Mollie	72	. Ellen	134
. Mary	216	. Luther	14	. William Alford	5	. Eva Jean	113
. Mary Elizabeth	216	. M.L.	205	NORTHCUTT,Abe	169	. Fannie Harrison	116
. Nathan	215	. Martha E.	205	. Adaline	186	. Franzina	168
. Percilla	215-216	. Martha Lee	51	. Anderson	200	. Herbert Andrew	145
. Priscilla	217	. Martha Paralee	205	. Bobbie Inez	41	. Hilda Iola	26
. Rhodie	215	. Mary	87,205	. Brenda Faye	200	. Hubert	26
. Saphronia	215	. Mary F.	205	. Callie	186	. Icie Lavone	18
. Sophrona	218	. Mary Ollie	34	. Caroline	186	. Isaac	231
. William	217	. Mollie Fay	45	. Cathy Rose	119	. James William	210
. Willie	215	. Patricia	72	. D.V.	115	. Jay	145
McWHORTER,Laura Lee	37	. Ruth	44	. Debora Ann	119	. Jess	117
Mildred L.	19	. Synthia	205	. Enoch	41	. John	132,257
NAILL,Velma	42	. Tabitha Ann	72	. Flora	169	. John Wesley	132,134
NASH,Carl Jr.	236	. William B.R.	205	. Frank Cheatum	114	. Juanita	57
Jennifer	236	. William H.	205	. Genevieve	231	. Laura	257
NEAL,Bertha	167	NEWMAN,Andrew J.	224	. Georgia Mae	50,200	. Lawson	257
. Betty Jo	27	. Andrew Jackson	221-222	. Hattie	104	. Lillie	132
. Calvin Anderson	219	.	239-240	. Hattie Almeda	221	. Lou Ann	111
. Carrie	54	. Anna	221	. Ida	200	. Louise	57
. Charlie	80,219	. Charley Mae	224	. J.A.	186	. Lucy	115-117,123,133
. Charlie Florence	15	. Clyve Haskell	243	. J.R.	221	. Lula	114
. Clayton Melvin	80	. Elizabeth	221-222	. Jo Ruth	119	. Maggie	132,134
. David	219	. Elizabeth P.	224	. John	119	. Margaret	132
. Dexter L.	44	.	239-240	. John Lawson	112	. Mary	114,122,127,129
. Ed	54	. Elizbeth	227	. Jonathan D.	112	. Mary Bershie	238
. Frank A.	15	. Elsie Flora	-	. Joyce	8	. Mary E.	132,134
. Hannah	44	. Beatrice	224	. Kathy Willene	8	. Mary J.	113
. Johnny	24	.	227	. Lillie	41	. Maude	116
. Josephine	24	. Emmett Lee	222,243	. Louisa Scott	120	. Minnie	145
. Lane	171	. G.S.	239	. Lucy Catherine	112	. Mylanda	231
. Lizzie M.	15	. George Edley	227	. Mary	169	. Myrick	116,134
. Madge	219	. George Edley Jr.	224	. Mary Frances	41	. Nancy	153
. Martha	54	. George Edley Sr.	224	. Matilda	186	. Nancy Ellen	134
. Mary Winnie	80	. Jemina	239	. Minnie Nye	112	. Oshie Mae	231
. Melvin Russell	15,219	. John Andrew	221	. Nannie	186	. Rachel	29,134,146,153
. Phillip Van	15	. Mable Claricy	221	. Ora	221	. Raymon Edward	113
. Ray Ambers	80	. Mary Frances	224	. Sam Dwayne	231	. Rice A.	57
. Sarah	202	. Nancy Waid	243	. Thelma Joyce	50	. Sarah	114,121
. Schuyler Glenn	24	. Sallie	243	. Thurman Lee	50,200	. Sarah Jane	134
. Susan Frankie	219	. Sallie S.	222	. Waymon	231	. Susan E.	129
. W.A.	15	. Willa Mae	243	. William A.	186	. Will	18
NEELY,Fuller	80-81	NEWSOM,Joe	108	. William N.	186	. Willis	153
. Louvernia	80-81	NICHOLAS,Irma A.	250	. William Ray	8,50	NUNNELLY,Charles	253
. Velma	39	Virgle	250	NORTHERN,Leatrice	15	. Eunice	253
NEIL,W.J.	108	NIEL,Eliza	102	Paul A.	15	. Joe Edward	253
NELSON,Elizabeth	157	NOBEL,Leatrice	213	NORTHUCTT,		NURNEY,Anna Eliza	99
Tennie	204	NOKES,		Kathy Willene	7	. Eliza	99
NERNEY,Ann	29	. Charlotte	-	NOVAK,Catherine Grace	15	. Hiram	99

==

O'BRIEN,Catherine	5	. John William	186	. Erma P.	115	. Hattie	214-216
O'NEAL,Alma	6	. Johnnie B.	184	. Etta Nunley	125	. Hulon	170
. Alma Grace	7	. Mary	1,138	. Francis Marion	144-145	. James Richard	197
. Margaret Malinda	6	. Mary J.	184	. Halie	164	. Jane	122
. Thomas J.	6	. Mary Jane	184,186	. James	112,131,143,145	. Jannie	217
OAKES,Bessie	54	. Nannie	138	.	164	. Jim	19
. Bobbye M.	54	. R.L.	138	. James Edward	150	. John M.	186
. Hunter	54	. Shelah Hatton	138	. Jodie Pauline	145	. Laura I.	49
OAKLEY,Addie	214	. Warren Edward	1	. John	143,149-150	. Lois	104
. Edmon	87	OWENS,Bluford	3	. John Cooper	5,144	. Maggie Dalena	67
. Isaac	65	. Cheryl Lynn	3	. Lafayette	143-144	. Martha Ann	186
. Lucy	254	. Dora Bell	27	. Lafayette F.	115,123	. Nancy	17
. Mary	65	. Ocie	6,36	. Lena Estelle	144	. Nancy Jane	186
. Minerva	87	. Sandra	3	. Lena Mae	144	. Nellie	13
. Ollie P.	65	PACE,John	211	. Leslie Waymon	144	. Patricia M.	52
. Sam	87	. Margaret	143,157,196	. Lila Mae	144	. Preston	215
. W.H.	254	. Sarah	211	. Lillie Ann	165	. Rebecca L.	67
. Will	214	. Susanna	211	. Lorena	144	. Ritter	215
ODELL,Vestie	169	PACK,Frances Ruth	49	. Maggie	123	. Robbie	19
ODINEAL,Rosalind	170	. Isabell	1	. Maggie Marie	149	. Robert T.	19
ODOM,Mary	138	. John W.	1	. Mary	115,143-144,147	. Sarah Hannah	197
OFFICER,Pauline	214	. Josie	50	. Myrtle Lula	144-145	. Terry Lynn	29
OGLES,A.J.	251	. Leona	24	. Noland Lorn	149	. Wayland M.	49
. Andrew G.	251	. Loretta Mai	49	. Sarah	145	PARKS,Carroll	121-122
. Andrew Johnson	251	. Minnie	42	. Sarah Jane	112,131,143	.	125
. Louise	251	. Othel	49	.	164	. Ella M.	121,147
. Ollie	251	. Othel D.	24	. Thomas	163-164	. Eulitia H.	121
. Rebecca	251	. Sam	24	. Wavie	144	. George W.	121,147
. Wight	251	. Sessie	1	PARIS,Betty	93	. Hixey	121-122,125
OGLETREE,Fannie E.	66	PADGETT,		. CLayton	245	. J.E.	121
OLIVER,Susan	66	. Lillian Louise	48	. Clifford	245	. James M.	121
ORNDORFF,Brace	234	. Wilbert Thurman	48	. Cornelia	239	. John M.	121-122
. Eli Christian	234	PAGE,Alex	2	. Della Elizabeth	22,25	. Loucretta	121-122
. Melba	234-235	. Andrew	102	. E.T.	171	. Mackey T.	121
ORRICK,Harriet	210	. Eliza	102	. Elizabeth	93	. Martha	122
. Lucy	211	. Emaline	2	. Frank	239	. Mary	122
. Luna	100	. Lula	2	. Georgia	25,239	. Mary L.	125
ORSBORN,Doris C.	39	. Mary Belle	231	. Hannah	14	. Vera	147
OSMENT,Andrew	52	. Myrtie	30	. J.Frank	25	PARRIS,Clayton	255
. Jennie	52	. Myrtle	31	. John B.	93	PARRISH,Beatrice Ann	66
. John E.	52	. Myrtle Gertrude	102	. John R.	224,245	PARSLEY,Amanda	12
. Pauline	52	.	105	. Joseph R.	93	.	103-104,227
. S.Clifton	52	. Ruth	8	. Lytle	224	. Calidonia	104
. Victoria	52	. Virginia Ruth	8,68	. Mary Josephine	224,245	. Estie	73
OUBRE,Celia A.	33	PALMER,Alice	114,126	. Maysie	93	. Georgia Alberta	10
OUTLAW,Cleo Bell	189	. Hazel S.	60	. Myrtle	239-240	. Homer E.	42
. Cora Bell	189	. Jane	252	. Pattie	207	. Inez	42
. Glen Thomas	97	. Monroe	252	. Ritchard	168	. James Alfred	251
. Leonard P.	189	. Tennie	252	. Rufus	224	. Jewell	73
. Lizzie May	97	. Thomas Hamilton	252	. Sarah	239-240	. Leona	24
. W.Tom	96	. W.Eston	252	. Sarah Catherine	91	. Martha Ethel	64
. William Thomas	189	. William Eaton	254	PARISH,Lon B.	4	. Mary F.	251
OVERALL,Ada	24	PANTER,Alma	149	. Mattie Irene	4	. Maudie Mae	42
. Bright	11	. Alma Lois	112,127	PARKER,Alfred	67	. Minerva Elizabeth	251
. Hazel Nadine	11	. Annie	143,163	. Aubrey	72	. Minnie	42
. Lebious B.	90	. Aubrey Maynard	144	. Benjamin Franklin	29	. Odell	73
. Minnie	11	. Audley Burris	144	. Bertha Mae	72	. Othel O.	42
. Rose Ada	90	. Charles Arthur	112,127	. Beulah J.	19	. Owen	42
OVERTON,Willie Mae	73	. Cleo	5,144	. Cecil Howard	52	. Pearl	10
OWEN,Bettie	138	. Clyde	131	. Darlene Renee	52	. Thomas P.	104
. Bob	138	. Cora	143,149-150	. Dovie	19	. William G.	10
. Dorsey Everette	184	. Dorothy Charlene	5	. Elaine	29	PARSON,Calvin A.	19
. J.B.	1	. Eliza J.	163-164	. Etta May	72	. Conger	19
. Jeremiah Jackson	184	. Elizabeth	164	. Hannah	199	. Marjorie	19
. John Balaam	184,186	. Erma Evelyn	150	. Hannah S.	197	. Mary	19

==

PARSONS,Anna Belle	99	PATTY,Florence	119	. Caroline	196	. Jesse	58
. Betty	99	. George E.	119	. Charley Clayburn	194	. Joetta	8
. Dallas	99	. William E.	119	. Claude Black	26	. John O.	221,247
PARTON,Lottie	208	PAYNE,Ardith	5	. Clayborn	196	. Johnnie	221
PATRICK,Amanda	128	. Della	39	. Clayburn	194	. Joseph Butcher	223-224
. Betty Jean	68	. Gloria Thelma	39	. Cleo	195	. Leonard	8
. Caroline	129	. Henry William	39	. Clifton Cantrell	26	. Lillie Bell	124
. Houston	128	. Margaret	255	. Clio Annie	101,103	. Maggie	15,224
. Joe P.	68	PEARSALL,Ada	29	. Clyde A.	31	. Manerva Elizabeth	238
. Lafayette F.	128-129	. Alice M.	29	. Delela C.	194	. Margaret	224,228,235
. Martha	119	. Annie	240	. Dora E.	52	.	238
. Mary Elizabeth	68	. Claude	29	. Eliza J.	138	. Margaret Edith	221
. Moses	129	. Fletcher C.	29	. Eliza Nora	103	. Margaret Frances	242
. Susan E.	129	PEARSON,Amanda	2,128-129	. Emaline	103	. Mary Katherine	237
. William	128	. Bertha	130	. Emma Mai	18	. Nerva Elizbeth	236
PATTERSON,Alma E.	31	. Beulah	66	. Flossie	17	. Phebia	237
. Amos	216	. Deliah	130	. Gaston	52	. Phebia Elizabeth	232
. Canzada	214	. Edith	190	. Gwyendelene	102	. Phelbia Elizabeth	236
. Connie Sue	53	. Elizabeth	30	. Henry	139	. Texann	223
. David C.	227	. George	119,128	. Hilda Iola	26	. Tommy Lee	142
. Elizabeth	213	. George Douglas	130	. Iron Howard	194-195	. Victoria	224,240
. G.A.	214	. Jadie	128	. Jodie Fred	17	. William C. Smartt	242
. Hattie	214-215	. James	130	. Joseph	17-18,26	. William J.	236,238
. Henry	213	. Lawrence E.	30	. Josephine M.	31	. William Thomas	242
. Herbert Bethel	31	. Nancy	119,128,130	. Joshua	138	. Willie Joe	232
. Isaac	213,215-216	. Sallie	119	. Josie D.	194	. Wilma Louise	123
. James	215	PEAY,Mary	108	. Judy Gail	52	PERKINS,Bertha Mae	72
. James T.	31	Thomas Terrell	108	. Louella	194	. Billy	68
. Jennie	31	PEDEN,Lucinda	5,56	. Margrit Azline	101	. Harold	72
. Jim	31	PEDIGO,E. Frances	36	. Mary	139	. James C.	72
. John Ann	56	. E.Frances	66	. Mary Elizabeth	188,194	. Lillie	72
. Jonah	72	. Ella	2	.	196	. Martha Jane	68
. Jones	214,216	. Fannie	35	. Mattie Ann	66,208	. Rosa	55
. Lillian	212-214,231	. Harvi	35	. Mattie Bell	26	. Rosa B.	68
. Lou Rhena	65	. Lillian	36,67	. Maudie Mae	103,107	PERLERI,Illumine	71
. Lucy	215	. Mable	36,67	. Melvina	211	PERRY,Alexander	154
. Mable Louise	214	. Oshie	35	. Mildred	106	. Annie Cordelia	142
. Mary	56	. Pleasant M.	36,67	. Millard J.	195	. Arkansas	155
. Rhena	66	. Thurman L.	66	. Nancy	138	. Athelia Arlene	142
. Sarah	213,215-216	. Thurman Z.	36	. Nancy Kay	52	. Bertha	112
. Shela	56	. Toy Ralph	36,67	. Nora	60,103	. Berthenia	150
. Sylva	215	PEEKS,Mary E.	30	. Octa	229	. Betsy	155
. Thelma	72	PEELER,Elizabeth	230	. Rose Gereldine	106	. Betty	6,228
. William C.	53	. Jesse	230	. Rowena	20	. Blanche Lemmer	6-7
PATTON,Annie Mai	9	. Roxie A.	230	. Ruby	52	. Charles E.	150
. Clarence D.	25	. Sarah	230	. Vernie Lena	60	. Charles Edward	142
. Dora	177	PELHAM,Avo	67	. William I.	60	. Charles T.	121
. Evaline	85-86	. Dewey	67	. William R.	103	. Delia Clara	142
. Flavil	28	. Sarah	256	. Winton Aubrey	103	. Dora	149
. Georgia	5	PENDERGRAPH,Harold U.	62	. mary	141	. Edward Hosmer	228
. J.B.	86	Mazel G.	62	PEPPER,Aaron A.	124	. Elizabeth	17,154
. James Hershel Sr.	9	PENDLETON,Charles	254	. Ann Payne	228	. Floyd	142
. James Porter	5	. John L. Sr.	57	. Austin Clark	237	. Frances E.	228
. Jessie Lee	230	. Judy Sharon	254	. Charles Otis	236	. Frances Elizabeth	118
. John	5	. Lillian	254	. Charlie William	232	. Frank	6,17,228
. John B.	25	PENEGAR,James	23	.	236-237	. Garry Steven	12
. Josie Henrietta	25	. Martha	23	. Cindy Rene	237	. George W.	118,121
. Lorraine	9	. Ola Betty Mae	23	. Cynthia	242	. Gertrude	14
. Mamie	25,86	PENNINGTON,Aaron	103	. Eleanor	223	. Grace	121
. Marietta	230	. Alice Elizabeth	17	. Eleanor E.	224	. Henry	155
. Ola Mae	28	. Allie	18,26	. Elish	228	. Homer O.	141
. Rebecca	10	. Annie	106	. Elisha II	224,242	. Horace Floyd	142
. Sarah	5	. Bobbie Lucille	101	. Elizabeth	221,251	. Isaac	150-151,155
. Thomas	230	. Calvin	106	. Garry Wayne	8	. Isaac Floid	155
. Thurman Edward	9	. Calvin T.	101,103	. James Eston	123-124	. Isiah	142

==

==

PERRY,(cont)		. Earl D.	8,68	POPE,Eliza Jane	67	. Glenn D.	10

PERRY,(cont)
. James T. 151
. Janie 27
. Joe Wheeler 155
. John 142,152,154-155
. 159
. John Boyd 17
. John H. 228
. John Houston 118,152
. Lela 155
. Lela Ruth 141
. Lemma 256
. Lizzie 142
. Malinda 142,152
. 154-155,159
. Mamie Ruth 17
. Marion Franklin 228
. Martha 152,155,159
. Mary 151
. Mary Rebecca 228
. Minerva 118
. Minerva Jane 121
. Napoleon Lonzo 142
. Rebecca 142
. Rebecca Caroline 141
. Robert 112
. Robert Lawson 142
. Royce L. 12
. Ruby 112
. Ruth 142
. Sarah Elizabeth 118
. Sepal 12
. Sherry Lorenzo 142
. Taylor 141
. Thomas Jefferson 118
. Velma Ida 29
. William Taylor 141-142
PERRYMAN,Alice 222
. Beulah Vista 222
. Henry E. 222
PETERS,Dale Denton 39
. Edith 39
. Frances 39
. Jack Denton 39
PETTUS,J.T. 108
PETTY,Ellenora 236
. James 108
PHARM,Fannie 46
PHELPS,Mollie 119
PHIFER,Albert 66
. Shannon 66
. Sue 9
. Susan 66
PHILLIPS,Angie V. 5-6
. Arthur Lester Sr. 44
. Belle 53
. Beulah 66
. Bonnie Sue 68
. Catherine 24
. Charles Wayne 52
. David Leon 8
. Deliah Belle 44
. Della 8
. Dollie Lorene 53
. Dorothy 54

. Earl D. 8,68
. Eliza 96-97
. Evelyn Elizabeth 13
. Flora Catherine 204
. Hazel Annette 66
. James Brownlow 44
. James Robert 13
. John 8
. John Floyd 54
. John Franklin 66
. Judy 8
. Lela A. 44
. Lizzie Ella 204
. Mary 204
. Millie C. 137
. Ola Mae 52,54
. Ruth 8
. S.B. 53
. Sarah 48
. Virginia Ruth 68
. W.V. Sr. 52
. William 54
. William Thomas 204
. William Virgil 52
PICKETT,Alice 165
. Erlene 165
. Frances 162
. Julia 184
. Mary 205
PIGG,Jeston 205
  Sarah 211
PIKE,Hugh P. 106
  Mary Emmaline 106
PINEGAR,Alice 254,256
. B. 254,256
. Beatrice 256
. Callie 70
. J.C. 256
. Ola 255
. Willie 254
PIRTLE,Hassie 187
PISTOLE,Catherine 253
. Catherine B. 241
. Charles 253
. Charles E. 241
. Charles Herschel 253
. Charles Hershel 241
. Rella Dell 65
PITTARD,Bessie 29,230
. Susie 230
. William 230
PITTMAN,James 189
. Nancy 189
. Vica Jane 191
. Vicie Jane 201
. Vicy Jane 189
PLOURD,Mary Lou 184
POGUE,Sarah Jane 253
POLLARD,Nancy Ellen 61
PONDER,Delton T. 64
. Eliza 29
. Enoch 29
. Novella 29
. Sarah 64
POORE,Lula 149

POPE,Eliza Jane 67
  Eula 66
PORTER,John Robert 4
  Rowena 32
POTTER,Anna P. 237
. Betty 233
. Dan S. 102
. Dorothy B. 55
. Ernest Samuel 51
. Ethel 102
. Eva 55
. Gladys 40
. Grady Alden 55
. J.C. 51
. Jackson 233
. Jennie Mae 237
. John Hackett 237
. John Houston 233
. John Huston 237
. Leander K. 10
. Leslie 55
. Lucinda 51
. Martha 233
. Mary Elizabeth 237
. Mary Etta 10
. Rebecca 10
. Ruth 51
POWELL,Charles 180
. Charlie 179
. E.Elizabeth 19
. Essie 180
. Inez 180
. John 175
. John F. 180
. Kitty Lorena 180
. Lettie 175
. Magnolia 179
. Martha Ann 242
. Martha Pearlee 242
. Mary 180
. Noma B. 175
. Thomas 180
. W. 242
. Willard F. 19
. Willard Franklin 19
. Wilma 19
POWERS,Howard T. 7
. Hubert 144
. Jo Ellen 7
. John Leonard 144
PRATER,Allen 183
. Arthur Huston 185
. B.H. 177
. Beatrice 183
. Benjamin 215
. Bertha Ann 151
. Bethia Ann 152
. Charles L. 64
. Cleva Dell 37
. Debra Faye 183
. Deletta Faye 183
. Emma Lee 45
. Faye 61
. Flora Dale 183
. Gearldean 185

. Glenn D. 10
. Ibie Jane 183
. J.Newton 186
. James 102
. James Edward 183
. James McKinley 31
. Jim 7
. Jimmie Lee 102
. Jimmy Lee 106
. Jo Ellen 7,64
. Joe 45
. Leonard 61
. Lesley Hoover 177
. Margaret Alice 7
. Martha E. 174,178-179
. Martha Ellen 31
. Martha Linda 186
. Mary 181
. Mary Ellen 12
. Maude 45
. Medford 183
. Millie 177
. Moses Ulyssis 12
. Oliver 61
. Ona 185
. Pauline N. 64
. Pearl 185
. Porter 45,185
. Quince 185
. Ronald Lynn 61
. Russell Irwin 61
. Ruth B. 31
. Sam Alrey 12
. Tennessee 12
. William Jasper 31
. Wilmer Curtis 183
. Zettie 111
PRESLEY,Betty 235
PRESTON,Betty S. 67
. Charley 138
. Elizabeth 67
. Gentry 67
. Harry M. 67
. Hervey 67
. Liza Parasada 200
. Mae Bell 185
. Mary Jane 138
. Verna 67
. William C. 138
PRIEST,Alice 26
. Flora Golda 149
. Goldie 149
. Joe 26
. Kenneth Ray 26
. Nettie 149
. Nola B. 26
. Ocie 26
. Seamon 26
. Tim 149
PRIOR,Howard H. 16
. Margaret J. 16
. Nelma K. 16
. Roger Arlington 16
PRUETT,Catherine 12
PRYOR,Josie Estella 25

===

Name	Page
PRYOR,(cont)	
. Mack Dean	49
. Martha T.	49
PUCKET,Rosanna	254
PUGH,Alonza	11
. Lizzie	11
. Nola C.	11
. Sarah T.	81
PURSER,Sallie	53
PURSLEY,Sara	126
Sarah	120,125
PYBURN,Carrie Jane	115
PYLENT,Callie	210
QUALES,Bill	170
QUICK,	
Martha Elizabeth	11
QUINN,Bertha	20
. Charles Vance	20
. David R.	20
. Lemuel Q.	12
. Leslie L. Sr.	12
. Martha Pauline	20
. Nellie	12
RADER,Joe B.	17
Louise M.	17
RAINS,Annie	189,193,196
.	198
. Annie Birdine	192
. Delphine	188
. Dorothy	31
. Dovie	195
. E.L.	189
. Elizabeth	173,188,192
. Elvira	253
. Enoch J.	189
. General Crit	189,193
.	198
. Jimmy Edison	30
. Josiah	255
. Larkin	173,188,192
. Lonnie M.	31
. Lorene	69
. Macon O.	74
. Marie G.	30
. Mary	31
. Mary Emma	30
. N.B.	173
. Nellie Jo	189
. Newton	69
. Ollie Mai	198
. Oscar	30-31
. Prisie	173
. Prudie	69
. R.K.	30,189
. Rufus J.	195
. Rufus K.	193,195
. Sam Ross	69
. Susan	189,193
. Susan C.	195
. Susie	30
. Tammie McGuire	189
. Virgil V.	74
. Wavie Louise	193
. William Presley	173
. Willie Thurmon	189
RAMBO,Annie D.	76
Murphy	76
RAMSEY,Allie	75
. Annie Mae	215
. Betty Jean	60
. Clyde William	75
. Dave	172
. David	225
. Donnie	217
. Elizabeth E.	225
. Emily	218
. Fonella	60
. Frances	238
. Hubert	217
. Ivy Joe	75
. Joe Edward	60
. Josephine	74
. Kenneth Edward	60
. Leola Johann	27
. Leonia	216
. Lucy	225
. Lucy Dean	215
. Lula Lillian	224
. Lytle	27
. Martha E.	225
. Mary A.	60
. Octavia	224-225
. Phronie	215
. Roberta	217
. Sam McCaslin	225
. Samuel McCaslin	224
. Saphronia	215
. Sara R.	27
. Sarah J.	75
. Shirley Jena	218
. Susie	215,217-218
. Will	215
. William	215,218
. William Hershal	172
RANDOLPH,Anderson	253
. Heney	253
. James Martin	253
. Lou	131
. Martha Josephine	253
. Mary Ann	253
. Sarah Jane	253
RANKER,Ed	42
Kathy Sue	42
RANKIN,	
. Annie Clarissy	223
. James Andrew	223
. John Calvin	223
. Louisa	223
. Texann	223
RAPE,Eliza Mae	86
RASCOE,Blanche Evelyn	79
.	85
. Edgar	40
. Ila	85
. Mabel N.	40
. Myrtle	40
. Stokley D.R.	79,85
. William Henry	40
RAWSON,	
. George Edward Jr.	51
. George Edward Sr.	51
RAY,John Thomas	224
RAYBURN,Annie	245
. James	245
. James G.	245
. Margaret Elizabeth	245
RAYMOND,Agnes	85
. Bob	49
. Ceva Lillian	49
. Georgia Winnie	58
. Jerry W.	85
. Lucy	80
. Lucy Ann	49
. Mary Winnie	80
. Nancy	29
. Nancy Missoura	80
. Nina	85
. R.W.	80
. Walter	85
REAGAN,Fannie E.	66
. Grace	66
. William G. Sr.	66
. William Porter	66
RECORD,Willis	250
REDMON,Amanda Leann	71
. Brenda	71
. Donna K.	73
. Ella	32
. Ella Mae	71
. Estelle Era	71
. Felix	32
. Felix Terry	71
. Henry	20
. John H.	71
. John Roy	52
. Keith	73
. Leonard Payne	52
. Leroy	71
. Mary Ella	52
. Mary Helen	52
. Mattie G.	32
. Patricia	72
. Robbie Jane	71
. Rowena	20
. Sarah	237
. Sue	20
REED,Alice	26
. America	234,250,252
. America Lee	254
. Annie Mae	18
. Bill	254
. Cecil A.	10
. Della Elizabeth	25
. Delta	234
. Dorothy Mai	51
. Early	64
. Elsie L.	25
. Ervin	87
. Fannie	10
. Faye	57
. Frank Allen	184
. George David	51
. Gladys May	87
. Haley	51
. Hannah	254
. Harrison Joseph	25
. Hattie	46
. Jones	10
. Lee	101
. Louise	32,130
. Lucy Emma	18
. Malinda	101
. Martha L.	10
. Mary Ethel	25
. Meadows	25
. Michael Brent Jr.	57
. Michael Brent Sr.	57
. Mollie	101
. Pence	175
. Robert Lee	10
. Robert Newton	32
. Robert Newton Sr.	25
. Ruby	254
. Ruby May	249
. Sam	51
. Sanford	18
. Sarah	197
. Stacy	87
. Thena	10
. Wauleen	10
. William Sanford	18
REEDER,Helen Marie	1
. Lillian	36,67
. Mary	27
. Melvina	71
. Nova Lee	27
. William C.	27
REEDY,Bulah	141
Elmer	141
REEVES,Blanche Evelyn	79
.	85
. Sallie	79
. Thomas	79
RENO,Earline	220
REYNOLDS,Alfred	191
.	200-201
. Elizabeth	206,226
. Franklin Cordell	7
. Georgia Mae	50,200
. James	81
. Janie Adelene	246
. John B.	7
. Johnie E.	7
. Lora Jane	7
. Mae	81-82
. Mareanie	7
. Mary Jane	200
. Mollie	81
. Niner Myrtle	191
. Pheba Mae	74
. Reba I.	53
. Rebecca	122
. Robert A.	53
. Roy L.	246
. Thomas Belle	71
. Thomas Leroy	71
RHEA,Arsey Womack	135
. Austin	135
. Bessie Elise	17
. Bill	111

===

ROBINETTE,(cont)		. Hollie	123	. Margaret	57	SADLER,Matthew	60
. Estella T.	45	. Hollie Claire	117,126	. Paul	57	. Maud	8,13
. Josephine	44	. Ira	20	ROLLINS,James	152	. Maude	20
. Nancy Margaret	45	. James	229,241	ROMANS,Ada	68	. Valley	60
. Reva Enole	46	. James Morgan	32	. Elish Paul	68	. Zeedler Pauline	60
. Stella	46	. James R. Sr.	221,241	. Horas Greely	68	SAFFLE,Mattie A.	196
. Stella T.	45	. Jeff	32,221	. Lillie Ella	68	SAFLEY,David	131
. Wilma	44	. John H.	43	RONE,A.R.	37	. George L.	131
ROBINS,Mareania	7	. Joyce	8	. Altus R.	37	. Hazel Dove	7
ROBINSON,Alton E.	27	. Judy	8	. Anna	37	. Jane	131
. Amanda	26	. Laura	107	. Grace	37	. Jesse	110,131-132
. Charles Whitt	64	. Lawrence Roy	254	ROPER,Marie	31	. John R.	131
. Charlie H.	69	. Leona Z.	221	ROSE,Sandra	41	. Leonedus	131
. Dorothy Jan	27	. Lettie Arvilla	229	ROSENBAUM,Gloria	123	. Lon	131
. Edith	37	. Lillie	43	. Jackolean	123	. Lou	131
. Elbert IV	27	. Lizzie	43	. Jake	123	. Mary	110,121,125,127
. Elbert William	26-27	. Lock	250	ROSS,Charlie	4	. Minnie	92
. Elizabeth	22	. Locke	229	. Charlie Austin	83	. Myrick	131-132,134
. Elsie	26	. Louise	50,254	. Drucilla C.	232-233	. Nannie A.	131
. Estell	74	. Louise Ray	254	. Elizabeth J.	232	. Phatha	110,131-132
. Flaura	57	. Lucinda Ann	139-140	. Harry Hugh	200	. Sarah Ann	131
. Frances	62,186	. Maggie Low	123	. Laurence M.	4	SAIN,Colene	51
. Frank	26	. Manerva Elizabeth	238	. Martha	83,232-233,255	. Eva Mae	135
. Gladys M.	27	. Martha R.	241	. Mary E.	233	. Fred Wesley Sr.	50-51
. Jesse	137	. Mary	135	. Mary Wilma	200	. James Blanton	135
. John	26	. Mary Bell	12	. Minnie Mae	200	. James Lafayette	50
. Kizzie	64	. Mary Belle	49	. Nancy	227	. James R.	135
. Martha	242	. Mary Wilsie	117,123	. Nelda Juanita	83	. Lillian	50
. Martha Carolyn	26-27	. Mattie	227	. Ophia Lee	83	. Raymond L.	51
. Mary	239	. Melba Jean	163	. Ophie	4	. Ruby Irene	50-51
. Mary E.	48	. Mollie	46,229,250	. Robert	83	SAMUELS,Hazel M.	57
. Naomi W.	26	. Myrtle Ellis	250	. Sidney	232-233	SANDERS,Britan	75
. Staley	26-27	. Nannie Bell	104	. Wesley Brown	4	. Cleveland S.	74-75
. Thelma A.	69	. Nerva Elizabeth	236	. William	227	. Edna Mae	100
. Violet Jane	137	. Nora	20	. William Michael	200	. Emogene	74-75
ROBIRDS,Mandy	152	. Oscar	104,227	ROWAN,Jennie H.	241	. Estell	74
. Margaret	152	. Oscar Sidney	221	Stokley D.	241	. Eugene	106
. William Thomas	152	. Pina Jane	135	ROWLAND,Billie Joyce	20	. Eula	43
RODHON,David	59	. Quim Northcutt	227	. Flora Bell	20	. Evelyn	70
. Dorina	59	. Ricky Lee	255	. Levan	20	. Flora	6
. Olive	59	. Rufe A.	254	. Paul J.	20	. J.Popie	6
RODRIGUES,Chole	33	. Rufus Anson	49-50	. Sarah Ellen	27	. James Pope	6
ROGERS,Almond Sage	229	. Saint Elmo	123	RUCKER,Jenny Sue	42	. Jim	75
. Arthur Lee	229	. Sidney Robert	104	RUELLE,Clara	39	. Jimmie	70
. Avis A.	227	. Susie	129	RUFFIN,Harold C.	15	. Julia Ann	57
. B.M.	194	. Tabitha	140	Lorraine Angela	15	. Lavander Pope	6
. Bessie	249	. Thelma Joyce	50	RUSSELL,Bessie	111	. Ollie Mae	75
. Cecil Albert	255	. Thomas	255	. Clara	20	. Robert	74
. Cora Laura	62,64	. Thomas Estes	221	. Della	8	. Tommye E.	6
. Dion	43	. Travis Jr.	194	. Elihu	111	. W.M.	106
. Dorothy Jewell	12	. Velma	32,221	. John Tillman	20	. Wayne	70
. Dorothy Marie	32	. Villa	229	. Ora Nelson	111	SANDS,Edna Mae	57
. Eliza Irene	43	. William	140	. Pauline	249	. Harry Miles	57
. Elsie Mae	40	. William Silas	12,49	. Permelia	79	. Hazel M.	58
. Florence	221,229,241	. Willie Irene	20	. Sue R.	20	. Hazel Marie	57
. Georgia	236	. Willie Thomas	12	. W.M.	20	SANTEE,Amelia	233
. H.Travis	194	. Wilma June	123	RUST,Dennie	170	SATTERWHITE,Jane	140
. Hallie	113	ROGGLI,Alma	33	. Mary	170	SAULS,Mandy	67
. Harrison	135	. John	33	. Tamor	170	. Mattie Pauline	67
. Harrison McKinley	117	. Louise	33	RUTLEDGE,Evelyn L.	22	. Samuel Jackson	67
	123	ROJAS,Diero	175	. Jim Dillard	29	SAVAGE,Allie	68,170
. Hattie	104	Hettie	175	. Levi	229	. Annie Bell	163
. Hattie Almeda	221	ROLLER,Velma Mai	82	. Martha	228	. Belle	54
. Helen	255	ROLLEY,Charles Irwin	57	. Martha Reams	99	. Ben	170
. Herman B.	32	. Lois Cleta	57	. Vivian May	207	. Brittania	161

SAVAGE,(cont)		. Howard	236	SHELBY,Billy Jack	63	. Willie Alvin	191
. Edward	41	. J.M.	81	SHELLGROVES,Mary	159	SHOCKLEY,Bertha	218
. Effa	170	. Jesse C.	199	. Mary Ann	160	. Herman	218
. Elizabeth	224	. Josephine	22	. Nancy Adaline	160	. James P.	212
. Ella	246	. Kitty	22	. Nancy Adeline	162	. Sarah	212
. Eva	171	. Letta	114,126	SHELTON,Belle	25	. Sarah Isbell	168
. Frank D.	167	. Lettie	139	. James	196	SHOEMAKE,Richard Lynn	71
. George	224	. Lottie	149	. Polly Ann	196	Robbie Jane	71
. Georgia	41	. Lourene	15	. Prisie	173	SHOOK,Zora Ethel	200
. Hillis	54	. Mary	81,115,143	. Rachel Ann	6,30,196	SHORT,Catherine	31
. James	171	. Mary Frances	68	SHEPHERD,Elizabeth	109	. Isaac Newton	31
. Josa	245	. Maude M.	75	. James	109	. James Fletcher	31
. Josephine Clark	224	. Norma Jo	201	. Pheobe	109	SHRADER,Clarissa	219
. Josie C.	245	. Odus	149	SHEPPARD,Elizabeth	108	. Florence	241
. Lucion	167	. Pauline	21-22	SHERRELL,Alton	197	. John Daniel	231
. Marjorie A.	54	. Roy Lenour Sr.	29	. Catherine	194	. Nancy	231
. Mary A.	60	. Sala Ann	158	. Dorothy	70	. Rosa Jane	231
. Nora	167,170	. T.Lenier	40	. Flora	70	SHRUM,Lillie	56
. Rufus	171	. Tennie	29	. Grace	197	SIDE,Jane	216
. Sam	169-170	. Thomas Edward	22	. Lela Lucille	199	SIMMONS,Agnes A.	4
. Sterling	161	. Thomas Franklin	22	. Roscoe	70	. Gertrude	106
. Susannah	156	. Thomas Luther	81	. Roy Clarence	70	. Howard	53
. Theodore	169	. Vesta	160	SHERRILL,Gaines	46	. Joyce Ann	53
. Vance Smart	41	. Villa	236	. Geneva Joyce	59	. Rebecca M.	200
. Will	167	. William	95,126,139	. Hattie	46	. Rufus Elmo	200
. William	169-170	. William Martin	199	. Mabel G.	46	. Sherman D.	3
SAYERS,Grada	191	. Zelma L.	46	. Roger	46	SIMON,Herbert D.	196
. Nola	191	SCROGGINS,Mary	137	SHIELDS,Alexander	99	. Hester A.	196
. Orval L.	191	SCRUGGS,Martha	163	. Everett Leon	104-105	. Windonia	196
SAYLORS,Harriet	50	SEALS,Josephine	74	. Faye	57	SIMONS,Addie	193
SCARBERRY,Jennie	76	. Mack	74	. Hassie Cillar	104-105	. Adelaide	62
SCHILZ,Bertha	68	. Pearl	74	. Hassie Ciller	99	. Andrew Jackson	62,193
. Herman	68	. Solomon	74	. Lewis F.	104	. Anna Bell	69
. Mary S.	68	SEITZ,Logan	110	. Lucy Virginia	99	. Aubrey Walling	69
SCHOENFIELD,Alta	62	Nellie	110	. Mary Melissa	105	. Benjamin Claude	62
SCHOLTZ,Lorraine	9	SELF,James	26	. Matilda	99	. Dora Grace	62
SCHRADER,Elizabeth	257	. Martha Carolyn	26-27	. Rhodman Kinner	99,104	. Ellen	62
Florence	221,229	. Mary	26	. Robert Bruce	99	. Harold Raymond	62
SCHRAGEL,Alexander	230	SELLARS,Elizabeth	206	SHIRLEY,Alfred D.	191	. James	11
William Pearl	229	Helen	83	. Alton L.	8	. John William	126
SCOTT,Adeline	95	SETTLES,Addie	169	. Annie	191	. Luella	126
. Ailene	29	Joe	169	. Autie Frances	192	. Martha Elizabeth	11
. Alex	75	SEVERT,Bland B.	66	. Delia	190,193	. Mary A.	62
. Alice Mae	71	Helen	66	. Emily	201	. Ruth	11
. Andrew Marshall	21	SEWELL,John T.	250	. Eula Pearl	189,197	. Suella	193
. Arlene	47	Sarah Elizabeth	250	. Harriet	194	. Susan	69
. B.Gail	41	SHAFFER,		. Harriett	189,191,199	. Taylor	69
. Bertha Cecil	199	Annie Elizabeth	50	. Hatten Roland	194	. Tessa	69
. Beula Mai	181	SHARP,Lurline	127	. Joe	189,194,201	. Walling Todd	69
. Bobby Joe	201	. Melba	47	. Joe N.	191,199	. Willard	126
. Caldonia	126	. Melba Jean	57	. Joelene	199	SIMPSON,Amanda Endora	93
. Candy Kay	149	SHARPE,Billy Allen	60	. John B.	8,191-193	. Andrew Jackson	210
. Delia	139	. Clifton B.	60	. John W.	191,201	. Annie Luther	210
. Dora	11	. Clifton Birt Jr.	46	. Lela	8	. Clara	232
. Douglas E.	22	. Clifton Birt Sr.	46	. Margaret	201	. Ernest W.	210
. Eliza A.	199	. Effie Mai	46,60	. Margaret E.	191	. Hermon Robert	210
. Elizabeth J.	158	. George	46	. Mary E.	201	. Irene K	210
. Ella	75	. Nora Jane	46	. Mary Jane	200	. Jo Ann	198
. Emma	21-22	SHAW,Addison Sr.	51	. Melissa	191	. Josephine	62
. Erby Sedberry	75	. Minnie	51	. Mollie	8,191-192	. Linnie	210
. Frances M.	95	. Thelma	51	. Nellie	8	. Lucille	33
. Gary Dale	201	SHCRADER,Clarissa	238	. Niner Myrtle	191,200	. Minnie Nye	112
. George W.	29	. John D.	238	. Rita	194	SIMRELL,Buelah	20
. Glenn Clemmon	236	. Mary Ann	238	. Roland H.	191	. Henry	20
. Henry Samuel	158	. Nancy	238	. Ruby May	194	. Martha Pauline	20

SIMS,Tressa	125	. Alpha	57	. Marcus	114	.	239
SINCLAIR,Laura	3	. Ann	245	. Margaret	225,245	. Willie C.	226
SINGLETON,Josephine	98	. Anna Bell	224	. Margaret McConnell	225	SMEAD,Carl	59
Willie	239	. Annie George	245	. Maria	170	. Carol A.	59
SINK,Emma	254	. Aseneth	245	. Marion	116	. Gordon Allen	59
Lot	254	. Benjamin Franklin	114	. Martha	132,224,242	. Jenny	59
SINKS,Albert	17	. Bennett White	239,247	. Martha E.	225,247	. Laurie	60
. Amanda	17	. Beulah Vista	222	. Mary	114,126-127	SMITH,Addie	169
. Bessie Elise	17	. Caldonia	126	.	135-136	. Agnes May	10
. Will	17	. Carlee	111,114	. Mary A.	247	. Alexander S.	168
SINSABAUGH,Grace	234	. Carlie	135	. Mary Ann	224-225	. Alice	222
SIPE,Bessie Marie	242	. Charles Hinkley	222	. Mary Catherine	247	. Alton	87
. John Paul	12	. Claude Calhoun	239	. Mary E.	126	. Ann	29
. Mary	242	. Claude Clahoun	222	. Mary Esta	226	. Anna Elizabeth	99
. O.H.	242	. Cleopater	225	. Mary Ester	222	. Ara	136
SISCO,Myrtle Troy	41	. Cordelia Adalaide	245	. Mary Frances	224	. Arthur	134
SISK,Bettie Florence	62	. Cornelia Adelaide	33	. Mary Jane	222-224	. Ava	134
SISSOM,A.J.	194	. Daniel Thomas	222	. Mary Josephine	224,245	. Azel	91
. Elizabeth	194	. Dewey C.	226	. Milton	126	. Bell	95
. Idella Emaline	194	. Doshie	129	. Myrick	116,134	. Bernice	42
SKELTON,John	138	. Easter	133	. Myrtle	222	. Bettie	172
. Mary	138	. Elizabeth	222,242	. Nancy	231	. Betty	65,78,99
. William J.	138	. Elizabeth H.	225	. Nancy Ellen	134	. Beula Mai	181
SLATTEN,Clara R.	51	. Elizabeth Hackett	245	. Octavia	224-225	. Blanch	190
Rayburn Van	51	. Elizabeth Lee	133	. Octavia Laughlin	226	. Brittania	161
SLAUGHTER,Ana	152	. Ella	246	. Pathie	225	. Button	65
. Angie	158	. Emma Maude	129	. Paul	116	. C.E.	29
. Charles Nolan	147	. Emma Queen	116	. Peggy	224,226	. Callie	32
. Cora	146,148	. Erastus C.	246	. Petty	225	. Carl Brown	99
. Cora J.	152	. Ester	122	. Rachel	133,135	. Charlene	32
. Cora Lee	155	. Esther	170,239,247	. Rachel Hampton	222,226	. Charles W.	168
. Daisa	156	. Frances	57,61	.	239	. Charlotte	95-96,98,100
. Emma Lou	34	. Francis Burwell II	226	. Reuben	114	. Clara Bell	105
. Euphania	155	. Francis Marion	134	. Robert White III	33	. Claude Ray	115
. Euphema	152	. Frank	116	. Robert White Jr.	33	. Collie	253
. Grace Lee	148,150	. Frank Burwell	225,245	. Rosie Bell	129	. Collie Belle	99
. Hallie	147	. Frank George	224	. Ruben	134	. Collier C.	10
. Hugh	152	. Frankie Lee	17	. Rushie	114,123,126	. Cudge	29
. Hughey	146	. George Madison	33,245	. Sallie	222,243	. D.M. Sr.	48
. Hughey J.	148	. George White	245	. Sally	226	. David Cordell	105
. James A.	146-147	. Harris	114,127	. Samuel Galiten	224-225	. Dennis	172
. Jess Eli	149	. Hattie Jane	133	.	242	. Dorothy Marie	32
. Jesse	155,158	. James Preston	247	. Samuel Thomas	222	. Earl M.	120
. Jesse Eli	148	. Jennie	127	. Sarah	114	. Edith	37
. Laura	163	. Jennie Rebecca	247	. Sarah Ann	245	. Edna L.	115
. Leon	148	. Jessie E.	114	. Sarah Jane	134	. Edward C.	211
. Lodema Lee	148	. Jessie Elizabeth	247	. Savannah	111	. Eleanor	37
. Lucinda	141	. Joan	33	. Steve	129	. Elizabeth	29,37,114
. Marilda	160	. John	133	. Sydney Aileen	223	.	122,124,132,134,231
. Sarah	155,158	. John Rose	242	. Temothy Kezer	226	. Ella	190
. Sarah Elizabeth	145	. Josie	224,245	. Thomas Calhoun	226	. Elmina P.	91
.	146,158	. Josie C.	245	. Vivian Equilla	129	. Elsie	70
. Wilma L.	149	. Katie	224	. W.Dick	245	. Emaline	103
SLIGER,Andy	50	. Laura	111	. W.G.	245	. Ericus	254
. Clara R.	50	. Lela	222	. W.K.	246	. Ernest Carl	59
. Harriet	50	. Lemma Lee	116	. Wesley	133	. Eupha Jennie	185
. Joseph Andrew	50	. Lena Frances	222	. Wiley S.	129	. Eva	123
. Rozelle	50	. Leonard Bill	113	. William	225	. Flora	131
SLUSHER,Marguerite	68	. Letta	114,126	. William Cheek	222	. Florence Louise	101
. Marguerite G.	68	. Lettie	123	.	224-226,245	. Frances Ruth	48
. Pearl Susan	68	. Lillie	114	. William Davidson	224	. Frank	169,171
. Peter B. Sr.	68	. Lizzie Hackett	224	.	245	. George	101
. William S. Sr.	68	. Lou Ethel	123	. William Hackett	222	. George Otto	99,105
SMARTT,Alex	170	. Lucien S.	245	.	223-224	. Georgia	9
. Alma	33	. Lucy	5,114,116	. William Thomas	222,226	. Georgie Lena	29

SMITH,(cont)
. Gladys   235
. Gladys Beatrice   253
. Golda   101
. Gracey A.   118
. Haley F.   10
. Haskell   10
. Hassie Bular   100
. Hence   115
. Hope   169
. Isaac   161
. J.Harris   109
. Jake   142
. James   171
. James Franklin Jr.   56
. James Marion   101
. Jess   134
. Jess Phillip   169
. Jim   237
. John   29
. John Eugene   32
. John J.   99
. John M.   29
. John W.   190
. Josie   28
. Kathleen   65
. Lem   91
. Lemuel   91
. Lena   56
. Leona   56,61
. Lillian   38
. Lissy   134
. Lithia Kiami   123,232
. Lizzie   131
. Lori Jean   105
. Lottie   101
. Louise   169
. Lucille   177
. Lucinda   218
. Lula Mae   237
. Luther M.   131
. Lynwood III   37
. Margaret   132
. Marion   131
. Martha Nell   105
. Mary   95,151,168,190
. Mary A.   247
. Mary Ann   98,124
. Mary Brown   109
. Mary E.   223
. Mary Ellen   48,105
. Mary Frances   35,41
. Mary Irene   91
. Mary Sanders   201
. Mary Wilma   30
. Matilda Frances   25
. Matilda Watley   29
. Mattie Elizabeth   9
. Minnie Mae   237
. Monroe Marion   134,136
. Myrl T.   105
. Nancy   122,142,238
. Nancy J.   193
. Nancy May   98
. Neal   78

. Nonne Ethel   28
. Ocie Pearl   59
. Odera C.   10
. Ollie   115
. Orvell B.   136
. Oscar   56
. Otto   32,253
. P.T.   181
. Paul Edward   181
. Phillip   169
. Phillip Jr.   41
. Phillip Sr.   65
. Phoebe   254
. Phronia   101
. Rebecca Caroline   141
                            142
. Richard John   98
. Robert   160
. Rosanna   208,211,254
. Rosie   247,252
. Roy T.   95
. Ruby   10,65,169
. Sallie   255
. Sarah   23,78
. Sarah Elizabeth   134
. Susannah   128,164
. T.B.   190
. Tabitha   103
. Tamor   170
. Tena   172
. Tennessee Caroline 190
. Tennie   52
. Thomas C.   134
. Thula   98
. Tom   48
. Tootsie   213
. Turner B.   95
. Velda Lee   59
. Vernie   136
. Virgil   59
. Wallace   105
. Wauleen   10
. Will   101
. William Butler   95-96
                          98,100
. William Joseph   98
. William Lynwood Jr.   37
. William Lynwood Sr.   37
SMITHSON,Alice M.   29
. Bessie May   185
. Bill   256
. Calvin   101
. D.C.   185
. David Reese   185
. Dellah   185
. Delter   185
. Docia   185
. E.W.   101
. Ed.W.   34
. Edger   185
. Effie   174
. Elizabeth   256
. Eupha Jennie   185
. Florence   185
. Hester Lucy   195

. Ida   30
. Ida Josephine   70
                        195-196
. Isaac Fletcher   185
. J.A.   256
. J.B.   185
. J.L.   185
. Jess   185
. Luann   101
. Mammie   185
. Marion A.   174
. Marion Jr.   174
. Mary   34
. Media   185
. Mollie   34,101
. N.B.   185
. R.A.   185
. Riston   195
. Robert Lee   34
. S.C.   185
. Sarah Jackaline   208
. T.G.   185
. William Calvin   101
SMOOT,Annie M.   51
. Annie Marie   51,192
. Brenda Faye   200
. Charlie P.   192
. Claud Martin   194
. Claude   188
. Cora   46,189
. Della Lorene   194
. Elizabeth   96
. Elizabeth F.I.   189,194
. Frances   -
.   Elizabeth I. 192
. George   46
. Illileen   201
. Isaac Newton   51,192
. James Madison   92-93,95
. Jennie Mae   95
. Jennie May   93
. Jessie May   92
. John Calhoun B.   89
. John Isaac   200
. Johnny Golden   200
. Josephine   44
. M.S.   59
. Margaret   92
. Mary   188
. Mary Elizabeth   96-97
. Mary Jane   194
. Mary Vera   59
. Matilda   92,96-97,191
. Matilda Ann   95
. Matt   92
. Minerva Elizabeth   189
. Myra Octavia   89
. Nancy P.   97-98
. Rayford Ray   46
. Reva Enole   46
. Rree   188
. Susan Sophia   96-97
. Thomas C.   188
. William   92,96-97
. William Clancy   192

. William Henley   96,189
.   192,194
. Willie Matt   93
SNEED,Emily   89
SNELLING,Mary   65
SNIDER,Smith L.   65
    Willie G.   65
SNIPES,Betty   91
. Lonzy Polk   93
. Mary Emmaline   106
. Mary Eunice   16
SOAPE,Zenohia   194
SOETIBIER,Grace Jane   15
. Henry   15
. Matilda   15
SOLOMON,Ava   132,134,136
. Bennett   131
. Bennett Jason   132
. Dora Alice   49
. Fatha   131
. James E.   131
. Joseph ALfred   49
. Lela Belle   49
. Luther Artman   49
. Mary E.   132
. Mary Elizabeth   134
. Myrick   131-132,134
. Nancy   131
. Willis   132
. Willis L.   131,134
SOLTYSIK,Christine   1
SOUTHARD,Bobby   32
. Christine   19
. Gloria Annette   32
. Mary Elizabeth   19
. William   19
SOUTHERN,Ollie   254
SOWDERS,Ellen   52
SPAIN,Benita   38
. Marshall Stacy   38
. Tommy   38
SPANGLER,
. Mary Elizabeth   188
. Ruth Jane   7
SPARKMAN,Dollie   49
. Elvin   79
. Frank   49
. Irvin   79
. Loretta Mai   24,49
. Melinda Josephine   89
. Myrtle   40
. Permelia   79
. Sarah   79
SPEARS,Eliza   96
    Frank   98
SPENCER,Bessie Jane   201
. Edna R.   65
. Lou Rhena   65
. Mildred   66
. Rhena   66
. Roy Smith   66
. Thomas Harrison   65-66
. Thomas Timothy   65
SPIVEY,Valley   60
SPRADLEY,Annie   181

==

SPRADLEY,(cont)		. Minnie	235	. Gladys	3	. Christopher Adam	54
. Minnie Belle	181	. Nancy	251	. Hattie	14	. Ed Hill	54
. William Bryant	181	STARNES,Addie	75	. Himey Robert	62	. Jennifer Leann	54
SPRY,Elvira	198	. E.C.	75	. Hugh West	9	. Vivian	54
SPURLOCK,Adam	87	. Mattie Lou	75	. Iona	46	STROUD,Barbara	56
. Allen Douglas	4	. Myrtis June	75	. Jessie M.	14	. Barry K	56
. Allie	75	. William L.	75	. Kate	62	. Beulah J.	19
. Billy	65	STEMBRIDGE,		. Laura Elizaeth	237	. Bryant	204
. Bob	172	. Alfred Joe	211	. Leburn R.	14	. C.Grady	9
. Charles	208	. Annie Frances	39	. Lucille	9	. Caroline	19
. Charles A.	138	. Bertie Lee	203	. Lucy Jane	51	. Edna	47
. Cindy Bell	64	. Brenda	71	. Martha	46	. Edna Alene	102
. Florence	169-170	. Charles Henry	211	. Mary	207	. George W.	9
. Helen	82	. Delilah	203	. Mary C.	208	. Harry Brown	232
. John	170-172	. Dorothy Ann	210-211	. Phillip R.	62	. James Gwin	47
. Judy	170-171	. Gladys Louise	211	. Robert Lee	49	. James T.	47,102
. Julia A.	172	. Hattie	210-211	. Roberta	7	. Margaret	9
. Leara	172	. Horace	203	. Samuel	49	. Nort	19
. Lillie	169	. James	203	. Tim	14	. Ora Lee	9
. Margaret	65	. James Houston	203	. William	3	. Ruth	47
. Mary	65,87,170	. Jennie	203	. Willie Archie	46	. Sarah Elizabeth	47
. Maurice	172	. John Henry	210-211	STILES,		. Sussie E.	204
. Narcisus	207-208	. John Marshall	210	. Chester Arthur	182	STUBBLEFIELD,	
. Parasada	138	. Johney	203	. E.J.	254	. Asa Faulkner	50
. Perseda	208	. Jules	203	. Flora	6	. Aubrey M.	144
. Rebecca	78	. Lida Myrtle	203	. Mary Ann	253	. Belle	12
. Robert	170	. Martha	211	. Pauline	182	. Belle Z.	11-12
. Ruby	65,169	. Martha Frances	210	. Phatha	110,131	. Bill	11
. Sindie	172	. Mary	203	STIPE,Netta Treva	4	. Bill W.	12
SPURLOCK,Lydia	66	. Ruth	203	STIZ,Jane	50	. Charlie	68
ST.JOHN,Annie	221,229	. Sarah A.	203	. Rellie	50	. Elisha J.	248
. Bettie	186	. Sharah Melinda	211	. Virginia Reline	50	. Elizabeth	248
. Betty	7,176	. Thomas Houston	203	STOCKSTILL,Mary	205	. Faye	61
. John	192	. Thomas Webb	203	STOKES,Susan	148	. George	12
. Margaret	192	. Tom	203	STONE,Aline	16	. Hiram B.	121
. Margaret Alice	7	. William Nelson	210-211	. Amma	35	. Janie	68
. Margaret Jane	192	. William Roland	203	. Dolly Coleman	157	. Juanita R.	68
STACY,Donnie Joe	144	STEPP,Carrol	168	. Joyce B.	35	. Loucretta	121-122
. L.D.	184	. Eliza	168	. Mary	95,190	. Mapoleon B.	125
. Lee Grover	144	. Emma	234-235	. Orris B.	35	. Margaret Ella	224
. Lena Mai	144	. Francis Earl	235	. Ronald Frank	35	. Martah	172
. Maria	184	. Francis M.	234-235	. Rose	65	. Martha Ella	248
. Minnie	144	. Francis Mariou	223	STONER,Amy Lee	13	. Mary C.	120
. Richard Howard	144	. Howry Orville	234	. Cellia	243	. Mary Catherine	115
. Rosanah	184	. Jack	168	. Jess	52	. Mary Ellen	50
. Wavie	144	. James Errett	234	. Jesse	13	. Mary Emeline	16
STANELY,Nedra Ann	60	. Mary Louise	235	. Leida	52	. Nancy Jane	110,125
STANLEY,Agnes	246	. Melba	234	. Maggie	127	. Napoleon B.	110
. Dorothy E.	72	. Nancy	223	. Martha Abigail	13,52	. Opal Lee	121
. Gentry L.	72	. William Carroll	223	. Oshia H.	127	. R.Douglas	11
. Henry J.	72	STEVENS,Aubrey Eston	235	. Robert Clinton	52	. Rebecca	122,125
. Rebecca	241	. Bertie	235	STORMS,Martah	230	. Robert L.	172
. Sarah	72	. Kelly	245	STOTTS,Dee Ida	31	. Ruby Irene	50-51
STAPLES,Gwendolyn	49	. Mazel Leona	235	. Henrietta	117	. Ruth	22
STARKEY,Abbigail	90-91	. Nicholas	-	. James	117	. U.L.	172
. Andrew	235	. Wellington	235	. Mary Magdalene	117	. William	110
. Casandra	190	STEWART,Annie Frances	62	STREET,Nancy	173	. William Jeffery	122
. Cassandra	91	. Arthur	237	STRICKLAND,Agnes	87	.	125
. Icie	235	. Bertha	49	. Clara	38	STUDER,John Budd	45
. Isaiah	91,190	. Dora Gladys	3	. Odis	38	. Norma J.	45
. Jarvis	251	. Edora	49	STRIEGEL,Blanche B.	33	. Paul J.	45
. Jennie	55	. Effie Mai	46	. Ida	33	SULLENS,Annie Frances	39
. Lois M.	2	. Emma	237	. John	33	. Jessie Noel	39
. Mahaley	6	. Evin	9	. Theodore E.	33	. Martha Ross	39
. Martha	251	. George	62	STRODE,		. Richy Howard	39

SULLENS,(cont)		. William A.	171	. Marvin H.	69	. Betty	55
. Walter	39	SWANN,Barney	30	. Maude	20	. Caldonia	182
SULLIVAN,Betty E.	202	. Celia Mae	30	. Maude E.	21,47	. Caldonia Ann	183
. Billie Sue	112	. Electie	30	. Melba	47	. Catherine	146-147
. Charlotte Faye	32	. Hester A.	196	. Melba Jean	57	. Cathran	160
. Daisy	202	. Ida	30	. Mildred L.	47	. Cathren	159
. Edna	111	. Ida Josephine	196	. Raleigh M.	20	. Charline	165
. Frances Cordelia	202	. Marie G.	30	. Roxie Ann	231	. Cherlene	165
. James	202	. Sam	30,196	. Thelma	47	. Clyde	44
. James A.	32	. Violet	191	. Thomas	21	. Cornelia	182
. Jonas William	32	. William Blair	44	. William Frank	92,242	. Creed	183-184
. Lucinda	202	SWEENY,Helen M.	4	TALLY,Hallie	231	. Daniel Clayton	52
. Sophia J.	112	SWEET,E.M.	91	TAMNER,Anna Bell	105	. Dannis Wayne	147
. Thelma	32	SWETTON,Rosa Jane	231	TANNER,Albert	168,171	. Della	149
. William Abraham	112	SWIFT,Annie Lowe	17	. Alta	168	. Della Pearl	143
. William Alton	112	. Claude M.	17	. Emma Maude	129	. Dorothy Ann	41
. William C.	202	. Daniel	17	. Fleming	167	. Edith	160
. William T.	32	. Flossye E.	17	. Harvey Lee	74	. Eliddie Ann	161-162
. Wilma Lou	112	SWINDELL,Daniel Loyde	10	. John L.	167	. Ellen	52
SUMMA,Elbert G.	35	. Edith	10	. Luther	168	. Ellen V.	183
. Mary E.	35	. Elva	10	. Margaret	159	. Elsie	30
. Nazareth Mary	35	. Hatton	10	. Martha	144,151,159	. Emma Ethel	74
. Victor Michael	35	SWOAPE,Annie	192,196	. Mary	167	. Eula Mai	225
SUMMERHILL,Annie	240	. Cora	196	. Mary Lee	74	. Floid Ianthis	159
George W.	240	. Samuel Ross	192,196	. Mattie Bell	71	. Floy	30-31
SUMMEROUR,Mamie	37	SWOPE,Prudie	69	. Newton	159	. Frances Evelyn	61
SUMMERS,Anna	199	TAFT,John Henry	23	. Pearl	163	. Frank	165
. Frances	53	. Laura Edna	23-24	. Tilda	167	. George W.	80
. George W.	199	. Mattie Marcella	23	. William	171	. Gertrude	105
. George William	92	. Maud Emily	18	TARTER,Bessie	19	. Gertrude Bernice	225
. Gwyn	199	. Theresa	18	TASSEY,Jennie Mai	16	. Glynn Concord	151
. Hannah	199	. Thomas M.	18	TATE,Adelaide	120	. Grady	31,160
. Hannah Mai	199	. William M.	24	. Bessie	34,37	. Harriet	35
. Hershell	79	TALBERT,Aubrie L.	11	. Clyde	37	. Harry Raymond	28
. Hoelene	199	. Lee Roy	11	. D.M.	120	. Henrietta	31
. Ida	207	. Mary Lou	11	. Daisy	50	. Herman Banks	34
. Jesse Tom	53	. Octia	11	. Deletta Faye	183	. Howard	35
. Josephine	92	TALLEY,Alma	255	. Gertrude	75	. Irene	151
. Lewis Clark	199	. Carletta	47	. Glenn E.	37	. Jake	165,225
. Linda	10	. Catherine	11	. Lucinda	3	. James A.	181
. Mary Dena	53	. Claud	20	. Richard Morton	34	. James O.	228
. Nancy	100	. Claude	47	. Susan Edna	120	. Joe R.	159
. Octa	79	. Claude Barbee	21	. William B.	75	. John A.	159
. Palmer	53	. Clyde Alton	47	. Willie Clyde	34	. John H.	162
. Rachel	53	. Columbus	230	. Wilma G.	113	. Joseph L.	181-182
. Robert	53	. Columbus Caleb	242	TATUM,		. Laura	143
. Susan Paralee	92	. Donna	57	. Clarence Bethel	245	. Laura Jane	146,151
SUTHERLAND,Mattie	9	. Elva	232	. Kelly	245	. Leona	61
SWALES,Eleanor	161	. Emily	106	. Lenora	245-246	. Lester Willard	160
. John	161	. Frank Parker	242	TAYLOR,Adell	181	. Livie Lonzo	165
. Susannah	156,161	. Hallie	232	. Alfred	61	. Lorena	28
SWAN,Barney	201	. Hazel	20	. Almer W.	179	. Margaret Novella	181
. Electie	201	. J.B.	253	. Anderson	183	. Margarette E.	183
. H.Evelyn	70,195	. Jack Reece Jr.	57	. Andrew	146	. Marie	52
. Ida Josephine	70,195	. Jack Reece Sr.	57	. Andrew J.	151,165	. Marilda	160
. Media S.	195	. Jack Reese Sr.	47	. Andrew Jackson	28,34	. Martha	54,159-160
. Mennie Bell	195	. James H.	242	. 41,143,146-147,160		. Martha Alice	159
. Minnie	70	. Jane	21	. Anna	41	. Martha Allona	160
. Sam	70,195	. Jeannette	69	. Anna C.	160	. Mary	159-160,177
. Stephanie J.	86	. Jerry	253	. Arthur	160	. Mary Ann	160,228
. Tennie	248	. John Lucas	232	. Beatrice	165	. Mary Cleo	160
. Vernon Stene	70	. John Robert	47	. Ben Lewis	74	. Mary E.	184
. Vernon Steve	195	. Josie	92	. Bertha	165	. Mary Elizabeth	61,182
SWANGER,Lucille	187	. Lela	253	. Bessie	26	. Maude F.	182
. Sallie Evelyn	171	. Martha Ann	242	. Bessie Caldonia	145	. Melissa	74

===

TAYLOR,(cont)		. Velma	39	. Nannie Lee	220-221	THROWER,Gregory L.	111
. Minnie B.	181	. William	39	. Susie	133	. James	111
. Murdis Marie	147	. William W.	135	. Will Annen	220	. James Thomas	16
. Nancy	160,183	. Wilson C.	39	. William A.	253	. Jeffery G.	111
. Nancy Ellen	61	TENPENNY,		. William Annen	221	. Lou Ann	111
. Nellie	160	. Bertie Lucille	29	. William Annen Jr.	221	. Lourine	16
. Nolia	47	. Bessie	29,102,230	THOMAS,Alice	45	. Mary Emeline	16
. Norman	159-160	. Bob	182	. Almira Jane	250	THURMAN,Betty Sue	29
. Oliver Cleveland	151	. Clarence	104	. Benjamin	238	. Charlie	208
. Paul	147,160	. Clarence N.	231	. Benjamin C.	239	. Charlie A.	211
. Peggy	151	. Dorothy Mai	51	. Betsy	250	. Elisha Marlin	211
. Randa Gustava	34	. Eppie	6	. Coreba	188	. Georgie Lena	29
. Roberta	179	. Ernest	6	. Emma	167	. Harold Thomas	29
. Sally	28	. Ernest Lemuel	29,230	. Frances W.	10	. Margaret Elizabeth	211
. Sam	105,159	. Flavil Hall	250	. Hazel	233	. Martha Elizabeth	208
. Samuel Nelson	147	. Flavil Hall Jr.	250	. Ida	207	TIDUS,Rosie	70
. Sarah	165,183	. George L.	6	. Joe	250	TIDWELL,Alfred	172
. Sarah Adeline	165	. Georgia	7	. L.L.	252	. Bettie	172
. Sarah Katherine	34	. Gregory Keith	7	. Lon Greg	10	. Henry	172
. Sarah Leweller	159	. Hattie Belle	229,250	. Margaret	219	. Mose	172
. Selma	166	. Homer F.	7	. Margaret D.	239	. Rebecca	172
. Sidney	159,162	. Homer Franklin	6	. Mary	238-239	. Sudie	172
. Stephen	52	. James Ernest	29	. Mary Lou	248	TILLETT,C.H.	220
. Steven K.	181	. James R.	230-231	. Mary lou	238	. C.H. Jr.	220
. Suella B.	147	. Joe David	250	. Minnie Mae	94	. Eva	220
. Susie	61	. Juanita	231	. Pamela Elizabeth	239	. Fred Fuston	220
. Thelma	47	. Kathy Willene	8	. Rachel Hampton	222,226	. George	220
. Thelma Norene	44	. Katy Willene	7	.	239	. Jennie	220
. Thomas	160	. Lannie Lester	250	. Robbie Lee	252	. L.M.	220
. Tom	165	. Lannis Lester	229	. Robert	207	. Lillian Gladious	220
. Vernon Floyd	41	. Lillian	231	. Sarah ELizabeth	250	TILMON,Cindy	36
. Vester E.	181	. Lou Phema	43	. Sarah Jane	55	. Craig	36
. William Arthur	160	. Louise	230	. Tommie	37	. Joshua Burnett	36
. William Lewis	61	. Lupema	15	. Tommie J.	207	TIPTON,Dessie	66
. William M.	61	. Luphema	182	. William H.	250	TITTLE,Bellie Gray	33
. Willie V.	181-182	. Malissie	182	THOMASON,Della	73	. Georgia Mai	33
. Willis	159-160	. Mary	230	. Georgia Elizabeth	19	. Hassie	176
TEAGUE,Anna M.	71	. Mary Lee	250	. Guy D.	19	. Herman Cantrell	38
. Bessie	71	. Maude	231	. Helen	19	. John Roy	176
. Levi	71	. Melissa	29,229	. Mamie	19	. Lana Mae	38
TEAL,Ann	195	. Robert	29	. Nelson	19	. Malissa J.	176
Annie	30,201	. Robert Brook	230	THOMISON,Charlie	21	. Roy Delta	176
TEETERS,Betty June	148	. Robert H.	229	. Mary Lodema	21	. Sam	176
.	149	. Roxie A.	230	. Mary Lou	81	. Sammie	16-17,19,45,188
. Eugenia	148	. Roxie Ann	231	. Maude G.	21	. Sarah Ann	176
. Gordon	148	. Ruth	29	. Nellie	42	. Tillman C.	38
TEMONEY,Jacquelyn	24	. Susie	28	. james M.	42	. William R.	33
TEMPLE,Media	191	. Virginia Ann	177	THOMPKINS,Georgia	239	TITTLSORTH,James N.	23
. Melissa	191	TERRY,Cindy Bell	64	Ida	16	. Nancy Audrey	23
. R.M.	191	. John Walter	64	THOMPSON,		. Sandra Lorene	23
TEMPLES,Delia	27	. Nathaniel	64	. Ernest Elmore	185	TITTSWORTH,Emily	87
. Lucy Virginia	99	. Priscilla	64	. Georgia Azzeline	183	. James N.	64
. Will	201	. Sarah	217	. Gladys	186	. James W.	64
TEMPLESS,Mable Lee	171	. Walter Joe	64	. Jessie E.	120	. L.Ray	24
TEMPLETON,		TETZKE,Bertha	2	. John Calvin	186	. Lillie Bell	197
. Audrey Aileen	17	THATCH,Hattie	240	. Lillie Mae	186	. Lillie Gertrude	24
. Billie Lois	61	THAXTON,Ada Eugina	221	. Lula Azzaline	15	. Nancy	64
. Dimple J.	61	. Claudine	253	. Maggie Arnetta	183	. Nancy Audrey	64
. Joseph Allen	17	. Cynthia Caroline	242	. Martha	208	TOBITT,Cyril Edgar	71
. Maggie	234	. Dovie Claudine	221	. Mary	159	Linda Rose	71
. Mark Deran	61	. George	133	. Maude	20	TODD,Albert Grace	90
. Pena Jane	135	. Ira Thomas	220	. Rachel	133	. Allen	176
. Pleas	61	. James Earl	253	. Ruben	183	. Alley	186
. Pleas C. Jr.	61	. Mary	228	. Willene	183	. Allie	7
. Rachel	39	. Minnie Flora	220	. Willie Ruben	183	. Anna Bell	69

==

Name	Page	Name	Page	Name	Page	Name	Page
VANDERGRIFF,Maude A.	63	Stene	113	. Zeltie	111	.	133
Roy J.	63	WAFER,Melissa	74	WALLACE,Elva	232	. Jansie	158
VANDORNE,		WAGGONER,Joseph	212	. Lela Bell	49	. Katherine	120
Lorraine Angela	15	. Sarah A.	212	. Rebecca	155	. Mary Ellen	133
VANHOOSER,Isaac	205	. Susan	212	WALLER,Collie	253	. Ruby	115
. Jeston	205	WAGNER,Edna L.	115	WALLING,Ada	248	. Stevie Lynn	133
. Mary Ann	205	. George	115	. Alfred	213	. Thurman	111
VANHOOSIER,Hattie	66	. Mary	115	. Alice	151	. Tim	115,120
VANNOY,Clara Elora	218	. Minnie Eugene	115	. Annie	213	WARREN,Alma Grace	7
. Lewis	218	. William Jacob	115	. Audrene	25	. Alma O.	6
. Matilda	218	WAID,Willa Mae	243	. Betty Lou	214	. Annie Laura	18
VANTIPP,Louise	248	WALDEN,Mary D.	65	. E.V.	25	. Beulah	230
VAUGHN,Della	63	WALDERN,Hallie	216	. Elizabeth	213	. Frankie	55
. Emogene	74	WALKER,A.Gordon	53	. James Harve	120	. J.Ed.	6-7
. Floyd	63	. Alean	52	. Joe	213-214	. Jesie Walter	18
. G.B.	106	. Alice	12	. Josephine	213	. John Tubb	7
. George David	233	. Alvin J.	111	. Laura	120	. Lela Mai	7
. Gertrude	106	. Belle	89	. Leatrice	213	. Mary	182
. Helen Marie	233	. Bobbie Jean	60	. Monroe C.	120	. Ollie May	18
. James Francis	234	. Brintley	149	. Oshia	213-214	. Zula	58
. Margaret	3	. C.Dottie	58	. Raymond H.	213	WASHINGTON,Esau	170
. Martha	23,234	. Callie	32	. Rutha	18,81	WATERHOUSE,Ann	245
. Media	23	. Catherine Bell	103	. Smith	213-214	. Elizabeth H.	222,225
. Phyllis A.	234	. Claude	26	. Thomas Dillard	248	. Elizabeth Hackett	245
. Reba Jo	37	. Collie Belle	99	. Violet Ann	120	WATERS,Lethia	148
. Ruby	38	. Cumilla	25-26	WALLS,Dorothy Jewell	12	WATKINS,Cynthia Allie	11
. Ruby L.	63	. Dovie M.	111	. John	12	Mary	13
. Ruth Bell	233	. Earl	80	. Maggie	51	WATLEY,	
. T.R.	23	. Edward	13	. Nancy	12	. Arthur Benjamin	49
. Thomas Woodrow	234	. Eidth Jane	236	WALSH,Mary	61	. Louise	49-50,254
VAUGHT,Alice	186	. Evelyn L.	22	. Nola C.	11	. Matilda	29
. Deborah	28	. Flora	131	. Vincent	61	. Maude	49
. Emogene	75	. Frances	13	. William	11	WATSON,Belle	22
. Rilla A.	149	. Isaac Clinton	149	WALTERS,Letha	158	. Benjamin Logan	236
VEAL,Amos Alvin	4	. J.R.	252	WANAMAKER,		. Bertha Almeta	72
. Laurene M.	4	. James L.	22	. Carl Cantrell	66	. Charles Louis	56
. Netta Treva	4	. James O.	62	. Hazel Annette	66	. Dinah	41
VERPLANK,Grover	41	. Jessie A.	26	. James	52	. Elizabeth	19,24,184
Margaret Dorothy	41	. Jewell	5	. Jimmie	30	. Ernest	22
VIANDA,Virla	123	. Joe	52-53	. Leida	52	. Fred Brown	24
VICKERS,Annie	171	. John	99,103,111	. Marguerite	127	. Grace	37
. Eliza	200	. John Thomas	236	. Nancy	30,52	. J.E. Sr.	24
. Jane	165	. Joyce Ann	53	. Naomi	166	. Janice L.	20
. Milton	171	. Lela Pearl	22	. Oshia H.	127	. Jerry Dale	148
. Nancy Jane	67	. Lloyd B.	22	. Pauline	113	. Jessie Mae	148
VINSON,Colonel C.	176	. Lois Pauline	46	. Sidney Jacob	66	. Joe L.	148
.	177	. Lula	149	. Tennie P.	30	. John Ann	56
. Colonel Jr.	176	. Maggie Marie	149	. Zoda Bell	66	. Lela Pearl	22
. Ella	243	. Marjorie	11	WARD,Alice M.	143	. Paul F.	20
. Ethel	177	. Martha Eveline	252	. Bessie	54	. Rebecca Lynn	41
. Gertrude	243	. Mary Lodema	21	. Cleo	234	. Robert Ernest Jr.	41
. Hattie Ann	175	. Mattie	99,236	. Fronia	67	. Sally Ruth	24
. Hettie	176-177	. Melvina	103	. Grace A.	74	. Virginia Ruth	55-56
. Ike	177	. Metta	22	. James A.	74	WATTS,Gordon D.	24
. Jodie Laymon	177	. Robbie	25	. Lodie	39	. Isabell	1
. John Woodrow	177	. Sallie	53	. Lucy	21,80,83	. Margaret Ann	24
. Leburn	176	. Sam	5	. Mattie Henen	35	WEBB,Ambrose	170
. Letha	177	. Samantha	252	WARE,Bell	12	. Andrew Jackson	13,34
. Lucille	177	. Sarah	5,58,72	. Bettie V.	181	. Annie E.	174,179
. Odis Lavor	243	. Silas Richard	58	. Ethel	111,120,132	. Billy Ray	13
. Shely	176	. Sterling H.	5	. Gilberta	111	. Bryan William	34
. Sterling Brown	243	. Thelma L.	62	. Isham	115	. Evaline	87
. Viola	177	. Thomas	22	. Isham W.	111	. Frances	39
WADDELL,Loe	112	. Tom	252	. Isham Wash	120	. Josephine	44
WADE,Ellen Lucille	218	. Vernal	26	. Isham Washington	132	. Josie	40

==

WEBB,(cont)	. Nathan R. 89	. Elizabeth 247	. Eleanor 37
. Kathryn 27	. Ollie 115	. Lina 247	. Henry 4
. Martha 248	. S.H. 157	. Pauline C. 247	. James Nicholas 4
. Mary 101,203	. Sarah 122,204	. Rachel 136	. Mamie 37
. Mary Evaline 79,84,86	. William F. 204	. Thomas Jr. 247	. Mary Lorene 4
. Muriel Dean 13	WHITAKER,Aaron 74	WILES,Florine 2	WILLIS,Betty 126
. Nancy 34	. Celia 74	WILKERSON,Mandy 63	. George T. 118
. Nannie 16	. Frances Ruth 48	WILKINSON,Cleveland 10	. Gracey A. 118
. Riley 79	. Ida 114	. Mary Etta 10	. Matilda 218
. Rutha 79	. Jimmie L. 74	. Robert Lee 10	. Venie 118
. Samantha 34	. Leona 48	. Tabitha Ann 10	. Vera 66
. Shellia Elfleta 13	. Mollie 58	WILLIAMS,Aubrey E. 230	WILMONT,Martha 252-253
. Susan 34	. Richard E. 74	. Calvin Henderson 197	WILMORE,Naomi 50
WEDDINGTON,Athelia 142	. Robert Aaron 74	. Daisy Lee 197	WILSON,A.F. 185
. Carl Gene 47	. Sidney 48	. Della Mildred 230	. Amanda Belle 207
. Clay 46	. Sidney L. 48	. Doc 145	. Anna Belle 99
. Daisy 47	WHITE,Dora 69	. Elizabeth 161,214	. Arnold 115
. Daisy Susan 46	. Elizabeth 223	. Ella 32	. Artie E. 209
. Fannie 46	. Esther 170	. Ella Mae 71	. Betty 138
. Hazel 46	. Flaura 57	. Ethel 93	. Brown Ramsey 196
. Luther Virgil 46	. John 172	. Fred D. 54	. Charles 171
. Pauline 47	. John Henry 57	. Georgia 256	. Charlie E. 209
. Robert Carl 47	. Katrina 57	. Hoyt Smoot 197	. Cheslie 69
. Roy 46-47	. Kenneth D. 57	. Ida 49,114	. Cindy Down 28
. Roy Laymon 46	. Malinda 101	. Jackie C. 36	. Clessie 138
. William 142	WHITEAKER,Alice L. 15	. Jemima 2,153,156,161	. Connie C. 188
WELCH,Barbara Jean 59	. Gertrude 14	. Jerry 256	. Cynthia 198
. Bell 59	. Leonard 14-15	. Jessie Lee 230	. Dorothy Jean 27
. Lee 59	. Smith 14	. Joe 197	. Dovie Marie 62
. Minnie 59	WHITLOCK,J.K.P. 211	. John Marion 114	. Edmon 138
. Minnie G. 60	. James 178	. Kate 62	. Elizabeth Jane 207
. William B. 59-60	. James Polk 6	. Linnie Frances 236	. Ella 1
. Willie 59	. James Thomas 6	. Margaret W. 63	. Ellen Cecil 105
WENZEL,Bernard Henry 20	. Laura Ethel 6	. Martha C. 102-103	. Emaline 211
. Flora Bell 20	. Lucy 211	. Mary 155	. Emeline 138,208
. Fredrick 20	. Mahaley 6	. Mary Ellen 49	. Ethel M. 209
. Lena 20	. Mary Frances 178	. Mattie 195	. Eula Pearl 188,197
WEST,Carolyn 43	. Sarah 178	. Maymie 197	. Evelyn Carrie 105
. Christine 63	. Sarah Abigail 211	. Minnie 145	. Fannie B. 94
. Clara 20	WHITMAN,Bunie 21	. Mollie 198	. Fannie Myrtle 3
. Daisy C. 5	. Nettie Lee 129	. Nancy 164	. Fate 171
. Hester L. 4-5	WHITMON,Nellie Jo 189	. Olive Alice 16,230	. Harold 28
. James 100	WHITTENBURG,Alice 115	. Sallie 224,256	. Harry C. 32
. Jane 209	. 120,122	. Samuel D. Sr. 51	. Huey Jackson 188,194
. Kathleen 254	. Jim 234	. Sidney Lee 16	. Hugh J. 196
. L.Shelton 43	. John 115,120,122	. Sidney S. 230	. Hughie Jackson 196
. Lucille 9	. Laura 120	. Sidney Sherwood 16	. James 252
. Nancy 100	. Lennie Pearl 122	. Stanley 230	. James C. 208-209
. Ricky Darnell 233	. Minnie 115	. Tempie 147	. Janie 27
. Sarah 174,186	. Susie 234	. Temple Ann 144	. Jessie J. 209
. Viola 100	. William Charles 120	. Tempy 152	. Joe Firm 208
WETZEL,Alonzo 12	WHITTIMORE,Lou Cindy 198	. Tempy Ann 146	. John 3,207
. Eugene L. 12	. Lucindy 199	. Tempy Bess 163	. John B. 208
. Minnie 12	. Malinda 197	. Tennessee 197	. John Bearl 32
. Ronalda 12	WHITTLEY,Henry 39	. Tilly 12	. Joseph Firm 66
WHEELER,Alice 120,122	WHITWELL,Georgia 66	. Tom 114	. Laura 3
. 174	WICKER,Mary 19	. Wallie 114	. Lillie Brown 207
. Dosia 204	WIGINGTON,Drucilla 119	. Wesley B. 63	. Lucy 211
. Holly 89	. Elizabeth 119	. William 155	. Malinda 28
. John 55	. James 119	. William Jr. 164	. Margaret 99-100
. Joseph Edward 89	. John Griffin 119	. William Sr. 161	. Martha Eveline 252
. Julie 55	WILBURN,Mollie 6	. William Toy 49	. Marvin E. Sr. 32
. K.T. 122	WILCHER,	WILLIAMSON,A.E. 37	. Mary 207
. Maggie G. 157	. Archibald Price 247	. Betty Ann 4	. Mary C. 208
. Martha Alice 54-55	. Bonnie Lee 247	. Edna 18	. Mary Elizabeth 188,194

WILSON,(cont)		WISEMAN,		
.	196	. Bertie Lucille	29	. Johnny C.	37	. Gilberta	111

WILSON,(cont)		WISEMAN,		. Johnny C.	37	. Gilberta	111
.	196	. Bertie Lucille	29	. Leth	52	. Gladys	126
. Mattie	99,255	. Earl Willis	127	. Louise X.	248	. Grover Lee	124
. Mattie Ann	66	. George Sr.	127	. Lucinda	88	. Henry Clay	116
. Maude	78	. Georgie	29	. Martha Adaline	83	. J.J.	22
. Mildred Culley	32	. Jewel Dee	127	. Martha Paralee	205	. James W.	127
. Muriel Dean	13	. Joetta	8	. Mary	234,237	. Jim	127
. Nancy P.	138	. Martin Tipton	123,127	. Mary Ann	82-83,204	. John Edward	9
. Nannie	138	. Mary	127	. Mary L.	248	. John L.	9
. Nellie	208	. Mary Edna	123,127	. Minnie Adeline	204	. Lemma Lee	116
. Offie Lillian	208	. Mary Helen	127	. Ola Mae	52,54	. Lemma May	124
. Ola Mai	66	. Minnie Louella	29	. Ophia P.	234	. Levi	126,168
. Pearl	10	. Wayman Tipton	127	. Orah P.	237	. Lillie	118
. Phebie Jane	208-209	. Wilma Louise	123	. Parker	234,237	. Malissa	9
. Phebie Janes	252	WISER,Anna A.	173	. Shirley Jean	87	. Marguerite	127
. Phronia	196	. Irva V.	173	. Tennie E.	26	. Mary	127
. Rebecca	94,96	. Lavie	173	. William	88	. Mary Ann	124
. Roxie	32	. Mollie	8,192	. Willie I.	11	. Mollie	122
. Roy J. Jr.	188	. Ollie	116	. Zettie	90	. Myrtle	124,127
. Roy Jackson Sr.	188	. Rachel	190	WOOD,		. Nelma	235
.	197	. Rebecca	192	. Alexander Hamilton	221	. Ollie Jones	9
. Ruby May	194	. Thomas	192	. Ambie	64	. Oshia	111
. Sharon	11	. William	173	. Amby	221	. Oshia H.	127
. Stanley Cecil	11	WITKOWSKI,Anastasia	6	. Anderson Jackson	98	. Ozra Ellis	127
. Sterling Brown	27	WITT,Charlie	202	. Annie	221	. Susan Ann	168
. Thena	10	. J.E.	117	. Annie Gladys	64	. Velma	22
. Wauline	197	. Mary	202	. Arzona	98	. William A.	124
. Willard Robe	105	. William	202	. Bertha Pauline	248	. Willie Andrew	22
. William	138,208,211	WOLCOTT,Elmina P.	91	. Cleveland	221	WOODLEY,Dorothy B.	57
. Willie	138	William	91	. Eva	87	Ely	216
. Willie Flora	19	WOLF,Caleb A.	58	. H.G.	98	WOODS,	
. Woodrow	8	. Caleb Alvin	58	. Jack	246	. Alexander Hamilton	229
WIMBERLY,Clara	151	. Caleb Alvin II	57	. Jessie M.	10	. Annie	229
. Edna	2	. Doretta	58	. Jossie D.	194	. Ben F.L.	171,176
. Oscar	151	. Hazel Marie	57	. Leslie P.	249	. Bertha	40
. Peggy	151	. Ida	58	. Lizzie	246	. Charlotte Faye	32
WINCHESTER,Elizabeth	120	. Joseph Laban	58	. Maggie Mae	60	. Cleveland	221
WINFIELD,		. Joseph Labon	58	. Mary	221	. Eden	215
. Burton James	103	. Leslie Albert	58	. Mattie Eunice	10	. Evelyn Marie	241
. Rose Geraldine	103	. Margaret	58	. Millie	92	. Gladys	107
WINFRED,Ida Mae	151	. Mary Kathleen	58	. Nannie M.	108	. Hattie Belle	229,250
WINNDAD,Ann Clara	229	WOLFE,Bessie W.	16	. Nettie	245-246	. James M.	32
WINNETT,Liza	54	. Fannie	16	. Robert L.	64,221	. James Mitchell	32
. Mattie Lee	54	. John M.	16	. Sophronia A.	98	. Jane Tryn	218
. W.C.	54	. Norma Jo	201	. Sophronia	-	. Jennie	53
WINNINGHAM,Della	7	WOMACK,Abner Denton	248	. Elizabeth	100	. John B.	53
. James	7	. Abner Monroe	83,204	. Walter Allen	68	. Josephine	218
. Lora Jane	7	.	248	. Willie	68	. Lucious	53
WINTON,Alfred	48	. Agnes May	10	WOODEN,Auvil	105	. Mabel	40
. Andy J.	21	. Alma	86	. C.R.	100	. Maggie B.	55
. Ara	21	. Anna	88	. Clint	100	. Malissa J.	176
. Clara Frances	215	. Arsey	124	. Fate	100,105	. Malissie	182
. Dessie Jane	21	. Charles D.	52	. Gertrude	105	. Martha Amelia	241
. Ettie	48	. Clavin	87	. Nan	100,105	. Mary Dee	184
. Hence	48	. Dora V.	237	. Viola	100	. Mattie G.	32
. Hollis	215	. Dorothy J.	37	WOODLEE,		. Melissa	29
. Horace Smartt	224	. Ella	124	. Andrew Bucher	116	. Michael	36
. Lillian	224	. Ella Elizabeth	248	. Betty	126	. Ocies	40
. Lillie	41	. Eva	87	. Charity Lee	124	. Pamela Lynn	218
. Maxine	48	. F.Ethel	248	. Charlie	170	. Patricia Ann	32
. Pleasant Henderson	224	. Frank	90	. Claud	111	. Peggy A.	36
. Roberta	217	. Jacob Ervin	52	. Elizabeth	154	. Richard Luther	32
. Sam Houston	21	. James J.	26,82	. Ester	22	. Rowena	32
. Thelma	66	. Joe Lee	83	. Fannie Harrison	116	. Ruby	229
WISEAN,Wilma Louise	124	. John C.	83	. Frank Smith	124,127	. Sallie Evelyn	171

WOODS,(cont)		. Elihu Burr	85	. Martha M.	243	. Margaret	181,183

WOODS,(cont)
. Sarah 171,176
. Thomas Fred 218
. Tina Belenda 32
. Tom Robert 241
. Ulysses 229
WOODSIDE,Edna 47
WOODSON,Nancy 206
WOODWARD,Herman Lee 83
WOOTEN,Anna Amelia 108
. Annie 171
. David Hampton 108-109
. G.F. 107
. G.J. 92
. Garvis 92
. Jonathan 108
. Leah 45
. Mabel 107
. Mable 92
. Martha Jane 108-109
. Myrtle Elizabeth 108
. Nancy 108
. Richard 107
. Richard Franklin 92
WORD,Martha 159-160
WORLEY,Harriet 210
. Ida 200
. Lorin Anderson 210
WORTHINGTON,
. Annie Edna 213
. Buford 213
. Clarence B. 213
. Etta 213
. Mary 118
WRIGHT,Addie 75
. Bertha 46
. Catherine 57
. George W. 57
. Hattie Elizabeth 76
. Lois Cleta 57
. Nancy 73,98
. Ronalda 12
. Wilson 76
WYATT,Bea 19
. Jewel 19
. Michael D. 19
. Ruth 51
. Theodore R. 19
WYDELL,Mary 60
West,Julie 55
YARBRO,Margaret 39
YELL,Tennessee W. 22
YORK,A.B. 27
. Alice Mitchell 83
. Alton 21
. Bertha 111
. Bertha Savanah 21
. Bunie 21
. Burr 83
. Cecil Burgess 27
. Clance Z. 35
. Cora K. 107
. Cora K.A. 102
. Delia 27
. E.B. 83

. Elihu Burr 85
. Eona 111
. Ethel Perry 85
. Frances 43
. Hanry 106
. Henry 102,111
. Jeanette B. 35
. Jesse Lee 85
. Landon 35
. Lela 85
. Liza 191
. Louise 83,85
. Mary Frances 35
. Nancy Paulina 94-95
. Nathaniel 102,106
. Ollie Mai 70,191
. Temperance 94
. Uriah Jaco 85
. Venus Christopher 83
. W.C. 228
. William 94
YOUNG,Ace 168
. Alex 182
. Alice 254,256
. Amanda 182
. Ann 195
. Ann Calra 229
. Annie 30,201
. Ardith Ethel 5
. Asa Overton 84
. Barbara Joan 229
. Barbara Louise 230
. Callie 236
. Callie Ann 40
. Donnie Robert 38
. Dovie 195
. E.M. 182
. Edd 243
. Electie 30,201
. Ellenora 236
. Emily 89
. Ester Marshall 84
. Eva May 182
. Evelyn 64
. Evia Ann 243
. Fannie Frances 4
. Florence 4
. H.Lester 84
. Holly 89
. Isaac 236
. James Wayne 200
. John Marion 168
. Johnnie William 35
. Joseph 89
. Julia 84
. Larry 23
. Lassie M. 4
. Lear 192
. Leona 5
. Loretta Lynn 38
. Lou Ann 63
. Luther Harlon 229
. Mandy 182
. Margaret J. 207
. Martha 23,46,89

. Martha M. 243
. Mary Etta 192
. Mary Hilda 63
. Mary Wilma 200
. Matilda E. 84
. Mattie Louise 230
. Nancy 91
. Naomie 235
. O.M. 5
. Oshie 35
. Pamela Annette 23
. Pauline 229
. Phillip W. 192
. Raymond Eugene 230
. Robert F. 63
. Robert Felix 38
. Ruby 38
. Ruby L. 63
. Sandra Lorene 23
. Sylvapia 23
. T.M. 229
. Thomas Dudley 5
. Tom 5
. W.C. 201
. Willard Edward 4
. William Calvin 30,195
. William Hill 4,230
. William Hillard 4
. Zora Ethel 200
YOUNGBLOOD,Allen 183
. Azlene 174
. Benjamin F. 182-183
. Bettie 16
. Billie Ruth 147
. Caldonia Ann 182
. Carrie Ann 174
. Charley Tullie 180
. Charlie Newton 181
. Claudia 178
. Clifford 201
. Daisy L. 181
. Dallas 174
. Dessie B. 17
. Dollie Lorene 53
. Emma Lee 45
. Ernest Main 19
. Eva 175
. Hettie Ann 175
. Ibbie Jane 183
. Ibby 187
. Illileen 201
. J.C. 201
. James A. 174,178-179
. James Otic 174
. James Robert 174
. Jesse Lee 147
. Joe 175
. John Henry 174,186
. Joseph 175
. Joseph E. 181
. Juanita 16
. Lebron 53
. Leonard H. 16
. Leslie 174
. M.A. 180

. Margaret 181,183
. Martha 233
. Martha E. 174,178-179
. Martha Sue 16
. Marvina 19
. Mary 178,186
. Mary Elizabeth 188
. Mary Lou 175-176
. Mattie 186
. Myrtle Ruth 181
. Otte Eldg 178
. Pearl 185
. Robert 16-17,19,45,188
. Roy 178
. Ruby Ventrice 179
. Samie 19
. Sammie 16-17,45,188
. Samuel B. 179
. Sandra 16
. Sarah 174,186
. Sepal 12
. Tennie 179
. Verlinne 183
. W.J. 180
. William Jason 147
YOUNGLOVE,
. Muriel Nadine 72
. Robert D. 72
. Robert S. 72
. Wave 72
ZACHARY,Sara Ann 245
ZADIE,Bertha L. 195
ZIKEFOOSE,Eleanor 69
ZULLIGER,Louise 33
ZUMBRO,Violet 245

www.ingramcontent.com/pod-product-compliance
Lightning Source LLC
Chambersburg PA
CBHW081429270326

41932CB00019B/3141

* 9 7 8 0 7 8 8 4 8 9 8 1 5 *